financial planning

2nd edition

financial planning

2nd edition

Warren McKEOWN

Mike KERRY

Marc OLYNYK

WILEY

First published 2014 by
John Wiley & Sons Australia, Ltd
42 McDougall Street, Milton Qld 4064

Typeset in 9.5/12 pt ITC Giovanni Std

National Library of Australia
Cataloguing-in-Publication data

Author:	McKeown, Warren, author.
Title:	Financial planning/Warren McKeown; Mike Kerry; Marc Olynyk.
ISBN:	9781118644836 (paperback)
Notes:	Includes index.
Other Authors/ Contributors:	Kerry, Mike, author. Olynyk, Marc, author.
Dewey Number:	332.024

Printed in China by
Printplus Limited

10 9 8 7 6 5 4 3 2 1

About the authors

Warren McKeown

Warren was the Senior Lecturer and Course Director of Financial Planning at RMIT University for 11 years, where he devised and taught a range of financial planning subjects in the undergraduate Financial Planning degree program and also subjects in the Master of Financial Planning program. He is currently a Teaching Fellow in Financial Accounting at the University of Melbourne.

He has degrees in economics and education and a business master's degree by research. He has 25 years' experience in financial planning as a Chartered Accountant and as a Certified Financial Planner. He maintains a small client base to ensure that his financial planning skills are up to date.

Warren prepared materials and presented workshops in financial planning for the Personal Financial Planning and Superannuation segment of the CPA program for over 10 years. He was also a panel member of the Financial Industry Complaints Service (now Financial Ombudsman Service) and is currently a subject expert for CFP1, the Professionalism module of the FPA's CFP program.

Mike Kerry

Mike is currently the Director of Learning Services at DeakinPrime. Prior to joining DeakinPrime he was a Senior Lecturer in Financial Planning in the Faculty of Business and Law at Deakin University. Mike has been instrumental in the development and growth of both the undergraduate and postgraduate Financial Planning programs at Deakin University. He has also been extensively involved in the development of financial planning curricula for the university's commercial clients. Mike's research interests include retirement planning and the use of computer-based technology to enhance planner–client communication. Mike has a Bachelor of Commerce and a Master of Finance (Honours) from the University of Melbourne. Mike is also a Fellow of the Certified Practising Accountants of Australia and a Financial Planning Specialist.

Marc Olynyk

Marc Olynyk is a Senior Lecturer in Financial Planning at La Trobe University and has held various roles within both academia and industry in the areas of financial planning, superannuation, and retirement planning and accounting. He has many years' experience in both teaching and program leadership positions and has played a key role in the development, growth and accreditation of the financial planning discipline at La Trobe University. Marc is a member of the Financial Planning Association and the Institute of Chartered Accountants, a foundation member of the Financial Planning Education Council and a member of the Financial Planning Academic Forum. Marc has published articles in financial planning, superannuation and financial literacy.

Brief contents

Contents

Preface

The odds of picking the six correct numbers in TattsLotto are about eight million to one. That means — for most of us — securing our financial future is more likely to be the product of good planning rather than good luck.

Over time, there is going to be an increasing need for all of us to better plan and manage our finances. The more financial knowledge we have, the more control we have and the better the decisions we're able to make about our financial future. However, the financial planning environment is highly dynamic and individuals increasingly rely on financial planning professionals to help them navigate the complex and ever-changing world of personal finance. The financial planning profession is expecting significant growth over the next few years and a number of people will look to make a professional career out of assisting others to achieve their financial goals and objectives. This text has been designed to provide students of higher education institutions with the knowledge and concepts required to be able to enter the exciting profession of financial planning.

This edition has been extensively revised from the previous edition to reflect changes in legislation and professional regulations, as well as developments in teaching and learning design. End-of-chapter questions have been thoroughly updated, and there has been an increased focus on learning and understanding through the use of practical case studies to illustrate concepts.

Throughout this edition, a significant amount of work has been undertaken to integrate the Future of Financial Advice reforms, referred to as FOFA, into the relevant chapters. The FOFA reforms had their genesis in a string of high-profile collapses that included Storm Financial, Westpoint and Opes Prime, which in turn led to a lack of trust and confidence in the financial planning sector. FOFA has radically changed the financial planning landscape — particularly in the way in which financial planners are remunerated for their services as well as in relation to the best interest duty now imposed on financial planners.

In this edition we have also included a new chapter on self-managed superannuation funds (SMSFs). This is the fastest growing sector of the fast growing, trillion dollar plus, superannuation industry. SMSFs were once the province of a relatively few high net worth individuals; however, this is changing. One million Australians now have an SMSF account. New members are attracted to the level of investment control and opportunities that SMSFs provide. The phenomenal growth of SMSFs is just one change to the superannuation industry — many other superannuation changes are also discussed in this new edition of the text.

Many financial advisers will ultimately choose to specialise in one aspect of financial planning; however, all financial advisers need an up-to-date overview of the financial planning environment. This book provides that overview.

We are grateful to our colleagues who took the time to review the developing manuscript and offer their constructive comments. We would particularly like to thank Peter Lennox (University of South Australia), Gabrielle Parle (University of the Sunshine Coast), Fariba Ahmadi-Pirshahid (University of Wollongong) and Adrian Lee (University of Technology, Sydney) for their valuable work creating the accompanying solutions manuals, PowerPoint teaching slides and test banks/practice quizzes respectively.

We would also like to extend our thanks to the publishing team from Wiley: Terry Burkitt (Publishing Editor), Catherine Spedding (Content Editor), Kylie Challenor

(Managing Content Editor), Beth Klan (Editorial Assistant), Olivia Clarkin (Publishing Assistant), Delia Sala (Graphic Designer), Renee Bryon (Copyright and Image Researcher) and Jo Hawthorne (Senior Production Controller).

We wish you well in your studies and hope that this book simulates a lifelong interest in financial planning.

Warren McKeown
Mike Kerry
Marc Olynyk
March 2014

Acknowledgements

The author and publisher would like to thank the following copyright holders, organisations and individuals for their permission to reproduce copyright material in this book.

Images

• Shutterstock: **2**/auremar; **10**/Noam Armonn; **16**/Syaheir Azizan; **35**/Phil Date; **39**/racorn; **40**/Monkey Business Images; **48**/Iakov Filimonov; **55, 220**/Darren Baker; **70**/Chookiat K; **82**/Lana K; **83 top**/szefei; **90**/bikeriderlondon; **97**/michaeljung; **113**/Andrew Rakoczy; **134, 419, 567, 605**/Goodluz; **136**/InnervisionArt; **137**/wavebreakmedia; **163**/James Steidl; **169**/JHershPhoto; **174 (top)**/Dragon Images; **178**/Lighthunter; **201**/Vectomart; **212**/Passion Images; **221**/OLJ Studio; **232**/pkchai; **245**/Andresr; **257**/GTS Production; **258**/Algefoto; **262**/wavebreakmedia; **280**/Fabio Berti; **286**/Santhosh Kumar; **304**/Andresr; **305, 326**/max blain; **310**/kezza; **340**/hxdbzxy; **345**/Hans Kim; **348**/epstock; **354**/PeJo; **356**/Brisbane; **364**/Feng Yu; **375**/wavebreakmedia; **392**/Kzenon; **396**/JHershPhoto; **402**/JonnyDrake; **415**/Tyler Olson; **438**/Alliance; **442**/Ragma Images; **466**/Robyn Mackenzie; **467**/Oleg Golovnev; **469**/Micra; **475**/Jorg Hackemann; **483**/GeorgeMPhotography; **488, 534**/Monkey Business Images; **493**/Nic Neish; **512**/absolut; **524**/michaeljung; **531**/Franck Boston; **548**/Mark Soon; **562**/baki; **569**/Jan S; **570**/Cheryl E. Davis; **574**/zimmytws; **585**/Paul Smith/Featureflash; **596**/Petr Kopka; **614**/YanLev; **618**/StockLite; **622**/Alexander Raths; **648**/nahariyani; **651**/merzzie. • Cambridge University Press: **4**/Hazel Bateman, Geoffrey Kingston, John Piggott, *Forced Saving: Mandating Private Retirement Incomes*, Cambridge University Press, 2001. • Australian Bureau of Statistic: **7**/© Commonwealth of Australia. • Newspix: **41**/Newspix/Megan Brayley. • ASIC: **64**/Australian Securities and Investments Commission Moneysmart. • iStockphoto: © iStockphoto.com/**83 (bottom)**/KristianSeptimiusKrogh; **142**/sturti; **174 (bottom)**/eyetoeyePIX; **275**/EdStock; **606**/Courtney Keating. • Creative Commons: **93**/© Australian Taxation Office for the Commonwealth of Australia; **404**/© Australian Prudential Regulation Authority 2013. • MLC: **150**/'How much returns vary through time', © MLC, reproduced with permission; **151**/© MLC, reproduced with permission. • Reserve Bank of Australia: **181**/© Reserve Bank of Australia; **182**/© Reserve Bank of Australia, 2013, 'The Australian economy and financial markets', Chart pack, May 2013, p. 18, rba.gov.au; **183 (top)**/© Reserve Bank of Australia, 2013, 'The Australian economy and financial markets', Chart pack, May 2013, p. 20, rba.gov.au; **185 (bottom)**/© Reserve Bank of Australia, 2013, 'The Australian economy and financial markets', Chart pack, May 2013, p. 25 top right, rba.gov.au; **185 (top)**/© Reserve Bank of Australia, 2013, 'The Australian economy and financial markets', Chart pack, May 2013, p. 25 top left, rba.gov.au; **186 (bottom)**/© Reserve Bank of Australia, 2013, 'The Australian economy and financial markets', Chart pack, May 2013, p. 21 bottom right, rba.gov.au; **186 (top)**/© Reserve Bank of Australia, 2013, 'The Australian economy and financial markets', Chart pack, May 2013, p. 21 top right, rba.gov.au; **192**/© Reserve Bank of Australia, 2013, 'The Australian economy and financial markets', Chart pack, May 2013, p. 23 top left, rba.gov.au; **193, 250**/© Reserve Bank of Australia; **194**/© Reserve Bank of Australia, 2013, 'The Australian economy and financial markets', Chart pack, May 2013, p. 26 bottom left; rba.gov.au; **195**/© Reserve Bank of Australia, 2013, 'The Australian economy and financial markets', Chart pack, May 2013, p. 23 bottom left, rba.gov.au; **197**/© Reserve Bank of Australia, 2013, 'The Australian economy and financial markets', Chart pack, May 2013, p. 24 top right, rba.gov.au; **198**/© Reserve Bank of

Australia, 2013, 'The Australian economy and financial markets', Chart pack, May 2013, p. 24 top left, rba.gov.au; **241** (bottom)/© Reserve Bank of Australia, RBA bulletin, December quarter, 2012, graph 3, p. 17. • Fairfax Syndications (Photos): Fairfax Photos **224**/James Davies; **319**/AFR Picture/Gabrielle Charlotte; **580**/SMH News/Peter Rae. • Housing Industry Association: **241** (top)/© Housing Industry Association, HIA Economics Group. • Morningstar Australasia: **279, 294**/© Morningstar Australasia Pty Ltd. • Westpac: **284**/ © Westpac Banking Corporation. • ASX: **339**/'© ASX Limited ABN 98 008 624 691 (ASX) 2013. All rights reserved. This material is reproduced with the permission of ASX. This material should not be reproduced, stored in a retrieval system or transmitted in any form whether in whole or in part without the prior written permission of ASX. • Alamy Limited: **608**/© Alamy/David Moore. •

Text

ASFA: **5**/© ASFA. • Copyright Agency Limited: **10–11**/© Copyright Agency Limited 'Rush to sign up as MySuper kicks off', Andrew Main, *The Australian*; **41–2**/© Copyright Agency Limited, 'Keeping Storm's victims in mind', SMH, 19 May 2010; **242**/Copyright Agency Limited, 'ABS and Canstar analysis shows home loans doubled in 10 years', Sophie Elsworth, news.com.au; **245–6**/Copyright Agency Limited, 'Houses becoming cheaper to buy than rent', Simon Johanson, *The Age*; **280–1**/Copyright Agency Limited, 'Lessons in liquidity', *The Sydney Morning Herald*; **326–8**/Copyright Agency Limited, 'Margin loans still on the nose', Lesley Parker, *The Sydney Morning Herald*; **354–5**/Copyright Agency Limited, 'You bet your life: health insurer's cheap DNA test could prove costly', *The Sydney Morning Herald*, Nick Miller; **419**/Copyright Agency Limited, 'Bridging the gap: How women can catch up on super', Matthew Smith, *BRW*; **548**/© Copyright Agency Limited, http://www.news.com.au/money/money-matters/how-to-rev-up-your-age-pension/story-e6frfmd9-1226475507896. • Money Management: **35–6**/© Money Management. • Financial Planning Association: **44–6**/© Financial Planning Association of Australia. • Canstar Cannex: **68**/© Canstar http://www.canstar.com.au/credit-cards/compare-occasional-spender/The star ratings in this table were awarded on 26 October 2012. • ASIC: **70–1**/Australian Securities and Investments Commission Moneysmart; **492, 617, 618**/© ASIC'S MoneySmart website. • Creative Commons: **98, 101, 124**/ © Australian Taxation Office for the Commonwealth of Australia; **446**/© Commonwealth of Australia, Australian Government Actuary, 2013; **457**/© Australian Government Actuary 2013; **537**/© The Commonwealth of Australia; **540**/© Commonwealth of Australia 2012; **595**/© Commonwealth of Australia 2013. • Key Media: **112–3**/Published with permission from Your Investment Property Online and Jimmy B. Prince, author, *Tax for Australians for Dummies*; **622**/Kathleen Payne, Wealth Professional. • ASX: **160**/© ASX Limited ABN 98 008 624 691 (ASX) 2013. All rights reserved. This material is reproduced with the permission of ASX. This material should not be reproduced, stored in a retrieval system or transmitted in any form whether in whole or in part without the prior written permission of ASX. • Conexus Financial: **163–5**/© Conexus Financial, Article by Frank Gelber, Professional Planner, issue 52, April 2013.Frank Gelber, Professional Planner, April 2013: http://www.professionalplanner.com. • Fairfax Syndications (Text): **212–5**/ © Fairfax Media/Zoe Fielding. • finder.com.au: **248**/finder.com.au. Sourced from one of Australia's biggest comparison websites finder.com.au. • Reserve Bank of Australia: **264**/ © Reserve Bank of Australia, RBA 2012, 5655.0 — Managed Funds, Australia, December 2012,

RBA, Sydney, rba.gov.au. • MoneySmart: **274–5**/© MoneySmart, 'Window closing for LM First Mortgage victims', says Slater & Gordon. • Commonwealth Bank: **322**/© Commonwealth Bank of Australia. • McMullan Conway: **356**/'Flood definition becomes law', taken from http://insurancenews.com.au/local/flood-definition-becomes-law. • Rice Warner: **364**/© RiceWarner Media Release: Life Insurance Gap Reducing. • Bauer Media Group: **402**/© Bauer Media Group. • Australian Taxation Office: **450, 451, 491, 511, 524, 526**/© Australian Taxation Office for the Commonwealth of Australia. • Vanguard Investments Australia: **512**/© 2013 Vanguard Investments Australia Ltd. All rights reserved. • Department of Human Services: **539, 541, 544, 545, 552, 553, 555**/© Commonwealth of Australia. Represented by the Department of Human Services. • Forbes Inc.: **584**/© Forbes.com, 'Amy Winehouse didn't have a will after all, but did have millions', Mayoras, Danielle & Mayoras, Andy. •

Every effort has been made to trace the ownership of copyright material. Information that will enable the publisher to rectify any error or omission in subsequent editions will be welcome. In such cases, please contact the Permissions Section of John Wiley & Sons Australia, Ltd.

1 Personal financial planning

LEARNING OBJECTIVES

After studying this chapter, you should be able to:

1. describe the concept of personal financial planning
2. explain why personal financial planning has gained importance over the past few years
3. recognise the role played by financial counsellors in the financial environment
4. describe the role of the National Financial Literacy Strategy
5. define various types of risk
6. describe the general features of the economic environment
7. outline the origin of the global financial crisis and describe its impact on Australia
8. describe the evolution of the financial planning environment in Australia
9. outline the regulatory framework that applies to financial planning in Australia
10. identify lessons from history that should be understood by investors and financial planners.

CASE STUDY

Kane, aged 22, was proud of the money he had saved in the 3 years he had worked since finishing his plumbing apprenticeship. He built his savings by making regular contributions to a savings account with his bank, but was concerned that the return on his investment was a fairly modest 3.0% p.a. He also had to pay tax on the interest when he did his tax return. Kane wanted to grow his savings at a faster rate and decided to find out more about investing. He saw an advertisement on TV about investments and decided to see the financial planner at his local bank. The financial planner, Maria, discussed Kane's financial goals with him and asked him to complete a questionnaire that was designed to help Maria determine what sort of investor Kane was likely to be. Maria studied the questionnaire that Kane had completed and determined that he was a long-term investor and that he had a relatively aggressive risk tolerance profile as his main goals for saving were for a deposit on a house in seven or eight years. Maria told Kane that she needed to write a formal proposal for him, called a Statement of Advice, regarding investments and would get back to him in the next two weeks.

After Kane had read the statement of advice provided by Maria and deliberated on his options, he invested his $10 000 in savings into the Australian share market in July 2012. Kane thought the advice he received was good: he invested in a share fund that had performed reasonably well over the past 5 years despite the worst of the global financial crisis. For the first few weeks after investing his money, Kane tracked the performance of the fund and was pleased with the gains. Later in the year, however, he realised that his investment was going down in value and contacted Maria. She suggested that the slight downturn was not unusual towards the end of a year and that his investments were planned for the long term, so short-term ups and downs should not be of concern.

Still dubious about Maria's comments, Kane was nevertheless relieved to discover that by the middle of 2014 the value of his share portfolio had risen to $13 500. He had read stories about the global financial crisis (GFC) and was concerned that it was going to happen again, but was grateful for Maria's advice that his investments were focused on the long term: that he should not be too concerned about the volatility of the market in the short term, but to keep faith that the market would maintain an upward path over the long term.

Some of the issues to consider in Kane's case include:

- what qualifications his adviser has obtained in order to give financial advice
- if Kane had been assessed as a short-term investor, would it have made a difference to the advice he was given?
- lessons that could be learned from previous share market downturns and the planned term of investment.

These issues are explored throughout this chapter.

Introduction

Financial planning is often said to be a 'new' profession. This chapter provides an overview of what financial planning covers and why personal financial planning is important. Whether you want to become a financial planner/adviser or want to know more about your own finances, this chapter provides a background of basic features that should be considered by all those interested in personal finance. It also includes an outline of the work of financial counsellors and the role played by the former Financial Literacy Foundation — an initiative of the federal government to address financial literacy issues in society which operates under the auspices of the Australian Securities and Investments Commission (ASIC) and is now known as the National Financial Literacy Strategy (see http://www.financialliteracy.gov.au).

The starting point of anyone's personal financial plan is the preparation of personal financial statements (including a cash budget), followed by the identification of financial goals and the classification of those goals into relative time frames. All investors must have some understanding of risk. Kane's situation described in the opening case study reflects the experience of many people and indicates the inherent risk in investing.

Included in this chapter is an examination of personal financial planning and why it is important. The regulatory framework that encompasses personal financial planning is also outlined. The chapter provides an overview of some of the recent events that have moulded the development of financial planning and which provide valuable lessons about investment markets and financial planning. Later chapters include discussion of personal financial statements and specific types of risk that investors face.

LO 1 What is personal financial planning?

The term 'personal financial planning' implies that a person intends to achieve something in a financial sense. Some people do not have a plan or any particular goal. However, when we consider what we would like to set out to do, we often make a 'wish list' of objectives and then apply ourselves to achieving those objectives. Often it makes good sense to consider the list of objectives or goals in three time spans: short, medium and long term. There is no defined length of time for these periods, but the general principle of shorter, medium and longer time frames is a useful approach to setting personal goals.

Short-term goals are those which we intend to achieve over a time frame of about 12 months. You may have a short-term goal of saving enough money to buy a newer car or to travel overseas at the end of your year of study.

Medium-term goals are those we intend to achieve over a period of 2 to 5 years. You may have a medium-term goal of saving enough money for a deposit on a house or to accumulate a share portfolio of, say, $20 000. The level of credit card debt in Australia is cause for some concern, with some people building up a hefty amount of debt and being unable to pay for their purchases soon after placing the debt on their card. So a medium-term goal may also include a plan to retire (pay off) credit card debt by a certain time.

Long-term goals may range from items intended to be achieved in 7 or 8 years up to 40 or more years. Your long-term goals may include the purchase of a two-bedroom home which you can sell in about 10 years to buy a three- or four-bedroom home. You may not have thought much about retirement yet, and with an expectation of 40 years of work ahead of you the matter of a certain level of retirement income may be of passing interest only. The thought of living another 30 to 40 years after retirement is one which is so far off that the concept of building up funds to last for your lifetime may not have been considered at all. However, the principle of financial planning includes consideration of all time frames. To be realistic, goals should have two components — they should be *specific* or *quantifiable*, and be *referenced to a time frame*.

LO 2 Why is personal financial planning important?

Personal financial planning is about helping people achieve their financial goals. In some respects, it concerns helping people to achieve short-term goals, such as establishing a savings program with the objective of buying a newer car, funding an overseas holiday, generating a deposit for a house or building up a certain amount of wealth by, say, age 40. In other respects, as in Jordan's case, it concerns the long-term objectives of the building up of a 'nest egg' or creating sufficient capital to fund retirement. In short, personal financial planning is about setting in place some personal objectives and arranging financial means to satisfy those objectives.

Personal financial planning has its roots in the 'life-cycle' theory of consumption and saving. This economic theory considers the matter of income and expenditure over a lifetime. For a number of years, while in their infancy and youth, people depend on others to expend money on their behalf. Then, during the years of their working lives, sufficient income should be generated to meet current expenditure needs and to provide for the time when little or no income is generated after they have finished working. Figure 1.1 illustrates that the consumption pattern is relatively smooth over a person's life cycle, but that a person's lifetime income profile is quite uneven. It may be argued that a person's expenditure pattern is likely to fall somewhat in retirement as some expenses are likely to be discontinued, such as mortgage repayments and work-related expenses. However, the person's income will also fall in retirement as assets are used to meet consumption needs.

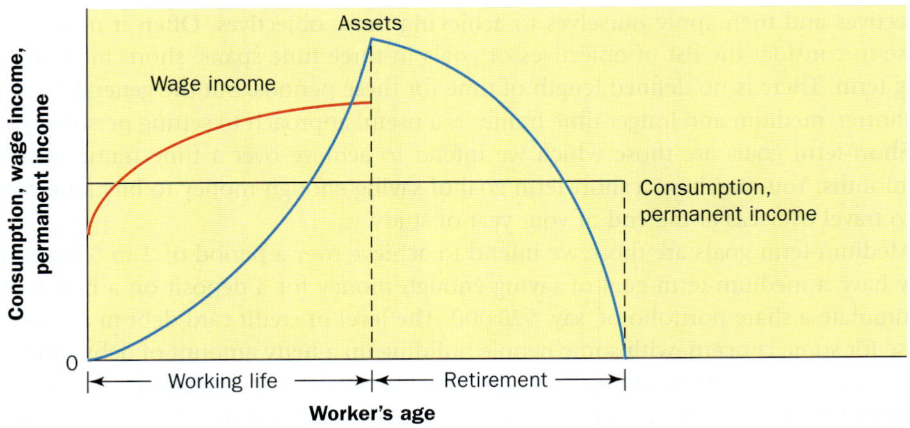

FIGURE 1.1
A theoretical representation of income and expenditure over a person's lifetime
Source: Bateman, Kingston and Piggott 2001.

However, the theory of saving sufficient funds to meet retirement expenditure is not always put into practice. Many people do not have specific savings plans and, rather than adopt a disciplined savings habit, are often persuaded through marketing campaigns to spend more than they earn. Compulsory superannuation contributions and more education about the need for savings are still required, in general, to make changes to people's savings behaviour. In the context of life-cycle theory, personal financial planning is about managing income, expenditure and savings to actively meet a person's short-term and long-term objectives.

The Association of Superannuation Funds of Australia (ASFA) regularly prepare a Retirement Standard (RS) which benchmarks the weekly and annual budget needed by Australians to fund either a modest or comfortable standard of living in the retirement years. The ASFA RS was developed to help people know how much they will need to spend each year to fund a lifestyle in their retirement. The standard includes spending needs on such things as communications, energy, food, leisure/recreation, transport, etc. A full explanation of the categories of expenditure is available on the website www.superannuation.asn.au. Table 1.1 provides an outline of two categories of lifestyle for both a single person and a couple. The table indicates the amount of expenditure needed on various items, on average, for a modest and comfortable lifestyle.

TABLE 1.1 Budgets for various households and living standards (June quarter 2013)

	Modest lifestyle — single	Modest lifestyle — couple	Comfortable lifestyle — single	Comfortable lifestyle — couple
Housing — ongoing only	$61.88	$59.40	$71.72	$83.14
Energy	$41.14	$54.64	$41.75	$56.62
Food	$74.31	$153.92	$106.15	$191.07
Clothing	$17.96	$29.15	$38.87	$58.30
Household goods and services	$26.21	$35.54	$73.73	$86.37
Health	$38.80	$74.89	$76.98	$135.87
Transport	$93.64	$96.29	$139.54	$142.20
Leisure	$71.04	$105.83	$215.27	$295.00
Communications	$9.49	$16.61	$26.08	$33.19
Total per week	$434.46	$626.27	$790.08	$1081.76
Total per year	**$22 654**	**$32 656**	**$41 197**	**$56 406**

Note: The figures in each case assume that the retiree(s) own their own home and relate to expenditure by the household. This can be greater than household income after income tax where there is a drawdown on capital over the period of retirement. Single calculations are based on female figures. All calculations are weekly, unless otherwise stated.

Source: http://www.superannuation.asn.au/resources/retirement-standard/

When a person has determined the retirement lifestyle they can be comfortable with, the next step is to determine what amount of superannuation capital they need to accumulate to fund that lifestyle. (Note that the modest lifestyle is regarded as marginally better than relying totally on the age pension.) Many Australians are not able to achieve the capital required and rely in varying degrees on the age pension (approximately 80% of retirees rely on the age pension to some extent).

The Financial Services (FSC) Council engages Rice Warner Actuaries to estimate the retirement savings gap (RSG), which is the value of the shortfall the working population will have in building an adequate or reasonable retirement benefit. On an aggregate measure the estimated gap is about $79 200 per person, indicating the reliance on the age pension for many who are currently close to retirement age. Rice Warner estimates that the average savings in superannuation for males between 55 and 59 is $86 601 and for females between 55 and 59 it is $72 308.

The accepted target benefit at retirement (which includes any entitlement to the age pension) is 62.5% of pre-retirement earnings for most of the working population. This is the chosen figure by the FSC because it is within the range nominated by an earlier Senate Select Committee on Superannuation and Financial Services within which people can maintain their standard of living in retirement. The AMP Retirement Adequacy Index suggests that the figure might be closer to 70%. However, the issue is complex as more spending appears to take place in the initial retirement years and reduces as retirees age. The AMP Retirement Adequacy Retirement Index study estimates that the average worker can now expect to retire on just under $49 000 per annum.

The focus on superannuation is an important factor behind the increasing importance of personal financial planning over the past few years. The main reasons for the growing importance of personal financial planning include:

- the increasing proportion of people in older age groups, including those who are about to retire
- the increase in longevity
- expected restrictions to reduce access to the age pension
- the introduction of compulsory superannuation
- a greater range of superannuation fund investment choices
- proposed changes to taxation on savings accounts and other government budget announcements.

In summary, an observation may be that the major reason for the increased importance of personal financial planning is the transfer of risk for providing for one's old age from the government (age pensions) and employers (defined benefit superannuation schemes) to individuals.

The increase in numbers in the older age groups

A study of demographic trends in Australia shows that we — like many countries throughout the world — are faced with an ageing population. This means that the proportions of the Australian population in the older age groups are increasing relative to the numbers in the younger age groups. Falling birth rates, falling death rates and changing rates of immigration have all contributed to a changing population structure. A significant feature of the structure of our population is the size of the group of people who were born in the period following WWII, from 1945 to about 1960. These people are often referred to as 'the baby boomers' (the name reflects a period of significant increase in the birth rate) and are now 55–70 years of age.

Australia's population will change between 2000 and 2050. Note that when Kane (the young man from the case study at the start of the chapter) is 75, it is estimated that the numbers in the 75–79 age group will exceed the numbers in the 0–19 age group. Some concern has been expressed about this trend because it is expected that Australia will have a sharp reduction in the number of people of working age compared to the number of retired people. The current ratio is about 5 workers for every person aged 65 years and over, whereas it is predicted that by 2050 this will decline to 2.7 workers for every person aged 65 and over. The expected dependence on fewer workers to supply sufficient taxation revenue to support the age pension and aged healthcare costs has led to a number of policy decisions in recent years, including compulsory superannuation, review of eligibility for the age pension, encouragement for people to defer their retirement, the introduction of the goods and services tax (GST), the government's co-contribution scheme and the changes to tax applied to interest earned on savings.

Figure 1.2 shows the age structure of the Australian population in 2014. Access the ABS website reference to see an interactive age structure where you can move the arrow at the bottom of the diagram to see the estimated changes to Australia's age structure over the years.

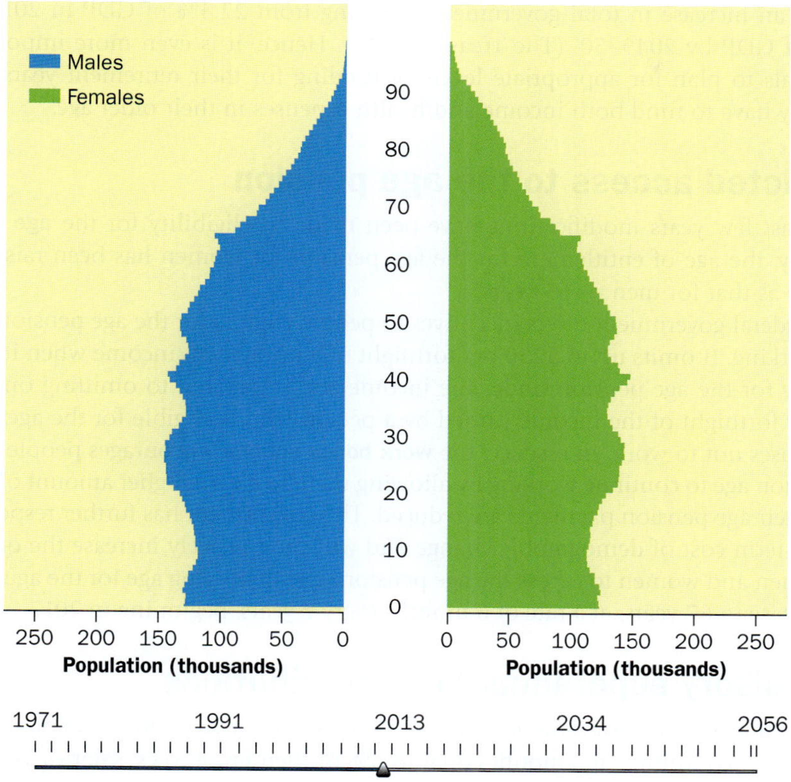

FIGURE 1.2 Age structure of the Australian population in 2014

Source: ABS 2013.

The increase in longevity

The 2010 Intergenerational Report, produced by the federal treasury, indicated that Australians' life expectancies remain among the highest in the world. Since 1901 life expectancies have increased from 55.2 to 79.2 years for men and 58.8 to 83.7 years for women. The report projects life expectancies to increase further, reaching 87.7 years for men and 90.5 years for women by 2050 (The Treasury 2010).

One reason for the increase in life expectancy is the vast improvements made in medical science, which have significantly reduced the impact of life-threatening diseases such as typhoid and diphtheria. Other reasons may include changes in dietary habits, with many people being far more aware of the impact of different foods. People are also more conscious of the damaging effects of smoking, as well as the need for regular exercise to reduce the risk of poor health. However, the present diet of many younger people and the reported incidence of childhood obesity may indicate a reversal of the trend to longer lives. To date though, despite the detrimental effects of increased levels of obesity and increases in mortality rates from lung cancer, cardiovascular disease, respiratory and other conditions associated with modern living, there is a gradual rise in the average life expectancy of males and females. The latest mortality rates indicate that, on average, a boy born in 2010 would be expected to live to 80.1 years, while a girl would be expected to live to 84.4 years (The Treasury 2010).

The increase in life expectancy has led to increasing numbers of people reaching 100 years of age. However, the increase in longevity has also been accompanied by increased costs of care for elderly people. 'Ageing and health pressures are projected to result in an increase in total government spending from 22.4% of GDP in 2015–16 to 27.1% of GDP by 2049–50' (The Treasury 2010). Hence, it is even more important for individuals to plan for appropriate levels of funding for their retirement years as they will likely have to fund both income and health expenses in their older age.

Restricted access to the age pension

age pension
a pension paid to eligible members of the community based on their age and subject to an income and assets test

work bonus scheme
a scheme that encourages people over age pension age to continue working by allowing them to earn a higher amount of income before their age pension payments are reduced

In the past few years modifications have been made to eligibility for the **age pension**. Gradually, the age of entitlement for the age pension for women has been raised to be the same as that for men — 65 years.

The federal government offers incentives to people eligible for the age pension to continue working. It omits up to $250 per fortnight of employment income when it assesses eligibility for the age pension under the income test, compared to omitting only about $150 per fortnight of the income earned by a person who is eligible for the age pension and chooses not to work. In essence, the **work bonus scheme** encourages people over the age pension age to continue working by allowing them to earn a higher amount of income before their age pension payments are reduced. The government has further responded to the long-term cost of demographic change and will progressively increase the qualifying age for men and women to access the age pension. The qualifying age for the age pension will increase to 67 years, at a rate of 6 months every 2 years, beginning in 2017.

Compulsory superannuation contributions

In 1992, the federal government introduced legislation that made it compulsory for employers to contribute an amount equal to 3% of their employees' salaries or wages to a superannuation fund. Conditions were attached to this rule:

- an employee had to earn more than $450 in a month
- no contributions were required for employees over 65 years of age
- an upper limit of income was applied to the requirement to contribute 3% as superannuation.

A graduated scale was introduced at the same time that required a steadily increasing rate of contribution by employers for the next 10 years. Since 2003 employers have been required to contribute an amount equal to 9% of an employee's remuneration to a superannuation fund.

The purpose of compulsorily requiring employers to contribute to superannuation is to spread the cost of funding retirement incomes to employers while people are actively working. However, estimates conducted by many sources indicated that contributions need to be 3–5% above 9% (i.e. 12–14% p.a.) over a period of 30–40 years of employment in order to produce a retirement income of about 70% of a person's final income from work. In the 2010 federal budget, the treasurer announced that the superannuation guarantee rate will increase progressively from 9% to 12% by 2019–20, commencing in 2013–14 with an increase to 9.25%. Thus, as the implementation of the increase in contributions is spread over the next decade it remains likely that a small age pension could still be claimed by people who are not able to accumulate sufficient funds in superannuation even after a lifetime of work. A worrying trend for the government is the need to encourage more people to contribute additional amounts to savings or superannuation as there appears to be an increase in the numbers of people relying on a part age pension. To illustrate, the proportion of the 65–69 age group receiving a full or part rate of age pension increased from 49 per cent in 1991 to 64 per cent in 2008 (ABS Social Trends, 2009).

Although self-employed people are not required to place any amount into superannuation, a tax deduction is allowed as an encouragement for people who do not have the benefit of employer superannuation contributions to make their own contributions towards their retirement income.

While the current rate of superannuation guarantee contribution may not be sufficient on its own for a person to accumulate the capital required to fund a comfortable retirement, the government encourages people to make additional contributions to their superannuation from their own resources. A salient point in financial planning for retirement is that individuals need to monitor their required income for their retirement years and to make contributions in the years prior to retirement to reach their goals. Many calculators are available on the internet to assist with this — people can nominate their required retirement income and input their contributions and superannuation balance to arrive at a recommended level of contribution to meet their target (see moneysmart.gov.au, ASIC's consumer advice website). Although people are unique and have different income needs, the documented guide is that people need between 60% and 70% of their pre-retirement income to meet their income needs in retirement.

Choice of superannuation fund

In 1997 the federal government proposed that individual members of superannuation funds should be given a range of choices for the investment of their superannuation benefits. Industry sources expressed concern about the levels of education being provided to members and the possibility of members making inappropriate investment choices. After lengthy debates, the legislation was passed to operate from 1 July 2005.

Over the period of the debate, many providers of superannuation funds reacted to the proposal by offering members a wider choice of investment within their existing superannuation fund. Many funds did not offer a choice to members or, at best, offered a range of three investment choices: a capital stable fund, a balanced fund and a growth fund. Now it is more common to find up to seven or eight different portfolio mixes and even some investment choices managed by different fund managers being made available to members of the fund. Hence, the main objective of offering a wider investment choice to members of superannuation funds was generally met before the introduction of member choice.

With the introduction of choice of superannuation fund, there was concern among regulators and industry observers that employees would be encouraged to change superannuation funds without proper advice. However, the Financial Planning Association took a strong stance by encouraging its members to ensure that high advice standards were maintained and that indiscriminate changing of funds did not occur. It was expected that many employees might decide not to transfer funds and would remain in the same fund. However, a great deal of marketing encouraged people to think about changing their fund, with new funds being promoted to the public. One expected benefit to consumers was that competition might force the underlying fees to be reduced. This has not occurred to any significant degree. Further, evidence indicates that less than 10% of those eligible to change funds actually did so at the time (Clare 2006; Fry, Heaney and

McKeown 2007). To accommodate the needs of employees who do not wish to or do not have the interest in their retirement fund, proposals have been made to provide a low-cost default fund. The 'Review into the Governance, Efficiency, Structure and Operation of Australia's Superannuation System' (commonly known as the Cooper Review), released in June 2010, recommended that a default superannuation fund — called 'MySuper' — be established. The fund is designed to have low fees, and asset allocations that are suitable to the individual employee's age and that reflect the expected term of investment (i.e. a shorter or longer time frame).

PERSONAL FINANCE BULLETIN

Rush to sign up as MySuper kicks off

The first two active elements of MySuper superannuation are now officially live, marking the start of a new superannuation system that experts hope will have some of the lowest costs in the world.

Local funds yesterday began making formal applications to the Australian Prudential Regulation Authority to register their MySuper funds, while pay offices around Australia are moving to make their compulsory superannuation payments online, rather than through the antiquated cheque system.

In 2012, APRA was given the authority to set the regulations for how MySuper would be managed, with the first MySuper funds being offered from July 1 this year. The last tranche of legislation setting the rules was passed by parliament on December 7.

Yesterday's applications were by funds seeking to be classified as registerable superannuation entities (RSTs).

Eight super funds, including CBus, lodged applications with APRA yesterday, on the first business day of the new regime, despite the fact that it will be almost six months before the funds can be formally offered to investors.

CBus chief executive David Atkin said: 'We were very keen to get in early, but we do not underestimate the amount of work that's going to be needed to achieve the new standards being set by the government'.

His industry fund, with $20 billion under management, has a relatively easy task ahead, since it will merely rebadge its main growth fund, where 90 per cent of its 700 000 members are invested, as a conforming MySuper fund. Its growth fund is a so-called default fund, where new members' money is invested unless they specifically request otherwise.

Mr Atkin said his fund had been exchanging drafts in recent months with APRA to make sure the relevant guidelines were followed.

Tom Garcia, policy manager at the Australian Institute of Superannuation Trustees, said that early applications 'will allow sufficient time for funds to have their systems in place for the January 1, 2014, deadline, when all default super contributions must flow into a MySuper product'.

The new online payment system is part of a software standard called SuperStream.

It will be brought in at the same time as MySuper as part of a move, recommended by the Cooper Inquiry into Australia's superannuation system in 2010, to make superannuation simpler and cheaper.

Before Superstream, the superannuation industry was the last place in Australia where cheques were widely used.

Under the improved financial and data transmission system, super funds will be required to publish their full portfolio holdings on their website twice a year. APRA will be able to publish data on the fees, costs and net returns of MySuper products.

Source: Andrew Main, *The Australian*, 3 January 2013.

Retirement benefits provided by many employers

Those employee groups that had the good fortune to expect retirement benefits from their employment before compulsory superannuation was introduced often were destined to receive their benefit in the form of a defined benefit or promise. In other words, employees would receive a retirement benefit based on a formula comprising the length of service and final average salary. With this type of fund, the employee was not involved in the investment decisions of the superannuation fund, as it was the employer's responsibility to place sufficient contributions into the fund to meet the expected retirement payments. In most funds, the benefit was in the form of a pension which was payable for life.

However, with the combined effect of increased longevity and the increasing numbers looking to retire in the next few years, employers were concerned about their future exposure to funding retirement benefits for an increasing number of years to an increasing number of retirees or their surviving spouses. The answer to this concern was the move to change the form of superannuation fund from a defined benefit or promise fund to a defined contribution or accumulation fund. With this type of fund, the employee receives a superannuation benefit which is the accumulation of the fund after the employer has made the compulsory, and sometimes additional, contributions to the fund. For example, BHP (before it became BHP Billiton) recognised the problem of paying pensions to members or their surviving spouses for longer than expected when the pension fund was established. In the early 1990s and through a series of seminars and information sessions, BHP offered members of the BHP Staff Superannuation Fund who were in receipt of a pension (many of them being the surviving wives of deceased employees) the opportunity to exchange the right to the lifetime pension for a lump sum.

A very important point to note is that along with this change in type of fund went a transfer of the risk of investment from the employer to the employee. With an accumulation fund, it is the member who ultimately bears the risk of the investment choice and the consequent performance of the fund. With the defined benefit fund, it is the employer who has to ensure payments are made to the member and hence carries the risk of both contributions and performance of the fund.

These changes to our socioeconomic circumstances indicate that:

- individuals must take responsibility for their own retirement
- planning must start at an early age
- the complexity of products, rules and decision making mean that people must become far better educated in regard to personal financial decisions.

LO 3 The role of the financial counsellor

financial counsellor a person who is not a financial planner, but who assists people who have difficulties with managing their money

In the process of helping people manage and plan their finances we discover that there are many people who require additional assistance. Before people may consult a financial planner some may need the assistance of a **financial counsellor**. Financial counsellors undertake casework with individuals and provide community education and community development activities. They provide a free, confidential and independent service for people experiencing financial hardship and are usually accessed via local government offices. Financial hardship can arise from any number of factors, such as family breakdown, depression, homelessness, physical and mental ill health, and financial stress.

The work of a financial counsellor involves an overall assessment of the individual's or family's financial situation, identification of options to address financial problems, and an exploration of the implications of the available options. The assistance that a financial counsellor can offer may include advice and advocacy on the implications of unpaid bills, debts and fines; assistance to work out payments with creditors; assistance with budgeting; and providing other relevant information.

Consumers live in an increasingly complex and expensive financial world and some financial practices impact adversely on low-income and marginalised consumers.

Financial counsellors assist clients across all ages with increasingly complex financial practices. The role of the financial counsellor is quite separate from that of the financial planner/adviser. Rather than advise on investing or dealing with superannuation matters, financial counsellors provide a valuable service to meet the needs of vulnerable people in the community.

reverse mortgage an arrangement to mortgage a home in order to receive payments from the fund provider in return for a percentage ownership in the home or an accumulated debt to be paid when the home is sold

Financial planners may refer some clients to a financial counsellor to assist in areas where a client may have little experience. Some of these areas include finding a home, particularly when housing is becoming more unaffordable for many; the use of credit card debt to furnish homes and to acquire the latest television sets; the difficulties of understanding mobile phone contracts and their charging practices; and the promotion of **reverse mortgages** among the elderly population.

Refer to the website for Financial Counselling Australia (FCA), the peak body representing financial counsellors (www.financialcounsellingaustralia.org.au) for more details about financial counselling. Search the media releases on the website to gain a deeper understanding of the work of the FCA.

LO 4 The National Financial Literacy Strategy

National Financial Literacy Strategy a body established by the federal government to act as a clearing house for resources to assist in the education of consumers about financial issues

The Commonwealth Government established the Financial Literacy Foundation in 2005 to provide opportunities for people to gain access to knowledge about finances and develop skills to manage their money better. The foundation, now known as the **National Financial Literacy Strategy**, works in partnership with government, industry, education bodies and community organisations to promote and advance financial literacy throughout Australia. The National Financial Literacy Strategy:

- focuses on promoting financial literacy issues to the Australian public via media campaigns
- operates a website (moneysmart.gov.au) as a reference point for information and resources
- runs education programs for schools and adult education centres
- conducts research into financial literacy matters.

The responsibility for administering the foundation has now been handed to ASIC.

The National Financial Literacy Strategy's website contains a substantial amount of advice about personal financial issues such as budgeting, reverse mortgages and savings plans. It also provides several calculators such as the 'regular savings' and 'superannuation contributions' calculators. See the website at moneysmart.gov.au.

LO 5 Understanding risk

A very important issue that must be considered in personal financial planning is the understanding of the term 'risk'. To start building an understanding of risk, consider the situation described in Illustrative Example 1.1.

ILLUSTRATIVE EXAMPLE 1.1

Oliver, aged 24, was given $50 000 from his grandmother's estate and decided to invest the money. 'I wanted to achieve a high return, so I'd have more money to use when I bought a house,' he said.

'When I found a managed share fund that had earned 20% in the last 12 months, and averaged over 15% a year over the past 3 years, I thought "Great — that's perfect!".' What Oliver didn't realise was that higher long-term returns usually go hand in hand with volatility.

In his situation, the share market represented a very risky investment choice. 'Six months later I had found a house and was ready to withdraw my money, but the value of my investment had fallen quite a lot. Of course, I didn't have time to wait for it to recover. I needed the money right away, so I had to accept a $5000 loss.'

In this example, Oliver failed to take into account the risk involved in a short-term investment.

Risk can mean several things. The Financial Planning Association of Australia (FPA) in conjunction with Macquarie Investment Management Ltd has produced a booklet entitled *The trade off: Understanding investment risk* which outlines different types of risk. The following meanings of risk have been adapted from the booklet.

- *Mismatch risk.* This is the mismatching of a person's objectives, investments and time frame. Oliver's situation is a prime example of mismatch risk. The general rule for a time frame and investments to match investment objectives is as follows.

Time frame		Investment
Short term	<1 year	Cash, e.g. cash management trusts
Medium term	>3 years	Emphasis on fixed interest with some cash and growth assets
Long term	>5 years	Emphasis on growth assets (shares and property) with some access to cash

- *Inflation risk.* This is the risk that the purchasing power of a person's money will be eroded by increases in the cost of living. For example, 50 litres of petrol for a car cost approximately $40 in 2006 but, with the increase in the cost of petrol a person needed about $75 to buy the same amount of petrol in 2013.

- *Interest-rate risk*. This risk may be considered in two ways.
  - *Reinvestment risk* — when fixed investments mature, an investor needs to consider the interest rates available at the time of reinvestment. If the interest rates have fallen significantly, the investor is faced with a lower income. This occurred in the early 1990s when investors who had invested for a 3- to 5-year period found that the reinvestment interest rate at the time of maturity had fallen from around 12% to about 6%. An investor relying on the interest of $12 000 from a fixed-term investment was then faced with an income of $6000. Similarly, investors who were able to obtain a 6% rate a few years ago are now faced with a fixed term rate of about 4% p.a.
  - *Market volatility* — fixed-interest investments usually have a set interest rate for the duration of the term. However, if you sold fixed-interest securities in an emergency and interest rates had risen since you invested, you may find that you would not receive the full value of the investment. For example, a 5-year bond worth $100 000 when interest rates are 5% would be worth approximately $96 000 if interest rates were to rise to 6%. So changes in interest rates can affect not only your reinvestment for income terms but also the capital value of your investment, unless you hold the investment until maturity.
- *Market risk*. All markets have ups and downs. Some are more volatile than others and it is important to be aware of the time frame of the investment in order to be able to ride out the bumps in the performance. Consider the graph in figure 1.3. In the short term the graph shows the effects of dramatic swings in volatility but the volatility needs to be seen in a longer term perspective, also seen in the graph. Figure 1.3 shows two sections of a graph of the Dow Jones Industrial Average over the period 2004–2013. In panel A an investor who is concerned in the short term about a portfolio of shares losing value would be very concerned as the index fell from over 12 000 in 2008 to a low of 6500 in 2009, but may have recovered some comfort when the index rose to 10 000 in 2009. Panel B shows that by holding on to the portfolio, by 2013 the index had reached a new high of nearly 15 000. This illustrates that it is best to hold on to a longer term strategy rather than to sell in the short term when panic sets in.

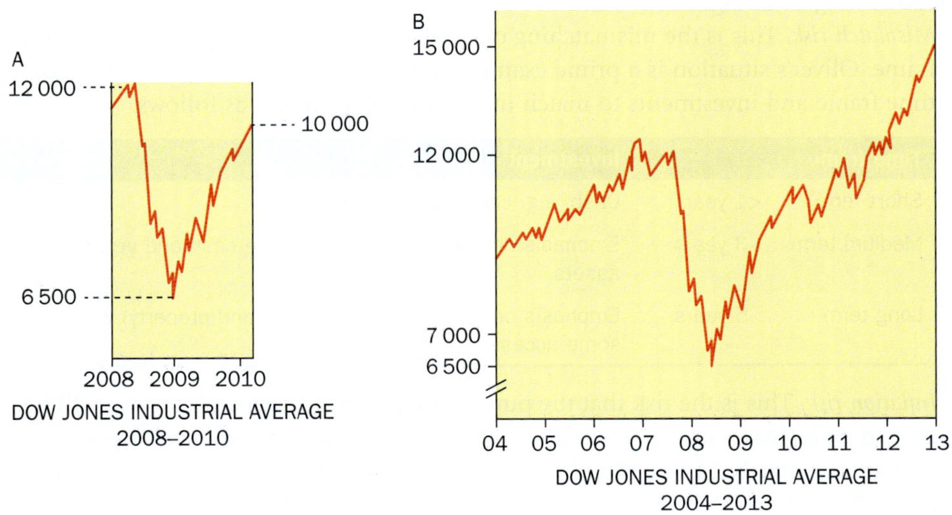

FIGURE 1.3
Don't lose hope in the short term.

- *Market timing risk.* Some people believe that they can time when to get into the market and when to get out of the market. In practice, this is very difficult to achieve and in many cases some market timers end up being worse off. History has shown that if investors missed the best single month over a 27 year period to July 2007 on the Australian Securities Exchange their $10 000 initial investment would have achieved the sum of $272 313, which is 14 per cent below the $316 332 if the funds had remained invested for the whole period. And if the investor missed the best 10 months over that period the accumulated sum would have been $102 948, which is 67 per cent less than if the funds had remained invested for the duration. The same principle applies for any period of time.
- *Risk of poor diversification.* The main benefit of diversification of investments is to reduce the overall risk of your investment portfolio. Although one market segment has a lower-than-expected return, other market segments may perform better than expected. The key to successful long-term investing with a lower level of risk is to ensure that your investment portfolio is diversified across a range of asset classes.
- *Currency risk.* This risk applies if you hold investments valued in overseas currencies. A rise in the Australian dollar relative to the currency of the country in which you hold some investments will see a fall in the value of your investments. For example, if you had invested A$10 000 in the US share market when the Australian dollar was worth US$0.90 your investment would equal US9000. When the Australian dollar rose in value to US$1.04, your investment would then be worth A$8654. Of course, if the Australian dollar falls in relation to the US dollar, then your investment would be worth more in Australian dollars.
- *Liquidity risk.* It is always important to have access to cash for emergency purposes. We can never foresee when we may need the cash, but it is very important to have either cash in the bank available at call or a credit facility that can provide cash at very short notice. Redeeming investments to meet such a need may mean paying an exit fee or selling an investment when market prices are low.
- *Credit risk.* Credit risk applies to investments such as term deposits, debentures, mortgage loans and bonds. It is the risk that the company to which you have lent money will become insolvent and will be unable to meet interest payments or repay your funds. You can guard against this to some degree by seeking information about the company's credit rating, past performance and ownership, which should indicate the quality of the organisation. The international ratings agencies Standard & Poor's (S&P) and Moody's rate various banks and managed investments. The highest rating is AAA. The agencies consider funds rated from AAA to BBB to be 'investment grade'; that is, they have the capacity to pay income and repay funds in a timely manner.
- *Legislative risk:* the risk of losing your capital or suffering reduced returns due to changes in laws and regulations. Governments may change laws, such as the carbon tax, which impact on the firms in which an investor places their money. In adapting to the changed laws lower profits may be available to be distributed as costs may have increased.
- *Gearing risk:* the risk involved in borrowing to invest. Such risks are twofold. First, there is the rate of interest to be paid by the investor which may go up and require an increased amount of repayment to the lender. Second, there is the risk of a severe falling in the value of the assets in which the funds are invested which may mean the loan or a portion of the loan may need to be repaid immediately.

PROFESSIONAL ADVICE

What advice would you give this person?

This is a letter to a financial adviser who responds to readers' queries in a daily newspaper.

Dear Financial Adviser,

I am a 20-year-old university student and have recently inherited $40 000 from the estate of my grandmother. I have decided to keep $10 000 in my bank account to spend on a number of things over the next year or so, but I wish to invest $30 000. My investment time frame is long term, as I do not need the money now. I intend to continue renting a flat with some friends when I complete my degree and start work. I may also go overseas for a year or so with my work or I may take a year off work to travel in Europe and South America. I am interested in capital growth but am not sure whether I should keep the money in a term deposit in the bank until I decide to use the funds as a deposit for a home unit, or to invest in shares. I am aware of the share market going up and down each day and would be prepared to invest some in this area. Interest rates seem to be fairly low at the moment and the share market seems to be rising despite its daily changes.

What advice do you have as to my best options for investing this money?

Yours sincerely,

A student with a money problem

QUESTIONS

1. Prepare a list of questions that you think should be asked of this student to clarify the meaning of 'my investment time frame is long term'.
2. Describe the investment option, or outline a number of investment options, that you would suggest for this student.

LO 6 Features of the economic environment

In the early 1990s, Australia had interest rates of 12%, inflation was running at 6%, unemployment was 9% and the annual growth rate was 2%. In mid 2007, Australia's interest rates were around 6%, inflation was down to 3%, unemployment was under 5% and the annual growth rate was around 3%. By 2011 Australia's interest rates, which had declined to below 3% in 2009 had risen again to 4.75%. But, in early 2013 it was again 3% p.a. after falling to 2.5% in late 2011. Inflation was 3.3% in 2011 but had fallen to 2.5% in 2013. Unemployment was 4.9% in 2011 but rose to 5.4% in early 2013. The annual growth rate of the Australian economy was 2.7% in 2011 but slightly less at 2.5% in 2013. The volatility in the economic features that occurred between 2007 and 2013 was somewhat due to the impact of the global financial crisis. It should be noted that

Australia suffered in a minor way compared to the rest of the developed world. This was a result of federal government stimulus spending and the strength of the demand from China and India for Australian minerals. Current rises in unemployment are considered to be the result of the higher Australian dollar which cheapened goods produced offshore and took away many manufacturing jobs in Australia.

We can see that the economic circumstances were quite different about 20 years ago. In the context of making financial plans, we need to be very much aware of the economic conditions existing at the time of preparing a plan and the trends which may be occurring in the economy. Over the longer time frame, we are able to see how economies have generally featured in a boom–bust business cycle, as shown in figure 1.4.

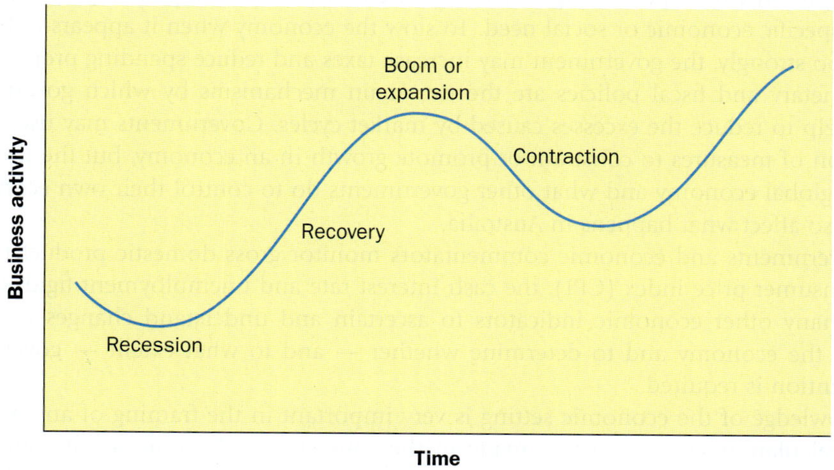

FIGURE 1.4
The business cycle

The business cycle may generally be viewed in four stages.

1. *Boom or expansion:* the phase of the business cycle when employment and economic growth are high. An increase in inflation becomes a concern.
2. *Contraction:* the phase when the economic growth rate starts to slow, sales begin to fall, and the level of unemployment starts to rise.
3. *Recession:* the phase when high unemployment is recorded and economic growth slows and may even be negative.
4. *Recovery:* the phase when unemployment begins to fall and economic growth starts to rise.

We cannot consider the Australian economy in isolation. We live in a global economy in which we rely on other countries to supply us with goods and services. Similarly, other countries rely on us for goods and services. We are able to invest in overseas markets and overseas investors can invest in the Australian markets. Decisions that we make can be affected by what goes on in other markets. Large amounts of capital can be transferred from country to country within a few seconds with no regard for the economic consequences to either country.

The federal government uses fiscal or budgetary policies to try to keep the economy from swinging wildly from highs to lows in business cycles through taxation and spending measures to inject into or withdraw money from the general community depending on the economic conditions at the time. Monetary policy, administered by the Reserve Bank of Australia (RBA), is concerned with control over interest rates and the amount of money in circulation. Monetary policy can be used to stimulate the economy by reducing interest rates or to slow the economy by increasing interest rates when needed. A reduction in interest rates tends to encourage spending and borrowing by consumers and so increases activity throughout the economy. On the other hand, an increase in interest rates tends to restrict borrowing and spending and is designed to slow the growth in the economy.

Fiscal policy is concerned with managing the economy through the use of government-controlled taxation and spending policies. To stimulate the economy, governments may reduce taxation and allow more spending power to remain in the hands of consumers. Governments may also be selective in their spending programs and allocate resources to specific targets such as the elderly or the young unemployed to meet some specific economic or social need. To slow the economy when it appears to be running too strongly, the government may increase taxes and reduce spending programs.

Monetary and fiscal policies are the two main mechanisms by which governments may help to reduce the excesses caused by market cycles. Governments may use a combination of measures to constrain or promote growth in an economy, but the influence of the global economy and what other governments do to control their own economies may also affect what happens in Australia.

Governments and economic commentators monitor gross domestic product (GDP), the consumer price index (CPI), the cash interest rate and unemployment figures along with many other economic indicators to ascertain and understand changes occurring within the economy and to determine whether — and to what extent — government intervention is required.

Knowledge of the economic setting is very important in the framing of any personal financial plan as any decision is made in the context of a dynamic set of conditions; that is, the conditions will change and any financial plan will need to allow for changes. For example, an investor wants to invest in fixed-interest securities for a 5-year period. If interest rates are relatively low and have been for some time, and economic observers note that there are pressures for interest rate rises, it may be advisable to invest for shorter time periods — say, 3, 6 or 12 months at the most — to take advantage of the rising interest rates that are expected at those maturity dates. In that way, the investor is not committed for the longer term of 5 years at low interest rates when higher rates of interest for the same degree of risk could be obtained at time intervals somewhere during the investor's time frame.

A brief look back at the events of recent years shows the changing economic, financial and social environment that Australians have had to work their way through. Investors must be aware of the need to be flexible and be able to adapt and make changes in response to changing economic circumstances. To develop an appreciation of this need to be aware of changing circumstances it is worth considering some of our recent investment market history. Following are brief descriptions of some major events that represent lessons from which we can learn.

- *1987 share market crash*. The value of the Australian share market fell by a dramatic 50% in the space of a few days. In the months leading up to 20 October 1987, funds managers placed advertisements which boasted annualised returns of 70% to lure investors to subscribe and financial planners to promote their products. Unaware of the possibility of a sharp correction in the share market, investors placed money into equities funds in the months leading up to October and left their money there after the crash ended. Some lost all of their money; for others it took a long time for their investments to return to their original capital value. Some funds managers went out of business and many investors had what remained of their investment portfolios taken over by older, established funds managers who were able to weather the storm with less fallout.

- *1990 property trust freeze.* Unlisted property trust investors faced a rude shock in the early 1990s when funds managers were unable to redeem investments without selling the properties held by the trusts. Large inflows of cash had been placed into unlisted property trusts in the late 1980s as investment yields were high at 8%. Many retirees had invested a great deal of their funds into the income units of the trusts in the belief that property investments were a reliable form of investment which paid a consistent rate of income. Unfortunately, the valuations of many of the properties were tested severely when some properties were placed on the market and it was discovered that commercial property, in particular, had been overvalued by up to 30 or 40%. Investors tried to redeem their investments but the only way managers could buy back the units was to sell the properties to raise the amount of cash required. To avoid releasing so much property into a falling market and exacerbating the fall in the property market price, the managers took action to freeze the units for a period of 12 months or more to avoid a fire sale of property stock.
- *1991 Pyramid Building Society closure.* Victorian investors seeking high interest rates had a very rewarding period with interest rates on their deposits in the Pyramid Building Society of 15–16% p.a. However, rumours started to circulate that the building society was not safe and that investors should get their money out. To avoid a panic rush on the building society and the consequent withdrawal of deposits from other financial institutions, the Victorian Government announced that the Pyramid Building Society was safe and there was no need to withdraw funds. In the next few weeks, however, the building society closed its doors, leaving deposit holders in a state of shock. The Victorian Government was held accountable to ensure that investors who held deposit accounts would receive their money back over an extended period of time. It was soon revealed that the building society had been lending money to property developers at rates of 20–21% but the developments began to fail and the developers were not able to pay either the interest or the capital they had borrowed. Of course, the capital had been sunk into land purchases and development, and the current market prices would not realise the capital injected into the projects so mortgagees' sales would have been fruitless.
- *1992 Japanese share market crash.* Investors in overseas share markets received another setback with the Japanese share market crash. Japan saw little of the 1987 crash which affected much of the world's share markets but suffered falls in asset values of some 40% or more 5 years later. Recovery of the share market in Japan has taken a much longer period than recovery from crashes in other parts of the world.
- *1994 bond market crash.* Concerned about the outbreak of inflation, the United States Government raised interest rates on US government bonds in February 1994. Immediately, the flow-on effect filtered through to Australia causing interest rates to rise sharply. The immediate impact was to cause a fall in the value of government bonds and fixed-interest securities. Such investments comprised large proportions of the portfolio of investment products known as capital stable or capital secure.

The more conservative investors who had invested in such products in the belief they were safe from falls in capital values were extremely upset. Many panicked and withdrew their funds, realising capital losses on their investment. The sad fact is that if they had retained their investments they would have found that the capital was restored to their investments within a 12-month period, as interest rates stabilised and began to fall again. Many financial planners also learned by bitter experience that capital values of bonds can go down as well as up. It was estimated that such a capital loss on these products may be a 1-in-25-year event but, nevertheless, it proved a learning experience for many of the new breed of financial planners and their clients.

- *1997 Asian crisis*. In 1997 the world currency markets were put to the test with the value of the currencies of many Asian countries being severely reduced. The fall in currency values put strains on the share markets in the region and called on central banks and governments to take positive action to restore value to their economies. In the early 1990s investors in Australia were advised to look to the developing countries of South-East Asia for investment. Spectacular returns were recorded for 5–6 years leading up to 1997 but then there was a dramatic fall. Investors who withdrew their funds to salvage some capital from their investments may have been wise to hold on as by 1999, with currency improvements and banking reconstruction under way, a number of the South-East Asian funds again showed strong returns. This was a sad lesson for those who went into the market on the strength of the immediate past performance.
- *2000–01 dot.com crash*. In mid April 2000, share markets around the world suffered sharp falls. Even though there had been some volatility in the markets prior to this date, the severity of the falls led to the comment that the 'technology bubble had finally burst'. For a number of years the Nasdaq, an index measuring technology shares in the United States, had been reaching new heights with price–earnings multiples between 60 and 100. However, in 2000, technology shares in the United States, in particular, were severely affected, with many shares suffering record-breaking losses of 50–60% from the highs of a few months earlier. Similar falls were recorded in technology shares around the world. Even solid blue-chip shares fell in price as investors retreated from the share markets to assess their situation in light of possible interest-rate rises and fears of inflation. In one day, the Nasdaq fell 9.67% and the Dow Jones Industrial Average fell 5.66%. In Australia, the All-Ordinaries fell 5.7%, closely approximating the fall in the US market. Since the record highs a month earlier, the Nasdaq had recorded a total fall of 34.2%. Many people who had borrowed money to buy speculative technology shares learned the harsh lesson that, in reality, markets can reverse suddenly and huge losses can be sustained as well as gains made.
- *2001 World Trade Center disaster*. The immediate effect of the September 11 terrorist strikes on the World Trade Center and the Pentagon was the closure of the US stock market for two days. This was done in an effort to avoid the dramatic sell-off of US shares in the aftermath of the attack. Stock markets around the world lost heavily in the following days.
- *2001–02 corporate collapses*. The collapse of major corporations such as WorldCom and Enron in the United States, and other companies such as HIH and One.Tel in Australia, focused attention on the role of auditors in verifying financial statements

on which the public could rely, and on the disclosures made to the public by company directors and executives.

- *2002 falls in world market shares.* In the United States in July 2002, Wall Street's S&P 500 was 45% below its March 2000 peak and 27% down for the year. London's FTSE 100 was 42.8% below its late-1999 high, including a 15.4% fall in July. The Australian market was 14.5% below its March 2002 high. The dramatic fall in share prices was precipitated by revelations of false accounting practices which had overstated profits and profit projections.
- *2004 share markets rebound.* Share markets in the United States and in Australia reached record highs towards the close of the year with consumer sentiment and other signs indicating a return to positive returns for shareholders.
- *2006 collapse of Westpoint Corporation.* An estimated 3000 investors lost money in a failed property developer which had developments in all capital cities in Australia. This was the first of at least another three property developers that were forced into administration, leaving investors with lost funds.
- *2006 housing affordability crisis.* Rising property prices in capital cities led to calls for governments to tackle the housing affordability crisis. Reports indicated that housing prices had risen by some 30% over the course of 2–3 years and this, coupled with slightly rising interest rates, caused a rise in mortgagee sales.
- *2007– 2013 crisis in the US subprime mortgage fund industry and the global financial crisis.* Share markets around the world fell by an average of 15% over a 2-week period as markets weighed up the effects of the **subprime mortgage fund** crisis in the United States. Action by the US president which provided support for low-income people with an inability to service their repayments helped the liquidity crisis to dissipate marginally. The US Federal Reserve and the RBA released funding into their respective economies to ensure markets returned to normal as soon as possible and mitigated the immediate concerns of the markets. However, the effects of the collapse of the US subprime mortgage market spread rapidly across the world causing share markets to fall by 50% and housing prices to fall in some parts of the world by 30–40%. This became known as the global financial crisis or GFC.

subprime mortgage fund
a fund that holds mortgage assets that are of low quality; that is, the mortgages have been given to people who are in danger of not being able to make repayments on their mortgage

- *2010 – (ongoing) European debt crisis.* In May 2010, the European Union was concerned about government debts in Greece, Portugal, Ireland, Belgium and Spain as the effects of the GFC became pronounced across European countries. In 2010 Greece (April) and Ireland (November) and in 2011 Portugal received bail-out packages by the larger European countries (Germany and France in particular). In return for such guarantees, the bailed-out countries were required to take measures to cut back on government debt and spending. As a flow-on effect, the concern over the crisis caused falls in share markets around the world. In early 2013, the worst of the situation seemed to pass as the European Central Bank and European governments put measures in place to stabilise their economies. However, just when the doom seemed to be over, another European country went into crisis mode. Cyprus emerged as having severe liquidity difficulties. Restrictions were imposed on access to bank accounts and a levy on deposits over 100 000 euros was proposed. The European Commission, the European Central Bank and the International Monetary Fund agreed to a 10 million euro deal with Cyprus to ease the crisis. As part of the solution, Cyprus's second largest bank was closed, with its assets transferred to the Bank of Cyprus.

LO 7 The global financial crisis and its impact on Australia

Anyone studying personal finance issues should have a basic understanding of the financial crisis that impacted on most countries throughout the world in 2007 and beyond. Students should be alert to the origins of the crisis in order to recognise how the genesis of a financial crisis can build up slowly and how it may take some years for the crisis to take full effect. To understand the credit crisis in the United States and its effects on the financial statements of banks, institutions and investors in mortgage-backed securities around the world — in what ultimately became the 'global financial crisis' or 'GFC' — it is important to understand the origins of the housing boom in the United States. To help build this understanding, a hypothetical case of Mr and Mrs Smith is used in the following step-by-step explanation.

Mr and Mrs Smith wanted to buy a house, and so they applied for a mortgage. They had low-paying jobs and no deposit. The bank would not lend to them so they went to a mortgage broker.

The mortgage broker arranged for a loan with no deposit and for a 'honeymoon' (low) rate of interest for 5 years. The broker justified the loan on the basis that 'housing prices always go up' and they could refinance the loan in a couple of years when the value of the house had risen. The mortgage broker duly received a commission for the 'sale'.

Five years later the honeymoon period was over and Mr and Mrs Smith received a letter requesting an increase in their loan repayments which was three times their original repayment. They struggled to pay the amount and also Mrs Smith lost her job so their income was below the amount of the repayment. They decided to sell their house.

However, the market experienced an increase in the number of properties available for sale and the prices were below what Mr and Mrs Smith paid for the house. So they decided to give the keys to the house back to the lender and walk away as they could not afford the repayments.

Meanwhile, the finance lenders decided that there were some risks in lending so much to so many people with no deposit and low income and decided to package a number of the loans together and sell the packages of loans to investment banks who could then 'on-sell' them to institutions and other investors. They argued that because some potentially bad loans could be mixed with good loans, the concept of diversification would 'hide' any loans that could not be paid and so the package overall could be considered to be 'low risk'. Recall that the packaged loans were able to offer a higher return because the 'honeymoon' low interest rates passed in the first 5 years and then the rate of interest increased substantially. Hence, the attractiveness of a 'higher return, lower risk' investment opportunity to many investors was soon to be undone!

The investment banks further divided the loans into categories of low risk, medium risk and high risk and were able to obtain favourable ratings from ratings agencies on the level of their security and bond insurance from insurance companies. Ratings agencies based their assessment of risk on the probability that most mortgages would be repaid and if a small number of mortgagees defaulted the loss could be spread over the many mortgagees that would continue to pay their debt. Up until that time, a severe shock in the home property sector had not been encountered for many, many years and it was considered to be a very unlikely event that so many mortgagees would renege on their obligations at the same time.

Thus, armed with the ratings agencies' approval and bond insurance, and with the backing of mortgage loans on houses, investment banks were able to sell packages of mortgage-backed securities, now called collateralised debt obligations (CDOs), with the promise of high returns (following the 'honeymoon' period) and low risk (based on home mortgages) to willing investors across the world.

However, when people like Mr and Mrs Smith could not afford the repayments on their loans, investors became worried about the interest payments that they were no longer receiving.

When these investors realised that the substance behind the CDOs was non-existent (i.e. no repayments were being made) and the bond insurance was totally inadequate, banks and lending institutions were forced to shut down. The effects of such a withdrawal of credit precipitated a global financial crisis, the scale of which had not been seen before.

While Australia fared better than most other economies, it was not entirely immune to the effects of the GFC. A number of institutions — local councils, superannuation funds and other investment institutions — invested in CDOs offered by the American investment institutions. Hence, such investments lost value. The most severe impact was felt when the Australian banks, which could not obtain funds from overseas banks to lend to businesses in Australia, had to stop lending. This action prompted many people to want to get their funds out of the banks in case the banks closed their doors. It also caused businesses to close because they could not get finance from their bank to carry on normal business practices. As a consequence, the federal government acted swiftly in a number of ways to counteract the effects of the GFC.

- It promised that deposits in banks would be guaranteed by the government.
- It put in place a number of projects to keep businesses going such as building projects in schools, the home insulation scheme, and an increase in first home buyers grants.
- It offered a $900 cash bonus to taxpayers in order to encourage spending in the community.

As a result of these measures, Australia survived the GFC far better than most other developed economies. It recovered far sooner and with far less long-term impact overall.

LO 8 The evolution of the financial planning environment

It is useful to reflect on historical developments as it helps us understand aspects of the present. Table 1.2 (overleaf) presents a summary of some of the major changes that have occurred in the financial planning industry since 1980.

Since the mid 1980s, numerous other changes to tax, social security and superannuation laws and various product developments have resulted in people seeking financial planning advice to better their financial situation. They also led to the continued development of the financial planning industry to the extent that financial planning may now be referred to as a profession. This involved the development of a wider range of skills, education and knowledge for financial planners. ASIC has raised the education standards of financial advisers by requiring them to meet minimum competency standards under regulatory guide RG 146 *Licensing: Training of financial product advisers* and undertake ongoing professional development.

TABLE 1.2 Evolution of the financial planning environment

Decade	Selected events in the development of financial planning as a new occupation
1980s	▪ 1983: Introduction of 'rollover' superannuation funds led to an expansion of superannuation products ▪ 1985: Introduction of capital gains tax led to planning to minimise effect of the tax ▪ 1986: Introduction of fringe benefits tax led to salary packaging ▪ 1987: Creation of imputation credits on company dividends
1990s	▪ 1992–93: Introduction of compulsory superannuation contributions, gradually rising from 3% to 9% ▪ 1997: Wallis Report recommended many changes to Australia's regulatory system and the operations of the range of financial services offered by institutions such as banks, insurance companies, managed funds, sharebrokers, superannuation funds and friendly societies that operated in the economy
2000s	▪ 2001: Financial Services Reform Act 2001 led to many changes in the way financial planning was carried out ▪ 2006–07: 'Simpler Super' proposals introduced by the federal government led to significant changes in superannuation rules ▪ 2007: Changes to the assets and income tests for age pensions ▪ 2008–2010: Three commissions by the federal government: the Ripoll Inquiry into corporate collapses and financial services; the Henry Tax Review to report on new taxation initiatives; and the Cooper Review into the superannuation industry
2010s	▪ 2011: Future of Financial Advice (FOFA) proposed a range of changes to the way financial planners are remunerated and how financial planners were to operate their business ▪ 2011: MySuper instituted by the federal government to provide a low cost alternative superannuation fund for investors ▪ RG 175 revision put into operation the changes required by FOFA

LO 9

The regulatory framework that applies to financial planning

As with any other profession, financial planners are subject to a wide range of regulations and controls. The principal legal regulations and controls that govern the financial planning profession are listed in table 1.3.

TABLE 1.3 Legal regulations and controls regulating the financial planning industry

Act	Administering body
Corporations Act 2001	Australian Securities and Investments Commission (ASIC)
Financial Services Reform Act 2001 (FSRA)	ASIC (incorporated into the *Corporations Act 2001*)
Insurance Contracts Act 1984	ASIC, the common law and the court system
Superannuation Industry (Supervision) Act 1993	The Act and its regulations and ancillary legislation are administered by the Australian Prudential Regulation Authority (APRA); other parts administered by ASIC
Superannuation (Resolution of Complaints) Act 1993	ASIC
Life Insurance Act 1995	Parts are administered by both APRA and ASIC
Australian Securities and Investments Commission Act 2001	ASIC
Future of Financial Advice 2011	ASIC (incorporated into the *Corporations Act 2001*)

Regulatory structure and influences

The recommendations of the 1997 Wallis Inquiry into the financial services industry led to some significant changes in the legislation and regulatory authority covering financial services activity in Australia. The thrust of the changes was to bring a range of financial services which were previously covered by different legislation under the one Act of Parliament. These changes were incorporated into the *Corporations Act 2001* and the *Financial Services Reform Act 2001*. These two Acts are explained in more detail in the next two sections.

Corporations Act 2001

The Corporations Act contains provisions that are in force to govern the financial planning industry. The main area of the Corporations Act affecting financial planners is the provision of financial products or financial advice to the public.

Licensing regime in the financial products and financial services advice industry

The Corporations Act states that financial products dealers and financial products advisers are required to be licensed (refer to Part 7.6 Division 5 of the Corporations Act).

According to ASIC's RG 36 *Licensing: Financial product advice and dealing* a person could provide securities advice in a number of capacities. These include:

- as a person conducting a financial product dealing or a financial product advice business
- as a representative of a financial product dealer or a financial product adviser
- as a person with a limited exclusion for certain types of activities, for example solicitors and accountants in public practice giving merely incidental advice.

(*Note:* ASIC Policy Statements (PS) were renamed Regulatory Guides (RG) from July 2007 and are updated from time to time.)

Authorised representatives

A licensee may appoint an authorised representative who acts and transacts on behalf of the licensee. Under s. 916A of the Act a natural person, a body corporate or a partnership may be an authorised representative. In the event that a body corporate is a representative, its employees may need to be appointed as authorised representatives of the licensee (refer to s. 916B).

Principals must keep a register of their authorised representatives. 'Principal' means 'licensee' under the Corporations Act, and these two terms are used interchangeably. A 'licensee' is a holder of an Australian Financial Services Licence (AFSL) under the Act.

Financial services business

A person will generally need to hold an AFSL if he or she carries on a financial services business other than as a representative of a licensee.

A person who provides financial services as a representative of a licensee will generally need to be authorised under the Corporations Act (unless the representative is an employee or director of the licensee or related body corporate).

Licensee's obligation

A licensee must monitor and supervise the activities of representatives to ensure they are complying with the law (refer to s. 912A(1)(ca)). Licensees must also ensure that their representatives are adequately trained and are competent to provide financial services (refer to s. 912A(1)(f)).

In RG 104 *Meeting general obligations*, RG 104.11 and RG 104.1 refer to the licensees' obligations under the Act. These obligations are intended to result in:

- consumer confidence in using financial services
- licensees providing financial services in a fair, honest and professional way.

The 'know your client' obligation

Licensees and their representatives who are providing personal financial advice to a retail client must generally:

- make reasonable inquiries into the personal circumstances of the client and have reasonable basis for the advice (s. 945A)
- warn the client if the advice is based on incomplete or inaccurate information (s. 945B)
- give the client a statement of advice (SOA) (s. 946A).

Under FOFA s. 961B was incorporated in the Act which places an obligation on financial advisers to act in the client's best interests. The 'best interests' rule was included to ensure that financial advisers did not just know the client and know the product but also were to dissociate themselves from any influence that the sale of a product might impose on their recommendations. The focus of the provision is for a financial adviser to provide advice that is likely to leave the client in a better position. RG 175.235 provides six examples of what a reasonable advice provider would believe is likely to leave the client in a better position if the client follows the advice.

RG 175 *Licensing: Financial product advisers — conduct and disclosure* provides specific guidance for advisers with regard to items to address when considering a client's best interest and when recommending a particular investment product. RG 175.291 states:

> Where advice relates to financial product(s) *with an investment component*, we consider that the 'relevant personal circumstances' of the client will normally include the client's:
> (a) need for regular income (e.g. retirement income);
> (b) need for capital growth;
> (c) desire to minimise fees and costs;
> (d) tolerance of the risk of capital loss, especially where this is a significant possibility if the advice is followed;
> (e) tolerance of the risk that the advice (if followed) will not produce the expected benefits;
> (f) existing investment portfolio;
> (g) need to be able to readily cash-in the investment;
> (h) capacity to service any loan provided for a financial product; and
> (i) tax position, social security entitlements, employment security and expected retirement age.

The section also states that this is not an exhaustive list as the client's circumstances may include any other matter that would reasonably be considered to be relevant to the advice and that the client considers is important. The items listed provide a checklist for advisers to ensure that they have addressed a wide range of features that may impact on the selection of investment products for the unique circumstances of that client.

In addition, in RG 168 *Disclosure: Product Disclosure Statements (and other disclosure obligations)*, RG 168.79 and 168.80 require advisers to disclose fees and charges in a clear, concise and effective manner. Where investment-based products are concerned, advisers must disclose investment returns and how those returns are calculated.

What is a financial product?

The term 'financial product' is defined in general terms in s. 763A of the Corporations Act. Each limb of the general definition is then further examined in ss. 763B to 763D. Section 764A provides a list of things which are financial products and s. 765A provides a list of specific things that are not financial products.

Items which are regarded as financial products include:

- a security (e.g. a share in a body corporate or a debenture of a body corporate)
- an interest in a registered scheme
- a derivative
- a contract of insurance
- a superannuation interest
- a deposit-taking facility
- a debenture, stock or bond issued by a government
- foreign exchange contracts.

Some items are specifically excluded from the definition of a financial product. Examples are health insurance, funeral bonds and reinsurance. This list of exclusions is extended to include exempt public sector superannuation schemes within the meaning of the *Superannuation Industry (Supervision) Act 1993*.

People deal in a financial product when they:

- make a financial investment (e.g. superannuation, securities, managed funds, bank deposits)
- manage a financial risk (e.g. insurance, derivatives, hedging)
- make non-cash payments (e.g. direct debit facilities, travellers cheques).

What is a financial service?

People provide a financial service if they:

- give advice in relation to financial products
- deal in a financial product
- make a market in a financial product
- operate a registered scheme
- provide custodial or depositor service.

A financial service is a statement of opinion, a recommendation, or a report on either of these that is intended to influence a person in making decisions relating to a particular financial product or class of products, or could reasonably be regarded as being intended to have such an influence.

An AFSL is not required by those people offering legal advice, or by tax agents and the media. It is not required for insurance quotes, for information about a product or for the provision of exempt documents (including financial services guides and personal disclosure statements).

Retail and wholesale clients

Chapter 7 of the Corporations Act provides a clear distinction between retail and wholesale clients. Generally, consumer protection applies to retail clients, as it is recognised that wholesale clients do not require the same level of protection, being better informed and better able to assess the risks involved in financial transactions. The definition of 'retail client' is provided in ss. 761G(5), 761G(6) and 761G(7). The Corporations Act s. 761G(7)(c) indicates that exceptions to retail investors are people with net assets of at least $2.5 million or a gross income of $250 000 per year for the last 2 financial years, or the value of the product is greater than $500 000. Note that these tests are subject to current review.

Professional investors are always considered wholesale clients. They include corporate superannuation entities, licensees and APRA-regulated bodies.

Financial services guide

A financial services guide (FSG) is a document that must be given to a retail client in relation to the provision of financial services, in accordance with Division 2 of Part 7.7 of the Corporations Act (also refer to s. 941A). A FSG is required to contain information so that consumers can make an informed decision about whether to acquire financial services. The information included in a FSG must be worded and presented in a clear, concise and effective manner (refer to ss. 942B(6A) and 942C(6A) of the Act).

A FSG includes information such as:

- who will provide the services
- the kind of financial services offered
- who the service provider is acting for when providing the financial services
- the means by which the service provider is remunerated for the services being offered to the retail client
- details of commissions
- details of any associations or relationships which might be expected to influence a service provider in providing the service.

Regulations may provide further detail about what information a FSG is required to contain (refer to ss. 942B(4), 942B(7), 942C(4), 942C(7) and 949B).

Generally, a FSG must be given to the client before providing the financial service (refer to s. 941D(1)). However, if the 'time critical' criteria are met, then the service provider may give certain information verbally before providing the service without giving the full FSG (see s. 941D(2) and (3)). A full FSG must be provided within 5 days after the client has been given the verbal statement or sooner if practicable (refer to s. 941D(4)).

Financial Services Reform Act 2001

The financial services reform legislation included the *Financial Services Reform Act 2001* (FSRA), the *Financial Services Reform (Consequential Provisions) Act 2001*, and Regulations. The FSRA (previously known as CLERP 6) represented the most significant corporate law reform experienced by the financial services sector in Australia. The legislation was supplemented by ASIC policy and guidance as to how it proposed to administer the law. The Act affected the general insurance, life insurance, superannuation and deposit-taking industries. It also covered investment advisers, dealers, responsible entities and market makers. The FSRA was incorporated as a new Chapter 7 in the Corporations Act.

Among its reforms the FSRA provided a single regulatory regime for financial services and financial products, financial markets and clearing and settlement facilities. Major aspects of the FSRA stem from the Wallis inquiry of 1996–97, which recommended the establishment of three agencies based on their individual functions. These are the RBA and the twin peaks regulatory model realised in the formation of ASIC and the Australian Prudential Regulation Authority (APRA). APRA has responsibility for financial safety and prudential regulation generally, and ASIC is responsible for market integrity, consumer protection and corporations.

The establishment of ASIC

The establishment of ASIC in 1998 combined the roles of the old Australian Securities Commission (ASC) and the Insurance and Superannuation Commission (ISC). ASIC aims to maintain public confidence by improving sales and disclosure practices in the financial advisory industry. It is committed to raising standards of financial services and products offered to Australian investors through policy, surveillance, industry campaigns and targeted enforcement. As indicated earlier, ASIC administers the following legislation:

- *Corporations Act 2001* (including the Corporations Regulations)
- *Australian Securities and Investments Commission Act 2001* (ASIC Act)
- *Insurance Contracts Act 1984*
- *Superannuation (Resolution of Complaints) Act 1993*.

The objectives of the Corporations Act

A key objective of the Corporations Act is to promote confident and informed decision making by consumers of financial products and services. It also promotes fairness, honesty and professionalism by those who provide financial services, and creates a fair, orderly and transparent market for financial products. The Corporations Act also aims to reduce systematic risk and provide fair and effective services by clearing and settlement facilities.

The Corporations Act adopted many of the Wallis report's recommendations in areas that include a single licensing regime for financial products advice, sales and dealings, and a single set of requirements for financial sales and advice. The latter includes minimum standards of competency and ethical behaviour, requirements for the disclosure of fees and advisers' capacity, rules on handling client property and money, and financial resources or insurance available in cases of fraud or incompetence. The Corporations Act also incorporated a uniform financial product disclosure system that brings consistency and comparability to all financial products, and a single authorisation procedure for financial exchanges, clearing and settlement facilities.

Types of licensing regimes under the Corporations Act

Three different licences can be issued: the Australian Markets Licence, the Australian Clearing And Settlement Facility Licence, and the Australian Financial Services Licence (AFSL).

The Corporations Act imposes general obligations on all licensees to:

- act efficiently, honestly and fairly
- comply with licence conditions
- comply with financial services laws
- ensure representatives comply with financial services laws
- have adequate financial, human and IT resources unless they are APRA-regulated licensees
- maintain competency to provide the services
- ensure representatives are adequately trained
- have a complying dispute resolution system in place where services are to retail clients
- have adequate risk management systems unless they are APRA-regulated
- have satisfactory compensation arrangements.

Who requires an AFSL?

An AFSL is required by an entity or its representative which engages in one or more of:

- provision of financial products advice
- dealing in financial products
- making a market in financial products

- operating a registered managed investments scheme
- providing custodial or depository services.

Applicants for AFSLs should have:

- the capacity to discharge obligations efficiently, honestly and fairly
- the capacity to demonstrate ongoing compliance, appropriate financial resources and internal controls
- the relevant competence, skills and experience
- adequate systems in place for training/supervision of representatives.

The Corporations Act requires people who provide financial services to be licensed. It also requires all others who provide such advice or who deal in financial products to be the representatives of a licensee and operate under his or her licence. This applies to advisers who provide such financial services to retail and wholesale clients. The AFSL also applies to corporate superannuation funds. It is not required for a managed investment scheme that provides only a custodial holding assets service to the exclusion of other financial services. Reinsurance is specifically exempt from the requirement to have an AFSL.

Regulatory guidance provided by ASIC

ASIC's regulatory guides provide ASIC's view of how it will interpret the legislation and provide more assistance to the industry in helping licensees and advisers to comply with the law. Some of the most important regulatory guides related to financial planning are:

- RG 104 *Licensing: Meeting general obligations*
- RG 105 *Licensing: Organisational competence*
- RG 146 *Licensing: Training of financial product advisers*
- RG 165 *Licensing: Internal and external dispute resolution*
- RG 166 *Licensing: Financial requirements*
- RG 167 *Licensing: Discretionary powers*
- RG 168 *Disclosure: Product Disclosure Statements (and other disclosure obligations)*
- RG 169 *Disclosure: Discretionary powers*
- RG 175 *Licensing: Financial product advisers — conduct and disclosure*
- RG 179 *Managed discretionary account services*
- RG 181 *Licensing: Managing conflicts of interest*
- RG 182 *Dollar disclosure*
- RG 183 *Approval of financial services sector codes of conduct*
- RG 184 *Superannuation: Delivery of product disclosure for investment strategies*
- RG 200 *Advice to super fund members*
- RG 229 *Superannuation forecasts*
- RG 246 *Conflicted remuneration.*

Training under the Corporations Act

According to RG 146, licensees must adequately train their representatives in relation to the financial services they offer and which are covered by their licence. All licensees must adhere to ASIC training standards specified in RG 146. All advisers must be Tier One qualified (i.e. have attained at least diploma level under the Australian Qualifications Framework (AQF)). A lower level of training is also recognised by ASIC for other staff advising in:

- general insurance products, other than sickness and accident insurance
- basic banking products, such as deposit accounts and some term deposits
- non-cash payment facilities, such as direct debit facilities or cheque accounts.

These people require Tier Two qualification, which is equivalent to a certificate level of education under the AQF.

Organisational capacity requirements under the Corporations Act

RG 104 requires licensees to:

- monitor and supervise representatives
- have sufficient financial, technological and human resources
- hold relevant competence, skills and expertise
- have competent and trained representatives (RG 146)
- have ASIC-approved internal/external dispute resolution procedures as stipulated under s. 912A(1)(g) of the Corporations Act and enforced in RG 165
- have adequate risk management systems
- have adequate compliance measures.

RG 105 requires licensees to display relevant competence, skills and expertise to hold a licence.

The Corporations Act disclosure requirements

There are three disclosure documents — the product disclosure statement (PDS), the financial services guide (FSG) and the statement of advice (SOA). On 11 March 2002 the PDS replaced the prospectus as the key disclosure document for managed investments. ASIC provides some guidance on the process of preparing such documents and the outcome that such documents should achieve (refer to RG 165). Under the Corporations Act, the FSG and the SOA must be disclosed by licensees.

The FSG must be given to a client at the earliest practicable opportunity before a financial service is provided, and as soon as it becomes apparent that a financial service will be, or is likely to be, provided (refer to ss. 941A, 941B and 941C of the Act for exceptions). The FSG provides information about the licensee, the services provided, remuneration and complaints handling processes.

The SOA is mandatory each time advice is given to a client. It must set out the client's personal circumstances, objectives, risk profile, financial needs, likes and dislikes and so on. The SOA must also disclose any benefits (such as fees, commissions, soft dollar arrangements) obtained which might reasonably be expected to influence the entity providing the advice.

Other disclosure requirements under the Corporations Act include:

- provision of additional information on request
- confirmation of transactions
- advice of material changes and significant events
- periodical statements for retail clients of investment products
- the content of advertising of a particular financial product or promotional material that is reasonably likely to induce people to acquire the product.

RG 168 recognises the PDS provisions and contains general guidelines to help product issuers and to promote the objectives of these provisions, that is, making informed choices and helping consumers to compare financial products. ASIC has also developed Good Disclosure Principles. These guidelines apply equally to PDSs, FSGs and SOAs. They require that disclosure should be timely, relevant and complete, promote product understanding and comparison, highlight important information and have regard to consumers' needs.

Some other changes included in the Corporations Act under the FSRA

Other changes included in the Corporations Act under the FSRA changes include:

- market misconduct provisions (e.g. insider trading)
- direct money handling requirements

- anti-hawking provisions
- cooling-off provisions for retail clients
- ongoing transaction confirmations and reporting requirements for certain financial products.

Some observations on the cooling-off period under the Corporations Act

The cooling-off period (14 days) has applied to most financial products since the commencement of the FSRA reforms to the Corporations Act. Exemptions to the cooling-off period exist only in relation to the sale of a risk insurance product that has a 12-month duration and is a renewal of an existing product on the same terms and conditions. The cooling-off period does not apply to a financial product offered or issued under a distribution reinvestment plan or switching facility. Nor does it apply to a managed investment product that is not liquid at the time the product is issued.

Treatment of real estate advice under the Corporations Act

Real estate agents selling investment properties must consider whether they provide financial services (advice), even if it is incidentally, in relation to financial products such as general insurance or real estate-based managed investment schemes.

Other relevant laws

In addition to the requirement to comply with the Corporations Act there are a number of other laws that financial advisers need to comply with. These include other Acts of Parliament as well as the common law of negligence and contract.

Common law

Common law deals with civil liability. The general application of common law provides remedies for such matters as contracts and negligent misrepresentation.

The common law provides that in a contractual obligation with a client, for example fee-for-service basis, if the financial planner's services are not performed satisfactorily, the client is entitled to contractual remedies for cost recovery and loss suffered.

Advisers who operate on a fee-for-service basis are under a contractual obligation to the client. If they perform those services in an unsatisfactory or negligent manner, or do not perform those services, the client can seek redress under common law. The adviser has a duty of care that must be exercised under common law. Otherwise, the person relying on that information may be entitled to damages for negligent misrepresentation.

Superannuation Industry (Supervision) Act 1993 (SIS Act)

Superannuation entities must comply with the SIS Act in order to attract concessional tax treatment. Failure by these entities to comply may result in a loss of tax concessions as well as risking civil and/or criminal legal action by an aggrieved person.

Three other pieces of legislation provide for the regulation of superannuation entities.

- *Superannuation Supervisory Levy (Amendment) Act 1995*. This Act imposes a levy on superannuation entities for the purpose of recouping the APRA and ASIC cost of supervision of the superannuation industry.
- *Superannuation (Financial Assistance Funding) Levy Act 1993*. This Act imposes a levy on superannuation entities, which is used to provide financial assistance to funds which have sustained losses due to theft or fraudulent activities.
- *Superannuation (Resolution of Complaints) Act 1993*. This Act established a complaint resolution scheme and the Superannuation Complaints Tribunal.

The SIS Act aims at providing the framework for the prudent management of superannuation funds. It provides the necessary checks, rules and standards that aim to minimise risks to ensure compliance. It sets out rules and clarifies the duties of the trustee, for example external audit requirement, complaints handling, and information disclosure and member participation in the management of superannuation funds.

APRA administers the SIS Act and its Regulations and ancillary legislation which regulate the superannuation industry. A main objective of APRA is to properly safeguard the benefits of members and policyholders.

Life Insurance Act 1995

APRA administers the Life Insurance Act which has specific reference to the operations of insurance companies offering life insurance. ASIC also administers the way in which advisers of life insurance conduct their business with clients.

Insurance Act 1973

This Act, administered by APRA, regulates the general way in which insurance companies conduct and operate their business.

Australian Securities and Investments Commission Act 2001

This Act establishes the regulations pertaining to the organisation of ASIC.

Statutory complaints resolution schemes

Financial advisory service providers are governed by various structures which regulate complaints and potential disputes with clients. They are as follows.

- *Internal complaints-handling mechanisms for superannuation funds.* Under SIS legislation, superannuation funds, other than excluded superannuation funds, must have internal complaints-handling mechanisms to resolve disputes. Under FSRA legislation, licensees must offer clients internal dispute handling as the first means of settling any dispute that arises.
- *The Superannuation Complaints Tribunal.* An external Superannuation Complaints Tribunal handles unresolved disputes in superannuation funds, other than excluded funds. A member who is dissatisfied with the internal complaints procedure can make a complaint about the decision of the trustee if:
  - the decision was not within the trustee's powers
  - the trustee did not exercise its powers properly
  - the decision was unfair or unreasonable.

  The Superannuation Complaints Tribunal can also deal with complaints in relation to the sale and management of superannuation-related annuity products acquired after 12 December 1995, to enable it to:
  - review and make determinations about complaints
  - refer a complaint, or part of a complaint, to another complaints-handling body, where the complaint is not within its jurisdiction, relates to misrepresentation by an insurer or its representative, or involves life office conduct and decisions.
- *The Financial Ombudsman Service (FOS).* This service operates as an external dispute-handling body for complaints by clients against advice and service provided by financial planners, life insurance advisers, managed investment schemes and stockbrokers. It was established to provide free advice and assistance to consumers

to help them in resolving complaints. There are jurisdictional limits on the type of complaint heard and also monetary limitations. If the person is not satisfied with the licensee's response, the service will investigate written complaints, provided they fall within its guidelines, and resolve those complaints by investigation or conciliation. The service's decision is binding on the company but not on the complainant.

The role of ASIC

It is the role of ASIC to ensure practitioners comply with legal requirements governing the financial planning industry. ASIC does not draft legislation — this is Treasury's role. ASIC's role is to implement the legislation. ASIC is the watchdog for consumer protection laws in financial products and services. Its powers relate to the client:

- receiving financial advice
- putting money into investments, superannuation, life insurance or general insurance, or depositing money with a bank, building society or credit union.

Its powers do not relate to the client in the following situations:

- borrowing money, which is governed by state or territory departments of fair trading or the Australian Competition and Consumer Commission
- having concerns about the actual level of fees; that is, where the client has been clearly told about them and has been charged only what the contract provides for
- buying health insurance
- the merging of banks or closure of their branches.

In meeting the challenge of implementing the reforms of the Corporations Act, ASIC has developed policy and guidance in consultation with industry members and industry bodies to help the advisory services industry apply the legislature provisions to their individual circumstances (refer to the ASIC website, asic.gov.au).

Remuneration

On the question of remuneration, ASIC's view is clearly expressed in the Corporations Act — licensed advisers have to inform their clients of the details of any benefit they or their representatives will receive if clients follow particular recommendations. Although permitting different remuneration systems, ASIC clearly instructs licensed advisers to disclose any commission, fee, benefit or advantage, whether pecuniary or not, direct or indirect, that they have received or expect to receive. This ensures that consumers are informed of potential influences on the services provided. RG 168 *Disclosure: Product Disclosure Statements (and other disclosure obligations)* foreshadowed further work to promote product comparability through the use of the new product disclosure statements. ASIC has also argued for new legislation to ban remuneration based on commissions. Under the Future of Financial Advice (FOFA) reforms, the federal government has legislated to ban conflicted remuneration. In brief, this means that advisers are not to be paid a commission from the investment products or platforms for new investments after 1 July 2014 (see RG 246 Conflicted remuneration). See chapter 15 for more detail.

Independence

In its licensing regime of securities dealers and securities advisers, ASIC directs that in order for holders of an investment adviser's licence to maintain their public 'independence' status, they may charge a fee only for giving advice. Only licensed dealers are permitted to charge commissions (brokerage).

Section 923A of the Corporations Act restricts the use of the word 'independent'. Licensees are prohibited from using 'independent' or similar words (e.g. impartial, unbiased) where ownership links and the means of remuneration could result in potential bias.

In determining whether a dealer's or an adviser's licence is required, ASIC provides the elements which characterise the distinction between a dealer's licence and a securities adviser's licence as follows: if the person has no personal interest in the outcome such as commission, brokerage or success fee, but receives a fee for service, he or she will be treated as an independent adviser under a single licensing regime.

ASIC defines different types of compensation and benefits received by a licensee, and establishes grounds on which they may create a bias. It also investigates the question of product ownership links and how this may adversely affect the independence of advice, and describes the legal consequences if an adviser misuses the word 'independent'.

The Corporations Act provides ASIC with the power to revoke or suspend a licence or ban a person from providing financial services or acting in the capacity of representative of a licensee. However, 'ASIC will have a power to exempt certain products from the licensing obligations, allowing flexibility in the application of the licensing provisions'.

PERSONAL FINANCE BULLETIN

FOFA leaves its mark on financial services

2012 will stand as a watershed year for the Australian financial planning industry — the year during which the various elements of the Future of Financial Advice (FOFA) legislation passed the Parliament and began the process of being translated into regulation.

As the year has drawn to a close, we have been witness to the industry accepting the reality of the FOFA changes, and in most instances, seeking to make the best of something which many people continue to view as a less than perfect outcome.

2013 is, of course, an election year, and if there is a change of Government and the Coalition lives up to its promises, then the changes being wrought via FOFA may not seem that bad at all and, indeed, as ultimately benefiting the industry.

As the industry enters the New Year it needs to accept that, for better or for worse, financial planning needed to move beyond a number of the practices and commercial models which had distinguished it over the prior two decades, not least conflicted remuneration.

However, the Government's approach to achieving its policy objectives with respect to both FOFA and its Stronger Super changes has been far from perfect, giving rise to a number of anomalies, and in some instances tilting the playing field in favour of the industry superannuation funds.

It is these anomalies and imbalances which will need to be addressed if the financial services industry is to achieve the objectives which originally gave rise to the development of the FOFA legislation.

2012 also proved to be a pivotal year for the Financial Planning Association (FPA) and its ambition to become a fully-fledged professional body.

»

»

While provoking the ire of other industry participants over the manner in which it dealt with FOFA negotiations, the FPA claimed this year that it had succeeded in moving back into the black.

Overcoming the considerable revenue black hole created by changing its membership structure represented a signal achievement by the FPA, which clearly continues to benefit from being the vehicle via which planners can access the Certified Financial Planner (CFP) designation.

The FPA also ends the year on a high note with the Minister for Financial Services, Bill Shorten, delivering on his promise to introduce legislation which will enshrine the term 'financial planner/adviser' in law.

However, the Association of Financial Advisers also recorded a strong year, leading the way on discussion around life/risk churn, securing the presence of the Shadow Assistant Treasurer, Senator Mathias Cormann, at its roadshow events and drawing record numbers of attendees to its national conference on the Gold Coast.

Both organisations already know they have a full workload in the opening months of 2013.

Source: Mike Taylor, http://www.moneymanagement.com.au/opinion/editorial/fofa-leaves-its-mark-on-financial-services, 8 January 2013.

LO 10 What investors and financial planners can learn from history

The history of the development of the financial planning industry since 1980 contains a vast range of issues that has led to the creation of the 'new profession' of financial planning. The Financial Planning Association (see the appendix to this chapter) is taking steps to lift the standards of financial planners so that members of the public will receive a more professional service. Legislative change, economic circumstances, a lack of general financial literacy and a deeper understanding of the risk of investment have all played a part in this development. Recent history contains many lessons for financial planners and investors, including the need for an awareness of:

- market cycles — shares, property and interest rates all experience cycles of high and low returns
- the risks accompanying high returns — recall the adage 'high return equals high risk'
- the benefits of diversification — the benefits of spreading investments over asset classes to reduce risk and obtain more reliable returns
- the underlying portfolio of investment products — a fixed interest return may not be what it seems; an investor needs to know how money is being invested as a product may have a different set of risks than is immediately obvious, even though it may be 'guaranteed'
- scams — they appear quite frequently and ASIC website's (moneysmart.gov.au) provides updates and examples to watch out for
- the need to review investments based on economic and legislative changes — changes in the rules and regulations occur frequently and may affect a person's tax

position or eligibility for age pension. Economic changes may indicate a time to re-allocate an investment mix; for example, rising interest rates may mean it is time to move some funds from shares to fixed interest investments.

- the need for financial planners to abide by established rules of conduct and regulations; otherwise, government is likely to impose new rules and regulations to address any misbehaviour or practices exhibited by financial planners that are to the detriment of consumers.

Summary

Personal financial planning is about setting in place some personal objectives and arranging financial means to satisfy those objectives. Preparing a personal budget is a starting point in helping people to assess their financial position. Some people need additional help, through the aid of financial counsellors, in dealing with the complexity of the range of financial services.

Personal financial planning is carried out in an economic environment and investors should be aware of the impact that changes in economic circumstances can have on their financial plans. Business runs in cycles and monetary and fiscal policies are the two main mechanisms by which governments may help to reduce large fluctuations in the business cycle.

Changes in legislation, such as changes to capital gains tax and superannuation rules, and changes in the regulatory framework, such as the financial services guide and the statement of advice requirements, have helped to shape the personal financial planning industry/profession. Economic changes over the last 20 or so years, such as share market crashes, overvaluation of property and overseas interest-rate increases, have provided some hard lessons and made both financial planners and investors more aware of market cycles, the risks of high returns, the benefits of diversification, the variety of available investment products and the need to regularly review investments.

Professional application questions

1.1 A client aged 50 says to you, a junior financial planner, 'I would like to retire with a comfortable level of income. Can you help me to do that?' How would you restate the client's request in more definite terms?

1.2 Prepare a table to summarise the different roles carried out by ASIC, APRA and the ATO.

1.3 The Superannuation Guarantee is one reason why personal financial planning has increased in importance in recent years.

(a) Why do you think that many people show a low level of interest in their superannuation fund?

(b) Will you make your decision about setting an investment portfolio choice in an accumulation fund or will you leave it to a default choice where the fund manager nominates one portfolio selection such as 'conservative' for all members who do not nominate their own selection? Write your opinion about making a choice of investments for your own superannuation fund.

1.4 Suppose you had a friend who lost his/her job and was unable to pay the electricity account when it was due and the electricity supply was disconnected. How could a financial counsellor assist your friend?

1.5 The Corporations Act requires financial planners disclose three documents to their clients. What are these documents? Describe the purpose of each.

1.6 Section 961B(1) and RG 175 both require a financial advice provider to act in the best interests of the client in relation to the advice they provide to the client. Describe 'best advice' in one or two sentences, using an example to illustrate your answer.

1.7 Consider the 1987 share market crash; the 1990 property trust freeze; the 1992 Japan share market crash; the 1997 Asian crisis; and the 2000–01 dot.com crash. What common features can you identify in such events?

1.8 What are your own short-term, medium-term and long-term financial goals? Name two for each of the time frames.

Professional application exercises

Basic	*
Moderate	* *
Challenging	* * *

1.9 The global financial crisis *

A friend of yours wants to know how the global financial crisis started. Using a diagram and in your own words, provide an answer to your friend.

1.10 A lesson from history — property trust freeze *

Suppose you were considering placing an investment in an unlisted property trust at a time when large amounts of funds were invested in the property sector and valuations of the properties held in the trust had increased by 30% over the past year. Explain whether or not you would consider investing in the trust at that time.

1.11 A lesson from history — price-earnings multiples * *

Based on the experience seen in the dot.com crash period, write an opinion giving advice to an investor who wonders if he should sell his investment when the price–earnings multiple reaches 60.

1.12 Assessing financial advice * *

RG175.160 says that where an adviser recommends replacing one financial product with another one the SOA must contain statements about:

(a) whether the investor's existing product has been considered;
(b) the cost of the change in product;
(c) the potential benefits that may be lost; and
(d) any other significant consequences of the switch for the investor.

Suppose Ferdie, a financial planner advises you that the superannuation fund that you are currently invested in is not suitable for you as it had a poor return and he can recommend a better fund. What items so you think Ferdie needs to include in the SOA to comply with the law? Search for articles on 'switching super' to assist you.

1.13 Financial planners — professionals? * * *

(a) Prepare a list of things that you regard are indicative of a profession.
(b) What characteristics suggest that financial planning is a profession. (You may consider the legislation and the role of the FPA as part of your answer.)

1.14 Retirement income ✱✱✱

On a personal level, assess the level of income you think you would need — at a minimum — when you retire. Do you agree with the notion of 62.5% of pre-retirement earnings to be an adequate measure? If a person earned $100 000 prior to retirement what level of capital is required to produce 62.5% of such an income? (Assume a rate of return of 6% p.a.)

CASE STUDY 1

Short-term goals

Tanya is 19 years old and has been working as a retail assistant for 2 years. She earns $33 800 per year in salary after tax. Because her family lives in a country town, Tanya had to leave home to find employment and learn to look after herself and her finances.

She shares a flat with two friends. Her weekly payments on average are: rent $150; public transport fares $50; food $140; utility bills $50; mobile/internet phone $30; clothing $50; and entertainment $60. She also makes sure that she is saving some of her income and for the past 2 years has arranged for an automatic debit of $400 per month from her bank account into a managed fund. The amount accumulated in the fund comprises the original $2000 she was given for her seventeenth birthday to start the fund when she left home and contributions and earnings of $8000, making a total sum of about $10 000. The managed fund is a balanced fund. Any money left over after expenses and investment is kept in her bank account, which totals $1000.

Tanya's main goal is to buy a car in the next 6 months if she can afford it. She will use some money in her managed fund if she has to, but hopes to buy a car valued at about $13 000 plus insurance of $750 p.a.

QUESTIONS

1. Clearly state Tanya's short-term goal.
2. How would a financial counsellor help Tanya to determine whether she may be on target to meet her goal?
3. Suppose the retail store proposes to reduce Tanya's hours and her annual pay will decrease to $31 000 p.a. How will this affect her living costs and savings target?
4. What advice might a financial counsellor give to Tanya in such circumstances? Is there any other advice you may offer to help her achieve her goal?
5. What are main three investment risks that Tanya faces given her short-term goal?

CASE STUDY 2

Disclosure requirements

The following is based on the article 'Retirees' nightmare: anything goes if you disclose' (www.abc.net.au/news/2013-03-04/long-prime-tust-betrayal-disclose/4551422).

The Prime Trust went into liquidation in 2011 with the loss of $550 million of investors' funds. How did the trust lose so much money when it was supposed to be invested in retirement villages and aged care facilities? The answer lies in the small print in the product disclosure statement that allowed the manager of the fund to change the constitution (rules) of the trust. The change allowed the manager to charge a range of fees to the trust to cover things like the listing fee on the ASX — some $33 million! The founder also charged management fees to the trust and then sold the management rights to another party associated with the founder of the trust for a total of around $100 million. The cash flow that went to the founder has been directed to family trusts so that the founder has no control over the assets but is a beneficiary. ASIC's response to an irate investor included: 'we note that the fees you complained of were outlined in the PDS prior to the trust's listing on the ASX. Accordingly, there is no evidence that there has been a breach of the trust's statutory obligations.' Similar things have happened in many mortgage funds and other managed investment schemes where investors have lost money. The main issue is whether the operations and fees are disclosed to investors. The writer states 'the absurdity of "disclosure" as a safeguard is evident in the billions that mainly elderly retirees have lost in such funds over the years'.

QUESTIONS

1 Why is the disclosure seen as an absurdity as a safeguard in this situation?

2 If a financial planner had recommended Prime Trust, what obligations under the Corporations Act are placed on the financial adviser in giving advice to a client?

3 The FPA's Code of Ethics (see appendix to Chapter 1) contain principles of how a financial planner should deal with clients. Select three from the FPA's Code of Ethics and discuss how they may have saved retirees from making the investment in Prime Trust or whether, in fact, the Code of Ethics would not have made any difference to the advice given to a retiree.

4 What do you think of the ethics of the founder of the trust by charging such a high fee for listing services on the ASX and changing the constitution of the trust without notifying investors?

CASE STUDY 3

Keeping Storm's victims in mind

The dogs bark and the caravan moves on. The former prime minister Paul Keating's aphorism about the transience of the public spotlight applies to the 3000 Australians who invested an estimated $3 billion through Storm Financial. These investors are now slipping from the public gaze as the caravan moves on.

There is little in the way of words that can explain the losses retirees who invested through Storm have faced since its collapse in late 2008.

But a petition launched by Storm Financial investors addressed to the Prime Minister, Kevin Rudd, at petitiononline.com/vfahmg goes close to expressing the frustration of those who trusted in the Townsville financial planner.

After 17 months, a parliamentary inquiry and a settlement with the Commonwealth Bank, there are still plenty of reasons for Storm Financial's investors to feel angry.

They fell for a business model they trusted. Many say they relied on the fact Storm Financial held an Australian Financial Services Licence administered by the Australian Securities and Investments Commission.

The business model didn't work, and the investors lost the lot. The Commonwealth Bank, to its great credit, has participated in a resolution scheme that nobody likes much but is better than nothing. Other banks — notably Bank of Queensland and Macquarie Group — have made no such public concessions about their treatment of Storm investors.

Sure, there are varying degrees in what went on. Those reasonably intelligent investors who thought they were on a rocket to the moon — well, really, what were they thinking? But those elderly and unsophisticated investors who were mis-sold products (some were given official Storm documents that said their new debts were 'Clayton's debts') have been given precious little assurance their post-collapse interests are being looked after.

Storm's founder, Emmanuel Cassimatis, has himself likened his model of financial planning to that of a Big Mac or a Ford production line. The model didn't care whether the client was rich, poor, mentally disabled or in the first stages of senile dementia — they all got the same rubbish.

Let there be no doubt, especially as Cassimatis uses this vacuum in any meaningful response by regulators to once again woo his former devotees, it really was rubbish: a house of cards waiting for the first serious downturn before it fell over.

Since the collapse, these investors have had nothing that could be classed as giving them comfort from ASIC. In March ASIC gamely said its investigation had moved from a 'recovery options' phase to a 'commercial negotiations' phase and ASIC set up — wait for it — a website.

On the plus side, there is a My Storm Investment back-end to the website, containing individual details for individual investors, that raises the hope ASIC is still on the case.

»

»

Also on the plus side, ASIC grasped the nettle last year and took the unusual step of recommending to the parliamentary inquiry a policy position that all forms of commissions for financial planners should be banned.

However, the watchdog is perpetually constipated when it comes to explaining what it is actually doing in live investigations, fobbing off media and investor inquiries with various excuses and downplaying any emerging reportage.

(When its investigation into Storm raised media reports that ASIC chairman Tony D'Aloisio may be taking a personal interest in the matter, D'Aloisio promptly hosed the report down. You have got to wonder about how ASIC plays the public relations game when the boss uses the media to say he is not taking an unusual interest in a case that affected the livelihoods of 3000 Australians.)

ASIC is due to release a statement about its Storm investigation this month and it is to be hoped its work results in a better outcome than the comfortless position statements delivered so far.

Picture it for yourself. All your retirement savings gone, and no meaningful words from the corporate regulator about the course of the investigation more than 17 months after you lost the lot. The delay lengthens. A fickle media switches its gaze to more diverting topics.

No wonder Storm Financial investors are angry. No wonder they are signing the petition in droves.

Source: Washington 2010.

QUESTIONS

1. Storm's founder likened his model of financial planning to that of a Big Mac or a Ford production line. What do you think he meant by that?
2. What part of the Corporations Act indicates that such an approach is not in accord with the legislation? Why do you think the approach by Storm was not consistent with the legislation?
3. What of the requirements of an AFSL holder do you think the Storm advisers did not meet?
4. Why do you think that the collapse of Storm occurred in late 2008? Describe the economic circumstances of the time and their coincidence with Storm's collapse.
5. What role does the writer ascribe to ASIC and why do you think he criticises ASIC's actions?
6. Why do you think ASIC recommended to the parliamentary inquiry that all forms of commissions be banned?
7. Research the Storm Financial collapse. What did Storm advise clients to do? What did they invest in? How much did they invest? What avenues of redress have clients available to them?

References and further reading

ABS 2009, *Australian social trends*, 4102.0.

ABS 2013, www.abs.gov.au/websitedbs/d3310114.nsf/home/Population Pyramid-Australia.

AMP 2009, *AMP retirement adequacy index, summary of trends June 2011–December 2011*, AMP.

ASFA 2013, *The ASFA retirement standard*, www.superannuation.asn.au.

ASIC 2013, Money Smart website, moneysmart.gov.au.

Bateman, H, Kingston, G & Piggott, J 2001, *Forced saving: Mandating private retirement incomes*, Cambridge University Press, Cambridge.

Clare, R 2006, *The introduction of choice of superannuation fund — results to date*, February, ASFA Research and Resource Centre, Sydney.

Clare, R 2007, *Are retirement savings on track?*, June, ASFA Research & Resource Centre, Sydney.

Connolly, E 2007, *The effect of the Australian Superannuation Guarantee on household saving behaviour*, Research discussion paper 2007–08, August, Reserve Bank of Australia, Sydney.

Financial Planning Association of Australia Limited 2008, *The trade off — understanding investment risk*, fpa.asn.au.

Financial Planning Association of Australia Limited 2009, *Code of professional practice*, fpa.asn.au.

Financial Services Council, March 2012, Retirement savings gap at June 2011 prepared by Rice Warner.

Fry, T, Heaney, R & McKeown, W 2007, 'Will investors change their superannuation fund given the choice?', *Accounting and Finance*, vol. 47, no. 2, June, pp. 267–83.

Higgins, E & Abey, A 2000, *Fortune strategy*, 2nd edn, Allen & Unwin, Sydney.

Long, Stephen 2013, *Retirees' nightmare: anything goes if you disclose*, The Drum ABC News, 4 March.

National Financial Literacy Strategy, www.moneysmart.gov.au.

Olsberg, D 1997, *Ageing and money: Australia's retirement revolution*, Allen & Unwin, Sydney.

Taylor, S, Juchau, R, Houterman, B & McDonald, T 2005, *Financial planning in Australia*, Lexis Nexis–Butterworths, Sydney.

The Treasury, Commonwealth of Australia 2010, *The 2010 intergenerational report*, treasury.gov.au.

Valentine, T 2007, *Modern financial & investment planning*, Pearson Education Australia, Sydney.

Washington, S 2010, 'Keeping Storm's victims in mind, *The Sydney Morning Herald*, 19 May.

APPENDIX

The Financial Planning Association of Australia (FPA)

During the late 1980s and early 1990s, the rate of growth in the financial planning industry led to the merger of two separate groups representing financial planners and investment advisers — the International Association for Financial Planning and the Australian Society of Investment and Financial Advisers — and in January 1992 the Financial Planning Association of Australia (FPA) was established. Based in Sydney, the FPA has a growing membership base, and currently has over 10 000 members of whom 7500 are practising financial planners. The FPA is also home to Australia's 5500 CFP® professionals.

The FPA represents the interests of the public and Australia's professional community of financial planners. The Association is unrivalled in its reach of the financial planning market, influence on government and regulators, standards set through a world-class Code of Professional Practice, unique position as the certification body in Australia for the global CFP® designation, and reputation for quality professional development. Building on a 20-year legacy, the FPA represents the changing face of financial planning from industry to a profession.

From 1 January 2007 the FPA raised the bar for entry into the professional program for those aspiring to become Certified Financial Planners. From that date, entry to the program required an undergraduate or masters degree. In 2013, practitioner membership was restricted to those who hold an approved university degree.

The FPA requires its members to undertake ongoing training and professional development through short courses offered by industry and universities. There are several educational programs designed to provide knowledge, and update skills and qualifications for financial planners. The FPA has also introduced a process of accreditation of people who are able to verify and certify the various educational programs designed to help the FPA's members gain continuous professional development (CPD).

In pursuing high standards of integrity and fair dealing, the FPA has not only raised the educational requirement expected of its members, but also considered the controversial question of advisers' remuneration by commission versus 'fee-for-service' in open discussion and has moved to a fee only basis from 2012. Currently, the FPA's policy is one of a full disclosure of all financial adviser benefits and other charges incurred by clients for services. The FPA has determined that remuneration must be disclosed whether it be commission or fee-based. This commitment to full transparent disclosure enhances financial advisers' positions as professionals, because it puts beyond doubt the fact that the financial adviser is acting in the client's interests and is not motivated by hidden rewards or incentives.

The FPA has continual liaison with government, ASIC and other regulators and industry bodies to work towards acceptable solutions to industry problems and issues as they emerge.

The role of the FPA

The FPA is a not-for-profit organisation with a vision to ensure that Australians have access to professional financial advice, so enhancing their financial wellbeing. The FPA promotes improved quality of financial advice and high standards of ethical and professional behaviour among its members. It does this by seeking a high level of integrity, largely based on compliance with ASIC regulations, among its members. As is the case with other professions, its members abide by a Code of Ethics and Rules of Professional Conduct. The association's website (fpa.asn.au) provides relevant financial planning information for both consumers and industry professionals.

The FPA Code of Ethics and Rules of Professional Conduct are part of the FPA's professional standards, by which all FPA members are required to abide as part of their membership. FPA's professional standards are mandatory and enforceable against all members, and non-compliance with the standards may attract FPA disciplinary action.

In addition, the FPA issues business tools and guidance notes from time to time to assist member practitioners in their day-to-day practice. Although not enforceable in themselves, the business tools and guidance notes may be used to assess alleged breaches of the professional standards. The FPA also has in place a complaints and disciplinary scheme which deals with complaints received against its members.

As with other professional organisations, the FPA uses its Code of Ethics to state to society and the field's professionals that it has its own professional charter. The norms of practice enforced by the FPA are, in general, stricter than legal requirements. The FPA Rules of Professional Conduct are specific standards and apply to all classes of members, that is general members, associate practitioners, senior associates, certified financial planners and principal members, unless otherwise stated.

The FPA's Code of Ethics includes general standards of conduct to be observed by financial planners. These include integrity, objectivity, competence and fairness. The revised code is enforceable from 1 July 2009 and is reproduced below.

FPA Code of Ethics

Principle 1: Client first

Place the client's interests first.

Placing the client's interests first is a hallmark of professionalism, requiring the financial planner to act honestly and not place personal and/or employer gain or advantage before the client's interests.

Principle 2: Integrity

Provide professional services with integrity.

Integrity requires honesty and candour in all professional matters. Financial planners are placed in positions of trust by clients, and the ultimate source of that trust is the financial planner's personal integrity. Allowance can be made for legitimate differences of opinion, but integrity cannot co-exist with deceit or subordination of one's principles. Integrity requires the financial planner to observe both the letter and the spirit of the Code of Ethics.

Principle 3: Objectivity

Provide professional services objectively.

Objectivity requires intellectual honesty and impartiality. Regardless of the services delivered or the capacity in which a financial planner functions, objectivity requires financial planners to ensure the integrity of their work, manage conflicts and exercise sound professional judgment.

Principle 4: Fairness

Be fair and reasonable in all professional relationships.

Fairness requires providing clients what they are due, owed or should expect from a professional relationship, and includes honesty and disclosure of material conflicts of interest. It involves managing one's own feelings, prejudices and desires to achieve a proper balance of interests. Fairness is treating others in the same manner that you would want to be treated.

Principle 5: Professionalism

Act in a manner that demonstrates exemplary professional conduct.

Professionalism requires behaving with dignity and showing respect and courtesy to clients, fellow professionals, and others in business-related activities, and complying with appropriate rules, regulations and professional requirements. Professionalism requires the financial planner, individually and in cooperation with peers, to enhance and maintain the profession's public image and its ability to serve the public interest.

Principle 6: Competence

Maintain the abilities, skills and knowledge necessary to provide professional services competently.

Competence requires attaining and maintaining an adequate level of knowledge, skills and abilities in the provision of professional services. Competence also includes the wisdom to recognise one's own limitations and when consultation with other professionals is appropriate or referral to other professionals necessary. Competence requires the financial planner to make a continuing commitment to learning and professional improvement.

Principle 7: Confidentiality

Protect the confidentiality of all client information.

Confidentiality requires client information to be protected and maintained in such a manner that allows access only to those who are authorised. A relationship of trust and confidence with the client can only be built on the understanding that the client's information will not be disclosed inappropriately.

Principle 8: Diligence

Provide professional services diligently.

Diligence requires fulfilling professional commitments in a timely and thorough manner, and taking due care in planning, supervising and delivering professional services.

Source: FPA *Code of Professional Practice*, November 2009.

2 Financial planning skills

LEARNING OBJECTIVES

After studying this chapter, you should be able to:

1. prepare personal financial statements
2. understand the purpose of analysing financial statements using ratio analysis
3. describe the importance of financial mathematics skills for financial planners
4. explain the concept of time value of money and the benefits of compound interest
5. understand the difference between nominal and effective interest rates
6. understand the concept of net present value
7. apply the time value of money concept to different investment choices
8. explain the effect of taxation and inflation on the rate of return.

CASE STUDY

Nina is aged 23. She has finished her apprenticeship and has now started her own landscape gardening business. Her uncle, an accountant, has suggested that she makes sure that she pays herself a small wage from the business and to keep the business income and expenses quite separate from her own bank account. She has had her own savings account for a long time, but when she left school she made regular contributions as personal savings throughout the four years of her apprenticeship. Nina has accumulated approximately $6000 from both savings and interest after withdrawing $3000 to buy items of equipment to set up her business. Nina also arranged to borrow another $3000 to buy other items before the prices increased. Her uncle has drawn her attention to the rate of interest that she needs to pay on the loan and the rate of interest that she earns on her savings. She is somewhat surprised to learn that she earns only 2% on her savings but has to pay 10% on her loan. However, she decided not to use all of her own money to start the business because she was a little uncertain that she would make a success of it. Nina's uncle also suggested using a credit card for the business expenses as a way of keeping business records, but to make sure that she paid the balance by the due date to avoid interest payments at 19%. While she was thinking about her finances she wondered how she could improve the rate of interest on her own savings. Her uncle suggested that she move most of her savings to an account where the interest is compounded every month rather than every six months as happens with her current bank account. He also said that the cost of living increases and the impact on tax on her savings meant that Nina probably wasn't really saving anything at all.

His comments raised a number of issues that Nina needs to consider. These include:

- the effects of interest rates on saved and borrowed funds
- the impact of increasing prices
- the use of a credit card
- the effect of taxation on her rate of return.

Illustrative examples used throughout this chapter will relate back to Nina's situation.

Introduction

Financial planning requires specialised knowledge across diverse areas including investments, risk management, taxation, estate planning, social security and retirement planning. This chapter looks at some of the technical skills that financial planners require in order to provide appropriate advice, particularly in the area of investments.

In this chapter we consider the essential data that an adviser needs to collect and the use that can be made of that data to advise clients. We also consider not only how compounding affects investments and examine ways in which comparisons of investment returns can be made, but also the impact of interest rates on credit cards. It is important that investments are considered in terms of their returns with regard to the frequency of interest payments, the time value of money in present value terms, the effects of inflation and the effects of taxation.

LO 1 Preparing personal financial statements

In chapter 1 you learned about personal financial goals and their relevant time frames. As you move through various stages of life, and as various events — such as a new job, marriage, the birth of a child, or the death of a parent — change your life, your personal goals may change. Such changes emphasise the importance of ongoing attention to the personal financial planning process and the need to periodically reassess financial goals.

Once we determine what our financial goals are we need to gather the necessary information and prepare working documents to determine whether such goals are achievable. These working documents involve the preparation of personal cash flow budgets and financial statements.

Personal financial statements consist of a set of information about a person's financial circumstances. Financial statements may be prepared in two parts:

1. a personal cash flow budget or statement, which aims to indicate all the sources of income and expenses to determine the amount of income available for savings or investment or whether, in fact, insufficient income is derived to satisfy the level of expenses
2. a personal **balance sheet**, which aims to indicate the assets or items of value owned by the person and all the liabilities or amounts owed to other people to derive a net worth value of that person.

balance sheet
a statement of assets and liabilities; the net result is the owner's value

Personal cash flow budget

The personal cash flow budget sets out the anticipated income from all sources and the items of spending or expenditure which will use up most or, in some cases, all of that income. The personal balance sheet involves listing a person's assets and liabilities.

Income consists of money received from salary, wages, interest, profits, bonuses, fees charged, dividends, distributions, social security pensions or allowances, or any other earnings. Expenditure consists of payments for food, clothing, gas and electricity, rent, interest on borrowed money, rates, entertainment, holidays, education, pay television, mobile phone and any other items of expense.

Assuming that income exceeds expenditure, the difference is regarded as savings. This may include regular transfers of money to a savings plan with a financial institution, the occasional purchase of shares, or the accumulation of savings in a bank account.

In some cases, there may be a period of negative savings where income does not meet the required level of expenditure. On these occasions, people will draw on past savings, use borrowed money or run up a credit card debt to meet the required level of expenditure. Examples of such circumstances include a period when one partner is out of work or when additional expenses need to be met when income flow is limited. Such a situation should be temporary; otherwise a drastic review of expenditure patterns is needed.

Your personal cash flow budget will be unique to your own circumstances as it depends on your stage in life, your occupation, your attitude to money management and your good fortune with regard to having wealthy parents or being a beneficiary of a deceased estate. Young singles living at home with no dependants are more likely to be able to save fairly high proportions of their income for some time and be able to accumulate some assets. Couples with a young family are more likely to spend more than they earn for a period of time and will have a different cash flow situation.

Suppose we are given the following information on income and expenditure prepared by Qinbo and Feilian Wong in 2013. Qinbo is employed as a telecommunications technician. Feilian works part-time at a migrant centre. Qinbo is aged 43 and Feilian is 42. They have two children aged 15 and 13 years.

The annual cash flow for the Wong family shows a positive result at the end of the year. Note that this illustration focuses on cash flow and does not take into account the end-of-year taxation issues which may result from the income and deductions allowed under the taxation rules for the investments; nor does it take into account any employer superannuation contributions that go directly to a superannuation fund.

Income (2013)	
Qinbo (after PAYG tax)	$85 000
Feilian (after PAYG tax)	35 000
Interest and managed fund distribution	3 000
Total	$123 000
Expenses	
Food, car, clothing, utilities and insurances	$55 000
School fees, uniforms, other activities, etc.	15 000
Loans and credit card repayments	22 000
Personal contribution to superannuation	6 000
Entertainment, holidays and miscellaneous expenses	18 000
Total	$116 000
Surplus/(deficit)	$7 000

The Wongs operate their finances with some savings in the bank but have access to additional cash through a home equity draw-down facility. This facility allows Qinbo and Feilian to draw additional cash through an agreement with their bank based on the level of assets they own. Qinbo and Feilian have not bothered to work closely with a personal cash flow statement before, as their joint income was in excess of their needs and they were able to accumulate some cash reserves and other assets before they had children. However, in the past couple of years they have noticed that they tend to have fewer savings available to spend and are more aware of the impact of school fees and the expenses of a growing family.

Projected cash flow budget/statement

To help the Wong family look ahead to their future cash flow position, we can also prepare a projected cash flow budget/statement which takes into account any significant changes we expect to occur over that time. When we look to the future cash flow position, we may refer to such a working sheet as a budget. A budget is a financial statement showing *expected* income and expenditure, and many people use a budget to help them keep a check on the 'cash in' and 'cash out' situation. The following shows an abbreviated 5-year cash budget based on forecasts made by the Wongs using a 3 per cent increase in income and expenses as an assumption.

	2013	2014	2015	2016	2017
Income ($)	123 000	126 690	130 490	134 405	138 438
Expenses ($)	116 000	119 480	123 064	126 756	130 559
Net cash flow ($)	**7 000**	**7 210**	**7 426**	**7 649**	**7 879**

In the context of considering the cash budget for the Wong family, we also need to consider their financial goals. In the short term, their objective is to take control of their finances and to show a decrease in the amount they owe the bank. This projection assumes that they do not change their current lifestyle and expenditure pattern. Their medium-term goal is to have sufficient savings to build up their investment portfolio. Their long-term goal is to accumulate sufficient assets to retire at age 65 with an annual income of about $75 000 in today's dollars.

Personal balance sheet

To complete the financial picture of the Wongs, we also need to consider their total financial wellbeing, not just their ongoing finances. To do this we need to know the health of their personal balance sheet. The preparation of a personal balance sheet requires the listing of all their assets and liabilities to indicate the equity they have, or their net worth (i.e. assets minus liabilities).

Assets are things of value we own. Assets include bank deposits, property, shares, managed funds, motor vehicles, antiques and any other item of value. The assets listed by the Wongs include their house and contents, cash, a managed investment fund, two cars and their superannuation funds.

The Wongs' net worth is the difference between their assets and their liabilities. The Wongs' personal balance sheet for 2013 is shown below.

Assets		
House and contents		$650 000
Cash in savings account		12 000
Motor vehicles (2)		32 000
Managed investment fund		23 000
Superannuation funds (combined)		240 000
Total		$957 000
Liabilities		
Credit card debt		12 000
Home equity facility		
Home mortgage	$250 000	
Car loans	22 000	
		$272 000
Total		$284 000
Net worth		$673 000

The Wongs have been able to accumulate net assets as Qinbo and Feilian have been working since their early twenties and they delayed having children until their late twenties.

Liabilities are those amounts of money we owe to other people or institutions. The Wongs' liabilities include the credit card debt, the home equity facility — which includes the mortgage on their home — and car loans. We need to ensure that we separate the assets from the liabilities so we can determine the difference, which is the person's or household's net worth.

Many people do not have the benefit of net assets like Qinbo and Feilian; they may have a much lower net worth position with fewer assets and a higher amount of debt. But, again, many may have a much higher net worth position. Personal financial planning is related to our own unique set of financial circumstances — some are more fortunate than others, but the general principle of using these basic data collection tools helps us put each person's financial planning needs into perspective for that person.

The use of a personal cash flow statement and a personal balance sheet is much the same as the use of similar financial documents in business. They are used to monitor the income and expenditure patterns of a business in terms of the goals that are set, and to consider the performance of the enterprise in meeting its short-, medium- and long-term objectives.

The next section considers the use of the information contained in the cash flow statement and the balance sheet, and applying such information using business management tools as a means of monitoring and assessing an individual's financial position.

LO 2 Using financial ratios as a planning tool

The two financial documents for the Wong family (as described earlier) can be used further to analyse the family's financial position. We will outline briefly four ratios which, in their various ways, provide useful information for evaluating a person's individual set of financial circumstances:

- equity, or net worth ratio
- liquidity ratio
- savings ratio
- debt service ratio.

You will be able to apply these ratios to exercises in the Professional Application Exercises at the end of this chapter.

Net worth ratio

The first of these ratios is the *equity or net worth ratio*. The equity/net worth ratio is the ratio of net worth to total assets, expressed as a percentage. It is found by dividing the net worth by the total assets and multiplying by 100. The formula is:

$$\text{Equity or net worth ratio} = \frac{\text{Net worth}}{\text{Total assets}} \times 100$$

Using the information in the Wong family's circumstances, we find:

$$\begin{aligned}\text{Equity or net worth ratio} &= \frac{\text{Net worth}}{\text{Total assets}} \times 100 \\ &= \frac{\$673\,000}{\$957\,000} \times 100 \\ &= 70.3\%\end{aligned}$$

This means that the Wong family owns 70.3% of the assets that they have acquired, and other people or institutions own 29.7%.

For a young person or couple, it is expected that their equity ratio would be relatively low as they are likely to have a high level of debt. An older couple nearing retirement would be more likely to have a high equity ratio, as they would be trying to eliminate debt completely or to reduce debt to a minimum by the time they retired. The equity ratio may be considered in terms relative to a person's stage in their working life.

Liquidity ratio

The *liquidity ratio* compares the amount of liquid assets with current debt, expressed as a percentage. Liquid assets are those assets which are in cash form or are likely to be converted to cash within a 12-month period. Assets which could be converted to cash could be included in this classification even though they are intended to be a long-term investment. However, in this case, the Wong family's managed investment fund is intended to be held for the long term, and so is not included in the liquid assets. The key to this matter is to be consistent in the application of the classification method used. Current debt represents that amount of debt which is to be repaid within the next 12 months. Thus:

$$\text{Liquidity ratio} = \frac{\text{Liquid assets}}{\text{Current debt}} \times 100$$

Assume that current debt comprises credit card debt, a commitment to repay debt on the home mortgage and repayments on the car loans of \$15 000 which total \$22 000. In this case we have liquid assets of \$12 000 (the cash in savings account) and total current debt of \$22 000. Thus:

$$\begin{aligned}\text{Liquidity ratio} &= \frac{\text{Liquid assets}}{\text{Current debt}} \times 100\\ &= \frac{\$12\,000}{\$22\,000} \times 100\\ &= 54.5\%\end{aligned}$$

This ratio shows the percentage of liquid assets available to cover current debt. It may be expressed in terms of months by multiplying the ratio by 12 (for months in the year). For example, suppose the ratio is 12% (or 0.12). Multiplying the ratio of 12% by 12 means there is 1.4 months of liquid assets available to meet current liabilities. In the Wong family's case they have 6.5 months of liquid assets available to meet their current liabilities (0.545 × 12). A higher liquidity ratio is important to those people who are fairly conservative and want the comfort of knowing that they have cash close at hand if needed. Others may be more inclined to have assets held in a more long-term form, such as property or shares, and rely on short-term debt by means of a draw-down facility to meet immediate cash shortfalls. In the Wong family's case, they know they can draw upon their home equity facility if immediate cash is needed. Income protection insurance would be advisable to provide income if Qinbo was unable to work due to illness or injury.

Savings ratio

The third ratio — the *savings ratio* — shows the level of savings expressed as a percentage of total income. In this case we need to be careful defining savings. It is not just the amount left over after deducting expenditure from income, since we would ignore any investments made within the expenditure items. We need to add back the items which may be regarded as investments, such as share purchases, extra superannuation contributions and additional bank deposits. The savings ratio (after tax) is calculated as:

$$\text{Savings ratio} = \frac{\text{Savings}}{\text{Net income}} \times 100$$

In this case we have an estimated $7000 increase in their bank account (savings) as they have a surplus of income over expenses for the 2013 year. The savings ratio for the Wong family after tax is calculated as:

$$\begin{aligned}\text{Savings ratio} &= \frac{\text{Savings}}{\text{Net income}} \times 100 \\ &= \frac{\$7000}{\$123\,000} \times 100 \\ &= 5.7\%\end{aligned}$$

It is likely that a young couple with small children may have a low or negative savings ratio. Similarly, an older couple may also show a low savings ratio. A couple whose children have left home and who are looking forward to 10 years or so of work before retirement may have a high savings ratio and so, too, might a young couple who have just married and are both intending to work for a few years before starting a family. There is no hard and fast rule about what the savings ratio should be; the savings ratio should be considered in the context of the set of circumstances under review. The Wongs' case may be similar to many people with teenagers at secondary school.

Debt service ratio

The monthly *debt service ratio* shows the monthly debt commitments expressed as a percentage of the after-tax monthly income. This ratio can be used to indicate the effect of a particular course of action such as the impact of a decision either to increase the level of debt significantly by undertaking a new major purchase, or to reduce drastically the level of income by one partner ceasing work or working part-time instead of full-time, or if a rise in interest rates occurs. The ratio is thus:

$$\text{Monthly debt service ratio} = \frac{\text{Annual debt commitments/12 months}}{\text{Annual net income/12 months}} \times 100$$

In the Wong family's case:

$$\begin{aligned}\text{Monthly debt service ratio} &= \frac{\text{Annual debt commitments/12 months}}{\text{Annual net income/12 months}} \times 100 \\ &= \frac{\$22\,000/12}{\$123\,000/12} \times 100 \\ &= \frac{\$1833.33}{\$10\,250} \times 100 \\ &= 17.9\%\end{aligned}$$

If the Wong family's income falls because Feilian's job is cut back to three days a week so that she earns only $15 000 after tax, the debt service ratio will show an increase from 17.9% to 21.4%. This is calculated by reducing total after-tax income for the family to $103 000 from $123 000. By indicating the effect of such a change on their ability to service their debt, Feilian may seek other employment to restore their level of income.

Note that some of these ratios use only the balance sheet and others use a combination of both the balance sheet and the cash flow statement. The use of the ratios on their own may not provide much useful information, but the trend over 2 or 3 years or more can be very useful together with information on the stage of life of the person who is the subject of the review.

Let us consider another view of debt ratios. If a family's balance sheet was similar to a firm's balance sheet we would clearly see what was regarded as short-term debt (current liabilities) and long-term debt (non-current liabilities). In this way we can see the proportion of short-term debt relative to the total assets and also the proportion of long-term debt relative to the amount of family assets. In the Wong family's case short-term debt may be regarded as their credit card debt and the car loans (total $34 000). This presumes that they want to pay them fairly quickly. As a proportion of their assets this means that their short-term debt is only 3.6% of their total assets; i.e. $34 000/$957 000 = 3.6%. In a strict accounting sense, short-term debt is that which is required to be paid within the next twelve month period. As it is expected that the Wongs will take about two years or more to pay the credit card debt and the car loans then the short-term ratio would be less than the amount illustrated above.

Their long-term debt, represented by their mortgage, is 26% of their assets; i.e. $250 000/$957 000 = 26%.

This example could be extended further if detailed monthly amounts for each type of debt were provided and a debt service ratio could then be calculated for both short-term and long-term debt.

Most people are aware of the power of using spreadsheets to make computations easier and to save time. However, the investment of time and thought to set up the spreadsheet properly will save even more time and provide for ease of auditing the cell formulae. To learn more about setting up a spreadsheet properly, see the appendix at the end of this chapter. It provides some very useful examples of how to set up a spreadsheet and how not to set up a spreadsheet to assist your financial planning.

PROFESSIONAL ADVICE

Newlyweds' net worth

Efram and Sofia, both aged 24, are newlyweds. Their after-tax salaries are $55 000 and $49 000, respectively. They have been renting a flat since they started work but have decided to buy a house. Their decision has been made easier because Efram's parents said that when they retire at age 65 in one year's time they would withdraw $40 000 from their combined superannuation funds and give the money to Efram and Sofia to help them to buy a house. When they approached the bank for a loan they had to provide details of »

»

their income, expenses, assets and liabilities to the lending officer. The items provided for their personal balance sheet were:

Assets	
Bank account	$45 000
Furniture/personal effects	$8 000
Managed investment fund	$20 000
Cars	$16 000
Superannuation — Efram	$26 000
Superannuation — Sofia	$21 000
Liabilities	
Credit cards	$5 500
Car loans	$3 000

They also advise the lending officer that their monthly commitments are:

- rent $1280
- car loans $290.

They would prefer not to cash in their managed investment fund at present as the value has fallen by 8% over the last 2 months. They have instructed the fund manager to reinvest the distributions rather than receive them in cash. Their intention is to leave the investment to accumulate to meet the education expenses of the children they hope to have in the future.

They anticipate paying off their credit card debt in full next month and they would also have paid off the car loans in the next 12 months. They also advise the lending officer that their current rate of household expenses (not including the rent and repayments) is about $2400 per month.

QUESTIONS

1. Prepare a net worth statement and ratio analysis for their current situation.
2. Prepare a net worth statement and ratio analysis for their estimated situation when they receive the gift from Efram's parents and purchase a house valued at $380 000 with repayments based on $2200 per month.
3. Discuss the impact on their savings and debt service ratio if Sofia was to cease working for a period of time to have children.

LO 3 Financial mathematical skills applied in financial planning

When will I be able to retire? Will my investments provide me with sufficient income for my retirement? How much will I need to invest so that I can afford to send my children to private schools? If I have $300 000 in my superannuation in 8 years, what is that equivalent to in today's money terms? Is it preferable to pay off my mortgage or invest any surplus funds? Financial planners are constantly faced with questions such as these. In order to provide answers to such questions, financial planners need to have a strong working knowledge of fundamental mathematical concepts that relate to investment and retirement planning as well as the taxation consequences of any investment decision. The skills required include a basic understanding of the nature of compounding and the time value of money. A simple example to demonstrate the need to understand the concept of 'time value of money' is the use of a projected superannuation balance or retirement income produced on some superannuation fund statements provided to members. When a projected figure of say, $1 million, is provided on such a statement it needs to be understood in the context of whether the impact of inflation has been taken into account in delivering such a figure. If the $1 million is a projected figure we need to know whether it represents $1 million at today's dollar value (the real value) or a dollar figure of some future time. The difference can be quite misleading. An understanding of these concepts will enable financial planners to determine both present and future values of capital amounts and to assess alternative income streams so that different investment options can be compared.

In practice, financial planners can often access computer packages which, with a click of the mouse, can determine present and future capital values, and compare alternative income streams. However, computer packages cannot equip financial planners with the skills to explain to clients the basis on which their advice is determined. Financial planning is a relationship profession built on trust and responsibility. It is imperative that financial planners provide clients not only with solutions but also with the assurance that the advice given is based on a thorough understanding of the factors that give rise to these solutions.

LO 4 Compound interest and the time value of money

Most financial decisions involve benefits and costs that are spread out over time. The concept of the time value of money establishes a relationship between cash flows received and/or paid at different points in time. If you are offered the alternative of receiving $1000 at the end of 4 years or receiving $1000 today, a rational response would be to choose to receive the money today. There are possibly three reasons you might prefer the money today.

1. The person promising you the money in 4 years may not fulfil the promise — there is an element of risk in that there is some uncertainty that you will receive the money in 4 years.
2. If you have the money now, you can invest the $1000 and earn a return — if you wait for 4 years, there is an opportunity cost (that is, the return you could have achieved in another investment).
3. If you have the money now, you can use it for present consumption.

Because there is risk, an opportunity cost and the postponement of present consumption, people prefer cash now rather than later. This is called the 'time preference for money' and it highlights the idea that a dollar today is worth more than a dollar to be received in some future period of time. In order for us to be indifferent to the receipt of the $1000 now or in 4 years, we would need to be compensated for undertaking the risk, forgoing the opportunity to invest the money now and delaying our ability to use the funds for consumption. The compensation we require is equal to our opportunity cost; that is, the best rate of return we could earn from investing the $1000 for 4 years. If we could earn 8% p.a. from investing these funds for 4 years, our opportunity cost would

discount rate the rate of return required by an investor from an investment

future value an amount of money at some future time

be 8% p.a. This compensation or opportunity cost is often described as the interest rate required, the rate of return required, the **discount rate** or the time preference rate.

We have discussed why a dollar in hand today is worth more than a dollar to be received at some future date. If we know what our opportunity cost (or rate of return requirement) is, we can determine what amount of money we would require in 4 years in order for us to be indifferent about receiving the $1000 now or receiving the $1000 plus compensation in 4 years. This can be termed the **future value** (often abbreviated as *FV*) of our investment. Using a financial calculator and this example, we can input the following values to determine the future value of the investment:

PV = amount of the present sum of money ($1000)
i = interest rate per period (8%)
N = number of periods (4).

If we select the future value key (*FV*) on the financial calculator, we will know that if our opportunity cost is 8% we will require $1360.49 in 4 years to be indifferent about receiving the money today or waiting for the 4 years.

This sum of money comprises the initial sum of money, $1000, plus interest earned over the 4-year period (see the table below).

Initial sum	$1000.00
Interest in year 1 = 8% × $1000	80.00
Interest in year 2 = 8% × ($1000 + $80)	86.40
Interest in year 3 = 8% × ($1000 + $80 + $86.40)	93.31
Interest in year 4 = 8% × ($1000 + $80 + $86.40 + $93.31)	100.78
	$1360.49

From this example we can see that in years 2, 3 and 4 we are earning a return not only on the original capital sum, but also on any accumulated interest. That is, in year 2 we earn interest on year 1's interest. In year 3 we earn interest on the interest from years 1 and 2. In year 4 we earn interest on the interest earned in years 1, 2 and 3. This is the nature of compounding. This is what Nina learned when she discovered that she was earning 'interest on her interest'. The longer the time that funds are invested and the higher the interest rate, the more significant is the effect of compounding on the value of those funds at some future period of time.

Table 2.1 shows future values at different interest rates. We can see that an investment of $100 invested for 2 years at 5% p.a. grows to $110.25, whereas that same investment will grow to $127.63 if it is invested at 5% p.a. for 5 years. If the time frame is 4 years, we can see that the higher the interest rate, the greater will be the value of our investment.

TABLE 2.1 Future values at different interest rates

	Future value of $100 at various interest rates			
No. years	5%	10%	15%	20%
1	$105.00	$110.00	$115.00	$120.00
2	$110.25	$121.00	$132.25	$144.00
3	$115.76	$133.10	$152.09	$172.80
4	$121.55	$146.41	$174.90	$207.36
5	$127.63	$161.05	$201.14	$248.83

We can also use a formula to determine the future value of an amount invested today. This formula is as follows:

$$FV = PV(1 + i)^n$$

where PV = amount of the present sum of money ($1000)
i = interest rate per period (8%)
n = number of periods (4).

$$\begin{aligned} FV &= \$1000(1 + 0.08)^4 \\ &= \$1360.49 \end{aligned}$$

Because of the nature of compounding, we can see why we say that money has a time value. That is, a dollar in one time period has a different value from a dollar received or paid in a different time period. This same notion of the time value of money can enable us to determine what an amount to be received at a future date is worth in today's money terms. Comparing the future value of two cash flow streams, or comparing the **present value** — that is, the value in today's money terms of those same cash flow streams — will always result in the same conclusion as to which is best.

present value
an amount of money at today's value

For example, Grace asks your advice about two options. Option A and Option B will generate the following cash flows:

	End year 1	End year 2	End year 3	End year 4	End year 5
Option A	nil	nil	$27 000	$8 000	nil
Option B	nil	nil	nil	nil	$40 000

In order to compare these investment options, it is necessary to consider the cash flows at a common time period. If we compare these two investment options at the end of year 5 — that is, the future value of both Option A and Option B — we can evaluate which investment option is preferable.

Using a financial calculator and this example, assume the opportunity cost is 8%. We can input the following values to determine the future value of the investment.

Option A

(We need to do this calculation in two parts.)
Part 1 — To calculate the future value of the $27 000 after 2 years
PV = amount of the initial sum of money ($27 000)
i = opportunity cost or interest rate per period (8%)
n = number of periods (2)
If we select the future value key (*FV*) on the financial calculator, we will know that, if our opportunity cost is 8%, $27 000 to be received in 3 years is equivalent to receiving $31 492.80 in 5 years.
Plus,
Part 2 — To calculate the future value of the $8000 in 1 year
PV = amount of the initial sum of money ($8000)
i = opportunity cost or interest rate per period (8%)
n = number of periods (1)
If we select the future value key (*FV*) on the financial calculator, we will know that, if our opportunity cost is 8%, $8000 to be received in 4 years is equivalent to receiving $8640 in 5 years.

The future value of both cash flows, $27 000 to be received in 3 years and $8000 to be received in 4 years is equivalent to receiving $40 132.80 in 5 years (adding Parts 1 and 2 together: $31 492.80 + $8640 = $40 132.80).

Option B

The future value of $40 000 to be received in 5 years is $40 000.

Our advice to Grace would be to explain that, because of the time value of money, she is better off accepting Option A because it provides her with more money in future dollar terms.

If we had compared Option A with Option B on the basis of the value in today's dollar terms, we would arrive at exactly the same conclusion. We can determine the present value of the investment by inputting the values shown below.

Option A

(Again, we need to work this out in two parts because of the different amounts of money to be received in different years.)

Part 1 — To calculate the present value of the $27 000 to be received in 3 years

FV = amount of the future sum of money ($27 000)

i = interest rate per period (8%)

n = number of periods (3)

If we select the present value key (PV) on the financial calculator, we will know that, if our opportunity cost is 8%, $27 000 to be received in 3 years is equivalent to receiving $21 433.47 in today's money terms.

Plus,

Part 2 — To calculate the present value of the $8000 to be received in four years

FV = amount of the future sum of money ($8000)

i = interest rate per period (8%)

n = number of periods (4)

If we select the present value key (PV) on the financial calculator, we will know that, if our opportunity cost is 8%, $8000 to be received in 4 years is equivalent to receiving $5880.24 in today's money terms.

The present value of both cash flows, $27 000 to be received in 3 years and $8000 to be received in 4 years, is equivalent to receiving $27 313.71 in today's money terms (adding Part 1, $21 433.47, and Part 2, $5880.24, = $27 313.71).

Option B

FV = amount of the future sum of money ($40 000)

i = interest rate per period (8%)

n = number of periods (5)

If we select the present value key (PV) on the financial calculator, we will know that, if our opportunity cost is 8%, $40 000 to be received in 5 years is equivalent to receiving $27 223.33 in today's money terms.

Again our advice to Grace would be to explain that, because of the time value of money, she is better off accepting Option A. In this analysis it is because it is providing her with more money in today's dollar terms.

The formula to determine the present value of future sums of money can be used to assess Grace's question. This formula is the inverse of the formula used to determine a future value from a present sum.

$$PV = FV(1 + i)^{-n}$$

Or it may be expressed as:

$$PV = FV/(1 + i)^n$$

where FV = amount of the future sum of money
i = interest rate per period
n = number of periods.

Applying this formula to the example for Grace, we can determine the present value of each cash flow stream:

Option A

$$PV = \$27\,000(1 + 0.08)^{-3} + \$8000(1 + 0.08)^{-4}$$
$$= \$27\,313.71$$

Option B

$$PV = \$40\,000(1 + 0.08)^{-5}$$
$$= \$27\,223.33$$

Obviously, our advice to Grace would be the same, as the lump sums are identical to those which we derived by using a financial calculator.

So far we have considered only the future value and the present value of single sums of money. A related issue is the determination of the future value and present value of an identical stream of receipts/payments occurring in every period for a specified time. A series of cash flows that are identical in amount and occur at the end of consecutive time periods is called an 'ordinary annuity'.

Consider the following annuity with an interest rate required of 7%:

End year 1	End year 2	End year 3	End year 4	End year 5
\$500	\$500	\$500	\$500	\$500

If we wish to find the accumulated value (future value) of this annuity at the end of 5 years, we can input the following values in our financial calculator to determine the future value of the investment:

PMT = amount of the annuity (\$500)
i = interest rate per period (7%)
n = number of periods (5).

If we select the future value key (FV) on the financial calculator, we will know that if our opportunity cost is 7% we will require \$2875.37 in 5 years to be indifferent about receiving \$500 each year for 5 years and receiving \$2875.37 in 5 years.

Alternatively, we can use the formula for the future value of an annuity to determine the accumulated value at the end of the 5 years. This formula is as follows:

$$FV = \frac{PMT[(1 + i)^n - 1]}{i}$$
$$= \frac{\$500\,[(1 + 0.07)^5 - 1]}{0.07}$$
$$= \$2875.37$$

Using the same example we can determine the present value of this income stream. To calculate the present value, we would input the following values into a financial calculator or use the formula for the present value of an annuity:

PMT = amount of the annuity (\$500)
i = interest rate per period (7%)
n = number of periods (5).

If we select the present value key (PV) on the financial calculator, we will know that if our opportunity cost is 7% we would be indifferent about receiving \$2050.10 today and receiving \$500 each year for 5 years. Using the formula:

$$PV = \frac{PMT[1 - (1 + i)^{-n}]}{i}$$

Hence:

$$PV = \frac{\$500[1 - (1 + 0.07)^{-5}]}{0.07}$$
$$= \$2050.10$$

Understanding the concepts of compounding and the time value of money enables us to consider the types of questions that might commonly be asked of a financial planner. Consider the following situation to illustrate how these concepts are applied.

ILLUSTRATIVE EXAMPLE 2.1

Lawrence has just turned 40 and is seeking your advice about his retirement plans. Lawrence would like to retire at 65, and wants to have \$1.25 million in an investment account by then in order to maintain his current lifestyle. He has determined that he can afford to invest \$9000 each year (for the next 15 years) towards his retirement. At age 55 he will need to withdraw \$25 000 as he intends to invest in a healthy food retail outlet venture. If Lawrence's retirement account earns 12% compounded annually, how much will Lawrence need to deposit into the account each year for the last 10 years (between ages 55 and 65) to meet his goal of having \$1.25 million? To tackle Lawrence's concerns, we could take the following steps:

Step 1

Determine how much Lawrence's account will be worth at age 55. We know:

PMT = amount of the annuity (\$9000)
i = interest rate per period (12%)
n = number of periods (15).

If we input these data and then select the future value key (FV) on the financial calculator, we will know that the value of Lawrence's account in 15 years when he turns 55 will be \$335 517.

Once we deduct the cost of the investment in the healthy food retail outlet (\$25 000), the balance of the account will be \$310 517.

Step 2

Determine the value of the \$310 517 left in the account until Lawrence reaches age 65. We know:

PV = amount of the present sum of money (\$310 517)
i = interest rate per period (12%)
n = number of periods (10).

If we select the future value key (*FV*) on the financial calculator, we will know that the amount left in the account, $310 517, will grow to a value of $964 419.

In order for Lawrence to have $1.25 million, he will need to accumulate a further $285 581.

Step 3

If Lawrence is to accumulate the extra $285 581 in the years between the ages of 55 and 65, he will need to deposit regular amounts (annuity) into his retirement account. We know:

FV = amount of the future sum of money ($285 581)
i = interest rate per period (12%)
n = number of periods (10).

If we select the payment key (*PMT*) on the financial calculator, we will know that if Lawrence deposits a regular amount (annuity) of $16 274 for each of the 10 years after his 55th birthday, he will achieve his goal of having $1.25 million in his retirement account at age 65.

Figure 2.1 provides an illustration of the impact of compounding interest and the time value of money in a different context. In this situation, the mortgagee has already paid off their home and at around age 70 decides to undertake a new mortgage called a '**reverse mortgage**' under which the lender will provide ongoing payments or a lump sum. In most cases, no repayments on the mortgage are made and the interest accumulates and therefore compounds over the period of the loan. Figure 2.1 illustrates the effect of compound interest for someone who takes out a reverse mortgage. Note the illustration which represents the percentage amount of the house that the owner has over a period of time and the increasing effect of the unpaid interest on the loan as the interest builds upon the previous unpaid interest. Go to moneysmart.gov.au and input different variables in the reverse mortgage calculator to see the impact of compound interest for people who commence a reverse mortgage.

reverse mortgage an arrangement to mortgage a home in order to receive payments from the fund provider in return for a percentage ownership in the home or an accumulated debt to be paid when the home is sold

The example in figure 2.1 (overleaf) is based on a 70 year old person living alone whose house is valued at $500 000 with an anticipated increase in value of 3 per cent per annum. The reverse mortgage rate is 8 per cent per annum. The person requires a lump sum of $100 000 in one month and the fee is $12 per month.

In another example, Nina's grandmother, Anne, is 80 years of age and living alone in a home worth $650 000. Instead of a lump sum, Anne requires an extra $300 per month to help with some medical and rehabilitation expenses as she is getting frailer in her old age. Anne does not have access to a computer so she asks Nina to help her to find out the effect on her estate if she goes ahead with the loan. Based on the reverse mortgage calculator, Nina discovers that in 5 years the total payments to Anne would be $18 000 with interest owing of $8399 and fees of $3500, and her total debt would be $29 899. Nina informs Anne that her home is now worth $753 528 but her equity is now $723 630, or 96% of the house's value. Nina also tells Anne that in 10 years her equity in the home will fall to 91% or $796 301 (assuming a growth rate in the home of 3% p.a.). Anne is quite pleased that her family will gain a large share of the house when she dies, so thinks that her life will be much easier if she goes ahead with the reverse mortgage.

Home equity = Home value LESS the amount borrowed and interest and fees ?

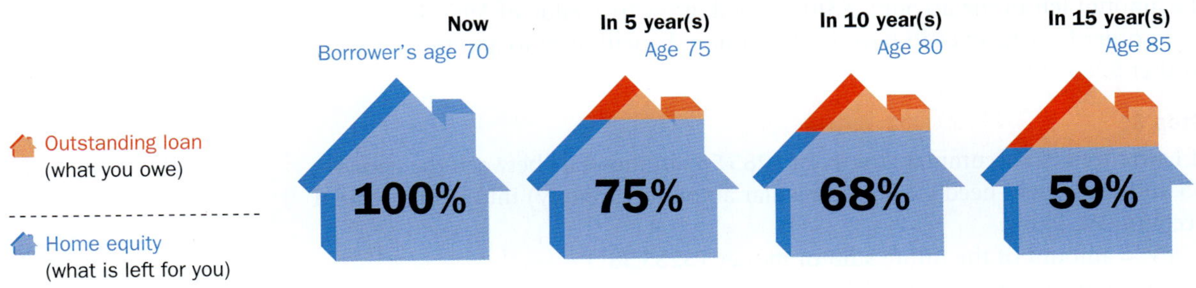

	Now	In 5 year(s)	In 10 year(s)	In 15 year(s)
Home value	**$500 000**	**$579 637**	**$671 958**	**$778 984**
Lump sum(s) borrowed	-	−$100 000	−$100 000	−$100 000
Payments to you	$0	$0	$0	$0
Interest owing	$0	−$46 149	−$115 234	−$217 080
Fees paid	$0	−$720	−$1 440	−$2 160
Total owing	**$0**	**−$146 869**	**−$216 674**	**−$319 240**
Home equity	**$500 000**	**$432 768**	**$455 284**	**$459 743**
Equity as % of home	**100%**	**75%**	**68%**	**59%**

The equity in your home might reach $0 when Borrower is **over 100 years old.**

This is an estimate, not a guarantee. You may end up with more or less equity in your home.

FIGURE 2.1

The effect of compound interest on a reverse mortgage over time

Note: To help borrowers better understand some of the (market) risks associated with taking out a reverse mortgage, the website provides two other scenarios for each set of conditions: one, if interest rates were 2 per cent higher and; two, if the house did not grow in value.

Source: MoneySmart 2013, Reverse mortgage calculator, www.moneysmart.gov.au.

LO 5 Nominal and effective interest rates

So far, we have assumed that compound interest rates are determined on an annual basis. These are the nominal or stated rates of interest that a bank might quote as the interest rate applicable to your mortgage. If, however, the interest is calculated more than once a year, the value of any investment or loan is affected by the frequency of those interest rate determinations. When nominal interest rates are compounded more than once a year, the convention is to determine the periodic interest rate, i, as:

$$i = \frac{j}{m}$$

where j = the nominal rate of interest

m = the number of compounding periods per year.

For example, the nominal interest rate for a year is $j = 0.09$ (or 9% p.a.) and we are told that interest is compounded each quarter. If $m = 4$ quarters each year in a 4-year period, you now have:

$$m \times n = 4(4) \text{ or } 16 \text{ periods of 1 quarter each}$$

with a quarterly interest rate of:

$$\begin{aligned} i &= \frac{j}{m} \\ &= \frac{0.09}{4} \\ &= 0.0225 \text{ per period of 1 quarter.} \end{aligned}$$

We can illustrate this concept by considering the situation of Leonie.

ILLUSTRATIVE EXAMPLE 2.2

Leonie is considering taking out a loan but is not sure of two main options that she has for meeting the repayments. One option is to take the loan of $100 000 with an interest rate of 9% p.a. compounded quarterly over a period of 5 years; the other is at 9% compounded monthly over the same time frame. She wants to know what the size of the repayments would be and what the effective interest rate would be for each option.

Using the formula for the present value of an annuity, we need to adjust the formula to reflect that the number of compounding periods is more than once a year.

$$PV = \frac{PMT[1 - (1 + i)^{-n}]}{i}$$

The same formula adjusted to reflect the fact that interest is compounded quarterly is:

$$PV = \frac{PMT\left[1 - \left(1 + \frac{j}{m}\right)^{-m \times n}\right]}{\frac{j}{m}}$$

$$\$100\,000 = \frac{PMT[1 - (1 + 0.0225)^{-20}]}{0.0225}$$

$$PMT = \$6264.21 \text{ per quarter}$$

When interest is compounded more frequently than once a year, Leonie is actually paying more than the nominal interest rate quoted. In order to have a clearer picture of how much interest she will pay, we use the measure called the 'effective rate of interest'. This is the interest rate that would be charged if the interest had been compounded once a year.

The formula to determine the effective interest rate is given by:

$$i = \left(1 + \frac{j}{m}\right)^m - 1$$

In our numerical example we have:

$$\begin{aligned} i &= \left(1 + \frac{0.09}{4}\right)^4 - 1 \\ &= 9.31\% \end{aligned}$$

»

»

The nominal interest rate of 9% p.a. quoted to Leonie is actually an effective rate of 9.31% p.a. when we take into account that the interest is compounded quarterly.

We need to compare the two options for Leonie by using the same formula and calculating the repayments based on 60 payments (5 years of 12 monthly payments). In this case the repayments are $2075.84 per month.

$$PV = \frac{PMT\left[1 - \left(1 + \frac{j}{m}\right)^{-m \times n}\right]}{\frac{j}{m}}$$

$$\$100\,000 = \frac{PMT[1 - (1 + 0.0075)^{-60}]}{0.0075}$$

$$PMT = \$2075.84 \text{ per month}$$

The effective interest rate for the monthly repayments is:

$$i = \left(1 + \frac{j}{m}\right)^m - 1$$

$$= \left(1 + \frac{0.09}{12}\right)^{12} - 1$$

$$= 9.38\%$$

In this case Leonie would have to choose either to pay an effective interest rate of 9.31% if she is able to make repayments of $6264.21 per quarter for five years, or to pay $2075.84 per month each month for 5 years at an effective interest rate of 9.38%. Note that the effect of the higher number of compounding periods per annum results in a lower total sum to be repaid ($124 550.40 = $2075.84 × 60 monthly repayments and $125 284.20 = $6264.21 × 20 quarterly repayments) despite having a higher effective interest rate (9.38% compared to 9.31%).

The following scenario illustrates the importance of understanding the difference between nominal interest rates and effective interest rates.

Consider the interest rates charged by two banks:

- Bank X charges 8.25% p.a. compounded daily.
- Bank Y charges 8.5% p.a. compounded annually.

To determine which bank is charging the lower interest rate we need to compare interest rates on an annual basis, that is, compare the effective interest rates being charged.

The effective interest rate being charged by Bank X is calculated as follows:

$$i = \left(\frac{1 + 0.0825}{365}\right)^{365} - 1 = 8.6\%$$

The interest rate of 8.5% p.a. charged by Bank Y is compounded annually so this will be identical to its effective interest rate, that is, 8.5% p.a.

We can see, therefore, that 8.5% compounded annually is lower interest than 8.25% compounded daily (with an effective interest rate of 8.6% p.a.).

If we extend this issue further we can illustrate the importance of understanding the difference between nominal and effective interest rates by considering the following interest rates quoted by three banks:

- Bank A: 15%, compounded daily
- Bank B: 15.5%, compounded quarterly
- Bank C: 16%, compounded annually.

The effective interest rates for these three banks are as follows:

$$\text{Bank A} = \left[1 + \frac{0.15}{365}\right]^{365} - 1 = 16.18\%$$

$$\text{Bank B} = \left[1 + \frac{0.155}{4}\right]^{4} - 1 = 16.42\%$$

$$\text{Bank C} = \left[1 + \frac{0.16}{1}\right]^{1} - 1 = 16\%$$

Which bank is offering the best rate? For a saver, Bank B offers the best (highest) interest rate. For a borrower, Bank C offers the best (lowest) interest rate. Nina would be delighted to know that, as a saver, a higher interest rate may be earned over the year when the interest is paid on a more frequent basis as well as the interest gaining the benefit of being compounded.

What we can see from this situation is that the highest nominal interest rate is not necessarily the best interest rate for an investor, and compounding during the year can lead to a significant difference between the nominal interest rate and the effective interest rate. Any comparison of interest rates should be made on the basis of effective interest rates.

To consider the notion of effective interest rates in a specific context that impacts on most people, let us look at the interest rates charged on the use of credit cards.

Credit cards

Credit card lending has grown strongly over the past two decades. Credit cards are offered by many organisations, not just banks, and nearly everyone has one if not two cards. Basically, they work this way — lines of credit are approved and can be drawn on by the borrower in the form of cash advances, or they may be used to purchase goods and services directly.

Credit card charges vary. Some charges are based on an annual fee combined with an interest charge on the outstanding balance after a certain interest moratorium period. For example, interest might not be charged to the account if the outstanding balance is settled within 30 days of the issue of the credit card statement. Additional fees are usually levied for cash advances.

Table 2.2 (overleaf) gives some examples of credit cards with some of the common features available today.

TABLE 2.2 Examples of credit cards with some of the common features available

Company name	Product name	Current rate	Star rating	Interest free days	Credit card fee	Speed to waive fee	Minimum credit	Maximum credit	Rewards program available
Qantas Credit Union	Lifestyle	12.34%	★★★★★	0	$0.00	N/A	$1000.00	$50 000.00	✓
Teachers Mutual Bank	Teachers Credit Card	11.50%	★★★★★	55	$0.00	N/A	$1000.00	$25 000.00	✗
Victoria Teachers Mutual Bank	Visa Classic Credit Card	13.19%	★★★★★	55	$0.00	N/A	$500.00	No max	✗
Australian Defence Credit Union	Low Rate Visa Card	10.99%	★★★★	55	$49.00	N/A	$500.00	No max	✗
ANZ	Low Rate	12.99%	★★★★	55	$58.00	N/A	$1000.00	$15 000.00	✗
Bankwest	Breeze MasterCard	11.99%	★★★★	55	$59.00	N/A	$1000.00	$25 000.00	✗
Bankwest	Zero MasterCard	17.99%	★★★★	55	$0.00	N/A	$1000.00	$25 000.00	✗
Bendigo Bank	Basic Black MasterCard	12.49%	★★★★	44	$45.00	N/A	$500.00	$50 000.00	✗
Bendigo Bank	Basic Black Visa	12.49%	★★★★	44	$45.00	N/A	$500.00	$50 000.00	✗
Bendigo Bank	RSPCA Rescue Visa	15.49%	★★★★	40	$24.00	N/A	$500.00	$50 000.00	✗
Commonwealth Bank	Low Fee MasterCard	19.74%	★★★★	55	$24.00	$1000.00	$500.00	No max	✗
Bank of Melbourne	Amplify Credit Card	18.74%	★★★	55	$79.00	N/A	$1000.00	$80 000.00	✓
Bank of Melbourne	Gold Low Rate MasterCard	15.99%	★★★	55	$79.00	N/A	$4000.00	$80 000.00	✗

Credit card facilities are provided by banks, building societies and credit unions. Australians have considerably increased both their available credit card limits and total credit card debt outstanding since the early 1990s. An interesting observation on the growth of credit card use in Australia is the increase in fees collected by the providers of credit cards. Fees on credit cards collected by banks from households jumped from $898 million in 2005 to $1.3 billion in 2012, with an average annual fee rising from $78.52 in 2008 to $92.45 in 2011; an increase of nearly 18 per cent over those three years. In fact, in 2012 banks earned more from credit card fees than the $1.2 billion from home loan fees. (RateCity, 2013).

Apart from this fee income, banks also collected merchant service fees for credit card transactions from businesses and, even though the RBA has forced reform of these fees upon the providers, the total of these two distinct sources of fee income is about $3.2 billion annually and growing (RBA 2010a).

Credit cards are a good example of open-ended lending. Such credit can be used repeatedly until a prearranged limit is reached. Credit cards are generally issued by financial intermediaries; similar instruments, technically charge cards, are issued by American Express, Diners' Club and bodies such as major retailers for use in their stores only, and by specific-purpose providers such as MotorCharge for vehicle fuel accounts and vehicle servicing. With all credit cards, the borrower decides the amount and timing of credit to use up to the prearranged limit.

Consumers are attracted to credit cards for automatic billing because of the convenience, the inducements such as frequent flyer points and customer loyalty rewards programs, and because they have more control over their spending.

Interest rates on credit cards are generally quoted as effective interest rates. Effective interest rates allow for the impact of compounding. Following on from the previous section on effective interest rates: if we owe $100 on a credit card which charges interest at the rate of 1.6% per month, at the end of the first month we will owe $1.60 in interest and our balance will be $101.60. At the end of the second month, we will owe interest on our original $100 and interest on our interest, which is the essence of compounding. This process would continue month by month until the end of the year. At the end of the year, we will owe $120.98 on the credit card, which means the effective rate of interest is 20.98% per annum. Recall the formula for the effective rate of interest:

$$\begin{aligned}\text{Effective rate of interest} &= (1 + 1.6\%)^{12} - 1 \\ &= 20.98\%\end{aligned}$$

A credit card might typically charge an effective annual rate of 20.98% on purchases (and a higher rate on cash advances), which means the monthly interest rate is 1.6%. Therefore, any outstanding balance on a credit card will grow by 1.6% per month. All credit card providers insist on a minimum monthly payment which is a percentage of the outstanding balance — the minimum will vary between card providers but 2% would be a typical figure.

The amount owing on a loan which increases by 1.6% per month and decreases (if only minimum payments are made) by 2% per month is unlikely to fall very rapidly, if at all. Indeed, if the credit limit has not been reached then even one or two credit purchases during the next month will most likely mean that the individual owes more this month than last month. The cycle can be a vicious one, with one commentator suggesting that people who mismanage credit cards will spend a year of their life working just to pay off the interest on their cards.

ILLUSTRATIVE EXAMPLE 2.3

Junia is 22 and owes $3000 on her credit card. The current interest rate is 1.6% per month. If Junia makes no additional purchases on her credit card and pays $60 per month off her debt, Junia will be 30 when she makes her last payment and she will have paid more than $3000 in interest. If Junia's credit card provider charges an annual fee of $59 to her account each December, after 8 years of payments of $60 per month, Junia, at age 30, will still owe more than $1000 and she will have paid more than $3600 in interest.

As we can see, minimum payments barely cover the ongoing interest commitment. Making minimum payments leaves the individual exposed to very high interest rates. Individuals need a plan which discharges credit card debt as quickly as possible. This might include:

- making payments greater than the minimum
- consolidating credit card debt with other debt which attracts a lower rate of interest
- switching to a credit card which offers a lower rate of interest, including taking advantage of cards that offer a low honeymoon rate — although clients must be clear on the interest rate consequences once the honeymoon period is over.

Using the Credit Card Calculator available on the moneysmart website we can inform Junia of the effects of a nominal interest rate. If Junia owes $3000 with an annual interest rate of 18.5% and minimal repayments of 2% or $20 per month then she will pay a total of $10 227 over 26 years and 9 months. The effective interest rate using the above formula is 20.152%. However, if she is able to increase her repayments to $148 per month she will pay only $3557 over two years and save a total of $6670.

PERSONAL FINANCE BULLETIN

Credit offers

Watch out for these credit offers as they can be debt traps.

Credit limit increase invitations

From 1 July 2012, credit card issuers are not allowed to send you invitations to increase your credit limit without first getting your agreement. This applies to both new and existing credit cards.

You can contact your card issuer at any time and ask them not to send you credit limit increase invitations. Even if you do agree to receive credit limit increase invitations, you can change your mind later by contacting your card issuer.

Whether you decide to opt in or out of receiving credit limit increase invitations, you can ask your card issuer for an increase to your credit limit at any time.

If you can't afford to pay off your balance in full each month, don't increase your credit limit. A higher credit limit makes it very easy to get into more debt — and you'll end up paying a lot more in interest too.

If you need extra money to make a special purchase, aim to pay the debt down quickly. Then lower your limit back to a more manageable amount.

Think carefully before getting a credit limit increase and don't live beyond your means. If you make only the minimum repayments on your card each month, you will pay more in interest and it will take longer to pay off your balance. See making repayments for more information.

Honeymoon rates

Sometimes cards offer an introductory or 'honeymoon' interest rate. Check how much the interest rate will rise at the end of the honeymoon period, and what fees and charges come with the offer. A card with higher fees might wipe out your honeymoon savings before long. The same principle applies to offers of 'no fees for 12 months'.

Cash back offers

'Cash back' credit cards give you back some credit on your account. But the benefits are quickly outweighed if the card has a higher than usual interest rate. If you don't pay the whole balance off each month, this kind of offer is not for you.

Balance transfers

This is when you transfer outstanding balances from one credit card to another, often at a lower interest rate for a certain time (for example, 4.9% for 6 months).

You can get the full benefit of this by paying off the balance transfer amount within the balance transfer period. Just make sure you check the interest rate that will apply once the balance transfer period is over.

If you use your new card to buy something, your purchase will attract the full interest rate of the new card (not the special balance transfer rate).

It is a good idea to check how different credit card features may apply when you transfer your balance to a new card. For example, you may be unable to take advantage of any interest-free period on new purchases until the balance transfer amount is paid in full.

When you make a payment on your new card, there are two ways it can be applied:

- the credit card issuer will apply it to the balance with the highest interest rate (for example, purchases you have made at the standard interest rate or cash advances at the cash rate, whichever has a higher interest rate)
- with the credit card issuer's agreement, you may request that payments be applied in a different way (for example, that any payments made during the balance transfer period will be applied to the balance transfer amount, even if the interest rate is lower).

When the balance transfer period is over, if you have not paid off the full balance transfer amount, the amount remaining will be charged at the standard interest rate or cash advance rate (which may be higher).

Check the conditions of your card to see what rate applies.

Source: https://www.moneysmart.gov.au/borrowing-and-credit/credit-cards#offers.

LO 6 Net present value

net present value the present value of a stream of income payments after deducting the cost of the stream of income payments

Net present value (otherwise referred to as NPV) is a means to determine whether an investment is worth undertaking. This concerns the comparison of what is proposed to be outlaid or invested in today's dollars with what the investment is predicted to return in today's dollars.

NPV is the sum of the present value of cash inflows less cash outflows. The expected future cash inflows are adjusted for the time value of money by discounting those cash flows by a discount rate — this gives a present value. The discount rate is usually determined by the rate of return on the investment required by the investor. It sometimes is referred to as the cost of capital. By undertaking this process we can make a direct comparison between alternative investments or investment projects.

NPV is calculated as follows:

$$NPV = PV\text{ (Future cash flows)} - \text{Investment today}$$

NPV may also be expressed in a formula as:

$$NPV = -CF_0 + \frac{CF_1}{(1+r)^1} + \frac{CF_2}{(1+r)^2} + \cdots + \frac{CF_n}{(1+r)^n}$$

$$= \sum^{i} \frac{CF_i}{(1+r)^i} - CF_0$$

where

NPV = net present value of the project
CF_0 = the initial outlay of the investment
CF_i = the future cash flows over the period i
r = the discount rate or cost of capital
i = number of periods
n = the number of the last year of the project.

Note that if the NPV of an investment is:

< 0 then the investment is generally financially unacceptable
$= 0$ then the investment may be regarded as marginal
> 0 then the investment is generally regarded as financially acceptable.

The process of discounting is based on the reverse of compounding. If you expect to receive $100 in 1 year with a discount rate of 10% p.a. the present day value of the $100 in 1 year is $91. So, if an investment costs $300 today and is expected to return $100 at the end of each of the next 4 years with an interest rate of 10% p.a. then we can see the NPV as follows:

$$NPV = -300 + \frac{100}{(1+0.1)^1} + \frac{100}{(1+0.1)^2} + \frac{100}{(1+0.1)^3} + \frac{100}{(1+0.1)^4}$$

Note the initial investment is shown as a minus figure to indicate that it is an outflow.

We can see the result in the following table:

Year	0	1	2	3	4
Cash flow	−300	100	100	100	100
Discount factor	1	0.9091	0.8264	0.7513	0.6831
Discounted cash flow	−300	90.91	82.64	75.13	68.31

Note: The discount factors may be found in tables in most finance textbooks. Alternatively, the discount factor can be calculated using the formula:

$$\frac{1}{(1 + r)^n}$$

Thus the discount factor for 1 year is:

$$\frac{1}{(1 + 0.1)^1} = 0.909\ 090\ 9$$

and the NPV in the above example is:

$$\begin{aligned} NPV &= -300 + 90.91 + 82.64 + 75.13 + 68.31 \\ &= \$16.99 \end{aligned}$$

Thus, as the NPV is a positive amount the investment proposal may be regarded as financially acceptable.

The NPV technique is widely used to compare and evaluate investment options for investors.

LO 7 Further applications of the time value of money concept

The time value of money concept has a number of applications further to the above situations and a financial adviser needs to be well versed in understanding the concept and how it may be applied. We will consider two of these applications in this next section, namely, the internal rate of return and the valuation of fixed-interest securities.

The internal rate of return

Often investors and financial advisers use the **internal rate of return** (IRR) on an investment as the investment yield or return on an investment. The IRR is the discount rate at which the NPV is zero. That is, the IRR is the rate of return at which the present values of cash inflows and outflows are equal. The discount rate at which the NPV is zero is given by the following formulae:

internal rate of return the rate of return at which the cash inflow and cash outflow of an investment is zero

$$NPV = -CF_0 + \sum \frac{CF_i}{(1 + r)^n} = 0$$

or:

$$-CF_0 = \sum \frac{CF_i}{(1 + r)^i}$$

where CF_0 = the initial outlay of the investment
CF_i = the future cash flows over the period i
r = the discount rate
i = number of periods
n = the number of the last year of the project.

The IRR is usually calculated by using a financial calculator or a spreadsheet package. However, it is possible to calculate IRR by using a linear interpolation method by following these steps.

$$IRR = r_A + \frac{(r_A - r_B) \times NPV_A}{(NPV_B - NPV_A)}$$

Step 1: Apply an estimated discount rate, say $r_A = 10\%$.
Step 2: Calculate NPV_A using this discount rate. In the example in the previous section, $NPV_A = \$16.99$.
Step 3: Estimate a second discount rate r_B that could produce a negative *NPV*; say 15%.
Step 4: Calculate NPV_B for the discount rate r_B (as shown in the table below).

Year	0	1	2	3	4
Cash flow	−300	100	100	100	100
Discount factor	1	0.8696	0.7561	0.6575	0.5718
Discounted cash flows	−300	86.96	75.61	65.75	57.18

Therefore:

$$NPV_B = -300 + 86.96 + 75.61 + 65.75 + 57.18 = -14.5$$

If the result does not produce a negative result you need to try again with another discount rate.

Step 5: Calculate the IRR using the formula provided above:

$$IRR = 10 + \frac{(10 - 15) \times 16.99}{(-14.5 - 16.99)}$$
$$= 10 + \frac{(-5 \times 16.99)}{-31.49}$$
$$= 10 + 2.7$$
$$= 12.7\%$$

The variation of NPV may be represented in figure 2.2 which shows that the NPV is positive at all discount rates less than the IRR (12.7%) and negative for discount rates above the IRR. The concept of IRR differs from the discount rate as the IRR is the return that will be made from the investment and the discount rate is the rate that is applied to compare different investments.

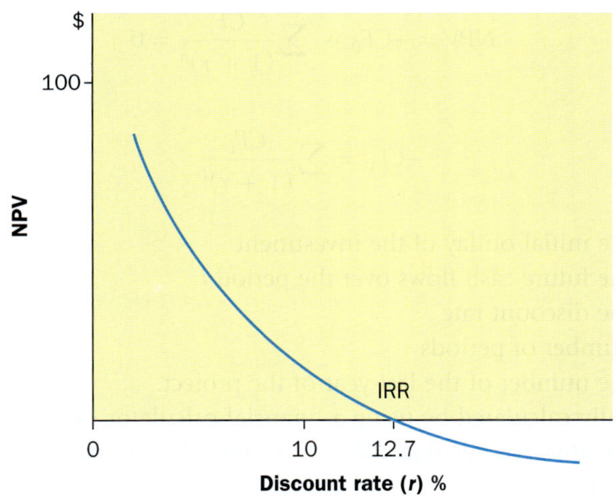

FIGURE 2.2
The variation in NPV at different discount rates

An investment is attractive when the investment's IRR has a positive NPV and its return is higher than the discount rate.

So, if the IRR of an investment is:

$< r$ then the investment is generally financially unacceptable

$= r$ then the investment is marginal

$> r$ then the investment is generally financially acceptable.

A note of caution: Where there is only one sign change in cash inflows and outflows there will be only one IRR value. When there are multiple sign changes in cash inflows and cash outflows this can result in multiple IRR values at which NPV = 0 or no IRR value at all. In these cases, a financial adviser should use NPV analysis rather than IRR.

Fixed-interest securities

Investors in fixed-interest securities lend money to the security issuer, so the investors are, in effect, investing in debt because the issuer will re-lend the funds for some purpose to another party. In return for their investment, the issuer will pay the investors a fixed rate of interest for a set period of time. The regular interest rate is termed the 'coupon rate'.

All goes well for an investor as long as the issuer pays the interest on time and repays the full amount at the maturity date. However, if the investor needed to sell the security prior to the maturity date then the value of the security may not be the same as agreed. The value that the investor may receive will depend on the interest rates prevailing in the economy at the time the investor needs to sell the fixed-interest security.

How the value of the security is determined again comes back to the time value of money concept as the method used to calculate the market value of the security is known as the discount method. This method refers to the rate of return required by the investor and is the rate at which future cash flows are discounted back to the present value.

ILLUSTRATIVE EXAMPLE 2.4

A security agreement is made on the basis of 12% interest (6% each half year) for a period of 2 years. Thus, during the course of the 2 years, the investor, Howard, will receive interest payments of 6% each 6 months and at the end of the 2 years he will also receive the amount of the original investment. Suppose Howard invests $1000 under the above terms.

The contract will stipulate the following payments:

Period	6 months	1 year	18 months	2 years
Future returns	$60	$60	$60	$60 + $1 000

However, only a few days after the security is invested the interest rates in the economy change and for a similar 2-year investment period the interest rate falls to 8% p.a. or 4% every 6 months. Howard's own situation changes too and he decides that he needs his $1000 for emergency expenses on his home. He decides to sell his security on the fixed-interest securities market.

Howard discovers that he will receive not $1000 but $1072.60. He is delighted at such a quick gain on his investment after only a few days and wonders how did it happen?

»

»

The answer is based on the time value of money concept of the future cash flows under the original agreement. The present value of the future returns is:

$$PV = \frac{FV}{(1+i)^n}$$

where PV = present value
FV = future value or cash flows
i = the interest rate per period
n = the number of compounding periods

In Howard's case:

Period	Formula	PV of cash flow ($)
1	$\frac{60}{(1+0.04)}$	57.70
2	$\frac{60}{(1+0.04)^2}$	55.50
3	$\frac{60}{(1+0.04)^3}$	53.30
4	$\frac{1060}{(1+0.04)^4}$	906.10
Total		1 072.60

Note that the future cash flows of $60 and the return of the principal amount of $1000 are set future cash flows. The difference is that the prevailing interest rate has changed and provides a lower discount rate. Hence, Howard is able to sell his security, nominally valued at $1000, for a market price of $1072.60. If Howard was able to hold on to his investment for the 2 years, then he would receive interest at a higher rate than the 4% the market offered *after* he had made his investment.

The critical point in this example is that the prevailing interest rates can affect the market price of the security and can result in a capital gain or a loss if the interest rates increase.

Suppose an investor is faced with the choice of two fixed-interest investments. Option A offers a fixed interest rate at 5% p.a. for 1 year and Option B offers a fixed interest rate of 6% for 2 years. Also assume that the investor wants to invest for a period of 2 years. Is it better for our investor to choose Option B and receive a guaranteed 6% for 2 years, or to invest in Option A to get 5% p.a. for 1 year and take a chance on the interest rate for the second year — which may be higher or lower than 5%? Which is the investor more likely to choose? How can a financial adviser offer advice to an investor facing such a choice?

forward rate
the interest rate that is required to be achieved in a later year when choosing between a short-term and longer term fixed-interest investment

One way of resolving this dilemma is to solve for the rate at which the second year of investment for Option A is expected to represent the same outcome as for Option B. This is known as the **forward rate**.

For this example, let f_2 be the interest rate for year 2 that an investor choosing Option A would need to obtain to receive the same outcome as an investor who chose Option B.

$$f_2 = \frac{(1 + r_2)^2}{(1 + r_1)} - 1$$
$$= \frac{(1 + 0.06)^2}{(1 + 0.05)} - 1$$
$$= 0.07 \text{ or } 7.0 \text{ (rounded)}$$

where f_2 = the future rate of interest in the second year for Option A
r_1 = the interest rate for the 1 year investment for Option A
r_2 = the interest rate for the 2 year investment for Option B.

To explain this further we will consider an investment of \$1. For Option B the compound interest for the two years is $(1.06)^2$ = \$1.12 (rounded). For Option A the return after one year is (1.05) = \$1.05. At the end of year 1 if the investor of Option A obtains an interest rate of 7.0% then (1.05) × (1.07) = \$1.12 (rounded). If the interest rate for year 2 went down to, say, 4% then the Option A investor would realise (1.05) × (1.04) = \$1.09 at the end of year 2. If the interest rate in year 2 went up to 8.0% then the Option A investor would receive (1.05) × (1.08) = \$1.13.

So, in the case described above there is no difference in the investment choices as long as the interest rate that is available for the second year at the maturity of the 1-year fixed term is at least 7.0%.

However, investment choice depends on the investor's view of the future interest rate. If interest rates move down after 1 year then Option B would be the better choice. If interest rates move up in the second year then Option A would be the better choice, as long as the rate increases to above 7.0%. So, it depends on the expectation of what the future interest rate is likely to be and, in many respects, the view about the trend of inflation. If for a 1-year term the interest rate is 5% and for a 2-year term it is 6% it may be likely that, at the outset, the view is that the future rate will be 7.5% after 1 year. By choosing the 2-year security an investor might miss out on possible higher interest rates.

The use of the forward rate approach may act as a guide in helping to resolve such a dilemma but economic conditions are changeable and future interest rates are difficult to predict with accuracy.

LO 8 Effect of tax and inflation on the rate of return

When advising clients an adviser needs to inform their client of the effects of both inflation and taxation on the net return on investments. In other words, an adviser needs to indicate the real rate of return after the *nominal* return is reduced by taxation and the effect of inflation. The nominal rate of return is the return stated by an investment; for example, 7% p.a. fixed interest. The real rate of return is the actual return to the investor after deducting the taxation to be paid by the investor and the impact of the rate of inflation. The repayments for fixed-interest investments, in particular, are prone to be overestimated when the effects of inflation and taxation are ignored. Table 2.3 (overleaf) indicates in simple form the effects of inflation and taxation on the real rate of return on a fixed-interest investment. Note that this table does not take into account the timing of the interest or tax payments which both may affect the real rate of return and indicate an even lower rate of return than that illustrated.

TABLE 2.3 Effect of inflation and taxation on the real rate of return on a fixed-interest investment

Tax rate %	20.5	34.0	38.5	46.5
Interest %	8.0	8.0	8.0	8.0
Tax on interest %	(1.64)	(2.72)	(3.08)	(3.72)
After-tax return %	6.36	5.28	4.92	4.28
Inflation %	(5.0)	(5.0)	(5.0)	(5.0)
Real rate of return %	1.36	0.28	−0.08	−0.72

Note: This example assumes: interest rate = 8% p.a., inflation rate = 5% p.a., tax rates include 1.5% Medicare levy and are based on the rates applying in 2010–11.

Assuming Nina was happy with a fixed interest rate of return she may be less happy when she considers that she may lose some of the value of her interest if she pays personal income tax and when the cost of living increases, which reduces what she can buy with her money.

Summary

Financial planners need to assist their clients in achieving their financial goals. They do this by helping clients to determine how much money is required and in what time frame. They then need to apply a number of skills such as the preparation of personal financial statements and applying ratio analysis to advise their clients on how they may reach their objectives and to assist clients to understand the impact of certain events on their family budget. Financial planners also need to explain to clients how money has different values in different time periods. A dollar in hand now is worth more than a dollar received in a year. This notion is referred to as the time value of money. The longer the time that money is invested, the greater will be the future value of that investment. The increase in value comes about because any interest received on the original investment will itself earn interest in subsequent time periods. This is the nature of compounding.

Other knowledge and skills that the financial planner needs to have in order to explain concepts of finance to clients include the need to understand the difference between nominal and effective interest rates and the use of the present value method to evaluate different investment choices. In particular, financial advisers need to alert clients about the effective interest rates charged on credit cards when the full amount is not paid by the due date. Finally, the financial adviser needs to understand and to relate to clients the effects of inflation and taxation on the returns that they will actually gain and how this may differ to the stated returns.

Professional application questions

2.1 Review the Professional Advice feature in this chapter. Consider the impact on Efram and Sofia's financial circumstances if both were to continue working but Sofia's after-tax income was increased by 40% for a period of 2 years while she takes on a more responsible position. How will this affect their savings ratio and their net wealth? (Assume that Sofia decided to delay having children until after the 2-year period of higher payment.)

2.2 Explain in your own words why $100 today will buy more goods and services than $100 in 3 years.

2.3 An advertisement offers a fixed term deposit for 4 years with an interest rate of 4.8% p.a. compounded annually or a fixed deposit for 4 years with an interest rate of 4.65% p.a. compounded quarterly. Which one would you choose? Explain why.

2.4 (a) A credit card is a virtual requirement in today's society. Do you agree or disagree with this statement? Explain.

(b) Find out the nominal interest rate on your own credit card and calculate the effective rate of interest.

2.5 Your uncle invested $50 000 in a 5-year fixed term security 2 years ago when the interest rate was 5.5% p.a. payable half yearly. He now needs to get his money back as an emergency situation has arisen. He asks a broker to sell the security on the securities exchange market and is delighted to receive the sum of $53 000. Explain why your uncle has received more than he originally invested.

2.6 Edmond has a dilemma. He has a choice of investing $10 000 for 5 years at an interest rate of 5.25% p.a. with interest payable quarterly or investing for 6 years at an interest rate of 5.5% p.a. with interest payable quarterly. Edmond does not need the $10 000 for a 6-year period. What will determine whether Edmond chooses one or the other investment period?

2.7 Wim and Dorothy are aged 79 and 75 respectively and they own their own home. They do not have much spare capital to undertake repairs and renovations on their home but intend to sell their home in the next 3 years and move into a residential unit where they will have easy access to care as they age. They believe that their home will gain a better price if they spend about $50 000 on updating their bathroom and kitchen and doing some painting. Consider the proposal of borrowing the funds as a reverse mortgage with no repayments made until they sell their house. What factors do they need to consider in making their decision?

2.8 Brad and Nerida are considering two alternative investments. Option 1 requires an outlay of $10 000 and after 2 years is expected to bring a cash flow of $1500 p.a. for the next 3 years. Then the investment would be terminated and they would get their $10 000 back. Option 2 requires an outlay of $15 000 and is expected to bring a cash flow of $1200 for each of the next 5 years. They would then expect to sell the investment for $17 500. Explain how net present value calculations would help them to decide on the best investment choice.

2.9 Cherie, one of your clients, invested $50 000 into a fixed term security at a rate of 6% p.a. Cherie earns income that puts her in the 34% marginal tax bracket. She wonders why you have mentioned that she needs to understand the effects of inflation and taxation on her 'real' rate of return. Calculate the real rate of return to Cheri if inflation is given as 3% and write a brief explanation to Cherie to demonstrate the real rate of return on her investment.

Professional application exercises

Basic	*
Moderate	* *
Challenging	* * *

2.10 Ratio calculations *

Tim and Laura provide the following financial information:

Assets	Home $400 000 Bank account $4000 Car $15 000
Liabilities	Home loan $300 000
Income p.a. (after tax)	Laura $58 000; Tim $80 000
Home loan repayments	$25 000 p.a.

(a) Calculate their net worth ratio.
(b) Calculate their debt service ratio.
(c) Calculate Tim and Laura's debt service ratio if a rise in interest rates causes their home loan repayments to increase to $30 000 without any change in their income.

2.11 Credit card switch ✱

Angie has received an offer in the mail to transfer her $5000 credit card balance to a new provider. The offer is 'low rate and no fees'. The rate offered is 3.99% p.a. compounded monthly for 6 months with no application fees or transaction fees. However, in the terms and conditions it says:

- after the 6-month introductory period, the interest rate will revert to 19.5% p.a., which is a variable rate
- the transferred balance will be repaid first
- government charges and a late payment fee may apply
- minimum monthly repayments are required to be 3% of the outstanding loan amount or $30, whichever is the greater.

(a) What advice can you give Angie?
(b) Why might Angie consider switching to the new provider?

2.12 Investment returns ✱✱

Effie has been given a chance to invest in her sister's frozen fruit juice company which needs some 'seed' capital so that production can commence. Her sister, Libby, estimates that an investment of $50 000 to buy 50 000 shares is needed. Libby estimates that each share will be worth $5.00 in 5 years.

(a) Nominally, what is the rate of return that Effie can expect to earn?
(b) What is the present value of the expected sum in 5 years if Effie sells her shares?
(c) On present value terms, what is the rate of return that Effie can expect to earn?

2.13 Savings needed ✱✱

Wanda wants to accumulate the sum of $30 000 in 3 years when she anticipates using the sum as a deposit on a home unit. She plans to have an annual holiday which she can fund from other savings. She has an initial starting amount of $6000 in an investment fund. If she expects an average annual rate of return of 7% on her investment, how much will she need to save each year for her to reach her objective?

2.14 Credit card interest ✱✱

Pedro always thought that his credit card company charged a monthly interest rate. He has just checked his credit card statement and was surprised to learn that the company charges a daily interest rate of 0.000 52%. Pedro believes that when you allow for 365 periods of compounding that the interest rate would be astronomical. What is the effective annual rate?

2.15 Evaluating a potential project ✱✱

New Growth Ltd's ambitious finance manager provides the following information with regards to a possible new project and wants you to evaluate whether the company should proceed with the project.

Purchase price of equipment	$6 million
Expected life of equipment	7 years
Tax depreciation of equipment	$1 million p.a.
Scrap value of equipment after 7 years	$350 000
Company tax rate	30% p.a.

Required rate of return	11% p.a.
Expected sales	$3.0 million p.a.
Operating costs (excl. interest and depreciation)	$1.5 million p.a.
Finance for the equipment	7-year bank loan with interest @ 9.5% p.a.

2.16 A savings plan ✱✱

Bruce and Karen have a newborn baby, Lisa. Generous grandparents have made a gift of $15 000 available for Lisa. Bruce and Karen have decided to invest this in trust for Lisa so that on her 21st birthday she will have a deposit to buy a one-bedroom home unit.

Bruce and Karen are considering making additional annual payments to the trust account, in order to increase the deposit amount to 40% of the expected price of the unit. Assume that the current price of a one-bedroom home unit is $220 000 and that property prices grow at 3% p.a. Assume that the trust account receives interest at 6.5% p.a.

(a) What is the projected amount that will be available to Lisa, when she turns 21, from the gift that is being held in trust?

(b) How much must Bruce and Karen contribute each year to achieve the desired deposit amount of 40% of the unit's expected purchase price?

(c) Discuss what factors may affect the achievement of Bruce and Karen's objective.

2.17 Choosing an investment term ✱✱

Your aunt seeks your advice about investing $40 000 for a period of 3 years with interest paid half yearly at a rate of 5.2% p.a. or for 2 years with interest paid half yearly at a rate of 5.6% p.a. Calculate the rate of interest your aunt would need to get in the third year to be content with either investment choice.

2.18 Changing interest rates ✱✱✱

Tom and Jane originally borrowed $80 000 from the bank as a mortgage loan to be repaid over 10 years, at a variable nominal annual rate of interest of 7.5%, compounded monthly. They considered fixing the rate because they were somewhat concerned about rising interest rates. However, the fixed rate of interest was set at 8.5% so the initial repayments were cheaper under the variable lending rate. However, because of a credit crisis overseas the bank now advises that it needs to raise interest rates on all its variable loans and advised Tom and Jane that their interest rate is to be increased to 9.5% p.a. compounded monthly. There are still 7 years to go before the loan is fully repaid.

Tom and Jane ask you to calculate how much extra they will need to pay each month after the interest rate rise.

2.19 Paying off a mortgage early ✱✱✱

Caitlin and Troy have settled on buying a new home for $600 000. They have sold their current home for $400 000 and after paying the balance on their first home mortgage have a deposit of $150 000 they can use against the mortgage on their second home. The details of their new home loan are:

Repayments	Monthly
Interest	8.00% p.a. (nominal)
Term of the loan	20 years

(a) What are Caitlin and Troy's minimum monthly payments?
(b) If they wish to pay their loan off within 12 years, what would be the new amount of the monthly payments in order to achieve their goal? (Assume there are no other changes in the loan conditions.)

2.20 Fixed-interest securities in a changing interest market ✱✱✱

Jacob invested $20 000 in a fixed-interest security for a period of 3 years on the basis of 9.0% p.a. with interest payments made every 6 months. After 1 year, calculate the market value of the remaining 3-year security if the prevailing interest rates in the economy for 3-year securities with interest paid every 6 months change to:
(a) 7% p.a.
(b) 12% p.a.

CASE STUDY 1

Assessing a financial situation

Albie and Debra are a young married couple who have one child, Noah, aged 3 years. They have plans to send Noah to a private secondary school when he is 12 years of age and have decided to undertake an investment plan so they can pay for the fees from their investments rather than pay the fees from their salaries at that time. They have not yet put into place any savings plans.

Albie and Debra are undecided about whether they should invest funds over the next 5 years and then let the investments grow for the remaining 4 years or whether they should wait until Noah is in primary school, when they may be able to afford more money to invest as their salaries should be higher. They are conscious that Debra may not be able to work full-time again until Noah goes to primary school so that is part of the reason why they may not save initially. Hence, they plan to invest $200 per week from now for such a purpose. They know which school they would like to send their children to and have been advised that the fees are $7000 per annum per student. The bursar at the school also advised them that the fees may be expected to rise by 3% per year. Albie and Debra expect to achieve a long-term rate of 6.5% p.a. on their choice of fund, one that is designed for education funding, because of its tax-free status.

QUESTIONS

1. Calculate the end benefit if Albie and Debra start investing $200 per week for the next 5 years and then leave the investment intact for the following 4 years.
2. Calculate the alternative approach, which requires them to invest nothing for the next 5 years but then $300 per week for the 4 years prior to Noah commencing secondary school.
3. Explain the difference in terms of the impact of compounding.
4. What other issues do you think they need to consider in their analysis?

CASE STUDY 2

Net worth statements and ratio analysis

Refer to the discussion of Qinbo and Feilian Wong in the chapter.

QUESTIONS

1. Prepare a net worth statement for the Wongs.
2. Undertake ratio analysis for the Wongs' current situation.
3. If the Wongs were given $50 000 from an inheritance, suggest three options (with reasons) that they may consider for the funds and prepare a new net worth statement and ratio analysis for their changed situation.

CASE STUDY 3

Reverse mortgages

Barbara is a widow aged 72 who lives alone. Barbara requires $50 000 to renovate her kitchen and bathroom and to undertake some additional repairs to the guttering on her home. She does not want to leave her home for at least the next 10 years.

Barbara's home is valued at $400 000. The only other funds she has available are a $20 000 term deposit with her bank and 400 shares in Telstra valued at about $1400. She has no other funds to draw on to enable her to undertake the upgrade on her house as she relies on the full amount of the age pension for her normal living expenses. Hence, Barbara has been advised to consider a reverse mortgage. She understands that if she obtains $50 000 as a reverse mortgage against her home that the interest rate would be 8.3% p.a.

Barbara seeks advice from a reverse mortgage provider and is given a package of documents to consider. The documents require Barbara to seek legal advice from a solicitor and also advice from a financial adviser before she can proceed with her application. Both the financial adviser and the solicitor are each required to sign a document in the package.

»

»

QUESTIONS

1. Calculate the debt that Barbara would accumulate over the planned 10-year period.
2. Calculate the estimated growth in the value of Barbara's home if the property market is estimated to increase in value at the rate of 6% p.a.
3. Write a memo to Barbara to outline the consequence of entering into a reverse mortgage in terms of the debt to be paid to the reverse mortgage provider and how much she would have left when she may sell her home in order to buy a smaller home in ten years or so.
4. Why do you think it is a requirement for a person seeking a reverse mortgage to consult with both a solicitor and a financial adviser and require them to sign about the advice they have given before making an application?

References and further reading

ASIC 2013, 'Credit card calculator', ASIC, moneysmart.gov.au.

ASIC 2013, 'Credit cards — buying on credit', ASIC, moneysmart.gov.au.

ASIC 2013, 'Reverse mortgage calculator', ASIC, moneysmart.gov.au.

Beal, D, Goyen, M & Shamsuddin, A 2008, *Introducing corporate finance*, 2nd edition, John Wiley & Sons, Brisbane.

Brealey, RA, Myers, SC & Allen, F 2008, *Principles of corporate finance*, 9th edition, McGraw-Hill, Sydney.

Gitman, L, Joehnk, M, Juchau, R, Wheldon, B & Wright, S 2004, *Fundamentals of investing*, 2nd Australian edn, Pearson Addison-Wesley, Sydney.

Higgins, E & Abey, A 2000, *Fortune strategy*, 2nd edn, Allen & Unwin, Sydney.

RateCity, 'Banks make nearly as much from credit card fees as home loan fees: households paid $1.3 billion in card fees in 2010', 11 July 2011, RateCity.com.au.

RateCity, 'Record $11.4 billion in bank fees: stop paying too much!', 21 June 2013, RateCity.com.au.

APPENDIX

Financial modelling

Financial advisers need to be proficient in the use of spreadsheets as a means of both 'crunching numbers' and communicating with clients. Many off-the-shelf spreadsheet products can be a 'black-box' for a client and in some cases a 'black-box' for the financial adviser — that is, users are uncertain about the processes applied by the product. If advisers and their clients rely unconditionally on off-the-shelf products where they do not understand the implicit assumptions and the mechanics of the calculations, there is danger of errors.

Most financial analysis can be quickly modelled by a financial adviser using a spreadsheet. Off-the-shelf products have their place; however, there will be many instances when the needs of a client will not fit the software and should not be made to fit the software. Further, financial advisers need to validate results produced by software using sound estimation skills and by having a thorough appreciation of any assumptions and calculations used by the software. Financial advisers also need to ensure that their clients understand and are comfortable with any financial analysis, whether it be the product of an off-the-shelf software package or the result of an adviser's own spreadsheeting skills.

Figure 2.3 is an example of a well-constructed spreadsheet. This spreadsheet can be contrasted with figure 2.4, which is a poorly designed spreadsheet. Take some time to compare the two spreadsheets. In the 'good design' spreadsheet the formulae used in row 30 are outlined in the box at the bottom of the spreadsheet. In the 'poor design' spreadsheet the formulae used in row 7 are outlined in the box at the bottom of the spreadsheet. From a client's point of view it should be readily apparent which spreadsheet is more effective in communicating the assumptions and calculations required to produce the final result. With more direct and easy-to-follow formulae, the client is in a position to understand and, if necessary, question any of the assumptions and calculations. The approaches taken by the two spreadsheets are compared in table 2.3.

It is beyond the scope of this appendix to review all the aspects of good financial modelling — advisers may spend many hours working on their spreadsheets and be satisfied with what they perceive to be a very elegant solution. However, other users of the spreadsheet, including clients, will not devote the same amount of time trying to understand the spreadsheet. Therefore, a spreadsheet should always be 'road tested' on naive users.

Perhaps the most powerful ally and most dangerous enemy in creating spreadsheets is the copy command. With a properly structured data section and working section, the copy command should enable the working section of the spreadsheet to be created quickly. The copy command is at its most powerful with a clear understanding of the difference between absolute and relative cell references. Placing a '$' symbol in front of a column letter or a row number fixes that column letter or row number; placing a '$' symbol in front of *both* the column letter and row number fixes *both* the column letter and the row number. For example, I16 is an absolute cell reference that can be copied anywhere on the spreadsheet and the reference will remain to cell I16. There is usually a shorthand way of fixing a cell reference. For example, on most laptops, a cell reference highlighted in the formulae bar can be converted to an absolute cell reference by pressing the function key F4. In the 'good design' spreadsheet, the rate of earnings growth of 4.2% is located in the data section in cell I16. At the bottom of that spreadsheet are the formulae displayed for row 30 — the formulae for earnings in row 30 are simply copied by virtue of the absolute cell reference I16 to rows 31 through 40. Indeed, once all the formulae have been correctly entered into row 30, the entire row can be highlighted and copied down to row 40 — this is a sign of robust spreadsheet design that is built on an intelligent combination of relative and absolute cell references working in conjunction with a data and working section.

A1	B	C	D	E	F	G	H	I	J	K
2							**Filename:**	Good Design		
3							**Author:**	Mike		
4							**Date created:**		10-Feb-2010	
5							**Time created:**		10.20 am	
6										
7										
8	**Data Section**									
9										
10										
11	Opening salary							90,000		
12	Opening salary index							1.0		
13	Opening balance of fund							75,000		
14	Age at commencement							45		
15	Year at commencement							2002		
16	Rate of earnings growth							4.2%		
17	Superannuation contribution tax							15.0%		
18	Superannuation earnings tax							15.0%		
19	Rate of employer superannuation guarantee contributions (SGC)							10.0%		
20	Rate of salary sacrifice							10.0%		
21										
22	**Working Section**									
23										
24										
25	**Age**	**Year**	**Salary**	**Opening**	**Earnings**	**Earnings**	**SGC**	**Salary**	**Contributions**	**Closing**
26				**Balance**		**Tax**		**Sacrifice**	**Tax**	**Balance**
27				**of fund**						**of fund**
28										
29	44	2001	90,000							75,000
30	45	2002	90,000	75,000	3,150	(473)	9,000	9,000	(2,700)	92,978
31	46	2003	90,000	92,978	3,905	(586)	9,000	9,000	(2,700)	111,597
32	47	2004	90,000	111,597	4,687	(703)	9,000	9,000	(2,700)	130,881
33	48	2005	90,000	130,881	5,497	(825)	9,000	9,000	(2,700)	150,853
34	49	2006	90,000	150,853	6,336	(950)	9,000	9,000	(2,700)	171,539
35	50	2007	90,000	171,539	7,205	(1,081)	9,000	9,000	(2,700)	192,963
36	51	2008	90,000	192,963	8,104	(1,216)	9,000	9,000	(2,700)	215,151
37	52	2009	90,000	215,151	9,036	(1,355)	9,000	9,000	(2,700)	238,132
38	53	2010	90,000	238,132	10,002	(1,500)	9,000	9,000	(2,700)	261,934
39	54	2011	90,000	261,934	11,001	(1,650)	9,000	9,000	(2,700)	286,585
40	55	2012	90,000	286,585	12,037	(1,805)	9,000	9,000	(2,700)	312,116
41										
42										
43	**Explanatory notes:**									
44	The earnings tax rate and the contributions tax rate are separate data items to allow for possible superannuation surcharge.									
45	It is assumed that SGC and salary sacrifice occur at year end and therefore do not attract earnings.									
46	Closing balance = opening balance + earnings − earnings tax + SGC + salary sacrifice − contributions tax.									

30	=B29+1	=C29+1	=D29*I12	=K29	=E30*I16	=F30*−I18	=D30*I19	=D30*I20	=(H30+I30)*−I17	=SUM(E30:J30)

FIGURE 2.3 Well designed spreadsheet

A1	B	C	D	E	F	G	H	I	J
2	Poor Design								
3									
4									
5									
6	45	2002	90000	75000	9000	9000	3150	3172.5	92977.5
7	46	2003	90000	92977.5	9000	9000	3905.055	3285.75825	111596.7968
8	47	2004	90000	111596.7968	9000	9000	4687.065464	3403.05982	130880.8024
9	48	2005	90000	130880.8024	9000	9000	5496.993701	3524.549055	150853.247
10	49	2006	90000	150853.247	9000	9000	6335.836376	3650.375456	171538.708
11	50	2007	90000	171538.708	9000	9000	7204.625734	3780.69386	192962.6398
12	51	2008	90000	192962.6398	9000	9000	8104.430873	3915.664631	215151.4061
13	52	2009	90000	215151.4061	9000	9000	9036.359055	4055.453858	238132.3113
14	53	2010	90000	238132.3113	9000	9000	10001.55707	4200.233561	261933.6348
15	54	2011	90000	261933.6348	9000	9000	11001.21266	4350.181899	286584.6655
16	55	2012	90000	286584.6655	9000	9000	12036.55595	4505.483393	312115.7381

7	46	2003	90000	=J6	9000	9000	= E7*0.042	=(H7*0.15)+((F7+G7)*0.15)	=E7+F7+G7+H7−I7

FIGURE 2.4 Poorly designed spreadsheet

Table 2.4, comparing the well-designed spreadsheet and the poorly designed spreadsheet, appears overleaf.

TABLE 2.4 Spreadsheet comparison

Characteristic	Good design	Poor design
Separation between data and workings	The spreadsheet has a data section and a working section. All literal values are defined in the data section and no literal values are included in the working section. If a literal value changes then only one cell will need to be changed (e.g. if the rate of earnings growth changes then the only cell that will need to be changed is cell I16).	There is no clear separation between the data and the workings — if the rate of earnings growth changes this value is embedded in cells H6 to H16. There are many other literal values embedded in the spreadsheet making it very difficult to perform 'what if' type analysis.
Spreadsheet looks ahead	The spreadsheet looks ahead and identifies potential future variables (e.g. the current assumption is that the salary will not increase in real terms but it could). By including an opening salary index and multiplying the salary by that index we can provide for this possibility.	The spreadsheet does not look ahead (e.g. if the current salary increases in real terms then the whole structure of the spreadsheet will need to be reworked).
Reference data	The spreadsheet has a filename, author name, date and time created.	No reference data is provided. Assuming that you print out the spreadsheet several times before you get it right, how can you be sure you (or the client) are looking at the latest version?
Column structure	Columns are clearly labelled and are logically organised from left to right. Including the SGC and salary sacrifice columns to the right of the earnings column reinforces the notion that these contributions do not attract earnings in the current year. This is also reinforced by explanatory notes on the spreadsheet.	The columns have no headings. If/when the user has decoded column H as representing earnings, it is not clear whether this is inclusive or exclusive of SGC and salary sacrifice.
Number of columns	Wherever possible a spreadsheet in a financial plan should be contained within an A4 page — if absolutely necessary it can be printed in landscape format. Use as many columns as can reasonably be displayed. Combining too many calculations within one column makes the spreadsheet less transparent. Many financial plans are prepared for people approaching retirement. (The font should not be too small.)	If you look at column I — too many calculations are performed here — the spreadsheet lacks transparency.
Number formatting	The formatting needs to be consistent. If the spreadsheet is calculating values in the thousands of dollars then displaying cents is unnecessary. Percentages should be displayed as percentages and the number of decimal places should be consistent. For large numbers, using a comma to separate the thousands improves readability. If items are to be deducted, show them as negative numbers rather than hiding the subtraction in the formulae.	

3 Taxation planning

LEARNING OBJECTIVES

After studying this chapter, you should be able to:

1. identify the source of Australian taxation law
2. outline the different components of taxable income
3. calculate net tax payable for an individual, including levies and tax offsets
4. outline the taxation implications associated with the returns generated from different forms of investment, including capital gains tax
5. identify a range of common tax-effective strategies
6. explain the taxation implications of income splitting
7. explain the taxation implications of income versus capital growth
8. identify the various taxable entities, and compare the tax advantages and disadvantages of these different entities
9. explain the concept of negative gearing
10. explain remuneration planning and understand the taxation implications of salary packaging and fringe benefits tax (FBT)
11. explain the goods and services tax (GST).

CASE STUDY

Frank runs a panel beating business as a sole trader and employs 2 workers. His pre-tax income after expenses for the current year is $140 000. Frank's spouse Angela works part-time selling sporting goods with a major sports chain. Angela's salary is $42 000 p.a. The couple have 3 children aged 17, 22 and 24.

The couple is seeking some advice on how they are able to minimise their tax and build upon their long-term wealth. They realise that they have not given much attention to their investments over the years but are now committed to building wealth for their retirement.

The couple advises that they are looking to buy a rental apartment close to the city for around $450 000 plus $25 000 of costs associated with the purchase. They would contribute $140 000 from their own funds and borrow the rest from the bank at a 6% interest rate.

The couple provides the following financial information.

Investment	Amount	Cost price	Ownership
Bank account	$70 000	$70 000	Frank
Term deposit	$30 000	$30 000	Frank
Share portfolio	$225 000	$160 000 (acquired 10 November 1994)	Frank
Superannuation	$80 000 $120 000		Frank Angela

The couple's debt amounts to $360 000 and consists of the following:

- home mortgage $320 000
- car loan $30 000
- credit cards $10 000

Some of the issues in this case to consider from a tax point of view include:

- how much income tax is the couple paying?
- are the couple's investments held in the name of the most appropriate person to minimise the imposition of tax?
- should Frank look at establishing a more tax-effective strategy for running his business, such as a family company or family trust?
- in whose name should the rental property and debt be acquired in? Would it make any difference if the rental property was expected to make a profit each year or not?
- from a tax point of view, is it preferable to pay off the home loan first or the rental property loan?
- could Angela restructure her remuneration package to minimise tax on her salary income?

Illustrative examples used throughout this chapter relate to Frank and Angela's situation.

Introduction

An important factor to consider with any investment or financial decision is the implications of taxation. The amount of tax payable can vary considerably depending on the type and timing of the income and deductions as well as who is liable for the tax. An investment which shows the best return before tax may not generate the best return after tax has been taken into account. Different strategies and investments can significantly impact upon the amount of tax payable.

Although tax is an important component, it should never be the sole determining factor. A taxpayer needs to weigh up all of the expected benefits compared with the total costs from an after-tax perspective. The investment or strategy must also be consistent with the risk profile of the client (refer to chapter 1).

Some people claim that there are two certainties in life — death and taxes. Death is certain but taxes are not necessarily so, as any tax planner will agree. What is certain, however, is that whatever the tax law is now, it will change — a risk that must be recognised by all investors. Because of the frequency and dimension of these changes, comprehensive tax guides may be useful for only a short time. This chapter concentrates on general taxation principles as they affect personal financial planning rather than the fine details.

As with financial planning, tax planning is very specific to the needs of an investor. For example, a particular tax structure may be of benefit to one investor but detrimental to another. It depends on the tax position of the investor in the years involved.

Taxation planning is the legitimate organisation of an investor's affairs in accordance with taxation laws to minimise tax. *Tax evasion* involves criminal falsification or non-disclosure as a means of reducing tax. *Tax avoidance* fits between the two and although it looks to minimise tax through legal means, the strategies employed are artificial and contrived and have no reason other than obtaining a tax benefit. Tax avoiders run the very real risk of having their schemes struck aside and heavy penalties imposed. Tax evaders run the risk of very heavy fines and long prison terms. In the context of personal financial planning, this chapter is about taxation *planning*, the organisation of an investor's affairs to minimise tax.

LO 1 The Australian taxation system

The primary function of most taxes is to redirect economic resources from the private sector to the government to enable it to conduct its various spending programs. Taxation represents the major form of government revenue raising in most countries around the world. Taxation has a number of different functions including:

- to finance the activities of government that modern society expects and that may not be adequately provided by the free-market — for example, defence, health, education and roads
- to achieve the government's economic objectives — for example, an increase in taxes can be used to reduce private-sector spending and therefore restrict inflation
- to achieve desirable social objectives — taxation can be used to encourage or discourage spending on particular types of products and services such as imports, tobacco, alcohol and heavily polluting goods
- to redistribute income and wealth — for example, to provide social welfare to families.

A short history of taxation in Australia

income tax
a tax levied on individuals and companies in proportion to the level of income earned

Although various forms of taxes have been around for many hundreds of years, the first **income tax** was introduced in England in 1799 to help finance the war against France. At that time, a taxpayer made his own assessments of assessable income and allowable deductions and paid 10% of this to the government. Various models of tax were imposed over the years in England to finance various wars and were withdrawn when hostilities ceased.

The first income tax in Australia was imposed in South Australia in 1884. By the early 1900s, income tax had been introduced by every Australian state. The first Commonwealth income tax Act was imposed in 1915 largely as a means of financing the war effort during World War I. The 1915 measures continued in force until the 1922 Act was introduced, which was superseded by the 1936 Act which remained in force for many years. Until 1923, both the states and the Commonwealth levied their own income taxes and taxpayers were required to prepare and lodge two sets of income tax returns. The two sets of income tax lasted until 1942 when, due to financial pressures arising from World War II, the Commonwealth Government took over the levying of income tax exclusively.

The Tax Law Improvement Project (TLIP) commenced in 1983 with the objective of redrafting and simplifying the *Income Tax Assessment Act 1936* (ITAA36) which had become cumbersome and complex. The first instalment of the program resulted in the enactment of the *Income Tax Assessment Act 1997* (ITAA97). However, the full number of instalments of this Act were never enacted which means that large parts of the tax law are still contained within the ITAA36 and taxpayers are required to work with two Acts.

In the latter part of the 1980s, a major reform of the income tax law began with a view to broadening the income tax base of the government and attempting to minimise tax avoidance. The statement known as the Reform of the Australian Income Tax System outlined a number of major policy developments including:

- introducing a capital gains tax
- introducing a fringe benefits tax
- introducing a dividend imputation system to eliminate the double taxation that existed on the taxing of dividends received by shareholders
- the non-deductibility of entertainment expenses.

All of these measures have become part of the Australian income tax system over the years and will be discussed in further detail in this chapter.

Taxation bases

In Australia, taxes are imposed at the Commonwealth, state, territory and local government levels. Over the years, taxation has been levied on a range of different activities, transactions and property. Some examples are a tax on income, profits, goods and services, the importation of goods, the production of goods and services, capital profits and even death. Most countries rely upon a range of taxes to raise government revenue and there is no developed country that relies upon a single taxation base.

Income tax (direct tax)

Direct tax is a tax paid directly by the person or organisation on whom it is levied and is payable on most forms of income and profits. Examples include wages and salaries, most forms of income derived from investments and business income. Since the initial Commonwealth income tax was levied in Australia in 1915, there have been calls for Australia to broaden its tax base away from just income tax.

Goods and services tax (indirect tax)

The **goods and services tax (GST)** was introduced into Australia effective from 1 July 2000. It is a broad-based value-added tax on goods and services and is charged at a flat rate of 10% on suppliers and importers. An indirect tax is defined as a tax levied on expenditures, that is, the tax is paid when the good or service is purchased. Examples include sales tax, goods and services tax, excise tax and value-added tax. Indirect tax is collected and paid by a supplier, but it is ultimately borne by the consumer through the charging of higher prices. Other examples include customs duty, which is a tax imposed on an importer for goods imported into Australia, and excise duty, which is a tax on the manufacture of certain goods such as alcohol, tobacco and petrol.

In this chapter, we will be focusing on the determination and calculation of income tax.

goods and services tax (GST) an indirect tax imposed on the purchase of goods and services at a flat rate of 10%

Sources of taxation law

The three basic sources of taxation law in Australia are:

- the *Income Tax Assessment Act 1997* (ITAA97) — since the Tax Law Improvement Project, which involved rewriting the old *Income Tax Assessment Act 1936* (ITAA36) into simple English, the readability and usability of the legislation has improved. Many of the improvements are included in legislation as amendments to the 1936 or 1997 Acts. References to law are sometimes to ITAA97 and sometimes to the old legislation, ITAA36, in addition to the relevant amendment
- case law, where interpretation of legislation by the courts sets precedent
- the Australian Taxation Office (ATO), which gives advice on the application of the law with rulings and determinations.

The ATO legal database website at law.ato.gov.au (see figure 3.1) provides easy access to all sources of taxation law.

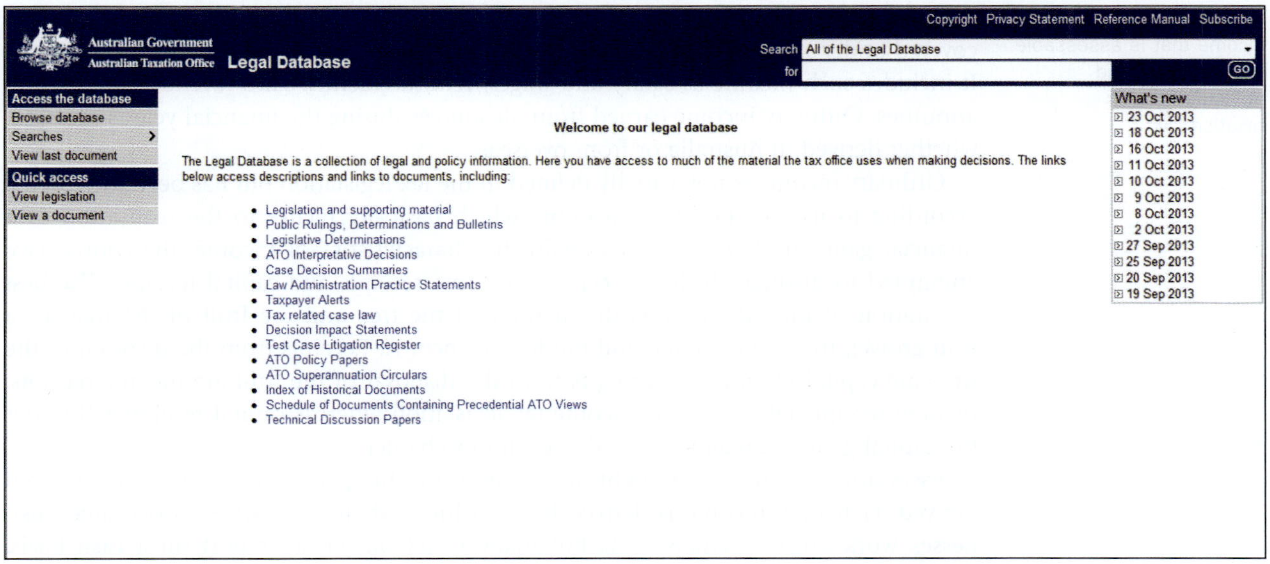

FIGURE 3.1
The ATO legal database
Source: ATO 2013a.

LO 2 The components of taxable income

Income tax in Australia is determined on a financial year basis, which is the period from 1 July to 30 June, and is levied on a range of different entities including individuals, companies, trusts and superannuation funds. The calculation of income tax requires certain tax rates to be applied to the taxable income of the particular entity. Net tax payable is determined as follows.

Determine taxable income
Multiply by a tax rate
= Gross tax payable
Deduct tax offsets and rebates
Add levies
= Net tax payable

Taxable income is worked out as:

Assessable income less allowable deductions

All taxpayers are required to lodge a tax return each year with the ATO. Each individual in Australia is assessed individually and is required to submit an income tax return for income earned and deductions incurred in their own name. Family members are assessed individually and not as a family unit.

self-assessment regime a system whereby the ATO initially accepts taxation information provided by a taxpayer for the purposes of assessing the taxpayer's tax liability

Since 1986, Australia has operated under a **self-assessment regime** where the ATO generally accepts information provided by taxpayers in their tax returns and issues tax assessments on this basis. Information supplied by taxpayers in their returns is subject to audits and other verification processes.

Assessable income

assessable income income that is assessable or recognised and measured under taxation law

Assessable income includes ordinary income and statutory income. Ordinary income is covered under s. 6.5 of ITAA97 and described as 'income according to ordinary concepts'. It includes such income as salary and wages, rent, dividends, sales revenue, interest and annuities. Ordinary income earned from all sources during the financial year is assessed, whether derived in Australia or from overseas.

Ordinary income is not actually defined in the tax legislation but has been interpreted according to its common-law meaning, which basically relates to the realisation of a financial gain. In attempting to explain the characteristics of income, the courts have attempted to distinguish the concepts of income receipts and capital receipts. The best illustration of the difference is the analogy of the tree and the fruit of the tree. To a fruit grower, the tree is capital and the fruit is income. Receipts from the disposal of the trees are capital receipts and receipts from the disposal of the fruit are income receipts. Income receipts fall under the income tax legislation whereas capital receipts fall under the capital gains tax regime covered later in this chapter.

Assessable income is brought to account in the period when it is considered derived. Generally income is derived by a business when it is earned. Most large businesses work on an accruals basis but many small businesses report on a cash basis. An important issue when considering the taxing of business receipts is whether the activity undertaken by the taxpayer constitutes carrying on a business, and is therefore subject to tax, or whether the taxpayer is merely undertaking a hobby where any receipts will be tax free. To determine whether an activity constitutes a business or a hobby, the courts have considered a number of issues, including the nature of the activity undertaken, its size, the amount of time and effort spent, whether a profit motive exists and the degree to which the activity is carried out on a commercial basis. Dividend income and interest income are considered derived when they are credited to the investor's account, that is, they do not have to be received in cash for them to be considered earned.

Employment income, including salary, wages, allowances, amounts received for unused leave etc. are all assessed when received. For all employment-related activities, an employer is required to detail the total income received by the employee as well as any tax withheld from their pay on a payment summary, which must be provided to the employee and the ATO by 14 August of each year. The taxpayer uses the information provided in the payment summary to prepare their tax return. Fringe benefits received by employees, such as cars, additional superannuation contributions, loans etc. are also required to be shown on the employee's payment summary despite the fact that they are not regarded as income of the employee. Fringe benefits are discussed in a later part of this chapter.

While a number of regular government pensions, allowances and benefit payments are assessable income, such as the age pension payment and the Newstart allowance, most support-type payments are exempt income. Some of the exempt government payments include:

- youth allowance
- family tax benefits
- disability support pension
- ABSTUDY
- carer allowance.

The year in which income is derived is important as it may impact upon when tax is payable as well as how much tax is payable. To minimise tax, it is generally advantageous to defer income to a later period. Consider the following example.

ILLUSTRATIVE EXAMPLE 3.1

Angela, who is employed as a retail assistant, is considering retiring on 30 June (see the opening case study). Upon her retirement, she expects to receive the following payments.

Salary	$6 000
Unused annual leave	$4 000
Employer termination payment	$12 000

From the point of view of minimising taxation, does it make any difference whether Angela retires on 30 June or 1 July?

It is likely that Angela will be better off if she retires in July of the next financial year. The reason is that Angela's taxable income in the year of retirement will be lower than in the current year when she is fully employed and receiving a salary of $42 000. With a lower taxable income, the rate of tax will be lower,

»

»

which means her tax payable will be lower. Income tax is charged on a progressive basis in Australia with the result that the more income a person earns, the greater the percentage of tax applied. As a general rule, it is normally advantageous to defer income to a later financial year. Not only does this defer income and the payment of tax, it may also reduce the overall amount of tax payable, as discussed earlier.

In the tax planning process, only income receipts are assessable. Capital appreciation of an investment is not generally regarded as income of the taxpayer. However, when the investment is realised or sold, the gain from the capital appreciation is subject to another form of tax called the capital gains tax (CGT). The CGT legislation is very complex and taxes the gains or profit made from the disposal of most assets and investments. Capital gains tax will be discussed further in a later section of this chapter.

Allowable deductions

allowable deductions expenses incurred by the taxpayer which are deducted from assessable income to derive taxable income

Allowable deductions include two types of expenses or outgoings: general deductions and specific deductions. Section 8.1 of ITAA97 covers general deductions and provides that an expense may be classified as an allowable deduction on the basis that it is necessarily incurred in gaining or earning that assessable income. There must be a sufficient connection between the expense incurred and the earning of the assessable income. Examples of the type of expenses that would be considered an allowable general deduction include: travelling expenses incurred in the course of an employee's work, subscriptions for professional journals related to the employee's employment, business deductions and interest paid in connection with an activity that generates assessable income. Deductions are not allowed for outgoings of a private, capital or domestic nature, or for expenses incurred in earning exempt income. For example, travelling costs to and from work are not tax deductible because they are considered to be of a private nature. Expenses incurred in connection with investments are normally allowable deductions as long as they are incurred in the course of earning assessable income from those investments. Thus, interest payable to the bank on funds borrowed to buy an investment property would be deductible as long as the property generated assessable income. On the other hand, interest on borrowings used to finance the purchase of a vacant block of land generating no income is unlikely to be tax deductible. Interest on borrowings used to finance the family home is not deductible as the home is of a private or domestic nature and does not generate assessable income.

The taxation legislation also provides for a number of specific deductions that would not normally be allowed under the general provisions but which have been specifically legislated to be an allowable deduction. Examples include tax preparation expenses with a tax agent, donations and gifts to approved charities, repairs and bad debts. All of these expenses are allowable deductions for a taxpayer, even though they are not directly attributable to earning assessable income.

Deductibility of expenditure is therefore important, and structuring a client's affairs to maximise deductions and therefore minimise taxable income and tax payable is of prime importance.

Substantiation of allowable deductions

Generally, a taxpayer is required to have written evidence for any expense they claim as a deduction, which normally takes the form of an invoice or receipt. Travel diaries are required to be used to verify travel claims. Employees are generally required to be able to substantiate any work-related claims they make in their tax returns, except where the work-related expenses are less than $300 in total.

PROFESSIONAL ADVICE

Travelling expenses

Phil Stewart joined Let's Fly Away Travel in 2013 as a travel agent. During the current year, he travelled overseas on four occasions and interstate twice as detailed below. The travel arrangements were either supplier-structured or self-structured. In broad terms, supplier-structured involves travel where the itinerary is structured by the supplier of the travel product. With self-structured travel, the traveller structures the itinerary themself. In the case of supplier-structured arrangements, the travel costs are borne by the supplier. The only cost to Phil is a participation fee and his own personal expenses. In the case of self-structured arrangements, he pays for all his travel costs, including fares and accommodation while on annual leave. In addition to four weeks annual leave, he is eligible for five days paid educational leave. Phil uses his educational leave for his supplier-structured travel.

Details of his travel during the year are as follows:

Date	Destination	Period	Leave type	Itinerary structure
August	Bali	1 week	Educational (& weekend)	Supplier-structured
October	USA and Thailand	1.5 weeks	Annual leave	Self-structured
December	Tasmania	1 week	Educational (& weekend)	Supplier-structured
February	Gold Coast	1 week	Educational (& weekend)	Supplier-structured
December	Thailand and Vietnam	2 weeks	Educational (& annual leave)	Supplier-structured
June	Around the world	2 weeks	Annual leave	Self-structured

Phil is claiming a portion of the travel expenses as a tax deductible claim for an amount of $8000. Phil's rationale for the claim is that on each of the trips he undertook holiday activities, he was employed to sell holiday-related travel

»

»
products and his employer's business model emphasised 'excellence of service to its customers' based on the personal experiences of the consultant. Phil argues that to survive in the travel industry, you have to be passionate about travel, which he says he is, and you have to travel at every available opportunity, which he does.

QUESTIONS

Answer the following questions based on the above facts.

1 Do you believe Phil is entitled to claim a tax deduction for the costs of the trips that he undertook during the year as a travel agent?

2 Would it make any difference to his claim if Phil took his family with him on the overseas trips?

3 What documentation would Phil need to keep in order to substantiate his claim?

Individual tax rates

marginal tax rates the percentage of tax paid on each additional dollar of income earned

Individual taxpayers pay tax at progressive rates where the rate of tax increases with the level of income. These are known as **marginal tax rates**. Marginal tax rates for resident individuals are shown in table 3.1.

As illustrated in the table below, no tax is payable if an individual's taxable income is less than $18 200, known as the tax-free threshold. A 19% marginal tax rate applies to income between $18 200 and $37 000, 32.5% on any income above $37 000 up to $80 000 and so on. With progressive taxation, the tax effect of additional income or additional deductible expenses depends on the level of taxable income earned.

pay as you go (PAYG) a system for paying instalments towards a taxpayer's expected tax liability

All individuals pay tax on total taxable income that they have earned during the financial year. Most individuals pay tax on a **pay as you go (PAYG)** basis where tax is pre-paid in instalments throughout the year to the ATO towards payment of their expected final tax liability. Most employers are required to deduct income tax from the pay of their employees on a weekly, fortnightly or monthly basis. At the end of the year, individuals — with the help of a Tax Pack, e-tax, a tax agent or an accountant — submit a tax return. Based on the total taxable income for the financial year, net tax payable is determined by the ATO and tax already paid under the PAYG system is deducted from this net amount. The taxpayer will either need to pay the balance of the amount of tax owing or will receive a refund of tax.

TABLE 3.1 Marginal tax rates

Taxable income	Marginal tax rate	Tax payable ($)
$0–$18 200	0%	Nil
$18 201–$37 000	19%	$0 + 19% on the excess over $18 200
$37 001–$80 000	32.5%	$3572 + 32.5% on the excess over $37 000
$80 001–$180 000	37%	$17 547 + 37% on the excess over $80 000
$180 000 +	45%	$54 547 + 45% on the excess over $180 000

Source: ATO 2013b.

ILLUSTRATIVE EXAMPLE 3.2

Janet earns assessable income of $84 000 consisting of a salary of $82 000 and bank interest of $2000. Her allowable deductions consist of work-related expenses of $500 plus $50 of donations. Accordingly, her taxable income totals $83 450.

Gross tax payable is determined as follows:

Janet's taxable income falls in the band of between $80 000 and $180 000. Therefore, her marginal tax rate is assessed at 37%.

Tax on $80 000 (detailed in table 3.1)	$17 547.00
Tax on excess income above $80 000	
$3450 × 37% marginal tax rate	**$1 276.50**
Total gross tax payable	**$18 823.50**

Residency

The imposition of taxation in Australia differs depending on whether an individual is regarded as an Australian resident or non-resident for taxation purposes. A person is regarded as a tax resident if they either permanently reside in Australia, as evidenced by setting up a home, studying or working within Australia, or they satisfy one of three tests. Generally a period of 6 months of work, study or setting up a home is used to determine tax residency. The consequences of being classified as a tax resident include the following.

- Tax residents apply the marginal tax rates detailed in table 3.1 above whereas non-tax residents do not get the tax-free threshold, nor are they entitled to receive a number of tax rebates and offsets.
- Tax residents are taxed on income from all sources, derived both within and outside of Australia, whereas non-residents are taxed only on income derived in Australia.

When an Australian citizen decides to work overseas for a period of time they may lose their Australian residency for tax purposes. Let us consider two examples. Emma takes up a 1-year contract to teach English in Korea. After her contract expires, she intends to travel for the following 3 months before returning to Australia. She will board with a family while she lives in Korea. Emma has a home in Australia that she will rent out while she is away. In the second example, Gail takes up a 3-year contract with an overseas firm with an option to extend for a further period. Gail and her partner decide to rent out their home in Australia while they are away. While overseas, Gail and her partner will rent a property and Gail will receive an accommodation allowance.

From the two examples Emma is likely to be treated as a resident but Gail is likely to be treated as a non-resident. The significant differences are the length of time that Gail plans to be away from Australia and the establishment of a new home outside of Australia. Being classed as a 'resident' or 'non-resident' for tax purposes needs to be determined on a case-by-case basis via specific tax advice.

Tax rates payable by other entities

Companies

Most companies are levied income tax at a flat rate of 30% on their taxable income for the financial year. There is no tax-free threshold.

Superannuation funds

Complying superannuation funds pay income tax at a flat rate of 15% on their taxable income. Non-complying superannuation funds pay tax at a flat rate of 45%. Again, there is no tax-free threshold for superannuation funds.

Partnerships

beneficiary
a person nominated to receive a payout from an insurance policy, a superannuation fund or the assets of an estate

A partnership is not a separate legal entity. Accordingly, partnerships are not assessed for tax even though they are required to lodge a tax return. Profits are allocated between the partners who are assessed on their share of the profits at their individual marginal tax rates.

Trusts

trustee
the person or entity that has the responsibility for holding and managing the assets of the trust on behalf of the beneficiaries.

All profits earned within a trust structure are generally required to be distributed between the various members having an entitlement to that income, called **beneficiaries**. The income received by a beneficiary is added to any other income earned and taxed at the beneficiary's marginal tax rate. Any income not distributed from the trust to beneficiaries is taxed by the **trustee** at the highest marginal tax rate, currently 45% plus Medicare.

LO 3

Calculation of net tax payable for an individual resident taxpayer

Once gross tax payable has been determined, an individual taxpayer may be entitled to a number of tax offsets or rebates, which are used to reduce tax payable. However, a taxpayer may also be subject to a number of levies and charges, which have the effect of increasing the amount of tax payable. As outlined previously, the calculation of net tax payable is determined as follows:

Gross tax payable
Deduct tax offsets and rebates
Add levies and charges
= Net tax payable

Tax offsets

tax offsets or rebates
reductions in tax payable provided by the government to support or assist individuals or activities

Individual taxpayers may be entitled to claim a reduction in their tax payable through the use of a number of **tax offsets or rebates**. Tax offsets are used by the government to provide social and welfare assistance and support to individuals and families in need, encourage certain kinds of activities and investment, and provide a credit for payments of tax.

Unlike an allowable deduction, which is subtracted from assessable income in order to determine taxable income, a tax offset represents a reduction in the amount of tax that is required to be paid by a taxpayer. Examples of tax offsets include the imputation credit or franking credit offset, low income tax offset, senior Australians tax offset and dependent spouse offset.

A complete list of possible tax offsets can be found on the ATO website (ato.gov.au). Generally, a tax offset can only be used to eliminate gross tax payable. That is, in the majority of cases, where a tax offset exceeds gross tax payable, the difference is not refundable, cannot be applied against the Medicare levy and cannot be carried forward to future years. One of the main exceptions to this is in respect of the imputation credit which will be discussed later in this chapter.

The low income tax offset

To assist low-income earners, the government provides a tax offset which has the effect of reducing net tax payable. For the 2013–14 year, the maximum tax offset is $445, payable for taxable incomes up to $37 000. Where the taxable income of a taxpayer exceeds $37 000, the offset is reduced by 1.5 cents in the dollar and cuts out completely at a taxable income of $66 667.

The effect of the low income tax offset is that a taxpayer can effectively earn a taxable income of around $20 540 and together with the low income tax offset entitlement of $445, have a zero tax liability.

Levies and charges

The Australian Government imposes a number of levies and charges on individual taxpayers. The most important of these are the Medicare levy, the Medicare levy surcharge and the higher education loan program (HELP) charge.

Medicare levy

Most resident individual taxpayers are required to pay the **Medicare levy** as part of their tax liability. For a number of years, the Medicare levy has been set at a rate of 1.5% of taxable income. The Medicare levy is used to fund Australia's national health system. From 1 July 2014, the Medicare levy will increase to 2% of taxable income to help fund the Disability Support Scheme. The Medicare levy is based on the taxable income of the individual. Low-income earners may be entitled to some relief from having to pay the Medicare levy. The Medicare levy is only applied once the taxable income of a single person with no dependent children exceeds $20 542 or to families with a taxable income of $32 279 and higher (2012–13).

Medicare levy
a levy on the taxable income of an individual taxpayer to help fund Australia's health system

Medicare levy surcharge

The Medicare levy surcharge is an additional levy imposed on individual taxpayers that are high-income earners without adequate private health insurance. As with the Medicare levy, the surcharge is applied on a sliding scale based on the taxable income of the individual. The rates are provided in table 3.2.

TABLE 3.2 Medicare levy surcharge

Taxable income		Levy payable
Single income	Family income	
Up to $84 000	Up to $168 000	Nil
$84 001–$97 000	$168 001–$194 000	1.0%
$97 001–$130 000	$194 001–$260 000	1.25%
$130 000 +	$260 000 +*	1.5%

*Add $1500 for each additional child after the first child.
Source: ATO 2013c.

HECS and HELP charge

In order to assist students pay their higher-education fees, the government provides support through making available Commonwealth Government loans. The system, called HELP (higher education loan program), assists students by allowing them to defer payment of their higher education fees and to repay them at a later time through the taxation system when their taxable income reaches a certain minimum income threshold. The government has proposed from 1 January 2014 that the discount that applies for students making upfront payments of their HELP debt will cease.

ILLUSTRATIVE EXAMPLE 3.3

Frank and Angela's daughter, Michelle, is employed as a journalist and earns a wage of $87 000 p.a. During the current year she also received $2500 in bank interest and $3000 from a Tatts lotto win. Michelle's expenditure for the year is as follows:

Travelling to and from work	$1200
Travelling costs incurred for work purposes	1000
Membership of Australian Journalists Association	800
Donation to hospital	200
Membership of local tennis club	200
Tax agent's costs (preparation of tax return)	600

Michelle is single and does not have any private health insurance. What is the net tax payable by Michelle for the current year?

Assessable income		
Salary	$87 000	
Bank interest	2 500	
Total assessable income	89 500	
Less **Allowable deductions**		
Travelling costs incurred for work purposes	1 000	
Membership of the Australian Journalists Association	800	
Donation to hospital	200	
Tax agent's costs (preparation of tax return)	600	
Total allowable deductions	2 600	
Taxable income	**$86 900**	
Gross tax payable ($17 547 + 37% of the excess over $80 000)		20 100.00
Add Medicare levy (2.0%)		1 738.00
Add Medicare levy surcharge (1.0%)		869.00
Net tax payable		**$22 707.00**

Notes:
- The TattsLotto win is considered to be a windfall gain and normally non-assessable.
- Travelling to and from work is considered to be expenditure of a private nature and not tax deductible.
- Donations or gifts of $2 or more have been specifically legislated to be an allowable deduction.
- Expenditure incurred by a taxpayer in managing their tax affairs has been specifically legislated to be an allowable deduction.
- As Michelle does not have private health insurance and her income exceeds the Medicare levy surcharge income threshold, she is liable to pay a 1% levy.

Taxation of minors

Special tax regulations are in place to prevent taxpayers avoiding tax by directing income to children. Minors are defined as unmarried persons under 18 years of age not in full-time employment. The special tax rules relate to the 'unearned income' of minors. This includes the income from most forms of investments, such as interest, rental income and dividends and income distributed from a family trust. However, income which is considered 'earned' by the minor is excluded from the special rules, and includes employment and business income.

Where a minor is in receipt of unearned income, the first $416 of taxable income is exempt from tax. A rate of 66% applies to income between $417 and $1307, and the top adult marginal tax rate of 45% applies to that part of the income above $1307. The aim of the shading between $416 and $1307 is to achieve a maximum overall rate of 45% — the same as the top marginal rate paid by adult taxpayers. It is evident therefore, that it is not particularly tax-effective to invest funds in the name of minors where income generated on unearned income exceeds $416.

Note that income which is considered earned by the minor, such as employment income, is taxed at normal adult marginal tax rates.

Effective from 1 July 2011, the government removed the ability of minors to access the low income tax offset to reduce tax payable on income other than employment income.

ILLUSTRATIVE EXAMPLE 3.4

Frank owns a term deposit with the XYZ bank for $30 000 which pays an interest rate of 4%. Should Frank invest the term deposit in the name of Grace, his youngest daughter who is aged 17 and working?

Grace can earn only $416 of unearned income before becoming liable to penalty rates of taxation on the interest. Therefore it would only be worth investing a maximum of around $10 400 of the term deposit in the name of Grace ($10 400 × 4% = $416).

LO 4 Impact of tax on investment income

Income received from most forms of investment, such as shares, property and bank accounts, are assessable for tax, although some differences in tax treatment do exist. The following sections explain the significance of these differences and helps explain the importance of understanding the tax impact on income received from different forms of investments. When buying an investment or constructing an investment portfolio, an investor should be analysing and comparing after-tax returns. Where a taxpayer disposes of an investment that was acquired after 19 September 1985, capital gains tax may also be payable on the gain or loss made. CGT is an important consideration in determining the net return from an investment. The provisions of the capital gains tax legislation will be considered in further detail later in this chapter.

Interest

Interest received by a taxpayer is normally treated as assessable income and subject to tax at the taxpayer's marginal tax rates. Interest is normally assessed when it is actually received by the taxpayer.

Tax is a significant determinant of the net return derived from interest-bearing securities. If an investor earns 4% on the money market, the after-tax return of an investor on a marginal tax rate of 45% is 2.2%. This ignores the effects of inflation. Once inflation is taken into account, the investor is likely to be making a negative real return.

In situations where there is a joint bank account, such as with a husband and wife, interest is normally brought to account based on the couple's beneficial (right to receive) share of the account. If the individual shares are not specified, interest received is normally assessed on a 50/50 basis.

Issues may arise in respect of interest earned on a child's bank account. There may be circumstances where the parent is assessed on the income even though the account is in the name of the child. This may arise where the parent provides the money and is seen to control the use of the funds. For example, a parent sets themself up as trustee for their child's bank account and makes all investment decisions. Where the ATO is satisfied that the funds really belong to the parent and the parent is the one that has a beneficial entitlement to the funds in the bank account, the parent will be assessed on the income, even though the bank account may be in the name of the child. Consideration should also be given to the penalty rates of tax that apply to the unearned income of minors as discussed previously.

Dividend income

Dividends are distributions of company profits to shareholders. Dividend income is fully assessed in the hands of the shareholder, regardless of the source of the company profits. The income is included within the assessable income of the investor when the dividend is paid, credited or distributed to them.

dividend imputation a system in which shareholders are entitled to tax credits for the relevant amount of tax paid by a company on its profits

Before the introduction of **dividend imputation** in July 1987, dividends were subject to double taxation — once by the company when the profits were earned, and again by the shareholders when the after-tax dividends were distributed to them. Since the introduction of dividend imputation, an investment in shares has been far more attractive in Australia.

The basis of the dividend imputation system is to ensure that company profits are in effect only subject to tax once in the hands of the shareholder at the shareholder's marginal rate of tax. If the company has already paid tax on the profits from which the dividend has been derived, the shareholder will be entitled to a tax offset for the tax already paid by the company. This is done in order to prevent the double taxation of the dividend.

Before describing the operation of the dividend imputation system, it is worth understanding some of the terms used.

- Where a company has paid full tax on the profits from which a dividend is derived, the dividend is known as a *franked dividend.*

- In situations where the company has not paid tax on its profits for the year, perhaps due to carried forward tax losses, any dividend paid is known as an *unfranked dividend*.
- Companies can have a situation where they have paid some tax on their profits, but not the full rate. Any dividends paid from profits in this situation are known as *partially franked dividends*.

The operation of the dividend imputation system is as follows. A shareholder in receipt of a franked dividend in a financial year will need to include both the dividend received plus a franking or imputation credit, representing the amount of tax previously paid by the company, within their assessable income. The total amount is then assessed at the taxpayer's marginal tax rate. However, to avoid double taxation, the shareholder is then entitled to a tax offset for the amount of the franking credit included within their assessable income. To assist the taxpayer with preparing their tax liability, the company paying the dividend will advise the shareholder of the amount of the attached franking credit. The franking credit is determined as follows:

$$\text{Franking credit} = \text{Dividend received} \times \frac{\text{Company tax rate}}{1 - \text{Company tax rate}}$$

$$= \text{Dividend received} \times \frac{0.30}{0.70}$$

Where the taxpayer is in receipt of an unfranked dividend, the cash received is fully assessable, but the franking credits do not apply. Illustrative example 3.5 illustrates the operation of the dividend imputation system.

Table 3.3 compares the impact of dividend imputation on investors with different tax rates.

ILLUSTRATIVE EXAMPLE 3.5

Assume that Angela decides to acquire $100 000 worth of shares in Tassie Devil Ltd which pays a dividend of 20 cents per share fully franked. The cash dividend is $2000 and the imputation credit is $857.14 ($2000 × 30/70). Angela also receives a salary of $42 000 for the year.

As Angela is on a 32.5% marginal tax rate, then the tax implication is as follows.

Salary		$42 000
Franked dividend received	2000	
Plus imputation credit	857	2 857
Taxable income		44 857
Gross tax payable		6 125.53
Less low income tax offset		(327.15)
Less imputation credit		(857.14)
Add Medicare levy		897.14
Net tax payable		5 840.38

»

»

To understand the benefit of dividend imputation, assume that the $2000 dividend is instead received as an unfranked dividend as follows.

Salary	$42 000	
Unfranked dividend received	2 000	
Taxable income	44 000	
Gross tax payable		5 847.00
Less low income tax offset		(340.00)
Add Medicare levy		880.00
Net tax payable		6 387.00

With the franked dividend, the taxpayer is better off by an amount of $546.62. This illustrates the importance of franking credits on the after-tax return to investors.

As can be seen by table 3.3, the benefits of the franking credits attached to dividend income vary depending on the tax position of the investor.

TABLE 3.3 Comparison of the impact of dividend imputation on investors

	Low-income investor	Mid-income investor	High-income investor
Dividend received	$700	$700	$700
Franking credit (dividend x 30/70)	$300	$300	$300
Taxable income	$1000	$1000	$1000
Marginal tax rate Gross tax payable Less imputation credit Gross tax payable (refund)	19% tax rate on $1000 $190 $300 ($210)	37% tax rate on $1000 $370 $300 $70	45% tax rate on $1000 $450 $300 $150
	Because the company has already paid tax at a rate of 30%, the low-income shareholder will be entitled to a refund for the difference between the tax already paid by the company and the tax rate of the shareholder.	Because the company has already paid tax at a rate of 30%, the shareholder will need to pay only an additional 7% tax to bring the tax payable to their marginal tax rate.	Because the company has already paid tax at a rate of 30%, the high-income earner will need to pay only an additional 15% tax to bring the tax payable to their marginal tax rate.

Dividend imputation means that the receipt of fully franked dividends by shareholders, particularly those on a low marginal tax rate, are particularly tax effective when compared to the receipt of income from most other forms of investment. However, not all dividends are fully franked and a financial planner must take into account variations in the level of franking when recommending and analysing Australian shares.

Dividend reinvestment

Some companies offer a scheme whereby instead of the investor receiving a cash dividend, the investor is offered the opportunity to acquire additional shares in the company to the value of the cash dividend. The price at which the additional shares are offered to the shareholder varies, but a common discount is around 2% on the average of the market price over the last 5 days. No brokerage or stamp duty is payable by the shareholder, so this is a relatively attractive way of building up a portfolio. It is also attractive for the company as a means of preserving cash within the business.

Regardless of whether the shareholder receives dividends in the form of cash or in the form of additional shares in the company, the dividend is still taxable and is required to be included in the taxable income of the taxpayer.

Rental income

Where a property is held for investment purposes, while any rental income is assessable to tax, any expenditure incurred in earning that income may be an allowable deduction. The main deductions for an owner of rental property are the interest payable on any borrowings used to finance the acquisition of the property, deductions for the decline in the value of certain furniture and fixtures, repairs, commissions paid to managing agents, bank fees, financial institution duties, insurance, rates and land taxes. A number of the more common complex deductions will be discussed in the following section.

Interest deductibility

Interest incurred on a loan used to finance any investment may be an allowable deduction as long as it is incurred in earning assessable income. The key issue to be considered is that there must be a clear connection between the borrowing of the funds and the earning of assessable income and the loan must not be of a private, capital or domestic nature. This goes back to s. 8.1 of the ITAA97, covered earlier in this chapter. Interest incurred on a loan used to buy a home which is used as the person's principal residence is not deductible because the expenditure is domestic in nature, nor is interest payable on a loan made to buy vacant land, because it has not generated any assessable income (unless the taxpayer is a land developer). On the other hand, interest payable on a loan taken out to buy an investment property that is generating assessable income will be tax deductible.

An important factor in accumulating wealth is to ensure that loans taken out for private purposes that do not provide any tax benefits, such as for a home or a car, are paid off as quickly as possible when compared to loans that do provide tax benefits.

Where the interest charge together with any other costs incurred exceed any income generated from an investment, this is known as negative gearing and gives rise to a tax loss. On the other hand, where income received exceeds the total costs incurred from an investment, including interest, this is known as positive gearing. Refer to chapter 8 for a comprehensive coverage of gearing.

Capital works deductions

Where construction on a residential building used for investment purposes commenced after 15 September 1987, a taxpayer is entitled to a capital works deduction at the rate of 2.5% p.a. This was previously a deduction of 4% where construction commenced between 17 July 1985 and 15 September 1987.

When purchasing a building to use for earning rental income, it is crucial to determine the date of construction, as this entitlement to a deduction passes to the purchaser upon sale. For example, an investor purchases a block of flats on 1 July 2001 for $1 million. The taxpayer will be entitled to an annual tax deduction of $25 000 ($1 000 000 × 2.5%).

Deductions for the decline in value of assets

The cost of acquiring an investment or asset (e.g. a kitchen stove for a rental property) is regarded as capital expenditure and therefore not generally tax deductible in the year of purchase. However, the decline in value of the asset over its effective life is an allowable tax deduction because of the loss of benefits to the taxpayer over time. The deduction comes under the provisions of the Uniform Capital Allowance System, and from 1 July 2001 this system applies to most depreciating assets.

Concessions provided to a small business allow an immediate write-off or tax deduction for assets costing less than $6500.

Income from managed investment schemes

managed investment schemes (managed funds) investment schemes where funds are deposited with a fund manager to manage on behalf of investors

Managed investment schemes, commonly known as **managed funds**, are unit trust structures that allow investors (unit holders) to pool their money together to invest into an investment which is managed by a professional fund manager. The funds within the structure can be invested into a range of different types of investments, such as shares, cash, fixed interest and property.

Managed funds are a very popular investment vehicle in Australia and can either be listed and traded on the Australian Securities Exchange (ASX), where they are known as a listed investment company (LIC), or they may be unlisted and not able to be traded on the ASX. Unlisted managed funds account for the majority of managed funds that exist in the market place. The structure of managed investment schemes is discussed further in chapter 7.

Managed funds are a particularly popular investment vehicle for investors who do not have the time or expertise to manage their funds themselves. Funds within the managed investment structure are managed by a professional fund manager and investors have a right to a share of any income and profits generated. Being unit trusts, the managed fund itself is not assessable to tax. All income earned within the fund, such as rental income, interest, fully franked dividends and capital gains made on the sale of investments are distributed to investors of the fund and taxed at the investors' individual marginal tax rates. As well as being taxed on the income and capital gains generated within the trust, the individual unit holder will be taxed on any realised capital gains or losses made on the disposal of the units they hold in the managed fund. The unit price of investing in the fund will reflect the value of the investments held within the managed fund and will increase and decrease over time.

To illustrate the taxation consequences of investing in an unlisted managed fund, consider illustrative example 3.6.

ILLUSTRATIVE EXAMPLE 3.6

On 1 July, Frank takes $10 000 from his savings account to invest into an Australian shares managed fund. However, by the end of the financial year he notes that his investment in the fund has fallen to $9500. He receives a tax statement from the fund which states that during the financial year he received a distribution from the fund consisting of $400 of income and $600 of capital gains. Frank wonders how he could be liable to a taxable capital gain when the value of the fund had fallen by year end.

The distribution of $400 of income reflects the fact that during the year, the fund generated income from investments held. In addition, the capital gain of $600 would have arisen from the manager selling some investments during the year. Tax will therefore be payable on any realised capital gains made within the fund. The fall in the value of the Australian shares managed fund at year end reflects the fact that investments held within the managed fund have fallen at that time. If the investor does not sell the units in the managed fund, the loss is unrealised and no gain or loss is brought to account at that stage. This shows that an investor may have to report income and a capital gain in a year even when the value of their investments has actually fallen.

Capital gains tax

capital gains tax (CGT) a tax applied when a profit is made on the disposal of a capital asset

Prior to the introduction of the **capital gains tax (CGT)** regime on 20 September 1985, profits made upon the disposal of any capital asset, such as shares, property, bonds etc. were not considered to be assessable under the ordinary income provisions of the Income Tax Assessment Act and were therefore tax free. The introduction of specific statutory provisions of the CGT regime in 1985 were designed to broaden the income base of the government, limit investment speculation and bring capital gains to account as assessable income of the taxpayer.

It should be noted that the CGT provisions do not apply to gains or losses made as part of the business activities of a taxpayer such as a property developer or share trader. Such gains and losses are considered as assessable income under the ordinary income provisions of the ITAA and are fully assessable.

CGT is a tax on realised capital gains. For CGT to apply there must be disposal of an asset that was acquired by the taxpayer after 19 September 1985. The CGT is calculated as the difference between the net disposal value and the net cost of the asset. The assessable capital gain forms part of the taxable income of the taxpayer for the year and is taxed at the taxpayer's marginal tax rate. Where the taxpayer incurs a net capital loss for the year, the amount cannot be claimed as a tax deduction; it can only be offset against a capital gain made in the same year, or if no capital gain is made, it can be carried forward indefinitely to be set off against future capital gains.

Certain items are exempt from the CGT legislation including:

- the taxpayer's main residence
- passenger motor cars
- gains from lottery wins
- gambling winnings
- insurance proceeds where the compensation is for personal injury
- proceeds from superannuation funds
- assets acquired prior to the introduction of CGT on 20 September 1985.

The CGT legislation is very complex and far reaching and over 50 different kinds of events may trigger a capital gain or loss, including disposal of an asset, a loss, cancellation or destruction of an asset and the end of an option to acquire shares. A disposal includes any change of ownership. Thus the transfer of shares from one spouse to another or from an individual to their private company or family trust would be considered to be a capital event. Once a capital event is triggered, the capital gain or loss is determined as the difference between the net proceeds from sale and the asset's net cost base. The net proceeds represent the amount of funds received upon sale of the asset less any incidental costs incurred upon the sale of the asset. Examples of incidental costs may include legal costs, brokerage charges and advertising fees. The net cost base of the asset represents the total funds paid to acquire the asset plus any incidental fees incurred in the process of acquiring the asset, such as stamp duty, valuation and legal costs. Other capital expenditure incurred during the period of ownership to increase or improve the value of the asset is also added to the cost base of the asset. Examples of capital expenditure relating to an investment property may include renovations, extensions, major repairs and painting. Expenditure undertaken on the property which is considered a repair rather than a capital expenditure would be treated as an allowable deduction.

Calculating the capital gain or loss

Once a capital gain or loss has occurred, the taxpayer needs to determine that amount to be included in their assessable income. This is known as the assessable capital gain. Where the asset has been held for less than 12 months, the full capital gain is brought to account as part of the taxpayer's assessable income. Where the asset has been held for greater than 12 months, the taxpayer may be entitled to a concession in the method of calculating the capital gain. The two possible methods of calculating the assessable capital gain include the indexation method or the discount method.

1. The *indexation method* allows for an increase in the cost base by applying an indexation factor based on the increase in the consumer price index (CPI) from the date of acquisition up to 20 September 1999. Under this method, the cost base is indexed by the percentage increase in the CPI for the period commencing from the quarter of the year in which the asset was acquired until the quarter ended September 1999 when the availability of this method ceased. CPI increases after the September 1999 quarter are disregarded so that indexation effectively became frozen at that date.
2. Under the CGT *discount method*, the capital gain is reduced by a discount factor to determine the net assessable capital gain. The discount factors used to determine the net capital gain are as follows:
   - individual or trust — 50% discount
   - complying superannuation fund — 33.33% discount
   - other entities including companies — 0% discount.

Thus, for an individual, once the 50% discount is applied to the capital gain made, only half of the capital gain is included in the assessable income of the taxpayer.

The selection of the two methods depends upon when the asset was first acquired.

- For assets acquired after 20 September 1985 and before 21 September 1999 the taxpayer has the choice as to which of the two methods they select — the indexation method or the CGT discount method.
- For assets acquired after 21 September 1999, the CGT discount method must be used.

The *normal assessable income rules* are used when the investment has been acquired and disposed of within a 12-month period. A taxpayer is only able to use the indexation method or the CGT discount method where the asset has been owned for at least 12 months.

A capital loss from the sale of an investment is made if the reduced cost base is greater than the proceeds from the sale of the asset. The reduced cost includes the costs of acquisition but excludes any amounts to the extent to which the expenditure is tax deductible. When a capital loss is incurred, no allowance is made for the effects of inflation under the indexation method, nor is the individual entitled to a 50% discount under the CGT discount method.

ILLUSTRATIVE EXAMPLE 3.7

Frank has decided to sell the share portfolio that he acquired on 1 November 1994 for $160 000. Frank sells the shares in July of the current financial year for $225 000. The costs of disposal are $5000. The cost base is $160 000 while the net capital proceeds amount to $220 000 ($225 000 – $5000). The capital gain is therefore $60 000.

As the shares were acquired prior to 20 September 1999, Frank can select from either the indexation method or the CGT discount approach to determine the net assessable capital gain that will form part of his assessable income. Under the indexation method, the value of the property is indexed by CPI from the date of purchase (CPI at that time was 112.8 for the December 1994 quarter) up to the September 1999 quarter when the indexation method was frozen (CPI was 123.4 at that time).

Net capital proceeds	$220 000
Less indexed cost base ($160 000 × 123.4/112.8)	$175 035
Net assessable capital gain	44 965

Under the CGT discount approach, the net capital gain is determined as the difference between the net cost base and the net capital proceeds less the discount factor.

Net capital proceeds	$220 000
Less net cost base	160 000
Capital gain	60 000
Less 50% discount	30 000
Net assessable capital gain	30 000

As the CGT discount method provides the lower net capital gain, an amount of $30 000 will be included in the assessable income of Frank and taxed at his marginal tax rate.

Tax planning and capital gains tax

Tax planning is an important consideration with the acquisition and disposal of investments in order to be able to minimise the imposition of any assessable capital gain. Issues to consider in the planning include:

- the structure used to invest
- the nature of the investment
- the amount of time the investment is held

- the timing of disposal
- the method used to calculate the capital gain or loss.

The structure/entity used to hold the asset is important. The capital gains discount for an individual taxpayer and a trust is 50%. The discount for a superannuation fund is 33.333%. There is no discount for a company. Therefore, it is generally not advisable to hold appreciating assets within a corporate structure.

Where a taxpayer disposes of a capital asset as part of normal trading or business activities, such as with share traders or property developers, capital gains will be fully assessable as ordinary income with no allowance provided for indexation or a discount factor. Just what constitutes a business activity is debatable, but the taxation authorities usually look at a number of factors including the frequency of transactions, profit motive and the commercialisation of the activity. Persons who regularly buy and sell shares or properties may be considered as traders. However, being classified as a share trader or property developer is not necessarily bad news. For an investor, capital losses can be offset only against capital gains, but if a trader makes a loss, it is deductible from the trader's assessable income.

In order to take advantage of the tax concessions available in calculating the assessable capital gain, an investor would be advised to hold an asset for longer than 12 months. Taxation is relevant not only in the decision to invest, but also in the decision to sell that investment as well as the timing of the disposal. If an asset has been held for longer than 12 months, the taxpayer may be entitled to utilise either the indexation method or the discount method, depending on when the asset was acquired. As indexation became frozen at September 1999 (when the index was 123.4), the passage of time will mean the discount method will normally yield the lower assessable capital gain. However, tax planners must consider the application of both methods and choose the one that provides for the lower capital gain. Different methods can be used for each asset sold. The index numbers are available on the ATO website (ATO 2013e).

The timing of the disposal of an asset is an important issue in terms of minimising the imposition of taxation. It is normally beneficial to dispose of an asset in the year in which the taxpayer's taxable income is lower, thereby reducing the marginal tax rate applicable. This might occur during the taxpayer's retirement, for example.

If during the year, capital gains have been made on the disposal of an asset, the investor may consider different strategies for reducing the impact of the capital gain on their taxable income. For example, the investor may be able to realise capital losses to offset other capital gains made during the year. The taxpayer may also look to see whether they are able to qualify for a tax deduction that can be used to reduce their taxable income. For example, a taxpayer may be entitled to a tax deduction for a personal contribution made to their superannuation fund. See chapter 11 for further details.

PERSONAL FINANCE BULLETIN

Tax headache: CGT and lodgers

Question: I'm about to sell my property and am looking for help on my capital gains tax situation. The problem is that I have had people paying board in my own property to bring in some extra cash and need to work out how much of my capital gain on the house is now subject to CGT.

I had one tenant for 30 weeks and one tenant for 47 weeks, with an overlap of about two weeks in the middle (I have two spare rooms, but only really wanted one boarder at a time). I'll have had the property for six years when I sell. Is there a formula for working out how much of my capital gain will be taxable? And what rate of tax will I pay?

Answer: Ordinarily your main residence is exempt from capital gains tax (CGT). To gain this benefit your home must be used primarily for private or domestic purposes, which means you cannot derive assessable income. If part of your main residence is used to derive assessable income (for instance you lease two rooms) you're only entitled to a part CGT exemption during the period your home is leased, and a full exemption during the period it's not leased.

The portion that's liable to CGT is normally determined on an area basis and time basis. For example, if your home consists of ten rooms and you use two rooms to derive assessable income over a 30 week period, under these circumstances, 20% of your main residence is liable to CGT during the 30 weeks the property was leased. Complications can arise where these variables (as in your case) are not consistent.

For more information you can read Tax Office publication 'Is the dwelling your main residence', and more particularly the section that sets out the formula for 'Calculating a part exemption'. You can download a copy from the Tax Office website (www.ato.gov.au).

Incidentally, as you had owned the property for more than 12 months (in your case six years), only 50% of the portion of the capital gain you make on sale is liable to tax at your marginal rates of tax (which can vary between 0% and 45%) plus a 1.5% Medicare levy. As this is a rather complex calculation (especially in your case) it's best that you seek advice from a registered tax agent.

Source: Your Investment Property, www.yourinvestmentpropertymag.com.au/article/tax-headache-cgt-and-lodgers-120888.aspx

LO 5 Taxation planning

One of the more important parts of the financial planning process in helping an individual to meet their financial goals is personal taxation planning. The aim of taxation planning is to develop strategies that will legitimately minimise the imposition of taxation on an individual. That is, it is the process of organising the affairs of a person or persons with a view to minimising the amount of income and other taxes that are payable.

The financial planning process requires financial planners to undertake a detailed consideration of a client's circumstances and financial position and to develop appropriate recommendations to deliver on the client's objectives.

The financial planner has a **best interest duty** under the Corporations Act to act in the best interests of the client, which includes taking into account the taxation position of the client and the tax ramifications arising from any recommendations put in place. This will mean that the advice must be based on sound principles and the client must be made

best interest duty the obligation placed upon the financial planner to act in the best interests of the client

fully aware of the consequences before acting upon the advice. However, taxation law in Australia is very technical and complex, and financial planners need to ensure that they do not provide taxation advice outside of their experience, training and qualifications. Prior to acting upon certain advice, financial planners may encourage the client to seek the advice of their accountant or tax adviser to confirm the taxation implications of the advice given.

While taxation planning forms an important aspect of the investment strategies developed for an individual, taxation should not be the overriding factor determining investment decisions. However, many people do invest in particular assets because of the tax advantages that type of asset offers. Towards the end of the financial year, in particular, various investment schemes and financial products are often promoted as an effective means of reducing the amount of tax a person will have to pay. Examples that have been promoted in the past include pine plantations, almonds, films, aquaculture and structured investments that have a capital protection element to them. It is important in assessing any investment to properly understand how the product works, its risk and return characteristics, and its role in achieving the person's overall financial objectives. While taxation may be an important issue to consider, the investment must stand on its own merits and have the potential to provide real after-tax returns.

The following taxation planning strategies are considered in the remainder of this chapter: income splitting, income versus capital growth, tax structures, negative gearing, and salary packaging and remuneration planning.

LO 6 Income splitting

income splitting shifting income from a person on a high marginal tax rate to a person or entity in a lower tax bracket

One of the most common methods of taxation planning is **income splitting** or transferring income from an individual paying tax at a high marginal tax rate to an individual or other entity that is on a lower rate of tax. A number of strategies are available that can assist in achieving the transfer of income. The decision to divert income to another individual, such as a family member, or into a particular tax structure will depend upon a number of factors including the cost, the benefits to be gained, other tax implications involved and the financial understanding of the individuals involved.

Salary or wage income cannot be split. Also, under the personal services income (PSI) regime, income that is earned predominantly from the personal activities of a person cannot be diverted or assigned to another person, entity or structure. In contrast, income derived from the carrying on of a business can be diverted. The range of different structures available to a person to operate a business activity will be discussed later in this chapter.

Normally, the easiest means of diverting income is by transferring investments and other assets to family members earning a lower taxable income. If the other taxpayer has no other income, this strategy will be particularly attractive because of the tax-free threshold of $18 200 that applies to individuals, as well as the opportunity for them to take advantage of tax offsets, such as the low income tax offset.

However, the transfer of investments or other assets may give rise to a number of issues and tax consequences.

1. Care needs to be taken with the transfer of income to children because of the special penalty rates of tax that apply to the unearned income of minors under the provisions of ITAA36 Div. 6AA (discussed earlier in this chapter). This does not apply to children and other family members over the age of 18.

2. The person to whom the income has been diverted is entitled to demand actual payment of the income and the asset (as it is in their name), which may not be intended or desirable.
3. The transfer of an asset to another entity or person, including a family member, is considered a disposal, and accordingly the impact of the CGT provisions must be considered. That is, the amount of any CGT payable on the transfer of the asset would need to be considered in determining the feasibility of the strategy.

LO 7 Income versus capital growth

In many situations, the benefit attached to holding an investment or an asset may be provided in the form of either income or capital growth. The preference for income over capital growth will depend upon a range of factors such as the cash flow needs of a person; their time horizon — that is, whether they are investing for the short term or long term; and the tax consequences associated with each option. From a tax point of view, income earned from an investment or other asset is fully assessable to tax. On the other hand, capital gains generated are taxable under the CGT provisions which might provide that the gain is assessed in a concessional manner. For example, for an investment that has been held for more than 12 months, an individual is entitled to a 50% discount on the gain under the CGT discount method.

The distinction between the receipt of income and the receipt of capital is therefore important in terms of the available tax concessions for a capital receipt.

LO 8 Tax structures

As discussed earlier, one of the important strategies available to an individual in minimising the imposition of taxation is to attempt to split or divert their investment, business and other income to another individual or tax structure. It is normally beneficial for the individual within a family on the lowest marginal tax rate to receive investment and business income. However, rather than an individual earning the income in their own name, it may be preferable to hold investments or to run a business under an alternative tax structure which might not only minimise the imposition of tax, but also provide other benefits to the investor. The main tax structures available to hold investments or operate a business include sole ownership, partnership, family company, family trust and superannuation fund.

Each tax structure has its own advantages and disadvantages which need to be carefully considered before their establishment. Two of the most important issues to be considered in deciding which entity should be used to receive income are cost and complexity. Establishing and administering alternative tax structures can be costly and complex. Before setting up an alternative tax structure, an investor needs to ensure there are real gains to be made. The different tax structures — and their advantages and disadvantages — are considered next.

Sole ownership

This is the simplest and cheapest entity for holding investments or running a business. The individual has complete control over the decision making, there are no set-up costs and individuals have an entitlement to an $18 200 tax-free threshold, a range of tax offsets and rebates and a 50% discount on the capital gains made on the sale of assets. Income splitting can occur through investments being held in the name of the individual on the lowest marginal tax rate.

However, sole ownership has a number of disadvantages and limitations. All of the income belongs to the individual and tax is paid at their marginal tax rate. In addition, there is limited asset protection for a sole-owner business and the business has a finite life (based on the owner's capacity to continue the business). When the owner dies, the business and any investments held by the business must be sold or transferred to another party.

Attempts to divert or transfer income to other individuals within a family may be difficult. If an investment is already held in the name of one individual, the transfer of assets to any other individual or entity may incur capital gains tax. In addition, while there may be opportunities to divert investment income to another member of a family, tax regulations do not permit the diversion of income derived from personal services income.

Partnerships

A partnership for tax purposes exists when two or more persons form an association for the purposes of either running a business as partners or for the purposes of receiving income jointly; for example, a couple with a joint bank account. Taxable income in these circumstances can be split between taxpayers — usually members of a family — to minimise tax.

Advantages of forming a partnership include the fact that it can be established quickly, cheaply and simply, and income can be split between the partners. For example, assume that the total investment earnings of the Rajasekaram family are $80 000 for the current year. This is their only source of income. Rather than either one of the couple owning the investments in their own name and having a taxable income of $80 000, the ability to split income between the husband and wife (i.e. $40 000 each) will result in a saving in net tax through each person being on a lower marginal tax rate and each having a tax-free threshold of $18 200.

Disadvantages of a partnership include the fact that it has limited asset protection, control of a business is shared and there is limited flexibility in being able to split income between the different partners. That is, each partner receives a share of the income of the partnership based on their share of their interest or ownership in the partnership.

With respect to investment income where ownership is in joint names, such as with joint bank accounts or a jointly owned investment property, unless the ownership share is specified, the income is normally divided equally between the parties who own the investment. The same principles would apply to income earned from carrying on a business. In conducting a business, normally a partnership agreement would be established to clarify roles, responsibilities and profit splits.

While a partnership is not a separate legal entity and therefore does not pay income tax, a partnership is still required to submit a partnership tax return in order to show to the Australian Taxation Office how the taxable income or loss of the partnership has been distributed among the partners in accordance with the partnership agreement. Income tax is then levied on the partners individually.

Tax payable by entity
— nil

Tax payable by individual partners
— individual marginal tax rates

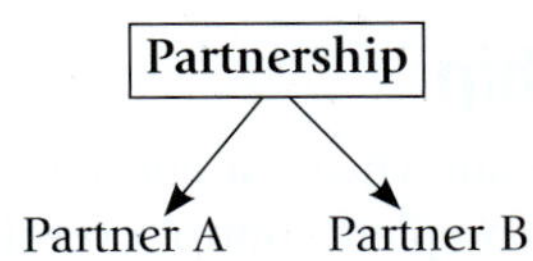

Companies

Companies are a separate legal entity where the directors of the company manage and administer the assets of the company on behalf of the company's owners, who are called shareholders. Companies are taxed in their own right. That is, a company is required to submit a tax return and pay income tax in their own right at a flat rate of 30%. There is no tax-free threshold or graduated level of tax as there is for individuals.

Profits of the company are available to be distributed to the shareholders of the company in the form of dividends. Capital gains on the disposal of assets held by a company are normally fully assessable. The indexing of the cost base or access to the CGT discount are not available for companies which means it is usually advisable for investors *not* to hold investments in a corporate structure.

The advantages of operating through a corporate structure include:

- limited liability of shareholders
- the ability to split income between family members through paying wages and salaries
- the company continues to exist regardless of the death of a shareholder or any changes in shareholders
- imputation credits can be passed onto shareholders through the payment of franked dividends
- profits of the company can be retained within the entity and do not need to be paid out as dividends in a particular financial year. The timing of the payment of dividends can be deferred to a period where the shareholders may be on a lower marginal tax rate, such as upon retirement.

The drawbacks of operating through a company structure include:

- a company is relatively costly to set up and to administer on an ongoing basis
- companies are subject to the rules and regulations of the *Corporations Act 2001* and *Australian Securities and Investments Commission Act 2001* which imposes time and dollar costs on directors and shareholders
- companies have no tax-free threshold, no entitlement to the tax offsets available to individuals and no entitlement to tax concessions on capital gains.

Tax payable by entity
— flat rate of 30%

Tax payable by individual shareholders
— individual marginal tax rates incorporating dividend imputation system

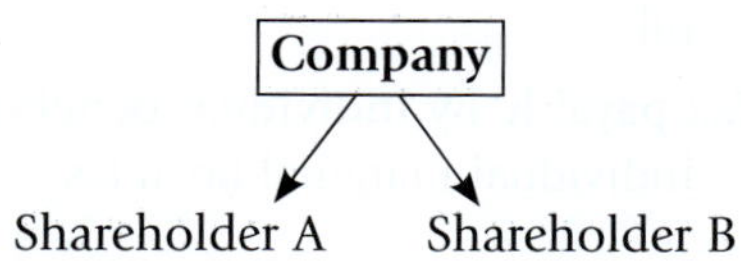

ILLUSTRATIVE EXAMPLE 3.8

Based on the opening case study, assume that Frank or Angela had acquired their share portfolio in the name of their family company rather than in their individual names.

For tax purposes, the company will make a capital gain of $60 000 which is taxed at 30% — a tax of $18 000. There is no discount available to a company. If Frank or Angela had invested in the share portfolio in their individual names, the capital gain would have been reduced by 50%. The tax saving to the individual would depend on their individual marginal rate of tax.

Trusts

trust
a legal structure where property is nominally owned and held by a trustee on behalf of beneficiaries

A **trust** is governed by a trust deed which sets out the various rights and obligations on the operation of the trust. A trust is a structure that can own and hold assets and investments, or run a business. It is controlled and managed by a person or company (trustee), for the benefit of other persons (beneficiaries). The trustee has legal control over the assets of the trust which means they can buy and sell assets but will never own or enjoy the benefits of ownership, such as the income generated from their use. While the beneficiaries do not legally own the assets within the trust, they are the ones that are entitled to the assets and profits of the trust.

There are four elements of any trust:

1. a trustee
2. property capable of being held in trust
3. one or more beneficiaries
4. a personal obligation attaching to the trust property.

There are two main types of trusts. A unit trust is divided into a fixed number of units, much like shares within a corporate structure, and profits are distributed according to the number of units held. Unit trusts are commonly used in non-family situations where it is important for the ownership of units and distribution of profits to be formalised to prevent disputes. In contrast, a discretionary trust is a far more flexible vehicle and particularly suited to family situations. With a discretionary trust, income is distributed according to the discretion of the trustee. This can be undertaken with a view to minimising the imposition of tax across the family members.

From a tax point of view, trusts are not separately taxed. While a tax return is required to be prepared, this is to show how the income of the trust has been distributed among the various beneficiaries. Trust income is generally taxed in the hands of the beneficiaries at their marginal tax rates. All income, gains and losses are required to be distributed to the beneficiaries, including any tax offsets or rebates associated with the income. This is because of the 'flow through' effect of all transactions to the investor in the trust.

Tax payable by entity
— nil

Tax payable by individual beneficiaries
— individual marginal tax rates

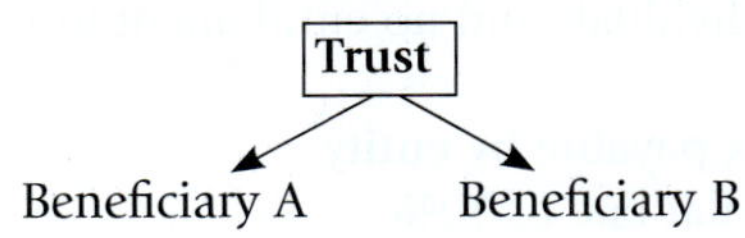

Superannuation funds

A superannuation fund is a scheme for the payment of benefits upon retirement or death. Savings are held in trust until the person retires or dies. It is an invaluable tool for the financial planner and client and is driven considerably by taxation concessions. Complying superannuation funds are levied with a concessional income tax rate of a flat 15% on the fund's taxable income. Employer compulsory superannuation contributions for their employees are generally deductible for the employer. Personal contributions are also deductible when the person making the contributions is self-employed, employed without superannuation support, or a full-time investor.

Tax payable by entity
— flat rate of 15%

Tax payable by individual fund members
— no individual tax implications

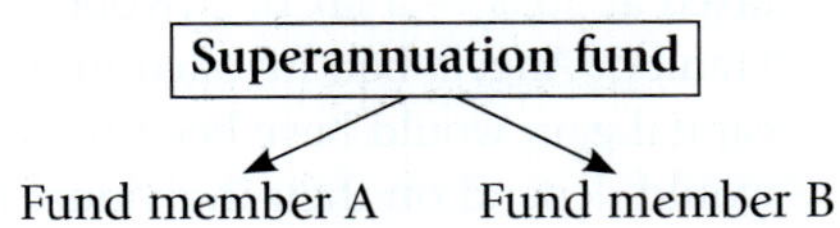

Table 3.4 shows the advantages and disadvantages of different tax entities.

TABLE 3.4 Advantages and disadvantages of different tax entities

Entity	Advantages	Disadvantages
Sole ownership	▪ Investment income can be split ▪ Main residence exempt from CGT ▪ 50% discount on capital gains ▪ A tax-free threshold of taxable income and a graduated tax scale depending on the size of taxable income ▪ Domestic losses can be carried forward to be offset against assessable income	▪ Not possible to split salary or wage income ▪ Minors subject to penalty tax ▪ Marginal rates climb to 45% ▪ Medicare levy at certain income levels plus possible Medicare levy surcharge ▪ Unlimited liability
Partnership	▪ Capacity to split income ▪ Capacity to direct property and therefore income to the partner with the lowest level of income ▪ Losses can be distributed to partners and used to offset against income they have earned from other sources ▪ Relatively simple to administer	▪ Minors subject to penalty tax ▪ Marginal rates climb to 45% ▪ Medicare levy at certain income levels plus possible Medicare levy surcharge ▪ No flexibility in sharing income as fixed according to partnership agreement ▪ Unlimited liability
Companies	▪ Flat rate tax of 30% ▪ Normally, losses can be carried forward ▪ Limited liability of shareholders ▪ The ability to split income between family members ▪ The company continues to exist despite the death of or changes in shareholders ▪ Imputation credits can be passed onto shareholders through the payment of franked dividends ▪ Earnings of the company can be retained within the entity thereby deferring the payment of tax on distributions of dividends	▪ No tax-free threshold ▪ Losses are kept within the company ▪ No concession on the calculation of capital gains tax ▪ Costs of administration ▪ Subject to a significant amount of government regulation
Trusts	▪ Capacity to direct income to the beneficiaries with the lowest tax rates ▪ 50% discount on capital gains ▪ The trust continues to exist despite the death of or changes in beneficiaries	▪ Losses are trapped inside the trust and can be offset only against future trust income ▪ Costs of administration
Superannuation funds	▪ 15% tax rate on earnings ▪ Possible reduction of capital gain by one-third *Note:* When a superannuation fund is in pension mode, it pays no tax on income or capital gains.	▪ Borrowing not allowed ▪ Costs of administration ▪ Funds cannot be accessed until the member has satisfied a condition of release such as retirement

LO 9 Negative gearing

negative gearing
a situation where the total deductions associated with an investment, including the interest charge, exceed assessable income generated from the investment; in this case, the loss can be claimed as a tax deduction

Negative gearing arises where the total deductions associated with an investment, including the interest charge, exceed assessable income generated from the investment. That is, a tax loss is generated from the investment which may be able to be claimed as a tax deduction. Negative gearing is a useful tax-effective strategy especially for those on the highest marginal tax rate as the loss can be used to reduce income from other sources, such as wages, and reduce the overall incidence of tax. However, there is little point acquiring an investment that simply generates a loss each year. To be effective, the investment must show an eventual and overall profit. An investor may be willing to generate a tax loss each year as long as there is the potential to generate a capital gain upon disposal of the asset of sufficient amount to compensate for the risk attached to the borrowing, and to cover the tax loss generated over the years from the negatively geared investment. As with any investment, although taxation is a significant factor to consider, the primary consideration is the ability of the investment to produce a real after-tax return for the investor. Negative gearing is covered in more detail in chapter 8. The benefit of the tax loss depends upon the marginal tax rate of the borrower. This is an important issue to consider when determining which family member should own the investment and take out the borrowing. Thus, in a situation where an investment is negatively geared and generates a tax loss, a family member on a high marginal tax rate (MTR) will receive a much higher tax benefit from the loss than a family member on a low marginal tax rate.

positive gearing
a situation where the assessable income generated from the investment exceeds total deductions incurred, including the interest charges; in this case, the tax is payable on the profit

A situation of **positive gearing**, where the assessable income in a year exceeds all allowable deductions, may still be attractive for an investor despite generating taxable income. Positive gearing is likely to be attractive for those investors requiring an ongoing income and/or where taxation is not a prime consideration. In this case, the debt and borrowing should be held in the name of the family member on the lowest marginal tax rate in order to minimise the payment of tax.

LO 10 Salary packaging and remuneration planning

salary sacrificing
where an employee asks their employer to take some of their income and redirect this to paying for a benefit on behalf of the employee; the most commonly salary sacrificed benefit is superannuation

Salary sacrificing, also known as salary packaging, is a common benefit made available by employers and is aimed at providing an employee with their salary in a more tax-effective manner. Salary sacrificing involves substituting part of an employee's future cash salary or wages for non-cash benefits provided by the employer, such as a car, additional super contributions or a laptop. While not all employers provide a salary-packaging option for their employees, enterprise bargaining is leading to more flexible remuneration packages being negotiated.

The principle behind salary sacrificing is that instead of an employee receiving all of their remuneration from employment in the form of a fully taxed cash salary or wage, they take part of their remuneration in the form of concessionally taxed or exempt non-cash benefits. Non-cash benefits received by an employee are not subject to income tax. For salary sacrificing to be effective for the employee, the combined after-tax benefit from the salary and non-cash benefits must be greater than the after-tax benefit from receiving just the salary. From an employer's point of view, the aim is to ensure that the total cost of an employee's remuneration package is no greater by providing salary sacrificing as an option.

Depending upon the employer, a number of non-cash benefits may be made available to an employee. The most common benefits provided include:

- superannuation contributions in addition to the mandatory superannuation guarantee (SG) contributions
- the use of a fully maintained car
- paying car-parking costs
- providing reduced-interest or interest-free loans
- paying school fees for the employee's children
- providing a laptop, mobile phone or other electronic device.

A number of these benefits are covered in the next section.

The question of whether a person should salary sacrifice a non-cash benefit, or whether an optimum combination of salary and non-cash benefits exists, will depend on the individual's circumstances. Each person has differing financial circumstances, goals and needs, and a financial plan should determine the 'optimum package' for each person.

ILLUSTRATIVE EXAMPLE 3.9

Angela earns a salary of $42 000 p.a. and her employer has given her the option of salary sacrificing into a $10 000 non-cash benefit. Angela is unsure whether she should salary sacrifice or not.

Some of the issues that Angela will need to consider include:

- Tax savings — by salary sacrificing, Angela's gross tax payable and Medicare levy will be based on a cash salary of $32 000 instead of $42 000 resulting in a saving in income tax.
- Need for the benefit — to what extent does Angela really need or want the non-cash benefit?
- Reduction in disposable income — can Angela afford the reduction in her cash salary?
- Fringe benefits tax payable — will the non-cash benefit be subject to fringe benefits tax (see below)?

Fringe benefits tax

Although the provision of non-cash benefits does not form part of the assessable income of an employee and is not subject to income tax, non-cash benefits may be subject to another form of tax called the **fringe benefits tax (FBT)**. The rate of the FBT is 47% (from 1 July 2014), based on the highest individual marginal tax rate plus the increased Medicare levy of 2% effective from 1 July 2014. While the tax is payable by the employer, the cost will be passed onto the employee as part of the employee's total remuneration package.

fringe benefits tax (FBT) a tax applied to the taxable amount of non-cash benefits provided to an employee

Fringe benefits tax (FBT) was introduced in 1986 to cover the loss of income tax to the government that resulted from employees being paid non-cash benefits instead of fully taxed cash salaries. The FBT legislation was introduced to ensure that the imposition of tax on the individual would be the same regardless of whether the employee receives a cash salary and pays income tax at their marginal tax rate or takes a non-cash benefit and pays the FBT.

Salary sacrificing and the payment of FBT is payable by employers as a result of there being an employer–employee relationship. Accordingly, sole traders cannot salary sacrifice. Employers are able to claim a tax deduction for both the cost of the benefit provided to an employee as well as the cost of any FBT paid. The FBT year is based on the period 1 April to 31 March.

FBT is determined under the following process.

Step 1 — Determine the taxable value of the benefit

Step 2 — Apply a gross-up rate
= Fringe benefits taxable amount

Step 3 — Apply FBT rate of 47%
= FBT payable

The taxable value of a fringe benefit is based on a set of valuation rules — different categories of benefits have specific rules for calculating the taxable value. The purpose of the grossing-up process is to convert the fringe benefits received by an employee to their pre-tax equivalent value so that there is little difference in the taxation treatment between an employee receiving a cash salary and paying income tax at the highest marginal tax rate of 47% or the employee receiving a fringe benefit and the employer paying FBT at 47%.

There are two gross-up formulae for calculating the fringe benefits taxable amount. The two gross-up rates are required because of the impact of GST on the cost of non-cash benefits provided to employees. Where an employer does not incur GST on the cost of a benefit, or is not entitled to claim GST credits back from the government, a gross-up rate of 1.8692 is applied. This is known as a type 2 benefit. In situations where GST is payable on a benefit and the employer is able to claim a GST credit from the government, a gross-up rate of 2.0647 is used. This is known as a type 1 benefit. The higher gross-up rate allows for the employer to recover GST credits from the government as a result of providing a fringe benefit to an employee. The amount of FBT payable is calculated on the GST tax-inclusive value of the fringe benefit.

It is most important when a salary package is arranged, that it is undertaken in accordance with Taxation Ruling 2001/10. The ruling reaffirms the ATO's stance that where an employee agrees to forgo future salary and salary sacrifice into a non-cash benefit, an agreement to salary sacrifice must be in force from the outset and not put into place after the employee has become entitled to income or benefit.

ILLUSTRATIVE EXAMPLE 3.10

Frank and Angela's second child, David, is provided with a type 1 fringe benefit of $2800 for holiday airfares. The fringe benefits taxable amount is calculated as follows:

$$\$2800 \times 2.0647 = \$5781$$

In addition, David is provided with a type 2 fringe benefit of $4000 for school fees for his child. The fringe benefits taxable amount is calculated as follows:

$$\$4000 \times 1.8692 = \$7477$$

David's aggregate grossed-up value of fringe benefits is $5781 + $7477 = $13 258.

The fringe benefits tax payable is $13 258 × 47% = $6231. This amount will be payable by David's employer to the ATO but the employer will deduct this payment from David's remuneration package.

A fringe benefit is defined broadly and is designed to capture most forms of non-cash benefits provided to an employee. Benefits are divided into four main categories for FBT purposes as follows:

- fully taxed fringe benefits
- concessionally taxed fringe benefits
- exempt fringe benefits
- excluded benefits.

Fully taxed fringe benefits

These are benefits provided by an employer where the actual cost or value of the benefit is fully assessable for FBT purposes. Examples of fully taxed fringe benefits include many types of private expenses incurred by the employee such as payment of mortgage loans, school fees, holidays and private telephone expenses.

There is generally no financial benefit to be gained by an employee salary sacrificing into fully taxed benefits. That is, either the employee will pay income tax at their marginal tax rate if they do not salary sacrifice or if they do salary sacrifice and have to pay FBT, a tax rate of 47% will be payable. From this it can be seen that an employee on a marginal tax rate of less than 47% is actually going to be worse off salary sacrificing into fully taxed fringe benefits which are taxed at the highest marginal tax rate.

Taxable value of benefit	$10 000
FBT on grossed-up amount	$10 000 × 1.8692 × 47%
FBT	$8785
Charge against package	$10 000 + $8785 = $18 785

Thus, to receive a $10 000 benefit, the charge against the pre-tax income of the employee is $18 785.

If the employee had paid for the $10 000 benefit themself from their after-tax income, the amount of pre-tax income they would have required can be determined by the following equation:

$$\$10000 \times \frac{1}{1 - \text{MTR}}$$

For an employee on a MTR of 34.5% (including the 2% Medicare levy), the amount of pre-tax income required would be $10 000 × (1/0.655) = $15 267. Thus, the employee would be worse-off salary sacrificing a fully taxed fringe benefit by $3518.

Concessionally taxed fringe benefits

These are benefits provided by an employer where the taxable value of the benefit is assessed at a lower amount than the actual monetary value. Concessionally taxed fringe benefits provide the most tax advantage to employees on the highest marginal tax rate. However, depending on the circumstances, they may also provide tax benefits for some employees on lower marginal tax rates.

As the provision of a car benefit is one of the most common types of concessionally taxed non-cash benefit provided to employees, this benefit will be covered in some detail.

Motor vehicles

A car fringe benefit arises when a car that is owned or leased by an employer is made available to an employee for private use. Private use arises in situations where the car is used for private purposes or is available for private use. Available for private use would include where the car is garaged at the employee's home overnight.

The value of the benefit is calculated either by the statutory formula method or the operating cost method as follows.

Statutory formula method

Under the statutory formula method, the taxable value of the benefit is determined by applying a statutory rate to the base value of the car. The statutory rate is based on the number of kilometres travelled. Prior to 1 April 2014, the greater the number of kilometres travelled annually, the lower was the statutory rate that was applied. For new contracts entered after 1 April 2014, a standard rate is applied as detailed in table 3.5 below. Under the statutory formula method, there is no requirement on the employer to establish the percentage of private use of the car by the employee. An allowance is made within the formula for situations where the employee may contribute towards the cost of the benefit.

The taxable value of the benefit is determined under the following formula:

$$\text{Value of car} \times \text{Statutory rate} \times \frac{\text{Days in the FBT year car used or available for private purposes}}{\text{Days in FBT year}} - \text{Employee contribution}$$

TABLE 3.5 Statutory rates based on kilometres travelled

	Statutory rate				
Distance travelled during the FBT year	Prior to 10 May 2011	From 10 May 2011	From 1 April 2012	From 1 April 2013	From 1 April 2014
0–15 000 km	.26	.20	.20	.20	.20
15 000–25 000 km	.20	.20	.20	.20	.20
25 000–40 000 km	.11	.14	.17	.20	.20
More than 40 000 km	.07	.10	.13	.17	.20

Source: ATO 2013f.

The taxable value of a car benefit is reduced by any employee contribution paid to the employer towards the cost of the benefit. Employee contributions can be an effective strategy for reducing the taxable value of concessionally taxed benefits and therefore the FBT payable for employees on a marginal tax rate less than the FBT rate.

Operating cost method

The cost method works out the cost of operating the car for the year (for example, petrol, servicing, insurance). From there, the employer (with the employee's help) establishes the percentage of private use (such as a weekend drive to the country) and percentage of income producing use (travelling from work premises to clients) of the car by the employee.

This is done on the basis of kilometres travelled on each activity by the employee. This is ascertained by the employee by keeping a log book of income producing trips for 12 weeks in the first year in which the employee had use of the car.

Once the percentage of private use is established, it is applied to the cost of the car to establish the taxable value of the benefit (for instance, the operating cost of $8000 with 40% private use would mean a taxable value of $3200).

The higher the proportion of private use of the car, the higher will be the taxable value of the benefit. The formula used for determining the taxable value is as follows:

$$\left[\text{Total operating costs of car} \times \left(100\% - \text{Proportion of business use for year}\right)\right] - \text{Employee contribution}$$

If the car is owned by the employer, rather than being leased, the costs are also required to include a depreciation charge at a rate of 25%. The costs are also required to include an imputed interest charge based on the statutory interest rate. The statutory benchmark interest rate is published annually in an ATO taxation determination. From 1 July 2013, the rate was 6.2%.

Both the operating cost method and the statutory formula method should be calculated to determine the most cost-effective alternative. Unless there is a large percentage of business use, the statutory formula method will usually result in a lower taxable value and therefore a smaller FBT liability. The operating cost method may provide a lower taxable value when the car does not travel many private kilometres in a year. However, even when the operating cost method does provide a lower taxable value, it still may not be the preferred option because of the need to maintain detailed records to substantiate the costs incurred and the nature of the kilometres travelled.

ILLUSTRATIVE EXAMPLE 3.11

Angela's employer provides her with a car benefit for the current FBT year. The employer leases the car which has a value of $32 000 for the FBT year from 1 April 2013. The car was available to Angela for private use for the full year. Angela agrees to pay the employer $1800 in respect of fuel costs incurred. Total kilometres for the FBT year were 30 000. The log book showed the car was used 40% for business purposes and 60% for private purposes. The following car costs were incurred for the year.

Lease payments	$8 200
Insurance	980
Registration	550
Repairs	1 000
Fuel	2 800
Total cost of car benefit inclusive of GST	13 530

Under the operating cost method the taxable value of the benefit is:

$$(\$13\,530 \times 60\%) - \$1800 = \$6318$$

Using the statutory formula method, the taxable value is:

$$(\$32\,000 \times 20\%) - \$1800 = \$4600$$

»

»

Calculating the FBT liability on the car benefit

Because the lowest value is used to calculate the FBT liability, the statutory formula method applies in this case. The FBT payable is calculated as follows:

$$\$4600 \times 2.0647 \times 47\% = \$4464$$

The total annual cost charged by the employer to Angela's salary package would be calculated as follows:

$$\$13\,530 \text{ (total costs)} + \$4464 \text{ (FBT payable)} = \$17\,994$$

Note that the employer may decide to reimburse the employee for the amount of GST included within the costs of the car.

Exempt fringe benefits

A number of fringe benefits provided to employees are exempt from FBT and, accordingly, are particularly attractive to salary sacrifice into. Some eligible work-related benefits include notebooks, laptops and other portable computers; protective clothing (required for employment); briefcases, mobiles and calculators. The FBT exemption will apply only if the benefits are primarily used within the employee's employment and the exemption is restricted to one item per year. Other common exempt fringe benefits include newspapers and periodicals used for business purposes, and minor benefits of up to $300 which are infrequently provided and/or are difficult to record and value, for example Christmas gifts or Christmas parties, the cost of a taxi for a single journey to or from work and certain other work-related items.

Excluded benefits

These are benefits that are specifically excluded under FBT legislation. One of the most common excluded benefits is superannuation which makes it particularly attractive as part of a salary sacrifice arrangement.

Superannuation

Superannuation contributions are an attractive form of salary sacrifice because an employee is provided with tax concessions to assist in accumulating wealth for their retirement. In the case of superannuation, the employee substitutes part of their cash salary through making additional contributions to their superannuation account. These contributions are in addition to the mandatory superannuation guarantee (SG) contributions that employers are required to make for their employees. SG contributions are discussed in more detail in chapters 10, 11 and 12.

FBT is not payable on superannuation contributions made to an employee's super fund as part of a salary sacrifice arrangement. However, it is important to note that all superannuation contributions made by an employer to a super fund are subject to a 15% contribution tax payable by the superannuation fund from the employee's account balance. Thus, for each $100 of superannuation contributions made through the SG scheme or through salary sacrificing, $15 is paid as tax to the Australian Taxation Office and only $85 will be left in the member's account.

For the majority of employees that are on a marginal tax rate greater than 15%, significant tax savings can be made through salary sacrificing into superannuation. While salary sacrificing into superannuation is an effective means of reducing income tax payable, generally the reduction in taxable income cannot be used to increase a person's entitlement to government benefits or to reduce their government obligations (discussed next).

Reportable fringe benefits

Where the total taxable value of fringe benefits provided to an employee is greater than $2000 in a FBT year, an employer is required to report the grossed-up taxable value on an employee's payment summary which is made available to the Australian Taxation Office. This is done to ensure that employees are not able to obtain certain government benefits or avoid their obligations for a number of government taxes and levies through salary sacrificing into non-cash fringe benefits and reducing their taxable income. Some of these government benefits and obligations include the government co-contribution, eligibility to make personal deductible contributions, spouse contribution tax offset (for the receiving spouse), Medicare levy surcharge, baby bonus, family tax benefits parts A and B, and income support payments under age-pension age.

In determining reportable fringe benefits, the employer is required to use the type 2 gross-up rate of 1.8692, regardless of whether the employer is entitled to claim GST input tax credits.

In addition to reporting the taxable value of fringe benefits, employers also need to include **reportable employer superannuation contributions (RESCs)** on the payment summaries provided to employees. Reportable employer super contributions include salary sacrificed superannuation contributions and contributions an employer makes on behalf of an employee, other than the mandatory SG contributions.

reportable employer superannuation contributions (RESCs) additional superannuation contributions salary sacrificed by an employee or made on behalf of an employee that are included in the definition of income for the purposes of determining entitlement to government benefits and obligations for government taxes and levies

LO 11 Goods and services tax

The goods and services tax (GST) was introduced in Australia in July 2000 as part of a major tax reform involving the abolition of wholesale sales tax and the reduction of income tax rates for individuals and companies. The government considered the existing tax system was inadequate to meet the needs of a community which, with its ageing profile, will place a larger and larger burden on the public purse. The GST is based on the value-added tax model adopted in several countries around the world. It is a 10% broad-based tax applied on the consumption of most goods, services and property, including those that are imported, but does not apply to goods or services which are exported or consumed outside Australia. The cost of some items has decreased, for example televisions and compact disc players on which there was a wholesale sales tax exceeding 20%, whereas other items, particularly services, which were not previously taxed, have increased in cost.

The investment which bears the greatest impact of GST is property and its impact is broken into four sections as follows.

Rents.

- Residential rents are not subject to GST.
- Commercial rents are subject to GST.

Expenses.

- GST is paid by both residential and commercial landlords on agents' commissions, insurance, investment advice, renovations and repairs. Investors in residential property cannot claim a credit for GST paid on the above expenses, but investors in commercial property can claim against the GST imposed on rent from commercial property.
- GST is not added to water and sewerage charges, council rates and interest costs.

Acquisition of investment.

- All new property, residential or commercial, attracts GST on the sale.
- The purchase of non-new property is not subject to GST if it is residential, but is subject to GST if it is commercial. Investors in commercial property can offset the GST paid on purchase against the GST charges on rental.

Realisation of investment.

- GST is not imposed on the sale of residential property by investors but it is imposed on the sale of commercial property. However, if the turnover, that is, annual rentals of commercial property, is less than $75 000, then investors do not have to register for GST. If they are not registered they do not have to charge GST on their rentals. However, if investors in commercial property are not registered, they cannot claim a credit for GST paid on inputs.

GST, therefore, must be taken into account in any decision on property investment. It is difficult to identify specifically the impact of GST, but investors considering investing in either residential or commercial property must now feel biased towards residential, which does not attract the GST. When considering investing in new or non-new property, residential investors must be biased towards non-new property, as there is no opportunity to offset the GST imposed on new property.

GST does not affect other forms of investment to the same extent, but it is payable on the brokerage charged on the purchase and sale of shares and on such inputs as computers and stationery.

Summary

Like most developed countries, Australia relies upon a range of taxes to raise government revenue. The Australian taxation system has four basic forms of taxation — income tax, capital gains tax, fringe benefits tax, and goods and services tax.

The taxable income of a taxpayer is determined by subtracting allowable deductions from assessable income. Assessable income is made up of both ordinary income and statutory income and includes income earned from all sources during the financial year, whether derived in Australia or from overseas. Expenditures incurred by the taxpayer will be an allowable deduction only to the extent to which they are incurred in earning assessable income during the financial year.

Individuals are assessed for tax purposes based on marginal rates of tax which means the greater the taxable income of a taxpayer, the greater the rate of tax that applies. Both companies and superannuation funds are assessed on a flat rate of tax regardless of the amount of taxable income earned.

The returns generated from all forms of investment are subject to tax. However, in attempting to maximise after-tax returns, it is important that an investor understands the different tax planning strategies associated with each form of investment. The gains and losses derived from the sale of all forms of investments are subject to the capital gains tax provisions. Due to the concessions attached to the calculation of CGT for individuals, it is important to distinguish between receipts of a revenue nature and those of a capital nature.

Taxation could be regarded as an investor's greatest threat as it has the potential to reduce substantially the actual return earned on an investment. Alternatively, it can be seen as an opportunity to increase the wealth of the investor through careful planning. With careful planning, taxpayers have some flexibility to structure their affairs so as to minimise the imposition of tax and maximise their after-tax returns.

One of the major decisions facing a taxpayer in establishing a business or acquiring investments is the form of entity that should be utilised. The major tax entities available include sole traders, partnerships, trusts, superannuation funds and companies, and each has its advantages and disadvantages.

Salary sacrificing involves substituting cash salary for non-cash benefits that are subject to a lower imposition of tax. While non-cash benefits are free from income tax, many are subject to the fringe benefits tax. Remuneration planning can be a very effective tool for creating long-term wealth and minimising the imposition of taxation.

The GST is a 10% broad-based tax applied on the consumption of most goods, services and property. The investment which bears the greatest impact of GST is property and it impacts rents, expenses, and the acquisition and realisation of investments. GST, therefore, must be taken into account in any decision on property investment. GST does not affect other forms of investment to the same extent, but it is payable on the brokerage charged on the purchase and sale of shares and on such inputs as computers and stationery.

Professional application questions

3.1 What are the general conditions that need to be satisfied for an expense to be considered an allowable deduction for tax purposes?

3.2 John and Eve are looking to make a gift of $15 000 to help pay for the future education of each of their three grandchildren. Should the payment be invested in the names of the grandchildren or their parents? Discuss.

3.3 Becky aged 17 receives income from a salary of $22 000 as a first year hairdressing apprentice as well as receiving dividends of $2000 from a share portfolio that was bought for her as a birthday present. How will Becky's total income be taxed?

3.4 Amanda and Chen have a joint account with the Westpac Bank and Chen owns a portfolio of Australian listed shares. Chen works full-time and pays tax at the highest marginal rate; Amanda is at home with twin boys. What is the best way of organising their affairs to minimise tax? Chen is considering transferring all their investments into Amanda's name. Identify the benefits of doing so and any possible costs.

3.5 What is the difference between the Medicare levy and Medicare levy surcharge? How are the charges determined and are the charges payable by all types of taxpayers?

3.6 Michael acquired a share portfolio last financial year consisting of 1000 shares in the CBA Bank worth $60 000. During the year he receives fully franked dividends of $3000 and, at the end of the year, the share portfolio has increased in value to $70 000. What amounts will be included in Michael's taxable income for the year?

3.7 Vivian is negotiating her salary package with her new employer, Spindex Ltd. She wants to salary package $10 000 to superannuation, $5000 for private expenses and $2000 for a laptop. Outline the FBT impact on each of the items including advantages and disadvantages.

3.8 Brigitte buys and sells shares on a regular basis. During the year, she makes a loss of $10 000. Can she claim the loss of $10 000 as a tax deduction?

3.9 Paul acquires a holiday home for an amount of $380 000 and borrows $200 000 at an interest rate of 7% p.a. His annual loan repayments to the bank amount to around $18 000 including interest of $14 000. Paul rents the holiday home out to friends during the year over the Christmas and Easter periods and earns rental income of $9000. Is the rental income from the holiday house assessable? Are the loan repayments of $18 000 to the bank tax deductible?

3.10 On 15 June 1992, Soo Chin bought $10 000 of Singmex Ltd's shares. On 20 February in the current year, they had tripled in value and Soo Chin realises that she could dispose of these shares to take advantage of this price movement. Given that her marginal tax rate is 32.5% and the CPI index number for June 1992 is 107.3, calculate CGT under both the CGT discount and indexation methods to advise her which method is most appropriate.

3.11 Patrick is considering purchasing an investment property for $350 000. The property was built in 2006. Patrick hopes to rent out the property for $350 per week. He expects that annual insurance, rates and costs to maintain the property will be approximately $4000 p.a. and interest costs on his loan will be $24 000 for the year. Patrick earns a salary of $40 000 p.a. while his wife earns $120 000 p.a. as an accountant. Outline the income and CGT implications of this investment, including in whose name the investment should be acquired.

3.12 Terry is a landscaper and operates as a sole trader in his business. He is aged 48 and married to Mary aged 46 who is a stay-at-home Mum. They have 3 children aged 22, 19 and 16. Terry's net income from the business is $140 000 and he also earns $12 000 a year teaching landscaping at the local TAFE College and $10 000 net income from an investment property. Terry is looking at ways of how he might be able to minimise his taxable income for the year. He wants to know the following:

- should his landscaping business be set up under a better tax structure?
- can he divert his salary income from the TAFE College to Mary?
- can he transfer the investment property to Mary so that she earns the income in her name?

Professional application exercises

Basic	*
Moderate	**
Challenging	***

3.13 Dividend imputation *

Monique has shares in an Australian mining company, JKL Ltd. She has received a final dividend statement for the year. Monique needs you to explain some things about the statement to her. The details are as follows:

Description	Dividend per share (A$)	Number of shares	Franked dividend	Unfranked dividend	Gross payment
Final	24 cents	750	$108.00	$72.00	$180.00

Franking credit = $46.29

(a) Explain the difference between 'franked dividends' and 'unfranked dividends'.
(b) What percentage of the shares is regarded as 'franked'?
(c) Explain how the 'franking credit' would be treated in the calculation of Monique's tax payable for the year.
(d) Suppose Monique earns a salary of $45 000, has no other income apart from the shares and does not have private health insurance. Calculate her tax payable in this situation.

3.14 Tax calculations ✷

George has just commenced employment as a teacher and his first year's income is $55 000. He also receives bank interest of $500. His expenses consist of $500 of subscriptions to the Teachers Association, $700 of car expenses in travelling to and from work, and donations of $100. Calculate his net tax payable.

3.15 Capital gains tax ✷

Gayle has just disposed of a property and received $550 000. Her costs of selling the property amounted to $5000. Explain the tax implications of the following scenarios.

- Gayle lived in the property as her principal residence for the total period of ownership.
- Gayle acquired the property for rental purposes in October 2000.
- Gayle is in the business of buying properties, renovating them and selling them off for a profit.

3.16 Tax calculations ✷✷

Toby and Emma are a young couple with no children. They are both employed — Toby as a computer programmer and Emma as an accountant. Toby earns a salary of $55 000 and incurs the following expenses:

- computer society subscription $500 p.a.
- technical journals $700 p.a.
- hobby magazines $500 p.a.
- donations $200 p.a.

In addition, Toby receives investment income of $4000 from investments in a managed fund. The fund distribution includes $1500 of fully franked dividends and assessable capital gains of $600.

Emma earns a salary of $63 000 and receives $2000 of fully franked dividends and $1000 from unfranked dividends. She also made a profit on the sale of her car recently of $1000. Emma's expenses comprise:

- technical journals $800 p.a.
- parking expenses (when visiting clients) $900 p.a.
- accountants' society subscriptions $800 p.a.
- local craft society subscription $200 p.a.

Calculate the tax payable for both Toby and Emma for the current financial year.

3.17 Tax structures ✷✷

Howard and Jeanette are planning to purchase an investment property in a bayside suburb of a capital city. The purchase price is $450 000. Jeanette was the beneficiary of the sale of her deceased mother's house and has the money available for investment. As Howard and Jeanette are in their mid fifties and expect to retire in the next 8 years or so, they are wondering how they should purchase the property. They could either buy it in Jeanette's name, in the name of a discretionary family trust or in the name of a family company. Jeanette is on a MTR of 37% whereas Howard is on a MTR of 32.5%. The couple has 2 children aged 13 and 15. During the period of ownership, the property is expected to earn a net return of 4% p.a.

(a) What are some of the issues you would consider in determining in which name or entity the property should be purchased in?

(b) Would there be any tax benefits to be gained in distributing income earned from the property to the couple's two children? Discuss.

(c) What difference would the tax structure have on the way that the capital gain on sale would be calculated and taxed?

3.18 Tax structures * *

Carol runs a successful restaurant as a sole trader and normally generates a net income of around $240 000 p.a. Her husband Keith is employed as an engineer and earns a taxable income of $85 000 p.a. The couple have two children, both aged under 16.

(a) Carol is looking to acquire a car and wants to know whether she is able to salary sacrifice into a car through her business.

(b) What are the benefits and drawbacks of running the restaurant through a family company?

(c) If the company structure was set up, Carol wants to know how profits are distributed and whether all the profits of the company need to be distributed each year.

(d) If the business was set up within a trust structure instead of as a company, would you recommend the establishment of a family unit trust or a discretionary trust? Explain.

(e) Would it make any difference which structure was set up in terms of the distribution of income to their children?

3.19 Tax strategies * *

Anthony and Kellie are aged in their late 40s and are seeking some advice on how they can improve their financial position. Kellie earns a salary of $140 000 p.a. while Anthony earns a taxable profit from his business as a self-employed land surveyor of $70 000 p.a. The couple's disposable income after tax is $22 000 p.a. The couple has 3 children — Jack, aged 14, Kim, aged 19, and Felicity, aged 22.

The couple's investments are shown as follows:

Item	Market value	Ownership
Bank account	$60 000	Kellie
Managed fund account (acquired in March 2000 for $70 000)	$100 000	Kellie
Shares		
▪ acquired 10 months ago for $50 000	$60 000	Kellie
▪ acquired in March 1998 for $50 000 (CPI factor at that time was 120.3)	$80 000	Kellie

The couple is looking to sell the entire share portfolio in a couple of months to pay off their home loan. Kellie has a carried-forward capital loss of $10 000 from

2 years ago when she sold an investment property. The couple is concerned by the large amount of tax they are currently paying and seek some advice on how they might be able to minimise tax and maximise wealth prior to retirement.

(a) Outline some of the tax-effective strategies that the couple might consider putting in place in order to minimise their overall tax liability each year.

(b) If the shares are sold, calculate the net assessable capital gain that would be included in Kellie's assessable income for the year.

(c) In order to minimise taxation, Kellie has been advised to sell the managed fund portfolio and transfer the proceeds into a family company structure. What would be the advantages and drawbacks of this strategy? Discuss.

3.20 Salary sacrifice and fringe benefits tax * * *

Wendy has decided to salary sacrifice into a car benefit through her employer. The cost of the car is $35 000 and Wendy expects to travel 30 000 kilometres each year, 30% of which are expected to be for business purposes. The costs incurred by the employer in providing the car are as follows:

Leasing costs	$11 000
Repairs	1 000
Petrol	3 500
Registration	600
Insurance	700
Total costs	16 800

All of the costs include GST except for registration. The employer is required to pay GST on the car costs but can claim GST input tax credits. The car is available for private use throughout the FBT year. Wendy contributes $1000 p.a. towards the cost of the benefits provided.

Wendy is also considering salary sacrificing $12 000 into her superannuation fund this year.

(a) Is salary sacrificing an effective strategy for all non-cash benefits and for all employees? Are there circumstances where you would not recommend a salary sacrifice arrangement for a particular employee?

(b) Calculate the FBT payable by Wendy's employer on the total non-cash benefits provided for the FBT year from 1 April 2014.

(c) What are the tax benefits of Wendy making a superannuation contribution as part of a salary sacrifice arrangement as compared to making a contribution from her after-tax income?

(d) Could Wendy's husband Dave also salary sacrifice into his superannuation account? Dave is a self-employed builder and is looking to build his superannuation balance in a tax-effective manner.

3.21 Negative gearing * * *

Carl and Karen are seeking some advice on accumulating wealth for their retirement. The couple has an aggressive risk profile and is prepared to take on further debt. Carl has a salary of $140 000 p.a. and Karen works part-time and earns a salary of $42 000 p.a. They have a home worth $520 000 and a home mortgage of $120 000 charging an interest rate of 7% p.a. They also have an outstanding credit card balance of $10 000 which has an interest rate of 17% p.a.

Carl earns $1500 from bank interest and has work-related expenses of $1200. Karen's work-related expenses total $400. The couple has private health insurance. The couple is looking to take out a bank loan for $100 000 to acquire a share portfolio. The bank loan would have an interest rate of 9.5% p.a. and it is expected that the shares will generate a 4% p.a. fully franked dividend and capital growth of around 5% p.a. The bank has advised that the annual loan repayments would be $15 900 p.a. with the first year's interest payment being $9500.

(a) In whose name would you recommend that the share portfolio be acquired in? Explain.

(b) Would the interest charged on the bank loan used to acquire the share portfolio be tax deductible? Explain. Would there be any circumstances in which interest charged on a loan used to acquire an investment would not be tax deductible to an individual?

Carl decides to take out the bank loan and acquire the share portfolio in his own name. In the following year, assume that the shares generate the expected returns and that there is no change in the salary, other income and work-related expenses of the couple.

(c) If the couple had surplus income after paying off all expenses and were looking to pay off their debt as quickly as possible, what would be the order that you would recommend for the repayment of the debt? Discuss.

(d) Based on the above information, calculate the tax payable for both Carl and Karen for the year using current tax rates.

CASE STUDY 1

Taxation planning

Nick and Selena are a married couple in their forties. They have three children — Tom aged 17, Kate aged 15 and Linda aged 14. Nick works as an office manager and earns $80 000. Selena is a partner in a law firm and earns a salary of $170 000 p.a.

Nick and Selena seek some advice from you in respect of reducing tax payable, especially by Selena, and also on generating wealth. They have not taken an interest in their financial planning to date but want to change this now. The couple provides the following details:

Balance sheet

Assets	
Home and contents	$800 000
Cars	$55 000
Holiday house (rental income of $4000)	$500 000
Bank account (interest rate of 3% p.a.)	$70 000
Share portfolio (fully franked dividends of 4% p.a.)	$120 000
Superannuation (after-tax return of 6%)	$400 000
Total assets	$1 945 000

Liabilities	
Mortgage on home (interest rate of 6% p.a.)	$350 000
Bank loan on share portfolio (interest rate of 8% p.a.)	$50 000
Credit card (interest rate of 17% p.a.)	$10 000
Total liabilities	$410 000

- All of the assets are owned in the name of Selena except for the bank account and holiday home which are jointly owned.
- The share portfolio was acquired for $100 000 in 2002. Selena took out an interest only loan (no payments are made against the principal owing). Selena has a carried forward capital loss of $7000 relating to some shares she sold 3 years ago.

Expenses

In addition to their interest and loan repayments, the couple incurred the following expenses during the year:

Expenditure	Nick	Selena
Work-related expenses	$1 000	$2 200
Travelling to and from home	$1 200	$1 500
Child care expenses	$0	$6 000
Donations	$500	$0
Living costs	$18 000	$18 000
Tax agents' fees	$700	$900

The couple does not have any private health insurance.

QUESTIONS

1 Determine the net tax payable for the current year for both Nick and Selena.

2 The couple is concerned with the amount of overall tax they are paying. Discuss some of the tax-effective strategies that the couple could use.

3 The couple has suggested salary sacrificing into their superannuation account. What is the benefit of salary sacrificing into superannuation and who would most likely receive the greatest tax benefit?

4 The couple is wondering whether they are able to claim any expenses incurred on the holiday house. Is this possible and how would any entitlement to a tax deduction be determined?

5 The couple has been disappointed with the growth in value of the share portfolio over the past few years and are now looking to sell the entire portfolio and invest the proceeds into an Australian bond fund. Based on the current market price and after taking account of estimated selling expenses of $2000, calculate the likely assessable capital gain.

CASE STUDY 2

Salary packaging

James Zocchi is 28 years old and single. After completing his degree in marketing, like many young Australians, he travelled overseas on a working holiday. After 18 months travelling through Europe and working for some of the time in London, he arrived back in Australia and was offered employment with a large food products distribution company for whom he had worked while overseas. To his surprise, and based on the references he obtained while working for the head office in London, he was offered a gross salary of $100 000 plus superannuation. The personnel manager met with him to work out details of how he would like to be paid as he was given the opportunity to request his employer to package his salary in ways that would benefit him.

James was told that his employer would contribute $10 000 of SG contributions to his superannuation fund regardless of whether James wanted to package any himself. Even though James is fairly young and knows that he is not able to access his superannuation until he is at least 60 years of age — some 32 years away — he knows that he needs to put money aside for his retirement and that by putting a bit more away at an earlier age the benefits of compound interest will work in his favour in the long run. So James decided that he would like to package $5000 to his superannuation fund in addition to the employer's contribution. When James left to go overseas he gave his laptop computer to a young nephew as it was about 5 years old. After speaking with the personnel manager he decided to take up the offer of salary packaging a new personal laptop computer costing $2000. He could have paid for it himself over a few months but decided to take advantage of the opportunity to acquire it without paying income tax on the amount needed to buy it and without any fringe benefits tax.

As a young marketing professional and with career advancement in sight he decided that there would be benefits for him if he became a member of the Young Marketers Association, which required a membership fee of $850 p.a. He decided that it would be very convenient to have his employer pay the fee on his behalf as a salary package item as he might forget to pay the membership fees when they fell due. So, even though he could get a full personal tax deduction for the membership fee, he decided that for convenience reasons he would package the amount from his salary.

When James arrived home from his overseas travels he found his old car waiting for him in the garage at his parents' house. His car was 15 years old, dripped oil, did not run smoothly and needed about $3000 spent on it to maintain its roadworthiness. He decided that with his newly acquired employment and with such a generous starting salary he should drive a more modern car. As he had just arrived back in Australia after spending the savings that he had accumulated, he wondered how he might acquire such a car. He did not have sufficient funds to buy a car immediately and did not want to borrow his mother's new car as she needed it almost every day. However, the personnel manager advised him that he could take up the option of salary packaging a car through his employment. The personnel manager gave him a list of vehicles from a car dealer and a list of various costs so that James could consider the type of car and range of costs that would suit him and his salary package. James considered the list and costs and concluded that the vehicle he would like to package required the following payments: cost of car $30 000; lease costs $12 000 p.a.; and petrol and service costs estimated to be $4000 p.a. He estimated that he will travel about 24 000 kilometres in the 12-month period and he will have the car for private use for the whole year. He selected a particular type and model of vehicle and gave the information to the personnel manager, along with his preferred colours for the car and interior. Within a few weeks, James was contacted to collect the vehicle and to complete all the required paperwork.

QUESTIONS

1 Why would the employer want to offer James the opportunity to enter into a salary packaging arrangement?

2 Under what circumstances would you recommend that salary sacrificing is not an appropriate strategy for a client?

3 Rather than salary sacrificing, what other options could James consider in order to obtain a new car?

4 Calculate the FBT liability for the FBT year from 1 April 2014 and the total cost charged by the employer against the salary of James if all of the above non-cash benefits are salary sacrificed.

5 What is the effect on the FBT if James decides to contribute $2200 of his after-tax income towards the cost of the vehicle package? Is it worth doing?

CASE STUDY 3

Negative gearing

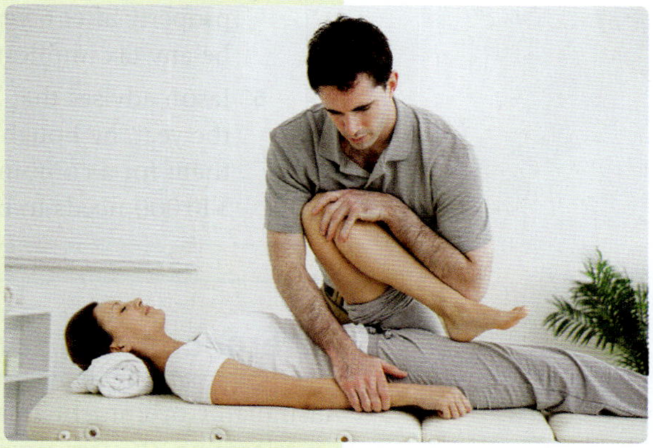

Jason, aged 32 and single, is employed as a physiotherapist earning $65 000 p.a. Jason has quite an aggressive risk profile and is looking to buy into an investment property. The plan is that after 6 years, Jason would move into the property himself and make it his home. Jason approaches you for some advice on how best to structure the purchase.

Jason is looking to purchase a property for around $400 000 and take out a bank loan for $280 000. Jason is able to get the loan for a period of 20 years at an

»

»

interest rate of 6.8% p.a. Jason has saved $120 000 which is currently sitting in a share portfolio. He inherited the majority of the shares 5 years ago from his grandfather who purchased them in 2001. The shares are currently worth $130 000 and have a cost base of $80 000. Jason provides the following information relating to the estimated income and expenses of the property in the first year:

Estimated rental income	$20 000
Estimated expenses:	
Rates	$2 000
Insurance	$600
Interest and loan repayments	$25 400
Depreciation on fixtures and fittings	$3 000
Painting of two of the rooms	$1 000
Installation of carport	$8 000

Jason also incurs the following:

- work-related expenses of $1500 and tax agents' fees of $600.
- Jason salary sacrifices a car through his work. The costs of the car benefit amount to $14 000 and the FBT payable is $5000.

QUESTIONS

1. Should the property be purchased in the name of a family company or trust or be acquired in the personal name of Jason? Discuss.
2. Discuss the likely tax treatment of the painting expenditure and the installation of the carport in respect of the property purchase.
3. Based on the above information, calculate the net tax payable by Jason for the year.
4. What would be the tax implications if Jason was to move into the property after 6 years and use it as his principal residence? Would there be any tax implications upon a future sale?
5. Jason advises that he loves sailing and he owns a small yacht. During the year, he bought 2 run-down yachts, fully renovated them and sold them for a combined profit of $10 000. Jason wants to know whether the $10 000 needs to be included in his assessable income for the year.

References and further reading

Australian Government Treasury 2011, *Reforms to car fringe benefits tax rules*, Joint media release no. 76, treasury.gov.au.

ATO 2013a, *Legal database*, law.ato.gov.au.

ATO 2013b, *Individual income tax rates*, ato.gov.au.
ATO 2013c, *Medicare levy surcharge income thresholds*, ato.gov.au.
ATO 2013d, *Introduction to capital gains tax*, ato.gov.au.
ATO 2013e, *The indexation method of calculating your capital gain*, ato.gov.au.
ATO 2013f, *Fringe benefits tax for small business*, ato.gov.au.
CCH 2013a, *Australian master financial planning guide 2013/14*, CCH Australia Limited, Sydney.
CCH 2013b, *Australian master tax guide 2013*, CCH Australia Limited, Sydney.
Mills, S 2007, 'Rent out your house and avoid capital gains tax', *Money*, March, money.ninemsn.com.au.

4 Investment choices

LEARNING OBJECTIVES

After studying this chapter, you should be able to:

1. consider the general attributes of investors
2. explain the broad investment classes
3. understand the risk and return relationship
4. understand the benefits of diversification
5. appreciate the performance history of the various asset classes
6. understand general investment strategies
7. be aware of investor behaviour
8. develop an awareness of investment scams
9. identify information sources for investment choices.

CASE STUDY

Alexander is 19 and a retail shop assistant in a large city department store. He is quite pleased as his manager has recommended him to become a trainee manager specialising in men's clothing. After going to the football one weekend with some friends they go to a bar to have a few drinks before heading to a night club after dinner. Tran, who works in real estate, started to talk about the capital gains that could be made by buying a property in the right location and 'doing it up'. He indicated that he was considering borrowing a large sum of money to do just that. Nick, who works in a bank, agreed it could be a good investment, but was cautious about the changes in the rate of interest that Tran would have to pay while he was doing up the house with no income coming in. Nick said a safer approach to investing would be building up a bank account first so Tran had a bigger deposit and would have to borrow less. Stravos, who is studying to be an accountant, thought that the property investment idea was good but it didn't allow for any flexibility if Tran needed to get some cash quickly out of his investment. Stravos said he preferred to be a bit more flexible and, if he was to borrow money for an investment, he would borrow and buy a parcel of shares so he could buy and sell shares depending on the need for cash or the ups and downs of the share market.

Alexander thought about what he had heard from his friends over the next few days and felt that he was fairly ignorant about investing. He asked his uncle, Pete, who worked in superannuation about investing. His uncle advised him to start learning about the different forms of investing himself so he would have some knowledge about what people were talking about when investment choices came up in conversation. So Alexander decided to buy some books and search on the internet to give himself some background knowledge for future discussions with his friends.

Issues to be considered from this case concerning investment choices include:

- the features of some of the major investment choices
- the return and risks to be expected from such investments.

These and other issues will be considered in this chapter.

Introduction

This chapter deals with investment choices. Just as there are different types of investors there is also a broad range of investments that consumers can choose. Broadly, investors may choose from two forms of investment: direct and indirect. Direct investment occurs when investors make their own decisions about where their funds are ultimately placed, be it in fixed-interest deposit accounts, shares, property or some other form of asset. Indirect investment is when investors place their funds with funds managers who use vehicles such as unit trusts and master funds to consolidate the funds of many investors and then invest the pooled funds according to their own stated investment strategies. Direct and indirect investments are discussed in chapters 5, 6 and 7.

To consider any investment choice, an investor should have an appreciation of the risk and return relationship to understand that the higher the return the higher the level of risk. This chapter also considers the means by which risk may be reduced. Such risks and returns for each investment category also need to be understood in terms of recent performance history and time frames. Such an understanding is fundamental to adopting an investment strategy, as is having an awareness of how investors behave and the danger of investment scams. The chapter concludes with an outline of the sources of information for investment choices.

LO 1 General attributes of investors

In 1949, Benjamin Graham, writing in the classic text on value investing *The intelligent investor*, distinguished between two main types of investor: the defensive investor and the enterprising investor. The defensive investor is focused on conserving capital — their main emphasis is on avoiding any serious mistakes or losses, and also on freedom from effort, annoyance and the need for making frequent decisions. The second type, the enterprising or aggressive investor, is characterised not by speculation, but by their willingness to devote time and care to the selection of sound and attractive investments even though they may not be fully trained experts in the field. In summing up his 'intelligent investor', Graham remarks that the enterprising investor will never embark on an investment choice which he does not fully comprehend and which he cannot justify by reference to the results of his personal study or experience.

In many respects, the classification that Graham observed is not dissimilar to the general range of classifications of investors used by financial planners today. Table 4.1 provides an insight into the general classification of investors that may be applied by financial planners. The table indicates some features that may be ascribed to different investment types such as stability of income, tolerance to risk and an approximate investment time frame. Investment classification is also usually matched to a typical asset allocation held by various investors. In the table, the 'growth' investments represent a combination of property investments and share investments which may be invested in domestic or international markets.

TABLE 4.1 A general investor classification

Investor classification	Features	Approximate asset mix
Very conservative	▪ Household income is unstable and insecure. ▪ No tolerance for loss of capital. ▪ Investing time frame is 2 years or less.	▪ Cash 60% ▪ Fixed interest 30% ▪ Growth investments 10%
Conservative	▪ Household income is somewhat unstable and insecure. ▪ Able to tolerate no more than 5% decline in capital value. ▪ Investing time frame is between 2 and 4 years.	▪ Cash 20% ▪ Fixed interest 40% ▪ Growth investments 40%
Balanced	▪ Household income is fairly stable and secure. ▪ Able to tolerate a 10% decline in capital value. ▪ Investing time frame is between 4 and 6 years.	▪ Cash 10% ▪ Fixed interest 30% ▪ Growth investments 60%
Aggressive	▪ Household income is substantially stable and secure. ▪ Able to tolerate a 15% decline in capital value. ▪ Investing time frame is between 6 and 8 years.	▪ Cash 5% ▪ Fixed interest 15% ▪ Growth investments 80%
Very aggressive	▪ Household income is very stable and secure. ▪ Able to tolerate regular fluctuations of 20% or more in capital value. ▪ Investing time frame is between 8 and 10 years.	▪ Cash 5% ▪ Fixed interest 10% ▪ Growth investments 85%

LO 2 Broad investment classes

When faced with deciding what to invest in an investor needs to have a sound understanding of the range of investment choices. This section provides an outline of the main investment choices:

- cash
- fixed interest
- property
- shares/equities.

Cash

A person uses cash to access funds for day-to-day living expenses and emergency situations. However, cash also plays an important role in an investment portfolio as it can be used to manage cash flows into other asset classes and as a safe haven if an investor feels that it is wise to withdraw from one asset class and hold it in cash to avoid a decline in value of that portion of a portfolio.

Cash investments aim to provide income, liquidity and stable returns. Cash investments can include savings accounts, money-market securities and cash-management trusts. Cash has the lowest risk of all asset classes and generally offers a relatively low rate of return. Cash investments are usually referred to as a 'risk-free' investment as there is a very low chance of default by the banking sector. For analysis of investments purposes the interest rate of the federal government's 90-day Treasury notes is generally regarded as the risk-free rate of return in Australia. Cash investments are less volatile than other types of asset classes because of their short-term nature. Most cash investments do not provide a capital guarantee although there was a short period of time during which the federal government guaranteed bank deposits as part of their response to the global financial crisis. Despite its relative safety, one aspect of cash investments is that there is the risk that capital will not keep pace with inflation and lose value in real terms. Income from cash investments is paid as interest and the amount paid varies as interest rates move up and down with expectations of inflationary trends.

Fixed interest

Fixed-interest investments are investments that are agreed for a certain period of time at a known interest rate. Interest is usually paid on a regular basis, but with some fixed-interest investments the interest payment is factored into the final payment and offered as a discount security or with accumulated interest paid on maturity. Some fixed-interest securities offer a reinvestment of interest to gain the benefit of compounding. Fixed-interest investments can be issued by banks, the Commonwealth Government, state governments, semi-government authorities, overseas banks and authorities, and other corporations. (*Note:* From 21 May 2013, Commonwealth government bonds commenced trading on the ASX and are now called exchange-traded Treasury bonds. This offers a way for investors to buy and sell these securities in the form of CHESS depository interests (CDIs).)

Fixed-interest investments usually have longer investment terms than cash investments. For example, Australian bond maturities range from one to 15 years while US bonds can extend up to 30 years. Investment in both international and Australian fixed-interest securities increases diversification and lowers overall investment risk. The main types of fixed-interest securities are:

- term deposits — issued by banks
- debentures — issued by corporations
- government and semi-government bonds — issued by governments to fund or help pay for major public projects
- corporate bonds or notes — issued by large public companies to fund business expansion. Corporate bonds usually offer a higher interest but have less security behind them. Sometimes corporations issue hybrid securities which have characteristics of both equity and fixed-interest securities. Convertible bonds/notes, for example, commence as bonds but can be converted into equity at a future date. These types of securities have higher risk than government or corporate bonds as they are less secured.

Fixed-interest securities can be traded on the secondary market before their maturity if an investor needs to convert their investment to cash. Fixed interest is a low- to medium-risk investment suitable for investors with a time frame of 3 years or more. As well as providing a regular stream of income, fixed interest can provide a stabilising effect on a portfolio during periods of share market volatility. In the next chapter, you will learn about the potential capital growth or loss that can occur if a bond needs to be sold prior to maturity.

A big issue for fixed-interest investors is credit risk, which is the risk of an issuer defaulting on repayment of capital. Fixed-interest investments offered by banks have a low level of risk, as such investments are backed by the strength of the banking sector. Some fixed-interest investments may be backed by a guarantee which is supported by the institution. However, the guarantee is only as strong as the institution itself and history has shown that some institutions have not been able to pay the interest and even have lost capital because the institution itself has become bankrupt. Investors should refer to credit ratings which provide a good indication of the risk level associated with the issuer. However, credit ratings are not a guarantee even though a high rating indicates a lower likelihood of the issuer defaulting on repaying capital. See the ASIC website moneysmart.gov.au and search for 'warning on fixed interest investments'.

Property

Direct residential property has been the traditional form of investment for many Australians and may be considered separate from an investment portfolio, as many people consider their home to provide shelter and lifestyle benefits rather than viewing it strictly in terms of an investment choice.

Leaving aside the family home, **property** investments can consist of rental properties (residential, commercial, industrial or rural); listed property trusts known as real estate investment trusts (REITs); and unlisted property trusts. Property trusts are pooled investments which hold a basket of properties in one or more of the property sectors and offer units to be purchased by investors.

property
an investment into the asset class that covers real estate in its many forms

Property is a long-term investment with higher risk than fixed-interest investments but slightly lower risk, historically, than shares. Direct property offers steady rental income, tax breaks via negative gearing and capital appreciation. At the same time, direct property has a number of drawbacks: it takes time to buy and sell; building a diversified property portfolio is an expensive exercise; property exposure is usually limited to one sector; locating and keeping good tenants can be difficult; and there is always ongoing care and maintenance. There is also the risk of capital loss and lower rentals during times of oversupply.

REITs and unlisted property trusts (both forms of managed investment) provide many of the benefits of direct property investment without some of the constraints. Returns from property trusts can include income in the form of rent received from the underlying properties and capital growth (or loss) from changes in the value of the unit price. Property trusts also offer tax advantages to investors in the form of tax deferred income distributions.

Some property trusts hold properties overseas which can provide a further level of diversification to an investment portfolio. Income is derived from rental payments and then distributed as income to unit holders. The income return can be compared to fixed-interest returns but may also vary from time to time depending on the quality of the tenants and the terms of the leases which are managed by the property trust.

Property trusts have similar risks to shares. The value of their units can rise and fall and is subject to changes in investor confidence and other factors affecting the property market. Property investments are usually funded by borrowings and interest is thus paid by the trust to the lender. If the level of borrowing is substantial and the demand for the property falls, the value of the units in the property trust can fall. During the global financial crisis, many property trusts suffered severe falls in value when they could not refinance debt and had to sell off development and other properties at low prices and even at prices lower than the purchase price.

Shares/equities

shares
an investment holding in a company

Shares are a unit holding (i.e. a share of the ownership of a company). Companies may be public or private, but generally when we consider investment portfolios we think of shares in public companies which are listed on the Australian Securities Exchange (ASX) or overseas stock exchanges.

Shares listed on the ASX are classified into industry sectors based on the Global Industry Classification Standard (GICS). The Australian share market sectors are energy, materials, industrials, consumer discretionary, consumer staples, healthcare, information technology, telecommunication services, utilities, property trusts and financials. Common measures used in evaluation of the performance of a share portfolio are the various indices created by the ASX, such as the S&P/ASX 200 Energy Index which comprises companies whose businesses are dominated by either of the following activities: the construction or provision of oil rigs, drilling equipment and other energy-related service and equipment, including seismic data collection; or companies engaged in the exploration, production, marketing, refining and/or transportation of oil and gas products, coal and other consumable fuels.

Shares are generally considered a high-risk and high-return investment and are suitable for longer-term investors. Historically, Australian shares have provided long-term growth well above inflation. But in the short term, share market returns have been quite volatile at times. Thus, share market investors can expect a negative return once in every 5 years, which is why shares are suited to longer-term investors (7 years plus). The length of time of the investment greatly reduces, but does not eliminate, the volatility in returns from shares. Share markets move in cycles, reflecting the underlying strength of the economy, political factors, industry trends and market sentiment. On any given day, interest rate and inflation expectations, company profits, dividends, economic growth figures and the rise or fall of the Australian dollar can impact share prices.

Shares provide a good source of income but are mainly the focus for capital growth. Most companies distribute a proportion of their profits in the form of dividends. Companies that pay high dividends tend to be blue-chip companies such as those in the banking, insurance and retail sectors. Some companies, such as those in the mining sector or newer industries such as biotechnology, may retain dividends to fund future research, expansion or exploration. Dividends can change from year to year depending on the company's profitability. Australian shares can provide tax-effective returns by means of the dividend imputation system under which, given companies have already paid tax at the company tax rate, investors can use franking credits to offset the amount of tax they pay on dividends. The higher the franking level the greater the benefit. Thus, the dividends are imputed to carry the tax credit to the shareholder.

Australian investors can also access international share markets. Investing internationally can increase diversification and provide access to industries and companies not available in Australia. Australia represents less than 3% of the total world share market. By diversifying some portion of an investment portfolio in overseas markets, an investor may benefit from returns generated in countries experiencing different phases of the business cycle than Australia at a particular point in time.

All of the different investment classes can be accessed by investors either directly or indirectly via managed funds.

LO 3 The risk and return relationship

We have all heard the expression 'the higher the return the greater the risk'. This section provides an overview of the relationship between risk and return. John Bogle (founder of the Vanguard Group of Investment Companies), wrote in 1994 that 'the message is to maximize your capital by earning the highest returns you can over the longest period possible ... However, risk is every bit as central as reward in the establishment of your investment portfolio, so you must carefully consider what risks you are prepared to assume.' The key determinants of the price of an asset are the risk associated with the asset and the returns that the asset is expected to generate. Consequently, all financial decisions must be evaluated in terms of expected risk and expected return. In order to adequately present investment options to clients, financial planners must be very clear about what is meant by investment risk and investment return, and how measures of both risk and return are determined.

Inflation-adjusted rates of return

When we consider the rate of return on an investment we need to consider the real rate of return not just the nominal rate. The real rate of return allows for the effects of inflation. Inflation causes investors to lose purchasing power when they sell their assets in the future and wish to buy goods and services with the proceeds. Inflation also causes the rate of return on an investment to fall in value. The real rate of return (R real) is calculated as:

$$R\text{ real} = \frac{1 + R\text{ nom}}{1 + h} - 1$$

Where: R nom is the nominal rate of return and h is the inflation rate.

So, if the nominal rate of return is 6.27% after tax and inflation is 5% the real rate of return is:

$$R \text{ real} = \frac{1.0627}{1.05} - 1 = 0.0121 \text{ or } 1.21\%$$

Definitions of risk

Some of the more common definitions of risk are the chance of loss of capital, the chance of loss of purchasing power or the variability of the returns associated with the given asset. Return is the total gain or loss experienced by the owner of a financial asset or investment over a given period of time.

The chance of loss of capital

The chance of loss of capital varies for different asset classes. In the past 60 years, a cash investment has always resulted in a positive return to investors, albeit small in some years. Some 20 years ago cash investments earned over 8% p.a. whereas at the time of writing interest on cash was under 3% p.a. There has been no chance of loss of value. Recall from the previous sections that investments in cash do not always generate a return which maintains its purchasing power. This occurs when the returns are not greater than inflation — the second definition of risk. Consequently, an investment in cash may result in a negative real return.

Investments in shares and some fixed-interest investments such as debentures can and have resulted in a loss of capital value over some time periods. Shares are therefore considered to be more risky than investments in cash. Share investments, although generating negative returns over some time periods, have a decreasing likelihood of negative returns as the time period increases. During the past 60 years, any period of 10 years generated positive returns. That is, as the length of time for the investment increased, the chance of loss for share investments decreased. However, the risk of some shares and debentures losing capital altogether remains as a risk of investing.

The chance of loss of purchasing power

Russell Investment Management Ltd (2004) provides an interesting comparison of the nominal and real returns of three asset classes commonly found in investor portfolios:

> A dollar invested in cash between 1937 and 2002 earned a 6.0% average annual return. Yet, according to the Australian Consumer Price Index, inflation during that same period averaged 5.5%. Cash's real return? Only 0.5%. A dollar invested in Australian bonds over the same period earned a 6.3% average annual return. Less inflation, the real return is 0.8%. Better than cash, but not by much. A dollar invested in Australian shares over this period generated an 11.2% average annual return. The real return: 5.7%. That's 7 times better than bonds and almost 12 times better than cash.

Most discussions on investment performance focus on nominal returns. Yet, an investor's personal 'bottom line' is how their investments perform after inflation has been allowed for and also after allowing for taxation.

The variability of returns

In order to understand what we mean by variability of returns consider the position of Gold Ltd and Silver Ltd shown below.

Gold Ltd and its competitor Silver Ltd generated the following returns over the past 5 years:

	Year 1	Year 2	Year 3	Year 4	Year 5
Gold Ltd	12%	17%	8%	11%	22%
Silver Ltd	12%	15%	13%	14%	16%

To determine the expected return for both these companies, we calculate the mean return as follows:

$$\text{Gold Ltd} \quad \frac{(12\% + 17\% + 8\% + 11\% + 22\%)}{5} = 14\%$$

$$\text{Silver Ltd} \quad \frac{(12\% + 15\% + 13\% + 14\% + 16\%)}{5} = 14\%$$

Both Gold Ltd and Silver Ltd have the same mean return or expected return $E(R)$.

In order to choose between the two companies, an investor must evaluate the returns in light of the associated risk. One measure of risk is the variability of returns. Clearly, Gold Ltd has returns which vary to a greater extent around the mean return or expected return than do the returns of Silver Ltd. In financial planning, we can measure this risk by calculating the **standard deviation** of the returns, which measures the variability of returns around the expected return. For Gold Ltd, we can calculate the standard deviation (s) in two stages: (1) calculate the variance, and (2) take the square root of the variance.

standard deviation a measure of the riskiness of an investment

$$\begin{aligned} s^2 &= \sum_{i=1}^{n} \frac{[X_i - E(R)]^2}{(n-1)} \\ &= \frac{(12-14)^2 + (17-14)^2 + (8-14)^2 + (11-14)^2 + (22-14)^2}{(5-1)} \\ &= \frac{122}{4} \\ &= 30.5 \end{aligned}$$

where s^2 = variance
X = value of each return
n = sample size
i = position of each return in the sample

The standard deviation is equal to the square root of the variance so for Gold Ltd the standard deviation is 5.52%, and by following the same process for Silver Ltd the standard deviation is 1.58%.

What does the standard deviation tell us? No analyst, sharebroker, mathematician or financial planner can tell with any certainty what the returns for a company will be in some future period. At best they can use their knowledge of past returns to estimate the probability of future returns. The standard deviation is based on probabilities. It is a statistical fact for normal distributions that if we know the standard deviation, we know that roughly two-thirds (66.7%) of the actual returns will lie in the range of expected return plus one standard deviation and expected return minus one standard deviation.

For Gold Ltd and Silver Ltd, this would tell us that two-thirds of the actual returns lie in the following range:

Gold Ltd	8.48% – 19.52%
Silver Ltd	12.42% – 15.58%

i.e. in Gold's case: 14% − 5.52 = 8.48% at the low end and 14% + 5.52 = 19.52% at the high end.

If we want more certainty about the likely range of returns that could eventuate, we can again use the standard deviation. To be 95% confident that the actual returns will lie in a given range, we simply determine the values of the expected return plus two standard deviations and the expected return minus two standard deviations, assuming the returns are normally distributed.

For Gold Ltd and Silver Ltd, this would tell us that 95% of the time we can expect the actual returns to lie in the following range:

Gold Ltd	2.96% – 25.04%
Silver Ltd	10.84% – 17.16%

Using the standard deviation as a measure of risk, we can see that although Gold Ltd and Silver Ltd have identical expected returns, Gold Ltd is far more risky as there is greater variability of the returns. The standard deviation shows the possible range of returns that may be expected given the history of returns of that asset. Investors in Gold Ltd are likely to receive higher returns in some periods than investors in Silver Ltd, but they are also likely to receive lower returns in some periods than investors in Silver Ltd.

This example highlights only the risk of individual shares. We can also see that the returns we can expect for different asset classes have different degrees of variability or volatility.

Figures 4.1 and 4.2 suggest that equity market volatility is a short-term phenomenon and that equity markets consistently rise over the long term. Figure 4.2 shows no negative result in any 10-year period over the 109-year period to the end of December 2008. (Note that 100% reinvestment of distributions is assumed.)

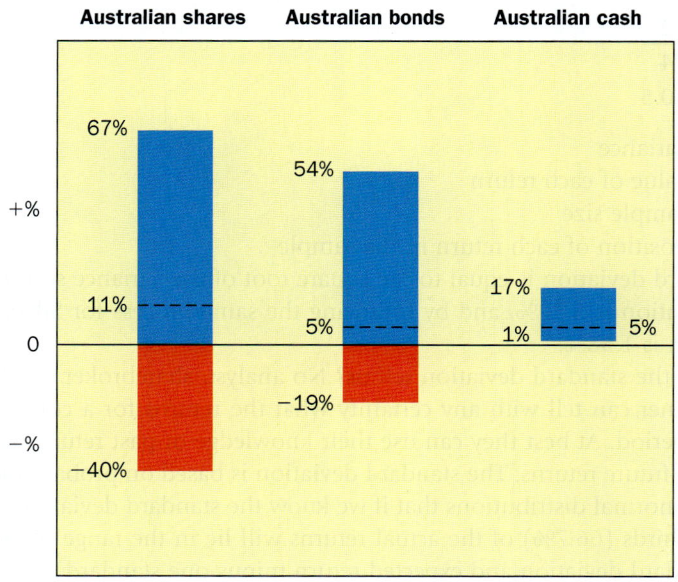

FIGURE 4.1
Range of 1-year returns over the previous 109 years, ending 31 December 2008. The median return is shown by the dotted line.
Source: MLC.

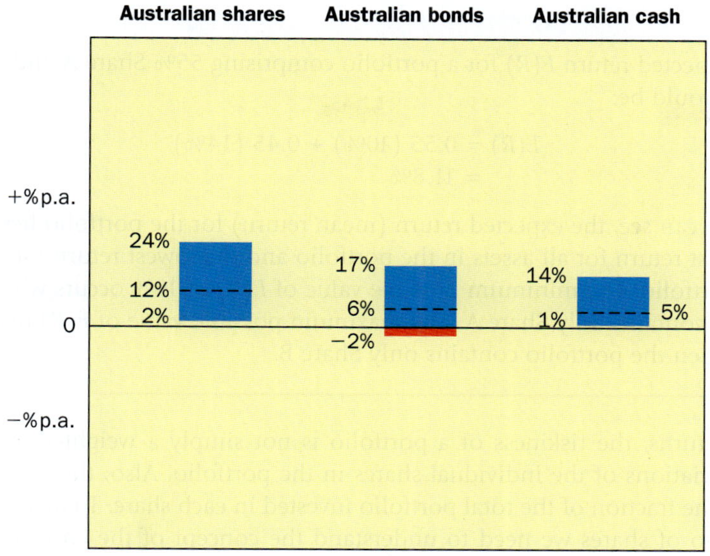

FIGURE 4.2
Range of 10-year average annual returns over the previous 109 years, ending 31 December 2008. The median return is shown by the dotted line.
Source: MLC.

As indicated in figures 4.1 and 4.2, the returns in the share market are more volatile over 1-year periods (a range of +67% to –40%) than 10-year periods (a range of +24% to +2%). Over longer periods of time, the different returns offset one another and the 10-year returns show much less volatility.

With an understanding of the variability of returns (volatility), most investors recognise the importance of diversifying their investments to minimise investment risk. In the next section, we examine how diversification actually results in a reduction in risk.

LO 4

The benefits of diversification

How can diversification reduce risk?

As outlined earlier, the risk of a share (the variability of the returns) can be measured by the standard deviation. When a portfolio of shares is held rather than shares in one company only, we have to consider the risk and returns of the portfolio as a whole.

The expected return on a portfolio is simply the weighted average return of the individual shares in the portfolio, where the weights are the fraction of the total portfolio invested in each share.

ILLUSTRATIVE EXAMPLE 4.1

Consider a portfolio that comprises two shares: Share A and Share B.

	Share A	Share B
Expected return	10%	14%
Standard deviation	3%	5%
% of total portfolio	55%	45%

»

»

The expected return $E(R)$ for a portfolio comprising 55% Share A and 45% Share B would be:

$$E(R) = 0.55\ (10\%) + 0.45\ (14\%)$$
$$= 11.8\%$$

As you can see, the expected return (mean return) for the portfolio lies between the highest return for all assets in the portfolio and the lowest return for all assets in the portfolio. The minimum possible value of $E(R)$ of 10% occurs when the portfolio contains only Share A. The maximum possible value of $E(R)$ of 14% occurs when the portfolio contains only Share B.

Unlike returns, the riskiness of a portfolio is not simply a weighted average of the standard deviations of the individual shares in the portfolio. Also, the weights used are not simply the fraction of the total portfolio invested in each share. To determine the risk of a portfolio of shares we need to understand the concept of the correlation between shares. To explain the concept of correlation, consider the following.

When the economy is growing, firms in the building and construction industry tend to do well. Firms which manufacture whitegoods also tend to do well. When the economy is declining, firms in both these industries tend to perform badly. We can say that the returns of these companies tend to move together in the same general direction. When one performs well, the other performs well. When one performs badly, the other performs badly. We can say that the returns from such companies are *positively correlated*.

In a strong economy, the Australian dollar may increase in value. This will have the effect of making our exports more expensive. Firms which rely on exports may not perform as well as they might do in a declining economy. Comparing the performance of companies in the building and construction industry with companies reliant on exports, we may find that when one company performs well, the other performs badly. We could say that the returns of these companies tend to move in the opposite direction. That is, the returns from these companies are *negatively correlated*.

The statistical measure which determines the extent to which two companies are positively or negatively correlated is called the *correlation coefficient*. This measure can take any value between +1 and –1, where +1 indicates that the companies move in exactly the same direction together. A portfolio consisting of two such shares would be just as risky as the individual shares.

A correlation coefficient of –1 would indicate that the two companies move counter-cyclically to each other. When the returns on one share rise, the returns on the other share fall, and vice versa.

With an understanding of the correlation between shares, we can return to the problem of determining the risk of a portfolio of shares. In combining two shares into a portfolio, where the individual shares are quite risky as measured by their standard deviations, it is possible that the risk of the portfolio as a whole will actually be less than the risk of the least risky share in the portfolio. In some situations, it is possible that the portfolio risk can be reduced to close to zero. This will occur when the returns of the shares are perfectly negatively correlated; that is, they have a correlation coefficient of –1.0.

In reality, most shares are positively correlated, but not perfectly so. On average, the correlation coefficient for the returns on two randomly selected shares would lie in the range +0.5 to +0.7. Under such conditions, combining shares into portfolios reduces risk but does not eliminate it completely.

If we return to our previous example, we can see the impact on the portfolio risk (standard deviation of the portfolio) for *different correlation coefficients* between Share A and Share B. (*Note:* The calculations to determine standard deviations of the portfolio are not provided as they are complex and lengthy. Students interested in calculating the standard deviation of a portfolio can find the workings for calculating covariance, correlations and standard deviations in any business finance text.)

	Share A	Share B	Correlation coefficient			
Standard deviation	3%	5%	−1.0%	0.2%	0.6%	1.0%
Portfolio risk (standard deviation of the portfolio)			0.6%	3.0%	3.5%	3.9%

An investor who wants to achieve the mean return of 11.8% by holding a mix of both Share A and Share B will be able to do so, and provided the correlation coefficient between the assets is less than +1.0, the risk of the portfolio will be reduced.

This discussion and Illustrative Example 4.2 highlight why the concept of diversification for investments is so important. An investment which has a portfolio comprising assets with less than perfectly positive correlation coefficients between the assets will generate weighted average returns but with reduced risk. So, if the correlation coefficient between Shares A and B is 0.2 it means that the standard deviation of the portfolio of the two shares is 3.0%. This is the same risk as having all shares in A, but much less risky than having all shares in B.

ILLUSTRATIVE EXAMPLE 4.2

Consider a different portfolio that comprises two shares: Share C and Share D.

	Share C	Share D
Expected return	10.5%	9.5%
Standard deviation	4.0%	4.0%
% of total portfolio	50.0%	50.0%

In this second example, the expected return for the portfolio comprising both shares is again the weighted average of the returns for each share.

$$E(R) = 0.50\ (10.5\%) + 0.50\ (9.5\%) = 10\%$$

The risk of the portfolio will not usually be the weighted average of the risk of each share (4%) but rather it will be less than 4%. Considering several correlation coefficients, notice that except when there is a perfect positive correlation between these two shares, the risk of the portfolio is less than the risk of either individual share.

	Share C	Share D	Correlation coefficient			
Standard deviation	4%	4%	−0.1%	0.2%	0.6%	1.0%
Portfolio risk (standard deviation of the portfolio)			0%	3.1%	3.6%	4%

Again, note that for a correlation coefficient of 0.2 the risk of the portfolio of Shares C and D is 3.1%, which is much below the 4% standard deviation for both Shares C and D; that is, the combination of two riskier shares results in a lower level of risk.

Diversification across asset classes

It is also important to diversify across asset classes — that is, to hold funds in cash, fixed interest, property and shares, because these asset classes are less than perfectly positively correlated. As such, the risk is reduced.

Reilly and Norton (2006) demonstrated the benefits of diversification of asset classes. They placed a $10 000 investment in each of two investment strategies over a 25-year period. Strategy 1 contained one asset only; Strategy 2 invested $2000 equally in five assets. In Strategy 1 the asset earned an average of 7% p.a. At the end of the period the total was $54 275 (rounded). Of the five assets in Strategy 2, one asset was a total failure with the $2000 lost completely. The second investment earned no return at all, but the $2000 remained. The third investment earned an average of 5% p.a. over the 25 years. The fourth investment earned an average of 10% p.a. and the fifth investment earned an average of 12% p.a. The total return of the Strategy 2 portfolio is $64 442 (rounded). So, even though some assets performed poorly the gain of the portfolio containing a number of assets (across asset classes) achieved a return of more than $10 000 over the single asset strategy.

Table 4.2 describes some of the risk, return and correlation attributes associated with the various asset classes. We can see that the asset classes are not perfectly positively correlated and as such we know that the overall risk of the portfolio will be reduced.

The big question, then, revolves around what proportions we place in each asset class. This is an important question because research evidence suggests that this decision is the major determinant of the performance of a portfolio. A study — that has long stood the test of time — by Brinson, Singer and Beebower (1991) examined US pension fund plans and found that the decision as to how much should be allocated between the asset classes explained 91.5% of the variation in a plan's performance. Later studies have confirmed the Brinson, Singer and Beebower finding with similar results.

TABLE 4.2 Risk, return and correlation attributes

	Cash	Fixed interest	Property (direct)	Shares	International investments
Risk (short-term volatility)	Very low	Low	Medium	High	Medium to high but excellent for diversification as natural hedge
Correlation with other asset classes	Low	Low	Low with cash, fixed interest; moderate with shares	Low with cash, fixed interest; moderate with property	Depends on asset class
Returns in the long run	Low	Low to medium	Medium to high	High	Depends on asset class
Ability to beat inflation	Very poor	Poor	Good	Very good	Depends on asset class

Application of the diversification decision

At this stage we need to consider briefly the theory about the best combination of investments for an investor. Figure 4.3 shows a curved line which reflects the trade-off between returns and risk to produce a combination of assets to minimise volatility in a portfolio. If investors limit themselves to low-risk securities, they will be limiting themselves to investments that tend to have low rates of return. So, for better returns, they should include some higher growth, higher risk securities in their portfolio, but combine them in a way so that some of their fluctuations cancel each other out. (In statistical terms, an investor should consider a combined standard deviation that is low, relative to the standard deviations of the individual securities.) The result should provide a high average rate of return, with less of the volatility.

The science of efficient portfolios was based on the research of Harry Markowitz, who received the Nobel Prize for Economic Sciences in 1990. His theory was to assume investors have return and risk data for a collection of securities and they graph the return rates and standard deviations for all the possible combinations of these securities. Markowitz showed that the result will be a region bounded by an upward-sloping, concave curve, which he called the **efficient frontier**. Higgins and Abey wrote in 2000, that there is no one 'best' portfolio. 'There are, in fact, any number of efficient portfolios, at different points in the trade-off curve' (p. 86). Thus, point A represents the combination of securities that provides the best possible return at the lowest risk. Point B shows the best possible return for the highest risk. Any point along the curve shows the combination of securities that gives the optimal return for the amount of risk that investors would tolerate.

efficient frontier the curved line that represents the optimal mix of return and risk for a portfolio of investments given a required level of risk

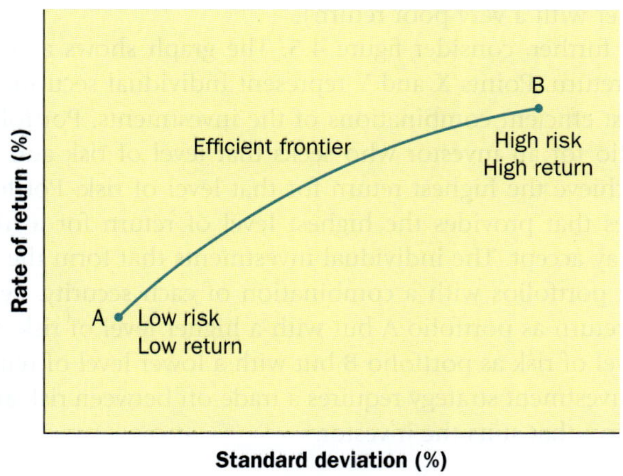

FIGURE 4.3
The efficient frontier

So, for any given value of standard deviation, investors would like to choose a portfolio that gives them the greatest possible rate of return; so they always want a portfolio that lies along the efficient frontier, rather than inside the curve. Inside the curve represents either a lower rate or lower return or both for the particular combination of the two securities. The first important aspect of the efficient frontier is that it identifies where the most efficient portfolios are. The second important aspect of the efficient frontier is that it is a curve. This is the key to how diversification lets investors improve their risk–return ratio. To illustrate, imagine a 50/50 allocation between two securities. Assuming that the performance of these two securities is quite different as their business cycles have not coincided, the standard deviation of the 50/50 allocation will be *less* than the average of the standard deviations of the two securities separately. Figure 4.4 (overleaf) indicates that this stretches the possible allocations of the two securities from a straight-line relationship *to the left* of the straight line joining the two securities and this forms a curve in the relationship between the two.

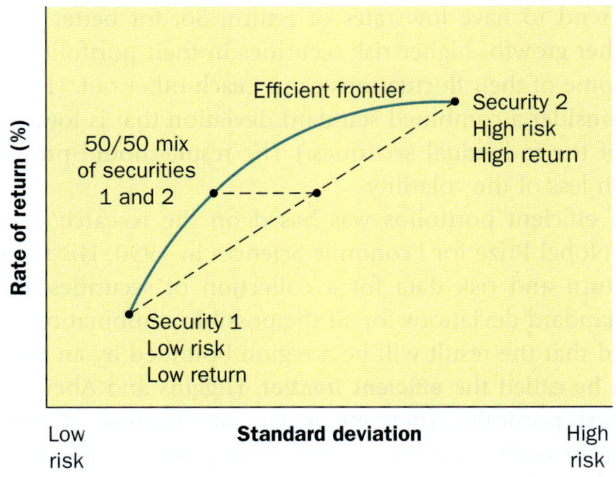

FIGURE 4.4
The efficient frontier for a combination of two securities

In statistical terms, this effect is due to lack of covariance. This means that the smaller the covariance between the two securities, the smaller the standard deviation of a portfolio that combines them. This indicates a lower level of variation and risk. The ultimate would be to find two securities with *negative* covariance (one security with a very good return and the other with a very poor return).

To explain this further, consider figure 4.5. The graph shows a conceptual trade-off between risk and return. Points X and Y represent individual securities. The curved line represents the most efficient combinations of the investments. Portfolio A is a low risk, low return portfolio for an investor who seeks that level of risk and indicates the best combination to achieve the highest return for that level of risk. Portfolio B is a combination of securities that provides the highest level of return for a higher level of risk that an investor may accept. The individual investments that form the portfolios are less attractive than the portfolios with a combination of each security. Security X produces the same level of return as portfolio A but with a higher level of risk. Investment Y produces the same level of risk as portfolio B but with a lower level of return. So, the objective of setting an investment strategy requires a trade-off between risk and return to get to the best combination that suits the investor.

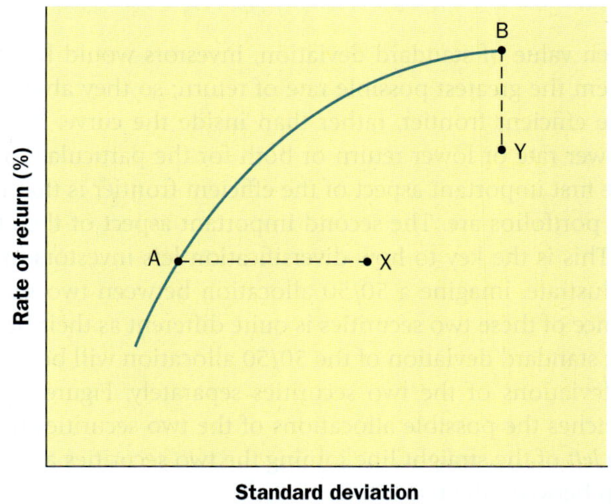

FIGURE 4.5
Risk and return with the efficient frontier

The curve of the efficient frontier shows where the most risk–return efficient portfolios are located but the Sharpe ratio identifies the best possible proportions of these securities to use in a portfolio.

The Sharpe ratio is defined as:

$$S(x) = \frac{(r_x - R_f)}{StdDev(x)}$$

where x = an investment

r_x = the average annual rate of return of x

R_f = the best available rate of return of a 'risk-free' security (e.g. the cash rate)

$StdDev(x)$ = the standard deviation of r_x

The Sharpe ratio is a direct measure of return to risk. To see how it assists an investor in creating a portfolio, consider figure 4.6 of the efficient frontier again, this time with cash drawn in. This ratio indicates the historic average differential returns (relative to a benchmark) per unit of historic variability of the differential return.

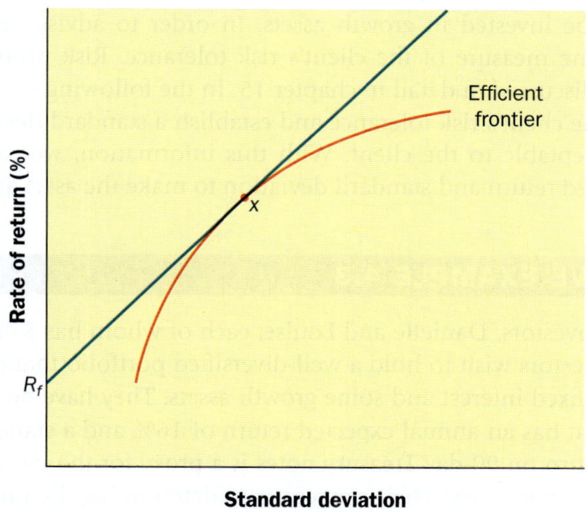

FIGURE 4.6
Relationship between the efficient frontier and the Sharpe ratio

There are three important things to notice in figure 4.6.

1. If you take an investment like x and combine it with cash, the resulting portfolio will lie somewhere along the straight line joining cash with x. (On this occasion, it is a straight line and not a curve because cash is riskless.)
2. Since investors want the rate of return to be as high as possible, they select the investment (indicated by x) that gives them the line with the greatest possible slope (as indicated in figure 4.6). The slope of this line is equal to the Sharpe ratio of x. So, in summary, this gives an investor the method for finding the best possible portfolio from this collection of securities. That is, first, find the investment with the highest possible Sharpe ratio. Second, take whatever linear combination of this investment and cash will give an investor for the desired value for standard deviation. The result will be the portfolio with the greatest possible rate of return.
3. Markowitz's modern portfolio theory assumes there are only two asset types: risky and risk-free. The key concern for investors is the determination of what proportion of wealth to invest in 'risky' assets and what proportion to invest in 'risk-free' assets. Because of the risk characteristics of cash, fixed interest, property and shares, we can

categorise these asset classes as relatively risky or risk-free assets. We can broadly call cash and fixed-interest 'risk-free' assets, although in reality some fixed-interest investments are not risk-free at all. Some fixed-interest securities are subject to credit risk and when interest rates change, substantial gains and losses can be made from investments in traded fixed-interest securities. Cash is not always risk-free either. In this sense, there is always the risk that a cash investment will not outperform inflation. Notwithstanding these limitations, we still consider both cash and fixed-interest securities as 'risk-free' investments within the context of modern portfolio theory. We can broadly call property and shares risky or growth assets. The risky assets have the potential to generate growth in the underlying value of the portfolio.

Financial planners need to help their clients make a decision as to what proportion of wealth should be invested in growth assets and what proportion in cash and fixed interest. The asset allocation decision will depend largely on the specific risk attributes of the client. Financial planners should try to help clients become more familiar with the client's own risk characteristics, as the risk characteristics will determine the proportion of the total portfolio that should be invested in cash and fixed interest, and the proportion that should be invested in growth assets. In order to advise on asset allocation, planners need some measure of the client's risk tolerance. Risk profiling by means of questionnaires is discussed in detail in chapter 15. In the following example, assume that we can quantify the client's risk tolerance and establish a standard deviation of portfolio returns that is acceptable to the client. With this information, we can use our understanding of expected return and standard deviation to make the asset allocation decision.

ILLUSTRATIVE EXAMPLE 4.3

Consider two investors, Danielle and Louise, each of whom has $100 000 to invest. Both investors wish to hold a well-diversified portfolio that comprises some cash and fixed interest and some growth assets. They have both selected a growth fund that has an annual expected return of 16% and a standard deviation of 12%. The return on 90-day Treasury notes is a proxy for the risk-free rate of interest and is currently 6%. Their concern is in determining the proportion of their investment that they will place in the growth fund and the proportion they will place in cash and fixed interest (risk-free assets). Danielle is relatively risk tolerant and you have been able to determine that she would be comfortable with her total portfolio having a standard deviation of 9%. Louise is relatively risk averse; she is comfortable with a standard deviation in her portfolio of only 5%.

From modern portfolio theory, we can state the risk–return relationship as follows:

$$E(R_p) = R_f + \left[\frac{E(R_{pi}) - R_f}{\sigma_{pi}}\right]\sigma_p$$

where $E(R_p)$ = expected return on the entire portfolio
$E(R_{pi})$ = expected return on the risky fund
σ_p = standard deviation of the entire portfolio
σ_{pi} = standard deviation of the risky fund
R_f = risk-free interest rate

Substituting the values for the risk-free rate, the expected return on the growth fund and the standard deviation of the growth fund, we can express the relationship between the expected return for the entire portfolio and the standard deviation for the entire portfolio:

$$E(R_p) = R_f + \left[\frac{16\% - 6\%}{12\%}\right]\sigma_p$$
$$= 6\% + 83.3\%\,\sigma_p$$

Using this formula, we can now substitute Danielle's and Louise's risk tolerances to obtain the proportions of wealth to be included in risky assets (growth assets) and risk-free assets (cash and fixed interest).

Danielle — risk tolerance is 9% standard deviation

$$E(R_p) = 6\% + 83.3\%\,\sigma_p$$
$$= 6\% + 83.3\%(9\%)$$
$$= 13.50\%$$

For a two-asset portfolio (risky assets, risk-free assets), the proportions are:

$$E(R_p) = (X)[E(R_{pi})] + (1 - X)R_f$$

where X = proportion of wealth in risky assets. The equation can be rewritten as:

$$E(R_p) = [E(R_{pi}) - R_f]X + R_f$$

If we substitute the expected return for a 9% risk into this model, we obtain:

$$13.50\% = [16\% - 6\%]X + 6\%$$

We can rearrange this expression to obtain the solution for X:

$$X = 75\%$$

Thus 75% will be invested in risky or growth assets. The remaining 25% will be invested in risk-free assets (cash and fixed interest). This combination is the best mix to try to achieve Danielle's target level of 9%.

Louise — risk tolerance is 5% standard deviation

Recall that Louise has a preference for a standard deviation of 5%.

$$E(R_p) = 6\% + 83.3\%\ \mathrm{op}$$
$$= 6\% + 83.3\%\ (5\%)$$
$$= 10.17\%$$

Again, for a two-asset portfolio (risky assets, risk-free assets), the proportions are:

$$E(R_p) = (X)[E(R_{pi})] + (1 - X)R_f$$

where X = proportion of wealth in risky assets. The equation can be rewritten as:

$$E(R_p) = [E(R_{pi}) - R_f]X + \mathrm{R}_f$$

»

»

Using the values we determined and Louise's expected return:

$$10.17\% = [16\% - 6\%]X + 6\%$$
$$X = 41.7\%$$

Thus 41.7% will be invested in risky or growth assets. The remaining 58.3% will be invested in risk-free assets (cash and fixed interest). This combination should achieve Louise's target risk level of 5%, if future returns mimic past performance.

From this analysis we can summarise the asset allocation decision for Danielle and Louise as follows:

	Cash and fixed interest	Property and shares	Standard deviation of portfolio
Danielle	$25 000	$75 000	9%
Louise	$58 300	$41 700	5%

However, some investors take a different view of investing in a small number of assets and monitor the small portfolio closely for performance; that is, they say 'put your eggs in a basket and watch that basket!'

LO 5

Recent performance of asset classes

In this section, we consider the recent performance of the various classes of assets. The ASX (periodically), many research houses, stockbroking firms, industry associations and fund managers examine the returns from the various asset classes. One set of results is given in table 4.3. Keep in mind that these data reflect diversified portfolios in each asset class. An undiversified portfolio may not perform in a similar manner.

TABLE 4.3 Percentage returns at 30 June 2012 over time

	10 year %	20 year %
Australian shares	6.1	8.7
International shares (hedged)	3.7	6.7
International shares (unhedged)	–3.1	4.8
Australian bonds	6.4	7.6
Listed property (A-REITS)	0.4	6.0
Cash	3.8	4.1
Consumer price index (CPI)	2.9	2.6

Source: Russell Investments/ASX long-term investing report June 2012.

These results are more or less what would be expected from finance theory. Over the longer time frames, returns for the risky asset classes are expected to outperform the less risky asset classes because they take more risk. Over the 10 and 20-year time frames, most asset classes experience returns above the CPI to indicate a real rate of return after inflation. The only asset classes to fall below inflation are the 10-year performance of A-REITs and the unhedged international shares. But over the 20-year time frame both asset classes have very positive returns on average per annum. The 20-year time frame takes into account a number of business cycles so that where we see the 10-year negative returns in A-REITs and unhedged international shares we can detect the significant effect of the global financial crisis over the 10-year period. This indicates the different business cycles that different parts of the world experience in terms of short-term performance, but it also indicates the benefit of long-term investment. Note that each year such figures will change on a rolling-time basis. Gradually the severe effects of the 2007–13 period will be diminished and long-term returns will even better reflect the benefit of riskier assets despite the short-term volatility that can depress returns over the shorter time frame.

LO 6 General investment strategies

Investment strategies take a number of forms. Individual investors may use one approach or another; some investors combine the features of several. The initial principle which investors are wise to adopt is *diversification*. Diversification merely reflects the old adage 'don't put all your eggs in one basket' if you don't want to run unnecessary risks. Modern portfolio theory is based on the same premise.

From earlier in this chapter, portfolio theory suggests that risk among a collection of investments, called a portfolio, can be reduced through the judicious selection of appropriate assets. Risk is reduced if the determinants of risk and return among the assets are related to different phenomena. Even more preferable for the risk-averse investor is the case where risk is related to the same underlying determinants but is related in the opposite direction. For example, if the Indonesian economy boomed when the French economy was depressed and vice versa, then an investor could reduce risk by investing in assets in both economies, rather than in one or the other. This reflects the principles of negative correlation.

If diversification is generally considered to be a good thing, then the question arises as to how an investment portfolio should be *allocated* to get the benefits of diversification. As outlined in the discussion of modern portfolio theory previously, investors have to make allocative decisions. Suppose Jane wins $100 000 and decides to invest it. What would she do?

- She might look around and decide *not* to invest in casinos, mining or pine plantations.
- She might decide she is interested in communications, medical technology and banks. She has, in effect, made some allocative decisions.

The top–down allocation approach is based on the idea that the whole investment scene should be analysed to determine attractive and unattractive areas, for example, sectors likely to enjoy future high growth and potentially depressed sectors, respectively. Once forecasts are made, decisions may then be made about how funds should be split between investment classes and sectors to match each investor's risk preference. For example, an ideal investment spread for an individual may be selected as:

- 40% Australian equities
- 20% international equities
- 30% property
- 10% fixed-interest securities.

Once the allocation decisions are made, the *selection* of appropriate investments, be they Australian listed shares, international shares, properties or fixed-interest securities, involves choosing a few from many thousands of available investments. How does an investor choose appropriate investments? And also, what long-term strategies may be adopted?

Matching investors to products

In portfolio theory, we assume most investors are risk averse, but that investors differ in their degrees of risk averseness. Apart from innate forces which dictate a person's tolerance to risk, it would be reasonable to expect that risk tolerance would be governed by a person's age, income, wealth, gender, years to retirement, past financial experiences and perhaps some other factors. For example, young people are often happy to take on more risk than older people. There are good reasons for this. Youth generally appear to be less risk averse, they have often had less chance of experiencing financial losses when investments have 'gone wrong', and they have usually more years to increase wealth before retirement and thus have more time to recover should things go awry.

Fixed-interest products appeal to more risk-averse people. There are two aspects of this which are worth consideration. First, there is the guarantee of the interest payment at a given level, so long as the borrower remains solvent. Selection within this category needs to be carefully scrutinised as many 'guaranteed' products are available. The 'guarantee' offered by some entities may end up being quite worthless. The entity may guarantee the interest and return of capital but if the entity fails then the 'guarantee' of return of income and capital is only as good as the assets of the entity offering the guarantee. However, overall there is usually little uncertainty about the income from these products. Second, many of these products are capital stable. That is, the value of the capital remains fixed and there is little chance of the loss of capital.

Investment in traded securities such as bonds remains an exception to this rule. A rise in the general level of interest rates will normally promote decreases in the capital values of traded fixed-interest securities. Conversely, holders of these securities will enjoy an appreciation in capital values when the general level of interest rates falls.

Notwithstanding the fact that more risk-averse investors are drawn to fixed-interest products, it is normal for many investors to hold some proportion of fixed-interest securities in their portfolios. The proportions will vary according to investment strategy. For example, a so-called capital stable portfolio might have 50% fixed interest whereas a growth portfolio may have less than 20%. Host Plus (a superannuation fund for employees in the hospitality, tourism, recreation and sports industries), for example, includes a range of between 30% and 50% fixed-interest securities in its conservative portfolio. Other funds managers may include different proportions in their portfolios, according to their assessments of their clients' risk preferences and the investment choices of the managers of the different portfolios in the fund.

Few investors with reasonable wealth do not own their own homes. Property thus often occupies a major position in possibly a majority of portfolios, as we saw earlier. Apart from the family home, property investment appeals to people because of its tangibility and its familiarity. In addition, people are aware that property values generally keep pace with inflation. Thus, unless investors are forced to sell during a downturn in the property cycle, they are likely to retain the purchasing power of their funds and can indeed make large capital gains. In terms of the risk–return trade-off, property appeals to people who can tolerate moderate risk, who are looking for medium rates of return and who have a medium- to long-term investment horizon.

Investors who favour the share market are generally less risk averse than those who favour property, and certainly much less risk averse than those who favour fixed-interest products. However, the range of shares is so large that a wide range of risk averseness can be accommodated by the appropriate selection of shares.

An investor wanting relatively lower risk, for example, might select a share in the consumables or retail sector, a class of listed investments which typically shows only small price variations. In contrast, the prices of biotechnology shares and mining stocks have varied tremendously in recent times.

Gibson (2000) studied the effects of **multiple-asset class investing** over a period of 26 years between 1972 and 1998. He used different portfolios of asset classes using cash, bonds, property (REITs) and shares. His research concluded that by using a combination of all four asset classes over a period of time, an investor would achieve a higher long-term average return with a lower level of risk. Gibson discovered that the combination of the four asset classes resulted in a compound average return of 13.77% compared with 13.61%, 13.30% and 12.46%, respectively, for portfolios of three, two and one asset classes. In addition, he found the risk of the portfolios was significantly decreased by holding the four asset classes. The standard deviation for the four-asset class portfolio was 10.55% whereas the standard deviations for the three-, two- and one-asset class portfolios were 11.92%, 14.45% and 20.04%, respectively. The lower risk of the four-asset class portfolio was confirmed by Sharpe ratios. The Sharpe ratios were: 0.66, 0.60, 0.50 and 0.37, respectively, for the four-, three-, two- and one-asset class portfolios. The Sharpe ratio calculation indicates a volatility-adjusted performance for each portfolio with the higher figure representing a higher risk-adjusted return.

multiple asset-class investing
a mixture of asset classes in an investment portfolio

Overall, an investor is faced with a vast range of investment choices and combinations. The determination of a strategy is the first step, followed by the combination of asset classes, and then by the selection of components of each asset class.

PERSONAL FINANCE BULLETIN

Get used to cyclical volatility and structural change

Get used to cyclical volatility and structural change. We'll have to live with a lot of those changes over the next 15 years as we adapt to rolling investment cycles, another major structural change and, most likely, punctuated by internal and external shocks.

These influences are not new. Certainly, this is a much bigger mining investment boom than we have experienced before. But we've been living with internally-generated investment cycles for a long time. These are long cycles.

How did we get here?

The latest cycle, dating from the peak of Australia's debt-driven investment boom of the 1980s, has yet to run its course. The excesses associated with that investment boom set up our very own financial crisis and recession in the early 1990s. This was followed by a long period when growth was constrained by weak investment as

»

»
we absorbed the excess capacity created during the boom. That underinvestment was not limited to the private sector. Governments around Australia cut investment as they focused on fiscal responsibility and reducing budget deficits.

The emergence of capacity constraints in 2002–03 underpinned a phase of generalised business investment and solid (balanced) growth. That was before the resources boom began. And the emergence of infrastructure bottlenecks mid-decade drove a phase of increased government investment.

The resources boom changed everything. In a market economy, there is little choice. The extraordinary increases in minerals investment, which have continued until recently, provided strong stimulus to the Australian economy, albeit focused in industries and regions servicing the investment boom.

The associated rise in the Australian dollar triggered a process of structural change, with the decline in non-mining, trade-exposed industries 'making room for the minerals boom' and allowing a shift of labour and resources to build capacity to service major investment projects. That process of structural change is ongoing as the impact of the high dollar on competitiveness works its way through the system.

Meanwhile, the global financial crisis (GFC) provided a substantial shock to the Australian economy. Despite fears to the contrary, there was no financial crisis or recession in Australia. Certainly, Australia had participated in a 'financial engineering' debt-driven boom with weight of money driving equity prices too high. However, unlike most other developed Western economies, investment had not yet gone over the top. Australia had a correction rather than collapse, a credit squeeze rather than a financial crisis, and a downturn rather than a recession. Nevertheless, the subsequent economic fears, pressure and deleveraging changed the psychology. Australian business, including industries sheltered from the impact of the high dollar, remains in survival/cost-cutting mode, containing expenditure and underinvesting. Australia still hasn't recovered from the impact of the GFC.

Solid growth

Through all of this period of uncertainty, Australia continued to experience solid growth on average, though there have been major disparities between the performance of different industries and regions. But now the economy is softening. The boost to government investment associated with the stimulus package is being wound back aggressively.

The extraordinary stimulus to GDP from minerals investment growth is rapidly receding as minerals investment peaks. That contribution will turn negative from now on as minerals investment recedes from peak levels. Even so, minerals investment remains extraordinarily high, at a level adding substantially to our capacity to produce and export.

What next?

Next cab off the rank is a phase of residential investment, with activity strengthening through the middle of the decade. That will be driven by strength in the undersupplied regions — notably Perth, Sydney and Brisbane. Oversupplied regions will miss this cycle. And that's not unusual. They'll probably lead the next cycle.

But residential alone won't be enough to offset the decline in resources and government investment. Waiting in the wings, the main driver of growth will be non-mining business investment. We don't think it will pick up for another year or two. However, given the extent of underinvestment, once it picks up momentum, it will constitute a long and strong upswing. Some sectors, notably commercial property, look like peaking around the end of this decade. The delay to the commencement of this investment is setting the preconditions for a strong cyclical upswing.

But let's not get ahead of ourselves. The economy has hit a soft patch. Confidence remains weak. Companies remain focused on reducing costs. The residential upswing is fragile, despite reductions in housing interest rates. The RBA knows that it needs to reduce interest rates sufficiently to kickstart residential property and investment — and given that inflation is not currently a problem, we'll probably see more cuts this year.

But the real problem is that there is still enough capacity to service demand in the non-mining business economy. That means that a significant recovery in investment is still one to two years away. Initially, it will be tentative, only building up momentum in the second half of the decade.

Meanwhile, the dollar remains high, continuing to drive structural change, further damaging the non-mining, trade exposed sectors. That won't always be so.

We don't expect that resources investment can continue indefinitely at these levels. And we don't expect commodity prices to remain this high indefinitely. Eventually, worldwide supply will catch up to demand. We don't know how precipitately that will happen. Our forecast is for an orderly decline in resources investment. However, the risk is that a fall in commodity prices will precipitate a much sharper decline in investment, leading to a substantial negative shock to the economy. In any case, much of the boost to the economy from strong minerals investment growth will be reversed.

The next structural shift

The next structural shift will come when the Australian dollar falls, most likely when commodity prices fall. Though the timing may not be precisely matched, it will offset the impact of declining resources investment. It will again involve a painful process of structural change at the industry and regional levels, and partially reverse the structural change we've been going through, with an improvement in the competitiveness of industries currently hit by the high dollar.

It means a boost to manufacturing, agriculture, tourism, education, finance and business services. But we are unlikely to go back to where we started. The question is how much of the damage done during the current episode is irreversible. Manufacturing may never recover lost ground — unless new highly capital intensive technologies change the game. Services are likely to be the major beneficiaries.

We are a long way from stable balanced growth. We'll have to cope with significant cyclical and structural shifts into the future — just as we have had to in the past. This economy will look very different in 15 years' time.

Source: Frank Gelber, *Professional Planner*, issue 52, April 2013.

LO 7 Investor behaviour

The traditional view of studying markets is that there is an assumption that the market is efficient. That means all publicly available information that exists about that company or product is known to all participants in the market and the price determined is an interaction between buyers and sellers. Efficient-market theory, modern portfolio theory and asset-pricing relationships (such as the capital asset pricing model or CAPM) between risk and return are all built on the assumption that investors are rational.

However, over the past 30 years, a number of academics have researched the concept of a relatively inefficient market. They have questioned the rationality of investor behaviour and developed a discipline of studies in behavioural finance. Olsen (1998) wrote that behavioural finance 'seeks to understand and predict systematic financial market implications of psychological decision processes ... behavioural finance is focused on the implication of psychological and economic principles for the improvement of financial decision making.' They have pointed to the bubbles that have occurred in economic history and argued that the occasional huge rise in prices could not have been the result of efficient or rational behaviour. One such bubble is the US dot.com bubble of 2000 as illustrated in figure 4.7. In early 2000, analysts were predicting that stock returns would be in the order of 15–25% p.a. over the next few years in response to the rapid and widespread use of the internet. Some companies, keen to get into the market, sold themselves to investors as the next 'hot stocks' as they provided the means to ride on the back of the internet revolution. When many of such companies were trading at 100 times earnings or more (price/earnings ratio), a crash was soon on the horizon. For example, Amazon.com traded at a high US$75.25 in 2000 but fell to US$5.51 in 2001–02 (a percentage decline of almost 93%). Many companies who started late in the 1990s to cash in on the new craze did not survive the crash and went out of business.

FIGURE 4.7
The NASDAQ Composite Stock Index, 1998–2004
Source: Malkiel 2007.

What history shows is that there are many periods when markets reached dizzying heights and then crashed to regain a more normal pattern for a few years. Students might care to research Dutch Tulip mania in 1636–37 and the South Seas bubble of 1720. These examples indicate that there are times when investors are less than rational. In 1979, the efficient market theory was challenged by two psychologists, Daniel Kahneman and Amos Tversky, who argued that people, at times, display some irrational behaviours. Since then, behavioural finance studies have identified and quantified a number of factors found to create irrational investor behaviour. We will consider four such factors in the following sections.

Loss aversion

Kahneman and Tversky (1979) described individual behaviour in the face of risky situations where investors faced the prospect of gains and losses. Hence they termed their theory 'prospect theory'. They argued that individuals place different values on gains and losses, and discovered that losses are considered far more undesirable than the desire for equivalent gains. They conducted experiments based on a gamble of winning $100 or losing $100. The found that losses were 2.5 times more undesirable as equivalent gains were desirable. Even when there was a choice of two losses — a sure loss of $75 or a 75% chance to lose $100 and a 25% chance to lose nothing — they found that people chose to take the gamble.

The studies of behaviour in taking a risk with losses was extended when the trading records of some 10 000 clients was studied and a 'disposition effect' was observed. That is, there was a clear disposition among investors to sell their winning stocks and to hold on to their losing stocks. Selling a stock that had risen enabled an investor to realise a profit. If they sold their losing stocks, they would realise a loss which hurt more than could be offset by the equivalent gain. In fact, investors with losing stocks tended to hold on to them in the hope (the gamble) that the stocks would recover. Hence, it was observed that investors have an aversion to losses which is counter to the efficient market and the rational investor theories. Efficient investor behaviour may be seen in an example where it would be advantageous for an investor to plan to sell losing stocks to offset the capital gains tax levied on winning stocks that they have sold and then later, if they believed that the losing stocks would eventually recover, they could repurchase the losing stocks before that recovery. Yet there seems to be a reluctance to implement this strategy as it would mean realising a loss.

Prospect theory may also be seen in practice in the large number of people who decided not to take any action to change their superannuation investments when 'choice of fund' legislation was passed. No action in such a choice was seen to be an avoidance of a potential loss situation.

Herding

Some behavioural finance research indicates that groups tend to make better decisions than individuals. This is based on the belief that if information is shared and all points of view are considered then, on balance, the wisdom of the group prevails in the decision-making process. This may provide a well-informed market and result in a relatively efficient market. Yet, group behaviour may lead to incorrect decision making and turn into 'group think'. This was illustrated by a study where a person stood on a street corner and looked up at the sky. A few people stopped to look up too but when five people stood and looked up the number of observers grew four times. When the researcher placed 15 people on the corner almost every passer-by looked up. The 2000 dot.com bubble was an example of when people made incorrect decisions and acted as a herd, forcing prices up to unrealistic levels. Many did not want to miss out on the action and bought stocks on the basis that they were rising and would keep on rising.

Robert Shiller, author of *Irrational exuberance* (2000) noted that the process feeds on itself in a 'positive feedback loop'. Fund managers are not immune from this behaviour: as the market rises, more investors may pour more funds into managed funds which may be seen to encourage the managers to invest further into a rising market when their other instincts may suggest that they should not. It is suggested that they may also succumb to the herd mentality despite their investment management responsibilities.

Overconfidence

Research indicates that people deviate from rational thinking in making judgements where there is an element of uncertainty. This can be seen in the overconfidence sometimes portrayed by people about their own personal beliefs and abilities or an overoptimistic view of the future.

Experiments where a class of students was asked about their level of competence in relation to the average driver in the group invariably resulted in about 80–90% of students estimating that they were above the average. Other experiments indicate that 25% of the class believed they were in the top 1% of the population in terms of getting along with others and in judging athletic ability, and at least 60% of the students believed they were in the top quartile. Such results have also been observed to explain investor behaviour. The results indicate that many individual investors are mistakenly convinced that they can beat the market. As a result, they tend to speculate more than they should and end up trading too much. In fact, research by Barber and Odean (2001) studying the trading records of a large discount broker discovered that the more individual investors traded the worse they did. The researchers also found that male traders did worse than female traders.

The fact that many investors exhibit levels of overconfidence may be based on hindsight bias; that is, it is argued that investors tend to have a selective memory of their own successes which translates into any future success being perceived as the result of their own attributes. Investors then rationalise that poor results were the product of external events over which they had no control. Observers of market performance note that there tends to be an overvaluation of 'growth' stocks because many investors think that those stocks will perform better and hence put their money into such stocks and drive the prices higher. When the forecasts of some stocks are not realised and the projected earnings are subdued, investors may decide to seek better value elsewhere and sell such stocks. Thus, the prices of such growth stocks are likely to record a fall in value and then, as often happens when projections are not realised, may underperform the more solid stocks (with less expectations of rapid growth) otherwise known as 'value' stocks.

Biased judgements

Investors' decisions are sometimes clouded by a bias which runs against sound probabilistic thinking. An illustration of this is shown in the famous Tversky and Kahneman (1982) experiment where a description was given of a young lady. The young lady was aged 31, single, outspoken and very bright. She majored in philosophy and, as a student, she was deeply concerned with issues of discrimination and social justice. She also participated in anti-nuclear demonstrations. Participants in the experiment were then asked to rate different statements about her. One statement was that she 'was a bank teller' and another was that she 'was a bank teller and is active in the feminist movement'. More than 85% of participants judged that she 'was both a bank teller and is active in the feminist movement' rather than simply a 'bank teller'. In terms of probability theory, the probability that somebody belongs to both category A and category B is less than or equal to the probability that she belongs to category A alone. Because the description of the young lady made her seem like a feminist, the choice that she was both a bank teller and a feminist was perceived as being more representative of her than just being a bank teller.

This 'representativeness' leads to a number of other biases in investors' judgement such as investors who chase 'hot funds' (those that have performed well in the past year or so) or who extrapolate from recent evidence. The bias towards investing in housing in the United States (prior to the global financial crisis) was seen in comments made by advisers that 'house prices never go down!'

PROFESSIONAL ADVICE

Investor behaviour

Max was having coffee with two of his old school friends, James and Simon, and the conversation turned to the share market. Both James and Simon said that they had bought into Slick Oil Company when the price per share was 25 cents and now the shares were worth $30 each.

'Wow,' said Max. 'That's for me. I'll buy some!'

James said that the shares were still on the rise even though the company had not paid a dividend yet, and that the company was sure to declare a distribution soon. Simon said the price–earnings ratio was about 120 to one but that was not really anything to worry about as it was a growth stock and did not need to worry about earnings in the short term.

QUESTIONS

1. What sort of investor behaviour do you think Max is exhibiting?
2. What sort of investor behaviour do you think James and Simon are exhibiting?
3. What advice would you offer to the three friends?

LO 8 Investment scams

This chapter is concerned with investment choices. So, it would be remiss if we did not consider the lessons from the past about investment schemes that have been promoted to investors and have, instead of being valid investment opportunities, in fact been **investment scams**. The following examples are sourced from MoneySmart, the Australian Securities and Investments Commission's (ASIC) financial tips and safety checks website (moneysmart.gov.au). The website lists scams relating to investors; superannuation; banking and credit; other scams; how to avoid and report scams and how to recover losses.

investment scam an investment opportunity that is promoted to investors which has no substance other than to benefit the promoter of the investment

Some factors are common to all investment scams. These include:

- they do not have a product disclosure document
- they promise high returns
- most require the prospective investee to provide a password or bank account details
- the investments are often based overseas or must be kept a 'secret', presumably so other people don't find out about the offer and make a killing as well.

The simplest, yet most effective (devastating) scams perpetrated on unsuspecting investors for many years have been 'Ponzi' schemes. Such schemes require only a few victims in their early stages to be successful. The promoter promises a very high return on the investment and says it is secure. Part of the money deposited by early investors is then used to pay the first dividend cheques or interest payments. The victims are more than happy to receive high dividends. The scammer continues paying dividends for a couple of months until the investors are more comfortable with their investments, and decide to invest more. Investors typically then begin to urge their friends and relatives to invest as well, usually at the behest of the promoter of the scheme. Soon there is a steady flow of funds into the scheme and the number of investors grows. (The classic and largest Ponzi scheme which came unstuck during the global financial crisis concerned the fund management activities of Bernard Madoff. Search the internet for details.)

Provided the scammer is disciplined about how much money is left in the account to pay 'interest' or 'dividends', the scam can continue for years. Theoretically, if the scheme continues to draw in new investors, it could go on indefinitely. In practice such schemes generally fall over because the promoter starts to spend the money too quickly or the pool of investors starts to decline. A classic Ponzi scheme was operated by Mr M who offered people investment returns of between 3% and 6% per month. Mr M's illegal scheme received $216.9 million from investors who ultimately lost $76 million. Many of the investors were from the local community who became aware of the scheme through family and friends. This is typical of how many people become involved in a Ponzi scheme. Mr M is currently serving a 5-year jail term. (Mr M received a 'Pie in the Sky' award outlined below.)

Another scheme in recent times concerns 'Nigerian letter scams' where letters or emails are sent from a person claiming to represent a government agency in Nigeria. The letter asks the person to give their bank account details so that their bank account can be used for offloading many millions of dollars offshore — for which the person will be paid a generous commission. ASIC's advice is to ignore these letters and not to give the scammers any banking details. All that happens is that the scammer withdraws the balance out of the person's account. ASIC reports that at least six people who provided their account details travelled to Nigeria to investigate the scheme and were murdered.

ASIC awards an annual 'Pie in the Sky' award to the scheme that has been most convincing. The purpose is to bring such scams to the attention of consumers. The 2010 'Pie in the Sky' award went to the Little Super Fund and its trustee, Mr L:

> Mr L illegally obtained the superannuation of the members of the Little Super Fund and then pocketed a high commission. ASIC's investigation of the Little Super Fund led to Mr L's conviction and imprisonment. (For more details see the ASIC press release 'Little super is pie in the sky', moneysmart.gov.au).
>
> This early release scam cheated people out of their hard-earned superannuation which is illegal with severe penalties. Victims of early release of superannuation scams are convinced by these promoters that accessing superannuation is a solution to their money problems. The reality is the promoters are looking for a way to scam people out of their superannuation savings.

As well as Mr M, other past winners of the award include the following.

> *Boxing Day tsunami estate scam*
>
> This advanced fee fraud email scam asked people to help a Togo barrister access US$17 million from the estate of a man who, along with his family, was killed in the 2006 Boxing Day tsunami. The barrister offered people a share of the wealth if they claimed to be the deceased's next of kin and paid a fee. People paid their money but received nothing.
>
> *Pegasus investment scheme*
>
> An illegal investment scheme promoted through wealth seminars across Australia, operated by CM. Pegasus Leveraged Options Group lured 90 unsuspecting investors

and raised $3.7 million. CM gambled and spent over $2.1 million of the funds. The NSW Supreme Court found Pegasus investors were promised astronomical returns of up to 8% per week. Investors were even issued a Certificate of Guarantee by a fictitious 'International Investment and Securities Commission'. CM was jailed in October 2005. (Search the ASIC website for more investment scams: www.moneysmart.gov.au.)

Despite warnings to the scam nature of the investment many people hang on to the belief that there is gold at the end of the rainbow and are prepared to take the risk. Even when alerted to the fact the money may have been transferred from their account, some people insist on the fact that the promised rewards will arrive. All consumers need to be aware of basic risk and return principles and be prepared to treat such offers with scepticism.

LO 9 Information sources for investment choices

When an investor undertakes their own research into appropriate investments they will be confronted with a wide range of information. The information can be considered in different categories:

- the economy — current and forecast economic conditions, both domestic and international
- the industry — background, competitors and outlook for a particular industry sector
- the institution/company — specific information about the background and prospects for an institution or company
- prices/quotations — current prices and the recent trend in prices/quotations of the specific investment alternatives.

Investors may gain information from a number of sources which may include:

- ASIC's website
- the business sections of the daily newspapers and finance journals
- monthly magazines focusing on investments and strategies
- government publications such as the Reserve Bank *Bulletin*
- stock exchange releases
- annual reports issued by companies and institutions
- analysts reports usually available by subscription or through stockbrokers
- published industry data
- ASX prices
- the internet using a search engine to find investment information websites, some of which may be free but otherwise by subscription.

Summary

There are many forms of investment, offering various promises of return and carrying varying degrees of risk. Investors carry their own individual attitudes to the risk and return features of investing. Whether investing directly or indirectly, an investor needs to understand the basic features of the asset class. To consider investment choices, an investor should have an appreciation of the risk and return relationship to understand that the higher the return the higher the level of risk. Risk may be reduced by diversification of assets. Efficient market theory describes the trade-off required between risk and return for the most efficient investment portfolio to achieve the highest return for a given level of acceptable risk by an investor. The risks and returns for each investment category also need to be understood in terms of recent performance history and time frames. Such an understanding is fundamental to adopting a suitable investment strategy. However, an investor's strategy may be influenced by certain types of investor behaviour. Behavioural finance research has found various reasons that many investors may not behave rationally in their investment choices at all times. A number of common investment scams take advantage of this fact.

Professional application questions

4.1 What are the main differences between a 'very conservative' and a 'very aggressive' investor?

4.2 What are the general features of a fixed-interest investment?

4.3 What is the significance of a standard deviation and how would you explain its meaning to a client? Write your response as if you were drafting a letter to a client.

4.4 Why doesn't a portfolio rely on assets that are positively correlated?

4.5 What was the main feature of Gibson's findings about multi-asset class investing?

4.6 Where there is an element of uncertainty 'people deviate from rational thinking in making judgement'. Provide an example when a person may exhibit a sign of overconfidence.

4.7 What does the efficient frontier mean for an investor who is considering a number of investment choices?

4.8 What are the four main factors identified as common to all investment scams?

4.9 From your reading of the Personal Finance Bulletin write a short briefing memo to Alexander (from the opening case study) about what investment sectors of the economy he should consider investing in over the next few years

Professional application exercises

Basic *
Moderate * *
Challenging * * *

4.10 Designing a suitable portfolio *

Construct a suitable investment portfolio for an investor who is considered to be a 'conservative' investor.

4.11 The ASX website *

(a) Prepare a table of the sectors under the GICS and search the ASX website to nominate two companies that fit into each sector.
(b) Identify the P/E ratios and year highest and lowest prices for each company.
(c) Provide an explanation for any differences that you observe.

4.12 Investment advice * *

Examine the following portfolio of Daisy and Donald.

	Year 1	Year 2	Year 3	Year 4	Year 5
Daisy	12%	20%	6%	8%	22%
Donald	14%	18%	5%	8%	18%

(a) Calculate the expected returns for both Daisy and Donald.
(b) Calculate the standard deviations for both Daisy and Donald.
(c) Discuss which is the safest security to invest in.

4.13 Nominal and real rates of return * *

Benedict told his friend Henry that he expected to receive an investment return of 9.5%. Henry suggested to his friend that 9.5% might not actually be the real return on the investment. Henry told Benedict that he had forgotten to consider the effect of inflation.

(a) Calculate the real rate of return for Benedict if inflation was 3.4%.

(b) Suppose the rate of return of another investment that Benedict was considering was 4.5%. What then would be the real rate of return?

4.14 Return expected from a portfolio ✱✱✱

Assume a portfolio has two investment funds as per below.

	Apples	Oranges
Expected return	8%	12%
Standard deviation	4%	7%
Percentage of portfolio	60%	40%

Calculate the expected return for the portfolio.

4.15 Portfolio efficiency ✱✱✱

The figure indicates two different portfolio choices, A and B. Explain why portfolio A is less efficient than portfolio B.

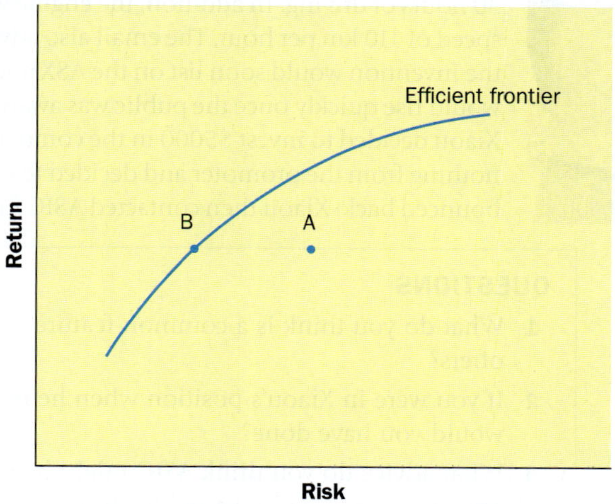

4.16 Choosing a portfolio ✱✱✱

Given the figure at right which indicates two different portfolio choices, C and D, explain why portfolio D is the preferred option to portfolio C.

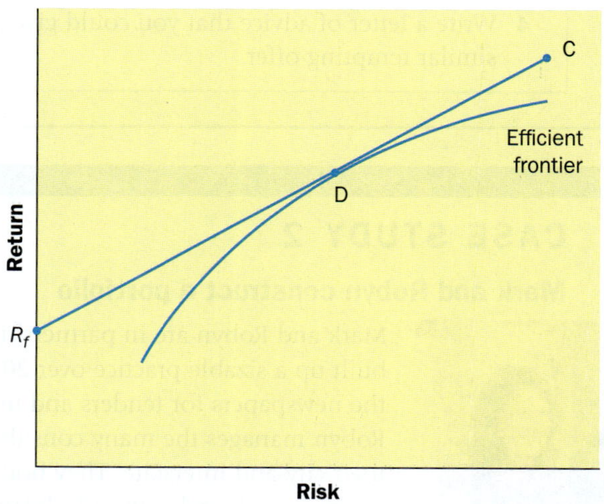

4.17 The behaviour of an irrational investor ✱✱✱

Distinguish between 'biased judgements' and 'overconfidence' as two forms of behaviour that indicate that investors do not always act rationally in making investment decisions.

CASE STUDY 1

An investment opportunity not to be missed

Xiaou got chatting with a man at the gymnasium who told him of a new motor engine that used revolutionary technology. Xiaou was interested in making money and gave his email to the man so he could get more information. In a few days, Xiaou received an email containing the business plan of the promoter and details of the revolutionary engine. Photos of the engine were attached along with details of how to invest in the new technology. The email gave a background of the development of the technology which was based on a powerful battery which needed charging only once a week and after 30 hours of driving. In addition, the engine would power a motor car at a top speed of 110 km per hour. The email also advised that the company behind the invention would soon list on the ASX and it was expected that share prices would rise quickly once the public was aware of the revolutionary technology. Xiaou decided to invest $5000 in the company. After six months he had heard nothing from the promoter and decided to email the company. His email bounced back. Xiaou then contacted ASIC for advice.

QUESTIONS

1. What do you think is a common feature of email-promoted investment offers?
2. If you were in Xiaou's position when he received the initial email, what would you have done?
3. What advice do you think ASIC might have given to Xiaou both prior to and after Xiaou had invested his money?
4. Write a letter of advice that you could give someone who is faced with a similar tempting offer.

CASE STUDY 2

Mark and Robyn construct a portfolio

Mark and Robyn are in partnership as psychologists and have built up a sizable practice over 20 years. Mark constantly trawls the newspapers for tenders and new consulting opportunities. Robyn manages the many consultants that they employ both in their city and interstate. They both work exceptionally hard in the business and rarely take a holiday. As they are both now in their mid forties, a friend has suggested that they take stock of their business and their lifestyle and attend to some of the things in life to restore some sense of balance. They decide to take a holiday to

Europe for 3 weeks and to take a week to review their personal assets and financial plans.

They discover, to their delight, that they have $300 000 in cash accounts and decide to invest the funds to achieve a better rate of return than cash at bank interest rates. They consult a financial planner who discovers at the joint meeting that they both wish to hold a well-diversified portfolio that comprises cash, fixed-interest, property and share investments. Their planner, Paula, provides some recommendations for them and they agree on a fund that is focused predominantly on growth of capital. The fund has an expected return of 14% and a standard deviation of 10%. Paula notes that the risk-free rate of interest on 90-day Treasury bonds is currently 7% and both Mark and Robyn agree that they are prepared to take some risks in achieving capital growth over the next 5 years. They know that they will both continue to work in the business for at least 5 more years before they consider selling it. However, they still want to maintain some measure of stability in their investment and do not want to subject their $300 000 completely to the wide swings of property and share investments. They discuss this matter with Paula. Their concern is in determining the proportion of their investment that they will place in the growth fund and the proportion they will place in risk-free assets, namely cash and fixed interest.

Robyn is relatively risk tolerant compared with Mark, and Paula has been able to determine that Robyn would be comfortable with her total portfolio having a standard deviation of 8%. Mark is relatively risk averse in contrast to Robyn and is more comfortable with a standard deviation in the portfolio of only 6%.

QUESTIONS

1. Using the formula for the risk–return relationship, calculate the expected return for the portfolio and the standard deviation for the portfolio.
2. Using the results from (1), substitute Robyn's risk tolerances to obtain the portions of funds to be included in risky assets (property and shares) and risk-free assets (cash and fixed interest).
3. Using the results from (1), substitute Marks's risk tolerances to obtain the portions of funds to be included in risky assets (property and shares) and risk-free assets (cash and fixed interest).
4. From the results calculated in your analysis, prepare a table as indicated below to summarise the asset allocation decision for Mark and Robyn.

	Cash and fixed interest $	Property and shares $	Standard deviation of portfolio
Robyn			
Mark			

References and further reading

ASIC 2010, MoneySmart, moneysmart.gov.au.

Barber, BM & Odean, T 2001, 'Boys will be boys: gender, overconfidence, and common stock investment', *Quarterly Journal of Economics*, February, pp. 261–92.

Bogle, J 1994, *Bogle on mutual funds*, Irwin, Chicago.

Brinson, GP, Singer, BD & Beebower, GL 1991, 'Determinants of portfolio performance II: an update', *Financial Analysis Journal*, May–June.

Gelber, F 2013, 'Get used to cyclical volatility and structural change', *Professional Planner*, April, pp. 42–3.

Gibson, R 2000, *Asset allocation — balancing financial risk*, Irwin, New York.

Graham, B 1949, *The intelligent investor*, HarperCollins, New York.

Higgins, E & Abey, A 2000, *Fortune strategy*, 2nd edn, Allen & Unwin, Sydney.

Kahneman, D & Tversky, A 1979, 'Prospect theory: an analysis of decision under risk', *Econometrica*, vol. 47, no. 2, pp. 263–92.

Malkiel, BG 2007, *A random walk down Wall Street*, 9th edn, Norton & Co., New York.

Olsen, RA 1998, 'Behavioural finance and its implications for stock-price volatility', *Financial Analysts Journal*, vol. 54, no. 2 (March–April), pp. 10–18.

Reilly, FK & Norton, EA 2006, *Investments*, 7th edn, Thomson South-Western, Mason.

Russell Investment Management Ltd 2004, 'Ten commandments of investing', russell.com.

Shiller, R 2000, *Irrational exuberance*, Princeton University Press.

Tversky, A & Kahneman, D 1982, 'Judgments of and by representativeness', in D Kahneman, P Slovic, & A Tversky (Eds). *Judgment under uncertainty: heuristics and biases*. Cambridge University Press, pp. 84–98.

Vanguard Investments 2007, 'Realistic sharemarket expectations', vanguard.com.au.

Vanguard Investments, vanguard.com.au.

5 Direct investment — fixed interest and shares

LEARNING OBJECTIVES

After studying this chapter, you should be able to:

1. distinguish between cash and fixed-interest securities
2. understand the nature of and participants in the fixed-interest investment market
3. understand the different forms of direct fixed-interest investments
4. appreciate the difference between discount and coupon securities and the effect of a change in interest rates
5. understand the nature of and participants in the share market
6. consider the influences on share prices
7. understand the capital asset pricing model (CAPM)
8. apply two basic valuation models — the Gordon dividend discount model and the price–earnings ratio — to value shares
9. appreciate the existence of other forms of direct investment.

CASE STUDY

Lila, now aged 28, graduated as a medical doctor and after 3 years working in a city-based hospital she decided to gain more medical and surgical experience by spending a year in the Antarctic as a medical officer on a government-sponsored scientific expedition. As a very busy person while working at the city hospital, Lila had not attended to all her personal financial affairs and her savings had accumulated to about $30 000 which she had sitting in a savings account held at her bank. In the week before she left, she transferred her savings to a 12-month term deposit at the same bank.

While Lila was in the Antarctic she gained the benefit of being in a low income-tax zone and much of her salary was saved because meals, accommodation and other items were supplied. So, at the end of her year away, she arrived home knowing that her savings had grown by another $100 000.

Lila now wants to offer her medical skills in a new field and has decided to work for the next 12 months in Africa with Médecins Sans Frontières. However, before she starts work she has decided to better order her finances and consults a financial planner about her savings and what alternatives she has. She is not interested in acquiring a property yet but wants her savings to grow more than the inflation level that eats into the value of her savings.

She consults Rebecca, a financial planner. Rebecca discusses matters of riskiness of investments with Lila and suggests that Lila is a reasonably conservative investor but willing to invest in shares that are in the top 50 companies. Lila's first thought is to maintain her term deposits with her bank but Rebecca suggests that instead of remaining as a customer of the bank she could become an owner of the bank by buying some bank shares.

Lila's situation raises some issues to consider about direct investments. These include:

- whether to hold fixed-interest securities directly
- whether to hold shares as the more risky securities directly
- the risks and opportunities of investing directly in the fixed-interest market
- the risks and opportunities of investing directly in the share market.

This chapter will explore these issues.

Introduction

This chapter deals with direct investment into two main asset classes — fixed-interest securities and equities or shares — and considers the investment issues of other forms of direct investment. Direct investment occurs when investors make their own decisions about where funds are ultimately placed, be it in fixed-interest deposit accounts, shares, property or some other form of asset. The opposite case occurs when investors place their funds with funds managers who use vehicles such as unit trusts and master funds to consolidate the funds of many investors and then invest the pooled funds according to their own stated investment strategies. A managed fixed-interest fund is a pooled investment in which the manager invests in a range of fixed-interest securities. Likewise, a share fund is where a manager invests in a range of shares and manages that portfolio by buying and selling shares to make a profit. A **master fund** is another form of managed fund where an administration manager receives funds from an investor and then invests that money into a number of other funds so that only one item of reporting to investors is carried out by the administration manager, that is, the administration manager provides investors with a consolidated report of all the different fund managers in which monies are invested for that investor.

master fund
an investment fund which enables investors to invest in a number of funds via the one fund; sometimes referred to as a fund of funds or as an administration fund manager

Most people have an account at a financial institution where some savings or working funds are kept. These may be savings or cheque accounts, or term deposits. Also, many people own shares directly such as in Telstra or the Commonwealth Bank as a result of subscribing for shares when government-owned institutions became public companies. Many people also own shares directly in a wide variety of companies in industries including mining, retailing, banking and pharmaceuticals as part of their portfolio mix of investments. Some people prefer to hold some investments in the form of coins, collectable items or works of art. These too are direct forms of investment and may have some different features even though investors hold such investments to achieve long-term capital appreciation. For example, collectables differ, in an investment sense, in that they often suffer from a market that has too few buyers (otherwise known as a 'thin' market); they are relatively scarce; and they may suffer from theft or deterioration.

Each section of the chapter attempts to give an appreciation of the nature and structure of the relevant markets, the participants in the markets and the products on offer.

LO 1 Cash and fixed-interest securities

Deregulation of the Australian financial system accelerated in the early 1980s in response to global financial forces. Deregulation was the removal of many legal controls and regulations which had stifled innovation and hindered the adjustment mechanisms and operations of the various financial markets. For example, the price of the Australian dollar, the exchange rate, had been fixed in terms of other currencies until December 1983 and the government managed its price by making periodic adjustments. After the floating of the dollar, the operations of the various foreign exchange markets set the price of the Australian dollar according to market forces. Volatility increased. The value of the Australian dollar in terms of the US dollar, for example, fell from the US80–90 cents range in the early 1980s to less than US50 cents in the early 2000s and experienced rises and falls over the next few years. It rose to a high point of US110.55 cents in July 2011, retreating to US106 cents in 2012 and further to US96 cents in June 2013.

Deregulation does not mean that the economy is entirely left to the market with no regulation at all of the financial system. There is still plenty of regulation or at least prudential oversight. Bodies such as the Reserve Bank of Australia (RBA), the Australian Securities and Investments Commission (ASIC) and the Australian Prudential Regulation Authority (APRA) are concerned with the stability of the economy, the achievement of macroeconomic goals and the maintenance of public confidence in the financial system and its institutions so that investors and others can participate in the financial system in a well-informed and confident fashion.

Partly as a consequence of deregulation, the 1980s saw rapid growth in all forms of debt in Australia, with both individual and corporate borrowers participating in the rush.

The dollar value of debt increased markedly. However, more importantly from the point of view of the investor, the range of fixed-interest products available to those people who wanted to place funds in these types of investments increased rapidly.

Before reviewing the types of products available to investors looking for fixed-interest rates underlying the income they earn on their funds, we need to explain the concept of cash and to develop an understanding of the participants in the fixed-interest markets and how all the pieces in the markets fit together.

Cash as a term in finance has many meanings. Cash can be the money in our pockets or purses, or the money held under our mattresses. This sort of cash earns no return. No one pays us a rent for the use of the money. Cash held in a short-term account, on the other hand, can be just as available and we can arrange our affairs so that people pay us for the use of those funds. Large investors typically are paid interest on funds lent overnight. Thus, the overnight rate of interest is the 'cash' rate. Accordingly, we will think of cash as a short-term loan rather than as coins or notes in our pockets.

Fixed interest is a term used to describe an investment whether it be for a short or longer time frame where a set rate of interest is agreed on for the fixed period of time of the investment. So, typically a bank may offer a term deposit at say, 5.3% p.a. for a 2-year time frame. The contract thus means that the investor lends money to the bank for 2 years in return for an interest return of 5.3% p.a. with the return of both interest paid either after each year or at the end of two years plus the return of the initial capital sum invested. Fixed interest investments may take some variation of the above and also be offered by different institutions seeking to borrow money from the public.

LO 2 The nature of and participants in the fixed-interest market

The nature of fixed-interest markets and products

The essential features of most fixed-interest securities are that:

1. the interest rate, which is the price of the loan of the funds to the borrower, is set at the start of the loan period
2. the face value (the principal) is fixed.

Interest is payable at the start, during or end of the period.

The interest rate on fixed-interest securities varies according to the maturity of the debt and the perceived riskiness of the borrower. All interest rates stem from the base of the *cash rate*, which is the interest rate paid on money lent between the commercial banks overnight. Margins are then added to compensate lenders for increased risk and time until maturity. However, we also need to consider the difference between the cash rate and the real cash rate after allowing for inflation. We are aware that the rate of inflation is more commonly measured by the Consumer Price Index (CPI) which means that $100 in the future will not buy as much as $100 today. So, we need to distinguish between the nominal rate of interest and the real rate of interest.

The general formula for converting a nominal cash amount at a future period t to a real cash amount is:

$$\text{Real cash amount } t = \frac{\text{Nominal cash amount}}{(1 + \text{Inflation rate})^t}$$

This means that if you were to invest $1000 in a 10-year fixed-term investment at 10% p.a. then when the term deposit matures your final payment would be $1100 ($1000 + $100) but, with an inflation rate of, say, 5% per year, the real value of that final payment in 10 years would be $675.30 i.e. the nominal amount of $10 000 plus $100 discounted by 5% for 10 years ($1100/1.05[10]). The formula for calculating the real rate of return is:

$$1 + R \text{ real} = \frac{1 + R \text{ nom}}{1 + \text{Inflation rate}}$$

Thus, in the example above:

$$1.0476 = \frac{1.10}{1.05}$$

In other words, if the interest rate is 10% and the inflation rate is 5%, you are only better off by 4.67% at the end of the year.

Figure 5.1 shows the cash rate and the real cash rate after allowing for inflation over the period 1993 to 2013. The cash rate is the interest rate which the RBA directly manages through its management of money supply. The RBA buys or sells securities to inject or withdraw funds from the Australian economy so that appropriate amounts of cash are available on a daily basis in the economy. The board of the RBA determines when the cash rate should change. For example, during 2006–07, the board announced two cash rate increases of 0.25% from 5.75% in order to damp down activity in the economy and to try to avert increasing inflation. On each occasion, the cash rate quickly settled on or near the new target as the managed supply of funds was closely matched with expected demand. In the period 2007–09, the RBA dropped the cash rate to encourage people to borrow and to stimulate the economy, but in 2009–10, the RBA sought to gradually increase rates again to contain inflation. However, in 2011 the RBA again reduced the cash rate from 5% to 3% to attempt to stimulate the economy once more.

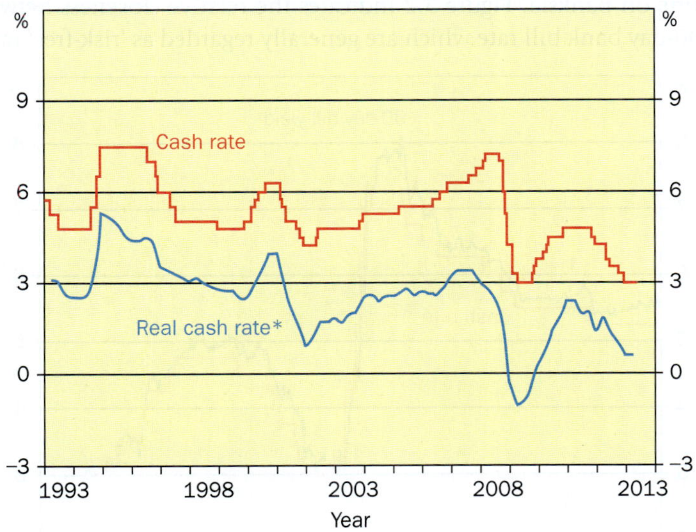

FIGURE 5.1
Australian cash rate and real cash rate (monthly)
* Real cash rate calculated using quarterly weighted-median inflation rate.
Source: RBA 2013, page 18.

Participants in the fixed-interest markets

The participants in the fixed-interest markets are principally the authorised deposit-taking institutions (ADIs) (including the banks and the non-bank financial institutions (NBFIs)), other finance sector firms such as insurance companies and funds managers, private individuals, trading companies ('ordinary businesses') and governments. Some of these participants come to the markets as lenders, some as borrowers and some as both. Many of the financial institutions act as intermediaries; that is, they facilitate the operation of the markets by, for example, collecting and pooling funds for investment in large projects or by matching lenders with borrowers.

It is worthwhile to note that, increasingly, the old divisions between market participants are becoming blurred. Twenty years ago, a bank housed itself in buildings of typical architecture that we knew meant a 'bank'; and it offered opening times that were somewhat restricted. Now, 'banks' or at least banking services can be found in supermarkets, department stores, fruit shops, petrol outlets, holes in brick walls and many other places, and service is available 24 hours a day, 7 days a week. Additionally, banking services are available from home or elsewhere via telephone or the internet.

LO 3 Different forms of fixed-interest investments

The terms of fixed-interest investments can vary from 'at call' (immediate access) to very long maturities of perhaps up to 20 years. There is a good deal of interdependence between all the instruments available in the markets, and this interdependence tends to keep interest rates reasonably tightly aligned, even though there may be significant differences in perceived riskiness and maturities. Some fixed-interest providers may offer higher rates of return to investors because the providers may use the funds for riskier projects such as lending to property developers. In these cases the rate of interest may be 3–4% higher than offered by the banking sector, indicating the relative riskiness of such projects — on occasions the rates of interest have failed to be met and a failure to repay the capital has occurred. A recent failure of the non-bank lending sector is Banksia Securities where investors may only receive 70–80 cents of every dollar invested. Search the internet for news reports on Banksia. Figure 5.2 indicates the relative closeness between the cash rate and the 90-day bank bill rate which are generally regarded as 'risk-free' rates of return.

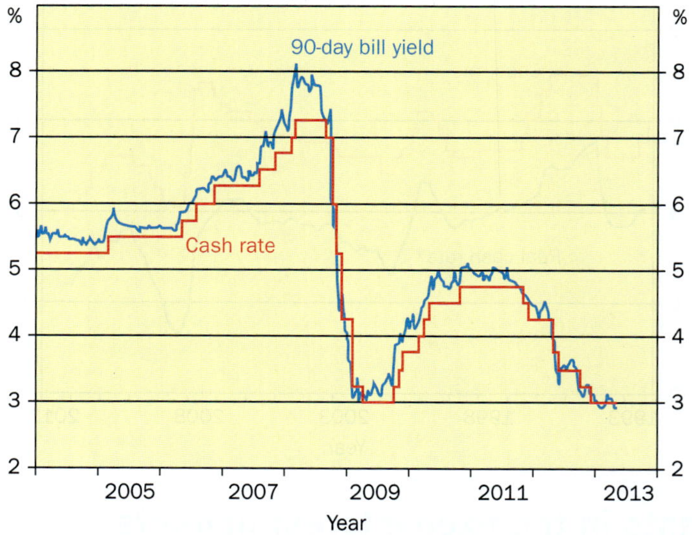

FIGURE 5.2
Comparison between the cash rate and the 90-day bank bill rate
Source: RBA 2013, page 18.

Figure 5.3 indicates the variation between a longer-dated bond (10 years) and the cash rate to illustrate the difference between the interest rates. To help clarify the nature of trading being undertaken, the fixed-interest markets are normally divided into two major classes — the *money market* where securities of up to one year's duration are traded and the *capital market* where longer-dated securities are traded.

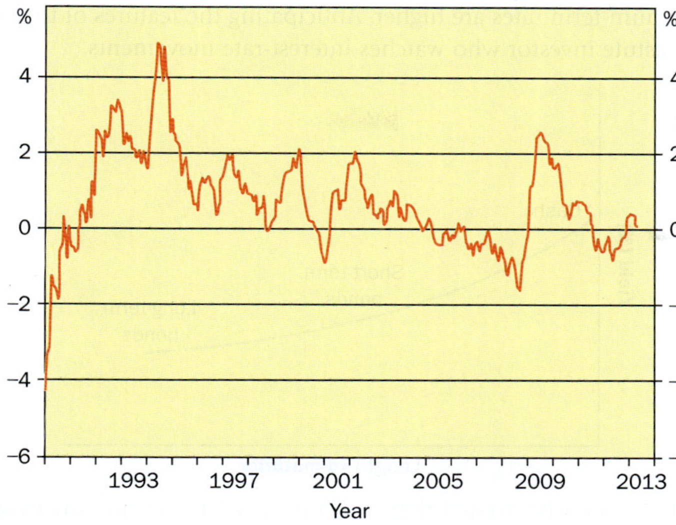

FIGURE 5.3
Spread between the Australian 10-year bond yield and the cash rate
Source: RBA 2013, page 20.

Longer maturity securities usually, but not always, offer a higher interest rate, because there can be higher risk attached to longer periods. Instruments with perceived higher risk such as personal unsecured loans attract higher interest rates than a bank-accepted (guaranteed) commercial bill or a government loan. The **yield curve** is a graph of interest rates related to maturity. Figure 5.4 shows the yield curve in a normal state which indicates that, generally, longer term investments attract a higher rate of interest. You will note that it is an upward sloping curve with shorter term securities offering a lower interest rate whereas longer term securities show an increasing yield.

yield curve
a line representing the interest rates for different time frames of investment

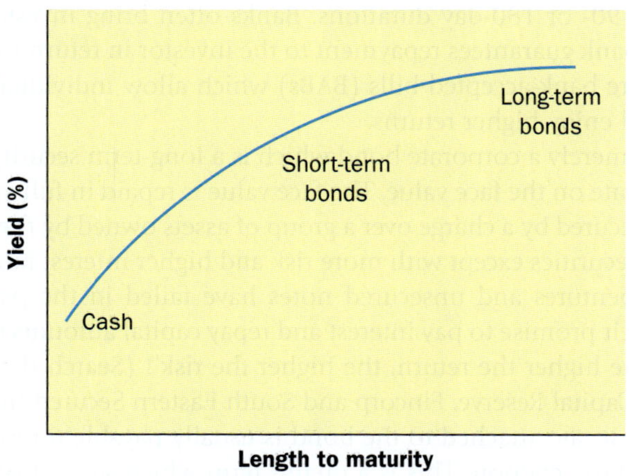

FIGURE 5.4
Normal yield curve

However, the yield curve does not always have a positive slope. Extreme monetary conditions such as a sudden change in monetary policy can affect the situation.

Figure 5.5 (overleaf) shows the yield curve for certain economic conditions where the curve takes on an inverted or downward sloping shape. This indicates that short-term interest rates are higher than long-term rates. This may occur when the RBA raises interest rates in the short term to curtail an inflationary trend. A higher interest rate for the short term will encourage people to deposit money in a bank and discourage people from borrowing, thereby reducing the pressure on prices. At other times the yield curve may be flat when short-term and long-term rates are virtually the same, and a humped yield curve may occur when medium-term rates are higher. Anticipating the features of the business cycle can reward the astute investor who watches interest-rate movements.

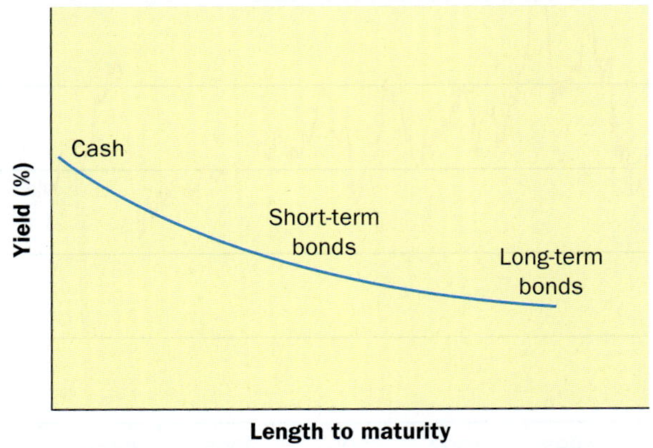

FIGURE 5.5
Inverse yield curve

Even though it could be argued that accounts at ADIs are not strictly direct investments, they act like direct investments. That is, current (cheque) and savings accounts at ADIs give investors immediate access to their funds, but very little return in the way of interest payments. Many of these products pay interest at between 0.00 and 1.0%.

Term deposits are available at ADIs for varying terms from 1 month to several years. The interest rates offered usually increase with maturity, although expectations that interest rates may fall will dampen the marginal increases in rates as terms increase. Because of the high credit ratings that Australian ADIs enjoy, there is little risk associated with these products.

Investors wanting higher risk and returns may invest in commercial bills, corporate debentures and unsecured notes offered by finance companies and others. Commercial bills usually have 90- or 180-day durations. Banks often bring investors and borrowers together and the bank guarantees repayment to the investor in return for a fee paid by the borrower. These are bank-accepted bills (BABs) which allow individual investors to take on higher risk and enjoy higher returns.

A debenture is merely a corporate bond which is a long-term security that pays regular interest at a fixed rate on the face value. The face value is repaid in full at maturity. Debentures are usually secured by a charge over a group of assets owned by the issuer. Unsecured notes are similar securities except with more risk and higher interest rates. However, some firms offering debentures and unsecured notes have failed in the past and have been unable to meet their promise to pay interest and repay capital amounts to investors. Recall the old maxim 'the higher the return, the higher the risk'! (Search the internet for news about Australian Capital Reserve, Fincorp and South Eastern Secured Investments Ltd.)

The fixed-interest rate attached to the bond is usually payable 6-monthly or annually, and is often called the coupon. This is a quaint term which stems from the old practice of having coupons (tickets or receipts) printed on the physical bond. When a periodic interest payment was made, the coupon was cut from the bond which the lender held and was given to the borrower as proof that the payment had been made. The coupon was thus a receipt for the payment.

Investors with reasonably large sums may invest directly in bonds offered by governments, semi-government authorities and corporations. In Australia, bonds offered by the government (Commonwealth government securities or CGS) enjoy very good security ratings, and the state governments and semi-government authorities have slightly lower, but still good, risk ratings. The Commonwealth Government in recent years has made it a budget strategy to repay outstanding debt, so that it has no net debt. As a result, access to Commonwealth bonds on issue has been limited; essentially only a few financial institutions hold CGS. Investors wanting to hold bonds have been forced to the corporate bond market. Corporate bonds have increased in popularity over the last decade as figures 5.6 and 5.7 show. Only a few years ago the Commonwealth Government introduced retail bonds to small-scale investors with a nominal value of $1000. Two types are available — Treasury Fixed Coupon Bonds and Treasury Capital Indexed Bonds — and investors may purchase bonds in lots of $1000 up to $250 000. They were available via the RBA until May 2013 and may now be purchased on the Australian Securities Exchange (ASX). These bonds are now known as exchange-traded AGBs (Australian government bonds) and can be purchased as either exchange-traded Treasury bonds or exchange-traded Treasury indexed bonds. They are purchased in the form of CHESS depository interests (CDIs).

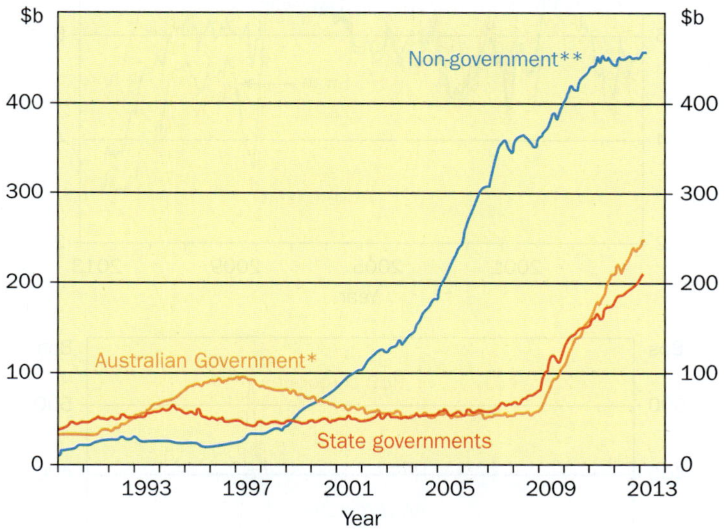

FIGURE 5.6
Australian bonds on issue (monthly)
*Excludes bonds purchased by the Australian Government.
**Excludes ADIs' self-securitisations, includes government guaranteed bonds.
Source: RBA 2013, page 25 top left.

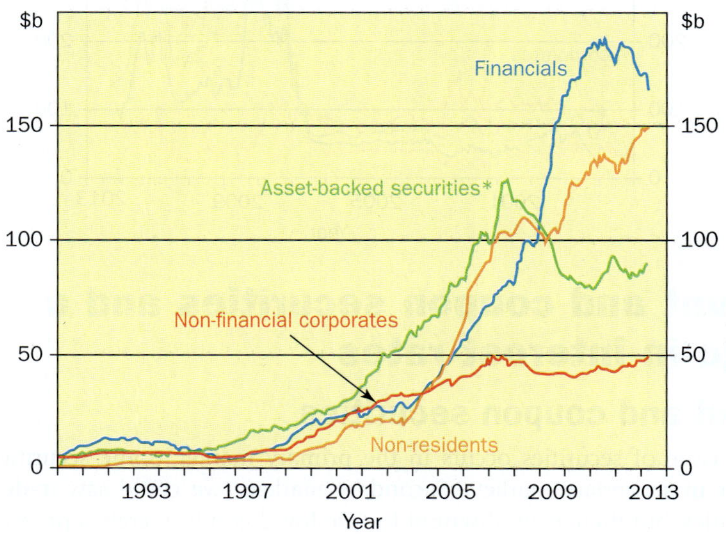

FIGURE 5.7
Non-government Australian bonds on issue (monthly)
*Excludes ADIs' self-securitisations
Source: RBA 2013, page 25 top right.

The yield from corporate bonds is higher than that from CGS, as can be seen in figure 5.8. Corporate bonds are rated for risk, with the lowest risks rated AAA and the highest BBB. The highest risk corporations must offer investors greater compensation, as figure 5.9 shows. Many banks and large financial institutions offer securities which have hybrid income qualities between fixed interest and the variable returns of equities. These are called floating rate notes (FRNs). These securities (FRNs) have a floating interest rate normally set 0.75% to 3% above the bank bill rate (to compensate for the higher risks involved) with interest paid quarterly and no fixed maturity date. They are listed on the Australian Securities Exchange.

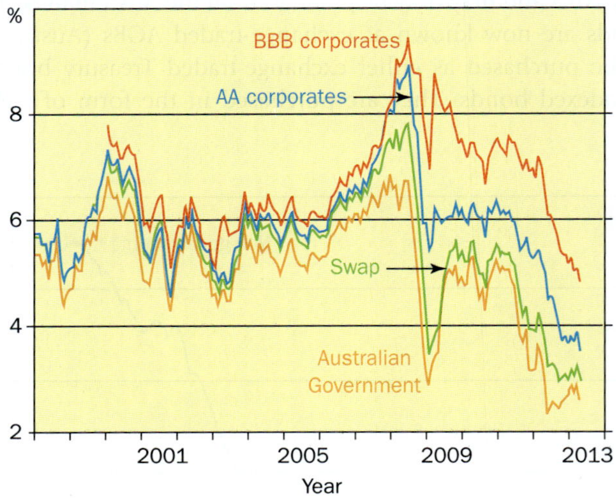

FIGURE 5.8 Australian corporate bond yields (monthly)

Note: Yields on bonds issued by the Australian Government and swap rates are 3-year maturities. Corporate bond yields are a weighted average of bonds with remaining maturities of 1 to 5 years; they include financial and non-financial corporates.

Source: RBA 2013, page 21 top right.

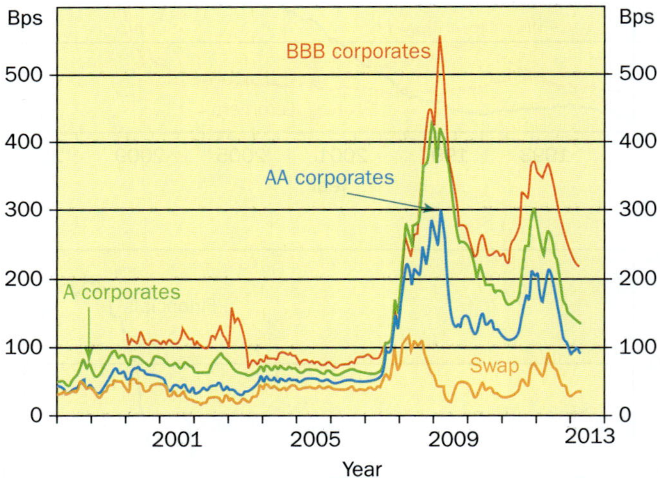

FIGURE 5.9 Australian corporate bond spreads (spread over government yields; monthly)

Note: Swap spreads are for 3-year maturity. Corporate bond spreads are a weighted average of bonds with remaining maturities of 1 to 5 years; they include financial and non-financial corporates.

Source: RBA 2013, page 21 bottom right.

LO 4

Discount and coupon securities and a change in interest rates

Discount and coupon securities

The initial issue of securities occurs in the primary market. Some securities are easily traded later in secondary markets. Secondary markets, we could say, trade in second-hand securities, but there is no discount for pre-loved goods, merely a price agreed upon according to quality. Secondary markets are very important to the efficient operation of the financial system. They give liquidity (the ability to convert easily into cash) to markets, promote confidence and provide a price-setting mechanism.

Accounts at ADIs such as current, savings and cash management accounts and term deposits are untraded products. The value of an individual's account changes only in response to additional deposits, withdrawals, the crediting of interest or the payment of fees. However, instruments such as BABs are discount securities in that their selling prices are less than (at a discount to) their face values. They are often traded. The difference between the selling price and the face value, which is redeemable at maturity, is the interest payment. Let us review the two main types of fixed-interest securities and examine the methods by which we can value the fixed-interest security. For simplicity sake we will refer to the fixed-interest securities as bonds.

First, we will consider the bonds that do not pay a coupon or interest payment but are referred to as **discount securities**. In other words, the face value of the bond is sold at a discount so that the amount paid on maturity is the face value of the bond. The formula to value the bond is based on the present value of the face value at the given rate of interest at the time of investment. Hence

discount securities fixed-interest securities are priced to include interest which is not paid in separate payments

$$V = \frac{FV}{(1 + r)^n}$$

where V = present value of the bond
FV = maturity or face value of the bond
r = interest rate
n = number of periods

ILLUSTRATIVE EXAMPLE 5.1

Imagine a $100 000 discount security with 3 years to maturity that may sell for $82 270.25. That is, the investor (buyer of the security) pays $82 270.25 to the borrower (issuer of the security). At the expiry of 3 years, the borrower pays the investor $100 000 in return for the note. In this case, interest is payable either upfront (the lender does not give the borrower the whole $100 000) or at maturity (the lender has lent $82 270.25 and gets $100 000 at the end of the period). The security in this example is thus sold at a discount on the face value of $100 000. An investor who requires a rate of return greater than 5% p.a. would pay less than $82 270.25. If the purchase price was greater than $82 270.25 then the investor would achieve a return of less than 5%. Remember from chapter 2, the method for calculating the price of a discount security is merely an application of the formula for the present value of a future sum.

To continue this example for an investor that has a much shorter time frame, suppose that an investor has a sum of money, say $100 000, that they want to invest for only 90 days. Assume an interest rate of 7% p.a. In this case, the purchase price is simply:

$$\text{Purchase price} = \frac{\text{Face value}}{1 + \left(\text{Interest rate} \times \dfrac{90}{365}\right)}$$

$$= \frac{\$100\,000}{1 + \left(0.07 \times \dfrac{90}{365}\right)}$$

$$= \$98\,303.26$$

»

»

And, if the investor did not know what the interest rate was when the financial institution offered a price for the $100 000 in 90 days then the investor's return on the investment is given by:

$$\text{Return on investment} = \frac{\text{Face value} - \text{Purchase price}}{\text{Purchase price}} \times \frac{365}{90} \times \frac{100}{1}$$

$$= \frac{\$100\,000 - \$98\,303.26}{\$98\,303.26} \times \frac{36\,500}{90}$$

$$= 7\%$$

coupon securities fixed-interest securities that pay interest at set periods of time during the life of the contract

Second, we need to consider the form of fixed-interest security that pays a coupon or interest payment at predetermined times. These are known as **coupon securities**. Such fixed-interest securities are more common and are often traded. They are initially issued in the primary market by the borrower, but may be sold later by the lender in the secondary market. Each time such a security is sold, the traders involved make a judgement about interest rates in general and the riskiness of the particular instrument. Regardless of the coupon rate, the price settled on at each trade governs the effective interest rate of the instrument. This is because the dollar value of the interest payments is fixed. Thus, the yield or effective interest rate depends on the price of invested funds. The price of a bond is calculated using the formulae for the present value of both a future sum and of an annuity.

ILLUSTRATIVE EXAMPLE 5.2

As an example, in 2010, a $100 000 bond is due in 2 years with a 5% coupon. It pays $2500 every 6 months for the remainder of its 2-year life. In addition, the bond issuer promises to repay the $100 000 principal at maturity in 2012.

The valuation of the bond is the present value (PV) of the interest payments (an annuity) and the PV of the principal due in 2 years. If the rate of return required by an investor is 6% then the PV of the annuity payments is $9292.82 and the PV of the future lump sum is $88 849.40. If we add the two together we get the sum of $98 142.22, which represents the present value of the bond at 6% and that is how much the investor requiring 6% will pay to acquire the bond paying coupons at 5% for 2 years. The investor will offer to pay less if an investor requires a higher rate of return, say 7%.

This calculation is based on a combination of the PV of a stream of interest payments and the PV of the face value of the bond. The formula to produce the above figures is thus:

$$PV = \frac{PMT}{i} \times \left[1 - \frac{1}{(1+i)^n}\right]$$

plus

$$PV = \frac{FV}{(1+i)^n}$$

Substituting the data into the equations:

$$PV = \frac{2500}{0.03} \times \left[1 - \frac{1}{(1 + 0.03)^4}\right]$$
$$= \$83\,333 \times 0.1115$$
$$= \$9292.82$$

plus

$$PV = \frac{\$100\,000}{(1 + 0.03)^4}$$
$$= \$88\,849.40$$

Total:

$$= \$98\,142.22$$

Accessing fixed-interest markets

Investors wanting access to these markets can approach many types of firms operating in the finance industry. ADIs offer current, savings, cash management and term accounts. Some institutions now offer a slightly higher-interest and fee-free internet account which attracts many investors.

Finance companies offer debentures and unsecured notes direct to the public. Semi-government and government notes and bonds are traded via telephone by professional bond dealers and Commonwealth bonds may be purchased directly via the ASX. Investors may thus gain access to these securities by purchasing in the secondary market or by buying when the securities are first issued.

The effect of a change in interest rates

We may make an assumption that most investors are risk averse, but that investors differ in their degrees of risk averseness. Apart from innate forces which dictate a person's tolerance to risk, it would be reasonable to expect risk tolerance to be governed by a person's age, income, wealth, years to retirement, past financial experiences and perhaps some other factors. For example, young people are often happy to take on more risk than older people. Youth are generally less risk averse, they have often had less chance of experiencing financial losses when investments have 'gone wrong', and they have usually more years to increase wealth before retirement and thus have more time to recover should things go awry. A retired person in their mid-sixties on the other hand may decide that fixed-interest investments will provide more security for their retirement than the risk of investing in shares that may not recover for some years after a share market crash.

Fixed-interest products appeal to more risk-averse people. There are two aspects of this which are worth consideration. First, there is the guarantee of the interest payment at a given level, so long as the borrower remains solvent. (*Note:* ASIC researched the profile of debenture holders to understand how better to protect small investors. They found that a typical investor was aged in their mid-sixties and was attracted by the perceived security of the rate of interest and capital protection of the investments.) However, generally there is usually little uncertainty about the income from these products. Secondly, many of these products are capital stable. That is, the value of the capital remains fixed, and there may be little chance of the loss of capital. However, investment in traded securities such as bonds remains an exception to this rule. A rise in the general level of interest rates will normally promote decreases in the capital values of traded fixed-interest securities. Conversely, holders of these securities will enjoy an appreciation in capital values when the general level of interest rates falls.

As an example, let us consider this situation. Suppose Wei buys a discount bond for $10 000 that will pay $15 000 in 5 years. The expected return is equivalent to an interest rate of 10%. However, imagine that Wei must sell the bond on the market in 2 years because she has an emergency need for the money, and the prevailing interest rates in 2 years have gone up to 15%. Wei will not be able to sell the bond for $12 000 which would represent the original 10% yield over the 2 years. A purchaser, Mo would offer Wei only the present value of the bond based on the maturity value and the present value of the remaining interest payment stream based on the 15% interest rate. If Mo paid $12 000 then he would get a return of only about 8% which is about half of the prevailing interest rate. The only way Wei could sell the bond is to lower the price so that the yield is equal to the prevailing interest rate. If she offered the bond at $10 400 this means that Mo would earn $4600 over the remaining 3 years to maturity which represents a yield of 15%. So Wei would make a return of only $400 or 2% instead of the 10% that she wanted when she bought the bond 2 years before.

This situation is an example of the fact that a very poor return may be made on a bond investment if a person has to sell prior to the maturity date. Then again, if the prevailing interest rates fall below the coupon rate, a seller can also make a gain on the sale. To follow Wei's example further, if the prevailing interest rates had fallen to 5% when Wei needed the money and had to sell the bond and Mo was able to buy the bond from Wei for $10 400, the bond would continue to pay coupons at 10%. If Mo then held the bond to maturity to obtain the $15 000 then this represents the return on his acquisition of the bond at the equivalent of 15% despite the fall in the prevailing interest rate. Of course, if Wei realised the impact on the bond value of the fall in interest rates, Mo would have to pay more than $10 400 to acquire the bond from Wei (as it would be in high demand) which would lower the return on his investment to equal the prevailing interest rate.

Notwithstanding the fact that more risk-averse investors are drawn to fixed-interest products, it is normal for many investors to hold some proportion of fixed-interest securities in their portfolios. The proportions will vary according to their own investment strategy. In addition to the funds which investors keep in their investment portfolios, many people also have separate accounts where they keep working funds and precautionary balances. Working funds for day-to-day living expenses may be kept in a current account with cheque and debit card access, and precautionary balances are kept in an easily accessed account such as a cash management trust (CMT). Precautionary balances are sums of money that people keep for emergencies. Although these working funds and precautionary balances may not be thought of as part of investment nest eggs, they do, in fact, increase the proportion of net wealth invested in fixed-interest products.

LO 5 The nature of and participants in the share market

Shares are also known as 'equities' in Australia and 'common stock' in the United States. Investment in equities or shares in Australia has become markedly more common in the last two decades. The increase in popularity is due to the almost unbroken steady climb in average share prices since the crash in October 1987 and the spate of privatisations of government businesses until the global financial crisis of 2007–13. The steep decline in prices following the September 11, 2001 terrorist attacks in the United States was quickly reversed by returning confidence and rising demand but was then washed away by the fall in global markets when the impact of the credit crisis across the world caused many investors to sell shares and withdraw to the safety of cash. The ASX200 has not yet reached its previous high point of 6829 in November 2007 even though the US stock market has overtaken its previous high point recorded prior to the global financial crisis.

Initial public offers (IPOs) of shares, including those issued in privatisations of government businesses, are often, but not always, a way of enjoying good capital gains. One reason for this is that, before a business is subjected to the scrutiny of the whole of the investing public, it is difficult to put a realistic price on the whole of it and consequently on its shares. IPOs are thus often underpriced in order to ensure that the 'float' of the business is a success.

initial public offer (IPO)
the first offer of shares to the public; sometimes referred to as a 'float' of shares

Another factor which has been important in government floats is that members of the government, who ultimately decide on the initial price of these shares, are unwilling to bear the electoral backlash that would ensue if shares were priced so highly that they traded on the market initially at a discount to the offer price. Even though initial investors need not sell and crystallise such losses, there would still be public protest. Take the case of Telstra, for example. The issue price for the second tranche at $7.80 per share was overoptimistic following the successful first sale of shares at $3.30 per share. For some years, prices in the secondary market for Telstra shares had been consistently about $3 lower than the offer price. Investors were not pleased. The third tranche was offered in two parts at a total price of $3.60. In December 2010, Telstra shares were trading at around $2.80 per share — far below the price paid by those who bought in the second tranche and below the price paid by those in the first and third tranches. But, by June 2013 Telstra's share price had risen to $4.70, a gain of 68% since December 2010.

The nature of the share market

Shares may be sold privately or by brokers who specialise in non-listed shares. However, the bulk of trading occurs on stock exchanges. In Australia, the ASX currently has a virtual monopoly on the trading of listed shares, but there are a couple of minor markets, such as the National Stock Exchange of Australia (formerly the Stock Exchange of Newcastle), which have only a fraction of the capitalisation and turnover of the ASX.

The ASX requires companies to satisfy its regulations before they can be listed and traded. For example, companies are required to meet the continuous disclosure rules so that the market can be fully informed of any significant events that might affect the decision making of investors about holding shares in that particular company. The market is clearly divided between the industrial sector companies in areas such as building, household goods, food processing, banks, transport, media and insurance (which collectively account for about 80% of the market) and the resources sector. Most trading is executed by members of the exchange on behalf of themselves or their clients.

The market price of traded shares is determined by the interaction of demand and supply, and the market is highly susceptible to movements of capital to and from Australia. There is normally a reaction in the value of Australian shares when there is a strong movement in prices on the United States' Wall Street. Additionally, the value of the Australian dollar and international demand for Australian products (commodities in particular) are major determinants of the strength of the market. Figures 5.10 and 5.11 show how the Australian market (ASX 200) has moved in relation to the US and world markets (S&P 500 and MSCI World, respectively). Figure 5.10 shows the changes since 1994 to 2013.

Each publicly listed company has a limited amount of shares which it can issue. This amount is specified in the company's constitution, and is known as authorised or nominal capital. This amount can be varied only with the approval of a majority of shareholders. At any point in time the amount issued to shareholders need not be the total authorised capital. Once issued in the primary market, the issued shares may then be traded in the secondary market. The forms in which capital may be raised are determined by the *Corporations Act 2001*.

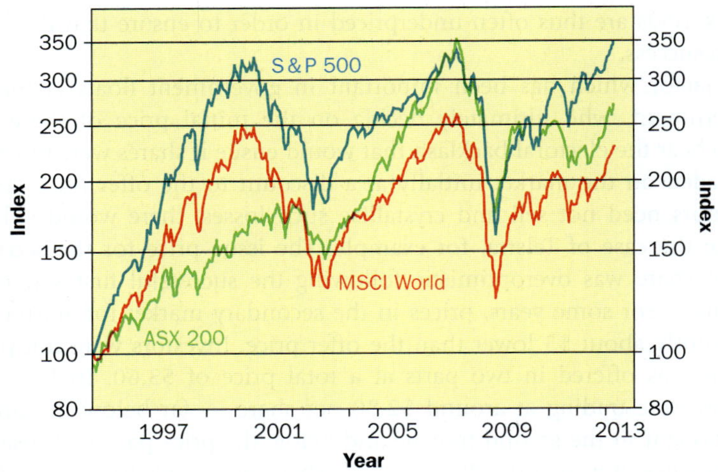

FIGURE 5.10
Australian, US and world share price indices, monthly (end December 1994 = 100)
Source: RBA 2013, page 23 top left.

Authorised capital may be issued in any of the following forms. Ordinary shares are the most common class of shares. Holders of ordinary shares share the ownership of the corporation with other holders of ordinary shares. Holders share the profits by receiving cash dividends or more shares in lieu of cash, or (theoretically) an increase in the value of each share where profits are not distributed. Holders also share losses through reductions in share prices or underlying value. Shareholders of limited liability companies risk only the amount of their investment; they cannot be made to repay debt owed by an insolvent corporation.

Contributing shares are not completely paid up when they are initially issued. A company may not require full payment immediately if it does not need the funds, and this makes the issue more attractive to potential investors. When the full amount owing has been called (requested) and paid, these shares become fully paid ordinary shares. As a variation of this theme, many of the large privatisations such as Telstra and Suncorp-Metway used a two-stage process to issue shares in an attractive manner to small shareholders. These have involved a fixed first payment which attracts either a dividend or interest, followed by a further payment, either fixed or set by the market, to complete the sale of each share.

Preference shares may be ordinary, cumulative, participating or redeemable. Preference shareholders have preference over ordinary shareholders with respect to claims on profits, dividends and the firm's assets should the company be wound up or liquidated. Holders of these shares usually have limited voting rights and shares have a fixed rate of return or dividend.

Characteristics of the various types of preference shares differ. Ordinary preference shareholders have a claim only on profits for a particular year. Cumulative shareholders retain priority over profits until all outstanding dividends have been paid. Participating holders have priority for dividends and have access to additional dividends after ordinary shareholders have been paid. Redeemable holders can have their shares bought back or redeemed at their face value at the discretion of the company at a certain date.

Deferred dividend shares are shares issued on the understanding that dividends will not be payable until a future specified date when a particular project becomes profitable. These shares usually trade at less than ordinary shares to reflect the dividend difference or the time shareholders must wait before they can expect to receive a dividend. In addition, corporations may issue options with varying conditions which grant rights to the holders to purchase new shares in the future.

Participants in the share market

The participants in the share market are listed corporations, investors and brokers who facilitate trading. Corporations are mainly interested in the primary role of the share market as a means of raising capital. They also use the secondary market to purchase shares in other companies, either for reasons of strategic alliance, takeover or for investment purposes. The latter is particularly true of institutional investors, such as managed funds, who play a critical role in the secondary market. Figure 5.11 shows equity (share) raisings by way of IPOs and other means (as well as buybacks where firms buy back, either on- or off-market, their own shares). Figure 5.12 (overleaf) shows quarterly net equity raisings 2001–13.

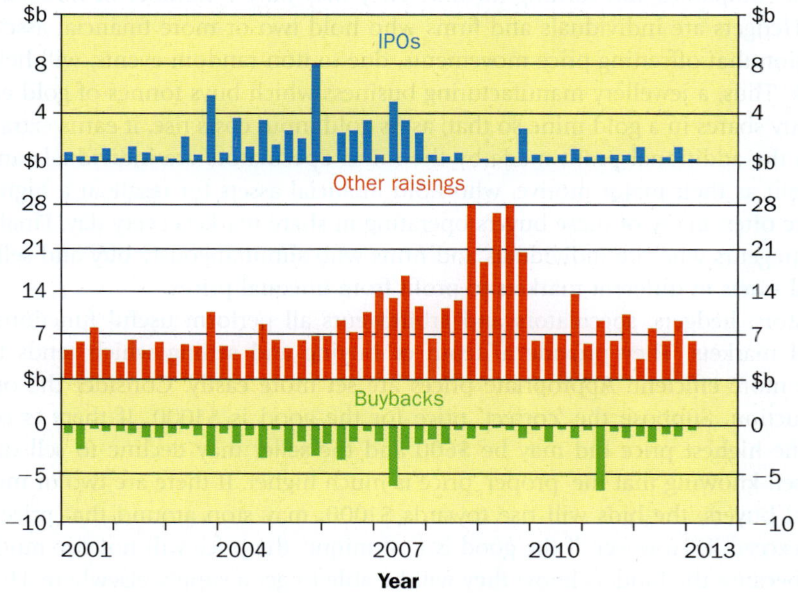

FIGURE 5.11
Equity raisings by way of IPO (all companies, quarterly)
Source: RBA 2013, page 26 top left.

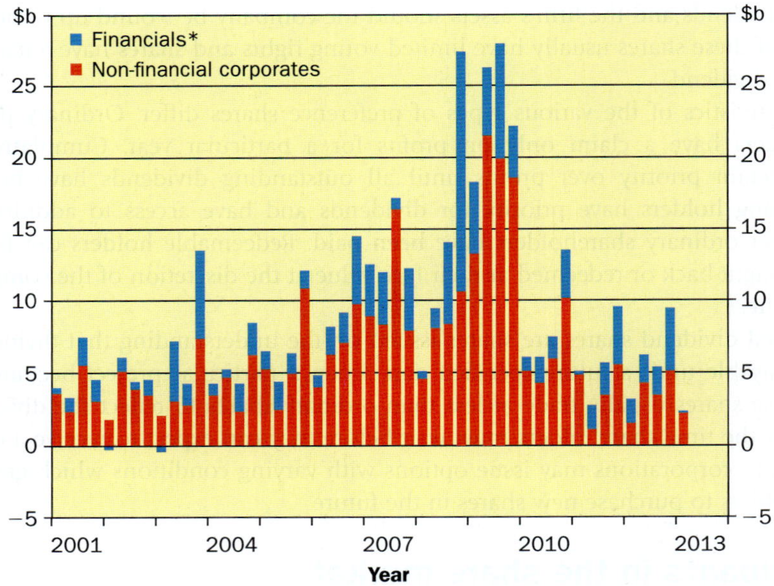

FIGURE 5.12
Quarterly net equity raisings 2001–13
*Includes banks and non-bank financials
Source: RBA 2013, page 26 bottom left.

Investors, as we know, are individuals and firms that buy and sell financial assets mainly for the income they receive from holding the asset. The Australian shareholder survey in 2010 found that typical shareholders were about 66% male and 34% female (up from 30% in 2008), tertiary educated and with household incomes exceeding $100 000. The survey also found that the peak age group for shareholding is the 55–64 age group and the 2010 study also found that there was a high level of share ownership among Australians over 65 increasing from 41% to 51% from the study conducted in 2008 (ASX 2011).

Purchasers of shares are not always involved for the purposes of participating in ownership of companies and earning income. They may have a number of different motivations. Hedgers are individuals and firms who hold two or more financial assets in the expectation that offsetting price movements, due to non-random events, will help eliminate risk. Thus, a jewellery manufacturing business which buys tonnes of gold each year might buy shares in a gold mine so that, as its gold input costs rise, it earns extra income through the additional profit made by the mine. Speculators are individuals and firms, with profit as their major motive, who hold financial assets for resale at a higher price. There are often many of these buyers operating in share markets every day. Finally, there are arbitrageurs who are individuals and firms who simultaneously buy and sell similar financial assets in different markets to profit from unequal prices.

Investors, hedgers, speculators and arbitrageurs all perform useful functions within financial markets. They provide a depth of buying and selling which tends to make markets more efficient. Appropriate prices are set more easily. Consider the operation of an auction. Suppose the 'correct' price for the good is $1000. If there is only one buyer, the highest price bid may be $600 and the seller may decline to sell or, if desperate, sell knowing that the 'proper' price is much higher. If there are two or more keen potential buyers, the bids will rise towards $1000, may stop around that price or may indeed exceed it. However, if the good is not unique, the price will not rise much above $1000, because the bidders know they will be able to get a supply elsewhere. Hence, the more depth there is in a market on both the buying and selling sides, the more accurate is the price-setting mechanism.

LO 6 The influences on share prices

Analysis of share prices

Market forces determine the prices of shares when traded in the secondary market. From 2000 to 2007 Australian share prices rose quite steeply as earnings increased and funds poured into the share market by superannuation funds managers. Figure 5.13 shows the rise in share prices of industrial, financial and resource companies. However, you can also see the fall in prices from late 2007 as the global financial crisis caused many investors both in Australia and overseas to withdraw from the market and to hold greater amounts in cash and fixed-interest investments. A slight recovery has been made since 2007 to 2013.

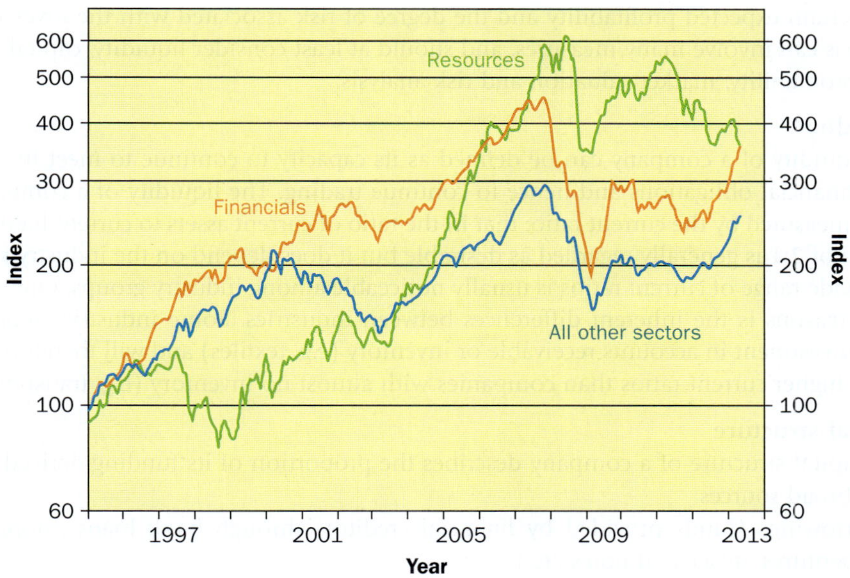

FIGURE 5.13 Australian share prices (end December 1994 = 100)
Source: RBA 2013, page 23 bottom left.

Many factors are likely to affect the price of shares. Essentially, however, if there is more buying than selling pressure, prices will rise. If the converse applies, prices will fall. It is difficult to list every factor which may influence an investor's decision to buy or sell shares, but rational decision making usually dictates that the following factors may be of some consequence:

- interest rate levels
- inflation
- taxation
- theoretical price levels
- earnings and dividends
- quality of management
- company reports and announcements
- profit reports

- changes in commodity prices
- industry events
- government policy and announcements
- takeover activity
- economic expectations
- domestic and international economic fluctuations.

Methods of analysis

There are two broad approaches to the analysis of share prices. Fundamental analysis uses objective measures to analyse a company's current financial situation. It also attempts to forecast the effects of future events on those measures. Technical analysis, on the other hand, is more concerned with how recent market perception of the worth of an investment has been translated into market prices.

Although it is important that individual investors are aware of macro factors likely to affect the return on an investment in a particular share, fundamental analysts think it critical that objective examination at the individual corporation level be conducted to ascertain expected profitability and the degree of risk associated with the investment. Analysis can involve many measures, and should at least consider liquidity, capital structure, profitability, market valuation and risk analysis.

Liquidity

The liquidity of a company can be defined as its capacity to continue to meet its short-term financial obligations and hence to continue trading. The liquidity of a company is often measured by the current ratio; that is, the ratio of current assets to current liabilities. A ratio of 2:1 is generally regarded as desirable but it does depend on the industry sector.

A wide range of current ratios is usually noticeable among industry groups. One of the main reasons is the inherent differences between industries. Some industries require a large investment in accounts receivable or inventory (e.g. textiles) and will therefore have much higher current ratios than companies with almost no inventory (e.g. transport).

Capital structure

The capital structure of a company describes the proportion of its funding derived from three broad sources:

1. borrowings (funds provided by financial creditors through bank loans, mortgages, debentures, unsecured notes etc.)
2. trade and other miscellaneous creditors
3. shareholders' funds.

Capital structure can be measured by the debt–equity ratio or, alternatively, by the proprietorship ratio which is the proportion of shareholders' funds to total assets.

Industry differences are again an important influence on capital structure. At one extreme are finance companies. Their business is to borrow funds in order to lend and they inevitably display a much higher dependence on outside financing than industrial companies. At the other extreme are companies in capital goods industries. Their fortunes are strongly influenced by the trade cycle and they must therefore adopt a conservative long-term financing structure.

Profitability

The most common measure of profitability for shareholders is the ratio of after-tax earnings to shareholders' funds. This is usually referred to as the return on shareholders' funds or rate of return on invested capital (RRIC), and is obviously an important ratio for investors. Again, there are wide differences in profitability between industries. Caution should be used in interpreting the figures because of differences in definitions and accounting procedures. Investors should be interested in the returns they receive from their shareholding — both in terms of dividend received and capital gain in the value of their shares, remembering too that different shares will carry more risk and may provide a higher return.

The profitability of a company can be measured in many ways. A useful measure of the return on a company's assets is provided by the EBIT ratio — EBIT (earnings before interest and tax) to total funds (shareholders' funds plus borrowings). This ratio allows comparisons between companies with different capital structures, as earnings are being considered before the impact of funding decisions. The ratio should also be compared with prevailing interest rates and, as a minimum (except in agriculture where returns are notoriously low), the company's return on funds should exceed the cost of borrowing. Short-term funding is often excluded in calculating the ratio to eliminate the distortions from seasonal funding fluctuations.

Investors are interested in dividends paid by corporations. Thus, dividend yield is an important measure. Dividend yield is dividend per share divided by the current price of the share. The value of dividend yields varies widely at any time over the range of listed corporations, from zero to perhaps 8%. This measure allows the returns from individual shares to be compared with those both of other shares and of other types of investments. Figure 5.14 shows average Australian and world dividend yields from 1988 to 2013. Note that Australian shares have generally provided higher average dividend yields. This does not necessarily mean that Australian companies have been more profitable. Dividend policy of companies is affected by taxation law and other issues. For example, US companies put less emphasis on dividends and more emphasis on capital gain as methods to reward their shareholders.

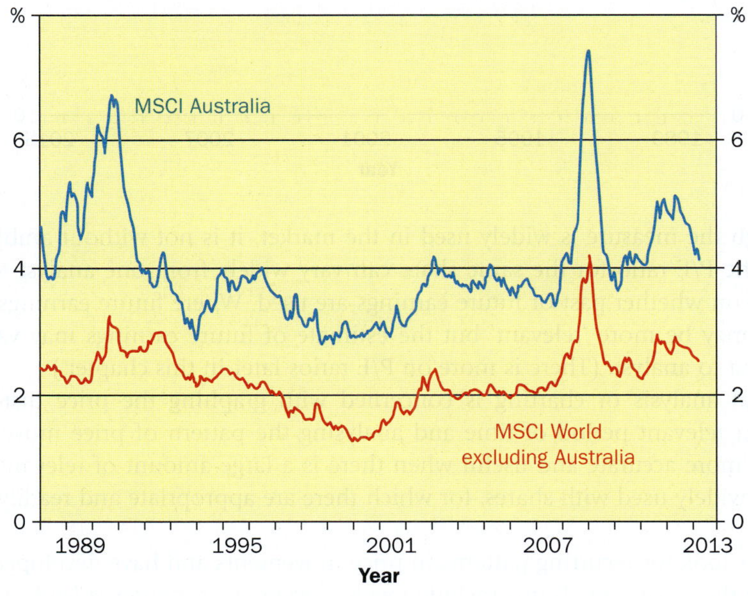

FIGURE 5.14
Average Australian and world dividend yields (monthly), 1988–2013
Source: RBA 2013, page 24 top right.

Market valuation

The market valuation (or capitalisation) of a company is the number of ordinary shares on issue multiplied by the market price per share. The market valuation represents the consensus of investor opinion as to the present value of the future dividends expected from the company. In practice, it varies according to the outlook for earnings, and thus dividends, and with takeover prospects.

A measure commonly used as an indicator of share market value is the price–earnings (P/E) ratio. The P/E ratio is the share market price of a company's shares divided by earnings per share. The ratio reflects investors' valuation of future prospects, rather than present performance. Where there is promise of strong earnings gains, the P/E ratio will tend to be high. When earnings growth is not expected to be strong, or where earnings in the industry are cyclical, the P/E ratio may be slow to respond to variation in earnings if investors hesitate to sell the shares. Figure 5.15 shows how, in 1998–2002 during the dot.com bubble, US investors allowed their exuberance to run ahead of earnings as they bid share prices up to far greater relative heights than investors in the Australian market.

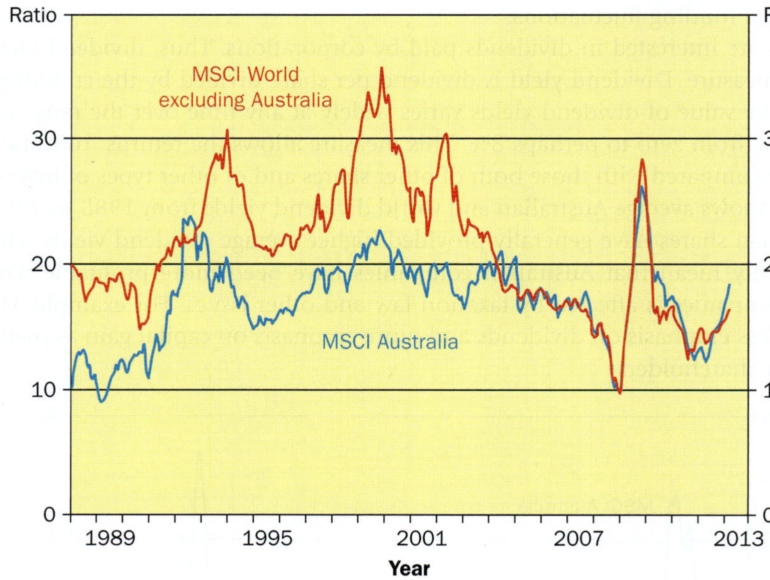

FIGURE 5.15
Trailing P/E ratios
Source: RBA 2013, page 24 top left.

Although the measure is widely used in the market, it is not without ambiguity. For example, the P/E ratio for the same share can vary widely from one analyst to another depending on whether past or future earnings are used. Where future earnings are used, the figure may be more 'relevant' but the estimate of future earnings may vary widely from analyst to analyst. (There is more on P/E ratios later in this chapter.)

Technical analysis or charting is concerned with graphing the price history of an asset over a relevant period of time and analysing the pattern of price movements. As graphs are more accurate and useful when there is a large amount of relevant data, the method is widely used with shares, for which there are appropriate and readily available price data.

Chartists look for recurring patterns in price movements and have developed a jargon to describe these patterns. Terms include *trends, support levels, resistance levels, symmetrical triangles, descending triangles, pennants, flags, shoulders* and *breakouts*. Supposedly all known market information is incorporated in these price movements and buy or sell points can be isolated.

Figure 5.16 illustrates one tool of the chartist — trendlines. A line is drawn between at least three points. In an upward movement the low points are connected to form an upward line. The trendline gains more importance when the number of price extremes that can be connected by a single line increases. In this analysis it is assumed that the market will continue in the direction of the trend until the trend is broken. In the case of an uptrend, buying opportunities are presented when the price is above the trend line. If the trendline has just been tested — which means that the price has moved down to the trendline, touched it and then rallied and moved higher — it may be taken as a signal to buy. Conversely, a break of that same upward-sloping trendline might be interpreted as a signal to sell. Hence, further research needs to be undertaken in a trading situation.

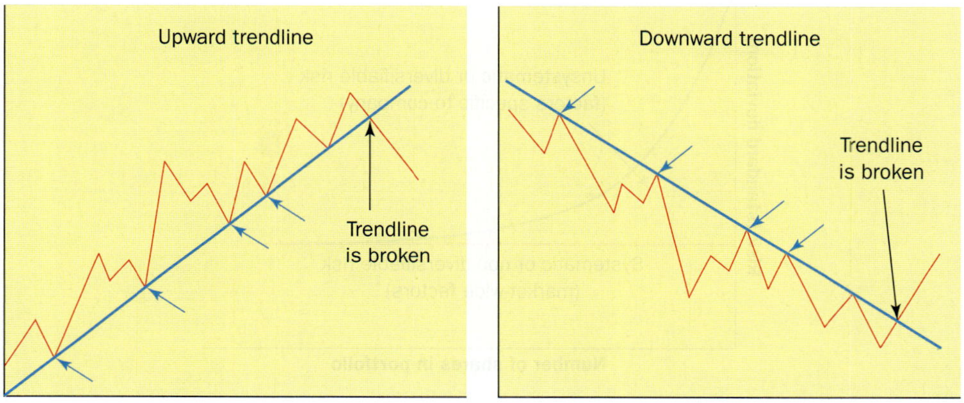

FIGURE 5.16
Trendlines

A chartist saying is 'Up by the stairs and down via the elevator'. This means that a falling market can often be extremely vicious. This is typical of a bear market, but a low point can often denote the end of a trend. Trendline theory argues that an investor should wait until the trendline is actually broken before it can be said that the up or down trend has finished. A trendline is broken when, in the case of the downtrend, the price moves above the trend. Some analysts use a 2-day rule to verify a break in the trend and require a close of the relevant price to be above the trendline, which will often save the trader from 'whiplash'. Whiplash means getting taken out of the market when a trend is 'broken' only to find the trend immediately resumes and had not really been broken.

Many people follow the chartist theories whereas others stick more closely to fundamental valuation methods. Some analysts focus on using fundamental analysis as a filter and then look towards technical analysis to determine buy and sell points.

Risk analysis

In recent years, portfolio managers have given increasing attention to the role of risk factors in constructing portfolios. This has been brought about by the development of portfolio theory which has supplied a rigorous framework of analysis where formerly intuition prevailed. In portfolio theory, investment risk is broken down into two components:

- 'market' or 'systematic' risk
- unsystematic risk.

The first, market or systematic risk, is the variation because of general market movement due, for example, to the impact of such general forces as interest-rate movements, a severe downturn in the global economy, a war, the collapse of a country's currency, or an event such as the tsunami that hit Japan in early 2011. The second component, unsystematic risk, comprises those factors which are peculiar to an individual company such as statements made by the chief executive officer, the decisions made by management or union activities designed to win a pay rise or better conditions. These latter elements are 'random' in their impact and their individual effects may be removed through diversification. The 'market risk', on the other hand, cannot be diversified away. Investment managers thus select shares to remove as much risk as possible. Figure 5.17 shows the conceptual relationship between risk and the number of investments held in a portfolio.

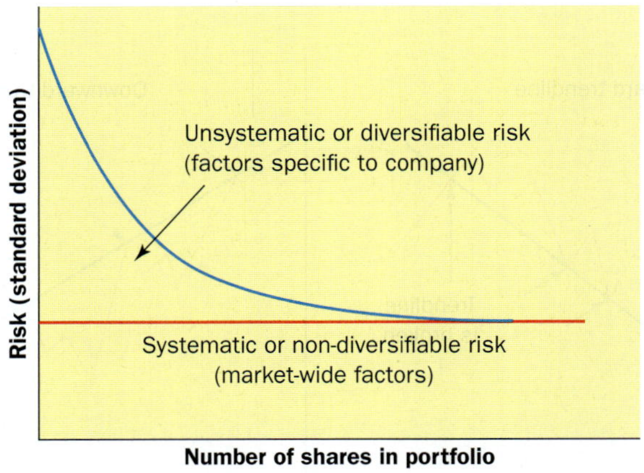

FIGURE 5.17 Systematic and unsystematic risk

Accessing the share market

Private investors access the share market through a sharebroker who will buy or sell shares on their behalf. Sharebrokers nowadays can generally be classified as full-service/full-price brokers or discount brokers. Discount brokers have made great use of the internet and modern technology to reduce their transaction costs and thus are able to reduce their fees. The distinction between the two types of brokers is blurring as full-service brokers cut fees and discount brokers add services such as research to enhance the value they can supply to clients.

In its role as facilitator, the ASX provides the technological platform which enables share trading to take place. In Australia, this system is known as ASX Trade. Simply put, ASX Trade can be thought of as a public auction, whereby market participants can place their orders to buy and sell shares by specifying a desired quantity and price. If you imagine a marketplace with thousands of such people continuously entering their 'bids' (if they are looking to buy) and 'offers' (if they are looking to sell), you will have a rough idea of the size and scale of the ASX Trade system.

Orders placed within the ASX Trade system are prioritised based on price-time priority. This is best illustrated with an example. If we have two investors looking to buy or sell a particular share, and each enters the desired quantity and price they are willing to pay or offer, the order with the 'best' price will have priority. The 'best' price is defined as the higher price if the person is looking to buy, or the lower price if they are looking to sell. The next logical question then is 'What if two investors are looking to buy or sell shares at the same price?' In this case, priority is based on a 'first come first serve' basis, whereby the order received in the market first will have priority.

The cost of trading shares ranges from $20 to $50 for a transaction up to $10 000 value to about 0.3–0.4% on large trades of, say, $1 million. Many brokers now insist that clients hold funds in accounts accessible by the broker to settle buy transactions and that they, the brokers, have proof that shares are owned before a sale transaction is effected. Transactions must be settled by the third day after the day of the transaction or a substantial fine is levied.

Because the old method of a printed share certificate has been abandoned, investors have their shareholdings substantiated by statements issued by registrars such as CHESS (Clearing House Electronic Subregister System), an electronic transfer and settlement system. Entries in this system are sponsored by the brokers with whom clients are registered. Alternatively, companies outsource or maintain their own electronic registers. Coupled with electronic transfer of cash, uncertificated holdings speed transactions and cut transaction costs.

The ASX is no longer located in a building with a trading floor where traders yell prices and share quantities at each other in order to make deals. When we see stories on television which involve the ASX and the picture shows floor-trading activity, it is file copy of another exchange such as the New York Stock Exchange (NYSE) trading floor which still operates by 'open cry'. This is because the ASX trades solely by way of linked computers and market activity can be viewed only on computer screens.

The effects of technological change and globalisation are nowhere more apparent than in the equity markets. Until the end of the 1990s, investors who wanted to expand and diversify their portfolios to include international equities were virtually forced to use the services of funds managers because it was difficult to obtain timely investment information and to trade on markets other than the ASX. However, during 1999, internet brokers started to provide investors with direct access to trade on US markets.

PROFESSIONAL ADVICE

Risk and return

Recall from the case study at the start of this chapter that Lila required some financial advice and consulted with Rebecca, the financial planner. They held a wide-ranging conversation about potential investments and the risks Lila was prepared to take. As a part of that conversation, Rebecca suggested to Lila that she buy some shares in her bank to become an owner rather than just a customer. As part of her explanation, Rebecca advised that the term deposit that the bank was offering for a 12-month period was 4.5%, but that shares in the bank were paying a dividend of 3.2%. At first Lila could not see that there was an advantage in investing where the return was lower and with more risk. But then Rebecca showed Lila a chart which showed the risk in interest rate returns over time and also that the dividend paid by the bank tended to rise by 3% p.a.

»

»

QUESTIONS

1. Suggest an argument why Lila might prefer to invest in the bank's term deposits.
2. Suggest an argument why Lila might prefer to invest in the bank's shares.
3. What would your advice be if Lila's investment time frame was at least 3 years?
4. What would your advice be if Lila's investment time frame was at least 7 years?

LO 7 The capital asset pricing model (CAPM)

So far, we have noted that there is a relationship between systematic risk and return. What we have not shown is the exact relationship. The capital asset pricing model (CAPM, pronounced 'cap-em') attempts to establish the relationship between systematic risk and return. The CAPM proposes a variable for *relative* systematic risk. This variable, beta (β), measures the risk of a share relative to the total market risk (remember, 'market risk' is 'systematic risk'). The variability of share returns relative to market returns is a measure of the share's systematic risk. The CAPM gives the following relationship between return and risk:

$$R_i = R_f + \beta_i(R_m - R_f)$$

where R_i = the expected or required return on share i

R_f = a risk-free rate

β_i = the beta of share i

$R_m - R_f$ = the risk premium (the margin for equity-market risk or, the difference between the market rate and the risk-free rate).

This model says that the expected return on a share is equal to the risk-free rate (the rate offered by a government security) plus the amount of risk (beta) multiplied by the price of risk (the risk premium). If investors wish to buy a particular share, the expected return must, at least, be equal to the return they would earn if they invested in a risk-free asset (such as a government bond or bank deposit). In addition, we know that owning shares is risky, so investors need to be compensated for that risk. They will not be compensated for total risk, just the systematic risk. Beta measures the systematic risk of the share and the risk premium measures the price of risk. These two variables multiplied together, plus the risk-free rate, provide the expected return of the share. In the CAPM, the beta of the market as a whole is always 1. Therefore, a share with a beta of less than 1 is less risky than the market as a whole, and a share with a beta of more than 1 is more risky than the market as a whole. Many mining and exploration companies have betas higher than 1 whereas companies providing more stability such as retailing or banking services have betas less than 1.

ILLUSTRATIVE EXAMPLE 5.3

A Ltd and B Ltd have betas of 0.8 and 1.2 respectively. The risk-free rate is 4% and the risk premium is 6%. What is the expected return on each share?

A Ltd
$$\begin{aligned} R_i &= R_f + \beta_i(R_m - R_f) \\ &= 4\% + 0.8(6\%) \\ &= 8.8\% \end{aligned}$$

B Ltd
$$\begin{aligned} R_i &= R_f + \beta_i(R_m - R_f) \\ &= 4\% + 1.2(6\%) \\ &= 11.2\% \end{aligned}$$

It is important to note that the only difference between these two shares is their beta. The risk-free rate and risk premium for the two are the same; indeed, they are the same for all shares on any particular market (but not for shares listed on different markets). The difference in expected returns is determined only by their betas.

When all shares are correctly priced as per the CAPM, we expect to see the relationship shown in figure 5.18.

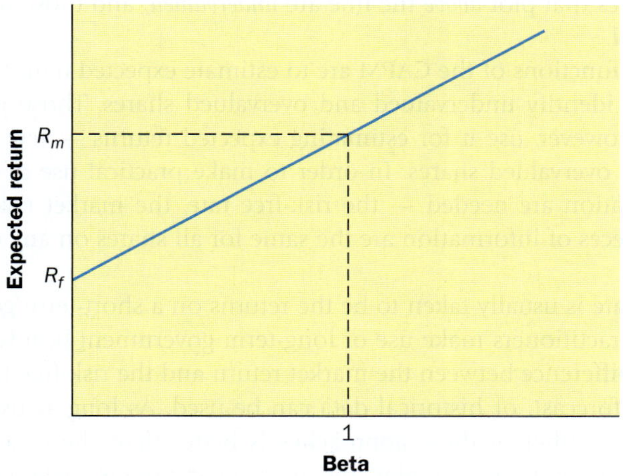

FIGURE 5.18 Graphical representation of the CAPM

In figure 5.18 we see an upward-sloping relationship between systematic risk and return. This upward-sloping line is called the *securities market line* (SML). Figure 5.18 also shows that the beta of the market return is 1. After all, the relative risk of the market as a whole relative to itself must be 1. The SML can be used to identify undervalued and overvalued shares. In the case of A Ltd and B Ltd, imagine we believed that A Ltd would actually provide a return of 15% and B Ltd would actually provide a return of 10%. Their expected returns given by the CAPM are 8.8% and 11.2% respectively. This situation is shown in figure 5.19 (overleaf).

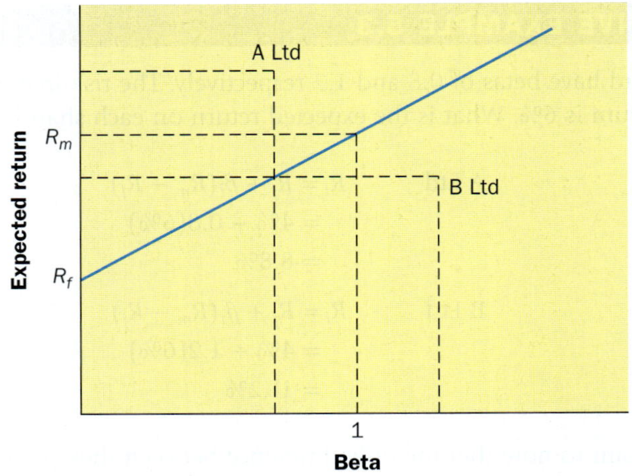

FIGURE 5.19
Undervalued and overvalued shares and the SML

As shown in figure 5.19, A Ltd is offering a higher return than we would expect given the CAPM. Similarly, B Ltd is offering a lower return than we would expect given the CAPM. Investors who discovered this would buy A Ltd because for low risk they can get high returns. As they continued to buy A Ltd, its price would rise and, for a given future price and future dividends, the return would fall until it was offering the expected CAPM return (8.8%). Similarly, investors would sell B Ltd. As they continued to sell, the price of B Ltd would fall. For a given future price and future dividends, the return of B Ltd would rise until it reached the expected CAPM return.

Looking at figure 5.19, we see that A Ltd plots above the SML, while B Ltd plots below the SML. All shares that plot *above* the line are *undervalued*, and those that plot *below* the line are *overvalued*.

The two basic functions of the CAPM are to estimate expected returns (using the basic formula) and to identify undervalued and overvalued shares. Those practitioners who use the CAPM, however, use it for estimating expected returns — few use it to identify undervalued and overvalued shares. In order to make practical use of the CAPM, three pieces of information are needed — the risk-free rate, the market risk premium (note that these two pieces of information are the same for all shares on any one market), and the share beta.

The risk-free rate is usually taken to be the returns on a short-term government bond, although some practitioners make use of long-term government bonds. The market risk premium is the difference between the market return and the risk-free rate. Each of these variables can be forecast, or historical data can be used. As long as usage is consistent, there is no reason either of these approaches is better than the other. Estimating the share beta, however, is more complex and most practitioners make use of a statistical procedure called regression analysis.

LO 8

Basic valuation models — the Gordon dividend discount model and the price–earnings ratio

In the following sections, two basic valuation models are introduced — the Gordon dividend discount model and the use of fundamental price–earnings ratios. Each of these models makes use of the CAPM as an input into the model and each requires an estimate of firm growth. We already have an understanding of the CAPM, so we now turn to a brief introduction to growth.

Estimating growth

There are two broad approaches to estimating growth rates:

1. making use of historical data
2. estimating growth from firm fundamentals.

The historical approach calculates what growth has taken place in the past and then extrapolates that growth into the future. Clearly, there are potential problems with this approach. For example, if the economy is recovering from a recession, the firm's growth may be very low, or even negative. Similarly, if the firm is just about to introduce a new product that will take the market by storm, historical growth will be underestimated.

When using historical growth figures, two approaches can be used to calculate the final growth estimate — the arithmetic average and the geometric average. The difference between the two is similar to the difference between simple and compound interest. The arithmetic average is simply the equally weighted average of past growth rates. The geometric average accounts for the impact of compounding in growth rates.

Let's have a look at the effects of using the different approaches with an example. Table 5.1 shows historical data for earnings per share (EPS) for C Ltd.

TABLE 5.1 Earnings per share for C Ltd

Year	Earnings per share ($)	Growth rate (%)
2003	0.20	
2004	0.35	75
2005	–0.10	–129
2006	–0.15	50
2007	0.05	–133
2008	0.10	100
2009	0.25	150
2010	0.33	30
2011	0.42	30
2012	0.55	30
2013	0.71	30

We can see some serious problems in table 5.1. First, which period do we use as our estimation period? If we use the 5 years from 2009 to 2013 (which seems a reasonable period), then:

$$\text{arithmetic average} = \frac{(150\% + 30\% + 30\% + 30\% + 30\%)}{5}$$

$$= 54\%$$

whereas

$$\text{geometric average} = \sqrt[5]{\frac{0.71}{0.25}} - 1$$
$$= 23\%$$

If we use the 10-year period (2003 to 2013), then the arithmetic average is 23% and the geometric average is 7%. First, note that the growth rates over 5 and 10 years have been very different. Second, however, is a far more serious problem. In the early period, earnings per share (EPS) for C Ltd were negative. Look closely at the growth rates for 2005, 2006 and 2007. They are not plausible. In 2006, the EPS was –0.15, down from –0.10 the previous year, but the calculated growth rate is +50%! Look at EPS in 2007, a positive 0.05, up from –0.15 the previous year. The calculated growth rate, however, is –133%. In short, the use of historical growth rates is complicated by negative EPS, which can happen from time to time. When using historical growth rates, a final issue to consider is that past growth rates have been shown to be (very) poor indicators of future growth rates.

One possible way to circumvent the problems of using historical data is to calculate a sustainable growth rate. This growth rate can be calculated as follows:

$$\text{Growth} = b(\text{RoE})$$

where b = retention ratio
RoE = return on equity.

The retention ratio measures how much of the firm's earnings are reinvested (as a proportion of earnings) in the firm as opposed to being paid out as dividends. Of the firm's total earnings (after tax), some is paid out as dividends (this amount expressed as a ratio of earnings is called the payout ratio), and the rest is reinvested in the firm's operations. If we assume that the firm earns the same return on this reinvested money as it does on all its other investments, then its incremental return (i.e. the firm's growth) is the two ratios multiplied together. The case of D Ltd demonstrates the use of this measure. This firm has a payout ratio of 60% of its earnings and an RoE of 12%. In this case, the retention ratio is 40% (the sum of the payout ratio and the retention ratio = 1). The sustainable growth rate will then be 40% × 12% = 4.8%.

It is rare to find a company that pays out all of its earnings as dividends. Shareholders expect the company to grow and achieve capital growth. Hence, shareholders are content to trade a higher share of earnings for a lower dividend and a higher level of capital growth.

The Gordon dividend discount model

We consider that financial assets have exchange value only. This means that the value of an asset is equal to the cash flow that we will earn from owning the asset. In the case of shares, this generally means that we will value the asset in relation to the sum of the dividends and the capital gains that we expect to receive. A dividend discount model explicitly incorporates this view. The share is valued by discounting future dividends to the present at the required rate of return. Generally, a dividend discount model would take the following form:

$$V_0 = \sum_{t=1}^{t=\infty} \frac{DPS_t}{(1+r)^t}$$

The problem with using this type of model is that we are required to forecast future dividends to infinity (or at least some distant point in the future). In order to overcome this problem, various 'shortcuts' have been proposed. The best-known shortcut is the Gordon dividend discount model. This model is a very special case of the general principle. In the case where a firm is in 'steady state' — that is, is in a mature industry and is not expected to grow dramatically over the foreseeable future — this model has practical use. The model takes the following form:

$$V_0 = \frac{DPS_1}{r - g}$$

where V_0 = the estimated value now

DPS_1 = the expected dividend per share in the next period

r = the required rate of return

g = the expected growth rate.

This model has some special features. First, the required rate of return must be greater than the expected growth rate. If this is not the case, then the model will estimate a negative value (which is impossible — share prices on the market are always positive). If the expected growth rate is really greater than the required rate of return, then the Gordon growth model is not appropriate for valuation. Second, this model assumes that the fundamentals of the firm will remain constant. If the firm changes its payout ratio, for example, the firm's growth rate will change and so the value of the firm will also change.

ILLUSTRATIVE EXAMPLE 5.4

Annsarita is interested in valuing XYZ Ltd. She knows that it has just declared a dividend of \$0.20. She estimates that XYZ Ltd, being a relatively risky firm, has a beta of 1.3. She has heard that over the next year or so the ASX is expected to have a return of about 13%. Government bond rates are expected to be about 7% for the foreseeable future. XYZ Ltd has a dividend payout ratio of 45% and an RoE of 15%.

Annsarita starts her valuation by calculating the inputs to the Gordon dividend discount model. She needs to calculate the required rate of return, the expected growth rate and the expected dividend in the next period. First, she uses the CAPM to calculate the expected rate of return:

$$\begin{aligned} R_i &= R_f + \beta_i(R_m - R_f) \\ &= 7\% + 1.3(13\% - 7\%) \\ &= 14.8\% \end{aligned}$$

She then calculates the expected growth rate. The payout ratio is 45%, which means that the retention ratio is 55%. The RoE is 15%. Using the formula:

$$\begin{aligned} \text{Growth} &= b(\text{RoE}) \\ &= 55\% \times 15\% \\ &= 8.25\% \end{aligned}$$

Next, she calculates the dividend per share in the next period. The firm has just paid a dividend per share of \$0.20, so the dividend per share next period, if the firm grows at 8.25%, must be \$0.22 per share, that is

»

»

$0.20(1 + \text{growth}) = 0.20(1.0825)$. With the inputs, she can now estimate the value of XYZ Ltd:

$$V_0 = \frac{DPS_1}{r - g}$$

$$= \frac{0.22}{0.148 - 0.0825}$$

$$= \$3.36$$

Now, what would happen if XYZ Ltd also announced that in future it would be changing its payout ratio from 45% to 75%? The retention ratio would now be 25% and the growth of the firm would be 3.75%. When Annsarita valued the firm, she would use the new growth rate and have the following result:

$$V_0 = \frac{0.21}{0.148 - 0.0375}$$

$$= \$1.90$$

Price–earnings ratio

One of the simplest valuation techniques used is the price–earnings ratio (P/E) approach. The P/E is simple to calculate and easy to understand:

$$\text{P/E} = \frac{\text{Price per share}}{\text{Earnings per share}}$$

Consider the P/E ratio in the situation of FGH Ltd and Stefano the analyst. If the price per share of FGH Ltd was \$10 and the expected earnings per share \$1, then we would say that FGH Ltd was trading at ten times earnings.

There are at least two ways this ratio can be used. The most common way is to calculate the P/E of a particular firm, and then assume that this P/E will be stable over time and use it as a forecast of whether prices are overvalued or undervalued on the market.

Stefano is valuing FGH Ltd which historically has had a P/E of 10. He has estimated that earnings per share (EPS) will be \$1.20 next year. He therefore expects that the share price should be \$12 per share. This is a very primitive form of valuation, which is, however, quite popular and widespread. A potential problem with this type of valuation is that there is no indication that P/Es are stable over time. Indeed, the evidence seems to suggest that they are not stable over time.

A more sophisticated approach is to relate the P/E to firm fundamentals. This can be done via the Gordon dividend discount model. Recognising that price and value are equivalent concepts, the Gordon dividend discount model can be written as:

$$P_0 = \frac{DPS_1}{r - g}$$

Recall that the dividend per share is that part of earnings that is paid out to shareholders, therefore $DPS_1 = EPS_0(\text{Payout ratio})(1 + \text{Growth})$.

$$P_0 = \frac{EPS_0\,(\text{Payout ratio})\,(1 + \text{Growth})}{r - g}$$

$$\frac{P_0}{EPS_0} = \text{P/E} = \frac{\text{Payout ratio}\,(1 + \text{Growth})}{r - g}$$

This relates the firm's fundamentals to the current P/E. If we wanted to make use of a prospective P/E — that is, relate price to the next period's EPS — then:

$$\frac{P_0}{EPS_1} = \text{P/E} = \frac{\text{Payout ratio}}{r - g}$$

P/Es can be used to tell if a firm is undervalued or overvalued using fundamentals. In general, there are some problems with the use of P/E analysis. There are various methods of calculating EPS, and these methods are all based on accounting conventions that are 'generally accepted', not standardised. Investors should also be aware that companies may use earnings management techniques to provide an earnings result that the analysts of the market were predicting. Companies may do so within the generally accepted accounting rules to 'tilt' a result favourable to the market. Also, EPS are often volatile over time and can often be negative.

ILLUSTRATIVE EXAMPLE 5.5

Valerie has compiled the following information:

Company	Market P/E	Payout ratio	RoE	Beta
ABC Ltd	9.06	55%	12%	0.8
DFC Ltd	7.01	60%	13%	1.2
MON Ltd	4.95	48%	10%	1.4
ZED Ltd	5.00	45%	11%	1.1
PES Ltd	9.00	50%	10%	0.9

She knows that the risk-free rate is 7% and the market risk premium is 6%. She wants to determine if any of these shares are mispriced by relating fundamental P/Es to the market P/Es. She needs to make use of the following formula:

$$\frac{P_0}{EPS_0} = \frac{\text{Payout ratio}\,(1 + \text{Growth})}{r - g}$$

To do so, she needs to determine the required rate of return and the growth rate. She makes use of the CAPM to calculate rates of return and the sustainable growth rate formula to calculate growth rates. (Refer back to Illustrative Example 5.4 for r and g calculations.) This exercise results in the following:

Company	r	g
ABC Ltd	0.118	0.054
DFC Ltd	0.142	0.052
MON Ltd	0.154	0.052
ZED Ltd	0.136	0.061
PES Ltd	0.124	0.050

She then calculates fundamental P/Es.

»

»

$$\text{ABC Ltd: P/E} = \frac{55\%\,(1.054)}{0.118 - 0.054}$$

$$= \frac{0.5797}{0.064}$$

$$= 9.06$$

$$\text{DFC Ltd: P/E} = \frac{60\%\,(1.052)}{0.142 - 0.052}$$

$$= \frac{0.6312}{0.09}$$

$$= 7.01$$

$$\text{MON Ltd: P/E} = \frac{48\%\,(1.052)}{0.154 - 0.052}$$

$$= \frac{0.5050}{0.102}$$

$$= 4.95$$

$$\text{ZED Ltd: P/E} = \frac{45\%\,(1.061)}{0.136 - 0.061}$$

$$= \frac{0.4775}{0.075}$$

$$= 6.37$$

$$\text{PES Ltd: P/E} = \frac{50\%\,(1.050)}{0.124 - 0.050}$$

$$= \frac{0.525}{0.074}$$

$$= 7.09$$

According to the calculations in the example, ZED Ltd and PES Ltd are not valued correctly. The market is valuing ZED Ltd at 5.0 times earnings whereas fundamentals indicate that it should be valued at 6.37 times earnings. Similarly, PES Ltd is valued in the market at 9.0 times earnings, whereas fundamentals indicate that it should be valued at 7.09 times earnings. If each of these firms had $1 of earnings, then we could argue that ZED Ltd is undervalued by the market (its price being $5 instead of $6.37) and PES Ltd is overvalued by the market (its price being $9 instead of $7.09).

Market practitioners often make use of P/Es by calculating a PEG ratio (price–earnings to growth ratio). This is calculated as follows:

$$\text{PEG} = \frac{\text{P/E}}{g}$$

Low values imply that a share is undervalued on the market. It is important to be aware of the pitfalls of this approach. It is not obvious what 'low values' are. As we have seen, P/E is a function of firm fundamentals — when comparing firms by P/E, make sure that they have similar fundamentals.

Other methods may also be used to value shares. Two of such methods, the free cash flow and residual income methods use fundamental accounting reports and a discounting approach to make estimations of the value of shares. The residual income method focuses on the net income figure minus a charge on the opening book value of the company, but, like the other methods, suffers from the infinite time horizon used to discount future earnings. Hence, when a time horizon is imposed, it too suffers from assumptions about estimates and forecasts. Thus, the valuation methods all rely on assumptions about future earnings. Generally, the valuation methods arrive at a similar outcome with reasonable consistency in the valuation of companies.

'Growth' vs 'value' investment

As we have seen, measures such as the P/E ratio and return or dividend yield have been deemed to be important guides to investment. However, opinions differ about the 'best' way to use these tools.

One school of thought is that *growth* investments with high P/E ratios and related low yields have potential for future high growth and therefore should be purchased now to enjoy future gains. In these cases, the market, through the extent of buying, has bid the price up so that the price has grown at a faster rate than earnings. This seems to indicate expectations of significant future growth. John Maynard Keynes, the famous economist, is said to have followed this investment principle to his financial advantage, even though he believed buying for value to be more rational. Success with this strategy depends on being able to sell the investment before other investors realise the price has outstripped the investment's ability to make a reasonable return on committed funds. For example, some US technology shares were priced so high in late 1999 that they needed to increase profits and dividends by 25% each year for the next 100 years in order to make average returns.

Consider a share like CSL (Commonwealth Serum Laboratories). In March 2002, its price was $42, its P/E was about 80 and its dividend yield was 0.62%. When CSL was privatised by the Commonwealth Government, the share became a 'darling' of the market and the price was pushed up by the weight of buying pressure. The price outran the growth in earnings at that time. Nevertheless, buyers still thought there was scope for the company to increase its profits in the reasonable future. However, the world price for blood products fell and CSL's earning potential was no longer so rosy. The share price fell to less than $20, but later recovered to about $30. In July 2005, the price was about $35, the P/E was 23 and the dividend yield was 1.2%. Two years later in July 2007, after much good news about vaccine sales and research results, the price was about $89, the P/E was 31 and the yield 1%. The share had been as high as $98 in the preceding 12 months. In October 2007, the shareholders approved a 3-for-1 share split which effectively tripled the number of shares and reduced the price per share by one-third. The share split was intended to benefit shareholders by increasing the liquidity and affordability to retail investors. By 2010, CSL's share price was around $33.75, its P/E was 18.2 and the dividend yield was 2.37%. By June 2013, the price was $59.60; its P/E was 27.5; and its dividend yield was 1.61. Some of the reasons for the growth in share price of CSL are: people are prepared to pay more for quality health products; there is a limited number of suppliers of such products (hence, few competitors); more products have been developed increasing the market share; and an ageing population requires more healthcare products. Hence, with the rise in price and fall in dividend yield the company may be seen as relatively expensive but investors are focused on the growth prospects of the firm.

The other investment strategy is to buy with *value* in mind always. Is the asset apparently underpriced in relation to value norms? If it is a business, how many years of current profits are necessary to pay back the purchase price? If it is a share, is the P/E ratio lower than the current market average and is the dividend yield higher than the current market average? If this is so, and the asset does seem to be priced so that its purchase would give good value, is there some known future detriment or liability that is depressing the current price? If not, then this asset may well be a good investment.

Many recent studies have suggested that portfolios consisting of shares which were purchased with low P/E and high dividend yields eventually perform well. Moreover, the selection of shares within those attribute constraints does not require any great skill — selection may be *random*.

If investing on the basis of value is such a sure winner, the question must be asked as to why 'value' shares languish on the market for extended periods of time before they start to enjoy price increases. The answer must surely be that there is a deal of fashion and herd mentality in all asset markets, and especially on the share market. Keynes observed that professional investors and speculators seemed to be far more concerned with forecasting short-term speculative gains which result from market enthusiasms. They are less concerned with real value and probable yields in the long term.

PERSONAL FINANCE BULLETIN

Risky moves: cash vs shares

Returns on offer from term deposits have been falling since the Reserve Bank of Australia started cutting interest rates about 18 months ago. At the same time, sharemarkets rallied strongly through 2012, rewarding those who had shifted into or rebalanced their portfolios towards riskier assets.

Having seen shares rise about 20 per cent in the past year, investors are now starting to regain their confidence in equity markets.

Advisers are finding for the first time in a long time that they are having to rein in some of their more conservative clients and remind them of the risks of moving out of defensive assets such as cash and fixed income.

'It's a normal emotional response', says HLB Mann Judd partner Jonathan Philpot.

'I'm very cautious with those people. I go back to: what are their financial requirements? Do they need to take that risk? Most of them don't.'

HLB Mann Judd, which is licensed by Lonsdale Financial Group, bases clients' asset allocation on a 10-year investment horizon.

The business appointed consultant Tim Farrelly to help redefine its investment processes following the financial crisis. The planners don't focus on how the sharemarket will perform in the next three to six months, but instead look at long-term trends.

Philpot says the 10-year focus gives a view of whether shares are over- or undervalued relative to the risk-free rate, which the advisers use as a benchmark for comparison.

The 10-year government bond rate used to serve as the risk-free rate. The advisers switched to using the cash rate available on term deposits as a reference when the federal government introduced a guarantee on cash deposits, effectively eliminating default risk for investors. Cash sums of up to $1 million were guaranteed from 2008 although the limit was cut to $250 000 in February last year.

Philpot locked some clients into five-year term deposits about three years ago when interest rates on offer in cash accounts were between 7 and 8 per cent.

'The 10-year outlook for cash is that we expect one to two more rate cuts. We think we are probably near the end of that rate-cut cycle but we don't expect to see them increasing quickly', he says. 'That's down to issues around the world where governments need to keep rates low to make a dent in their debts.'

Philpot says it's foolish to react to rallies and falls in the market, but he believes it is still a good time to be moving money from cash into equities. Yields of around 6 per cent are still available and the advisers assume capital growth will be in line with economic growth in Australia, at around 3 per cent, giving a total expected return of around 9 per cent. That represents a premium of about 5 per cent above the 4 per cent cash rate, Philpot says.

'It's not really until that premium drops to 3 per cent that we would be starting to limit our exposure', he says.

'If our outlook for Australian equities went to 7 per cent and the risk-free rate was at 4 per cent we would say it was fairly priced and would stop adding to it.'

John Hollyman, a planner at RK Financial Planning, which is licensed by Fortnum Financial Planning, isn't so sure.

'We're concerned that maybe the market has been running a bit too well and it's not cheap anymore', he says.

Hollyman does not recommend clients move out of cash investments to seek higher returns. He admits that interest rates of 4 per cent available on term deposits aren't great, but says that if there's any correction in the sharemarket, that rate could be an attractive alternative to potential capital losses on equities.

Some of Hollyman's clients are still buying shares but it depends on the individual's goals and whether they already have exposure to the markets.

If clients are holding equities, Hollyman says he doesn't want to top up their allocations just now.

'Last year we were buying equities', he says. 'We were looking at a yield focus. The yield-focused equities have gone pretty well now ... the banks, Telstra, that

»

»
were paying upward of 6 to 7.5 per cent dividends — they've all had some pretty significant performance and I don't know if there's a lot left in those stocks.'

If clients haven't already boosted their exposures to equities, it's usually because they were ultra cautious and couldn't handle the heat in the sharemarket, he says.

Rather than seeking yield by investing in more risky credit, Hollyman says that he has been suggesting his clients look at investing in growth assets with capital protection.

Fortnum has a unified managed account with a product called Eclipse that includes a protected option. The investment uses futures to protect clients' capital.

'People want to move out of cash but they're still frightened from 2008 and 2009 so protection is something that's becoming more and more important', he says.

Shadforth Financial Group private client adviser Bruce Chisholm has consistently helped his clients maintain a focus on strategic asset allocation.

Chisholm educates clients about the need for a diversified portfolio through risk management processes, and modelling their cash flows to make sure they can achieve their objectives.

'In the good times, clients sometimes get a bit too enthusiastic and don't want to rebalance their portfolios and you've got to remind them of what we're doing and why we're doing it', he says. 'One of the other things we do is look at lifelong cash flow modelling, sitting down with clients during the GFC to show them that they're still able to meet all of their objectives through to age 100, for instance. It's reassuring for clients to know that what has happened, happened, but that it doesn't affect what we were going to do.'

Except where clients have had short-term cash requirements, they have been fully invested right through the GFC.

'We're not really in a position where we've had clients sitting on lots of cash', Chisholm says.

Most of Chisholm's clients are retirees or people approaching retirement. There are a few accumulators who are the children of those clients.

'We have a range of strategic asset allocations with standard strategic asset allocations for each risk profile', Chisholm says.

A typical balanced client would have 60 per cent in growth assets, including 30 per cent in Australian equities, 20 per cent in international equities, 10 per cent in global property. About 30 per cent of the portfolio would be held in global fixed interest, capped off with about 10 per cent in cash.

More conservative clients might have 30 to 50 per cent invested in growth assets and the remainder in fixed interest and cash.

Prior to the GFC, Chisholm kept rebalancing his clients' portfolios, taking money out of equities and putting it into defensive areas to maintain their strategic asset allocations and reduce risk.

'We said, "Look, when markets turn the other way I'll be asking you to take money out of the defensive assets and rebalance back up to growth assets". They were prepared for that', he says.

Allen Private Wealth certified financial planner Steve Allen has been using the recent market rally as an opportunity to take profits and rebalance clients back to their original risk profiles. He says he'll be continuing that process over the next few months.

Allen holds the view that clients shouldn't sell their shares in the downturns.

'In the last 12 months [the S&P/ASX 200 Index] has spent more time closer to 4000 than 5000 so clients' cash probably needs a bit of topping up', he says.

'I'm more likely to have clients that have been running with a growth asset mix that is higher than they could tolerate just because I didn't want them to sell at 4000. But now it's 5000 I'm definitely happy to take profits and bring them back into line with where they should be.'

In mid-2012, when the All Ordinaries Index was sitting below 4000 points and dividends were strong, Allen was highly supportive of shifting from cash into shares. He's not suggesting clients chase sharemarket returns now.

'The horse has bolted', he says. 'Things like Telstra and the banks, they had some amazing dividend yields six months ago but I wouldn't put anyone's money into Telstra at the moment. It's a crowded space. Everyone is in there but they're too late, as far as I'm concerned.'

All of Allen's clients are over 50. He specialises in retirement planning.

Clients generally hold the minimum amount of cash needed to fund pension payments plus a cash buffer for emergencies.

He says that for the defensive parts of the portfolio, term deposits are still the best option.

'Even though [term deposit] rates don't look that great — it's about 4.4 for 12 months — relative to the cash rate it's still historically a massive premium', Allen says.

Australian and overseas government bonds are trading on 100-year low yields even though conditions in Europe and the US have stabilised.

Various industry commentators have suggested cash rates could remain lower than historical averages for a longer period of time than before.

MLC Investment Management portfolio manager, debt, Stuart Piper, says wider bank margins, more conservative household finances and fiscal consolidation may allow for much lower real cash rates in future. Similarly, government bond yields are likely to remain lower for longer.

In that environment, many clients will need to look to a higher-risk source of yield than cash or sovereign bonds.

Piper says the parts of the fixed income market that look most attractive lie at the non-investment grade end of the risk spectrum.

'The global financial crisis cleared out the weak credits', he says. 'Those [corporate borrowers] that were going to default died and failed. Those that survived didn't.'

Default rates on high-yield bonds are significantly below the long-term average. Meanwhile the returns from the bonds are above the long-term average, meaning that investors are being rewarded with above-average returns for their risk.

Piper advocates diversification in clients' fixed income exposures but notes that high-yield bonds are no substitute for cash. They sit more comfortably as a source of diversification within the growth component of a portfolio.

Source: Zoë Fielding, *ASSET*, pp. 30–3, March 2013.

LO 9 Alternative direct investments

'Alternative investments' is the name currently being generally applied to investments in assets such as infrastructure (e.g. toll roads, railways, airports, water supplies), property development trusts, residential property trusts, private equity and hedge funds. Where the vehicles owning these assets are listed, such as listed property trusts, they may be considered by the potential investor as much the same as listed equities. Where the assets are owned by entities set up as unit trusts or managed investment funds, these vehicles will be considered in the chapter on managed funds. Another alternative investment, private equity, will now be considered.

While private equity has received a great deal of media attention in the last few years because of the raising of high levels of debt, the takeover of well-known companies and brands, and the increase in risk for all stakeholders, this sort of private equity investment is outside the world of the personal investor. In contrast, private equity, in the sense of owning your own business (e.g. owning a service station, newsagency or bottle shop, or running your own accountancy firm, dental practice or legal firm) has always been in the realm of the private investor. In many cases, the owner(s) may organise their business as a company with the shareholding held by one or two or more people. The value of the shares will then represent the value of the entity. When a small business owner wishes to sell their business it is likely that the shares in the company will be sold to another small business operator and the business will continue on.

Other markets

Precious metals such as gold, silver and platinum are used as investment assets. It is possible to accumulate these metals in the form of collectables such as coins and crafted wares including jugs and plates, but people also collect ingots which have value but not much beauty. Precious metals are seen as a hedge against inflation, but their prices are also subject to supply and demand pressures and do not rise in a consistent fashion.

In addition to the conventional asset classes, there are other types of assets where people invest funds. Many of these markets started as hobbies which grew and 'got out of hand'. Some of these markets trade wines, art, antiques, stamps, bank notes, coins and various other collectables. Things become assets with market value when several people are willing to buy them. For example, the share certificates (scrip) of nineteenth century railway schemes, gold mines and like ventures were often highly ornate. Collectors became interested in collecting these intrinsically worthless pieces of paper and a new asset class was born. The hobby is called scripophily (love of scrip). Another example is the bond certificates issued by the Confederate States of America to finance the fighting of the American Civil War in 1861–65. These are worth nothing even though the South still owes money to the holders, but they are actively traded among scripophiles. The problem with markets of such items is that they may be quite 'thin', where the price may be made by relatively few buyers.

Another class of investment involves various agricultural schemes. These schemes have a long history in Australia and have involved emus, ostriches, goats, stud cattle, stud sheep, racing horses, llamas, trees for timber, trees for pulp, paulownia, aloe vera, nuts, jojoba, and the flowers, foliage and fruits of Australian native vegetation species. The schemes are often promoted as a means of having access to the simpler and more 'pure' country lifestyle with the added attraction of reducing tax. Many of these schemes have resulted in losses rather than increases in wealth. Government rulings have taken away significant tax advantages and, combined with the effect of the global financial crisis, where very little new money was invested in the schemes and loan money was not available to support the schemes, many schemes went into administration and liquidation.

Ethical investment

Reflecting a shift in societal values, ethical or social investment has emerged as an identifiable force in the last decade or so. The term 'ethical investment' tends to be used in the United Kingdom and Australia, whereas alternative names such as environmental, 'green' and socially responsible investment (SRI) are used mainly in the United States.

Ethical investments have characteristics which allow investors to integrate their personal values and social concerns with their investment objectives. Thus, businesses actively supported by such investments ('investees') operate in industries or carry out activities the investors approve of and want to support.

Ethical investors interested in putting their funds to work in companies they approve of are rather limited in the scope of activities and number of investees. Additionally, the lack of ready information about all the activities of corporations is a constraint to investment. Investors may invest directly in the primary or secondary market when they find a company they approve of, they may use the growing number of investment brokers who offer a service in screening the corporate world for likely ethical investments, or they may invest in trust funds especially set up to attract the ethical investor.

Surveys have found that environmental concerns are high in priority for Australian ethical investors. The issues with highest priority are active rather than reactive in nature, being environmental protection, sustainable land use, forest logging/woodchipping, reafforestation, and efficiency of energy and resource use. Of lesser importance, but still of concern, are the screening out of armaments, repressive regimes, unfair work practices, uranium and nuclear industries, and racism and discrimination. One issue to consider when choosing to invest in ethical investments is that an investor might increase the risk of investment because of a reduction in diversification; that is, the investor is choosing a portfolio based on a restricted number of shares in the total market.

Summary

Direct investment occurs when investors make their own decisions where funds are placed. Direct investments may be made in two main areas — fixed interest and shares — as well as in niche markets.

The fixed-interest markets are dominated by the financial institutions and governments. The financial institutions principally act as intermediaries which facilitate the operations of the markets by pooling funds for large projects and matching lenders with borrowers. Fixed-interest securities come with different terms, different rates of interest and features. Interest rates on fixed-interest securities are fixed for the contracted maturity and may be of two types — a discounted security or a coupon security. Fixed-interest investment generally appeals to more risk-averse investors.

Share investment has gained increasing interest by investors over the past two decades. This interest stems from the privatisation of public assets, a rising share market for most of the recent past, the internet boom, increased numbers of flotations of corporations and more general interest in investment. Shares in listed Australian companies are traded on the ASX and investors are able to buy and sell their shares by using the service of sharebrokers. Investors decide on the shares they will trade after undertaking analyses of current prices and current and future earnings. Investors attracted to shares are generally less risk averse than other investors. The capital asset pricing model (CAPM) can be used to estimate the level of systematic risk and expected returns associated with shares. The CAPM can be applied as an input into two valuation models — the Gordon dividend discount model and the price–earnings ratio, which estimate the value of a firm based on firm fundamentals.

Other forms of direct investment include coins, stamps and works of art. The markets for such investments may be rewarding but also may suffer from lack of depth and liquidity.

Professional application questions

5.1 Why is a nominal cash return not equal to the real return on a cash investment?

5.2 What does the inverse yield curve represent?

5.3 Why does an investor gain a greater level of security with a commercial bill compared with a corporate debenture?

5.4 Why do corporate bonds rated as BBB yield higher returns than corporate bonds with a AAA rating?

5.5 What effect is the likely effect of the general prices of shares of an announcement by the RBA of a decrease in the cash rate?

5.6 Provide a reason why an investor might buy shares that are selling on a very high P/E ratio.

5.7 In technical analysis, what is meant by breaking away from a trendline?

5.8 What does it mean if a company's share has a beta of: 0.8; 1.0 and 1.5?

5.9 From the Personal Finance Bulletin, explain what the commentator means when the risk premium falls from 5% to 3%.

5.10 Explain why an Australian platinum platypus investment coin weighing one ounce and denominated as $100 AUD in 2011 may be worth $1540 in today's prices (go to www.perthmintbullion.com.au, then search for coin traders).

Professional application exercises

Basic	*
Moderate	**
Challenging	***

5.11 Real gain from a term deposit *

Assume that you invest $75 000 in a 1-year term deposit at 6.5%. How much is repaid to you at maturity? If inflation is 2.75%, what is your real gain in today's prices?

5.12 Calculating the price of a 90-day bond *

A 90-day $100 000 BAB (Commercial Bill) security yields 6.6%. Calculate its price.

5.13 Calculating the price of a 180-day bond *

A 180-day $100 000 BAB (Commercial Bill) security is sold for $98 120. Calculate its yield.

5.14 Choosing a share to invest in *

Fiona is considering investing in either Share Apple or Share Pear. She has the following information.

Economy	Share Apple	Share Pear	Probability
Slowing	7%	8%	.25
Steady	19%	17%	.6
Expanding	27%	28%	.15

What is the expected return on each share?

5.15 Does the price of a bond change? ✱✱

A 6%, 10-year bond pays a coupon once a year and yields 5% per annum. If the yield remains unchanged, what will be its price in 1 year?

5.16 Expected return ✱✱

Camel shares have a beta of 0.8 and Lion shares have a beta of 1.3. The risk-free rate is 5% and the equity risk premium is 4%. What is the expected return of each share?

5.17 Growth and dividends ✱✱

A company reports the following data:

Year	Payout rate (%)	Return on equity (%)
1	50	11
2	55	16
3	60	15
4	85	9
5	80	12
6	45	18

(a) Calculate the growth rates for each year.
(b) What factors can you suggest are affecting dividend policy and dividend payouts?
(b) Comment on the usefulness of the calculated growth rates in this case.

5.18 What changes can take place for a 10-year bond? ✱✱✱

A 10-year bond is issued with a face value of $20 000 paying interest of $450 per annum. If market yields increase soon after the bond is issued, what happens to the bond's:

(a) coupon rate?
(b) price?
(c) yield to maturity?

5.19 The value of a share ✱✱✱

What is the theoretical value of the shares of a company where the dividend is expected to be 50 cents, its RoE is 17%, its payout ratio 45%, its beta 1.4 and the market return is 14% while the risk-free rate is 5%?

5.20 Buy or sell? ✱✱✱

Two firms report the following data:

Firm	RoE (%)	Payout (%)	Beta	Growth rate (%)	Earnings (c/share)
COW	9	65	0.9	2.5	110
PIG	13	45	1.3	5.5	210

The risk-free rate is 4.5%, the market risk premium is 5%, the price of COW is $7 and PIG is $14.

(a) Compute the fundamental P/E ratios.

(b) Classify the shares as either a 'buy' or a 'sell'.

CASE STUDY 1

Considering a term deposit

Kate Turner has sold her house and, after repaying the amount outstanding on her home loan, has $200 000 available to invest. Kate does not want to buy another house for at least three years as she has decided to work overseas for that time. However, she does not want to take undue risks with her funds and does not want to put the money in the share market. Kate goes to her bank and asks for the interest rates on term deposits for the 3-year period. She is given a rate chart that shows:

Term	Interest rate (per annum)
30 days	6.3%
6 months	6.2%
12 months	6.0%
24 months	5.9%
36 months	5.7%

Kate wonders what she should do with her $200 000. Should she put it all into a 3-year term deposit and forget about it until she returns or should she consider putting it into shorter-term fixed interest and then communicate with the bank as the term expires?

QUESTIONS

1 How would you describe the interest rate yield curve? Explain why.

2 Calculate the amount of interest that Kate would receive if she invests it all in the three-year term.

3 Calculate the present value of the interest and return of the principal in 3 years if the inflation rate is 3% p.a.

4 Suppose Kate decides to take the highest return and invests all her money for 30 days. What risk does she take when the term matures and she then needs to reinvest the funds?

5 Suggest a possible solution to assist Kate with her investment plans.

CASE STUDY 2

Chantal has been given $20 000 from her grandmother with the instructions to invest it wisely. She seeks the advice of a share broker who gives her a list of 5 different shares. However, as she is a finance and accounting student she wants to test some of the things she has learnt in her courses of study.

She gathers the following information about the 5 companies suggested by the broker. From the annual reports she finds the following:

	Albie Ltd $m	Julie Ltd $m	Sujay Ltd $m	Roslynn Ltd $m	Fei Ltd $m
Net income	5	29	8	12	25
Shareholders' funds	25	102	45	96	145
Dividends paid	2.5	20	4	8	13
Dividend per share	0.2	0.18	0.35	0.95	0.76

From the above Chantal is able to calculate the RoE based on net income/shareholders' funds and the payout ratio based on dividends/net income. Assume the growth rate of dividends is 5% per annum.

From an internet finance company she obtains the information about the expected market return of 10% and the beta of each company.

	Albie Ltd	Julie Ltd	Sujay Ltd	Roslynn Ltd	Fei Ltd
Beta	1.3	0.95	1.2	0.8	1.1

From the RBA website Chantal finds that the cash rate is 3.5%. From the business pages of the daily newspaper she finds:

	Albie Ltd $	Julie Ltd $	Sujay Ltd $	Roslynn Ltd $	Fei Ltd $
Market price/earnings ratio	13.4	21.8	15.1	19.8	35.2

»

»

QUESTIONS

1. Use the above information to calculate:
   (a) the payout ratio
   (b) the return on equity for each firm.
2. Use the above information to calculate:
   (a) the expected rate of return
   (b) the growth rate
   (c) the dividend per share for the next period.
3. Use your findings to calculate the fundamental price/earnings ratios.
4. Explain which shares Chantal would consider to be part of her share portfolio.
5. Explain which shares Chantal would consider not to be part of her share portfolio.
6. Discuss what features may cause the fundamental P/E ratio to be inaccurate.

References and further reading

ASIC 2009, *Investing in corporate bonds?*, www.moneysmart.gov.au.

ASX 2011, *2010 Australian share ownership study*, asx.com.au.

Beal, D, Goyen, M & Shamsuddin, A 2008, *Introducing corporate finance*, 2nd edn, John Wiley & Sons, Australia.

Bell, N 2012, *Why CSL is a top 10 business*, www.smh.com.au, April 30.

Brailsford, T & Heaney, R 2003, *Investments: concepts and applications in Australia*, 2nd edn, Harcourt Brace, Sydney.

Brealey, R, Myers, S & Allen, F 2008, *Principles of corporate finance*, 9th edn, McGraw-Hill, New York.

Collet, J 2012, *Regulations failing debenture holders*, www.smh.com.au, 19 November.

Fielding, Z 2013, *Risky moves: cash v shares*, ASSET, March 2013, pp. 30–3.

Jones, CP, Shamsuddin, A & Naumann, K 2006, *Investments: analysis and management*, John Wiley & Sons, Australia.

Malkiel, B 2004, *A random walk down Wall Street*, 8th edn, Norton & Co., New York.

RBA 2013, 'The Australian economy and financial markets', *Chart pack*, May 2013, rba.gov.au.

Wilkins, G 2013, *Greater returns on losses for investors in failed rural lender Banksia Securities*, www.smh.com.au, 5 April.

6 Direct investment — property

LEARNING OBJECTIVES

After studying this chapter, you should be able to:

1. outline the qualities and characteristics of property for investment
2. describe the different forms of property investment
3. describe the features and benefits of property funds
4. explain the taxation effects of investing in property
5. apply valuation methods to an investment in property
6. identify advantages and disadvantages of home ownership
7. discuss financial implications of home ownership versus renting
8. discuss financing a house purchase
9. understand the taxation implications of home ownership.

CASE STUDY

Charli is 24 years of age and has just graduated with a law degree. She lived at home with her parents while she was at university. Charli is about to commence her first job as an articled clerk before she is admitted to the bar as a fully fledged lawyer. Charli has taken a leaf from her parents' book and has built up some savings from her part-time work and invested in some blue-chip shares.

Charli now has a dilemma: should she stay at home with her parents and pay a modest board or rent a flat with a friend for a couple of years? She knows that if she rents with a friend it will be close to her work and she will become more involved in the inner-city social scene. Her decision is compounded by her need to save for a deposit so she can afford to buy her own home unit in a few years before prices become too expensive. She expects to earn $65 000 in her first year of employment but her salary will increase to $80 000 after she has obtained her practising certificate. If she rents a flat with a friend she knows she will be paying about $300 per week or $15 000 p.a. to a landlord. If she stays at home then she will pay $100 per week or $5000 p.a. to her parents to help meet the costs of the family household. However, if she stays at home, she will have additional travel costs of about $50 per week or $2500 p.a. as well as the burden of 2 hours travel time each day. Charli rationalises that the travel time may also be productive time where she can do some extra work-related reading and thinking. So, by staying with her parents, she thinks she will save a deposit more quickly than if she rents with a friend. Another complicating factor is that Charli may have an opportunity to work overseas for a couple of years where she hopes to earn extra savings by working in a low-tax country.

The issues that Charli and other young people need to consider that are explored in this chapter include:

- the dilemma of renting or buying
- whether to buy an investment property or invest in property funds
- how to value a property.

Introduction

The term 'property investment' covers a wide asset class with many ways in which a person may invest as part of a broad-based investment portfolio. An obvious property investment is in one's own home, which will be discussed later in the chapter. Another form of property investment is to purchase an investment property and use negative gearing as the financing method. This is discussed in chapters 3 and 8. Of course there are other ways of investing in property: it could be in the form of an investment company or an investment trust. There is a wide range of property investments to consider.

Although investment in property principally consists of an investment in buildings to produce an income stream and capital growth in the longer term, it has a great deal to do with the scarcity of land. In capital cities, we often see the purchase of a property followed by the demolition of the building and the construction of a new building. In many such cases, the purchase has been based solely on the position of the land and hence its value, and not on the building. So, it is the scarcity value of land that is the substantial reason for the escalation in prices of many properties.

Property is an asset class with many features. This chapter considers the many forms in which a person may invest in property and the range of property types that may be included in a property investment portfolio. In addition, the chapter considers the various taxation impacts on property investment and the methods used to calculate the value of a property.

This chapter will also consider some aspects of home ownership. Homes, or main residences as the Australian Taxation Office (ATO) calls them, are an extremely popular investment in Australia. Many people expect to be able to purchase their own home at some stage during their life. This chapter will provide an overview of the various types of housing available and will deal with some of the issues, such as the advantages and disadvantages, relating to home ownership. In addition, the chapter examines the financial and taxation effects of various decisions relating to home ownership.

LO 1 Qualities and characteristics of property

Property, as an asset class for investment, has a number of particular characteristics. The main characteristics of property include the following.

- It is generally regarded as a solid, tangible form of investment — some investors argue that they are investing in 'bricks and mortar' rather than a piece of paper representing a share certificate.
- Land is a scarce commodity and subject to changes in value according to demand.
- An investment in property is generally illiquid — part of it cannot be sold easily.
- Diversification is limited if a large proportion of a portfolio is invested in one location.
- Returns are less volatile than dividends paid from shares and capital values are relatively stable compared to shares.
- Returns may comprise both capital and income.
- Entry costs and exit costs can be relatively high.
- Management and maintenance costs can be expensive.
- A higher level of gearing is possible as lenders prefer to lend against property investments.
- Taxation advantages, such as depreciation allowances, provide investment incentives.
- Some property investments can offer diversification across a range of property classes as well as diversification of asset portfolios.
- Property market values are not subjected to daily valuations, unlike the share market.
- Property markets exhibit pronounced cycles which may not coincide with other sectors of the share market such as media, retailing, beverages or consumer services.
- Property markets may be affected by different cycles of values. For example, holiday houses tend to take a longer time to recover from a slump in the economy or rise in interest rates than residential property.

Higgins and Abey (2000) provide an excellent overview of the property market and the strategy of investment both in terms of the macro cycle (based on long time frames) and the micro cycle (based on demand and supply in the short term).

LO 2 Different forms of property investment

When deciding to invest in property, a person has a wide range of choice. They can invest in a direct form or an indirect form and can select from a range of options within these forms. The decision to invest directly or indirectly is based, principally, on the amount of funds available for investment and also on the requirement for diversification.

Direct property investment

A person may own property directly in freehold form when they have bought a property at auction or by private sale and they, or a related entity such as a trust, are the 'registered proprietor'; that is, the person or entity whose name appears on the title.

Direct property investment can be broken down into a variety of classes. These include residential (the most numerous and familiar type of direct property holding), retail, commercial, agricultural and industrial properties. Then it is also possible to identify types of each class of property. For example, commercial property can be divided into suburban strip commercial, regional shopping centres, CBD office buildings, hotels, motels, entertainment centres and so on.

Indirect property investment

Indirect property investments are other forms of property investments where the property is owned via a third party. Indirect property investment is most frequently seen in the following forms:

- listed real estate investment trusts (REITs): formerly known as listed property trusts (LPTs), these are property trusts that are traded on the Australian Securities Exchange (ASX)
- unlisted property trusts (UPTs): property funds that are not listed on the securities exchange
- property securities funds: unlisted trusts that hold investments in listed property trusts and other unlisted property trusts
- mortgage funds: trusts that hold mortgages over properties
- mixed funds: funds that hold some properties, as well as a range of other asset classes such as convertible notes
- private property syndicates: small groups of investors who form to purchase property.

These entities tend to invest in property other than residential property, although in recent times some small property syndicates have formed to buy and hold residential properties. Indirect property investment provides the means by which people can invest small amounts of capital but gain the benefits of diversification of investment in the property market.

As property investment can cover a very wide field, this section of the chapter will focus on property investment that financial planners are more likely to consider as part of a financial plan for most clients. Residential property is a favoured form of property investment for many people and is usually undertaken directly. The more favoured indirect form of investing in property is conducted via funds that focus mostly on commercial property. These two types of property investment are considered more closely next.

Residential property

Residential property has, generally, had a significant rise in capital value since the early 2000s. Traditionally, in the long term, residential property has provided rates of return lower than Australian and international shares. However, downturns in share markets and a boom in housing prices have seen some areas of residential property attain high rates of capital growth in recent years. The rapid rise in some housing areas may be considered to be a study of land economics. In brief, this consists of a limited supply of undeveloped land for housing development (based on government zoning plans); the cost of local government charges; costs of surveying; infrastructure costs, such as street lighting, drainage and road construction (some of which may be subsidised by government); and availability of finance at low interest rates to undertake the total development. Some argue that a rise in capital city house prices is because state governments limit supply of land around capital cities by means of zoning (which means that tracts of land are not available for housing development); others argue it is a function of our high levels of immigration with many people settling permanently in Australia; and others suggest it is a consequence of policies such as the continuation of negative gearing and a lowering of the capital gains tax which encourage investment in property as part of an investment strategy. The truth may be that it is a mixture of all three.

residential property property which is designed for and occupied by residents as a home

Of course, not all sectors of the residential property market have seen substantial rises in values. Many houses in regional towns have not experienced such growth and some areas in capital cities have only experienced modest growth in prices. The point to note is that different sectors of all property markets have cycles of demand and supply peculiar to the sector and not all types of property perform equally at the same time.

Residential property can range in price from under $100 000 in some cases to $10 million or more. The relatively low starting price range enables investors to purchase properties directly according to their particular financial circumstances. Charli (from the opening case study) will most likely be looking at a residential property within a price range determined by the deposit she is able to save. Many young people like Charli will have little option but to start at the lower price range.

Commercial property

Commercial property investment is largely the domain of institutional investment groups or high net-wealth individuals. This is largely due to the capital required to undertake a commercial property acquisition and the knowledge and experience that is necessary to determine a sound investment.

Commercial property includes a wide range of real estate — CBD, suburban strips, regional centres — such as office, retail, industrial factory, warehouse, farming, infrastructure, or leisure and tourism properties. Each has different risk and return characteristics and income and capital growth features. Commercial property can range in price from around $200 000 to $50 million or more, which means that most investors are unlikely to invest directly with such large sums of money required to purchase these buildings. Roth and Lang (2005) outline a means by which small investors can participate in private property syndicates of up to 20 members to acquire higher priced properties and potentially higher yields on their investment.

There are several factors to consider in buying a commercial property, such as the local geographic area, the trend in consumer demand and labour supply, lease covenants, zoning restrictions, redevelopment potential and specific information relating to the property itself (such as the amount of rent, terms of leases, vacancy levels and expected yields). In addition, the purchaser needs to have a comparative basis for the value of the property or some other means to ensure the property is purchased at a fair value.

It is interesting to note that the yield (the return of income expressed as a percentage of the value of the property) and the income security available from commercial property is usually superior to residential property. The highest yields generally are available from industrial property at 9% to 10%; a well-located retail or office property may yield 7% to 8%; while residential property usually commands about 5% to 6%.

Income security is also greater with longer-term leases, which in general have built-in rent increases and provisions to recover outgoings. In some cases, leases are secured with bank guarantees to cover up to 6 months rent in case of a lessee default.

An investment risk is that the tenant may cease trading, or that for some reason the tenant will not renew the lease at the expiry of the current lease. This means a big part of the investment decision process is finding out about the current tenant as well as how easy it may be to obtain another tenant for the property if for any reason the property becomes vacant. Hence, the property manager considers the matter of 'future maintainable rent'; that is, not the current rent but the rent that could realistically be achieved if the property was placed on the market should the current tenant leave.

Property funds are growing in popularity and provide for easy access in terms of low-cost entry and wide diversification benefits. Whereas chapter 7 deals generally with managed funds, in this chapter we will consider property funds as a major form of investment in property.

LO 3 Features and benefits of property funds

Property funds are pooled investments where the property assets are divided into units for investors. They are set up as trusts with investors as 'unit holders' and beneficial owners of the properties in the trust, with the legal owner of the properties as the trustee of the trust. The sections which follow describe the features and different forms of property fund. Property Investment Research (2007) provides an extensive outline of the features of property trusts that investors may consider for investment as part of their overall property portfolio. Such features are discussed in the following sections.

Real estate investment trusts

The units in a listed real estate investment trust (REIT — formerly known as a listed property trust or LPT) are listed on the ASX like shares in companies. In Australia, such a trust is referred to as an **A-REIT**. The owners of the trust — unit holders — can trade their units on the ASX in the same way as they would any share or other listed security. Investors owning units in the trust receive benefits from **distributions**, tax advantages and capital gains in the price of traded units. The managers of the trust (otherwise known as the responsible entity or RE) buy, sell and manage property assets with a view to maximising returns for unit holders.

A-REIT
a property fund listed on the Australian Securities Exchange

distributions
the amounts distributed from an investment to unit holders; it can include both income and capital gain

To measure the performance of A-REITs, investors can compare the performance of a particular A-REIT against the property trust average and against other assets. The most appropriate measure is the S&P/ASX 200 Property Trust Index, which is a weighted average of unit prices in A-REITs listed on the ASX.

Unlisted property trusts

An **unlisted property trust (UPT)** is not listed on the securities exchange. They are usually 'open-ended' trusts; this means they can expand by issuing new units which can then be used to purchase new properties or to retire debt. Some UPTs require a notification period for withdrawal of an investment amount; it may take between 10 and 30 days and, in some cases, some months to redeem an investment. In that sense, a UPT is a relatively illiquid investment. Whereas A-REIT unit prices may constantly change as units are publicly traded on the securities exchange and may act a bit more like shares, the prices of UPTs reflect a more stable form of investment value and may be likened more to that of a fixed-interest investment.

unlisted property trust (UPT)
a property trust that is not listed on the Australian Securities Exchange

UPTs are usually smaller than A-REITs, hold a less substantial property portfolio and, generally, carry higher amounts of debt to fund the purchase of properties. It was the relatively high amount of debt carried by UPTs that led to the fall in the unit value for many UPTs in the past few years. In the early stages of the global financial crisis some firms needed to refinance loans they had taken out to develop properties in their portfolios. When their sources of finance could not refinance the loans, many UPTs had to sell some properties in their portfolio, often at a lower price than otherwise expected, to repay outstanding loans.

UPTs suffered severe setbacks in the late 1980s and early 1990s when record high interest rates and falling demand for property saw most UPTs facing serious liquidity problems. When investors tried to redeem their investments and get their money back, the managers could not sell the properties without realising a loss and, in fact, some could not even find a buyer. Most managers froze redemptions for up to 2 years and some unlisted property trusts closed altogether, leaving some investors with a significant capital loss. Again, in the recent global financial crisis, some UPTs curtailed redemptions from the fund which restricted a possible closure of the funds altogether. Some funds only allowed redemptions to be made by investors over a period of 2–3 years to avoid dramatic losses for the investors who remained in the fund.

As a result of past liquidity problems, most UPTs now have strategies in place to deal with a repeat of a rush of redemption requests. In many cases, such funds have evolved into hybrid funds where significant amounts are invested in A-REITs as well as direct property. The A-REIT investments are principally held in property but since the units are traded on the ASX they are far more liquid, which in turn makes the UPT a relatively more liquid investment than previously was the case.

Property syndicates

The high entry price for commercial property means it is often purchased by pooling the resources of more than one investor. Property syndicates are designed to have a shorter life than UPTs (typically 5 to 7 years) and invest in office, retail and industrial properties. Examples of the types of commercial property a syndicate might invest in include entertainment venues, caravan parks, healthcare projects and retirement villages. Consider an example of a small investor syndicate. To illustrate the workings of a syndicate assume four people join together to buy a factory costing, say, \$2 000 000. Each contributes \$100 000 of their own money (possibly borrowed from their bank against the security of their home), then they each borrow \$400 000 from a separate bank secured against the factory and the owners' personal guarantees.

An advantage of this arrangement is that each of the four owners has been able to access an investment that may have been beyond them individually. However, they need to agree to hold the investment for a stated period of time as they would be relying on each other to buy the other out if some issue arose and they needed to sell their share within the agreed time frame.

Usually property syndicates are formed for a set period of time with an objective of selling the property at the end of that period, after realising an expected capital growth and high levels of rental income during the period. A feature of the small property syndicate is that, provided certain conditions are met, a small number of investors may combine to buy one or more properties without having to satisfy the *Corporations Act 2001* rules regarding licensing of responsible entities and the issuing of product disclosure statements and other regulatory requirements.

Property securities funds

Property securities funds hold a portfolio of units in A-REITs, other types of property funds and cash. They offer liquidity to investors as they do not hold property directly but provide for an investment in property to fit an investor's portfolio. Some specialise by sector, such as retail properties, but most are diversified.

Some of these funds do not try to outperform an index but are passive investments as they track an index of A-REIT performance. They suit most investors as they provide for diversification without having to choose or monitor an individual A-REIT and without an additional level of fees.

Mortgage funds

mortgage fund
an investment fund in which the assets are based on first mortgages over property

Mortgage funds enable investors to invest in a fund which holds a number of mortgages over property. Investments in mortgage funds are relatively illiquid with many requiring a 12-month investment period before redemption of the original investment. They are unlisted funds which hold mortgages over property against borrowers of the funds raised by the mortgage fund.

Returns are provided to investors in the form of a fixed interest payment based on the repayments of interest and loans by the mortgagors (borrowers). No capital growth is expected from an investment in a mortgage fund. The unit holder shares in the risk of default by a mortgagor and the effectiveness of the manager of the fund to lend responsibly to borrowers. Mortgage funds usually hold first mortgages up to 65% of the loan-to-valuation ratio (LVR) to limit the exposure to any default.

Mezzanine funds

mezzanine fund
a fund that offers a higher rate of return to investors based on a higher rate of return charged to borrowers — typically, borrowers invest in property development and are unable to borrow the full extent of the funds needed; hence they offer a higher return to investors to obtain more funds but the returns are subject to the developers' aims being achieved

A **mezzanine fund** lends money to developers who need to borrow more than they can borrow from the banking sector. Banks lend to a certain level of the value of a property development but the developers may require additional borrowings to fund the project. Such funds may be raised from investors with the promise of higher rates of interest as the manager of the fund lends the money to developers at a higher rate. However, the prospect of higher returns comes with an additional level of risk that the developer may not succeed with the plans of the project on time, if at all.

Recent collapses in some property funds have seen a loss of capital for some investors who loaned money to the funds at higher interest rates quite unaware of the risk involved (search the internet for articles about the Westpoint Corporation failure).

Hybrid funds

A **hybrid fund** is one which invests in a mixture of units in A-REITs, UPTs, syndicates and other forms of property funds, convertible notes, as well as cash. These funds offer diversification of property investment across listed and unlisted property funds and also between debt and equity forms of investment. A hybrid fund may also gear the fund by borrowing funds to achieve a higher rate of return.

hybrid fund
an investment fund that provides the benefit of both income and capital gains from a variety of sources

Relatively new to the market, a hybrid fund offers investors the chance of comparable returns of property fund investment but, above all, the benefits of liquidity and diversification.

Unit pricing of property funds

To invest in a property fund, an investor purchases units in the fund. Most funds require an initial investment of $5000, which buys a certain number of units. The price of each unit depends on the type of property fund but generally represents a portion of the market value of the properties in the fund.

A-REIT unit prices are determined by the same market forces that determine the price of any security. The unit price is equal to the market value of the underlying properties less any debt, divided by the number of units on issue. For example:

Market value of property held by the fund	$40 000 000
Less: mortgage debt owed to lenders	$15 000 000
Equals net asset value	$25 000 000
Divided by number of issued units	12 500 000
Equals price per unit	$2.00

Because properties are not revalued on a daily basis, units of A-REITs may trade at a premium or discount to the net asset value of the fund depending on the market's assessment of the property trust's prospects. (In practice, the net asset value used is the net tangible asset (NTA) backing of the fund. The NTA is derived from the net asset value by deducting intangible assets such as goodwill, brand names and copyright.)

Factors relevant to the market's assessment of unit prices may include:

- the A-REIT's income yield — that is, net income expressed as a percentage of the property's current market value, relative to some benchmark such as current interest rates
- expected rental growth and capital growth, which largely depends on the quality of the underlying properties and the strength of the A-REIT's management team
- general economic conditions in Australia and the rest of the world.

Units of UPTs are bought and sold via the manager; that is, a management company appointed by the unit holders to manage the property trust's affairs including the transfer, issue and redemption of its units and the maintenance of all unit-holder records.

An unlisted property trust's unit price will be set by the manager in a similar way as the determination of an A-REIT unit price. However, the fund manager deducts a manager's fee for handling the redemption or transfer of units.

The value of units in mortgage funds usually does not change as they reflect the characteristics of a fixed-interest investment whereby the original capital invested at the start is returned at the expiry of a predetermined period of time.

Summary of benefits of investing in a property fund

Property funds provide the opportunity to invest in a number of properties, allowing investors to diversify their portfolio by location, size and sector (e.g. office, industrial, shops, hotels) and also to avoid cyclical fluctuations in unit prices by owning properties in several of these categories. The cost of such diversification may be gained for a relatively small initial outlay. As Charli (from the opening case study) intends to work overseas for a period of time, a property fund enables her to obtain a diversified portfolio of investments in the property class of assets and provides the ability to sell part of her fund investment if she needs to or add to it if she wishes. It may be an ideal way for Charli to spread her investment over shares and property while she is overseas and before she buys her own home.

An investment in a property fund is a 'unitised' investment, allowing the buyer to purchase a parcel of units representing a pro rata entitlement to the distribution of income — derived generally from rent from the fund's properties. If an investor chooses to reinvest the distribution of income they will be allocated more units in the fund.

In addition, property funds do not require management by the unit holder because the ongoing maintenance and management of the trust is undertaken by the responsible entity. The manager of the fund does not own properties. The properties are owned by the unit holders and are held in trust on their behalf by the manager/responsible entity. The manager of a property fund is, in effect, a contracted employee of unit holders and can typically be removed by a majority vote of unit holders. Management fees vary from about 0.5% to 1.5% p.a. of the gross value of the assets of the trust. In addition, the manager may be entitled to property management fees and performance incentives. Such fees are an extra layer of costs that are levied. The manager, for example, may obtain a fee for arranging new leases, monitoring tenants to ensure the building is well maintained according to their contract and dealing with other such property management matters. The only decisions required by the investor are the buy or sell decision and those related to voting at general meetings.

PROFESSIONAL ADVICE

Another apartment?

Bruno is a 36-year-old middle manager with a no-nonsense attitude in a large firm. He says he has been too busy attending to his career to be much concerned with his finances, but over the Christmas holidays has decided to take stock and make some wealth accumulation plans. He is single and has no plans for marriage in the near future. He wants to take an annual holiday to Europe and he can comfortably afford to with his salary level. He expects promotion within his firm in the next 2 years, where he anticipates an increase in his salary of about 25%. He currently is paid a gross salary of $85 000.

Bruno lived with his parents until he was 25 years of age, when he purchased a one-bedroom apartment for $120 000.

He has now paid off the outstanding loan and has even more income surplus to his needs as he can now save the mortgage repayments that he was paying to the bank. He has about $15 000 in a cash account and, in a special savings account (established since he repaid his loan some months ago), he has $5000 available for investment.

He has now come to you for advice. Bruno estimates that his apartment is now valued at about $320 000 and that he can allocate about $500 per fortnight to his next venture into wealth accumulation. For his superannuation fund, he has nominated the Australian shares option so he considers that he has enough exposure to shares. He decides that he wants to invest more in the property market as he has seen how the value of his apartment has increased in the past few years. He is wondering if he should invest in another apartment in the same building where he lives as an apartment has just come onto the market for $300 000.

QUESTIONS

1 Calculate the interest that Bruno would have to pay based on an interest-only loan of 7.5% p.a. when he has to borrow the full amount. Identify other costs that he would be required to pay, both upfront and ongoing.

2 Suppose Bruno was able to let the property for $300 per week and allocate the extra savings of $500 per fortnight to the financing of the project. Ascertain whether it is affordable without consideration of any taxation advantages.

3 Prepare a table to illustrate the advantages and disadvantages of the proposal in question 2 (draw on the information in question 1) compared to an alternative proposal to invest the savings into a property trust (or property trusts) assuming that Bruno borrows 100% of the $300 000 on an interest-only basis to invest in the alternative proposal.

LO 4

Taxation of property investments

Property investments are subject to the same income and capital gains tax rules as other investments. Property investors benefit from the discount available on capital gains before tax and they also benefit through the depreciation allowance rules to reduce assessable income. Thus, there are two specific taxation advantages of investing in property.

Property funds are in the legal form of trusts. Trusts provide a 'flow through' of the income and capital gain derived by the trust, and provide tax benefits in the form of tax-free and tax-deferred income. They are very tax effective for investors. Consider the tax consequences of someone who has an investment property. The income to be declared in the income statement is the gross rental or lease income from the tenant. The deductions that can offset the income include:

- loan interest — most property investors borrow money to acquire an investment property and, under taxation rules, are allowed to deduct the interest as a cost of earning the income
- borrowing costs of loan — the set-up costs of borrowing funds are allowed to be deducted over a 5-year period

- depreciation — depending on when the property was built, a capital depreciation allowance of 2.5% of the cost of the building is allowable for 40 years
- depreciation of furniture, fittings and appliances according to the various depreciation rates (between 7.5% and 15% p.a.) laid down by the ATO
- rates and insurance
- agents' fees
- repairs (but not capital expenses, which must be depreciated)
- other costs that may be incurred in earning the rental income.

In many situations, investors purchase an investment property as a negative gearing strategy where the expenses will exceed the income. The ATO allows for the loss to be claimed because it is assumed that in the long run, when the property is sold, tax will be levied on the capital gain. Refer to chapter 3 to review the capital gains tax rules and taxation on real estate. With this strategy, however, there is the matter of the **cost base** of the property. When the property is sold, the cost base or original cost is reduced by the accumulated depreciation for the building that has been claimed as an expense over the years of ownership. The reduction in the cost base tends to increase the capital gain and hence the amount of tax to be paid on sale of the property. Of course, while it is assumed the property will be held for the purposes of achieving a capital gain there are occasions when the sale of a property may result in a capital loss.

cost base
the various costs of an asset that are included in the calculation of a taxable capital gain; these include the initial cost of the asset plus any other costs that are added to the initial cost

Tax advantages of a property fund

Trusts are not taxpaying entities, so cannot benefit from tax deductions that arise in the normal course of business. Therefore, the passing on of these tax benefits to the unit holder gives rise to a 'tax advantaged' component to dividend distributions received by the investor. The tax-free component relates to certain deductions available to the trust and the tax-deferred element derives from building depreciation allowances. In this case, tax is paid including the tax deferred component only when the unit holder disposes of their units. The value of this tax-advantaged component compared with the distribution actually paid can be quite high for investors in high tax brackets.

Illustrative example 6.1 shows both the tax for a year's income and the tax on the gain on sale of the property after holding the property for 5 years. It illustrates the effect of the reduced cost base when units in an unlisted property trust are sold. When income is distributed from a property trust, the income is assessable income to an individual. However, some of the income is classified as tax-exempt and some is tax-deferred. To repeat, the tax-deferred income is, in effect, the depreciation allowances for the building that need to be deducted from the original cost base when the units are sold.

ILLUSTRATIVE EXAMPLE 6.1

Sally wanted to invest in a property so she could increase her long-term wealth. She purchased a newly constructed unit which cost $300 000 and $12 000 for stamp duty and associated legal fees. Sally had $62 000 of her own money and borrowed $250 000 on the basis of interest-only at a rate of 8% p.a. She asked her accountant about how the income from the unit would be taxed and the after-tax cash flow effect. The accountant produced a schedule to show the income received and the deductions allowed for Sally's newly constructed rental property.

Cash flow	**$**
Gross rent $300 000 @ 7%	21 000
Less property expenses paid in cash (e.g. rates, repairs etc.)	(8 000)
Less interest payments on loan	(20 000)
Net cash flow before tax	(7 000)
Tax effect	
Net cash flow before tax	(7 000)
Less depreciation of building $300 000 @ 2.5%	(7 500)
Less depreciation of furniture, fittings etc. (assume)	(3 500)
Less allocation of one-fifth of borrowing costs (assume $1200)	(240)
Taxable income	(18 240)
Tax loss (i.e. tax savings) assuming 46.5% tax rate	8481.60
After-tax cash flow ($8481.60 – $7000)	**1481.60**

You will note that in this situation, if Sally has negatively geared the investment, she is able to use the tax loss as a tax deduction against other income, resulting in tax savings to offset the negative cash flow (refer to chapter 3).

Sally decides to sell the property after 5 years and the sale price is $390 000. Her accountant now produces a schedule to show the taxation liability and the after-tax proceeds on the sale of the property.

Net sale proceeds before tax	**$**
Sale proceeds	390 000
Less selling costs (assume)	(15 000)
Net sale proceeds	375 000
Less repayment of loan	(250 000)
Net proceeds before tax	125 000
Tax liability	
Net sale proceeds	375 000
Less purchase price (including stamp duty)	(312 000)
Less accumulated building depreciation (5 years)	(37 500)
Reduced cost base	(274 500)
Capital gain (net sale proceeds less reduced cost base)	100 500
Taxable gain (capital gain less 50% discount)	50 250
Tax on capital gain (assuming 46.5% tax rate)	(23 366.30)
After-tax proceeds on sale of property	**101 633.70**

Note that if the investor's marginal tax rate is lower than the highest rate then the tax savings are less.

Tax-advantaged distributions

Unlisted property trusts pay distributions most often on a quarterly basis, while some pay monthly distributions. Often a significant proportion of the distributions paid to investors is tax-deferred. The tax-deferred distribution is often a selling point made to investors, as most investors are keen to defer — if not avoid — paying income tax. However, the tax deferral is often not understood clearly, as the real basis for deferral lies in the impact of the depreciation and consequent reduction in the purchase price of the asset itself when it comes to calculating the tax to pay in the future.

Tax-deferred distributions are not required to be declared as taxable income by the investor in the year they are received, but they will reduce the closing tax value (previously known as the cost base) of the investor's units in the trust. This reduction in the closing tax value is likely to result in, depending on the investor's marginal tax rate, a higher taxable capital gain on disposal of the investment.

If the units are held by a superannuation fund and it is in pension phase (i.e. all assets of the fund are being used to support the pension payments), the income and capital gains of the fund are not assessable for income tax, making such investments very tax-effective. Thus, for a superannuation fund investor there is the likelihood of tax-deferred distributions while the fund is in the accumulation phase and nil tax on the distributions and capital gains when it is in the pension phase.

The impact of tax deferral

The distribution of income in a tax-deferred form may be seen as a relatively efficient form of investment. In fact, a trust may undertake property investments to gain the advantages of tax-deferred income and can offer up to 100% tax-deferred income for the first few years based on the substantial depreciation charges available from building refurbishment. To illustrate, suppose a trust invests in a commercial property and an investor on the highest marginal tax rate invests $100 000 into the trust. The fund can provide both tax deferral and tax halving. Table 6.1 shows the projected returns over a 5-year period.

TABLE 6.1 Projected returns over a 5-year period

	Year 1	Year 2	Year 3	Year 4	Year 5	Totals
Forecast returns	8.00%	8.00%	8.00%	8.00%	8.00%	
Forecast tax deferred	80%	80%	80%	80%	75%	
Amount distributed	$8000	$8000	$8100	$8200	$8320	$40 620
Tax-deferred distribution	$6400	$6400	$6480	$6560	$6240	$32 080
Assessable income	$1600	$1600	$1620	$1640	$2080	$ 8 540
Tax payable	$ 736	$ 736	$ 753	$ 763	$ 967	$ 3 955
Net after-tax distribution	$7264	$7264	$7347	$7437	$7353	$36 665
After-tax yield	7.26%*	7.26%	7.35%	7.44%	7.35%	
Equivalent pre-tax yield	13.6%*	13.6%	13.7%	13.9%	13.7%	

*Calculated as 7.26%/(1 − 0.465) (The after-tax yield is divided by 1 minus the highest marginal tax rate, 45% plus 1.5% Medicare levy, to determine the equivalent before-tax return for an investor on the highest marginal tax rate.)

In the first year of income, the amount forecast to be distributed is 8%. The tax deferral means that the income is 80% sheltered from tax in that year. The investor can then use that income for other purposes such as investing or reducing debt. Suppose then that the investor sells their units in the property trust and that the value of the investments at the end of year 5 is $120 000. In that case, the capital gains tax calculation is as follows:

Step 1: Establish the cost base

Purchase price	$100 000
less total tax-deferred amount	(32 080)
= Reduced cost base	$67 920

Step 2: Establish the taxable capital gain

Sales proceeds	$120 000
less reduced cost base	($67 920)
= Taxable capital gain	$52 080

Step 3: Apply discount to taxable gain

Taxable capital gain	$52 080
less 50% discount	$26 040
= Assessable amount	$26 040

Step 4: Calculate tax

Assessable amount	$26 040
× tax rate	46.5%
= Tax on capital gain	$12 109

So, the total tax paid by the investor in this case is $12 109 plus $3955 = $16 064. Compare this with other investments, such as simply placing the funds in fixed interest for 5 years at an interest rate of 8.0%; the amount of tax on the income over 5 years at the highest marginal tax rate totals $18 600. So, not only has the investor gained income each year with minimal tax payable, but the tax on the capital gain after the 5-year period is also very tax-advantaged and the investor has benefited by capital growth in the amount of the original investment.

However, if the trust bought and sold properties within the 5-year period, the investor may have to pay capital gains tax, as the capital gains are distributed to the investor as they occur. So, if Charli invested in a property fund and did not sell any of her units in the fund but the fund actually sold a property held in its portfolio then Charli may have a capital gains item to declare in her own tax return even though she did not make the decision to sell the property. Such is the hidden issue faced by investors in a managed fund.

LO 5 Valuation of property investments

Valuing property is different to valuing shares and bonds — each property is unique; the actual terms and conditions of a sale may vary substantially; information conveyed to the market such as projected yields and capital growth forecasts may be less than perfect; properties may not be readily saleable; and buyers may need to purchase a property relatively quickly without being able to establish a comparative price. Given all these factors, the 'actual' value of a property may not really reflect the market price. So, to offset such features, how do property investors place a value on a real estate investment? There are two main ways — estimating a market value and performing an investment analysis.

Estimating a market value

Three methods that may be used to estimate a market value are as follows.

1. *The cost approach.* The basis of this approach is to determine the cost of building the property at current costs of the land, labour, design and materials. However, for older buildings this approach provides a less than perfect valuation method; it is difficult to place a value on the uniqueness of some older buildings, including such considerations as their heritage value. Also, a valuation of older buildings needs to allow for depreciation of the structure.
2. *The direct comparison approach.* Although every property may have unique qualities, some properties may be quite similar in design, location, age and condition. Comparable sale prices can provide a representation of a market value for a particular property.
3. *The capitalisation approach.* An estimated market value is made by comparing recent sales figures to provide a rate of return currently required by investors based on the income stream paid to investors (i.e. the rent charged to tenants) less normal operating expenses. The market value can then be estimated by the following formula:

$$\text{Market value} = \frac{\text{Annual net income}}{\text{Rate of return (market capitalisation rate)}}$$

As an example of the capitalisation approach, suppose there were three recent sales of rental property recorded in a similar location, as follows.

Similar property	Net income	Sale price	Rate of return (capitalisation rate)
123 Smith Street	$15 000	$180 000	0.0833
139 Smith Street	$16 500	$200 000	0.0825
151 Smith Street	$16 250	$190 000	0.0855

Using this information, the capitalisation rate on average is 0.0837. So, if the net income for the property is projected to be $15 700, then the market value would be calculated thus:

$$\begin{aligned}\text{Market value} &= \frac{\$15\,700}{0.0837}\\ &= \$187\,575\end{aligned}$$

Similarly, this method can be used to determine the net income that can be demanded from a tenant. Suppose a person paid $250 000 for a rental property and required a return of 8.5% p.a. from the investment. By rearranging the formula we can determine the net income to be:

$$\begin{aligned}\text{Net income} &= \$250\,000 \times 0.085\\ &= \$21\,250\end{aligned}$$

(Note that an estimate of expenses would need to be made and added to the net income to arrive at a gross rent figure to be required from a tenant.)

Net present value investment analysis

As well as considering the estimates of market values of property, investors may also use methods of investment analysis which principally revolve around a net present value (NPV) approach. From chapter 2 you may recall the time value of money concept — how a dollar today is worth more than a dollar in the future. So, to calculate a net present value we need to know the future cash flow arising from a rental contract and then discount the future dollar amounts based on a discount rate representing the rate of return available on similar forms of investment.

ILLUSTRATIVE EXAMPLE 6.2

Stella wants to invest in a property (Property A) for a 3-year time frame. She intends to outlay $100 000 now and then to sell the property at the end of 3 years for $150 000. Stella expects to receive rising net income each year, starting with $5000 in year 1. She is also considering an alternative property (Property B) for the same amount which has a lower expected sale price ($140 000) at the end of year 3 but a higher income stream over the 3 years. By considering these two investment choices we can see how the investment analysis method can be applied. If Stella did not want to invest in either of the two properties then she would invest the $100 000 in a managed fund which is expected to pay a rate of return of 8% p.a. The expected net income flows are as follows.

	Year 1	Year 2	Year 3
Property A	$5000	$5250	$5500
Property B	$7000	$7500	$8000

Recall the formula to arrive at the present value of a lump sum from chapter 2. The following provides an example of application of the formula:

$$\text{NPV of Property A} = (\$100\,000) + \frac{\$5000}{1.08} + \frac{\$5250}{(1.08)^2} + \frac{\$5500}{(1.08)^3} + \frac{\$150\,000}{(1.08)^3}$$

Note that the denominator is taken to the power based on the number of years because the net income needs to be discounted to a present value. So, in year 2 the net income needs to be discounted from the end of year 2 back to the start of year 1 to enable Stella to compare the two investment choices. The initial outlay is in brackets as it represents an outlay of funds and the $150 000 sale price after year 3 is a positive figure as it represents a return of funds at the end of year 3. Thus

$$\begin{aligned}\text{NPV of Property A} &= (\$100\,000) + \$4630 + \$4499 + \$4367 + \$119\,100 \\ &= \$32\,596\end{aligned}$$

$$\begin{aligned}\text{NPV of Property B} &= (\$100\,000) + \frac{\$7000}{1.08} + \frac{\$7500}{(1.08)^2} + \frac{\$8000}{(1.08)^3} + \frac{\$140\,000}{(1.08)^3} \\ &= (\$100\,000) + \$6482 + \$6428 + \$6352 + \$111\,160 \\ &= \$30\,422\end{aligned}$$

»

»

This analysis using the net present value method tells Stella that it would be better to invest in Property A than Property B as it is expected to return a positive and higher current cash value than the other property. Also, because it shows a positive return, the investment should be proceeded with. If the NPV was negative, which may occur if the sale price after 3 years was estimated to be a much lower figure, then the investment proposal may be abandoned and Stella should then invest in the managed fund.

This analysis assumes a known projection of income, a future sale price and a stable rate of return for an alternative investment. However, it does provide a means of evaluating an investment proposal despite its assumptions. By substituting other figures for expected sales prices, income projections and a rate of return, this method can provide a means of considering the value of prospective investments under different scenarios.

LO 6 Advantages and disadvantages of home ownership

A significant feature about housing in Australia by world standards is the high proportion of home ownership by occupiers. The proportion of Australians living in their own homes has remained at about 70% for some decades. However, the proportion of those under 35 years of age who own or are paying off a house is about 60%, which indicates that the younger age groups tend to hold off home ownership until later.

An interesting article is 'Housing turnover and first-home buyers' (Reserve Bank of Australia 2010). This article indicates an increase in demand for houses by first-home buyers as a result of the Commonwealth Government's First Home Owners Boost in 2008, but then a subsequent decline when the grant was phased out. Another interesting article is 'Dwelling prices and household income' (Reserve Bank of Australia 2012) which provides an examination of the relationship between house prices and income.

It is clear that there is a distinct trend for young Australians to reach the milestones traditionally accomplished in early life (e.g. finishing education, leaving home, entering the labour force, taking a partner and having children) at slightly later ages. It is also well known that house prices have risen dramatically over recent years and housing affordability had dropped but then risen again in early 2012 by some 18% over the previous year. Figure 6.1 shows this change in housing affordability. Affordability is measured as the ratio of average household income to the income necessary to meet repayments on an average dwelling purchased by first-home buyers.

Figure 6.2 shows the ratio of median house prices to average household income from the early 1980s to 2010. In the mid-1990s, house prices were around four times average annual income; by the end of the housing boom in late 2003, this ratio had risen to almost eight times in capital cities. It then declined for a couple of years, as house prices stabilised while incomes grew, but more recently house prices have again been rising. The conclusion that can be drawn from the graph is that the measures of housing affordability since the mid-1990s are almost entirely due to the rise in house prices relative to incomes.

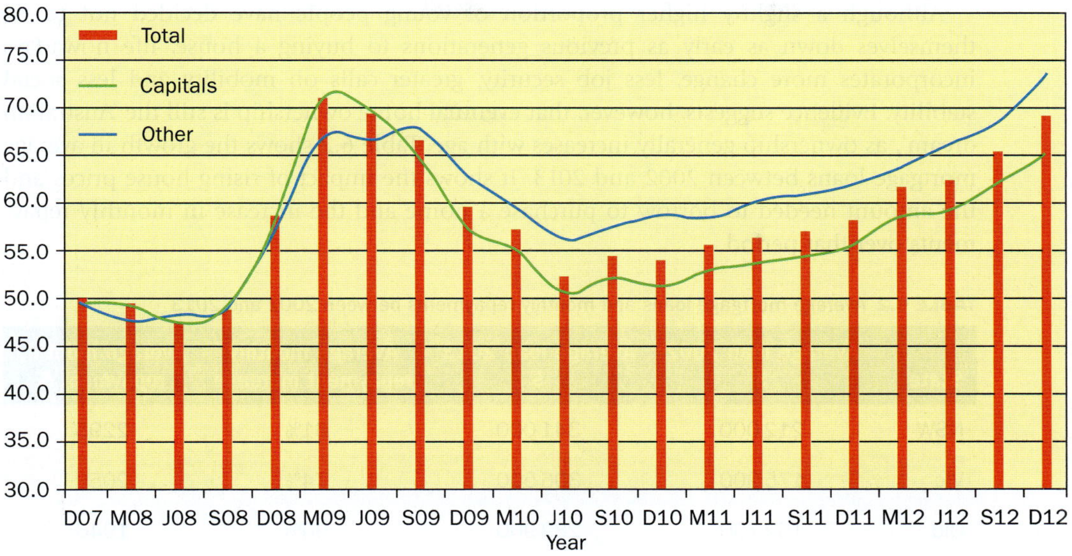

FIGURE 6.1
Housing affordability index, Australia
Source: Housing Industry Association, March 2013.

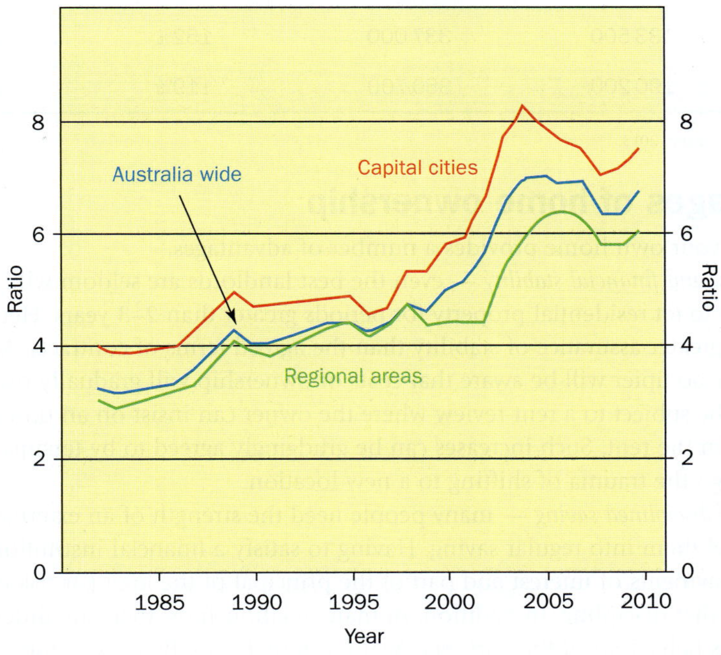

FIGURE 6.2
Dwelling price-to-income ratios
Source: RBA bulletin, December quarter, 2012, graph 3, p. 17.

However, a very recent ABC News Report claimed that 'Bureau of Statistics figures show, on average, that rent and mortgages take up the same proportion of household income as they did in 1994–95. Economists say that strongly rising incomes and substantially lower interest rates are the main factors maintaining housing affordability despite steep increases in house prices' (ABC News, 28 August 2013).

Although a slightly higher proportion of young people have decided not to tie themselves down as early as previous generations to buying a house, life nowadays incorporates more change, less job security, greater calls on mobility and less social stability. Evidence suggests, however, that eventual home ownership is still the 'Australian dream', as ownership generally increases with age. Table 6.2 shows the growth in average mortgage loans between 2002 and 2013. It shows the impact of rising house prices and the amount needed to borrow to purchase a home and the increase in monthly repayments over that period.

TABLE 6.2 Average mortgage loans and monthly repayments between 2002 and 2013

State	Average loan 2002 $	Average loan 2013 $	Average monthly repayment increase	Average monthly repayment $
NSW	212 000	341 000	61%	2295
Vic	175 900	306 500	74%	2058
Qld	152 700	289 900	90%	1946
SA	124 900	249 400	100%	1674
WA	141 000	302 500	115%	2031
Tas	94 800	218 100	130%	1464
NT	133 500	337 000	152%	2262
ACT	190 200	350 700	119%	2354

Source: ABS and Canstar, 2013.

Advantages of home ownership

Purchasing your own home provides a number of advantages.

- *Locational and financial stability* — even the best landlords are seldom willing to enter contracts to let residential property for periods greater than 2–3 years. Hence, tenants have no greater assurance of stability than the agreed terms of contracts. Additionally, an owner-occupier will be aware that costs of ownership will gradually rise, but will not be subject to a rent review where the owner can insist on an unreasonable increase in the rent. Such increases can be grudgingly agreed to by tenants unwilling to undergo the trauma of shifting to a new location.
- *A form of disciplined saving* — many people need the strength of an external force to compel them into regular saving. Having to satisfy a financial institution with regular payments of interest and part of the principal of the loan (or risk expulsion) provides that discipline. In addition, in many relationships, there are differences in savings behaviour of the partners. Again, externally applied discipline can help achieve savings where otherwise it would not be possible.
- *A useful asset base* — houses usually rise in value over the long term and therefore are often a good investment in themselves. Many successful businesspeople have started businesses with little capital but good ideas. Having a fully paid house or at least substantial equity in a house can help to finance business development and expansion. The house equity reassures financial institutions that applicants

for loans have financial discipline and, additionally, it can be used as security for a loan. Generally, it is not advisable to use the security in your home for a business loan.

- *Personal freedom regarding living conditions* — an owned home can be altered or added to at the whim of the owner, subject to local government regulations and any covenants entered into at purchase. For example, owners who want to install spa baths or swimming pools may do so, but tenants may not.
- *Taxation concessions and advantages* — there is no capital gains tax (CGT) on the main residence or improvements to it. However, if the homeowner needs to move from their home and rent it for a period of time then a portion of the gain on sale may be taxable. Also, if the homeowner uses their home for business purposes and makes claims for deductions for improvements then, again, when the house is sold a portion of the gain may be subject to capital gains tax. We will examine these issues in more detail later in the chapter and elsewhere in this text.

Disadvantages of home ownership

As with most things in life, there are costs as well as benefits, or downsides as well as upsides. Home ownership has several disadvantages.

- Property investment is best suited to medium- to long-term planning horizons and owner-occupied homes are no different from other property investments. Hence, an owner forced to sell for various reasons at an inopportune time can lose capital, especially if the investment has been held for a relatively short time. Over the longer time frame, and assuming there have been some periods of relatively high inflation, however, property prices generally will rise, usually to match or exceed inflation.
- Property investment is non-liquid, so owners needing ready cash are disadvantaged relative to, say, owners of shares. On the other hand, cash can be quickly gained by application for a loan on the security of home equity.
- Property investment is commonly the major asset in the total basket of individual wealth with owner-occupied housing comprising about 60% of average household assets in Australia. This is no doubt too high a proportion for appropriate risk management, but cannot be avoided until individual net worth increases sufficiently to allow a greater spread in assets held. Moreover, many people who are aware that their mix of assets is less than ideal are still happy to retain home ownership to gain the perceived subjective advantages.
- There is an opportunity cost in having wealth tied up in a home. Whether there is net cost or net benefit (taking into account forgone alternative investment benefits, avoided rental payments, costs of ownership etc.) depends on individual circumstances. However, it is true that rents are closely tied to housing costs, so owners who have $400 000 invested in their homes must remember that rents for comparable housing may be $300–$400 per week.
- Some people with particular income streams and financial circumstances find it beneficial to rent their main residence but to own other residential property. These strategies rely usually on taxation advantages rather than the pure economics of the situation. For example, negative gearing brings income tax deductions on income-producing property but not on owner-occupied housing. However, negative gearing often requires asset price inflation to be a reasonable proposition and brings additional risk for the investor. On the other hand, there are CGT advantages stemming from owner-occupation of residential property.

LO 7 Financial implications of home ownership versus renting

In this section, we look at the actual decision to rent or buy, assuming the householder has satisfied concerns about the given location, size of dwelling and so on. The decision to rent or to buy can depend on a number of factors. These are the sorts of things that Charli (from the opening case study) has to consider. First, there may be a cultural or environmental determinant. A new householder raised in a family which always lived in its own home perhaps cannot imagine living for very long in rented premises — 'A waste of good money!' On the other hand, the newly fledged householder may have other priorities — 'I'd rather go surfing, swimming, bowling, cycling, play footie . . . than mow the lawn every weekend'. In contrast, a person raised in rented premises may not think of buying a home even when it is financially possible.

Second, purchase decisions are more likely to be carried to completion when a reasonably sized deposit is available to give the new home purchaser some immediate equity in the house. What's a reasonable size? Around 20–30% of the total purchase costs would be useful. A deposit of 10% should be considered an absolute minimum.

Why would it be unwise to enter a house contract, supposing you could arrange finance, with less than 10% deposit? Over the more than 100 years since the Federation of Australia, there have been many housing schemes implemented by both state and federal governments. These have been given many names, but their goals have been the common one of trying to help people get started in paying off a home. Some of these schemes have been more successful than others. The least successful have been the 'no-deposit' schemes, where low-income earners with no saved funds are assisted. There are at least two reasons for this lack of success. People with no saved funds are less likely to have learned the skills which enable them to save. You might argue that they can't save because they do not have enough income. The counterargument to this is that people who are savers manage to save no matter what their income. People on relatively small pensions save, if they are savers. Thus, people without saving skills are likely to suffer financial emergencies when they are unable to pay the housing instalments and fall behind in their payment schedules.

People falling into arrears in their payment schedules may soon find that they owe more than the amount of the original loan if the shortfall in payments occurs early in the loan period. This is because the interest on the loan continues to accrue and is capitalised, thus increasing the total amount owed. Should the property market be falling at the same time, the question of equity in the home (the proportion of the total value of the house actually owned by the householder) becomes important. It is possible for the budding homeowner to owe more than the house is worth.

Equity provides a buffer between the market value and the loan principal. If the market is falling, the householder's equity falls, because the financial institution's stake in the house is a fixed dollar value (the loan principal), which falls only as the loan is repaid. If the market rises, on the other hand, the householder enjoys a windfall gain and equity rises. However, a householder's equity of reasonable size keeps the financial institution happy, because it is assured of being repaid should the house have to be sold. Financial institutions prefer the loan-to-valuation ratio (LVR) — that is, the value of the loan divided by the value of the asset — to be no more than 80–85%.

A further advantage of a larger equity in your home is that financial institutions insist on mortgage insurance if the equity value falls below a certain level. The premium for the insurance cover is paid by the householder. It thus increases costs and reduces the amount of savings which can be applied to the reduction of the loan principal and loan period.

Finally, there are the financial considerations. As we have seen earlier, rented residential property returns 3–6% to the property owner. Assuming costs amount to another 2% of the capital value, then gross rents may be up to 8% of the capital value. This means that a $200 000 property could rent for up to $300 per week.

Even though these figures reflect the *average* situation over time and at many locations throughout Australia, the values at any particular location at any given time will depend on the supply of and demand for unoccupied housing and for rental housing. It is quite possible and, indeed, likely that the values can slip out of synchrony for extended periods. Thus, the budding householder should examine the actual values for particular situations if confronted by this decision. Other factors apart from supply and demand which will have a significant impact are the interest-rate structure and expectations of future interest-rate changes.

PERSONAL FINANCE BULLETIN

Houses becoming cheaper to buy than rent

Low interest rates and flat home prices have seen a three-fold jump in the number of suburbs in which it's cheaper to buy a house than rent one.

Residents living in apartments in Carlton, Ballarat North and Bendigo's Kangaroo Flat may be better off buying than lining their landlord's pockets, according to the latest RP Data *Buy v Rent* report.

Renters in houses in Mildura, Moe and Norlane might benefit best from a mortgage, it said.

At the same time as historically low interest rates are prompting a rising number of borrowers to take out a mortgage, the RP Data figures show there are 692 towns and suburbs in which homes are cheaper to own than rent, up from 179 at the same time last year.

A rise in home loan approvals in May was a sign the Reserve Bank of Australia's cuts to official rates were stimulating the housing market, economists say.

Rates have fallen by 100 basis points since June last year.

The *Buy v Rent* report suggests prospective house buyers will be doing their sums to determine if they are better off paying a mortgage or their landlord.

National research director Tim Lawless said it now may be a good time to consider buying.

'In some suburbs it may actually be cheaper than renting especially where we are seeing evidence of tight rental markets resulting in rental increases and lower home values', he said.

The report analyses the difference between monthly mortgage and rental payments based on the median value of houses and units and median rents.

»

»

Property specialists have, in the past, criticised it for being too simplistic in comparing the costs of buying and renting.

Queensland, with 242 suburbs, and NSW with 193 offered the most opportunities to owners paying off principal and interest on a variable mortgage.

Victoria (45), South Australia (45) and Canberra (6) trailed behind Western Australia (78) and Tasmania (54).

The rise in loan approvals is unlikely to change expectations of an August rate cut.

Westpac senior economist Matthew Hassan said they showed the housing recovery was slower than expected.

'Given the degree of stimulus that we've seen, particularly from interest rate cuts, you might expect a stronger recovery at this stage', Mr Hassan said.

Mortgage numbers rose 1.8 per cent in May, according to the Bureau of Statistics.

ANZ head of property research Paul Braddick said low interest rates were working, especially in NSW after eight years of struggle.

'The market forecast was slightly higher but I'd still characterise this as a pretty strong number and it stands in pretty stark contrast to the weakness we've seen in a lot of the broader economic data over the last month', he said.

Source: The Age, 18 July 2013.

ILLUSTRATIVE EXAMPLE 6.3

Kumar is contemplating renting a house in the outer suburbs at $350 per week. Alternatively, he could purchase a house. Kumar has saved $60 000. A house will cost $360 000 so he will need a $300 000 loan. Suppose a standard variable interest rate for a home loan could be contracted at 7.85% plus fees and charges, bringing the rate to an equivalent of 8.00%. The repayment will be about $2316 per month over 25 years. In addition, there are other costs to be considered. Rates are $2400 p.a. or $200 per month. Insurance is $40 per month. Total cash costs so far are $2556 per month. Additionally, Kumar could earn about 6% or $300 per month as interest on the deposit if it were invested elsewhere. The opportunity cost of making the deposit on the house is thus $300, making costs so far $2856 per month or $714 per week for the ownership option. On purely present day financial considerations, Kumar would rent.

Market conditions can change the figures and make some propositions more attractive. However, perhaps the biggest consideration of all is not the financing decision, but the accumulation of an asset. The renter has nothing at the end of an extended rental period; the purchaser has an asset or a significant share in an asset which can be realised at any time.

LO 8

Financing a house purchase

If a buyer has the necessary funds, the easiest way to finance a house purchase is with the buyer's own cash. The advantages of this approach are the speed of settling the transaction, the freedom to make decisions without being fettered by a financial institution, and the absence of the fees associated with loan approvals. There are tax advantages in paying cash for an investor's own home and borrowing to invest elsewhere, rather than investing cash elsewhere and borrowing to purchase the home.

Unfortunately, the majority of investors are not in a position to purchase a house for cash — they must obtain a loan. The usual method is by way of mortgage loan. The word 'mortgage' stems from Old French *mort* meaning 'dead' and *gage* meaning 'pledge'. Thus, a mortgage is a 'dead pledge'. What, then, is a 'live pledge'? A live pledge is one where both the capital asset and its income are pledged to the lender. In contrast, with a mortgaged property the lender has rights only over the capital asset, not the income from it or the use of it or, in this case, the right to live in it.

Matching financial capacity to borrowings

How does a potential borrower decide the amount to borrow under a mortgage loan? Does it depend on the amount needed, personal income or current savings? The amount needed depends on the price of the house. How should a buyer decide which houses are too dear? Are some houses too cheap and unsuitable for a buyer with given financial worth?

Let us look at the last question first. Some houses may be too cheap. They may be in poor condition and need much expenditure to bring them up to standard; they may be in an unsuitable area for the buyer; or they may be of an unsuitable design for the buyer's needs.

Can a house be too expensive? Yes, many houses, although suitable in size and condition, are too expensive for the potential buyer's financial capabilities. How do we know the right price? It all comes back to affordability. Affordability relates the repayments to the borrower's income. As figure 6.1 shows, affordability in recent years has increased significantly from only 3–4 years ago. Another factor which must be considered is other indebtedness. If borrowers have no other debts, then they can afford higher mortgage repayments and hence can contract for larger loans. There are many ways to judge affordability. Some financial institutions prefer that a borrower's contracted mortgage repayments do not exceed about 30% of before-tax income and that the total of all loan repayments does not exceed 35% of before-tax income. Others suggest the mortgage repayments should not exceed 50% of the surplus funds after normal living expenses and taxes are met. These ratios set the upper limits of available contracted loans.

The use of the term 'normal' in the affordability criterion is interesting. Financial institutions are aware that many people lack financial discipline. Thus, whereas some people are able to make an extraordinary effort to save money and pay off a larger-than-usual loan, others cannot sustain the effort for very long and eventually default. Lenders bow to the inevitable for the community as a whole and suggest loans should be smaller or loan periods should be longer so that regular repayment amounts are smaller. Notwithstanding the norm of community behaviour, some people make an extraordinary financial effort and pay off loans very quickly. This sort of effort, incorporating supreme savings endeavour (i.e. cutting consumption), an appropriate loan structure and perhaps additional work to increase income, is the basis for books with titles like 'How I paid off my mortgage in five years'. People with this discipline can acquire assets very quickly.

The amount of current savings will determine the size of the deposit and thus the amount which can be paid for a property. Financial institutions prefer people to have a sizeable deposit. As many young people find it difficult to raise the deposit required to buy a home — and as prices rise, a higher deposit is required — many parents use some of their superannuation money or mortgage their own home to help their children raise the required deposit. The availability of a good deposit (about 20% or more) will influence the loan decision in a positive manner and will also reduce costs, in that mortgage insurance to cover the lender against default may not be required. In calculating the amount of savings which can be used as a deposit, buyers should remember that there will be loan establishment fees (up to $1000), conveyancing fees, and other transaction costs such as survey fees and stamp duty to be paid. In addition, an emergency cash balance should be kept to insure against unforeseen circumstances.

Loan types

Once all the side issues have been looked after, there are the major issues of interest rates and types of loans available:

variable loan
a loan that may vary in terms of interest rate charged to the borrower

fixed-rate loan
a loan whereby the interest rate is fixed by a length of time and/or by a fixed interest rate

- standard **variable loans** *(SVLs)*, usually for 20–25 years but allowing faster repayment, with the interest rate varying with the market (variations in types of variable loans also may exist from providers)
- **fixed-rate loans**, with rates and repayments fixed for 1–5 years, then becoming variable, and with penalties for earlier repayment
- *capped loans*, with a cap on rate increases that can be applied for 1 year, then defaulting to SVL conditions
- *introductory 'honeymoon' loans*, with about 1.0% lower rates for 1–2 years, then reverting to SVL conditions
- *all-in-one* or *100% offset loans*, allowing speedy repayment by applying all funds to repayment but drawing down for living expenses
- *combination fixed and variable loans*, allowing spreading of interest-rate risk
- *home equity loans*, allowing funds to be withdrawn against equity for other expenditure and enjoying lower interest rates than personal or credit card loans. The ability to re-borrow funds without going through the approval process, and at a competitive interest rate compared with personal loan rates of 11–14%, makes home equity loans very useful financial products. The major disadvantage of this type of loan is that increases in equity accrued through increases in asset value may be frittered away by expenditure on other goods and services.

Table 6.3 gives a sample of a range of interest rates and loan conditions at August 2013 for a two year fixed rate of interest. Mortgage insurance is charged by most institutions where LVRs exceed 80–85%. Mortgage insurance protects the lender should the borrower not be able to meet their repayments. Mortgage insurance on a $300 000 loan may cost around $2000 p.a.

TABLE 6.3 Sample of 2-year interest rates, LVRs, fees and borrowing limits at August 2013

Institution	Interest rate (%) 2-year fixed	Maximum LVR (%)	Establishment fees ($)	Minimum borrowing	Maximum borrowing
Aussie	4.64	80	Nil	100 000	2 000 000
Westpac	4.89	80	Nil	150 000	10 000 000
NAB	4.89	80	Nil	150 000	10 000 000
St George	4.94	95	600	10 000	1 000 000
CBA	4.89	80	600	10 000	10 000 000
ANZ	5.04	90	600	20 000	10 000 000

Source: Finder 2013

Home equity conversion loans

Home equity conversion (HEC) loans or **reverse mortgages** allow older people to use the wealth they have tied up in their homes to support a more comfortable retirement, either by the occasional expenditure of lump sums or the regular expenditure of small sums to fund consumption which could not be sustained by their regular disposable incomes. A borrower normally borrows a lump sum secured by the equity in their house. This lump sum may then be used to purchase an annuity, if regular increments to income are desired, or managed to supply intermittent lump sums. Rather than receive a lump sum, some prefer to arrange a direct monthly payment to supplement their normal income. Regardless of the method of tapping into the equity of the home, a loan is created with interest charged at a compounding rate. No repayments are made during the term of the loan, as the principal and interest owing are repaid when the borrower dies or decides to leave their home.

home equity conversion (HEC) loan (reverse mortgage) a loan or an amount by which a home owner may draw funds based on the equity or ownership value of the home

Issues which must be considered and written into the loan contract include:

- no negative equity guarantees — theoretically, interest on a loan could accrue to the extent that the value of the principal plus the interest exceeds the value of the house. The contract needs to state that the borrower, no matter how long they live, will not end up owing a net debt, and the lender cannot seek extra repayments from either the borrower or their estate.
- who is responsible for repairs and maintenance on the house
- what standard of repair to the house will be maintained.

In addition, borrowers need to consider the views of their families who may have expectations of inheritances. In approving loans, lenders need to consider whether the value of the underlying security will change. Normally, values of houses increase, but it is possible in the short term for values to decrease.

After an extended period of discussion and market research, several financial institutions now offer HEC loans. The interest rates charged are usually 1.0–1.5% higher than SVL rates. Most lenders are reluctant to have loan principals exceed 35–45% of the assessed property value to ensure there is a considerable margin to accommodate the accruing interest.

The value at maturity of a HEC loan is a simple application of compound interest. The financial institution normally will quote a nominal annual rate, compounded daily but charged monthly. The formula for the future value of a single-principal loan, as you know from chapter 2, is:

$$FV = PV\,(1 + i)^n$$

Consider Dave, who borrows \$100 000 under a HEC arrangement at 9.0% interest, compounded monthly. (We will assume compounded monthly for ease of calculation.) The LVR is 20%. Dave lives 18 years after taking out the loan and the loan is settled at exactly 18 years. What is the settlement value?

$$FV = PV(1 + i)^n$$

$$i = \frac{0.09}{12}$$

$$= 0.0075$$

$$n = 18 \times 12$$

$$= 216$$

$$FV = 100\,000(1.0075)^{216}$$

$$= \$502\,263$$

Will the sale of Dave's house cover this value? Very likely, as there almost surely would have been appreciation of prices over the 18-year period. In fact, over 18 years at an average of 5% growth rate per annum Dave's house grows in value to $1 203 310. Hence, there will be the sum of $701 047 left over for his estate.

Interest rates and repayments

Interest rates vary between loan providers and loan products. For example, in August 2013, rates for SVLs ranged from 5.2% to 5.884%, depending on the provider. Fixed 2-year rates ranged from 4.64% to 5.04%. Figure 6.3 indicates SVL rates for the period 1993 to 2013 and shows that interest rates increased gradually until 2008, fell as a result of the global financial crisis, then started to move up again in 2010, but have fallen again since 2010.

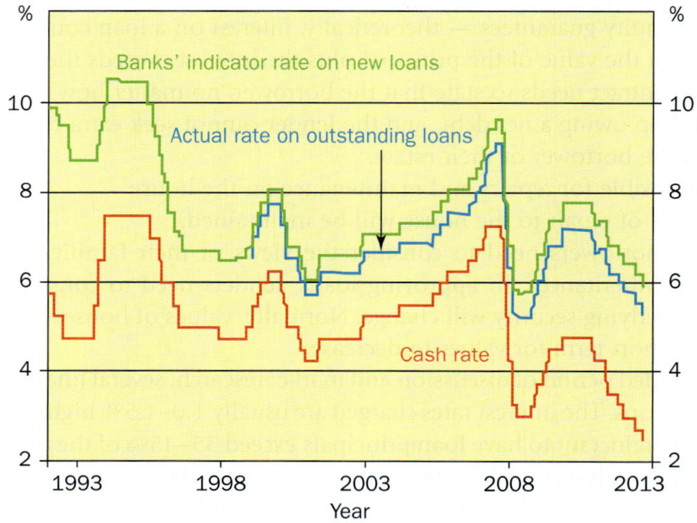

FIGURE 6.3
Australian housing interest rates 1993 to 2013
Source: RBA. Chart Pack, 2013.

Given an interest rate of 6.55% for a $100 000 loan taken out over 30 years, how is the required monthly repayment calculated? This is an annuity calculation. The $100 000 is the present value of an annuity. The formula, as we saw in chapter 2, is:

$$PV = \frac{C[1 - (1 + i)^{-n}]}{i}$$

where PV = present value
C = regular payment (or PMT if using a financial calculator)
i = interest rate per period
n = number of periods.

Thus

$$C = \frac{PV}{[1 - (1 + i)^{-n}]/i}$$

The first thing to calculate is the interest rate per period, which is the annual rate (6.55%) divided by 12 months for 12 monthly payment periods per year:

$$\frac{0.0655}{12} = 0.005\,458\,333$$

There are 360 months in 30 years, so n is 360. Substituting into the equation:

$$
\begin{aligned}
(1 + i)^{-n} &= (1.005\,458\,333)^{-360} \\
&= \frac{1}{(1.005\,458\,333)^{360}} \\
&= \frac{1}{7.046\,889} \\
&= 0.140\,906\,797
\end{aligned}
$$

So

$$
\begin{aligned}
\frac{-(1 + i)^{-n}}{i} &= \frac{1 - 0.14\,906\,797}{0.005\,458\,333} \\
&= 157.391\,13
\end{aligned}
$$

Thus

$$
\begin{aligned}
C &= \frac{\$100\,000}{157.391\,13} \\
&= \$635.36
\end{aligned}
$$

To help Charli solve her dilemma about buying or renting, such a calculation as above provides information to Charli about the monthly repayment required to buy the apartment. To make a comparison, Charli would need to consider the rent costs over such a period of time which effectively provide no asset after 18 years. A comparison would need to be made based on an equal series of payments per month. When considering the rent option, Charli would need to invest the balance over the rent payments for the 18 year period and then compare the investment value at the end of that time with the value of the apartment.

LO 9 Taxation and housing

This section deals with several aspects of taxation and the home. In particular, the following aspects are considered:

- the impacts of the GST on housing
- the taxation consequences of renting all or part of a home
- the taxation consequences of using part of the home as an office
- the taxation aspects of selling the main residence
- the taxation impact of selling the home after the owner's death
- the taxation effects on the family home as a result of a family breakdown.

Impacts of the GST on housing

The goods and services tax (GST) is payable on new houses supplied after 1 July 2000 to the first occupiers by builders and developers. From that time new house prices rose by up to 10%, depending on the proportion of content which had sales tax removed. However, as a form of compensation the government moved to offer a rebate of \$7000 to first-home purchasers. GST also applied to the sellers of land for new home building after 1 July 2000 but the GST only applied to the increase in value since 1 July 2000.

Sales of secondhand houses are not subject to GST. Some owners will have made extensions or repairs during the course of their ownership and GST will have been paid on these inputs. These owners are not able to claim GST credits when their home is sold. GST is payable on the services supplied during the sale of the house, including advertising, real estate agent fees, conveyancing fees and search fees.

Taxation consequences of renting part or all of a home

Owner-occupiers may rent out part of their houses. Rent received is assessable income and pro rata expenses are legitimate tax deductions. There are capital gains tax (CGT) consequences of renting out part or all of a main residence/home as the full CGT exemption on the home may be no longer available. Generally, the CGT liability will accrue proportionately (computed in days) for the part of the whole period where the property was not the taxpayer's main residence. People who are transferred on a temporary or permanent basis may decide to rent their former home. There are income tax, CGT and social security entitlement implications. This situation is treated in a similar fashion to normal investment property. However, the CGT legislation allows a concession in that a main residence may retain its exemption status even while producing rental income for up to 6 years if no other residence is claimed as a main residence in Australia.

Taxation consequences of using part of the home as an office

Some people work wholly or partly from home, and often have one room or several fitted up as office space. There is a great temptation to claim repairs, maintenance, electricity and other expenses for the office part of the house as a tax deduction in order to reduce income tax. Although these expenses are legitimate expenses incurred in earning assessable income, the ATO has stringent requirements which must be fulfilled for these deductions to be allowed. Many people deem it not worth the worry of an argument with the ATO and do not claim these deductions.

Where deductions have been claimed for use of part of a home for gaining assessable income, there are CGT consequences when the house is sold. A proportion of any gain, calculated relative to the space and time used for producing income, is liable to tax. Expert taxation advice should be obtained on this matter.

Some taxation aspects of selling a home

A CGT liability may arise when an investment house purchased after 19 September 1985 is sold at a price which yields a capital gain. In contrast, a capital gain made on the sale of a house used solely as the main residence is exempted under the CGT legislation. Note that for CGT purposes a main residence can be a caravan, houseboat or residential shed, as well as more conventional dwellings. However, as noted, the CGT exemption can be compromised by using part or the whole of the house for some time during the period of ownership for income-producing purposes. CGT can also be triggered by the owner ceasing to be an Australian resident.

Stamp duty (a state-levied tax) is payable on the sale of property including houses. Fortunately for sellers, this duty is payable by buyers. The rates of duty vary between states but range between 1.5% and 2%. Some states have concessional duty rates for main residences and/or first-home purchases.

Implications of the death of a homeowner

There are now generally no death taxes in Australia. However, CGT provisions may act like a quasi-death tax in some circumstances. No CGT liability is triggered by the fact of the death and transfer into the hands of an executor. A house registered at the Titles Office in joint names (joint tenancy) is not an asset of the deceased; title passes automatically to the surviving joint tenant. Thus, there are no CGT consequences in this situation.

The exemption from CGT of any gain made on the sale of a person's main residence (MR) during life continues after death, provided that it is sold within 2 years of death or is used as the MR of the deceased's spouse until the time of disposal. The CGT exemption extends also to a beneficiary inheriting a house, provided the beneficiary also disposes of the house within 2 years. There are further exemptions where sales take place after the 2-year period has elapsed when the beneficiary or a spouse uses the house as the MR.

Beneficiaries who do not qualify for any of the exemptions are liable to CGT when selling the property. A house which had been acquired by the deceased before 20 September 1985 should be valued at the date of the death, so that this market value forms the cost base in any future CGT calculations. On the other hand, a house which had been acquired by the deceased after 19 September 1985 takes the cost or indexed cost as its cost base in any future CGT calculations.

Family breakdown and the family home

Nowadays, marriage breakdown results in more equitable splitting of the combined assets of the separating partners than was the case before the most recent developments in family law. As the family home is normally the largest asset of the average family, the dwelling is usually involved in any property settlement.

If a transfer of property title occurs (i.e. the title in the home passes from one party to another), normally CGT liability would be incurred. However, CGT rollover relief is available on marriage breakdown. If there is a transfer of the property to a spouse or former spouse and a court order under the *Family Law Act 1975* or under law relating to a de facto relationship, CGT rollover relief applies automatically. The rollover relief means that no CGT liability arises from the transfer, pre-CGT assets retain that status in the hands of the transferee and post-CGT assets retain their original cost base. Essentially, the transferee gains title to the asset with exactly the same CGT characteristics as the transferor enjoyed.

Any subsequent CGT considerations are based on the transferee's use of the house. Thus, a divorce is able to turn a rental property after transfer into a family home with its CGT exemption. This is shown in Alan and Enid's situation. Alan and Enid own a rental property as well as their family home. They separate and, under a Family Court order, the rental property is transferred to Enid. Had they sold the rental property, CGT would have accrued on any capital gain realised. However, Enid moves into the house and uses it as her MR. The CGT situation now is more complex. On any subsequent sale and realised capital gain, Enid will be liable for CGT on (her original) part of half the capital gain, calculated on the number of days the property was rented over the whole period of ownership, and exempt from CGT on the half share she received under the Family Court order. (The 50% discount for the CGT liability is a separate issue.) Again, this is a complex legal area and specialised advice should be sought in such a situation.

Summary

Investment in property is an essential ingredient of a diversified investment portfolio to achieve both income and capital growth objectives. Property investment covers a wide range and includes residential, commercial, agricultural and industrial and the many variations of property contained within those broad classes. The development of property trusts and the growth in the numbers of property funds offered on the market has enabled many investors with limited means to invest indirectly in a diversified range of properties both in Australia and overseas. The advantage of being able to make relatively small investments coupled with the liquidity aspects of investing in property funds has led to the significant diversity in the property trust industry. Investors in property obtain taxation benefits to minimise the taxation effects of their investment.

Home ownership is often a major financial goal for many people. Currently, Australia has a high incidence of home ownership, but this may change in the future for a variety of reasons, not least of which are reduced job security and housing affordability. There are several advantages of home ownership, including being able to use the equity in a house, and the CGT taxation concessions it receives on sale. However, there are also disadvantages — property investment is non-liquid, there is an opportunity cost in having wealth tied up in a home, and losses may have to be borne if the owner needs to sell at an inopportune time.

Decisions have to be made on whether to rent or buy a home. Financing a 'buy' decision involves matching financial capacity to borrowings, and investigating the variety of loans available. Taxation issues include the impact of the GST; whether the home is partially or completely exempt from CGT when sold by the owner or by the owner's executor; and the circumstances when CGT rollover relief applies on a family breakdown.

Professional application questions

6.1 If you were planning to invest in property as a general asset class, list three positive characteristics and two negative characteristics that property investments are likely to possess.

6.2 Jodie wants to invest in an unlisted property trust. Explain how the units are valued.

6.3 Compare the features of investing in an A-REIT and a UPT.

6.4 Why might an A-REIT that holds a number of commercial properties in its portfolio be considered to be a safer investment than one that holds a single commercial property?

6.5 Describe the risk and return of investing in a mezzanine fund.

6.6 In your own words, write a paragraph of the advantages of home ownership.

6.7 Explain why a mortgage lender might refuse to lend over 90% of the price of a new home.

6.8 A financial institution offers Fatima the choice between a standard variable loan (SVL) of 5.23% or a 2-year fixed rate at 4.89% and then SVL after 2 years. Advise her of the issues and which loan to accept.

6.9 If your grandparents were considering a HEC loan contract, what are the main things that you suggest they should take into consideration?

6.10 Edwina bought her house in September 1984 for $54 000. She died in 2012 and left the house to her only daughter, Claire. Claire wants to rent it but is worried about the CGT implications. What advice would you give her?

Professional application exercises

Basic	*
Moderate	* *
Challenging	* * *

6.11 Calculating rental returns *

Nerida recently purchased a rental property for $350 000. She expects that she should be able to charge a rent based on a gross return of 6% p.a.

(a) What is the amount of gross rent that she would charge?

(b) If Nerida is told that ongoing costs of owning the property (without considering the interest costs on a loan) amount to $3500 p.a., calculate her net income return after costs.

(c) Assuming Nerida has not borrowed any funds to acquire the property and her marginal tax rate is 30% (ignore Medicare levy), calculate her after-tax return on the rental income.

(d) If, instead, Nerida borrowed $200 000 on interest-only terms to acquire the property and has to pay interest of 6.5% p.a., what is the taxation implication for Nerida?

6.12 Calculating the value of a property *

Foula has inherited a rental property from her father. The property is in a regional town that Foula visits only occasionally so she is not familiar with the prices of property in the area.

She visits a local real estate agent who advises that if she wants to rent the property, then she could expect to receive a rental income of $180 per week. Foula also wonders what the value of the property is expected to be if she decides to sell it. The agent advises that according to recent sales of similar properties, an average capitalisation rate of 7.0% could be applied.

(a) Calculate the expected market value of the property.

(b) How might the agent have arrived at an average capitalisation rate of 7.0%?

(c) List the factors that Foula is likely to take into account in making her decision to rent the property or to sell it.

(d) If you were in Foula's position, what might you decide to do? Explain.

6.13 Which loan is most suitable — 25 or 30 years? * *

Monique needs a loan of $250 000 as she has saved $100 000 to use as a deposit on a house. The interest rate is 8.0%. She has selected a standard loan for 30 years rather than 25 years, because the regular payments are smaller compared to her present income. For 30 years (360 payments) she will pay 0.667% compound interest per month and the monthly payment is $1835 and a total of $360 600 will be paid in interest. For 25 years (300 payments) she will pay the same interest rate and the monthly payments are $1930 per month and $279 000 in total interest. Monique wants the ability to make extra payments when she can afford to and would prefer a loan that would allow such extra payments to be made to reduce the amount owed. Monique earns $1500 net of all deductions and taxes each fortnight, but spends $500 of that on living expenses during the period to the next pay. She asks your advice on the following questions.

QUESTIONS

1 If a fortnight passes before Monique is able to deposit her first pay of $1500, how much is the loan balance at the end of the fortnight?

2 If Monique spends $500 on living expenses during the fortnight to the next pay, approximately how much is the loan balance just before the next pay deposit?

3 Discuss the effect of making extra repayments on the total period of time to pay the loan and the total interest costs.

6.14 Tax and property investments ✱✱

Than has purchased a newly built rental property for $350 000. He has borrowed $300 000 for the purchase at an interest rate of 9.0% p.a. on an interest-only basis. In the first year of the investment he gives you the following additional information: gross rent $25 000; property costs (rates, insurance, minor repairs, agent fees etc.) $4000; depreciation of building at 2.5% (assume cost of building $300 000); depreciation of fittings $3800; and borrowing costs $1500. Than's marginal tax rate is 45% (ignore Medicare levy).

(a) Prepare a table to show the after-tax cash flow that Than may expect to receive on the investment.

(b) Assume Than sells the property for $485 000 after 4 years. His selling costs are 3.0% of the selling price. Prepare a table to show Than the proceeds available to him on the sale of the property after tax and after repayment of the loan.

6.15 The effect of low interest rates on the decision to buy or rent ✱✱

Read the Personal Finance Bulletin and summarise the main points which indicate why it may be seen to be cheaper to buy a home rather than rent. Outline the process that prospective house buyers will follow to determine if they are better off paying a mortgage or a landlord.

6.16 Repayments on a home loan ✱✱

Georgie and Teresa are contemplating buying a house for which they will need a $200 000 loan. They find a suitable lender who offers them the funds at a nominal annual 6.5% fixed rate and advises a 25-year loan.

(a) What is the monthly repayment for a 25-year loan?

(b) How much interest is paid over 25 years?

6.17 Paying off a loan early ✱✱

Deng decides to pay off his $200 000 20-year 6.0% loan faster by paying fortnightly instead of monthly. By how much will the loan term be shortened (to the nearest full year) if he pays about the same amount per month in total, but pays fortnightly instead of once per month?

6.18 Repayment frequency ✱✱✱

Therese contracts for a $250 000 loan at 6.5% p.a. nominal interest rate. What would the periodic repayments be over 25 years if the repayments were made:

(a) fortnightly?

(b) monthly?

6.19 Home equity conversion loans ✱✱✱

Graham takes out a $120 000 home equity conversion loan on his fully owned $600 000 house. The interest rate is 8.5% compounded monthly. Graham dies and the house is sold after exactly 10 years. How much is the outstanding debt?

6.20 Capital gains tax on an investment property ✱✱✱

Joyce and Fergus bought an investment property on 1 July 2000 for $200 000. After they separated in 2005, they obtained a Family Court order that Fergus should receive the investment property to live in from then on. He moved in on 1 July 2006. After living there for exactly 5 years, Fergus sold and moved interstate. The property sold for $550 000. Discuss the capital gains issues that Fergus faces.

CASE STUDY 1

Retirement income streams

Victor comes to see you as a financial planner. Victor is 40 years old and is a marketing executive. He is dressed in a $1000 suit, bright blue shirt and a vibrant coloured tie. Victor is single, has been very successful with his marketing role, and earns a very good salary from which he is able to enjoy a reasonably lavish lifestyle and save to build up his bank account balance. The marketing industry is somewhat volatile and susceptible to ups and downs in the market. Yet, Victor has been lucky and has moved into different marketing positions at opportune times. He had a very successful period in the years 2003 to mid-2007 and received substantial bonuses in those years. He invested some of his bonuses in a range of companies listed on the share market but got badly burnt when the prices of some of those companies which were highly geared fell dramatically during the global financial crisis. Despite having lost some $50 000, Victor has not been dispirited altogether and has since invested and holds some $50 000 in blue-chip shares from the top ten share market picks.

He now has accumulated about $40 000 in spare cash and is seeking a higher return than the banks are currently offering for term deposits. He wants to invest about $20 000 into the property market as he is very much aware that many property funds had suffered severely in the global financial crisis and had been trading at below 50% of the prices that they had reached before the crisis. He wants an exposure to the property market but also wants to be able to get his money out quickly if the world suffers a 'double dip' and goes into another period of recession. As he is a busy person he does not want to manage his investments and considers that a property fund would suit his purposes best. He likes the idea of a fund that holds some of the largest CBD buildings in the major capital cities as he believes that these would be the safest funds to invest in. As he doesn't get time to review his investment regularly he has decided to ensure that he adds to his investment portfolio on a regular basis. Thus, he arranges to add $12 000 per year to the fund by contributing $1000 per month as a regular direct debit investment.

QUESTIONS

1 What sort of property funds might suit Victor's investment wishes?

2 Suggest reasons why Victor might consider investment into A-REITs rather than UPTs.

3 Consider whether investing $1000 per month into the same fund is a reasonable investment decision.

4 Do you agree with Victor's view that investing in assets that suffered severe price falls in the global financial crisis would prove to be a wise investment decision?

CASE STUDY 2

Comparing property investments

Todd and Wesley are two friends who met at university and, during their summer vacation, decided to develop a property together. Their plan is to buy a property that they can renovate and paint, then obtain a tenant and sell the property in 3 years when, with improved value, the property could be sold for a substantial gain.

They are currently considering two property choices. The anticipated net income for each property for each year is shown in the following table.

	Year 1	Year 2	Year 3
Property A	$22 000	$23 000	$24 000
Property B	$24 000	$25 000	$26 000

Todd and Wesley will borrow most of the funds required to purchase whichever property that they decide to develop, but regardless of interest payments they want to know which property is the best value for them to invest in.

- Property A requires an outlay of $280 000 to acquire the property and initial costs of $60 000 to upgrade the property before it could be rented. It is expected that they can sell the property at the end of the 3-year period for $420 000.
- Property B requires an outlay of $250 000 and initial costs of $40 000. They expect to sell the property in 3 years for $390 000.

The rate of return that they could obtain from an alternative investment choice is 8% p.a. Using the information provided:

QUESTIONS

1 Calculate the net present value of acquiring, developing and selling property A.

2 Calculate the net present value of acquiring, developing and selling property B.

3 Which property would you advise them to purchase? Explain why.

4 What questions would you consider if they decided not to undertake the property purchase but to invest in the alternative investment choice?

References and further reading

ABS 2010, *House prices indexes: eight capital cities, September 2010*, cat. no. 6416.0, abs.gov.au.

Ellis, L 2010, 'Recent developments in the housing market and its financing', Reserve Bank of Australia, Financial Review Residential Property Conference 2010, 18 May, Sydney, www.rba.gov.au/speeches/2010.

Elsworth, S 2013, 'ABS and Canstar analysis shows home loans doubled in 10 years', 12 April, News.com.au.
Featherstone, T 2010, 'Ten top A-REITs', *ASX investor update*, April, asx.com.au.
Finder 2013, Best home loans, 27 August, http://finder.com.au/home-loans/best-home-loans.
Higgins, E & Abey, A 2000, *Fortune strategy*, 2nd edn, Allen & Unwin, Sydney.
Housing Industry Association Ltd 2013, 'Housing affordability continues to surge', 21 March.
Janda, M 2013, 'Housing just as affordable as in 1994: ABS', ABC News 28 August.
Johanson, S 2013, 'Housing becoming cheaper to buy than rent', *The Age*, 13 July.
Property Investment Research Pty Ltd 2007, *Property funds investment for financial advisers*, training course, October.
RBA 2010, 'Housing turnover and first-home buyers', *Bulletin*, June, rba.gov.au.
RBA 2012, 'Dwelling prices and household income', *Bulletin*, December quarter 2012, rba.gov.au.
RBA 2013, 'Australian housing lending rates', *Chart pack*, 7 August 2013, rba.gov.au.
Roth, M. & Lang, C. 2005, *How investing in commercial property really works*, 2nd edn, John Wiley & Sons, Brisbane.

7 Managed funds

LEARNING OBJECTIVES

After studying this chapter, you should be able to:

1. discuss the growth and characteristics of the managed fund industry in Australia
2. explain the regulatory environment and the structure of managed investment schemes (MISs) in Australia
3. outline the advantages, downsides and risks associated with investing into managed funds
4. explain the typical fee structure of a managed fund
5. determine how to select a managed fund for investing
6. differentiate between different management and investment styles
7. explain the taxation implications of investing in managed funds
8. outline some of the methods used for measuring returns and analysing performance of managed funds.

CASE STUDY

Jake and Sarah acquired three different Australian equity managed funds a number of years ago on the advice of a financial planner. However, they have never understood the types of funds they have invested into or why they needed to invest in three different funds. The couple is looking to dispose of two managed funds (B and C) and invest all into Fund A on the basis of it producing the best 1-year return. The fees and returns for all three funds, together with a summary of their investment style, are provided below.

Fund	Total return		Management fee
A	1 years	46.71%	0.85% p.a.
	3 years	−4.38%	
	5 years	3.6%	
B	1 years	18.2%	0.5% p.a.
	3 years	−4.10%	
	5 years	7.79%	
C	1 years	14.4%	1.22% p.a.
	3 years	−3.35%	
	5 years	7.1%	

Fund A

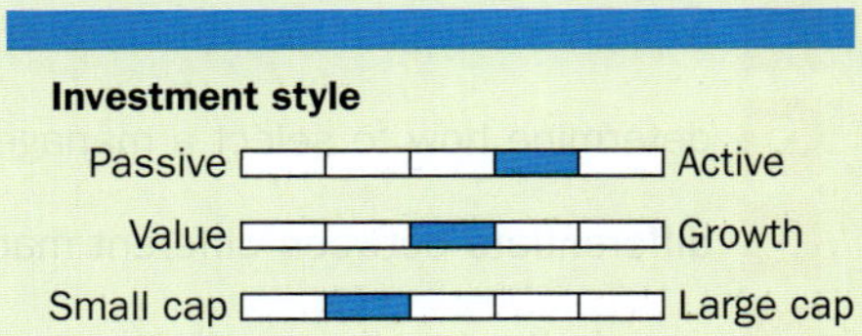

Fund B

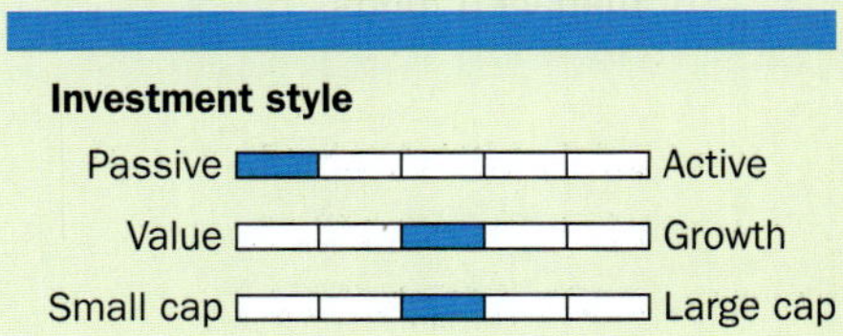

Fund C

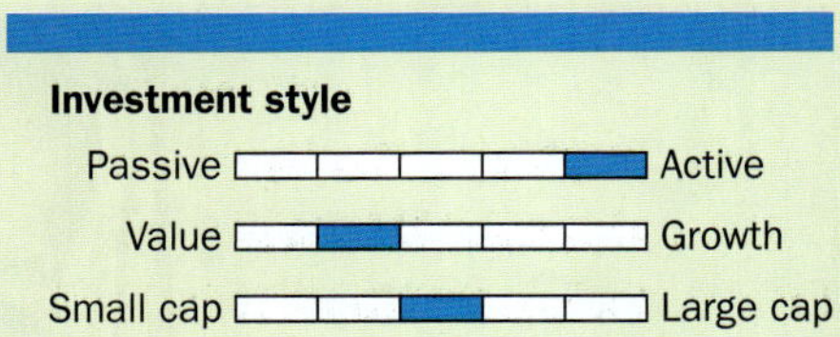

Some issues to consider from this case include the following.

- What are the benefits of investing into a managed fund?
- What do the different investment styles refer to within the three managed funds?
- Is there any value in the couple retaining all three managed funds or should all monies be consolidated into the one managed fund account?
- What issues would need to be considered if the couple decided to sell one or more of the funds?

Illustrative examples used throughout this chapter will relate back to the information contained within this case study.

Introduction

The managed fund industry is that part of the investment sector that is made up of superannuation funds, the statutory funds of life insurers, **public unit trusts** and managed investment schemes. Managed funds allow investors to pool their money together and invest into a variety of asset classes. The fund is managed by a team of professional fund managers. This chapter introduces this sector of investment markets in Australia and explains the role and use of managed funds within a portfolio of personal investments.

public unit trust
a trust that issues units to the general public for the purpose of investing monies raised

The modern managed fund industry gained impetus from the development of the unit trust which offered a vehicle for the funds of many small investors to be pooled so that relatively large amounts of funds could be raised and invested. Managed funds have evolved into investment vehicles that allow investors to invest into a wide range of asset classes and management styles, to make either periodic payments or lump-sum contributions, and to determine the desired level of risk they are prepared to accept within their investment portfolios.

LO 1 Growth and characteristics of managed funds

According to the Australian Securities and Investments Commission (ASIC), a managed investment scheme (MIS), commonly known as a managed fund, exists where:

- people are brought together to contribute money to obtain an interest in the scheme ('interests' in a scheme are a type of 'financial product' and are regulated by the *Corporations Act 2001*)
- money is pooled together with other investors (that often number in the many hundreds or thousands) or used in a common enterprise
- a responsible entity operates the scheme. Investors do not have day-to-day control over the operation of the scheme.

A managed fund operates under a trust structure where investors pool their money with many other investors in order to buy into a portfolio of assets that are managed by a professional manager. The funds are managed on behalf of the investors according to the stated investment goals of the fund. For example, the objective of an equity fund may be to invest in a concentrated portfolio of Australian shares that aims to offer long-term returns in excess of the cash rate plus 4% p.a. over a rolling 5-year period.

beneficial interest the entitlement to receive benefits generated by assets held in the name of another entity

Investors buy units in a fund, similar to buying shares in a company, and as the value of the investments within the fund rises or falls, the price of the units moves accordingly. Investors have **beneficial interest** in the pool of investments based on the proportion of the total investments they hold. Income and capital gains generated within the fund are distributed to investors in proportion to the number of units held. Unit holders may also incur capital gains and losses when they sell their units.

For example, Fund M collects $10 million from investors to invest into Australian shares. The fund manager will issue 10 million units each at $1. If an investor invests $10 000, they will receive 10 000 units in the fund. Let's say after 5 years the value of the fund is now $20 million due to an increase in the value of the investments held. Thus the investor's investment has doubled from $1 per unit to $2 per unit, which has resulted in an effective doubling of the original worth of their investment. In addition to the capital growth during the period, Fund M is also likely to have earned and distributed income to its investors based on the proportion of units held.

The growth of managed funds in Australia

The managed fund industry in Australia has grown at a significant rate over the last 30 years. Reserve Bank of Australia (RBA) figures as at December 2012 show that total domestic funds under management was around $2009 billion. The break-up of domestic funds under management within Australia is represented in table 7.1.

TABLE 7.1 Domestic funds under management within Australia

Funds under management	$ billion unconsolidated	Share of total
Superannuation	1457.1	72.5%
Life insurance	245.2	12.2%
Public unit trusts	265.3	13.2%
Other managed funds	42.2	2.1%
Total funds	**2009.8**	**100%**

Source: RBA 2012.

While the investment structure of the various types of managed investment funds are similar, they each have their own characteristics in terms of the way they are controlled, regulated and taxed. The focus of this chapter will be on funds classified as a managed investment scheme. While superannuation funds also operate as a trust structure, where funds are managed on behalf of superannuation fund members, they are not classified as managed investment schemes.

The managed funds sector has grown strongly over the past 20 years. Aggregate funds under management have increased from around $204 billion in 1990 to over $2009 billion at the end of 2012, representing an average annual rate of return of nearly 11%. Within the managed funds sector, superannuation funds account for the majority of funds managed at 72.5% of the total domestic funds under management, while public unit trusts account for 13.2% of funds. A public unit trust is a fund which is open to the general public to acquire units in. Public unit trusts took 30 years to reach $1 billion under management in 1980 (Foster 1996). These funds grew in the next decades to $28 billion in 1990 (Foster 1996), $123 billion in 2000 and $264 billion in 2012 (RBA 2012).

The main contributors to the overall growth in funds under management have been the deregulation of financial markets in the 1980s and the increase in superannuation contributions made by employers since 1990. Managed funds are now a cornerstone of wealth creation in Australia, and own a vast array of wealth-creation instruments.

Characteristics of managed funds

A managed fund is an unlisted investment vehicle where a financial organisation invites investors to invest monies with them with the objective of purchasing and managing a portfolio of investments in order to generate returns for the investors. The fund is managed by a professional fund manager who charges a management fee for undertaking their work. The fund generates earnings from its investments and distributes the earnings to the unit holders in the form of income, capital growth or a combination of both. A managed fund is characterised by the type of assets the fund invests in, the management structure, the tax concessions and tax structure available, and the regulatory structure required for the operation of the fund. A managed fund is purpose-built, where the rules and regulations for the operation of the fund, including the assets to be invested in, are established within a **trust deed** before potential investors are invited to invest. Interests in a managed investment scheme are a type of financial product and are regulated under the Corporations Act.

trust deed
a legal document used to establish and regulate the operation of a trust

Managed funds, over time, may collect a substantial amount of funds from investors. Some of the large funds manage portfolios worth over $750 m. The significant amount of funds raised allows a fund manager to invest into a large and varied range of different types of investments, some of which would be difficult for the individual investor to invest into directly. Examples include international shares, office property, ethical investments, commodities and infrastructure assets such as airports, tollways and wind farms. Managed funds offer investors the potential to invest into all of the main asset classes including:

- cash management trusts
- Australian and international equity (share) trusts
- Australian and international property (REITS) trusts
- Australian and international fixed interest
- alternative investments such as commodities and infrastructure.

These funds will be discussed further in a later section of this chapter but it's worth noting that the same risk and return relationship exists for investing into the various asset classes no matter whether investing directly or indirectly through managed funds.

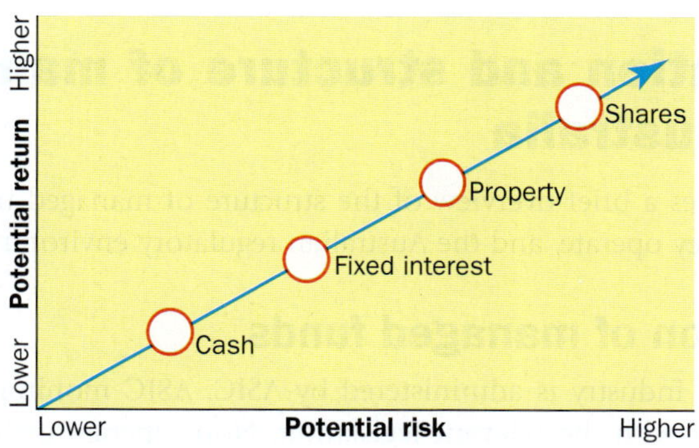

FIGURE 7.1
Risk/return relationship

Managed funds are popular because they allow investors to gain access to a wide range of different asset classes (cash, fixed interest, property and shares), gain exposure to different industry segments (e.g. commercial property or Asian shares) and gain effective diversification across a range of different investment types (e.g. a balanced fund which invests across all of the main asset classes).

In the absence of this type of investment vehicle, many of these assets or portfolio mixes would be unavailable or difficult for the individual investor to acquire.

However, many investors prefer to invest into investments directly, that is, they invest directly into the actual asset such as shares, retail property or term deposits. There are a number of benefits in investing directly into investments including the ability to control the actual investment (what to buy, when to buy and when to sell); management and administration costs may be less in many instances; and the investor has the ability to better control the taxation aspects of their investments (the decision of when to sell and incur capital gains tax will impact upon the taxation position of the investor). Figure 7.2 contrasts direct and indirect investments.

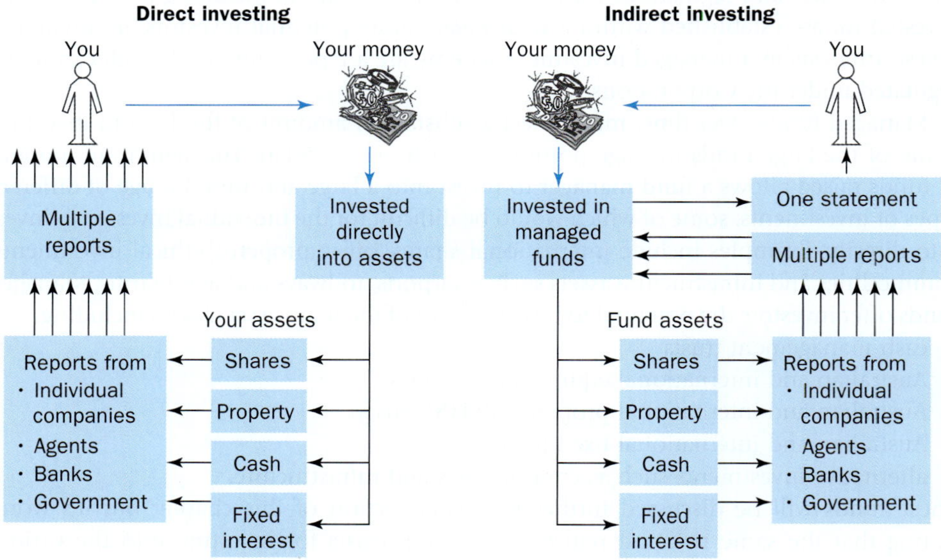

FIGURE 7.2
Direct versus indirect investing

LO 2 The regulation and structure of managed funds in Australia

This section provides a brief overview of the structure of managed investment schemes (MISs) and how they operate, and the Australian regulatory environment for MISs.

The regulation of managed funds

The managed fund industry is administered by ASIC. ASIC monitors the industry and ensures compliance with the relevant legislation. Non-superannuation managed funds (the focus of this chapter) fall under the Corporations Act. ASIC regularly issues policy statements and policy proposal papers to industry participants, outlining changes and alerting the industry to areas of concern.

Chapter 5C of the Corporations Act regulates the operation of an MIS. If it is intended that a managed investment scheme is to be available to retail investors, s. 601ED of the Corporations Act requires that an MIS with more than 20 members be registered with ASIC. As will be discussed later, a registered MIS must be operated by a responsible entity. The responsible entity of the fund is required to be a public company and hold an Australian Financial Services Licence (AFSL) under s. 601FA. Accordingly, MISs are subject to a number of general obligations that apply to all AFSL holders under s. 912A of the Corporations Act. Investment products available to retail clients are subject to the disclosure requirements set out in Chapter 7 of the Corporations Act, including the need to provide a **product disclosure statement (PDS)**.

product disclosure statement (PDS) an offer document designed to provide information about a managed investment scheme to investors, including its risk, cost, return objectives and other information

In addition to ASIC's involvement in the regulation of managed funds, the Australian Prudential Regulation Authority (APRA) has the role of supervising the banking and finance industry in Australia and of regulating the superannuation industry under the *Superannuation Industry (Supervision) Act 1993* (SIS Act). The regulation of superannuation will be dealt with in chapter 11. Combined with the RBA, ASIC and APRA make up the 'three pillars' of Australian financial services regulation (see figure 7.3).

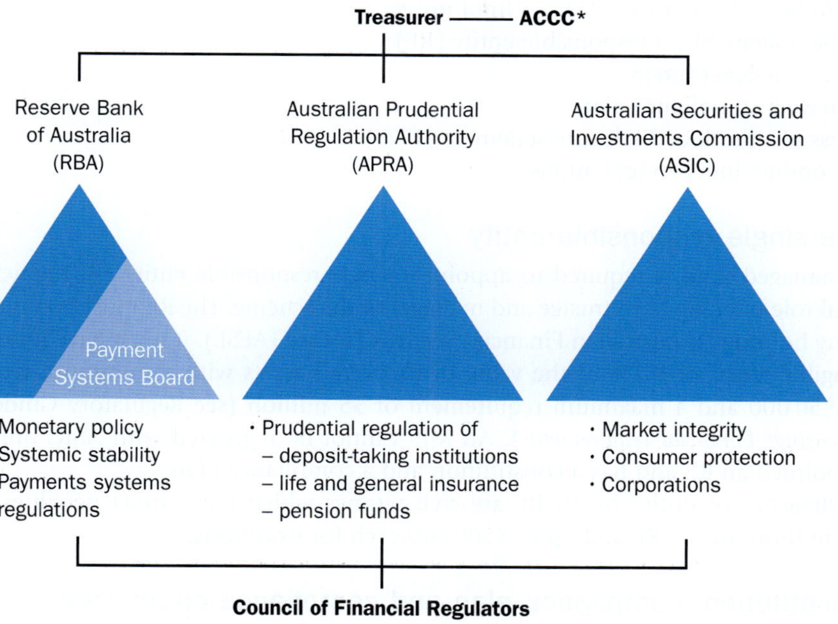

FIGURE 7.3
The three-pillar institutional framework for managed investments and securities in Australia
* ACCC = Australian Competition and Consumer Commission.
Source: Axiss Australia 2000.

In June 1998 the Australian Government passed the *Managed Investments Act 1998* (MIA) which made changes to the way managed funds report to their investors, to the structure and management of managed funds, and to the taxation of those funds. The changes to the legislation affected unit trusts with more than 20 members, but did not affect regulated superannuation funds. The aim of the Act is to ensure any investment vehicle that has prescribed interests (investors) is regulated in a more uniform manner. In 2001, the Corporations Act incorporated the Managed Investments Act into Chapter 5C.

The *Financial Services Reform Act 2001* (the FSRA) was introduced by the federal government to enhance the financial services industry and to have it regulated by one set of laws. The FSRA inserted a new Chapter 7 into the Corporations Act. One of the clear objectives of Chapter 7 is 'to promote confident and informed decision making by consumers of financial products and services while facilitating efficiency, flexibility and innovation in the provision of those products and services' [s. 760A(a)]. The enactment of the FSRA and the MIA has been the most significant legislative change to the Australian funds management industry since the deregulation of financial markets in the early 1980s.

The structure of managed investment schemes

responsible entity (RE) a public company that holds an Australian Financial Services Licence authorising it to operate and manage a registered managed investment scheme or managed fund

constitution a set of rules and regulations that govern the conduct of an entity

The Managed Investments Act introduced the MIS to the Australian investing public on 1 July 1998. An MIS must be registered with ASIC where the scheme has 20 or more members or the promoter is in the business of promoting such schemes. The chief changes the new Act introduced were the appointment of a single **responsible entity (RE)** instead of a trustee and a manager; the use of a constitution to replace the trust deed; and lodgement of a compliance plan to help ASIC ensure the MIS continues to meet its goals and objectives on behalf of the investors.

To be registered with ASIC, a fund must:

- be operated by a responsible entity (RE)
- have a **constitution**
- have a compliance plan
- issue a product disclosure statement (PDS)
- conduct independent audits.

The single responsible entity

A managed fund is required to appoint a single responsible entity (RE) which has the dual role of being both trustee and manager of the scheme. The RE must be a public company holding an Australian Financial Services Licence (AFSL). It must have minimum net tangible assets of 0.5% of the value of its overall assets with a minimum requirement of $50 000 and a maximum requirement of $5 million (see Regulatory Guide RG 166 *Licensing: Financial requirements*). An MIS cannot be registered with ASIC unless it has appointed an RE and has a constitution and a compliance plan.

Breaches of duties by an RE are civil wrongs which may attract penalties of up to $1 million for the RE and up to $200 000 each for its officers.

Constitution, compliance plan and compliance committee

Each MIS must have a constitution which sets out the rules of the investment scheme including matters such as:

- how much it costs to buy interests in the scheme
- the investment powers of the RE
- how to resolve complaints by investors
- the rights of investors to withdraw from the scheme.

An MIS is also required to prepare a compliance plan as part of its responsibilities. The compliance plan sets out how the RE will ensure the scheme complies with the

Corporations Act and the scheme's constitution. It covers such matters as ensuring scheme property is clearly identifiable, held separately from other assets and is regularly valued. It also covers the keeping of adequate records pertaining to scheme property. In addition to a compliance plan, an MIS must appoint a compliance committee if fewer than half of the directors of the RE are external directors.

Product disclosure statements

Holders of AFSLs who wish to offer units in an MIS to retail investors must provide investors with a product disclosure statement (PDS). The purpose of a PDS is to disclose such information as might reasonably be expected to have a material influence on a potential investor's decision about whether to invest in the product or not. Under s. 1013D(1) of the Corporations Act, a PDS must meet certain criteria to be accepted by ASIC. Some of the requirements include:

- details of the significant benefits of the product
- details of the risk of the product
- the cost of the product
- disclosure of all fees and charges (plus a worked example if the amounts are unknown because costs are calculated on the amount invested)
- whether the product will generate a return to the investor
- significant characteristics and features of the product
- information about dispute resolution systems investors can use if they are unhappy with the product or the performance of the product.

The details that must be included in a PDS are contained in Part 7.6 of the Corporations Act and RG 168 *Disclosure: Product Disclosure Statements (and disclosure obligations)*. The significant impact of this section of the Act has been a substantial increase in the amount of written information investors receive. Many in the industry claim that the volume and detail of information provided within a PDS is making it hard for investors to understand and be able to make an informed decision on the key matters relating to the financial product. Others argue for a comprehensive PDS on the basis that investors need to fully understand all the risks and benefits associated with the financial product they are seeking to invest into.

From 22 June 2012, all issuers of certain financial products must comply with requirements for shorter PDSs under the shorter PDS regime. The shorter PDS requirements apply to all PDSs for most superannuation products and simple managed investment schemes. The aim is to make PDSs shorter and simpler, and help consumers compare financial products more easily. ASIC has published an information sheet entitled *Shorter PDSs: Complying with requirements for superannuation products and simple managed investment schemes* (INFO 155) to provide concise guidance for industry on technical issues related to implementation of the new shorter PDS regime.

Unit holders

Unit holders are the investors in the fund or scheme and are the beneficiaries of the fund. They do not own the assets of the fund; they are simply investing in the ability of the fund's assets to generate a return. Unit holders have prescribed interests (or paid-for interests) in the assets and the income of the fund.

The structure of managed funds with more than 20 unit holders is explained in figure 7.4 (overleaf).

Current managed fund structure — managed investment schemes

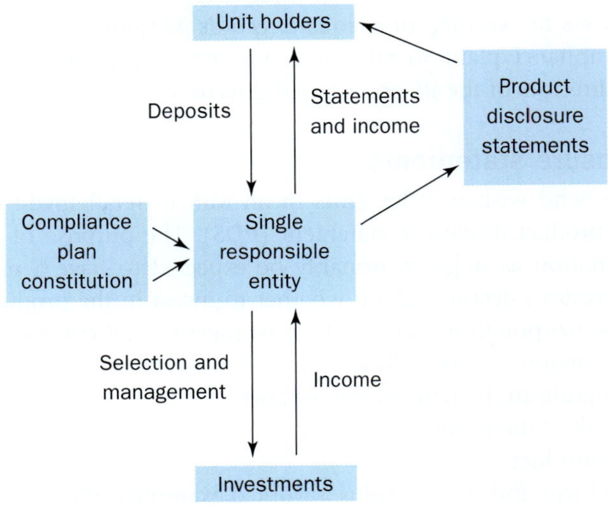

FIGURE 7.4
Structure of managed funds with more than 20 unit holders

LO 3

Investing into managed funds — advantages, downsides and risks

Advantages of investing in managed funds

The benefits of investing through a managed fund can be summarised as follows:

- able to access investments with only a small amount of funds
- provides access to a wide range of asset classes and investments
- provides investment opportunities that would normally be out of reach to the average investor
- funds are managed by a professional fund manager
- consolidation of reporting
- ability to achieve effective diversification.

Most asset classes can be invested either directly, where the asset is owned and controlled by the investor, or indirectly, where the investor has a beneficial interest in the investment through a managed fund structure. With indirect investing, total control over the purchase of the initial investment, the ongoing decision making and the final disposal of the investments is undertaken by the fund manager. While many investors prefer to have control over their investments, the task of selecting appropriate investments and managing them effectively is often a very resource- and time-intensive exercise. Also, many individual investors do not have the experience or expertise to manage investments themselves. For these investors, managed funds may be a viable alternative to direct investing as these funds are managed by professional investment managers who are paid for their skills, experience, processes and resources. Further, managing the administration, reporting and taxation aspects of direct investments can be difficult and time consuming. Managed funds consolidate the reporting on transactions, balances, withdrawals, income, capital gains and taxation for investors of the fund, thereby making the record keeping associated with investing a lot easier.

Perhaps the main benefit of investing indirectly through managed funds is the effective diversification able to be achieved by the investor — diversification across asset classes, fund managers with different styles, investment sectors and countries.

Using managed funds as a diversification strategy

Investing in managed funds provides investors with a greater choice of assets for a given amount of capital than can be achieved through direct investing. By investing in managed funds, investors can build a diversified portfolio of investments because they are able to access a range of investments across many asset classes.

The choice in the managed fund industry today is limited only by the variety of investments worldwide. An analysis of the managed fund industry at 31 December 2012 indicates that around 67% of the assets of managed funds were invested in financial assets, around 11% in land, building and property, and nearly 17.4% invested in overseas assets (RBA, 2012).

Benefits of diversification

Diversification is the spreading of investment capital across different asset classes with the view that if one sector performs poorly another sector will improve. Diversifying a portfolio into different investments allows the investor to take advantage of the full cycle of growth in an economy, and helps reduce the effect of a negative return from holding any one particular sector or asset class.

The large pool of funds controlled by a managed fund also allows the investor to access investments that they may not otherwise be able to afford or that may not be available to individual investors. Thus, by investing into an Australian share fund, an investor may have an interest in the top 300 Australian shares. Similarly, with a property fund, an individual investor may have access to commercial property, such as shopping centres that would normally be unaffordable or unattainable.

A managed fund allows access to a widely diversified portfolio with only a small amount of capital. Most retail funds (those funds open to investors with relatively small amounts of money) have a minimum initial contribution of $2000–$5000. Most managed funds also provide a regular savings or investment plan. Thus, an investor does not need to wait to save a significant amount of money before they can invest.

Diversification and risk

One of the ways investors are able to minimise risk associated with their investments is through diversification. Investing through a managed fund is one of the ways that investors are able to gain exposure to a number of securities, asset classes, countries and management styles regardless of the amount of funds an investor has at their disposal.

However, while some risks can be eliminated through diversification, other risks cannot be so easily eliminated. The total risk associated with a security or portfolio of securities is comprised of the following:

$$\text{Total risk} = \frac{\text{Systematic risk}}{\text{(market-related risk)}} + \frac{\text{Unsystematic risk}}{\text{(firm-specific risk)}}$$

Systematic risk represents the risk associated with the general market or broad economic factors such as market risk, inflation risk and interest rate risk. It is the risk common to all securities. Systematic risk cannot be diversified away because the value of all securities is affected by macroeconomic factors.

systematic risk
the risk associated with the overall market and which cannot be eliminated by diversification

unsystematic risk the risk associated with individual securities and which can be eliminated through diversification

On the other hand, **unsystematic risk** is the risk associated with holding individual securities and relates to factors specific to an industry or a company. This risk can be diversified away by adding further securities to a portfolio.

The total risk associated with a portfolio can be illustrated as in figure 7.5.

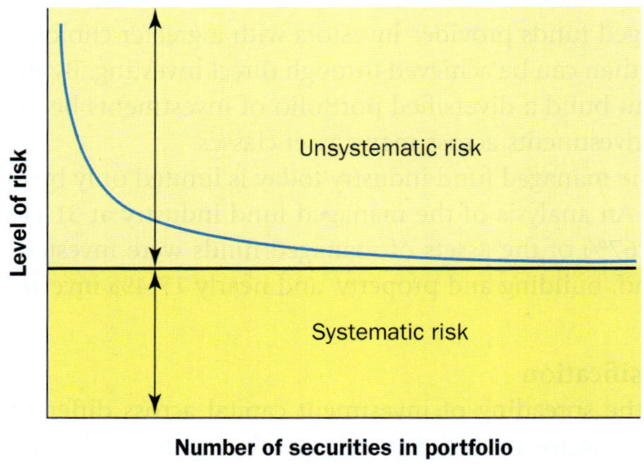

FIGURE 7.5 Total risk of a portfolio

Diversification exists at different levels

Diversification across asset classes

Whilst all investors would like to invest in the best performing asset class, evidence shows that it is virtually impossible to predict which asset class is likely to perform the best in any particular year. Investors should construct their investment portfolios based on their particular goals and objectives and the level of risk they are prepared to accept. Evidence from portfolio theory suggests that investing across a range of asset classes enables an investor to reduce risk for a given level of return.

Constructing a diversified investment portfolio across all asset classes is extremely difficult unless the investor has large amounts of money to invest. Most managed funds specialise in individual asset classes where the investor is provided with exposure to a number of securities within the particular asset class. A number of managed funds also offer balanced or mixed asset funds that invest in more than one asset class. This is a simple and effective way for investors to be able to achieve effective diversification.

Diversification across managers with different management styles

There are thousands of different managed funds in the marketplace. Investors have the ability to select from different funds and fund managers based on the particular management style that suits their goals, needs and objectives. Some of the styles available include:

active investing an investment approach which is based on an investment manager selecting and trading in securities with the goal of outperforming an index

passive investing an investment approach which is based on selecting investments within a portfolio based on replicating an index

- holding and managing a large number of securities within the fund or concentrating on just a few securities
- adopting an **active investing** approach to investing or a **passive investing** approach to investing
- selecting investments based on a value or growth approach or a combination of both
- utilising a tactical asset allocation approach, where the manager times the entry and exit of investments to take advantage of changes in the economic and market outlook.

Examples include the Vanguard Australian Shares Index Fund, which uses an index or passive approach to investing, and the Bennelong Concentrated Australian Equities Fund where the manager concentrates their efforts and skill by investing in only a relatively small number of Australian equities and attempting to identify mis-pricings in the marketplace.

Diversification across investment sectors

Using a managed fund to diversify across asset sectors means that the investor can achieve exposure to the cycle of returns from different asset classes. Thus, investors may wish to invest into a particular segment of a particular asset class. Examples may include healthcare, consumer staples, financial services or construction. Examples of managed funds that allow investors to invest in particular asset sectors include the AUI Wholesale Healthcare Property Trust, which invests in healthcare-based properties, and the Colonial First State Global Resources Fund, which allows investors to invest in global resource companies.

Diversification across countries

Research into international investing has shown that investors can enhance the returns of their portfolio by diversifying investment capital across countries. This can be achieved if the countries chosen have different economic cycles. The benefits of this strategy are evidenced by the significant ownership of Australian assets by international investors. Examples of this form of diversification include the Aberdeen Asian Opportunities Fund and the Fidelity India Fund.

Downsides of investing in managed funds

The downside of investing into a managed fund can be summarised as follows.

- Fund managers charge fees for managing and administering the investment portfolio.
- There is a lack of control over investment and timing decisions.
- There is a lack of transparency in a number of aspects including determining fees, returns and investment approach.
- The variety of managed funds in the marketplace makes it difficult to select and analyse an appropriate fund.

Investing indirectly through managed funds does come with a few downsides. Firstly, investing into managed funds can be costly. Many funds charge an entry fee and/or exit fee, charge an annual management fee (known as the **management expense ratio**) which typically falls in the range from 0.5% p.a. to 2% p.a., and the fund may also pay the investor's financial adviser a fee out of the fund balance as payment towards the cost of providing advice. A further disadvantage of managed funds is that the investor has no control over what investments are acquired by the managed fund or the timing of acquisitions and disposals. The sale of investments by the fund manager may lead to assessable capital gains and the payment of tax by the investor. Investing directly, on the other hand, gives control over timing decisions to the investor, which provides greater flexibility and control over the timing and payment of tax. Thus, the disposal of an investment in a period where the investor is on a lower marginal tax rate, for example upon retirement, may lead to a reduced tax liability on any realised capital gains.

management expense ratio
a ratio of fees charged to the value of the assets under management

Another problem that investors face when investing into managed funds is that there is now such a variety of investing combinations that it is often difficult for individual investors to choose the most appropriate fund manager for their circumstances. There are a number of ways of analysing and assessing an appropriate managed fund, and these are discussed later in this chapter.

In deciding whether to invest directly into asset classes or indirectly via managed funds, the main issue an investor has to consider is whether the benefits of having the investment managed by a professional fund manager across a diversified range of investments exceed the fees paid to the fund manager.

Risks of investing in managed funds

By investing into a portfolio of different securities, managed funds can effectively reduce the risk of being exposed to a single security, country or asset class. However there are a number of risks associated with investing into any investment or investment structure that investors need to be aware of. The risks will be determined by the nature of the asset class and in the selection of the investments made by the fund manager. Some of the risks that investors need to be aware of include:

- *market risk* — all markets and asset classes are subject to the risk of price and return volatility
- *security risk* — the individual securities or investments selected within a managed fund's portfolio will be subject to specific risks that will affect the performance of the fund
- *currency risk* — international investments are subject to movements in the exchange rate which can adversely impact upon the value of the investment portfolio
- *liquidity risk* — there is a risk in investing in unlisted managed funds in that the investor may not be able redeem their units because of lack of liquidity held by the fund. This applies particularly to property and mortgage funds. Listed investments generally have low liquidity risk because of the ability to transact through the Australian Securities Exchange (ASX)
- *gearing risk* — some managed funds have the ability to borrow funds which can magnify potential gains made by a fund. However, gearing also has the potential to magnify potential losses
- *taxation risk* — there is a risk that the government may change laws as they relate to the taxing of managed funds that may negatively impact upon the after-tax returns received by investors
- *beta risk* — investments in an index fund, such as exchange traded funds which are discussed later in the chapter, will only match the performance of the specific index that it tracks. There is no chance of the fund manager's selection skill generating returns above the market's performance.

PERSONAL FINANCE BULLETIN

Window closing for LM First Mortgage victims, says Slater & Gordon

Australians who invested in the collapsed LM First Mortgage Income Fund on the basis of bad financial advice could soon lose their window of opportunity to recoup losses, Slater & Gordon has warned.

Slater & Gordon commercial litigation lawyer Mark Walter said many Australians lost their life savings after advisers recommended investing in products managed by the fund, which went into administration last week.

The law firm said the six-year time limit, which generally applied for anyone wanting to sue, was closing for advice given in 2007 during the pre-global financial crisis (GFC) boom. Investors wanting to recoup losses needed to seek legal advice immediately, it said.

'We believe there is a large number of viable claims against financial advisers who recommended this and other high-risk products that will be affected by the time limit', Walter said.

'It's important that people exercise their right to hold their advisers to account and seek legal advice before it is too late.'

LM was particularly popular among advisers in communities with large populations of retirees, he said.

The same applied to a number of other funds that collapsed as the GFC took hold, including the Basis Capital funds and the Premium Income fund, according to Walter.

'The people we are talking about are typically risk averse and conservative and have relied on the professional advice of financial advisers to invest in these funds', he said.

'It is debatable whether these funds were appropriate for them, given their conservative needs.'

Investors were often in the dark about how to recoup losses from advisers due to bad advice, Walter said.

Since the GFC, Slater & Gordon said it had helped a number of investors recoup costs and had also issued a number of legal proceedings against advisers on behalf of investors who invested in LM.

Source: Money Management, 25 March 2013.

LO 4 Typical fee structures of MISs

ASIC has released a number of Regulatory Guides (RGs) and other guidance notes to assist REs in issuing adequate and comparable fee information to investors. RG 168 gives guidance on the framework and detail necessary to be disclosed in PDSs. RG 182 *Dollar disclosure* explains the minimum disclosure standards for fees and commissions. With few exceptions, all funds managers and advisers must disclose as a dollar amount all of the fees plus commissions that may affect the returns to investors. The intent behind RG 182 is to allow clients to compare fees more easily. In March 2005, the enhanced fee disclosure regulations were made. These provisions require PDSs for investment-linked financial products to include:

- a standardised fees and costs template (with accompanying explanation)
- an example of annual fees and costs for a balanced or similar fund
- a boxed consumer advisory warning that small differences in the performance of funds and fees charged can have a significant difference in the long-term value of the investment.

The enhanced fee disclosure regulations applied to PDSs for MISs from 1 July 2006.

The contemporary regulations ensure all significant fees are explained in a single table in an easily understood format in the PDS. The table shows:

- the fee type
- the actual amount in dollars or in percentage format with examples where the actual value is currently unknown
- how and when the fees are charged.

Types of fees

Various fees have enjoyed different names over the years. In its enhanced fee disclosure documentation, ASIC has suggested standard names to aid comparison.

- *Establishment fee.* An establishment fee is charged for processing the investor's application and establishing the investor's account. This is often nil, but may be a percentage of the initial deposit or a flat entry fee as a dollar amount.
- *Contribution fee.* Contribution fees are for the initial and every subsequent investment to cover the cost of processing. This fee may vary from nil to up to about 4%. It is deducted from each contribution. A portion may be paid to a financial planner as a fee.
- *Withdrawal fee.* These are fees charged by the fund for each withdrawal. Each fee may be nil up to a flat dollar amount of, say, $50.
- *Termination fee.* This is the fee charged for closing the account. It is often nil, but a withdrawal fee may be charged.
- *Ongoing fees or management costs.* These are fees charged for the ongoing maintenance of the investor's account and cover such things as investor updates, account management, taxation summaries, and overheads for the management of the fund. They are normally charged as a percentage of asset values (and vary depending on the complexity of the investment strategies.
- *Switching fee.* This is a fee charged when investors change their asset mix or their fund within the same managed group.
- *Adviser service fee.* Some funds managers pay financial planners ongoing fees for every year a client's funds remain in their MIS.

The payment of any fee reduces the overall returns to the investor and should be considered when choosing to invest in a fund or to withdraw from a fund. Investors should keep PDSs for future reference once a decision has been made to invest in a fund. Due to increasing competition and transparency within the industry, few fund managers now charge an establishment or contribution fee.

Indirect cost ratio

Among the individual fees listed in the previous section, you will have noted ongoing fees or management costs. These are the costs that funds managers incur to finance the operation of the fund and this must be disclosed to investors. They include costs of purchasing investments, external funds management, and custodial and valuation fees. They are deducted from investment returns before the returns for any period are declared. The indirect cost ratio (ICR) is the ratio of management costs not deducted directly from investors' account balances to the average net assets of the fund. ICRs vary from about 0.4% to 3% p.a. Some MISs call these costs 'management costs'. Some problems encountered in calculating the ICR include valuing current performance bonuses and the period to which costs relate.

Management expense ratio

The management expense ratio (MER) is similar to the ICR and is a ratio of fees charged to the value of the assets under management. The MER was the principal parameter used to compare the cost effectiveness of funds managers. It is no longer required in the official documentation for an MIS, but still may be seen quoted in the marketplace. The usual range for MERs is 0.5% to 3% of the value of the contributions or funds under management. The MER helped potential investors to determine how much of the contributions were used towards the operating costs of the fund and how much was actually invested in income- and growth-producing assets. Some analysts still use MERs to compare funds.

When assessing the performance of a fund, it is important to ascertain whether the manager is reporting returns gross or net of fees as this can make a significant difference to the distribution actually received by the investor. Most funds report returns net of fees and some report returns net of fees and taxes. When assessing the performance of a fund and determining performance relative to its competitors, the investor has to be able to determine how the return is being reported and to compare like with like.

ILLUSTRATIVE EXAMPLE 7.1

Referring to the case study presented at the commencement of this chapter, the three different funds (Funds A, B, and C) each have a different management expense ratio (MER). Is it better to always select the fund with the lowest MER and avoid the expensive funds?

Whilst a consideration of the MER is important, it is also important to note that it is only one of a number of issues that must be considered. The investments undertaken by some funds are, by their nature, more expensive to operate than others. Managing a fund that invests overseas, especially in emerging markets, is a lot more expensive than investments undertaken in Australia. Other factors to consider include the returns the fund generates, its management style and investment objectives.

LO 5 Selecting a managed fund for investing

There are a vast number of managed funds in the marketplace that have been established to suit the needs, objectives and risk profiles of most types of investors. Managed funds can be categorised based on a number of criteria such as:

- the unique investment objective and philosophy of the fund
- the nature of the fund's investments
- whether the funds are listed or unlisted
- the type of investors the fund attracts
- the investment structure of the fund.

These differences will determine the particular investment decision-making processes adopted by the managed fund and impact upon the type of investments selected, the fund's overall performance, its risk characteristics and its costs. It is important that investors properly understand and appreciate these issues before they invest.

Investment objectives

Each managed fund has a specific investment objective. It is important that the fund's particular investment objective and philosophy is detailed so that investors can determine the extent to which the fund is likely to satisfy their needs. Investor attitude to risk can vary and, as a result, it is important for fund managers to set out their specific investment strategy in advance, allowing investors to select funds that are consistent with their risk profile and invest into assets classes and investment segments that suit their needs. Fund objectives cover a wide range of issues including the time horizon; whether the emphasis is on income, growth or a combination or both; the level of volatility attached to the fund; and the type of investments targeted by the fund.

Differences in the investment objectives of managed funds can be illustrated by the following two types of funds.

1. *Australian share fund.* Objective: to provide long-term growth with moderate tax effective income. The assets are actively managed with a focus on flexible sector management and adequate diversification to minimise risk. The investment philosophy is to target both mid and small cap stocks which possess potential for superior growth
2. *Australian bond fund.* Objective: to provide investors with fixed-interest returns from investment grade Australian bond investments with an aim to outperform **benchmark** returns over any rolling 3-year period.

benchmark
normally an index or other measure against which the performance of a managed fund or other investment portfolio is measured

Listed and unlisted managed funds

Investors have the choice of investing into managed funds that are listed on the Australian Securities Exchange (ASX) or unlisted. Before investing into either of these structures, investors need to have a very clear idea of what they are investing into, the type of scheme being offered, the nature of the investments available and whether the fund meets the particular needs and objectives of the investor.

Unlisted managed funds

Unlisted managed funds are the most common type of managed investment scheme available in Australia. **Unlisted managed funds** are not listed on the ASX and investors deal directly with the managed fund itself. They are open ended structures, meaning that the fund itself can continually issue new units when new monies are invested into the fund and buy back existing units when an investor wishes to sell their units. Unlisted managed funds operate as trust structures and issue units to investors. An investor will purchase and sell units in the fund directly from the fund itself rather than from existing members or unit holders. As a result, unlisted funds need to be concerned with their holding of liquidity and their ability to fund redemptions from available cash or from selling investments.

unlisted managed funds
managed funds that are not listed on a stock exchange

Unlisted managed funds do not pay tax in their own right but are required to distribute all surplus income as distributions to unit holders, including a share of any capital gains made and franking credits received within the fund.

The underlying value of the units in the fund is based on the prevailing market value of the fund's investment portfolio. Whenever new monies are invested into the fund, new units are created to match the current market buying price. This is represented by the fund's net asset value. The net asset value (NAV) is the value of the fund's assets less the value of its liabilities. Each time units are sold or redeemed, investments within the fund are sold at current market selling prices.

The NAV is determined as:

$$\text{NAV} = \frac{\text{Fund assets} - \text{Fund liabilities}}{\text{Number of units issued}}$$

ILLUSTRATIVE EXAMPLE 7.2

A fund manager provides investors with the following information.

	($ million)
Assets	
Cash	30
Bonds	60
Equities	120
Property	30
International equities	60
Liabilities	
Debentures (loans)	35
Number of current units issued	16 101 324

The unit price of the fund is therefore:

$$\text{Unit price} = \frac{\$300\text{ million} - \$35\text{ million}}{16\,101\,324}$$
$$= \$16.46$$

Most unlisted funds have a separate buying (offer) price and selling or (bid) price. This is known as the fund's **spread** or **bid-offer spread**. The buying price is higher than the selling price to allow for transaction costs incurred by the fund in buying and selling investments, which is passed onto incoming unit holders.

spread or **bid-offer spread** the difference between the buying and selling price of units in a managed fund or other security

Figure 7.6 is an extract from Invest SMART (investsmart.com.au) which lists a number of unlisted managed funds ranked by the 1-year historical returns of funds rated three stars or higher by Morningstar Research.

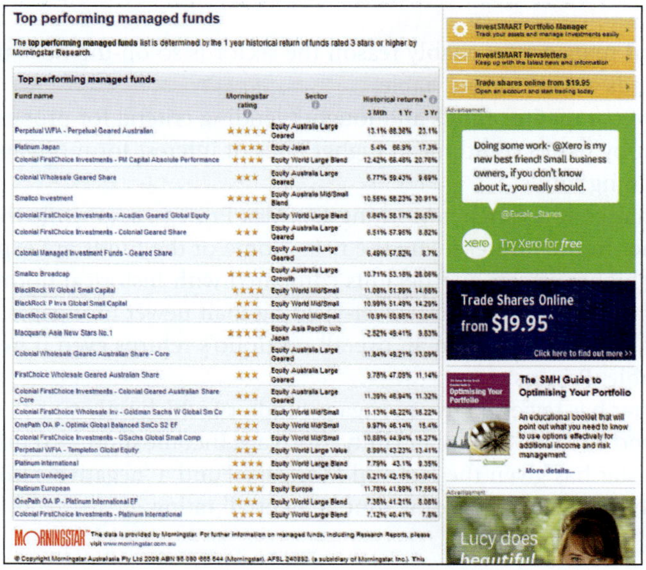

FIGURE 7.6 Unlisted managed funds
Source: Invest SMART 2013.

During the global financial crisis, a number of unlisted managed funds that had invested into property and mortgages experienced significant liquidity issues, forcing a number of funds to suspend redemption requests by investors. Hence, unit holders were left with illiquid assets. Listing overcomes this impediment.

PERSONAL FINANCE BULLETIN

Lessons in liquidity

The freeze on withdrawals from mortgage funds has thawed, at least for those funds that remain open to investors. But there are still billions of dollars of retirees' savings locked up in them.

Mortgage funds took investors' money and offered them daily liquidity while lending the money to property developers and holders of residential mortgages. The mortgages were to be paid back over several years.

In normal times the liquidity mismatch is not a problem, but in October 2008, to shore up confidence in Australia's deposit-taking institutions during the worst of the GFC, the federal government guaranteed bank deposits, including term deposits, but not mortgage funds.

Many mortgage-fund investors wanted their money back to put into term deposits. But the long-dated nature of the mortgages held by the funds meant they could not raise enough cash to repay investors in full.

Most funds allowed investors to withdraw money to a certain limit once a month or quarter, or under hardship conditions, while mostly continuing to pay interest to investors.

Some funds are in the process of closing and are not accepting investor contributions.

These fund managers probably reason the sector is so on-the-nose that their mortgage funds are no longer viable.

The exit of competitor funds and tougher lending criteria for property development by banks could mean higher rates of interest for mortgages supplied by the remaining funds.

A fund analyst at researcher Morningstar, Alex Prineas, says while the returns may be higher in the future, so are the risks. Some of the funds are experiencing significantly higher arrears and defaults compared with historical norms.

Existing mortgages, which are lower-yielding than newer mortgages, will take a while to clear and be a drag on an overall portfolio's returns even if new loans are more profitable, Prineas says.

Morningstar has reviewed five mortgage funds, of which only two — the Howard Mortgage Fund and the Australian Unity Mortgage Income fund — remain open. But Morningstar has given the Howard Mortgage Fund a 'negative' rating and the Australian Unity Mortgage Income fund a 'neutral' rating.

There is always the risk of another spike in investors wanting their money back, and returns need to compensate investors for that risk as well as the risks of an increase in defaults.

Over most time periods, the mortgage funds reviewed have underperformed the rate of return on cash as given by the UBS Bank Bill Index or delivered only a tiny premium to cash for the added risks, Prineas says.

That's hardly a ringing endorsement for mortgage funds. What remains of the mortgage-fund sector faces an uphill battle in replacing those leaving the funds by a greater number of new investors.

Source: The Sydney Morning Herald, 26 September 2012.

Listed managed funds

The objective of **listed managed funds** is similar to that of unlisted funds with these schemes also providing investors with the opportunity to invest into a diversified portfolio of investments managed by a professional fund manager. The main difference between listed and unlisted funds is that investors can buy and sell units or shares in listed structures through the ASX in the same way they can with shares and other listed securities. Listed funds offer investment opportunities across a wide range of asset classes and management styles to suit the particular investment requirements of most investors.

listed managed funds managed funds that are listed and traded on a stock exchange

The four main types of listed managed fund structures operating through the ASX are:

1. listed investment companies (LICs)
2. listed investment trusts (LITs)
3. real estate investment trusts (REITs)
4. exchange traded funds (ETFs).

A **listed investment company (LIC)** raises funds by issuing shares in the same way as any other listed company. The funds raised are used to invest into a portfolio of investments. The fund operates with a fixed number of shares on offer and a fixed amount of funds under management. It does not regularly issue new units or cancel existing units. This type of fund is known as a closed-end structure. Just like any other listed company, the fund may, over time, decide to raise more funds by issuing more shares or reduce the size of the fund by cancelling shares. Managers of listed funds are not as concerned with their liquidity holdings as unlisted funds as they do not have to worry about paying money out of the fund to investors wanting to redeem their units because investors wanting to sell their units in a listed fund trade through the ASX. LICs pay returns to investors in the form of dividends, which may be franked or unfranked. Two of the largest LICs listed on the exchange are Australian Foundation and Argo Investments.

listed investment company (LIC) an investment company listed on a stock exchange that has the objective of managing investments on behalf of investors

listed investment trust (LIT) an investment trust listed on a stock exchange that has the objective of managing investments on behalf of investors

A **listed investment trust (LIT)** operates in similar manner to a LIC, except that the fund issues units rather than shares. LITs can be both open-ended structures, where investors buy and sell units through the fund itself, or closed-end structures that allow investors to trade through the ASX.

real estate investment trust (REIT) an investment trust listed on a stock exchange that has the objective of managing a portfolio of property on behalf of investors

Real estate investment trusts (REITs) provide investors with the opportunity to invest into a managed portfolio of diversified Australian real estate. The manager selects and manages the investment properties. Returns to investors are distributions of rental income plus increases in the underlying value of the properties contained within the fund. REITs provide investors with the opportunity to gain exposure to property that would normally be inaccessible due to such factors as cost, size and geographic region. The types of property available within REITs include industrial, office, retail, hotels and leisure, and aged care, as well as diversified holdings across all property types.

exchange traded fund (ETF)
a fund listed on a stock exchange that has the objective of managing investments on behalf of investors based on tracking a particular index

Exchange traded funds (ETFs) are relatively new in Australia but represent one of the fastest growing investment products around the world. ETFs are listed on the ASX and trade in the same way as any other share. The investment style of most listed and unlisted managed funds is for the fund manager to select and trade in individual shares that they believe will outperform the market. This is called an active management style. The objective of an ETF is to track and duplicate as closely as possible the performance of a selected share market index. This is known as a passive or index management style. The different management styles are discussed in greater detail later in this chapter. Thus, ETFs provide investors with the opportunity to invest with a single transaction into a broad and diversified portfolio that is similar to a particular market index.

While the value of a listed managed fund portfolio is generally based on the value of its NAV, its actual value on the ASX is determined on a day-to-day basis by a range of demand and supply factors. Accordingly, depending on such factors as current market conditions, expectations and sentiment, the value of listed managed funds may trade at a discount, premium or at par to its NTA.

Types of investments undertaken by funds

Single sector funds

These funds concentrate on a specific asset class.

1. *Cash management funds* invest in:
   - overnight or 24-hour cash deposits
   - short-term government securities
   - a mix of short- and medium-term government securities
   - an international mix of short-term government securities
   - a mix of short-term government, banking and corporate debt, which may be either within Australia or internationally.
2. *Fixed-interest funds* invest in:
   - short- to medium-term government bonds
   - government bonds across all maturities
   - international government bonds
   - mortgage loans
   - a mix of government, banking and corporate bonds.

   In addition, fixed-interest funds may hedge their international portfolios (i.e. reduce the exposure to changes in interest rates) using swaps, options or futures, if allowed for in their constitution and compliance plan.
3. *Property funds* are usually divided into the category invested in, such as commercial, industrial, retail or residential. Most property funds hold a diversified portfolio of assets spread by location and activity undertaken within the property category. Large property funds are sometimes involved in the development of new properties such as housing estates or retail shopping centres.

4. *Share or equity funds* can be divided into the many different categories of shares that are available, including:
   - index funds — the manager exactly matches a share market index (such as the All Ordinaries)
   - sub-sector funds — the manager chooses equities from a particular type of company such as from the industrial, telecommunications, property development or banking sector
   - developing markets funds — the manager chooses equities from countries where the share markets or capital markets are still developing
   - high-growth funds — the manager chooses equities that are likely to experience high growth in the short to medium term; they are just as likely to achieve no growth in the same period, so these funds are high-risk funds and the returns should compensate the investor for that risk
   - small cap funds — the manager chooses companies that have a small capitalisation compared with the larger companies on the stock exchange, hoping to see the companies grow to larger firms of the future; the largest small caps market in the world is the Nasdaq market in the United States
   - ethical funds — the manager applies ethical, social or responsible screening to the selection of investments within the fund which may involve actively seeking out commercial activities that bring social or environmental benefits, and avoiding investments in activities which are socially or environmentally harmful.
5. *International funds* can be divided into:
   - regions — such as Asia–Pacific, Asian Tigers, European, G7, Americas, Emerging Markets
   - countries — such as local neighbours of Australia, major trading partners of Australia, or simply the United States, the United Kingdom or Europe
   - sectors — within the country the manager may choose specific types of investments such as property in the central business district, industrial equities, mining and resources equities, or government bonds.

Diversified (multi-sector) funds

While the majority of funds are single-sector funds (i.e. they invest their funds into one particular asset class such as Australian shares), a number of diversified or multi-sector funds do exist that invest across all or a number of different asset classes. The fund manager determines a broad asset allocation and determines the proportion of funds to be invested into each asset class. The advantages of this type of fund are that the investor can achieve effective densification across all or a number of asset classes within the one managed fund and the manager periodically re-weights the investments within the fund to ensure the specified asset allocation is maintained. This reduces the need for the investor to rebalance their investments themselves. The drawback with diversified funds is that the fund manager may not have the appropriate level of experience and expertise to manage each asset class.

Various types of diversified funds exist, covering a range of investor risk profiles.

- *Conservative funds* are designed for investors with a low risk profile who require investments with relatively low volatility and a low chance of negative returns. The funds aim to provide investors with income and some short- to medium-term capital growth through exposure to a diversified investment portfolio that holds a significant amount of their funds in cash and fixed interest. Typically around 40–60% of the fund is invested into such defensive investments.

- *Balanced funds* aim to provide investors with a mix of medium-term capital growth and income. The aim is to generate a return higher than conservative funds while restricting the level of risk or volatility by holding a portfolio of both growth-type assets, such as shares and property, and defensive-type assets, such as cash and fixed interest. Generally, around 50–70% of the fund's assets are invested into shares and property.
- *Growth funds* aim to achieve long-term capital growth and some income through investment into a diversified investment portfolio with an emphasis on share investments. The fund may also invest into a range of other, more high-risk investments such as small companies, private equity funds and emerging markets in order to chase higher returns. Because of the nature of their investments, the risk exposure of growth funds is relatively high and suitable, therefore, for more aggressive investors willing to take on risk in order to potentially achieve higher returns. Typically, around 70–90% of the fund's investments are allocated to growth-type investments.

Figure 7.7 provides an example of an asset allocation for a growth fund.

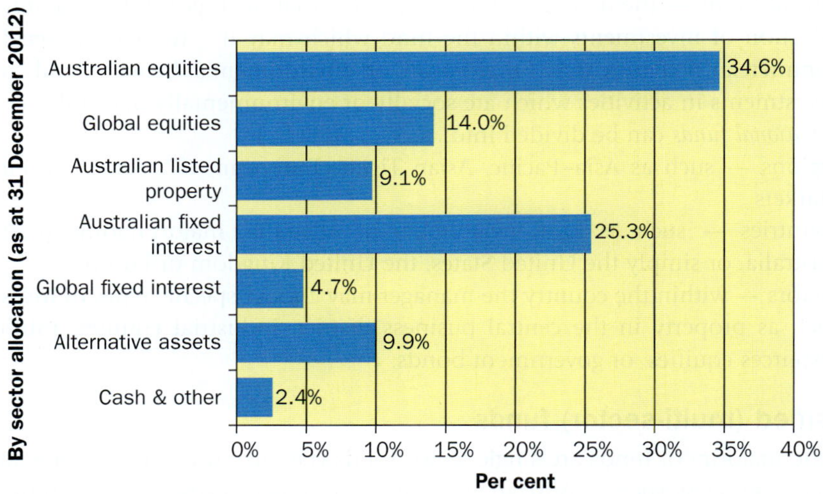

FIGURE 7.7
Example of an asset allocation for a growth fund
Source: Westpac Balanced Growth Fund – NEF: December 2012.

Another option for an investor who desires a fund that diversifies across all or a number of different asset classes is a multi-manager fund. This type of fund outsources the investment of funds and the investment decisions across a number of fund managers and packages them into a single fund providing diversification across a range of asset classes, management styles and specific management expertise.

wholesale managed funds
funds that are targeted at institutional investors or individual investors that are deemed to be professional or financially sophisticated with large amounts of money to invest

retail managed funds
funds that are targeted at individual retail investors with small amounts of money to invest

Retail and wholesale managed funds

Unlisted managed funds are typically offered to investors at a retail and/or a wholesale level. There is very little difference between **wholesale managed funds** and **retail managed funds** as they often have the same names and invest into exactly the same investments. The difference is that wholesale managed funds charge lower management fees and have a higher minimum entry amount. Managed funds offered at the retail level are typically open to the general public with most of these funds having a low minimum entry amount, often as low as $1000. Because retail managed funds spend a relatively high proportion of their fees in processing transactions of small value, they charge a higher MER, typically from 1.5% p.a. to 3.0%. p.a.

Funds offered at the wholesale level, on the other hand, have a typical minimum entry amount in excess of $100 000, some up to $500 000. These funds are aimed at investors with large amounts of money to invest, that is, professional investors or institutions, such as superannuation funds. These funds take in larger sums of money in single transactions. These economies of scale mean that they can charge a lower management fee to their investors. MERs for wholesale funds typically range from 0.5% p.a. to 1.5% p.a.

Investment structures and platforms

A recent phenomenon in investment markets is the introduction of a one-stop shop providing the facility for investors to invest into a range of investment products under the one administrative umbrella. Investing into a diversified range of investment products, whether directly into shares, term deposits or bonds, or indirectly investing into a number of managed funds can be costly, time consuming and administratively messy in keeping track over the various reports and statements. In the 1980s, ASGARD launched its Master Trust allowing investors to invest into a range of different managed funds under the one administrative structure with access to wholesale managed funds. Through these administrative structures, investors with small amounts of funds to invest are able to pool their money with a large number of other investors within the structure, and with the large pool of funds now available, are able to invest into wholesale managed funds that have much lower MERs. Since that time, a number of other product providers have entered this market and offered similar products across a range of investment types and fund managers. These products are commonly known as *investment platforms*. Investment platforms allow investors to access a range of different investment options under the one administrative structure. Not only do many of these platforms offer a range of different managed funds covering different asset classes and fund managers, they also commonly allow investors to invest directly into shares, term deposits and even property syndicates. Investment platforms provide investors with the ability to select from a wide range of investments that suit their particular needs, objectives and risk profile.

The two main types of investment platforms are master funds and wrap accounts, described in the following two sections.

Master funds

A **master fund** is an administration service that pools money together from investors and provides access to a range of different fund managers and other investment options. Within this structure, investors are able to access wholesale managed funds. The master fund provider may have a product list containing many different managed funds to select from. The funds selected by the investor from this approved product list are consolidated under the one account and held on behalf of the investor by the trustee of the master fund who is the legal owner. The investor receives one consolidated report covering all investments held within their account.

master fund
an investment fund which enables investors to invest in a number of funds via the one fund; sometimes referred to as a fund of funds or as an administration fund manager

wrap account
an administration service that provides access to a range of different managed funds and other direct investment options and wraps the various investments into the one account for an investor

Wrap accounts

Wrap accounts are similar to master funds in that they also provide an administrative structure to hold a diverse range of investments under the one account.

However, wrap accounts are different in their structure. Investments held within a wrap account are held in the name of the investor. As a result, investments within a wrap account can be transferred between different wrap providers and even to the direct ownership of the investor without triggering any capital gains tax. A modern wrap account can provide investors with access to not only a diverse range of different managed funds, but also to a number of direct investments such as shares and term deposits.

Benefits and drawbacks

The benefits of investing through a master fund or wrap account is that the investor:

- only deals with the one organisation for all of their investment transactions
- cost savings result because the managed funds can be accessed at wholesale MERs
- the investor can access funds that may not be available at a retail level
- the investor receives one consolidated report detailing all of their investments held within the master or wrap account and summarising overall asset allocation, performance and tax reporting.

While some investors are happy to manage their investments themselves, many are happy to pay for the administrative service provided by investment platforms. The main drawback of these types of products is that they come at a cost. Apart from the MER charged by each individual fund manager, the platform provider will also charge an administration fee. This fee will vary depending upon the funds under management but will typically range between 0.5% and 1% p.a., although some providers have recently reduced their costs by providing investors with fewer investment options. Thus, while investors in a master fund or wrap account will reduce costs by accessing managed funds at wholesale MERs, they will need to pay an additional administration fee to the platform provider. It is crucial for investors to weigh up the benefits and costs of the different investment options for their particular circumstances.

PROFESSIONAL ADVICE

Setting up an investment strategy

Barry works with the local council as a leisure services manager. He is aged 42, married with two young children and earns a salary of $75 000 p.a. Barry's wife is not currently employed. Barry would like to start investing into quality investments outside of his superannuation account to fund his children's education, to pay for a home extension that will be required in the next few years as the children get older, and to put some money aside to support his retirement.

Barry believes he has a moderate risk profile. He has little investment experience and is busy with his job and family. He does not have much of an interest in managing his finances. He is prepared to take on some risk in order to chase higher returns but would not want to borrow or invest into high-risk products. He owns a few shares in the Commonwealth Bank and has $10 000 in a cash account.

Barry will shortly inherit a small investment portfolio from his grandmother consisting of $30 000 cash and $40 000 in three managed funds as follows:

Australian Share Index Fund $20 000	(MER 2.5%)
Australian Bond Fund $10 000	(MER 1.6%)
Australian Infrastructure Fund $10 000	(MER 2.7%)

Barry is looking to sell all three managed funds, and invest the money into a share portfolio. He doesn't know anything about managed funds but believes he has the ability to successfully select and trade in ASX-listed shares in order to make reasonable gains.

QUESTIONS

1 Determine the type of investments that an Australian infrastructure fund would invest into.

2 Would it be worth Barry holding his investments within a master fund or wrap account structure? What are the advantages and disadvantages of this approach?

3 Would you recommend that Barry sell the three funds in order to trade in direct shares?

LO 6 Management and investment styles

Differentiating between the ways the funds are managed can help investors match their own risk profile to that of the fund. A manager's style or investment philosophy is a reflection of their fundamental approach to investing. The PDS and constitution of a fund will provide details of the particular management style adopted by the fund. The main investment styles are categorised under the headings of active and passive management styles. Figure 7.8 illustrates the relationship between the various active management styles.

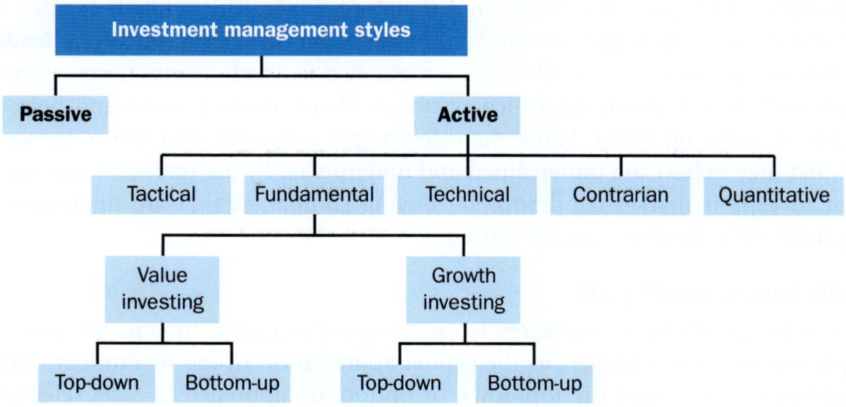

FIGURE 7.8 Investment management styles of fund managers in Australia

Active fund management styles

An active management style refers to a strategy that involves the fund manager selecting specific investments to be held within a portfolio with the objective of outperforming the market or the particular benchmark index. A traditional active-managed fund attempts to meet this goal through a combination of stock picking, market timing and asset allocation decisions. The active fund manager's style is generally categorised as either value or growth oriented, although a number of other styles exist in the marketplace. The active fund manager uses a particular method to determine the appropriate asset mix for the fund. Some examples of these methods include the following.

- *Tactical analysis*. Fund managers use two main methods when they purport to be tactical managers or tactical asset allocators (TAAs). The first is to over-weight or under-weight (increase or decrease the percentage of the portfolio's holding) an individual asset to take advantage of likely future changes in the asset's value. The second is to try to 'time' the market to determine when it is best to buy or sell an asset.
- *Fundamental analysis*. Fund managers evaluate the available accounting and reported data with a view to determining those companies or other specific investments that may be undervalued for the given circumstances (and therefore the fund manager would buy these assets), or overvalued given the information available in the market (and therefore the fund manager would sell these assets). These data are known as 'fundamental data' (see chapter 4 for more details).
- *Technical analysis*. The oldest form of analysis is to predict future price movements from past price movements. Technical analysis is the study of price and value data to determine patterns in past price movements. Decisions to buy or sell an asset are based on past history. This method, however, has few supporters in the academic finance community.
- *Contrarian analysis*. This is where fund manager buys when prices are falling and sells when prices are rising. Managers are not trying to pick the top or the bottom of the market — overall, they are hoping their average buy prices will be lower than their average sell prices.
- *Quantitative analysis*. 'Quants' use statistics and models to measure risk and expected returns from an investment/asset, with a view to constructing a portfolio of the highest expected return for the lowest possible risk.

Value funds managers

A basic method of assessing the value of an asset is to determine if the asset is undervalued (and therefore a buy) or overvalued (and therefore a sell). This analysis focuses on the ability of the asset to generate income, both now and in the near future. **Value funds managers** believe that markets are affected by many factors, such as emotion, momentum, rumours and market sentiment which results in shares trading above and below their fair value at differing times. Value managers target neglected and out-of-favour companies that they believe are undervalued and underpriced by the market. Value managers attempt to exploit market conditions by buying companies that are underpriced and selling them once they become overpriced.

value funds managers an investment management style where investments are selected and traded based on the extent to which they are believed to be under- or overpriced

growth funds managers an investment management style where investments are selected and traded on the basis of superior future growth

Growth funds managers

The focus for **growth funds managers** is capital growth or gain. Income streams are not as important to these managers as the capital appreciation of the investment. This style of fund manager also uses the top-down or bottom-up approach to asset selection and analysis. With a top-down approach, the fund manager studies macroeconomic variables and trends relating to an individual country as well as the global economy such as GDP, trade balances, currency movements, inflation and interest rates in order to determine where to invest and in what types of assets. A bottom-up approach concentrates on the fundamental analysis of the company and examines factors such as the company's sales growth, profitability, market share, cash flow and debt position. Growth managers concentrate on shares that have the potential to provide superior future growth. Typically, growth managers search out companies in high-growth or developing sectors and industries and also concentrate on the quality of the management of these companies to continue to provide continued excess growth.

While the majority of managers tend to categorise their style as either value or growth, a number of other styles have arisen over the past few years. One of these, which incorporates the characteristics of both the growth and value styles, is **growth at a reasonable price** or **GARP**. A fund manager using the GARP approach aims to invest into shares that offer good growth prospects but at a reasonable price.

growth at a reasonable price (GARP) an investment management style that incorporates both growth and value styles

There is often a debate as to which style provides the best returns for investors. Over differing periods in the market cycle, value managers will outperform growth managers and vice versa. While some investors may prefer to invest into a particular investment style, others may decide to blend value and growth investments by either selecting a combination of value and growth fund managers within their portfolio or otherwise selecting a fund that already combines the two types of investment styles. Some analysts argue that categorising investment styles is simply a way of fund managers attempting to differentiate themselves from each other when in fact value and growth are simply two sides of the same coin, meaning that all managers will consider both value and growth considerations in their investment selections.

ILLUSTRATIVE EXAMPLE 7.3

Referring to the case study detailed at the commencement of this chapter, one of the factors which Jake and Sarah will need to consider in determining which funds to keep and which to dispose of is whether they have a preference for value managers, growth managers or some other variation. Which of the investment styles provides better long-term returns and is it better to stick with one investment style or invest so as to capture both styles?

One of the factors affecting the performance of a particular investment style is the state of the economy and financial markets. In times of market growth and expansion in the economy, growth managers may tend to outperform because they invest into corporations and market segments that have the potential for significant future growth. Examples may include technology, healthcare and the resources sector. In times of economic and market contraction, there is usually a trend toward the more secure safer blue-chip companies that value managers typically invest into. As it is extremely difficult to forecast future economic and market conditions, it may be advisable to select funds that utilise different investment styles. This utilises the principles of diversification. Within the case study, reference to the investment styles of the three funds reveals that whereas Fund C is more value oriented, Funds A and B are very similar and therefore holding both funds may not significantly improve the diversification benefit.

Passive fund management or indexed funds

Passive funds managers do not attempt to outperform an index or benchmark; they simply try to replicate the performance of the benchmark. The main object of an index fund is to produce returns in line with the index of that particular asset class, minus their fees. However, most passive funds managers need to involve themselves in some active trading to ensure that their portfolio stays consistent with an ever-changing benchmark. Benchmarks change when the value of an individual asset within the benchmark portfolio changes, requiring either an increase in the number of shares in the investment portfolio (when the share price falls) or a decrease in the number of shares in the portfolio (when the share price rises).

The argument for adopting a passive investment style is that the average performance of all investors is the same as the market (the benchmark index) and therefore the aggregate return of all investors in the market will equal the market return. That is, it is impossible for everyone to beat the market — half the investors will beat the market while half will receive returns lower than the market return. Thus, while active managers attempt to beat the market and incur trading fees in attempting to do so, only half will generate returns (before fees) in excess of the market. Once fees are taken into account, active funds as a group will underperform the index.

'Indexing' involves building a portfolio of investments that replicates a widely publicised index. The index should be easily recognised in the market and information about its construction should be readily available to all market participants. The index should reflect all securities available in a market sector; for example all federal government bonds, all equities, all property. Exchange traded funds (ETFs), discussed previously, are a form of index fund. Examples of well-known indexes are the UBS Warburg Bank Bill Index, the ASX All-Ordinaries Accumulation Index, the suite of S&P/ASX indices and the Dow Jones industrial index. Most of these indexes are reported in the daily financial media.

ILLUSTRATIVE EXAMPLE 7.4

Again referring to the case study of Jake and Sarah detailed at the start of the chapter, the investment profile of managed Fund B indicates that it has a passive investment style whereas Fund C has an active management style. Fund A adopts a management style that is predominantly active. Which management style is preferable? Is one management style better than the other? Is it necessary to have funds covering all management styles?

This issue of which management style outperforms the other has been the subject of academic debate for many years. To date, there is no conclusive evidence one way or the other. A number of financial planners have adopted an investment process known as a core-satellite approach which looks to invest the major share of the investment portfolio (the core) in cheap index funds, especially in asset classes where it is difficult to outperform the market such as cash and fixed interest and shares in large companies. The planner may then invest a proportion of the portfolio in a number of funds that use an active management style (the satellite funds) in an attempt to find returns in excess of the market. Examples may include investments in the shares of small companies and in emerging markets such as China and India.

LO 7 Taxation issues for investors in managed funds

The taxation of returns from managed funds is often a complex area for the potential investor to understand. The basic tax principle the ATO adopts for managed funds is that investors should pay the same tax rate on returns from managed fund investments as they would if they undertook the investments directly.

Under current tax legislation, income generated from the investments held within the managed fund is passed straight to unit holders. The MIS itself pays no tax whilst unit holders pay tax on the income distributed to them at their own marginal income tax rate. Investors receive a proportionate share of all income received by the fund, including a share of all credits and tax offsets, such as franking credits and foreign tax offsets, as well as a share of all capital gains made within the fund. Although capital gains tax is dealt with differently by different fund managers, the details of how capital gains tax is distributed to unit holders must be outlined in the fund's PDS.

At the end of the financial year, MISs issue tax advice statements to investors. These advice notices show the amounts of trust income (ordinary assessable income), tax-deferred income (non-assessable), capital gains, tax credits, franking credits, foreign-source income and foreign tax credits that need to be included within the investor's tax return. Tax-deferred income received from a fund is not assessable to tax at the time of receipt, but does reduce the cost base of the investment so that upon disposal of the units in the fund there is a larger capital gain and therefore a greater tax liability.

LO 8 Measuring returns and analysing the performance of managed funds

A number of methods are used to assess the performance of a managed fund. Some methods are aimed at assessing the absolute return of the fund, whereas other methods analyse the overall performance of the fund relative to a benchmark or in terms of the risk taken by the fund managers to generate that return.

Measuring returns from a change in unit price

For the investor, information about the performance of the fund is contained in the daily unit price. The absolute returns from investing in a managed fund are calculated as:

$$r = \frac{\text{(Sale price or current market value)} - \text{Purchase price}}{\text{Purchase price}} \times 100$$

ILLUSTRATIVE EXAMPLE 7.5

Sam purchased 2000 units in the Infrastructure Trust on 30 June 2013 at a unit price of \$1.85. The market value 1 year later is \$2.36. The absolute return is:

$$r = \frac{\text{Current market value} - \text{Purchase price}}{\text{Purchase price}} \times 100$$

$$= \frac{\$2.36 - \$1.85}{\$1.85} \times 100$$

$$= 27.57\%$$

Of course, this is not the real return — Sam would need to sell his units at \$2.36, then subtract taxes and fees to determine his real return.

A more sophisticated formula for measuring the fund's return is:

$$R_p = \frac{(MV_1 - MV_0) + D - C}{MV_0} \times 100$$

where R_p = return on the fund

MV_1 = market value at the end of the evaluation period

MV_0 = market value at the beginning of the evaluation period

D = any distribution (redemptions or income distributions) from the portfolio to the client during the evaluation period

C = contributions to the fund during the period

Once a fund's return has been calculated, it is compared with the return on the benchmark portfolio or index for the same period. Many sources are available to investors to keep up to date with the performance of their funds, including the financial press, the finance pages of the general press, the fund's webpage, and the unit holder statements distributed by the fund.

ILLUSTRATIVE EXAMPLE 7.6

The following information is available.

Market value of the portfolio at 1 March 2013	$6960 million
Market value of the portfolio at 1 March 2014	$7260 million
Contributions to fund during the year	$320 million
Distributions paid during the year from the fund	$300 million

The return on the fund can be calculated as:

$$R_p = \frac{(\$7260 \text{ million} - \$6960 \text{ million}) + \$300 \text{ million} - \$320 \text{ million}}{\$6960 \text{ million}} \times 100$$

$$= 4.02\% \text{ p.a.}$$

As discussed earlier, it would be important to determine if the return of the fund is inclusive or exclusive of fees.

Analysing and assessing managed fund performance

With the hundreds of managed funds in existence, investors require a means of properly reviewing, assessing and comparing the risk and return characteristics of the various funds. Investors need to be able to assess which managed funds should be acquired, and review and monitor ongoing fund performance. Investors need to be able to:

- compare the performance against the fund's objectives
- compare the performance against that of other managed funds
- compare the performance against benchmarks
- refer to managed fund research
- undertake an assessment and interpretation of financial ratios.

In analysing the performance of a fund and determining whether the benefits of investing outweigh the costs, there are a few techniques an investor can employ. All managed funds provide regular performance reports, often on a monthly or quarterly basis, and these reports provide the basis for the investor's analysis. There is a natural tendency to concentrate on the short-term performance of the fund, whether good or bad, and use that as the basis for analysing fund performance and making investment decisions. However, assessing returns over a longer time frame may provide the investor with a better indication of long-term average performance. Choosing a longer time period that covers different economic cycles and market conditions will provide the investor with a better historical assessment of how the manager has performed under different economic and market conditions and therefore how they may perform in the future.

Another technique available to an investor is to compare the performance of a fund to other similar funds. Thus, while the average return of a fund might be low, if the majority of other similar funds performed worse over this time period, the performance of the fund might be considered good in relative terms. However, many investors judge the performance of a fund on its ability to provide good, long-term, absolute returns and would not be satisfied with a low return regardless of whether it was reasonable relative to its peers. A number of other techniques are considered in the following sections.

Comparison of performance against benchmarks

Looking at total returns from a fund does not provide much information about how the returns were generated by the fund manager. Using a benchmark, which is simply a point of reference used for comparison purposes, investors can compare the funds manager's performance with the performance of the market overall and determine how much of the declared return comes simply from being invested in the asset class. Excess return above that of the benchmark is often attributed to the skill of the funds manager. To be a fair and accurate comparison, the benchmark index must be consistent with the fund's management objectives and the structure of the index must be well known. Common benchmarks used to compare the performance of a particular fund against market index are as follows:

Australian shares	ASX All Ordinaries Accumulation Index
International shares	MSCI World Index
Property	S&P/ASX 300 A-REIT Accumulation Index
Fixed interest	UBS Warburg Composite Bond Index
Cash	UBS Warburg Bank Bill Index

The fund's stated objectives will be based around the benchmark and usually expressed in the form of outperforming the benchmark by a percentage or over a rolling period. For example, a fund's objective may be to outperform benchmark returns over any rolling 3-year period.

ILLUSTRATIVE EXAMPLE 7.7

With the vast array of managed funds covering different asset classes, markets, management styles and investment styles, how does an investor determine which is the best fund to invest into? This is the problem facing Jake and Sarah in the case study at the start of the chapter. One of the techniques that Jake and Sarah can consider is to determine what asset classes their three funds invest into and, by comparing the fund's performance against the appropriate benchmark referred to above, determine the extent to which the cost of the fund outweighs the returns generated relative to the index. Thus, if Fund C's performance prior to fees is 7.1% over the past 5 years whereas the index or benchmark is 7.5%, the fund has underperformed and an investor may feel that the relatively high MER being charged is not justified.

Reference to managed fund research

A number of research houses exist in Australia with the aim of researching and providing recommendations on the main managed funds in the marketplace. These research houses undertake extensive research on managed funds covering such aspects as performance, financial viability, the quality of the management team, whether the fund is true to its label (i.e. whether it sticks to its management style), and the financial backing and resources of the organisation.

Some of the research house players in Australia include Lonsec, Standard & Poor's, van Eyk and Morningstar and they provide a significant amount of detailed information on many managed funds. Much of the detailed information is, however, only available through a subscription service to financial planners and investors.

Figure 7.9 is an example of managed fund data typically provided by research houses to subscribers.

Trailing	6 Mth	1 Yr	3 Yr	5 Yr	10 Yr
Quartile					
Total %	22.31	23.68	6.46	2.93	12.99
Income %	3.07	5.13	4.22	3.83	3.80
Growth %	19.25	18.55	2.24	-0.89	9.19
Tax-Adj %	NAv	NAv	NAv	NAv	NAv
Index %	20.85	24.19	8.03	2.86	10.97
Category %	21.24	21.39	6.27	1.85	10.56

Index: S&P/ASX 200 Accumulation Index

Category Risk Meter (3 Year Standard Deviation)

Low	Moderate	High

Fund: Moderate; Category: Moderate

Risk	Std Deviation	Rel to Category
3 Year	14.62	Average
5 Year	17.31	Average
10 Year	16.19	Above Average

Portfolio 28 Feb 2013

Composition (28 Feb 2013)

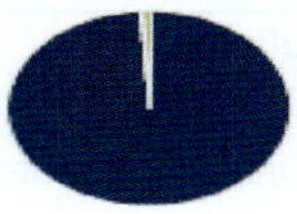

	% Assets
Domestic Equity	99.05
Int'l Equity	0.00
Listed Property	0.13
Unlisted Property	0.00
Mortgages	0.00
Dom Fixed Interest	0.00
Intl Fixed Interest	0.00
Cash	0.83
Other	0.00

Morningstar Style Box

Equity

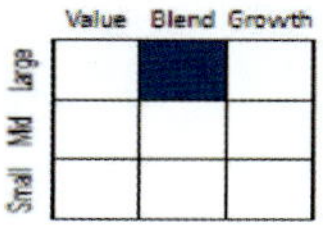

Large Blend
These funds own a mixture of larger-sized growth and value companies, or companies which exhibit both characteristics.

Top 10 Stock Holdings	Sector	% Assets
BHP Billiton Ltd		10.85
Westpac Banking Corp		9.42
Australia and New Zealand Banking Group Limited		9.23
Commonwealth Bank of Australia		7.76
National Australia Bank Limited		5.67
Telstra Corp Ltd		5.60
Wesfarmers Ltd		4.09
News Corporation DR		3.37
Rio Tinto Ltd		3.24

Top 5 Sector Weightings	% Assets
Financial Services	38.92
Basic Materials	19.48
Consumer Cyclical	13.82
Industrials	8.24
Communication Services	5.64

Top 5 Countries	% Assets
Australia	96.61
U.S.	3.39

Fees	
One-time	
Entry Fee/Contribution Fee	0.00%
Exit Fee/Withdrawal Fee	0.00%
Buy/Sell Spread	0.50%
Annual	
ICR pa (30 Jun 2012)	0.90%
Performance Fee pa (30 Jun 2012)	0.00%
Management Fee pa	0.90%
Max Ongoing Adviser Fee pa	0.00%

FIGURE 7.9
Excerpt of a research report provided by Morningstar on an Australian equities fund

While this chapter thus far has looked at some basic techniques to analyse managed funds, a range of more sophisticated techniques are available and can be beneficial in revealing further information concerning the risk and return characteristics of the fund. The following discussion will draw on the information provided in table 7.2.

TABLE 7.2 Equity fund performance (period ending 31 June 2013)

Analysis	1 year	3 year	5 year
Performance (% p.a.)	12.8%	1.8%	10.2%
Standard deviation (% p.a.)	16.5%	16.0%	17.2%
Excess return (% p.a.)	4.1%	3.04%	6.52%
Tracking error (% p.a.)	5.8%	5.5%	6.7%
Information ratio	0.7	0.6	1.0
Sharpe ratio	0.5	–0.2	0.3

Note: The benchmark used for the calculation of ratios is the S&P/ASX 300 Accumulation Index.

Table 7.2 is an example of the type of information typically provided by the research houses on managed fund performance and risk. The data in table 7.2 relate to a hypothetical Australian share fund. What does the information tell us about the performance and risk characteristics of the fund? Apart from the performance over time, a number of measures are provided. These measures can be utilised by both financial planners and clients to help improve their investment decision making in respect of a particular fund as well as relative to comparable funds.

Assessment and interpretation of ratios

Standard deviation

Standard deviation is used to quantify the risks associated with possible returns. It is a statistical measure of the variability of a particular distribution of values, in this case the historical returns of a managed fund. The higher the standard deviation of an investment, the greater the relative riskiness of the fund because of uncertainty associated with the amount of the return. The standard deviation can be used to illustrate that in approximately two-thirds of the time, the returns over a particular period will vary plus or minus one standard deviation from the average return, while approximately 96% of the time, the returns will vary plus or minus two standard deviations from the average.

standard deviation a measure of the riskiness of an investment

Thus, based on the information in table 7.2, the returns over a 5-year period will vary on average between a return of 10.2% plus or minus 17.2 percentage points for two-thirds of the time (i.e. between 27.4% and negative 7.0%).

Excess return

The excess return is the return generated by the fund relative to its benchmark. Thus for the 5-year period, the particular fund has achieved a return that is 6.5% over the particular benchmark used by the fund.

Tracking error

The **tracking error** is a measure which looks at how closely the returns of a managed fund follow the returns of the index to which it is benchmarked. It is calculated as the standard deviation of the differences between the return on the portfolio and the return on the benchmark. Tracking error is used to measure consistency of outperformance against

tracking error a measure which looks at how closely the returns of a managed fund follow the returns of the index to which it is benchmarked

the index and is an indication of active risk or how actively managed the fund is. An actively managed fund will have a high tracking error while an index fund will have a tracking error close to zero. If a fund has a relatively high MER because it is actively managed, an investor would normally expect to see a high tracking error. A low tracking error would simply mean that the fund is basically following the index. The managed fund expressed in table 7.2 has a relatively high tracking error over the period of analysis indicating that the fund is actively managing its investments and its selection of equities is not closely aligned to the benchmark index.

Information ratio

information ratio
a measure that considers the extent to which a fund has outperformed its benchmark after adjusting for risk

The **information ratio** is used as a risk-adjusted measure of the relative performance of a portfolio. The information ratio takes away the effects of market movements from returns and adjusts for the risk undertaken. It helps to answer the question, 'Was the manager sufficiently rewarded for the risk incurred by deviating from the benchmark?'

The higher the information ratio, the higher the active return of the portfolio given the amount of risk taken, and accordingly the better the manager. Better fund managers typically achieve information ratios of around 0.5 or greater.

The information ratio is calculated as:

$$\frac{\text{Excess return}}{\text{Tracking error}}$$

Based on the information provided in table 7.2, over a 5-year period, the information ratio is calculated as:

$$\frac{6.52}{6.7} = 0.97 \text{ (rounded to 1)}$$

Over the various periods analysed in table 7.2, the fund manager has been consistently able to outperform the benchmark relative to the amount of risk undertaken.

Sharpe ratio

A considerable amount of academic research since the early 1950s has provided investors with the means of breaking down returns into:

1. the return generated by simply being invested in particular assets
2. the return generated by any additional risk the manager is prepared to take.

By adjusting returns for the risks taken, investors can assess whether the return has been worth the risk.

Sharpe ratio
a measure of the risk-adjusted performance of a managed fund that considers the size of the return relative to the risk undertaken

The most widely accepted risk-adjusted return measure is the **Sharpe ratio** or index, which was first documented by William Sharpe in 1966. The Sharpe ratio compares the return of the fund with a risk-free rate of return to calculate the excess return that is attributed to the risk taken by the manager. The ratio is used to determine how well an investor is compensated for the amount of risk taken on by the fund. The higher the ratio, the better is the performance of the manager. To calculate the Sharpe index, the following formula is used:

$$SI_p = \frac{R_p - R_f}{\sigma_p} \times 100$$

where SI_p = Sharpe index
R_p = return on the fund or portfolio
R_f = risk-free rate of return (usually the short-term Treasury note interest rate)
σ_p = standard deviation of the returns from the fund or portfolio

ILLUSTRATIVE EXAMPLE 7.8

Universal Equities Fund has provided the following information to unit holders.

Start of year value	\$3.95 per unit
End of year value	\$4.08 per unit
Standard deviation of the fund (σ_p)	0.91
Risk-free rate (R_f)	3.10% p.a.

Return on the fund is calculated as:

$$R_p = \frac{\text{End value} - \text{Start value}}{\text{Start value}} \times 100$$

$$= \frac{\$4.08 - \$3.95}{\$3.95} \times 100$$

$$= 3.29\%$$

The Sharpe index is calculated as:

$$SI_p = \frac{R_p - R_f}{\sigma_p} \times 100$$

$$= \frac{0.0329 - 0.0310}{0.91} \times 100$$

$$= 0.21\%$$

Another fund that produced a Sharpe index of 0.40% over a 5-year period would be considered to have a superior performance relative to the amount of risk undertaken.

Summary

An MIS is a generic term to describe an investment structure which is designed to pool together funds from various investors for the purpose of purchasing and managing a portfolio of investments. An investment into a managed fund is an indirect investment in the assets held by a particular fund. Investors contribute money to managed funds in order to gain the benefits of diversification and to have their funds managed by a professional fund manager.

The non-superannuation funds industry is regulated by ASIC under the *Corporations Act 2001*. The Act changed many aspects of regulation including the way managed funds report to their investors, the structure and management of managed funds and the taxation of those funds.

Due to the large and varied range of managed funds that exist within the market place, investors thinking of investing in managed funds may need guidance on the selection of appropriate funds for their needs. The fees and taxes of managed funds can significantly reduce the returns to investors, so before investing in a fund it is important for investors to examine the fund's associated costs, past performance and asset allocation.

Some fund managers maintain an active style of management; others remain passive and merely attempt to mimic or follow a performance index. Some managers purchase shares with value potential (income generation); others concentrate on capital growth.

The taxation of returns from managed funds is a complex area. All income and gains generated by the fund are distributed to investors, included in their assessable income and taxed at their marginal tax rates.

Returns from managed funds can be analysed in various ways:

1. by a change in the unit price
2. by comparing the fund's returns with a benchmark portfolio or index for the same period
3. by calculating and analysing performance through statistical measurement formulae.

Professional application questions

7.1 What are the advantages and disadvantages of investing in managed funds?

7.2 What factors should an investor consider before deciding to invest into a particular managed fund?

7.3 Why have some unlisted property and mortgage managed funds suffered from liquidity problems in the past?

7.4 Are there reasons why an investor would not simply invest all their funds into the managed fund that has delivered the highest return to investors over the past one year?

7.5 What is the difference in management style between an active fund manager and a passive (index) fund manager? Why would an investor want to invest into an actively managed fund if its MER was higher than that of an index fund?

7.6 Why have wrap accounts and master funds become such popular investment vehicles with clients and especially financial planners?

7.7 What is the purpose of a product disclosure statement? Is there an argument for scrapping PDSs on the basis that most investors are financially illiterate and don't read or understand the documents?

7.8 How would your selection of a portfolio of managed funds differ between a conservative investor and an aggressive investor?

7.9 What are the advantages of investing into one managed fund that invests across all asset classes compared with investing into a number of different managed funds that each invest into a separate asset class?

7.10 What does the standard deviation of a managed fund indicate about the fund?

7.11 Would you recommend that an investor allocate their entire international share exposure to an emerging markets fund, such as China or India? Provide reasons.

Professional application exercises

Basic	*
Moderate	* *
Challenging	* * *

7.12 Managed fund characteristics *

A managed fund owns the following assets:

Cash/fixed interest	$60 million
Property	$15 million
Shares	$25 million

(a) What type of investor is likely to be attracted to this particular fund, on a scale of 1–5 with 1 being very risk averse?
(b) What long-term real return objective (in excess of inflation) would you expect this fund to have?

7.13 Managed fund characteristics *

Explain what the following information tells you about the type of managed fund that you are reviewing:

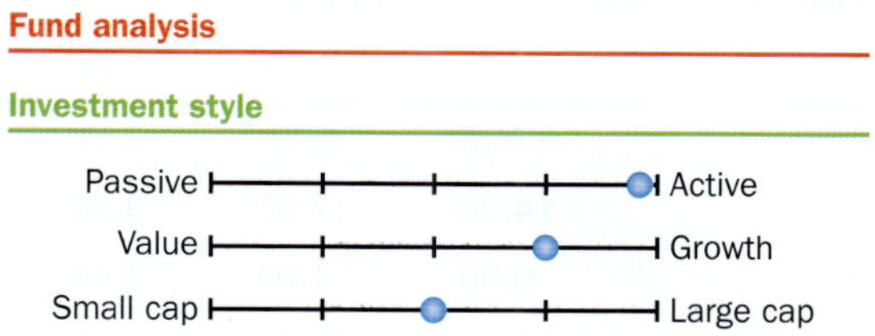

MER is 1.2.

7.14 Measuring performance *

Calculate the unit price of this fund using the following information:

	$ million
Asset allocation	
Cash and deposits	30
Short-term securities	30
Long-term securities	50
Equities and units in trust	175
Land and buildings	10
Liabilities	110
Number of units issued	11 109 657

7.15 Management styles *

You receive the following query from a friend.

I have just inherited $140 000 and wish to invest the amount into managed funds. Although I require a little income from the funds, I am mainly interested in long-term growth so have decided to invest in Australian domestic shares.

I have no other shareholding in my investment portfolio. I would classify myself as a moderately aggressive investor.

There are three funds that I am interested in investing into:

- the Second State growth fund — an 'active growth manager'
- the Syndal value fund — an 'active value manager'
- the Rearguard index fund — a 'passive fund manager'.

Explain to your friend the difference in styles between the three funds. Advise them on whether it is better to invest the $140 000 into one fund or across all three funds and, if so, in what proportions. Explain your advice.

7.16 Analysing managed funds ✱

You are looking to invest into a managed fund but note that the MER is 1.18% which you believe is quite high. You have seen another fund that invests into fixed interests that has an MER of only 0.6%.

After researching the managed fund you're looking to invest into, you note the following information:

Net assets (mil) — $623

The management style of the fund is described as a 'long-term high-conviction portfolio that differs markedly from the index'.

Returns	6 Mth	1 Yr	3 Yr	5 Yr
Total %	14.35	17.67	9.96	6.53
Income %	0.00	1.94	3.44	2.64
Growth %	14.35	15.72	6.52	3.89
Index %	15.97	11.70	4.42	0.19

Risk	Standard deviation	Risk relative to category
3 year	9.73	Below average
5 year	15.07	Above average

Break-up of investments	% assets
Domestic equity	0.00
Intl equity	97.97
Listed property	0.00
Unlisted property	0.00
Mortgages	0.00
Dom fixed interest	0.00
Intl fixed interest	0.00
Cash	2.03
Other	0.00

(a) What does the information provided tell you about the nature and characteristics of the particular fund?

(b) What are the reasons behind why this particular fund might have a higher MER than a fixed interest fund?

(c) Describe the management style of this fund which describes itself as a 'high conviction' fund.

7.17 Analysing performance ✱✱

(a) Calculate the Sharpe index for the following funds:

Fund A	
Unit price at start of year	$6.54 per unit
Unit price at end of year	$7.18 per unit
Standard deviation of the fund (σ)	0.76
Risk-free rate (R_f)	3.50% p.a.

Fund B	
Unit price at start of year	$2.25 per unit
Unit price at end of year	$2.75 per unit
Standard deviation of the fund (σ)	0.98
Risk-free rate (R_f)	3.50% p.a.

(b) Explain the difference in the two results to a potential investor.

(c) Which fund would you invest in? Explain.

7.18 Selecting managed funds ✱✱

Toby is aged 42. He recently inherited $180 000 from his uncle's estate and is looking to invest the funds. He wants to invest the funds outside of his superannuation account in order to provide access to liquidity if required. With the additional funds that he now has, he is prepared to take on more risk in order to try to generate a higher rate of return. He would like to use $60 000 to build a swimming pool in around 4 years.

Toby earns a salary of $120 000 p.a. and his spouse Melanie earns a salary of $52 000 p.a. They normally have a disposable income of around $10 000 p.a. after all expenses. The couple has 2 children aged under 16. They have minimal debt and their investments other than superannuation consist of $40 000 held in their bank account and $55 000 held in a term deposit. Toby has $320 000 held in his industry superannuation fund and invested in a conservative investment option. Toby wants to ensure that these funds are secured for his retirement and therefore wishes to minimise the risk associated with his superannuation monies.

(a) What would be the benefits of Toby investing the inheritance into managed funds?

(b) Given his risk profile and financial situation, how would you construct an appropriate asset allocation for Toby? Provide recommended proportions across the various asset classes.

(c) What issues would you consider in determining which particular managed funds would be appropriate for Toby to invest into? Toby advises that he does not require any further annual income.

(d) How would an investment in managed funds affect Toby's tax situation? Should the funds be invested in the name of another person or entity in order to minimise taxation? Explain.

7.19 Analysing performance ✱✱

The fund return, benchmark performance and standard deviation are provided for the following three funds:

Fund	Average 3-year return	Benchmark (index) performance	Standard deviation	Tracking error
Fund A	12%	10.1%	11.1%	2.6%
Fund B	12.5%	13.6%	12.3%	0.6%
Fund C	12.8%	14.2%	13.5%	6.1%

(a) Explain what the standard deviation tells an investor about the performance of each of the three managed funds.
(b) Does the information contained within the table provide any indication of the likely management investment style adopted by each of the three managed funds? Explain.
(c) Does the information in the table provide us with the basis for selecting the most appropriate fund?

7.20 Taxation issues ✱✱

The Phillips Managed Fund sends an investor the following tax statement at the end of the financial year relating to their holding in the Balanced Fund:

Tax return	Amount ($)	Tax return label
Non-primary production income	1466.55	13U
Other deductions relating to distributions	0.00	13Y
Franked distributions	102.44	13C
Franking credits	31.06	13Q
Credit for TFN amounts withheld	0.00	13R
Total current year capital gains	210.28	18H
Net assessable capital gain	82.78	18A
Assessable foreign source income	15.76	20E

(a) How much does this investment add to the investor's taxable income for the year?
(b) What type of income might the fund manager have classified under the 'non-primary production income' category?
(c) Is the investor likely to be able to claim a separate tax deduction for management fees and expenses charged by this fund? Explain.
(d) The investor is querying why he has to include a net assessable capital gain in his tax return when he has not sold any units during the year. Explain.

7.21 Analysing performance * * *

You are provided with the following information in respect of two funds, A and B.

Analysis	Fund A	Fund B
2-year performance	15%	12%
Standard deviation	14.4%	12.5%
Excess return	2.7%	0.1%
Tracking error	5.3	0.1

(a) Explain the nature of the tracking error.
(b) Calculate the information ratio and explain what it tells the investor about the fund.
(c) To what extent is it important for an investor to know the investment objective of a fund prior to investing and also whether the fund is true to its 'label'?

7.22 Selecting managed funds * * *

Investors have the choice of investing indirectly into securities through either listed managed funds or unlisted managed funds.

(a) There are approximately 30 ETFs and ETCs accessible through the ASX. Explain the difference between an ETF and an ETC. (Reference can be made to the Australian Securities Exchange — asx.com.au.)
(b) What are some of the reasons that might account for the increasing popularity of ETFs both in Australia and internationally?
(c) Explain how a listed investment company might be listed on the ASX at a market price of \$5.20 but have a net asset backing (NAB) of \$5.95. What does this tell us about the attractiveness of purchasing units in the fund?
(d) What factors should be analysed in determining the attractiveness of acquiring shares in a listed investment company?

CASE STUDY 1

Giving investment advice 1

Damien These is 32 years old and single. He is a civil engineer who was born in England but was brought up in South Africa. He and his two brothers went to boarding school because his parents travelled a great deal due to his father's mining construction job. Damien went to the University of Witwatersrand to complete his undergraduate education. He later travelled to England to complete diploma studies at the Imperial College, which helped him to specialise in concrete constructions. This specialist education placed him in high demand in the engineering field, especially in remedial engineering. After some time back in South Africa, he decided to migrate to Australia because he thought the political situation in Australia was attractive when compared with the state of affairs in South Africa.

»

»

Damien owns his own house, which he bought immediately on arrival with the help of a mortgage loan, and his car, and has about $20 000 in financial assets. He recently received a cash bonus from work after the successful completion of a large infrastructure job where he was called upon to determine why the driven piles were cracking in new sections of a major toll road and why the older sections were showing possibly dangerous cracks. He used the bonus to finish paying off the house.

He now earns over $120 000 p.a. gross and has put in place a salary-sacrifice scheme whereby he sacrifices $500 per fortnight to superannuation. He says he has the ability to save at least $25 000 p.a. although this normally doesn't occur as he tends to spend a lot on travel and entertainment.

Damien's father returned to England after his mother died quite early in life, and has recently died. After the sale of their father's house and the settlement of his estate, Damien and both his brothers each received a lump sum of the equivalent of A $250 000.

Damien wonders if he should buy another house and rent it out, buy shares or purchase units in a managed fund. He doesn't know a lot about investing and due to work commitments, doesn't have a lot of time to devote to managing his finances. He has been looking around casually for an investment house, but is not sure whether he is ready to be a landlord. He has seen two reasonably priced houses near the local university which he could buy, 'do up' a bit and rent out to students. He has been told that there is a good return to be had by doing this, but he is still unsure. With regard to investment in managed funds, his father always told him indirect investments were no good because 'you lose control' and the managers are only doing it for the fees.

Damien comes to you for advice. After some discussion and answering the standard questionnaire, together you decide that he has a fairly high tolerance for risk.

QUESTIONS

1. Given Damien's age, risk tolerance, financial position and personal preferences, what sort of asset allocation would you recommend? What are the arguments for Damien investing through an indirect investment (managed funds) as against via a direct investment?
2. With regard to Damien's thought of buying an investment property, what financial concept(s) would he be neglecting if he did this, even if a property deal appeared on paper to be a good investment option? On this basis, would you therefore recommend that Damien should not invest into property at all?

3 What are the arguments for and against investing into a property company listed on the ASX, such as Westfield, as compared to investing into an unlisted property managed fund.

4 A friend has suggested to Damien that he could borrow against his home to invest into shares. He asks your view on this. What benefits does this strategy bring?

5 If Damien decides to invest some of the inheritance into an unlisted property managed fund, what factors should be considered in deciding which particular fund he should invest into?

CASE STUDY 2

Giving investment advice 2

Heidi and Scott have a reasonable knowledge of investments and over the years have put together an investment portfolio consisting of direct shares, term deposits and a range of managed funds. The couple's investments are contained within the Alright Wrap account which was done upon the advice of their previous financial planner. The couple runs their own small business and holds very little within superannuation. Heidi is aged 45 and is married to Scott, aged 48. Both are self-employed in a business and earn a combined taxable income of around $170 000 p.a. The couple has three children, all under the age of 20.

The couple feels that they would like to fully retire in around 10 years. The couple has some interest in the financial market and are prepared to take on some risk in order to achieve a higher rate of return. They realise that there will be some short-term volatility in financial markets and are prepared to invest for the long term. They also realise that their current investment allocation and plan is unlikely to provide them with an appropriate nest egg upon retirement.

The couple is not particularly happy with the performance of their investments and is seeking some assistance.

From the website of the Alright Wrap Service, the couple's investments consist of the following:

Direct shares:

Commonwealth Bank (cost $45 000 in 1999)	$80 000
ANZ Bank (cost $18 000 in 2001)	$32 000
Bank of Queensland (cost $24 000 in 2009)	$18 000

»

»

Term deposits (fixed interest):

6-month term deposit (4.0% p.a.)	$50 000
12-month term deposit (4.1% p.a.)	$85 000

Managed funds:

Name of fund (wholesale)	Cost price	Current value	Management style	Tracking error	MER
Allcash cash fund	$52 000	$52 000	Invests in wholesale money market	0.5%	0.2%
ABC Australian share fund	$32 000	$25 000	Active value manager investing in large caps	2.4%	1.5%
BEB Australian share fund	$27 000	$32 000	Active value manager investing in large caps	2.2%	1.4%
China share fund	$45 000	$62 000	Active value manager investing in large caps	5.2%	2.1%
The Shopping Centre Retail trust	$30 000	$12 000	Active manager investing in shopping centres based in the United States	8.2%	1.4%

All returns from the managed funds are invested directly into the Allcash cash account. The Alright Wrap account charges an annual administration charge of 1.1% p.a. All managed funds were acquired in 2006, except for the BEB Australian share fund that was purchased 9 months ago.

QUESTIONS

1 Given the couple's financial circumstances and needs, determine what you believe is the risk profile of the couple and assess whether their current overall asset allocation is consistent with their risk profile.

Prepare a table of their existing investments allocated across the main asset classes. You should use the following table to determine the allocation:

Name of investment	Cash	Fixed interest	Australian shares	International shares	Property
Total funds – $ – %					

2 Based on your assessment of the couple's risk profile and financial circumstances, determine what you believe is an appropriate asset allocation for the couple (detail in overall dollar and percentage terms).
3 Explain the advantages to the couple of investing through a wrap account.
4 Analyse the investment holdings of the couple and provide recommendations for change or improvement.
5 Calculate the assessable capital gains if the couple were to dispose of all of the managed funds held within the Alright Wrap Service.

References and further reading

ASIC 2013A, *Managed Funds*, moneysmart.gov.au.

ASIC 2013B, Information Sheet (INFO 155), *Shorter PDSs: Complying with requirements for superannuation. products and simple managed investment schemes*, asic.gov.au.

ASIC 2013C, Regulatory Guide (RG 182), *Dollar disclosure*, asic.gov.au.

ASX 2013, *About exchange traded funds (ETFs) and exchange traded commodities (ETCs)*, asx.com.au.

Axiss Australia 2000, *Investment management in Australia: executive briefing*, axiss.com.au, p. 20.

CCH Australia, 2013, *Australian corporations and securities legislation*, CCH Australia, Sydney.

Foster, RA, 1996, *Australian economic statistics 1949–50 to 1994–95*, RBA, Sydney.

Fund Pick, 2012, 'Lessons in liquidity', *The Sydney Morning Herald*, 26 September, smh.com.au.

Moore, B, 2013, 'Window closing for LM First Mortgage victims, says Slater & Gordon', *Money Management*, 25 March, moneymanagement.com.au.

RBA 2012, 5655.0 — Managed Funds, Australia, December 2012, RBA, Sydney, rba.gov.au.

Treasury 2001, *Review of the Managed Investments Act 1998 — final report*, Treasury, miareview.treasury.gov.au.

Valentine, T, 2007, *Modern financial & investment planning*, Pearson Education, NSW.

8 Leveraged investments

LEARNING OBJECTIVES

After studying this chapter, you should be able to:

1. explain the concept of leveraged investing
2. outline how gearing can be used to magnify returns
3. discuss the income tax consequences of gearing
4. discuss the capital gains tax consequences of gearing
5. explain how mortgages work
6. outline margin lending
7. explain the benefits and risks of margin lending
8. outline how derivatives can be used to create leverage.

CASE STUDY

When Jill was about 10 her parents borrowed a large sum of money and purchased a sheep station in outback New South Wales. As a teenager growing up she really enjoyed helping her parents with the work around the farm.

Over the years she often heard her father say that they were 'long' in wool without really knowing what 'long' meant. She did however notice that her father was very happy when the price of wool was increasing and therefore concluded that it was good to be 'long' when prices were going up. There were also plenty of years when the price of wool was falling and her dad was not so happy.

More recently her dad had started using a broker and she often overheard conversations between her dad and the broker about going short in wool — which just didn't make sense when there were 5000 sheep running around the paddocks outside waiting to be shorn.

Jill is about to head to Sydney and commence her commerce degree. She is worried about how her parents will be able to manage the farm by themselves and how they will be able to meet the commitments associated with the large debt that still exists. She is also concerned for her own financial future and wonders whether borrowing money to fund an investment is a sound strategy.

Some of the issues that Jill needs to consider include the following.

- What does it mean to be 'long' in an asset?
- What does it mean to be 'short' in an asset? How is it possible to be short?
- When her dad goes 'short' in wool is he gambling and taking more risks than he should?
- Is it wise to borrow money to fund the purchase of an investment? What are the potential gains and what are the potential risks?

These issues are explored throughout this chapter.

Introduction

leverage
use a small amount of capital to access a larger amount of an asset

To **leverage** an investment means to use a small amount of capital to access a larger amount of an asset. A 'leveraged position' usually refers to borrowing money to add to the investor's capital in order to buy an asset. Borrowing money is also known as gearing. In Australia, most people's first experience of gearing is via the purchase of their first home; few people can accumulate enough capital to buy their first house and, as a result, use gearing to assist with the purchase. Investors can also use gearing to invest in income-producing assets. In this chapter, we will review how investors can take a leveraged position by borrowing money.

A leveraged position can also refer to the use of derivative instruments, where a small amount of capital can be used to create an exposure to significant gains (and losses). Derivative instruments include contracts for difference, futures, options and warrants. These will also be discussed in this chapter.

LO 1 Leveraged investing

The fundamental tenet of all investing is to own an asset if you believe the price of the asset will increase. For example, if an investor believes the price of National Australia Bank (NAB) shares will increase in the future, it would be good for them to own some NAB shares. Owning an asset is also sometimes referred to as being 'long' — you want to be long in an asset when prices are rising. We will see in this chapter that there are a number of ways that an investor can be long. The most conventional way is to simply buy and hold the asset. The purchase might be funded by a combination of the investor's capital and debt, thereby creating a geared investment. There are, however, a number of other techniques by which an investor can be long, including the use of contracts for difference, futures and options.

On the other hand, if an investor believes the price of an asset is going to decrease, they would prefer to not own that asset. Further, if they do own the asset, they should sell it. For example, if an investor believes the price of NAB shares will decrease in the future, it would be good for them to sell any NAB shares they currently own — they may be able to buy them back later at a cheaper price. To sell is to go short. There are a number of ways an investor can go short, including the use of contracts for difference, futures and options.

We have used the term 'investor' above but sometimes 'investors' have different motives. Some investors will be investing to make a profit — if they speculate that prices will rise they will go long and if they speculate that prices will fall they will go short. Any profit or loss that they make is not offset by any other position they may hold. Some 'investors' will be investing in order to manage risk; that is, they are trying to **hedge** a risk (protect a position) to which they are currently exposed.

hedge
to use a financial product to reduce or eliminate a risk to which an investor is currently exposed

In determining the appropriate leveraging strategy it is important to know the motivation of the investor — are they hedging or are they **speculating**? If the investor is hedging then it is vital to understand the current position that is being protected. If the investor is hedging a long position they should go short. If the investor is hedging a short position they should go long. If the investor misunderstands their current position they may, in fact, exacerbate the risk rather than reduce it. Identifying the current risk position is not always as easy as it seems.

speculating
using a financial product purely to achieve financial gain, that is, not to reduce or eliminate a risk

LO 2 Gearing

Gearing describes the use of borrowed money to buy assets. 'Gearing' investments might sound like a peculiar use of a word that is more often used with your bike or car, but the concept is actually exactly the same. Gearing essentially changes the ratio of inputs to outputs. With bikes or cars, a high gear allows you to get higher speed out of the engine. With investments, high gearing allows higher returns (either positive or negative).

gearing
the use of borrowed money to assist in the purchase of assets

In using borrowed funds, investors aim to achieve a return higher than the cost of those borrowed funds. The return can come by means of annual income and by means of a capital gain when the asset is eventually sold.

As we mentioned earlier with respect to the family home, gearing allows an investor to buy an asset they otherwise could not afford from their capital alone. Investors most commonly use gearing to assist with the purchase of share portfolios, managed funds and investment properties.

ILLUSTRATIVE EXAMPLE 8.1

Kevin believes that the price of two-bedroom units in his suburb is likely to increase so he decides to go long by buying a $300 000 unit. He already has a substantial asset base, so his bank is happy to provide an interest-only loan up to the full purchase price at a rate of 8% p.a.

Kevin expects that he can rent the unit for $400 per week. He also expects that the unit will appreciate in value over the next 12 months by 10%.

Kevin is not sure how much of his own capital he should contribute to the purchase.

If Kevin sells the unit in 12 months, what is the expected return on capital invested for various levels of gearing (ignoring the impact of taxes at this stage)? This is shown in table 8.1.

TABLE 8.1 Kevin: no taxes, and returns > costs

	All equity (ungeared) $	Low $	Medium $	High $
Capital	300 000	200 000	100 000	30 000
Borrowing	–	100 000	200 000	270 000
Total	300 000	300 000	300 000	300 000
Rental income	20 800	20 800	20 800	20 800
Less interest	–	8 000	16 000	21 600
Net income	20 800	12 800	4 800	–800
Capital gain	30 000	30 000	30 000	30 000
Total return	50 800	42 800	34 800	29 200
Capital invested	300 000	200 000	100 000	30 000
Return on capital invested	17%	21%	35%	97%

As long as the rate of return, which includes both income and capital gains, is greater than the cost of borrowed funds then increasing the level of gearing will increase the percentage return on capital invested. In this case, the rental income was 7% ($20 800/$300 000) and the capital gain was 10% for a total return of 17%. The cost of borrowed funds was 8%.

If Kevin could be guaranteed the returns outlined above then he should borrow as much as possible to fund the purchase of the unit. However, guaranteed investment returns are very hard to find — if the total return falls below 8% then increasing the level of gearing will, in fact, magnify Kevin's losses.

If we assume that Kevin's rental income is only $5000 and that the capital appreciation is only 3% what is the expected return on capital invested for various levels of gearing (ignoring the impact of taxes at this stage)? This is shown in table 8.2.

TABLE 8.2 Kevin: no taxes, and returns < costs

	All equity (ungeared) $	Low $	Medium $	High $
Capital	300 000	200 000	100 000	30 000
Borrowing	–	100 000	200 000	270 000
Total	300 000	300 000	300 000	300 000
Rental income	5 000	5 000	5 000	5 000
Less interest	–	8 000	16 000	21 600
Net income	5 000	−3 000	−11 000	−16 600
Capital gain	9 000	9 000	9 000	9 000
Total return	14 000	6 000	−2 000	−7 600
Capital invested	300 000	200 000	100 000	30 000
Return on capital invested	5%	3%	−2%	−25%

In this case the rental income was 2% ($5000/$300 000) and the capital gain was 3% for a total return of 5%. The cost of borrowed funds was 8%. Gearing has magnified losses rather than gains.

LO 3 Income taxes and geared investments

When an investor invests in an income-producing asset, that income is assessable for tax purposes. The expenses associated with the income-producing asset are tax deductible. Where an asset is highly geared, interest will be a significant deductible expense. Depending on the nature of the asset there will be other deductible expenses, particularly where the investment is in property. The Australian Taxation Office (ATO) provides details of all the expenses investors may claim against the income of a rental property. These include, among other things, council rates, cleaning, repairs and maintenance. An expense will be deductible when it is an outgoing necessarily incurred in earning income. Taxpayers must be able to produce the source documentation which proves that the expense has been paid, if they are asked to do so by the ATO, or risk fines.

Positive gearing

When the annual income from an investment is greater than the deductible expenses it is said to be **positively geared**. The excess income is taxed at the investor's marginal tax rate. Because annual income exceeds expenses, positive gearing is considered less risky than negative gearing which we will discuss shortly. Positively geared investors are able to meet their interest commitments through their investment income. Where interest-only financing is used, no call is made on any other income of the investor during the investment period. Positively geared investors can undertake a number of positively geared investments at the same time. If we refer back to the example of Kevin in table 8.1 the 'low' and 'medium' scenarios are examples of positive gearing; that is, the net income is positive.

positive gearing
a situation where the assessable income generated from the investment exceeds total deductions incurred, including the interest charges; in this case, the tax is payable on the profit

Consider the case of Sally. Sally has noticed that houses in the suburb of Deadville are very cheap compared to neighbouring suburbs. After checking with local real estate agents she has found out that the capital appreciation of the houses in Deadville in the last 10 years has averaged 1% p.a. Demand for rental accommodation, however, is high in Deadville with rental yields averaging 10%. If Sally can borrow at 8% and use the purchased house as security she can produce positively geared returns. Moreover, Sally might be in a position to buy several houses in Deadville.

Negative gearing

negative gearing
a situation where the total deductions associated with an investment, including the interest charge, exceed assessable income generated from the investment; in this case, the loss can be claimed as a tax deduction

tax shield
where the net deductible expenses of an investment reduce the amount of tax payable

When the annual income from an investment is less than the deductible expenses it is said to be **negatively geared**. This loss provides a valuable **tax shield**. The value of this tax shield should be added to the other cash flows associated with holding the asset in determining the net gain from holding the asset.

If we refer back to the example of Kevin in table 8.1, the 'high' scenario is an example of negative gearing; that is, the assessable income of $20 800 and allowable deductions of $21 600 result in negative net income of $800. If we assume Kevin earns a salary of $100 000 p.a. and his marginal tax rate is 37%, then this $800 'loss' can be used to reduce his assessable income from $100 000 to $99 200 and save him $296 in tax ($800 × 0.37). This $296 saving is effectively a positive cash flow which emerges from Kevin holding the income-producing asset — if he did not own the asset, he would be $296 worse off.

Table 8.3 shows the tax Kevin would pay on the 'all equity', 'low' and 'medium' scenarios. Paying tax reduces the total return. Comparing the return on capital invested for each of the three scenarios in table 8.3 to table 8.1 shows that the percentage returns have decreased. Table 8.3 also shows that the negatively geared 'high' scenario results in $296 less tax being paid than would otherwise be the case. This effectively improves Kevin's annual return on the investment.

TABLE 8.3 Kevin: impact of income tax

	All equity (ungeared) $	Low $	Medium $	High $
Capital	300 000	200 000	100 000	30 000
Borrowing	–	100 000	200 000	270 000
Total	300 000	300 000	300 000	300 000
Rental income	20 800	20 800	20 800	20 800
Less interest	–	8 000	16 000	21 600
Net income	20 800	12 800	4 800	–800
Tax paid/shielded	–7 696	–4 736	–1 776	296
Net income after tax	13 104	8 064	3 024	–504
Capital gain	30 000	030 000	30 000	30 000
Total return	43 104	38 064	33 024	29 496
Capital invested	300 000	200 000	100 000	30 000
Return on capital invested	14%	19%	33%	98%

The value of the tax shield is a function of the investor's marginal tax rate — the higher the marginal tax rate, the more valuable the shield. This is illustrated in table 8.4.

Negative gearing produces a valuable tax shield; that is, the annual losses on the investment are less than they otherwise would have been without the tax shield. Nonetheless, why would an investor want to hold an investment, which on an annual basis loses money? The investor must be hoping for a capital gain which will more than offset the accumulated annual losses associated with the investment.

TABLE 8.4 Tax dollars saved where deductible expenses exceed assessable income by $10 000

Marginal tax rate	Tax dollars saved
19.0%	$1900
32.5%	$3250
37.0%	$3700
45.0%	$4500

Risks of negative gearing

The primary risk associated with gearing, particularly high levels of gearing, is that borrowing repayments need to be serviced. The burden of repayments can be reduced if the lender is prepared to lend on an interest-only basis; however, sooner or later, the principal amount of the loan will have to be repaid. The risk for an investor of not servicing the loan is that the lender has the right to sell the asset at its current market value if the investor breaks the loan terms and conditions. The current market value may be less than the purchase price or the amount of debt outstanding. The investor/borrower is then obliged to repay the balance of the loan outstanding or face bankruptcy.

The risks of gearing are almost the opposite of the benefits of gearing, and include the following.

- The anticipated annual income is lower than expected. For example, a company may pay lower than expected dividends; a rental property may be vacant for a period of time.
- The anticipated annual expenses are higher than expected. For example, variable interest rates might rise; a rental property might need significant repairs.
- If the loan must be rolled over, the lender may change the rules or conditions of the loan which will affect the benefits of the gearing exercise. An example is an increase in the amount of capital the investor/borrower must contribute.
- The investor loses their job or earns less income resulting in a lower marginal tax rate which in turn makes the tax shield benefits of negative gearing less attractive. The investor might also struggle to generate the cash flow to service the outgoings, particularly loan repayments.
- Circumstances force the investor to sell the asset in less-than-favourable conditions.
- Asset specific factors adversely affect the investment asset. For example, bad tenants significantly damage a rental property; changes in government legislation negatively impact a listed company.
- The asset does not generate the capital gain anticipated. This is the critical success factor, particularly for negatively geared investments — why sustain annual losses unless the ultimate capital gain more than offsets them?

Gearing ratio and loan-to-valuation ratios

gearing ratio the ratio of debt to capital

The **gearing ratio** is used to measure the amount of debt in relation to the current market value of the investor's capital contribution. Some lenders set a gearing ratio as part of their debt agreement for borrowers to maintain during the life of the loan. A lower gearing ratio means there is a lower level of risk for the lender. The gearing ratio is calculated as follows:

$$\text{Gearing ratio} = \frac{\text{Borrowed funds}}{\text{Current market value of the investor's capital contribution}}$$

Returning to the example of Kevin, table 8.5 shows the gearing ratio for the various scenarios we have discussed.

TABLE 8.5 Kevin: gearing ratios

	All equity (ungeared) $	Low $	Medium $	High $
Capital	300 000	200 000	100 000	30 000
Borrowing	–	100 000	200 000	270 000
Total	300 000	300 000	300 000	300 000
Gearing ratio	–	0.5	2	9

The gearing ratio, as its name suggests, generally expresses the ratio of debt to capital. As shown in table 8.5, in the 'high' scenario, Kevin had $9 of debt for every $1 of capital.

loan-to-valuation ratio (LVR) the amount of debt expressed as a percentage of the total asset value

Many lenders prefer to use the **loan-to-valuation ratio (LVR)** measure as their means of determining an appropriate limit for the amount of borrowing by the investor. The LVR uses the same inputs as the gearing ratio; however, contrary to what its name suggests, it is generally expressed as a percentage. The LVR is calculated as follows.

$$\text{LVR} = \frac{\text{Debt}}{\text{Current market value of the investor's capital contribution} + \text{Debt}}$$

For Kevin, the LVR for the 'high' scenario is 90%.

LO 4 Capital gains tax and geared investments

As we discussed earlier, leveraged investments may result in net positive assessable income. That is, assessable income is greater than allowable deductions. In this case, tax will have to be paid at marginal tax rates. Alternatively, leveraged investments may result in negative assessable income. That is, assessable income is less than allowable deductions. In this case, the amount of tax the investor would have otherwise had to pay will be reduced, and the higher the investor's marginal tax rate the greater the value of this tax shield. Whether an investor has positive or negative assessable income on an annual basis, all investors will be hoping to make a capital gain on the disposal of an investment asset.

Investors can choose when to sell an asset (unless circumstances force them to sell). Therefore, they are able to time their capital gains so as to achieve a tax-effective outcome. Assets purchased prior to 19 September 1985 are not subject to capital gains tax.

Assets purchased after 19 September 1985 and before 21 September 1999 are subject to capital gains tax. The gain can be determined by the **frozen method** or the **discount method**. These methods were discussed in chapter 3.

Assets purchased after 21 September 1999 are subject to capital gains tax. Where the asset is held for less than 12 months the full gain is assessable. Where the asset is held for more than 12 months the discount method is used to determine the assessable gain. For individuals, 50% of the **capital gain** is **assessable income** and 50% is **exempt income**. Capital losses can be offset against capital gains. If there are capital losses but no capital gains to offset these against in a particular financial year, the capital losses can be carried forward to offset against future capital gains (they cannot be written off against other assessable income in the current year).

An investor may choose to sell their investment asset(s) and realise a capital gain during a period where their income is reduced e.g. upon retirement. One of the advantages of a share portfolio, unlike a house or commercial property, is that investors may also choose to sell a part of their portfolio and realise a smaller and more manageable capital gain in a single period.

Refer back to the example of Kevin and table 8.1. Let's assume that Kevin sells the asset that he has held for just over a year. His capital gain is $30 000, that is, 10% of $300 000. Half of this gain ($15 000) will be assessable income and taxed at his marginal tax rate which we will assume to be 37%. Half of this gain will be exempt income.

Table 8.6 shows the impact of capital gains tax on each of the scenarios. Capital gains tax reduces the total return for each scenario and therefore reduces the return on capital invested for each scenario.

frozen method
a method of determining a capital gain using CPI index numbers from the date of purchase and the date of sale

discount method
a method of determining a capital gain by including a percentage of the gain as assessable income

capital gain
a gain that arises when the price of an asset increases

assessable income
income that is assessable or recognised and measured under taxation law

exempt income
income that is not counted by the ATO and not taxed

TABLE 8.6 Kevin: impact of income tax and capital gains tax

	All equity (ungeared)	Low	Medium	High
Capital	300 000	200 000	100 000	30 000
Borrowing	–	100 000	200 000	270 000
Total	300 000	300 000	300 000	300 000
Rental income	20 800	20 800	20 800	20 800
Less interest	–	8 000	16 000	21 600
Net income	20 800	12 800	4 800	–800
Tax paid/shielded	–7 696	–4 736	–1 776	296
Net income after tax	13 104	8 064	3 024	–504
Capital gain	30 000	30 000	30 000	30 000
Assessable capital gain	15 000	15 000	15 000	15 000
Tax cn capital gain	5 550	5 550	5 550	5 550
Capital gain after tax	24 450	24 450	24 450	24 450
Total return	37 554	32 514	27 474	23 946
Capital invested	300 000	200 000	100 000	300 000
Return on capital invested	13%	16%	27%	80%

LO 5 Mortgages

mortgage a contract between a lender and a borrower which pledges real estate as security for a loan

mortgagee the person who receives the mortgage — the lender

mortgagor the person who offers the mortgage — the borrower

Mortgages are secured geared investments where the mortgage document is the contract between the lender and the borrower. A mortgage contract is a pledge of real estate to secure the payment of a loan. Mortgages can be secured by either residential or non-residential real estate. The mortgage contract gives the lender (**mortgagee**) the right to foreclose on the loan and take ownership of the property in order to ensure that the loan is paid off if the borrower (**mortgagor**) fails to make the contracted payments. Lenders prefer borrowers to have substantial deposits so that the loan-to-value ratio (LVR) is less than 80–85%.

In Australia, the most common mortgage loans are standard variable-rate loans and fixed-rate loans. A standard variable-rate mortgage (SVL) is one in which the interest rate on the loan is adjusted periodically. Recent trends have shown that the trigger for changing interest rates is the announcement of a change (an increase or a decrease) in the cash rate by the Reserve Bank of Australia (RBA).

Fixed-rate loans have fixed rates of interest for an agreed period. At the end of this period they generally convert to variable-rate loans. Normally, borrowers must decide what period, up to about 10 years, to contract for a fixed rate. After the expiry of that period, an investor may refinance and contract for a fixed rate for a further period. The decision, of course, rests on the likelihood of a rise in interest rates and the premium being charged by the lending institution for the fixed rate over the current variable rate.

With the deregulation of the finance industry, the use of mortgages for investing has become quite sophisticated at the retail level. Some variations on the standard interest-and-principal mortgage repayment schemes include:

principal the amount of a loan which is outstanding

equity the client's capital as opposed to borrowed funds

- interest-only loans with the entire **principal** payable at the end of the loan
- **equity** release loans, where surplus equity above agreed levels may be withdrawn
- reverse mortgages, where no repayments are made until the contract is settled when the homeowner dies or leaves the property
- second-mortgage loans for investing in other income-generating assets such as shares or other property.

All these styles of lending for investing using mortgages have the same underlying operational characteristics as a standard mortgage including:

- the pledging of real estate to the lender until the debt is repaid
- the need to service the debt regularly (e.g. monthly, annually), at the beginning of the loan (e.g. up-front interest payments) or at the end of the loan (e.g. reverse mortgages).

security the promise of assets, including real estate, in the case of loan default

There are a number of benefits of using assets as **security** for borrowings.

- It reduces the risk to the lender that the capital will not be returned. Should the borrower default on the loan, the lender has the right to sell the asset that is securing the loan at its current value, using the proceeds to repay the loan and to cover any costs incurred in selling the asset.
- It allows the borrower to access funds that would not normally be available if the borrower was providing only a promise to repay the loan.
- It allows the borrower to access funds at a cheaper rate than if the borrower was only providing a promise to repay the loan.
- It provides both borrower and lender with a safety net of value. As long as the asset is worth more than the loan, there is a barrier between the value of the debt and the amount that could be raised to repay the debt once the asset is sold.

The disadvantages of using assets as security for borrowing include:

- the increased risk for the borrower that the particular asset will be seized and sold by the lender
- the increased costs of preparing documentation for the loan — for example, the additional costs in obtaining an independent valuation for the asset.
- the borrower cannot use the asset that is used as security for the loan for any other purposes without the express written permission of the lender; for example, to secure another loan, to sell the asset, or to demolish and rebuild the property.

PERSONAL FINANCE BULLETIN

Buy versus rent only

The rent versus buy decision for the first home can in some ways be very simple.

Rental yields over the last 30 years have averaged around 4.5%. Over a similar period variable home loan interest rates have averaged around 8.5%.

If a young couple were to rent a $500 000 house in Sydney they could expect to pay approximately $430 a week in rent [($500 000 × 4.5%)/52]. If the same couple were to buy the house they could expect to pay approximately $820 a week in interest [($500 000 × 8.5%)/52].

If houses in Sydney were not expected to increase in value over time then renting would obviously be a much better financial choice than buying. However property prices in Australia over the last 30 years have increased by around 8.4% per annum. Buying allows the purchaser to capture this price increase whereas renting obviously does not.

If a $500 000 property increases in value by 8.4% in a year this represents an increase in value of $808 per week [($500 000 × 8.4%)/52]. Capital gains on the principal residence are exempt from capital gains tax in which case the homeowner gets to keep all this gain. Arguably this gain of $808 can be offset against the interest cost of $820 a week in which case the net cost of owning per week is only $12 compared to a rental cost of $430 a week.

Is it really this simple? The short answer is no.

We have used averages above and averages can be very misleading.

- We noted that the average property price increase was 8.4% for the last 30 years; however, for the period 1990 to 1995 the average increase was only 2.8%. Moreover the average increase in some areas/suburbs will be significantly different to others.
- We also noted above that average variable home interest rates were 8.5% over the last 30 years. However, this has included periods when the rate was as low as 5% and as high as 17%.
- If buying a house is a long-term 'buy and hold' strategy then there is a greater likelihood that long-term averages might be achieved provided the short-term pain of departures from the average can be survived e.g. meeting the loan commitments associated with variable interest rates of 17%. However, there is

»

»

no guarantee that averages recorded over the last 30 years will be replicated in the next 30 years.

Renting provides some advantages that cannot be achieved by buying:

- A number of property costs including maintenance and rates are covered by the rental whereas when buying these costs must be covered by the purchaser.
- Renting has very few transaction costs whereas buying and selling include considerable transactions costs including agent's fees, stamp duty and so on that can add up to 10% to the purchase price.
- It is much easier for a renter to relocate (e.g. if they do not like their neighbours or work forces them to relocate) than it is for a purchaser.
- Meeting interest and principal repayments means that a purchaser is often unlikely to be able to borrow more money to pursue other investment opportunities, whereas renters may decide to use their borrowing capacity to pursue other investments.
- Some renters may be able to afford only the rent ($430 in the example above). Some renters might be able to afford the cost of the interest ($820 in the example above) but not afford the repayments of the principal associated with the loan.

Buying provides some advantages that cannot be achieved by renting:

- Meeting mortgage repayments, which include a repayment of the principal component, is a form of enforced saving that renters might find difficult to otherwise achieve.
- There is no financial incentive for renters to make capital improvements to a property. However, buyers will often gain personal satisfaction from completing such work while at the same time improving the capital value of the property.
- The desire to own your own home runs deep in the Australian psyche. Australians have one of the highest rates of home ownership in the world, with approximately 70% of households living in a dwelling that they either own or are buying.

In the end buying a home is a decision that straddles both investment and personal considerations. To the extent that it represents an investment decision, it requires all the due consideration that is normally associated with a property investment. Buying a home is a long-term investment decision, so timing becomes less critical. However, considerations such as location, access to public transport and schools and so on remain very important if capital gains are to be ultimately achieved to help justify the buy versus rent decision.

Buy versus rent and invest

We mentioned above that the interest and principal commitments associated with repaying a loan on the family home may well crowd out the ability to borrow money for investment purposes.

A renter may well use their 'unused' borrowing capacity to borrow money to finance a non-family home investment. The income and capital gains from these investments need to be offset against the cost of renting when making a rent versus buy decision. It is important to remember that capital gains on the principal residence are exempt from capital gains tax whereas capital gains from other investments including other property investments (even when the person is renting) are subject to capital gains tax.

There will be circumstances where it makes more sense to rent and invest rather than buy. For example, a young couple may well have the financial resources to enter the property market. However, they:

- need to be able to relocate easily for work purposes
- are unsure of where they might want to live in the longer term
- think there are better investment opportunities than what a family home might offer
- want to continue to live and rent in an area where they can't afford to buy.

Conclusion

Buying and owning a family home for a relatively short period of time leaves the purchaser vulnerable to bad timing and high transaction costs.

To buy a home is to fundamentally make a leveraged investment decision. As with all leveraged investment decisions, if the return on the investment (the capital appreciation of the house) is greater than the cost of the borrowed funds used to finance the purchase of the house positive investment returns will be magnified.

As in the example we have discussed, even if the rate of capital appreciation (8.4%) is somewhat less than what was hoped for and somewhat less than the cost of borrowed funds (8.5%) it still may well be sufficient to justify the buy decision and avoid the costs of renting.

Buying and owning a family home for a relatively long period of time is rarely viewed as a poor investment decision.

LO 6 Margin lending

Margin lending is a geared investment where the lender advances funds to the investor/borrower and the amount borrowed is secured by the investment assets themselves rather than by a mortgage over property. Typically, margin lending is offered to share market investors, although it is not limited to share market investing. As with most loans there is interest to pay, but usually the loans are not for any fixed maximum term and principal repayments are optional during the life of the contract. Interest on margin loans is normally 1–2% higher than mortgage loan rates. Lenders seek to limit the amount of risk investors are exposed to by using conservative loan-to-valuation ratios (LVRs).

margin lending
lending for investment where the loan is secured by the investment

Margin lending increased dramatically in the 2000s. In September 2000, outstanding margin lending debt was $7 billion. By December 2007, pushed on by a buoyant share market, this amount had risen to $38 billion (RBA 2013). However, the falls in world share markets in 2008 had a significant impact. First, in an environment of falling share prices, it became less attractive to commence a new margin lending facility. Second, falling share prices resulted in people with existing margin lending facilities receiving margin calls (discussed later in the chapter) which led to the repayment of debt. By September 2009, the level of outstanding margin lending debt had contracted to $18 billion (RBA 2013). The rapid growth of the industry followed by the sudden contraction is not unexpected and reflects the inherent risk in any form of geared investment. While asset prices are increasing and investor confidence is high, the level of margin lending would be expected to increase. When asset prices are falling and/or investor confidence is not so high, the level of outstanding margin lending would be expected to decrease. By December 2012 margin lending had further contracted to $12 billion (RBA 2013).

With a margin loan a borrower must maintain a given LVR of the assets used as security. For example, if a lender specifies an LVR of 80% the value of the loan cannot exceed 80% of the value of the asset pledged as security. The specified LVR varies slightly between lenders. Generally, lenders set LVRs according to their perception of the underlying risk and inherent price volatility of the individual asset. The less the perceived underlying risk and the lower inherent price volatility the higher the LVR; that is, the more the lender is willing to lend. Typically, LVRs range from 40% to 80%. The significant reduction in margin lending in 2008 was accompanied by a widespread reduction in LVRs as lenders reassessed the inherent price volatility of all assets in the market and this lower level of LVRs has persisted as world economic conditions remain uncertain. Any widespread reduction in LVRs must constrain the growth of the margin lending market.

All of the major banks provide margin lending facilities. Table 8.7 shows a selection from the Commonwealth Bank's extensive list of Australian Securities Exchange (ASX) listed equities that are approved for margin lending purposes.

TABLE 8.7 Selected LVRs for CBA margin lending as at 1 April 2013

ASX Code	Company	Portfolio LVR
BSL	BlueScope Steel	60%
FMG	Fortescue Metals Group Limited	55%
IAG	Insurance Australia Group	75%
JBH	JB Hi-Fi Limited	70%
NAB	National Australia Bank	75%

Note: Portfolio LVR is applicable to stocks in a diversified portfolio with 5 or more approved securities.
Source: CommSec 2013.

ILLUSTRATIVE EXAMPLE 8.2

Penny wishes to create a $100 000 share portfolio by using some of her own capital and by commencing a margin loan facility. She intends to use $35 000 of her own money and borrow $65 000 through a margin lending facility.

She wishes to invest in the shares of two publicly listed companies, Newstock Bank and Bright Copper. Her lender advises that Newstock has an LVR of 70% and Bright Copper has an LVR of 60%.

Penny wishes to buy $50 000 of Newstock shares and $50 000 of Bright Copper shares. Her lender will recognise the following security.

Stock	Current value	LVR	Security
Newstock	$50 000	70%	$35 000
Bright Copper	$50 000	60%	$30 000
Total	$100 000		$65 000

One of the benefits of margin lending is that borrowers can also pledge existing assets as security for a margin loan provided they are on the lender's approved list.

If Penny already held $35 000 in shares, $17 500 in Newstock and $17 500 in Bright Copper, the analysis would be exactly the same as the above.

From the point of view of the lender, Penny is offering $65 000 as security for a $65 000 loan. If the value of her shares increases then the value of the security she is offering will also increase. If the value of her shares decreases then she needs to be careful that the amount of security she is offering does not fall below $65 000. If it does fall below $65 000, her lender will make a margin call. Moreover, the total value of the portfolio could remain the same; however, the movements in individual share prices could affect the amount of security offered. For example:

Stock	Current value	LVR	Security
Newstock	$25 000	70%	$17 500
Bright Copper	$75 000	60%	$45 000
Total	$100 000		$62 500

Borrowers must actively monitor their margin loan accounts. By regularly checking changes in the portfolio value, individual security value and loan balance, customers can better manage the chance of receiving a margin call. Naturally, lenders will monitor this as well.

Safety margin

safety margin a margin of security which must be maintained above the level required to meet the outstanding value of the loan

Most lenders will insist that an investor maintains a **safety margin** of security over and above the value of their loan. The size of the margin will vary from lender to lender. For example, a client might need to maintain a safety margin or buffer of 5%. The safety margin or buffer is there to protect the lender, particularly when asset prices are volatile. If prices fall, the lender will make a margin call to ensure that the safety margin is re-established.

The safety margin is also a source of comfort and reassurance for the individual investor. While the lender might insist on a safety margin of 5%, the individual investor may have a safety margin which far exceeds this in order to further reduce the likelihood of margin calls.

We can calculate the safety margin as follows:

$$\text{Safety margin} = 1 - \frac{\text{Borrowing}}{\text{Security recognised by lender}}$$

If we return to the example of Penny, and assume that the stock market has been performing well and she now has the following portfolio:

Stock	Current value	LVR	Security
Newstock	$60 000	70%	$42 000
Bright Copper	$75 000	60%	$45 000
Total	$135 000		$87 000

Penny's safety margin would be:

$$\text{Safety margin} = 1 - \frac{\$65\,000}{\$87\,000}$$
$$= 25.3\%$$

Margin calls

margin call
where a lender asks for an additional contribution by a borrower because the current level of the security they are offering has fallen below an agreed threshold

If the value of the security pledged falls below the value required by the lender, a margin call will be triggered. **Margin calls** normally have to be satisfied within 24 hours. Margin calls can be satisfied in one of three ways.

1. The borrower contributes cash which effectively reduces the outstanding balance of the loan and re-establishes a safety margin.
2. The borrower uses existing assets which are not currently pledged as security for the loan to increase the level of security offered and increase the safety margin.
3. The borrower sells some of the assets which are currently pledged as security for the loan and uses the cash proceeds from these sales to reduce the outstanding loan and increase the safety margin.

In a rapidly falling stock market the margin calls can be large and frequent. Highly leveraged individuals may find it hard to satisfy a margin call by the first two means above. This means that they may be forced to sell their assets during a period of falling market prices. Moreover, if a large number of individuals are in a similar position, the selling pressure in the market will drive prices lower and increase the likelihood of further margin calls. If we return to the example of Penny, and assume that the stock market has been performing poorly and she now has the following portfolio:

Stock	Current value	LVR	Security
Newstock	$45 000	70%	$31 500
Bright Copper	$43 000	60%	$25 800
Total	$88 000	-	$57 300

her safety margin would be:

$$\text{Safety margin} = 1 - \frac{\$65\,000}{\$57\,300}$$
$$= -13.4\%$$

In this situation, the lender will make a margin call which Penny must satisfy within 24 hours by one of the following means.

- Reducing the outstanding value of the loan by paying $7700 in cash to reduce the balance from $65 000 to $57 300.
- Pledging additional assets as security:

$$\text{Amount needed to be pledged} = \frac{\text{Cash required}}{\text{LVR}}$$
$$= \frac{\$7700}{0.7} \text{(assuming LVR is 0.7)}$$
$$= \$11\,000$$

- Selling existing assets and using the proceeds to reduce the value of the loan:

$$\text{Amount needed to be sold} = \frac{\text{Cash required}}{1 - \text{LVR}}$$

If Penny sold Newstock:

$$\begin{aligned}\text{Amount needed to be sold} &= \frac{\text{Cash required}}{1 - \text{LVR}} \\ &= \frac{\$7700}{1 - 0.7} \\ &= \$25\,667\end{aligned}$$

Alternatively Penny may sell some Bright Copper or some combination of Newstock and Bright Copper.

LO 7 Benefits and risks of margin lending

There are a number of benefits of margin lending for an investor, including greater access to wealth-creating assets, diversification, liquidity, tax benefits and direct investing opportunities. The main risk of margin lending is associated with meeting margin calls. A number of others risks are also associated with margin lending for the investor.

Benefits of margin lending

Margin lending allows investors to purchase assets that are of a higher value than they could afford using their existing funds. This increases the wealth-creation potential for the investor. Margin lending allows investors to spread their risk across a number of asset types and sectors. The ability to spread the investment capital across different asset types is known as **diversification**, which is a common risk-reduction strategy undertaken by investors.

diversification the spread of different assets held in a portfolio

Selling shares and repaying a margin loan takes less time than selling property, and can be achieved for a much lower transaction cost. Although most margin lenders charge a fee for early repayment of a loan, most also allow the full repayment of the loan without penalty after a certain period has elapsed. This allows investors ready access to any gains made on their portfolio.

There may be some income tax benefits of margin lending through deductibility of the interest charged on the loan, as well as deferring capital gains tax by not selling shares in a certain financial year. Margin lending allows investors to choose which shares they will invest in (within some limits set by the lending institution) and therefore allows investors to be actively involved in the management of their share portfolio. This may be preferable for some investors to using managed funds, and may also reduce management fees.

Risks of margin lending

In addition to the risks associated with meeting margin calls there are a number of others risks associated with margin lending for the investor.

Traditionally, Australian shares have provided between 60% and 80% and managed funds between 20% and 40% of the security for margin loans. For the investor, using shares or managed funds as security for a margin loan provides the assurance that only the investment assets subject to the margin loan are at risk and there is no **recourse** to other

recourse where the lender can seize a particular asset pledged as security for a loan if the borrower defaults on their payments; an unsecured loan is a non-recourse loan

assets owned by the investor. Post global financial crisis (GFC), however, we did see the increased use of margin loans secured by residential property. Partially, this was a response to the GFC-induced share market falls where investors with significant margin lending exposure were unwilling or unable to meet their margin call commitments through the various means we have described in this chapter. It could also be argued that residential property has seen less price volatility than the equity markets and, as such, provides a more stable level of security and therefore reduces the likelihood of margin calls. However, it is vital that investors understand that their residential property investments, including possibly the family home, are at risk when they are pledged as security for a margin loan.

There are three sources of risk for interest payments on margin loans — timing, servicing ability and tax.

- Timing issues arise when investors use dividend payments to pay for the interest expense on a margin loan and the dividend payments do not coincide with when the interest payments are due.
- The loan servicing ability of investors for repayments of the loan from existing income is also a risk to be considered, particularly where variable interest rate loans are used.
- Investors often negatively gear a margin lending facility and therefore derive a tax shield from the annual losses incurred. The tax shield is more valuable the higher the marginal tax rate of the investor. While the investor might have the cash resources to service the loan, any sudden and significant reduction in the client's marginal tax rate could seriously diminish the attractiveness of the overall investment.

Finally, the LVR must be maintained at an agreed level. Fluctuating values in the share market are normal and require constant monitoring by investors. Lenders mostly assign the onus of monitoring daily LVRs to their clients and clients must immediately rectify the situation, under the terms of the contracts, even though the lenders may not have issued margin calls. The effect of this condition is a high level of stress for borrowers if their LVRs are close to the contracted levels; they must monitor the trading results of the share market every day. The way to alleviate the situation is, of course, for borrowers to maintain a comfortable buffer or cushion between their actual or expected LVRs and the contracted levels.

PERSONAL FINANCE BULLETIN

Margin loans still on the nose

Margin loans are still out of favour, more than three years after the global financial crisis (GFC) began, with fewer investors than ever inclined to use them — and those that do opting for much more conservative levels of borrowing.

Total margin loan borrowings are at their lowest in seven years, Reserve Bank of Australia (RBA) data shows. Investors have less than $16 billion in margin loans, down from a peak of almost $42 billion in December 2007, nine months before the GFC first took hold.

On average, investors are borrowing about 35 per cent of the value of the securities their margin loan is funding, RBA data shows, well down on 60 per cent-plus gearing during the sharemarket boom and the 60 per cent loan-to-value (LVR) ratios many lenders still allow.

Financial advisers canvassed by *Money* last week said that if they suggest margin lending at all to clients, it is to a maximum of 50 per cent gearing: that is, clients must have a minimum 50 per cent 'deposit' for the shares or managed funds they are buying.

Margin calls

'It's not that it's being entirely disregarded but the appetite for margin loans is down, definitely', the national manager of advice strategy for ipac Securities, John Dani, says.

'We've seen a drop-off in two areas: the sheer number of people wanting to pursue margin loans as a wealth-accumulation strategy, basically as a result of the impact of the GFC, and those clients who are interested in being much more conservative in the level of debt they want to take on.'

'Before the GFC, while some investors were comfortable with 60 per cent to 70 per cent gearing, now 40 per cent to 50 per cent is probably more typical of what investors are comfortable taking on', Dani says. 'They want to avoid the dreaded margin call.'

Margin calls are made when the falling value of a portfolio means the borrower breaches his or her maximum loan-to-value ratio (LVR) and must bring the loan back into balance by topping up with cash or by selling investments, in all likelihood at the worst time to do so.

The rate of margin calls peaked at an average of 8.6 a day per 1000 clients in December 2008, up by only 0.6 a day on a year earlier. The average is now about two calls a day per 1000 clients.

'My attitude is that margin lending remains reasonable for a certain cross-section of investors who have the income certainty to service the debt and the discipline to remain invested when markets fall', a certified financial planner with Align Financial, Darren Johns, says, adding that clients are less inclined 'to borrow . . . at higher than reasonable interest [rates] to invest in an asset class whose short-term outlook is uncertain at best'.

Interest rates

Among the margin loans on the database of researcher RateCity, interest rates range between 8.1 per cent and 9.7 per cent (with some of the difference depending on the term and the sum involved). At the top end, this is a margin of 5.4 percentage points over the Reserve Bank's official cash rate.

The alternative of dipping into your home equity to fund investments, perhaps using a redraw facility, means you can access a mortgage rate, in theory as low as 6.5 per cent. 'With markets going nowhere for several years, clients aren't prepared to borrow at 8 per cent-plus through margin lending', a planner with Centric Wealth, Dean Easterby, says.

He says the irony is that the markets are offering reasonable value at the moment 'and for clients that have the cash flow to support a gearing strategy, reliable income, a minimum seven-year time frame and a clear plan to repay or eliminate the debt in the future, now is not a bad time to at least be looking at this strategy'.

»

»

Anne Graham, of McPhail HLG Financial Planning, says those clients who are still interested in margin lending tend to be more 'aggressive' investors, in a high tax bracket and without property as security for gearing.

'[They] are generally greater risk-takers and will want a higher LVR, say 70 per cent, but usually we convince them to manage risk better by reducing the LVR', Graham says.

Other options

Kate McCallum of Multiforte Financial Services isn't a fan. 'Our view is that margin lending is too risky for the potential return', she says.

'In most cases we can find alternative strategies that can add value for a client without exposing them to the risk of capital loss, and sleepless nights, that the combination of margin lending and a market downturn can bring.'

Jonathan Philpot of HLB Mann Judd says an alternative is using home equity.

'If the client's circumstances are appropriate — that is, good cash flow, low level of home mortgage debt, investing for a period of at least 10 years and understanding the volatility of sharemarkets — I don't have a problem recommending to clients they utilise the equity in their home to borrow to purchase shares', Philpot says.

'This avoids the risks of margin calls and lowers the cost of borrowing.'

Ipac's Dani agrees, adding that people should build at least 50 per cent equity in their home before borrowing against it.

He also suggests people stagger any geared investment, buying into the market gradually rather than investing a lump of borrowed money in one go. This way the 'timing risk' is lowered.

As for other gearing avenues, Ray Albrighton of Announcer Financial Planning says capital-protected products tend to be expensive.

'The protection mechanism is built into the ongoing interest rates, which can be in excess of 15 per cent. You can't have your cake and eat it, too', Albrighton says.

Centric's Easterby says structured products have three potential pitfalls: complexity, cost and illiquidity. 'It can be very difficult for retail investors to understand what they're actually investing in and if we have all learnt one lesson from the GFC, it has been to only invest in what you understand.'

Key points

In the current market, margin lending is too risky for the potential return, some advisers say.

It's hard to recoup the relatively high interest you'll pay for a margin loan.

Advisers are telling clients not to borrow more than 50 per cent of a portfolio's value.

They also suggest an investment horizon of at least seven years.

Using equity in your home to fund investments is a cheaper alternative.

Source: Lesley Parker, *Sydney Morning Herald*, 8 February 2012.

LO 8 Derivatives

If an investor directly owns an investment then they gain or lose by holding that investment. For example, if you own NAB shares and the price of NAB shares goes up then you gain; if the price goes down, you lose. Assume that you and I decide to have a side bet on the price of NAB shares (neither of us owns any NAB shares). If the price of NAB shares goes up today I will give you the amount by which they go up; if they go down you will give me the amount by which they go down. The bet itself has no intrinsic value — the value of our bet is *derived* from the underlying asset, in this case the price of NAB shares.

A number of investment products or instruments in the market derive their value from underlying assets, including contracts for difference (CFD), futures contracts, options, warrants and other complex leveraged investments. These **derivative** products allow the investor to be exposed to the price movements of these underlying assets without paying the full purchase price of these assets. In this way, they are a form of leveraged investment. We mentioned earlier that some investors will use derivatives purely for speculative purposes; that is, they are not trying to manage the risk associated with some pre-existing position. Other investors will use derivatives to hedge risks that they currently face. Whether the investor is speculating or hedging, the mechanics of how these derivatives work does not alter.

derivative
a financial product that has no inherent value; its value or price is derived from some other asset

Contracts for difference (CFD)

A **contract for difference (CFD)** is an agreement between a buyer and seller to exchange the difference in value of an underlying asset. The buyer of a CFD is going long and expects the price to increase. The seller is going short and expects the price to fall.

contract for difference (CFD)
an agreement between a buyer and seller to exchange the difference in value of an underlying asset

For example, assume the price of PIX shares is currently $10. A buyer and a seller agree to exchange the difference in the value of PIX shares. At the end of day 1, if the price of PIX shares has increased to $11, the seller will pay the buyer the difference of $1 ($11 – $10). As long as the contract remains open the buyer and the seller agree to continue to exchange any future differences in the value of PIX shares. If the price of PIX shares continues to increase and has reached $12 at the end of day 2, the seller will pay the buyer the difference of $1 ($12 – $11). If the price of PIX shares falls to $9 on day 3, the buyer will pay the seller the difference of $3 ($12 – $9). If the price of PIX shares increases back to $10 at the end of day 4, the seller will pay the buyer the difference of $1 ($10 – $9). In this example, PIX shares started at $10 and four days later ended at $10. If the contract was held open for four days both parties are back where they started because there was no difference in price. However, the buyer might have decided to close out the contract after two days and lock in their gains. Conversely, the seller might have been worried about their losses and decided to close out the contract after two days. If the contract had remained open after the second day the seller might have decided to close the contract after day 3 and lock in their gains and so on. The various possibilities are illustrated in table 8.8 on the next page.

For an individual investor to find a suitable counterparty to a contract for difference would be extremely difficult: markets bring buyers and sellers together. Most CFD markets around the world are **over the counter markets (OTC)** which are managed by private providers. OTC means that the terms and conditions upon which the CFDs are issued are not standardised and, as a result, OTC CFDs are not traded on stock exchanges. The first CFDs emerged in Australia in 2002. From 2002 to 2007, OTC CFDs were the only type of CFD available in Australia. In 2007, the ASX began offering listed-ASX CFDs. While

over the counter markets (OTC)
informal arrangements where non-standardised financial products are traded, as opposed to the trading of standardised financial products on exchanges such as the ASX

the listed-ASX CFD market is still a relatively small percentage of the total CFD market in Australia, examining how CFDs are traded on the ASX provides an insight into how CFDs work and how they are traded.

TABLE 8.8 Contract for difference, PIX shares

Day	Price	Buyer daily gain (loss)	Buyer cumulative gain (loss)	Seller daily gain (loss)	Seller cumulative gain (loss)
0	$10	$0	$0	$0	$0
1	$11	$1	$1	($1)	($1)
2	$12	$1	$2	($1)	($2)
3	$9	($3)	($1)	$3	$1
4	$10	$1	$0	($1)	$0

ASX-traded CFDs

The ASX lists the following CFDs:

- over 60 of the top listed stocks on the ASX
- the S&P/ASX 200 index and the Dow Jones Industrial Average
- the commodity of gold.

To buy or sell a CFD on the ASX market the buyer and seller must pay a margin to the ASX. The size of the margin is a function of the price volatility of the underlying asset. Margins typically range from 5% to 10% of the value of the underlying asset — the higher the price volatility of the underlying asset, the higher the margin.

If we assume that PIX shares are an ASX-listed CFD, their price would be quoted in cents as 1000 rather than $10. If the margin required was 10% then this is the equivalent of 100 cents or $1. For $1 a buyer and a seller can gain exposure to the price movements of a share which currently trades at $10, hence the leveraged nature of CFDs. If we assume from table 8.8 that the contract is closed out at the end of day 1, the buyer would receive $1 from the seller (via the ASX). For a $1 margin outlay the buyer gets a $1 return — a 100% return on their money in a single day. Conversely, the seller has lost 100% of their margin in a single day. If the contract remains open at the end of the first day, the ASX will make a margin call on the seller so that the seller can re-establish their margin. Margin calls have to be settled within 24 hours.

Unlike options and futures which will be discussed shortly, CFDs do not have an expiry date and remain open until such time as the buyer or seller closes out their position. A buyer will close out their position by selling a comparable contract. A seller will close out their position by buying a comparable contract.

ASX CFDs compared to OTC CFDs

ASX CFDs are similar to OTC CFDs; however, there are some important differences.

- *Market*. The ASX is independent and is required under the *Corporations Act 2001* to provide a fair, orderly and transparent market. The ASX is separate from the brokers who provide advice to the buyers and sellers of CFDs. This separation does not necessarily apply to OTC CFDs, although all OTC CFD providers are required by law to hold an Australian Financial Services Licence which does impose standards on the quality and independence of advice given.

- *Novation.* Once a buyer and a seller of a CFD have come together via the ASX CFD market the contract is novated. **Novation** in contract law means to replace an existing contractual obligation with a new contractual obligation. The ASX via the Sydney Futures Exchange Clearing Corporation (SFECC) substitutes the SFECC as the counterparty to all trades. Therefore, for the buyer, the seller is now the SFECC. For the seller, the buyer is now the SFECC. This process of novation gives confidence to buyers and sellers that their counterparty (which is always the SFECC) will always meet its obligations under the CFD. The SFECC is able to manage their own risks via the initial margins and margin calls required from buyers and sellers. As part of its capital adequacy, the SFECC also maintain a Clearing Guarantee Fund which could also be used to fund its novated obligations should one of the market participants default on their obligations. OTC CFDs are not novated.
- *Trading information.* ASX-listed CFDs are more transparent than OTC CFDs. Information such as bids, offers, last sale and volumes are readily available in exactly the same way they are for other assets traded on the ASX. All trades take place via a central market order book — the first person to enter the best price is always traded first.

novation
to replace an existing contractual obligation with a new contractual obligation

Despite the advantages associated with exchange-traded CFDs, the market in Australia is still dominated by OTC CFDs. The ASX only offers a limited range of CFDs, whereas the OTC market covers a wider range of CFDs including CFDs on shares listed on overseas exchanges. The standardised terms of ASX CFDs which facilitate efficient trading can also be seen as a weakness when those standard terms do not meet the needs of individual buyers and sellers. As a result, the non-standardised nature of the OTC CFD market remains one of its attractions.

CFDs have attracted their share of criticism. As a highly leveraged investment, CFDs have the capacity to magnify gains and losses. Much CFD promotional material is heavily biased towards the magnified gains and pays little attention to the risks involved. Table 8.9 shows that when we aggregate the gains and losses of the buyers and sellers of PIX shares, CFD trading is a zero-sum game.

TABLE 8.9 CFD gains and losses aggregated, PIX shares

Day	Price	Buyer daily gain (loss)	Seller daily gain (loss)	Buyer and seller combined daily gain (loss)
0	\$10	\$0	\$0	\$0
1	\$11	\$1	(\$1)	\$0
2	\$12	\$1	(\$1)	\$0
3	\$9	(\$3)	\$3	\$0
4	\$10	\$1	(\$1)	\$0

Why do people play zero-sum games? Presumably because they believe that they have some greater insight into the price movement of the underlying asset than the counterparty they are contracting with.

Hedging or speculating

We described buying and selling CFDs as a zero-sum game previously, but this really only applies when the CFD is used for speculative purposes. When a CFD is used to hedge a **physical position** it becomes a valuable risk-management tool.

physical position
when an investor is currently exposed to a financial risk

Consider the case of Jamie. Jamie runs a large jewellery business. Given the prices that he can charge his customers for finished jewellery he is happy to pay US$1500 an ounce for gold. Jamie is worried about the price of gold increasing above US$1500. He decides to go long in gold by buying an ASX Gold CFD. If we assume:

- the margin is 5%
- the standard contract is for 1 ounce of gold
- the current value of an ASX Gold CFD is US$1500

then for $75, Jamie can buy a standard contract.

If the price of gold goes up to US$1800 and Jamie closes out the contract, the seller will pay Jamie the difference (i.e. US$300). Jamie has made a US$300 return on a US$75 investment. While this is a good outcome for Jamie he now has to enter the physical market for gold and buy the gold that he needs for his jewellery business at US$1800 per ounce. The CFD has effectively provided Jamie with gold at US$1500 per ounce and, as such, has been a valuable risk-management tool.

If the price of gold goes down to US$1200 and Jamie closes out the contract he has made a US$300 loss. Jamie will have lost his initial US$75 margin plus another US$225 in margin calls. While this does not appear to be a good outcome for Jamie he can now enter the physical market for gold and buy the gold that he needs for his jewellery business at US$1200 an ounce. The CFD has effectively provided Jamie with gold at US$1500 per ounce and, as such, has again proved to be a valuable risk-management tool. With the benefit of hindsight Jamie would have been better off in this case if he did not buy the CFD; however, risk management does not come with the benefit of hindsight.

basis risk
the risk that the risk-management product used does not exactly match the risk that is being hedged

Given that the ASX standard contract which facilitates trading does not exactly match the needs of the hedger some **basis risk** will remain. In the foregoing example, Jamie may need to buy 1.5 ounces of gold to produce the jewellery that he needs for his customers. The use of an ASX Gold CFD will provide a valuable but imperfect risk-management tool; that is, some basis risk will remain.

The ASX provides a range of free and publicly available online short courses that take individual learners from basic concepts through to more complex and sophisticated analysis of particular products traded on the ASX. Go to http://www.asx.com.au/resources/asx-listed-cfd-courses.htm to access the ASX CFD courses and their first course, 'Market fundamentals'.

Futures contracts

futures contract
a futures contract is an agreement to trade something in the future, either to buy or sell a specific amount of a specific asset

A **futures contract** is an agreement to trade something in the future, either to buy or to sell a specific amount of a specific asset. A futures contract is very similar to a CFD. One key difference, however, is that futures contracts have defined expiry dates, whereas CFDs do not.

Futures trading began in the sixth century BC in Greece where it was used as a form of insurance against failed delivery of goods and commodities traded in open markets. Modern-day commodities futures markets emerged in the United States in the 1850s with exchanges in Chicago trading agricultural commodities. The first interest-rate futures started trading on the Chicago Board of Trade (CBOT) in October 1975 with a futures contract on the federal government mortgage market (whimsically called 'Ginnie Mae's'). As financial markets have developed globally, the use and acceptance of futures contracts have also developed.

The Sydney Futures Exchange (SFE) was established in 1960 as the Sydney Greasy Wool Futures Exchange when the Australian economy 'rode on the sheep's back'. The SFE soon diversified into other contracts and, in 1979, introduced the first financial futures contract: the 90-day bank accepted bill (BAB) contract. The SFE has been at the forefront of innovation with the introduction of screen-based trading, electronic clearing, electronic registries and electronic settlement. In July 2006, the SFE merged with the ASX to form the ninth largest listed securities exchange in the world.

The ASX via the SFE trades futures contacts over the following:

- index futures including the ASX SPI 200
- commodities including greasy wool, wheat, barley, sorghum and canola
- short- and long-term interest rates including 90-day bank bills and 10 year bonds
- energy futures including electricity, gas and renewable energy certificates (RECs).

New leveraged products

The emergence and growth of electricity and RECs trading highlights how financial managers and ultimately financial market makers such as the ASX and the SFE innovate and respond to changed circumstances. The privatisation of many electricity suppliers and the creation of a national grid for electricity have increased the need for suppliers to manage the future price of electricity and futures markets are an important part of this solution.

The Federal Government introduced an Emissions Trading Scheme on 1 July 2012. Initially carbon units will have a fixed price; however, it is anticipated that in 2015 carbon units will move to a fully flexible pricing structure. An essential underpinning of a flexible price structure is to have a market in which the future price of carbon can be readily traded and it is to be expected that the ASX will offer carbon futures contracts as carbon emitters seek to manage the future price of carbon.

A futures contract is a standardised contract which facilitates trading on the ASX. The specification will depend on the particular futures contract being traded. For example, the broad specifications for the SFE Greasy Wool Futures 21 Micron contract specification are as follows:

SFE Greasy Wool Futures 21 Micron contract specification	
Contract unit	The greasy equivalent of 2500 kilograms clean weight of merino combing fleece (approximately 20 farm bales).
Contract months	February, April, June, August, October, December up to 18 months ahead.
Minimum price movement	Prices are quoted in cents per kilogram clean weight. (The minimum fluctuation of 1 cent per kilogram is equal to A$25 per contract.)

More detailed specifications can be found on the ASX website asx.com.au.

Futures contracts have a set expiry date. A series of futures contracts might be on offer in the market at any one time with a range of expiry dates. For example, the SFE Greasy Wool Futures 21 Micron contract might be available with the following expiry dates: 10 April, 10 June and 10 August.

An investor may wish to buy an SFE Greasy Wool Futures 21 Micron contract with an expiry date of 10 April. There must be a similar investor prepared to sell the same contract. Buyers and sellers effectively come together through the process of demand and supply until such time as a price is agreed. The buyer could be a speculator or a hedger.

Similarly, the seller could be a speculator or a hedger. The SFE novates the contracts in much the same way that it novates the CFDs.

Assume that a buyer and a seller agree to trade 2500 kilograms of greasy wool on 10 April for a price of 950 (cents per kilogram). If the price exceeds 950 on 10 April the buyer will gain on the contract; if the price is less than 950 on 10 April the seller will gain on the contract. The pay-off profile of the buyer and seller of a SFE Greasy Wool Futures 21 Micron contract is shown in figure 8.1.

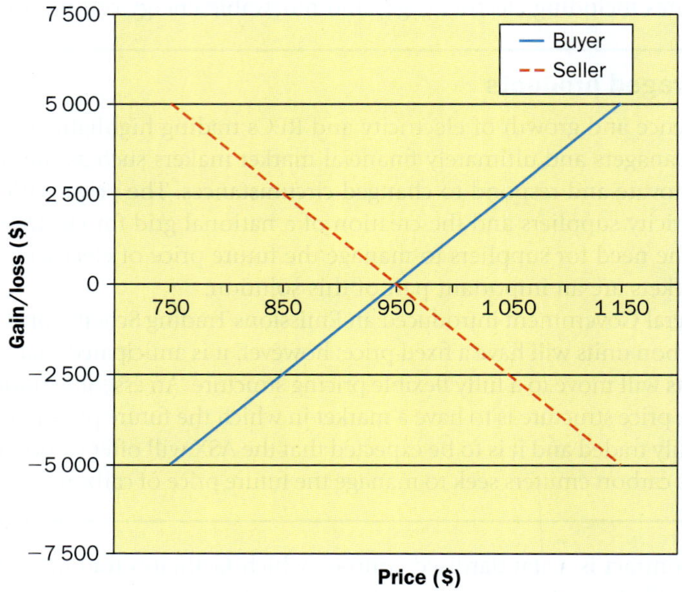

FIGURE 8.1
Pay-off profile of the buyer and seller of a SFE Greasy Wool Futures 21 Micron contract

If the price of the wool is 1050 on 10 April the buyer will gain $2500. Conversely, the seller will lose $2500. Similarly to CFDs, buyers and sellers of futures contracts pay a deposit or initial margin to the SFE which might range from 2–10% of the face value of the contract, hence the leveraged nature of the investment. Also similarly to CFDs if the price of the underlying asset changes the SFE will make a margin call against the investor — if the price goes up the call will be against the seller, if the price goes down the call will be against the buyer. This process is known as **marking to market**.

marking to market
constantly reassessing the financial obligations of buyers and sellers as the market price of an asset changes

Very few futures contracts end in the physical delivery of the assets which are the subject of the contract. Few sellers of an SFE Greasy Wool Futures 21 Micron contract, for example, would actually hold 2500 kilograms of greasy wool which meets the detailed specifications. Even hedgers would probably not be able to exactly meet the contract specifications. As a result, almost all futures contracts are **reversed out** by taking an opposite contract; for example, the buyer will sell a corresponding contract which leaves the investor with no residual obligation.

reversed out
taking out an equal and opposite contract which effectively cancels out the original obligation

Options

An **option** is an agreement that gives the buyer (holder) of the option the right but not the obligation to buy or sell something in the future at a fixed price. The holder of the option must pay an option premium to obtain this right, hence the leveraged nature of the investment.

option
an agreement that gives the buyer (holder) of the option the right but not the obligation to buy or sell something in the future at a fixed price

Options have a set expiry date. In Australia, share options allow the holder to exercise the option at any time up to and including the expiry date. These are known as American style options. In Australia, index options can only be exercised on their expiry date. These are known as a European style options.

There are only two types of options: a call and a put.

Call options

If an investor buys a **call option** by paying the option premium they have the right but not the obligation to buy the underlying asset. The investor has a long position, or, to be more technically correct, a potentially long position. By taking a long position, the buyer of a call is hoping for the price of the underlying asset to rise. The seller of the call option receives the option premium and is in a short position. The seller is hoping the price of the underlying asset will fall.

call option
a security that gives the buyer (holder) of the option the right but not the obligation to buy something in the future at a fixed price

ILLUSTRATIVE EXAMPLE 8.3

Fred thinks the price of PHC shares is likely to rise but is not sure by how much. He does not currently own any PHC shares but he is keen to speculate. He checks the financial press and finds the following option premiums.

Call option prices: PHC shares — last sale $27.61

Expiry date	Strike price ($)	Option premium per share — last sale ($)
1 month from today	28.50	0.42
1 month from today	29.00	0.24
1 month from today	31.00	0.03
2 months from today	28.50	0.51
2 months from today	29.00	0.30
2 months from today	31.00	0.04
3 months from today	28.50	0.66
3 months from today	29.00	0.54
3 months from today	31.00	0.13

A standard option contract is for 100 shares. Fred could buy a call option on PHC shares with a **strike price** of $28.50 per share which expires one month from today for $42 ($100 × 0.42). During that month, if the price of PHC shares rises above $28.50, Fred could exercise the option. If the price of the shares rose to $30.00, Fred could exercise the option and the seller of the option would have to deliver to Fred 100 PHC shares at a price of $28.50 each. If the price of the shares did not rise above $28.50 during the month Fred would not exercise the option. The loss for Fred in this case is the cost of the option premium and the gain for the seller is the option premium income.

strike price
the price at which an option contract will be transacted if the option is exercised

»

»

Figure 8.2 outlines the pay-off for the buyer of the call option (Fred) and the seller of the call option.

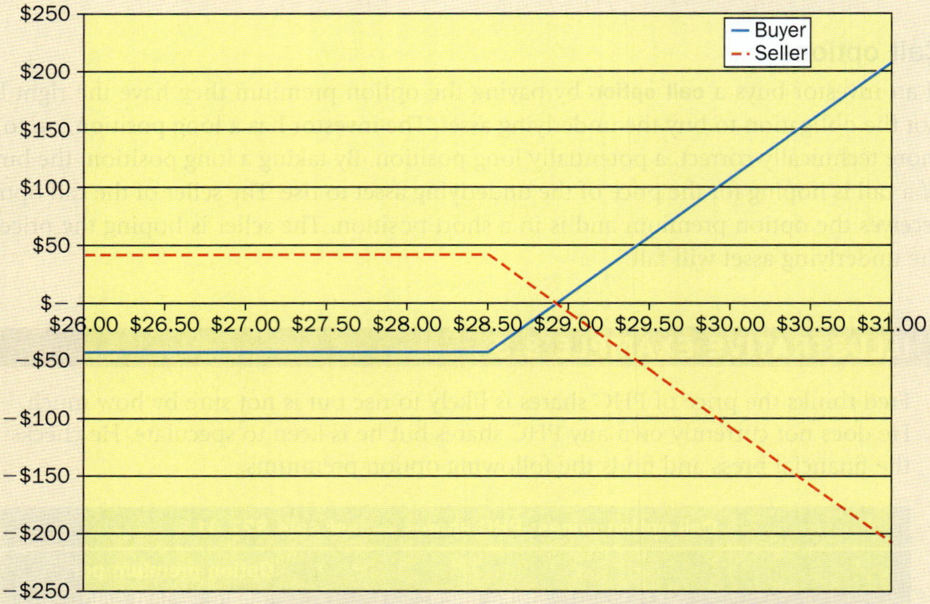

FIGURE 8.2
Pay-off profiles for the buyer and seller of a call option

The price of PHC shares will need to increase to $28.92 cents for Fred to at least cover his option premium. If the price of PHC shares rises above $28.50 but not above $28.92, Fred should still exercise his option in order to minimise the loss he has made on the option premium. If, for example, the price of PHC shares rises to $28.75, Fred should exercise the option — the seller of the option will sell him 100 PHC shares at the agreed strike price of $28.50 each which Fred can then promptly sell in the market at $28.75. Fred makes a profit of $25 which helps him recoup some of the $42 he spent on buying the option.

Fred might be confident that the price of PHC shares will rise but may not be sure if this will happen in the next month or soon thereafter. Fred could buy a call option on PHC shares with a strike price of $28.50 per share which expires 3 months from today for $66 (100 × 0.66). During those 3 months, if the price of PHC shares rises above $28.50, Fred could exercise the option. The longer an option is open the greater the chance that price volatility will push the share price above $28.50 and therefore the higher the option premium.

If Fred was very confident that the price of PHC shares was going to rise substantially in the next 3 months, he might buy a call option on PHC shares with a strike price of $31.00 per share which expires 3 months from today for $13 (100 × 0.13). In this case, Fred has limited his exposure to $13. The higher the strike (exercise) price is above the current price, the less likely it is that the option will be exercised and the lower the option premium.

The factors affecting the call option premium are described in table 8.10.

TABLE 8.10 Factors affecting the call option premium

Factor	Effect
Strike price compared to last sale price	The higher the strike price is above the last sale price, the less likely the option will be exercised, and the lower the option premium.
Duration of the option	The longer the buyer has the option the greater the chance price volatility will push the market price above the strike price, the greater the chance the option will be exercised, and the higher the option premium. As time passes as the buyer holds the option, the duration decreases and the market value of the option premium begins to decline.
Price volatility of the underlying asset	The higher the price volatility of the underlying asset, the greater the likelihood it will exceed the strike price during the period the option is open, and the higher the option premium.

As with CFDs and futures contracts, investors may use call options for speculative or hedging purposes.

Put options

Put options give the buyer (holder) of the option the right to sell an underlying asset. The holder of a put option is therefore in a potentially short position. If an investor believes that prices were going to fall they might buy a put option.

put option
an agreement that gives the buyer (holder) of the option the right but not the obligation to sell something in the future at a fixed price

Consider the case of Sam. Sam has just inherited 100 BRC shares. He is worried that the price of BRC shares might fall so he buys a put option with a strike price of $12.50 in order to hedge his exposure. The price of BRC shares subsequently falls to $11.28 during the life of the put option and Sam decides to exercise it. Sam can sell (put) his shares to the seller of the put for $12.50, making a profit of $122 on the transaction ([$12.50 – $11.28] × 100). Sam has, however, paid a premium for the put option and the cost of this premium will need to be offset against his $122 gain.

As with call options, investors may use put options for speculative or hedging purposes.

The ASX Options Market

Options are traded worldwide either through a registered exchange such as the ASX or over the counter. To facilitate trading on the ASX, exchange-traded options have standard terms; for example, a standard parcel of shares for option trading on the ASX is 100 shares.

The ASX Options Market trades options over the following:

- over 100 stocks listed on the ASX
- index options including the S&P/ASX 200
- interest rates including 3-year and 10-year Treasury bonds
- selected commodities including wool.

Similarly to the trading of CFDs and futures contracts, the ASX Options Market is a novated market where counterparty risk is removed.

Most options are not exercised. Some options will lapse because it is not profitable for the holder of the option to exercise the option. For those options that are worth exercising, the holder of the option may not wish to take delivery of the underlying asset (in the case of a call option) nor to deliver the underlying asset (in the case of a put option), in which case the investor will reverse out their position by taking an equal and opposite transaction to their opening transaction. It is estimated that less than 15% of options are exercised on the ASX.

Warrants and other complex leveraged investments

warrant
a leveraged investment that gives the investor the right to buy or sell a particular asset

trading-style warrant
a warrant which is traded actively for a relatively short period of time as compared to an investment-style warrant

investment-style warrant
a warrant which is less actively traded and held for a relatively longer period of time as compared to a trading-style warrant

endowment warrant
where an investor pays a deposit on a share and borrows the rest to finance its purchase; the investor then uses the dividend income stream as the means by which to pay off the balance owing

instalment warrant
where an investor pays a deposit on a share and then pays off the balance by one or more instalments

Warrants are another form of leveraged derivative instrument. The holder of a warrant has the right to buy or sell the underlying asset, so, as with all investment assets, the investor wishes to be long if they expect prices to rise and short if they expect them to fall.

In many ways, warrants can be seen as another form of option. However, whereas options are a highly standardised product which facilitates trading, warrants vary greatly in their terms and conditions, and the individual investor needs to be very careful in checking the product disclosure statement which must accompany any warrant issued.

All warrants have an expiry date. Some warrants will be American in style which means that they can be exercised on any day up to and including the expiry date. Some warrants will be European in style which means that they can only be exercised on the expiry date.

Warrants can broadly be disaggregated into **trading-style warrants** and **investment-style warrants** although some warrants will display characteristics of both styles.

Trading-style warrants tend to have a higher risk/return profile compared to investment-style warrants. They include warrants which are traded on stock market indices, foreign currency, and individual shares and portfolios of shares. Trading-style warrants tend to be short dated; that is, the warrants are only open for a relatively short period before their expiry date, and are frequently traded to try to 'beat' the market.

Investment-style warrants tend to have a lower risk/return profile compared to trading-style warrants. An **endowment warrant** is an example of an investment-style warrant. Endowment warrants normally have maturities of about 10 years. In effect, the investor pays a deposit on a share and borrows the rest to finance its purchase. If the dividends are not as high as expected, a final payment will be necessary to clear the debt and interest before the shares will be transferred to the investor. On the other hand, if the dividends clear the debt earlier than expected, the contract will be terminated and the shares transferred before the expiry of the contract period. Investment-style warrants tend to be longer dated and less frequently traded as investors using these warrants are more likely to adopt a buy-and-hold strategy.

Perhaps the most widely known warrant is the **instalment warrant**. Instalment warrants are similar to the depository receipts or partly paid shares issued by Suncorp-Metway Ltd and Telstra Ltd when they were privatised. The issue price is generally about half the full price with the second instalment due 18 months to 2 years later.

ILLUSTRATIVE EXAMPLE 8.4

Underlying instrument	DBR shares
Warrant type	Instalment
Expiry date	14 October 2015
Exercise price	$12
Exercise style	American

Assume that the current share price of DBR is $20 and the investor has already paid $10 for this warrant. If the investor exercises the warrant their full purchase price is $22, which is greater than the current share price of $20. The excess of the full purchase price over the current market price represents the interest component implicit in the transaction. Indeed, many warrant issuers will seek a product ruling from the ATO which recognises explicitly the interest component inherent in the transaction so that the investor may seek a tax deduction for the interest.

If the purchaser of the warrant decides to keep the warrant and eventually exercise it they are using the instalment warrant for investment purposes. If, however, a fluctuation in price of the underlying asset causes the purchaser to sell their warrant they are using the instalment warrant for trading purposes. If, for example, the current market price of DBR shares jumps to $30, a warrant to buy it for $12 is worth a lot more than the $10 the purchaser initially paid for the warrant. If the warrant is traded on an exchange the process of demand and supply will ensure that the price of the warrant increases.

A wide range of complex warrants have evolved over time to meet the needs of investors. Warrants can be exchange traded (the ASX has traded warrants since 1991) or traded OTC. Warrants vary significantly in terms of their degree of leverage and it is vital that the investor understands the risks associated with the individual warrant product.

Figure 8.3 highlights the risk/reward trade-off associated with warrants.

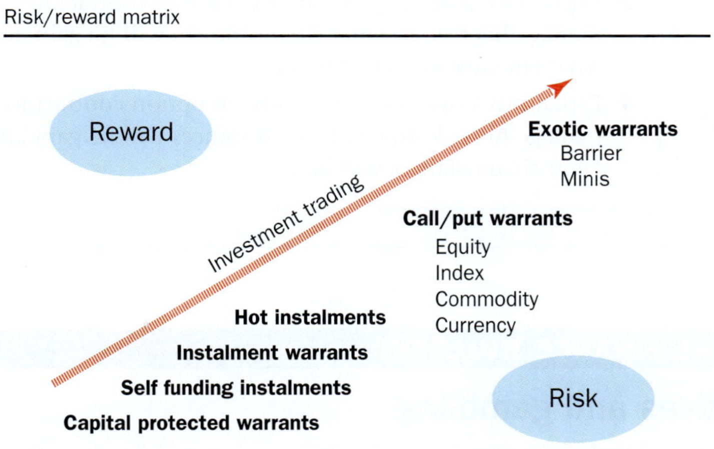

FIGURE 8.3
Warrant risk/reward trade-off
Source: ASX 2013a.

In this discussion of derivative products and markets we have concentrated on CFDs, futures, options and warrants. While this captures the bulk of derivative products on offer, many other products are available in the market, including collateralised debt obligations and credit default swaps. A detailed discussion of these products is beyond the scope of this chapter. In the case of an investment need that cannot be satisfied by existing derivative products, highly innovative and responsive product providers will financially 'engineer' a suitable product.

The Australian Securities and Investments Commission (ASIC), via its MoneySmart website (moneysmart.gov.au), provides advice on the use of complex investment products.

PROFESSIONAL ADVICE

There are many similarities between the various derivative products available.

An investor may wish to go long or short and it is possible that a number of different derivative products could fulfil this need.

An investor could go long by buying a CFD, a futures contract, a call option or an instalment warrant.

Alternatively an investor could go short by selling a CFD, a futures contract or by buying a put option.

Consider the case of Mark who has a well diversified share portfolio. He is worried about global economic conditions and wants to hedge the risk associated with his share portfolio.

WHAT ADVICE WOULD YOU GIVE MARK?

1. Should Mark use derivatives to go short or long?
2. If Mark does not want to use a derivative instrument for each individual security in his portfolio what alternative is available to him? What additional risk does this represent?
3. Explain to Mark how he can use a future contract to manage his risk. In what circumstances will he gain and in what circumstances will he lose?
4. Explain to Mark how he can use an option contract to manage his risk. In what circumstances will he gain and in what circumstances will he lose?

PERSONAL FINANCE BULLETIN

Derivatives and gambling

The line between trading in derivatives and engaging in gambling is sometimes hard to draw.

The distinction was further clouded when several years ago bookmakers began offering financial bets including bets over the ASX 200 and RBA interest rate changes.

A bookmaker might argue that in gambling the value of the bet is known and any potential winnings are determined by the odds. The event either happens or it does not happen i.e. it is determined by chance and as such any bet on whether, for example, interest rates go up or down is simply a bet that should be regulated under the relevant gambling legislation. This can be contrasted to derivatives trading where often the value of the bet and any potential winnings are unknown and the outcome, rather than being determined by chance, is 'derived' from the movement in the price of a financial instrument.

ASIC does not accept this distinction and argues that these financial bets are derivatives and as such this implies that the provider is running a financial services business for which a financial service licence is required. Bookmakers, however, continue to offer financial bets.

Alan Kohler (2012) has suggested that rather than bookmakers holding financial services licences, financial services business should have gambling licences. While the comment was perhaps made a bit provocatively in response to some of the more extreme use of derivatives associated with the Lehmann Brothers collapse, it does reaffirm the point that the distinction between trading in derivatives and engaging in gambling is sometimes hard to draw and that the excessive and reckless use of derivatives warrants further regulation and control.

To further reinforce this point the ASIC MoneySmart website which deals with complex investment products that we referred to earlier includes the following warning: 'some complex products attract investments with the potential to make quick money. This can be tempting for people with personality types that are attracted to gambling'.

The website then goes on to provide a link to a Gambling Hotline!

The use of derivatives to hedge a physical position is a prudent investment practice and difficult to criticise as 'gambling'. Speculators add depth and liquidity to derivative markets to allow them to operate more efficiently. The spate of corporate collapses that have been linked to the use of derivatives is perhaps not so much a criticism of derivatives themselves but how they have been used, including:

- a lack of understanding by users of the inherent risks
- the asymmetric payoff for the individual that is often associated with their use, for example the upside might be a large bonus; however, the downside might be no bonus
- the unethical and opportunistic promotion of derivatives by some financial institutions
- a lack of regulation.

Summary

It is worth reflecting on the case study of Jill that we introduced at the start of the chapter. Jill was confused by the notion of being 'long'. In this chapter we have outlined how owning an asset means that you are 'long' and when you own an asset you wish the price of that asset to increase. Sometimes investors who believe the price of an asset may increase will borrow money to assist in the purchase of that asset. Sometimes investors who believe the price of an asset may increase may buy a derivative such as a CFD, future, option or warrant in order to create a long position.

Jill was even more confused about the notion of being short. In this chapter we have outlined how derivatives can be used to adopt a short position. A hedger who has a long physical position may well decide to go short in order to manage their price risk — we saw that Jill's father went short in wool derivatives to offset his long position in wool. A speculator may believe that the price of an asset is likely to fall and wishes to gain from this fall in prices.

Jill was also concerned about borrowing money to fund the purchase of an investment. The fundamental principal of borrowing to invest is that the invested funds generate a return greater than the cost of those funds — it doesn't really matter whether that money is borrowed to fund the purchase of a business as is the case with Jill's father or whether it is used to fund the purchase of financial investments. Borrowing money does, however, bring with it the commitment that the money is repaid regardless of how the investment performs.

Using derivatives exposes the investor to significant gains but also significant losses. It is vital that the financial concepts underpinning the derivative are thoroughly understood by the investor and that any derivative exposure is carefully monitored and managed.

Professional application questions

8.1 What is the difference between positive and negative gearing?

8.2 What are the risks associated with gearing?

8.3 An investor wishes to buy some shares by using a combination of their own money and borrowed funds. They are unsure whether they should take out a margin loan which is secured against the shares or take out a mortgage against the family home. What are the advantages/disadvantages of each approach?

8.4 Outline three ways that an investor can satisfy a margin call.

8.5 Mohamed has 10 000 CSL shares in his portfolio. Mohamed is currently working full-time but plans to retire before the end of the current financial year. He plans to sell his CSL shares to help fund his retirement; however, to sell them now would mean that he would realise a significant capital gain. Therefore Mohamed has decided to sell his CSL shares in the next financial year. Mohamed is, however, worried that the CSL share price might fall in the near future. How can Mohamed use a CFD to hedge his risks?

8.6 'Trading in CFDs is very similar to playing roulette. With roulette basically half the wheel is red and half the wheel is black with a very small margin for the house. If it comes up red you win and if it comes up black you lose. With CFDs if the price goes up you win and if it goes down you lose. Half the people around the roulette table will go home happy and the other half will go home sad. What is the point of roulette? Where is the reward for skill? What is the point of trading CFDs? In fact, CFDs are worse than roulette. With roulette the most you can lose is your bet on the table; however, with CFDs you can lose your bet on the table and the money in your pocket as well. Most investors, or should I say gamblers, don't understand the leveraged nature of CFDs. My investment advice is that serious investors should stay away from CFDs.' Do you agree with these sentiments? Is the analogy between CFDs and roulette appropriate? Name any circumstances in which you envisage a serious investor should trade CFDs.

8.7 Critically evaluate the following statement: 'Most futures contracts do not end in the physical delivery of the underlying asset, in which case they have no value as a hedging device.'

8.8 Outline what impact each of the following events would have on a call option premium:
- higher strike price
- increase in the last sale price of the asset
- decrease in the duration for which the option remains open
- increased price volatility in the underlying asset
- being able to choose an American option in preference to a European option.

8.9 WWF shares are currently trading on the stock exchange for $40. WWF shares are also offered as an instalment warrant; the current market value of the warrant is $20. This warrant gives the holder the right to buy one WWF share for $22 in 12 months. Why would you effectively pay $42 for a share that you could buy in the market today for $40?

8.10 Selling a call option and buying a put option are both short positions. Does this mean that the payoff profiles for investors are the same?

Professional application exercises

Basic	*
Moderate	* *
Challenging	* * *

8.11 Impact of gearing on returns: magnified gains *

Your client, Jason, wants to start a share portfolio using the $50 000 in equity that he has already saved and possibly combine this with some borrowed funds. Assume the following:
- interest rates at 8%
- grossed-up dividend income of 6%
- annual capital gain of 4%
- MTR 37%.

What will be Jason's net return in both dollar and percentage terms for the following levels of gearing if he sells the investment asset a year and 1 day after he buys it?

(a) 100% equity ($50 000 in equity)
(b) 50% equity ($50 000 in equity and $50 000 in debt)
(c) 10% equity ($50 000 in equity and $450 000 in debt)

8.12 Impact of gearing on returns: magnified losses *

Recalculate your answers to exercise 8.11 on the following assumptions:
- interest rates at 9%
- grossed-up dividend income of 5%
- annual capital gain of 2%
- MTR 37%.

8.13 Safety margin *

Your client, Malala, has the following portfolio which she has financed through a $200 000 margin loan. What is her safety margin?

	Market value	LVR	Security
AGK	$80 000	75%	$60 000
BOQ	$80 000	70%	$56 000
DOW	$80 000	65%	$52 000
CSL	$80 000	75%	$60 000
	$320 000		$228 000

8.14 Margin call ✷✷

Assume that the stock market has suffered considerable falls. Malala's portfolio from exercise 8.13 is now:

Company	Market value	LVR	Security
AGK	$70 000	75%	$52 500
BOQ	$65 000	70%	$45 500
DOW	$85 000	65%	$55 250
CSL	$50 000	75%	$37 500
	$270 000		$190 750

Her lender has made a margin call. Malala does not have any cash to meet the margin call nor does she have any additional assets to pledge as security. For each of the shares in her portfolio, calculate how much she would need to sell to satisfy the margin call.

8.15 Reverse mortgage ✷✷

Your client, Chris, is a 75-year-old male. He currently lives independently in his own home and hopes to do so for another 10 years. He relies on the single age pension as his only source of income. He estimates that his home is currently worth $600 000. He would like to take out a reverse mortgage to release some cash; however, he wants to ensure that in 10 years at least half the equity in his house remains so that he can leave this as an inheritance for his grandchildren and/or afford to move to alternate accommodation. If we assume that house prices will increase by 5% and the interest rate on the reverse mortgage is 10%, how much would be a prudent amount for Chris to borrow?

8.16 Contracts for difference ✷✷

Sandy wishes to buy RNC CFD contracts. RNC shares are currently trading at $15.00 and the ASX requires a 10% margin to be paid upfront. How many RNC CFDs can Sandy buy? What is Sandy's gain/loss in dollar and percentage terms if the contract remains open and the price of RNC shares moves to:

(a) $12.30?
(b) $17.25?
(c) $15.00?

8.17 Futures contracts ✷✷

Wal is a sheep farmer from out west. When he shears his flock in 3 months he will have approximately 9000 kilograms of wool. The current price of the SFE Greasy Wool Futures 21 micron contract is $11.20 per kilogram for delivery in 3 months. Wal decides to sell four SFE Greasy Wool Futures 21 micron contracts at $11.20 per kilogram. What is Wal's gain/loss on the futures contract in dollar terms if in 3 months the price of wool is:

(a) $13.75?
(b) $10.12?
(c) $11.20?

8.18 Futures contracts with hedging ✷✷

From exercise 8.17, what is Wal's overall gain/loss when his physical position is netted against his futures position for each of the prices listed above?

8.19 Options ✱✱

Don believes that the current market price of TLE mining shares will skyrocket. He has decided to buy an American-style call option with 90 days to expiry. The current share price of TLE shares is $8.27 and the 90-day call option with a strike price of $12 is trading at $0.04. What is Don's gain/loss in dollar and percentage terms if the price of RUKRZ shares is:

(a) $6.27?

(b) $14.30?

8.20 Warrants ✱✱

Bashar pays $20 for a European-style warrant which gives the holder of the warrant the right to buy one share in CRU for $22, 1 year from today. If the price of CRU shares is currently $40 what is the implicit interest cost in both dollar and percentage terms contained within the warrant?

CASE STUDY

Taking out a margin loan

Carly is 26 and has just received a promotion at work. She now earns $10 000 more than the threshold at which the 37% marginal tax rate cuts in. Carly is unhappy at losing 37% of her money in tax. She hopes that by investing in a share portfolio she will be able to reduce this tax liability.

Carly has spoken to a margin lender who has suggested that she negatively gear her share portfolio by concentrating on stocks that place more emphasis on capital gains rather than income. The lender has recommended a portfolio with a weighted LVR of 70% and Carly is happy to contribute $60 000 of her own money and borrow the maximum amount that this equity contribution allows using an interest-only loan.

Carly lives with her partner in rented accommodation. They like renting as this gives them the freedom to move around, take holidays and not worry about maintaining a house and meeting mortgage repayments. Carly believes that her investment time horizon is about 7 years and would like you to do some financial projections on this basis.

Carly provides you with the following information and assumptions.

- Grossed-up dividend income will be 2% p.a.
- Capital gain will be 10% p.a.
- Interest cost will be 8% p.a.
- For the sake of arithmetic simplicity, MTR will stay at 37% even when capital gains are realised.

»

»

QUESTIONS

1 If Carly does decide to take out the margin loan what will be the:

(a) net annual gain or loss?

(b) accumulated net annual gain or loss over 7 years?

(c) compounded capital gain over 7 years?

(d) compounded capital gain net of CGT based on the assumption that she sells the share portfolio after 7 years?

(e) total net gain (the accumulated net annual loss and the compounded capital gain net of CGT) after 7 years after the principal of the loan has been repaid?

(f) annualised rate of return on equity?

2 Redo the calculations in question 1, above, based on the assumption that Carly does not borrow any money and instead invests her \$60 000 in equity only.

3 How does the annualised return on equity differ between scenarios 1 and 2 above? Write a brief report to Carly which explains why these figures differ.

4 Outline to Carly the risks inherent in her margin lending strategy.

5 Assuming that Carly is not satisfied with the annualised return on equity via the margin lending strategy, what leveraged derivative instruments are available to her in order to pursue a more aggressive strategy?

References and further reading

ASIC 2013, https://www.moneysmart.gov.au/investing/complex-investments.

ASX 2008, *Introduction to index futures and options*, asx.com.au.

ASX 2009 *Understanding ASX Listed CFDs*, asx.com.au.

ASX 2013a, *Warrants: understanding trading and investment warrants*, asx.com.au.

ASX 2013b, *Understanding options trading*, asx.com.au.

CommSec 2013, *Accepted ASX listed equities as at 1 April 2013*, comsec.com.au.

Kohler, A 2012, *Throw the Gaming Act at derivatives bookies*, *Business Spectator*, 26 September 2012.

RBA 2013, D10 Margin Lending.

9 Risk management and insurance

LEARNING OBJECTIVES

After studying this chapter, you should be able to:

1. explain how risk can be classified and describe the risk management process
2. explain the key concepts which underpin insurance
3. identify and evaluate the personal risks to which individuals are exposed
4. identify and evaluate property risks in relation to house and contents
5. identify and evaluate property risks in relation to motor vehicles
6. identify and evaluate personal and property risks with respect to sickness and accident, consumer credit and travel insurance
7. identify and evaluate liability risks
8. explain the need for an ongoing review process.

CASE STUDY

Simon Carter and Vikki Brown are both 28 years old and have recently purchased their first home in Brisbane. The house cost $500 000 and they have a mortgage of $420 000. They have insured the house for $300 000 and the contents for $20 000.

In Simon's opinion the house was a bargain. Recent record floods came close to inundating the property and the previous owners decided to sell. Vikki was very worried about this; however, Simon reassured her that all household insurance now includes flood cover so there is nothing to worry about.

Vikki is also concerned that they have only $20 000 in contents cover. Simon has reassured her that with all the security systems they have in place any thief would be unlikely to get away with more than $20 000 worth of goods so extra cover would be just a waste of money.

Simon and Vikki plan to start a family within the next 4 to 5 years and they expect that Vikki will cease work and stay home to look after the children. Simon has decided he should increase his life insurance but is unsure whether he should do this inside or outside his superannuation fund. He is worried that his past medical history might prevent him from getting additional coverage.

Vikki has a very basic level of life insurance cover through her superannuation fund. Simon has suggested that because she plans to cease work that extra life insurance is probably not worth it.

Issues to consider from this case include the following.

- Is flood cover now included in all house insurance policies?
- To the extent that flood cover is included in a policy, is all flood cover the same or do different insurance companies provide different types of cover?
- Is their contents coverage of $20 000 adequate? If a thief does steal $20 000 worth of goods is the insurance company likely to pay out $20 000? If fire, flood or some other disaster were to hit would $20 000 be adequate insurance?
- Should Simon organise his life insurance inside or outside his superannuation fund?
- Should Simon accurately declare his past medical history in his life insurance application? What are the possible consequences if he doesn't?
- How would Simon meet their mortgage repayment obligations over the next 5 years if Vikki were to pass away?
- When Vikki has stopped work does that mean that she does not need life insurance because there is no income stream that needs to be replaced?

These issues will be explored in this chapter.

Introduction

Planning is easy in a world without risk. However, risk comes in many forms and unexpected events disrupt our plans. Sometimes the disruption is a minor inconvenience and by working a bit harder or spending a few extra dollars the inconvenience can be overcome. However, there are times when the disruption is more than minor and it has a significant impact on our lives and the lives of people that we care for.

A financial plan sets out the steps by which a person can obtain financial security. This plan must take into account the possibility that risks such as disability and premature death may occur, thereby disrupting the plan. Part of the development of the plan will, therefore, include the analysis of those risks and steps to minimise or eliminate their occurrence or reduce the effect of those risks should they occur.

In this chapter we will identify the types of risk that can occur, and consider a systematic approach that can be used to manage those risks. The process is known as risk management. We will primarily concentrate on personal risks in terms of health, property and liability (a detailed analysis of business risk is beyond the scope of this chapter, with the exception of the health-related risks of business owners and key employees).

LO 1 Risk and risk management

Risk can be classified in a number of ways. Speculative risk and pure risk are two classifications.

Speculative risk arises where there is a chance of a loss or a gain. Gambling is a good example of a speculative risk. Once the bet is placed, there can be only a win or a loss. Setting up a business comes into the same category — the business will succeed or fail. The risks associated with investments fall into this category.

speculative risk
where there is a chance of a loss or gain, for example, in gambling or investing

Pure risk arises where there is only a possibility of loss or no loss. Pure risks are normally provided for by insurance. Pure risks can arise from the premature death of the breadwinner, which leaves the dependent family without an income, or loss or damage to an asset such as a house or car. The event will either occur or not occur.

pure risk
where there is chance of loss or no loss, for example, your house might burn down this year or it might not

Within a financial plan, both types of risk are experienced.

Pure risk can be categorised as follows.

- Personal — matters that affect the individual. Death, illness, incapacity or unemployment cause income to cease or be reduced.
- Property — loss or damage to property, such as a building burning down or car damage in an accident.
- Liability — losses suffered as a result of a legal liability incurred.

Risk management is a branch of management that has gained considerable prominence over the last 30 years and provides a systematic approach to the management of pure risk. Personal risk management is the adaptation of this process to the individual. The greatest benefit it provides is the systematic approach which helps ensure that all risks are identified and addressed.

risk management
a branch of management that provides a systematic approach to the management of pure risk

The risk management process can be divided into five broad steps as follows.

1. The identification of risk — what risks is the client exposed to?
2. The evaluation of risk — what is the likely cost of the risks the client is exposed to?
3. The control of risk — what measures can be put in place to reduce or avoid risk?
4. The financing of risk — will the client retain some risk and finance this through their own resources or will they seek to transfer this risk through the use of insurance?
5. The review of risk management program — working back through steps 1 to 4 above on a periodic basis.

Shortly we will discuss the risk management process in relation to personal, domestic property and liability risk. However, before we do that we should review a number of important concepts that underpin how insurance can be used in risk management.

LO 2 Key concepts in insurance

This section reviews a number of key concepts in insurance including how risk is pooled (shared), how the insurance market is structured, the obligation to act in the utmost of good faith and the use of terms, conditions and severity limitations in insurance contracts.

The pooling of risk

Insurance is based on the principle of pooling risk where individuals contribute resources to a fund that is used to pay for the adverse consequences suffered by some members of the pool. Such insurance is normally organised through an insurance company and the contribution to the pool is generally referred to as a **premium**.

premium
the cost of taking out insurance

Pooling is based on the premise that each entrant into the fund comes with a similar level of risk. If we know the mean risk level of the population and if our pool is a sufficiently large random sample selected from that population, then actuaries can estimate with reasonable confidence the likelihood of claims being made against the pool and can set premiums accordingly. For example, if we know that 1% of vehicles are likely to be involved in a major accident each year and our insurance pool covers 100 000 vehicles then this gives actuaries enough information to determine the applicable premiums.

We did note above that we assume that each entrant into the pool has a similar level of risk; however, this does not mean that they have an identical level of risk. As we know, inexperienced drivers under the age of 25 have a greater likelihood of being involved in an accident than older drivers, and therefore they can expect to pay a higher than average premium and/or be subject to other limiting conditions such as having a higher *excess* on their policy. Separating the pool into risk categories and charging different premiums is known as *underwriting*.

If a particular insurance company did not charge higher premiums for inexperienced drivers then it is likely that inexperienced drivers would be attracted to that fund and this in turn would mean that the mean risk profile of the fund would be higher than the mean risk profile of the population. Inexperienced drivers are making an *adverse selection against the fund*, that is, they are increasing its mean risk profile. More experienced drivers in the fund are effectively *subsidising* the less experienced drivers. Eventually premiums would have to increase to match the increased level of risk in the fund, which in turn will eventually drive away the more experienced drivers who could obtain the same level of insurance more cheaply elsewhere in the market. All general insurers in Australia charge higher premiums for inexperienced drivers.

The insurance market in Australia is very competitive and if an insurer prices a premium too high they are likely to miss out on business. One way of keeping premiums lower is to reduce the average risk profile of entrants to the pool. For example, if people over 50 are more likely to be retired or semi-retired and therefore likely to spend more time at home it is also likely that their risk with respect to home contents insurance would also be lower. In this case the insurer has narrowed the size of the pool; however, the pool is still large enough for actuaries to estimate the likely losses and therefore set premiums accordingly.

Selectively reducing the size of the pool can reduce the average risk profile of the fund but there is a limit to how small the pool can be reduced to. As we noted above, pooling is about sharing risk and applying probabilities to outcomes in order to determine premiums. The smaller the pool the less confidence actuaries will have in determining the likely commitments of the fund. As a result, premiums would eventually have to rise to reflect that uncertainty. In the theoretical extreme the pool reduces to one — for example, an opera singer may wish to insure their voice for an upcoming tour — such insurance is available through insurers such as Lloyds of London. However, the premiums are likely to be far in excess of what the probability would suggest that they should be simply because actuaries have no way of averaging this risk over a larger pool where they can have more confidence in the amounts they are likely to have to pay out.

Reducing the size of the pool to reduce the average risk profile of the fund also raises issues of equity. Should we discriminate on the basis of race, gender, age, lifestyle and so on? In some cases discrimination is a valid ingredient of the insurance offer; for example, life insurance should be more expensive as people get older and the mortality risk increases. However, sometimes the notion of what is acceptable discrimination is harder to determine. Federal Government regulations prohibit certain types of discrimination for some insurance products, for example, registered health insurance providers are not allowed to charge an additional premium for people who smoke, drink or are obese. A November 2012 Health Insurance Research report by CoreData (http://www.coredata.com.au) indicated that 73% of respondents believed that smokers should pay more for health insurance than non-smokers.

The insurance marketplace

This section briefly considers the players in the marketplace, their role and a broad view of the legislation governing the marketplace. The marketplace comprises insurers, intermediaries, clients and regulators.

Insurers

There are broadly three types of insurers operating in the market.

1. Life insurers provide a range of risk and investment products. Risk products include those where a benefit is paid in the event of death or disablement of the person insured. Today, the major part of a life insurer's business relates to investment products which include superannuation. The *Life Insurance Act 1995* relates to the licensing, control and, to some extent, the conduct of insurers.

   Life insurance products are examples of *non-indemnity* type products; that is, the amount paid out by the insurer does not necessarily relate to the actual loss incurred. For example, a life insurance policy may pay out $1m on the death of the insured — there is really no way of relating this amount to the actual loss incurred, nor does the amount paid out vary according to the circumstances relating to the loss. This can be contrasted to most general insurance products which are *indemnity* type products where the payout by the insurer is directly related to the actual loss incurred. For example, a person might have their household contents valued at $100 000 under a general insurance policy; however, they will be able to claim only the value of their actual loss.

   Life insurers were traditionally mutual companies. *Mutual* companies or organisations are businesses owned by their members and run for the benefit of their members. Over the last 20 years most life insurers have *demutualised* and listed on the stock exchange, so they are now owned by their shareholders and run for the benefit of those shareholders. Some of the life insurance companies that operate in Australia include AMP, AXA, Allianz Australia, MLC and OnePath.

2. General insurers provide risk products. The policies cover all types of risks, including disability risks but excluding life covers. Examples of the types of risks covered are property insurance, which covers damage to property by a range of different perils and liability insurance, which provides cover for situations where the insured is legally liable to others as a result of injury/damage or having given wrong advice. The legislative licensing and control measures for general insurers are contained in the *Insurance Act 1973*. Some of the general insurance companies that operate in Australia include AAMI, GIO, NRMA, RACV and CGU.
3. Health insurers provide hospital and medical benefits cover. Medicare Private is the largest private health insurer in Australia and is owned by the Federal Government. The other providers include a mixture of for profit (e.g. Australian Unity) and mutual organisations (e.g. BUPA). The legislative licensing and control measures for health insurers are contained in the *Private Health Insurance Act 2007*.

Intermediaries

intermediaries
those who arrange insurances for a client; that is, agents and brokers

agent
insurer's representative who directly organises insurance for clients

broker
insured's representative who determines the client's insurance needs

Intermediaries arrange insurances for a client; that is, agents and brokers.

The **agent** is the insurer's representative whose function is to arrange covers for clients with the insurer. The **broker** is the insured's representative whose function is to ascertain the client's needs and, being an expert in the insurance market, arrange the best terms for the client.

These intermediaries are controlled by the FSRA. The Act provides a framework for a single licensing regime and for disclosure standards. The provisions of the Act were covered in more detail in chapter 1. The Act seeks to protect the public. It does this by requiring full disclosure on the part of those in the financial services industry and by making organisations responsible for the actions of their agents and representatives. When an agent has acted beyond his or her authority, the principal is liable but can seek redress from the agent or representative.

Clients

The consumerism which swept through most areas of commerce in the 1970s and 1980s came to the insurance market also. A number of pieces of legislation were introduced and industry codes of practice were established. The objective of these was to produce an environment where the client could be reasonably sure of the solvency of the insurers and intermediaries and that the conduct of insurers and intermediaries would be fair.

The *Insurance Contracts Act 1984* governs practice in the insurance market and provides protection to the client. The Act states that its purpose is to reform and modernise the law in relation to insurance contracts so that a fair balance is struck between those insured and insurers, and that policy provisions and insurers' practices operate fairly.

During the late 1990s the insurance industry developed self-regulatory codes of practice. The codes had similar aims and objectives and sought to establish standards that ensured that the customer was placed in a position to make an informed choice. The codes promoted high-quality advice to customers and tried to ensure that advisers met adequate competency levels and followed the principles of fair dealing. The codes also established an inquiry and complaint-handling mechanism which ensured that customers were able to have their complaints adequately heard. The Life Insurance Code of Practice was superseded by the FSRA as the elements of the Code were incorporated into the legislation. The General Insurance Code of Practice covers advisers who are not covered by the FSRA but offer advice on general insurance. The Code may be found at www.codeofpractice.com.au.

Regulators

The insurance industry is controlled by two main regulators — the Australian Prudential Regulation Authority (APRA) and the Australian Securities and Investments Commission (ASIC). ASIC deals with consumer-oriented matters and APRA handles prudential regulation. ASIC is responsible for the FSRA and liaises with industry bodies in relation to improving the services provided by advisers to consumers.

Insurance policies and the principle of utmost good faith

A fundamental feature of an insurance policy is that it is a contract between the insurer and the insured. The contract relies on the principle of each party entering the agreement with the **utmost good faith**. Section 13 of the *Insurance Contracts Act* states that:

> *A contract of insurance is a contract based on the utmost good faith and there is implied in such a contract a provision requiring each party to it to act towards the other party, in respect of any matter arising under or in relation to it, with the utmost good faith.*

utmost good faith
under the *Insurance Contract Act 1984* both parties to an insurance contract must display the highest degree of honesty

This means that the highest degree of honesty is imposed on both parties to the insurance contract. Insurers accept the contract for insurance at certain rates of premium under certain terms and conditions based on statements made by the applicant for insurance. Likewise, the applicant enters into an insurance contract in reliance on the promise by the insurer to pay if loss occurs according to the terms and conditions stipulated in the insurance contract.

Thus, there is a duty of disclosure on the applicant to disclose to the insurer all the **material facts** that would influence a reasonable and prudent insurer in accepting a risk or in setting a premium given those particular facts.

material fact
a fact that would influence a reasonable and prudent insurer in accepting a risk or in setting a premium given those particular facts

The duty of disclosure requires the applicant to disclose all material facts except:

- facts known to the insurer, or those which it may reasonably be presumed are known to the insurer
- facts which diminished the risk insured against
- facts of public notoriety
- facts which the insurer decided to personally ascertain
- facts which may be regarded as superfluous by reason of an express or implied warranty in the policy which covers the circumstances
- facts of which the insurer was deemed to have constructive knowledge (e.g. facts the insurer would have discovered in its ordinary course of business).

The duty of disclosure exists during the negotiations and up to the time when a binding contract of insurance is concluded. It also exists at the time of renewal of the contract. If the applicant does not reveal a material fact to the insurer or deliberately withholds material information from the insurer the contract may be voidable at the option of the insurer. The insurer may also be entitled to reduce the level of liability that the insurer would otherwise be liable for if a claim is made under the contract.

Misrepresentation occurs when an inaccurate or untrue statement is made by the insured or the insured's agent prior to the conclusion of the contract. Two types of misrepresentation are recognised:

1. **innocent misrepresentation** — where the statement is inaccurate but made without fraudulent intent

innocent misrepresentation
an inaccurate statement made without fraudulent intent

fraudulent misrepresentation an inaccurate statement made knowingly believing it to be untrue, or an inaccurate statement made recklessly

2. **fraudulent misrepresentation** — where the statement was inaccurate but made knowingly, believing it to be untrue, or where the statement was made recklessly.

Innocent misrepresentation of a material fact renders the contract voidable at the option of the insurer; fraudulent misrepresentation renders the contract void from inception of the contract.

Section 21A of the *Insurance Contracts Act* requires the insurer to inform the applicants for insurance of their duty of disclosure. It also requires the insurer to assist the consumer to discharge their duty by requesting the applicant to answer specific questions relevant to the insurer's decision to accept the risk. In addition it requires the insurer to request the consumer to disclose any exceptional circumstance known to the insured that a reasonable person in the circumstances could be expected to know would be relevant to the insurer's decision.

PERSONAL FINANCE BULLETIN

You bet your life: health insurer's cheap DNA test could prove costly

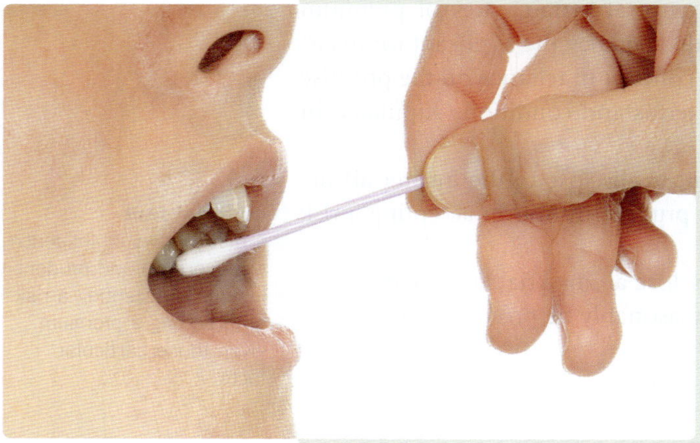

The insurer NIB has begun offering its customers cut-price genetic tests which could unwittingly expose them to higher premiums or even leave them unable to get life insurance or insurance payouts.

But the company says it has no ulterior motive and wants to help its members manage their health.

In an Australian first, the company has sent a selected group of customers a letter inviting them to take a DNA test to assess their risk of getting preventable illnesses such as diabetes, heart attacks and some cancers.

However, experts warn that taking up the offer could lead to privacy and financial risks — which the company only admits to in fine print at the end of the letter.

NIB has arranged a half-price deal with a US company, Navigenics, for a full genetic test that usually costs $1000.

It is understood that a select group of 5000 customers received the offer, but if it is successful it may be expanded.

In the letter, the NIB chief executive, Mark Fitzgibbon, reveals he has had such a test himself. 'I found it to be an invaluable experience and believe it could be something that you would be interested in, too.'

But a Sydney academic, Kristine Barlow-Stewart, a key government adviser on genetics technology, said the move was concerning. 'It certainly raised red flags for me,' she said.

Once someone has taken a test they can be forced to reveal the results to obtain life insurance, income protection or mortgage insurance and even membership of some superannuation funds which include life insurance.

Insurers can then use the information to increase premiums. If a customer concealed the fact they'd had the test, the insurer may refuse to pay out the policy.

Associate Professor Barlow-Stewart sits on the federal government's Human Genetics Advisory Committee. She has been researching cases of 'genetic discrimination', in which healthy people have been denied insurance cover due to the content of their DNA.

A spokesman for NIB said the genetic test results would remain strictly confidential between Navigenics and the policy holder.

He said customers were warned of the implications in fine print on the letter saying 'you may be required to disclose genetic test results, including any underlying health risks and conditions which the tests reveal, to life insurance or superannuation providers'.

The company also offered a counselling service for people who were worried or confused about the genetic test results.

Source: Miller 2010.

Terms, standard terms and severity limitations

Purchasing insurance requires the client and the insurer to enter into a contract of insurance. All contracts have terms and conditions which set out the rights and responsibilities of the respective parties. All contracts are based on the principle that both parties have willingly entered into an agreement and are aware of the terms and conditions which apply. Unfortunately often the first time a client reads the terms and conditions associated with their insurance policy is when they want to make a claim. Insurers have made significant improvements in recent years in improving the way they communicate the applicable terms and conditions; however, insurance contracts do rely on very detailed terms and conditions which inevitably produce a considerable volume of 'fine print' which most clients find daunting.

As we discussed earlier the *Insurance Contracts Act 1984* governs practice in the insurance market and provides protection to the consumer. Section 35 of the Act prescribes a range of insurance policies for which standard cover will be assumed to be part of those policies. For example, home contents insurance is a prescribed policy under the Act. The Act also outlines the range of cover for each of the prescribed insurance policies. For example, a home contents insurance policy is assumed to cover loss that is caused by '. . . storm, tempest, flood, the action of the sea, high water, tsunami, erosion or landslide or subsidence'.

The standard terms and conditions that fall under the standard cover are enacted via the *Insurance Contract Regulations 1985*. The consumer can therefore have confidence that the standard terms and conditions which have been drafted and enacted by government, in consultation with the insurance industry and consumer groups, represent a 'fair' basis upon which to enter into an insurance agreement.

The use of standard cover and standard terms and conditions does not, however, obviate the need for the consumer to be thoroughly aware of the extent of the cover and the terms and conditions which apply. As we noted above standard cover for a home contents insurance policy includes storm, tempest, flood etc. However, until recently there was no standard definition of flood in the regulations which many people in Queensland and New South Wales found out to their peril.

PERSONAL FINANCE BULLETIN

Flood definition becomes law

The standard definition of flood is now law, after the Federal Government this morning enacted the regulations to give effect to the definition.

Financial Services Minister Bill Shorten says the regulations provide for a two-year transition period, which 'will provide insurers with a sufficient lead time to update the content of product disclosure statements, retrain staff and implement any necessary system changes'.

The standard definition was finalised last November and has since been awaiting ministerial approval. It applies to home building and contents, small business and strata title insurance contracts across Australia.

Mr Shorten says under the regulations the word 'flood' in an insurance contract will mean:

> 'The covering of normally dry land by water that has escaped or been released from the normal confines of: any lake, or any river, creek or other natural watercourse, whether or not altered or modified, or any reservoir, canal or dam'.

He says the standard definition makes it easier for people to know what they are covered for, and what is not covered.

'A flood is a flood', he said. 'Never again do Australians want to see a situation — as we saw during the Queensland floods of 2011 — where neighbours hit by the same flood get different levels of cover because of technical definitions in an insurance contract.'

Mr Shorten says the Government recognises that many insurers have already adopted the standard definition. He urged all insurers to now do the same.

Insurance Council of Australia CEO Rob Whelan welcomed the move, saying this afternoon that the standard definition 'has long been a goal of the general insurance industry' and will give property owners and insurers greater clarity and peace of mind.

'Though the standard definition is welcome, it is one part of a complex issue', he said. 'Insurance can only help communities recover from the impact of floods. Governments are responsible for protecting at-risk communities in the first place.'

'Urgent investments in permanent, well-designed physical mitigation measures — such as levees, barrages, floodgates and improved drainage — are still required.'

Source: © insurancenews.com.au, 18 June 2012.

A consumer reading the above article may believe from its title that they are now protected from flood as it is defined in the regulations. However, it is still at the discretion of the individual insurers as to whether they adopt this definition.

An insurer is able to limit or exclude their liability which would otherwise be provided under standard cover provided they clearly inform the consumer that such cover is limited or excluded. Generally the inclusion in a Product Disclosure Statement (PDS) that the level of standard cover has been modified is seen as sufficient notification notwithstanding the fact that PDS documents are often long, complicated and unread by the consumer.

It is also worth reiterating that not all insurance contracts are prescribed under the Act. For those insurance contracts which are prescribed under the Act, not all contingencies for which the consumer seeks cover might be captured under the standard cover and standard terms and conditions. It is still very much a case of buyer beware.

The terms and conditions included in insurance contracts are one means by which insurers seek to limit their liability. Insurers may also seek to limit their liability through the use of severity limitations such as the use of policy excesses and waiting periods. Severity limitations mean that some of the risk is retained by the individual rather than transferred to the insurer. For example, a policy might have a $1000 **excess**. For a $5000 claim this would mean $1000 is paid (retained) by the individual and $4000 is transferred to the insurer. On a disability policy, a person may elect to exclude the first 4 weeks of any incapacity — the incentive for doing this is a reduced premium under those policies.

excess
the amount of insurance risk which is retained by the individual rather than transferred through insurance

LO 3 Life, disability, trauma and health risks

This section discusses the identification and evaluation of life, disability, trauma and health risks as well as the control and financing measures for these personal risks.

Identification of personal risks

The following areas need to be considered in the scope of personal risk: premature death, prolonged illness or injury, medical costs and business risks.

Premature death

The effects of a premature death will vary according to a person's responsibilities as far as **dependants** are concerned. A dependant is a person who relies on another, financially, emotionally or in some other capacity. The definition of dependant will vary dependent on, for example, legislation and trust deeds. Generally, dependants are treated more generously than non-dependants with respect to insurance and superannuation payouts.

dependant
a person who relies on another, financially, emotionally or in some other capacity

Consider the following situations.

- Single person, no dependants. There is little need for cover. An allowance for final medical and burial expenses is the extent of any need. Where there are any debts to be met, these need to be included also. In most but not all cases, the party to whom the debt is owed will either have security for the debt or have already required a term life cover to be effected for the amount of the debt.
- Single-parent family. This category has a considerable need. The income producer has dependants who need to be provided for in the event of premature death. Unlike the situation in two-income families, no alternative income is available should the income producer die prematurely. Although the loss of one income stream in a two-income family will leave a reduced income, at least there is still some income. In the event of the death of a single parent, there needs to be a provision for the children until they reach an age when they can become self-supporting. This provision needs to include an allowance for education and other such expenses to ensure a reasonable standard of living. Many in this category have a low income and their ability to provide for losses (meet insurance premiums) is limited.

- Two-income families. The majority of families with dependants fall into this group. In the event of the premature death of either or both breadwinners, the family will suffer a loss of income and with it a fall in living standard. Provision needs to be made so that funds are available to provide ongoing support for the family.
- One-income families. The same need that existed for two-income families exists here. The need may be seen to be greater, since if the sole breadwinner dies the sole income stream is lost. At least with two-income families, if only one of the breadwinners dies, one income stream remains.
- Additional dependants. Dependants are normally thought of as children, but they can be parents or other relatives. This needs to be taken into account when assessing future provisions, as these dependants may not always be clearly identifiable, since they may not be dependants at the time the assessment of future income needs is made.

Prolonged illness or injury

For illnesses of short duration, most people are able to call on existing resources and not suffer any significant fall in their standard of living. But when the incapacity is of longer duration, the living standard can be affected. The extent to which people are affected depends on whether they are employees or self-employed.

Employees are normally provided with sick leave by their employer and receive full pay, but how long this is provided for is the significant factor. In the event of a workplace accident, workers compensation benefits are provided. In contrast, those most exposed are the self-employed. Their income can be directly dependent on their efforts, and when their efforts cease, such as with illness, their income may cease also. It may be that the business can still function and provide the same income by employing someone to continue it, but funds will be needed to employ that person.

Medical costs

Medical costs can vary considerably, depending on the injury or illness suffered. Where an injury is work related or arises from a motor accident, then the medical costs arising from those injuries may be met by workers compensation insurance or by compulsory third-party insurance. These schemes set out the level of benefits payable and the extent of medical expenses to be paid and should cover most, if not all, costs. In the case of self-employed people, however, workers compensation insurance may not apply. Outside these areas, the choices are to use the public health system, have some type of health insurance cover or meet the costs from the individual's own funds.

Each option has its own problems. It is argued that the public health system is overburdened; there can be extensive waiting lists for treatment unless the condition is life threatening. Private health insurance comes at a cost. If people meet their own costs it can be very expensive, and it would be necessary to have funds set aside for this purpose.

Business risks

There are several risks for business, and these need to be recognised and provided for.

- *Partnership*. A partnership agreement may specify that, in the event of the death of a partner, the remaining partners will buy out the deceased partner's share of the business. In most cases, the remaining partners may not have the ready funds available to meet such a cost. If term life policies are taken out on the lives of the partners, the funds are then available to enable the remaining partners to buy out the deceased partner's share.

- *Key employee*. Where a business has a key employee, i.e. one who would be difficult to replace, a term life cover can be used to meet the cost of hiring and training a replacement employee. Multiple replacements may be needed, or a significant amount of training may be necessary.
- *Business loans*. Cover can be effected to meet the outstanding amount of a business loan. Take, for example, a small business where the involvement of the owner, manager or a key employee is vital for the success of the business. The business may be able to obtain a loan at more attractive interest rates or a **creditor** may feel more secure in providing a loan if there is a term life cover in force for the amount of the loan. Should the principal or key employee die, then the loan can be repaid from the policy proceeds. These policies are often referred to as 'key person' policies.

creditor
a person to whom money is owed

Evaluation of personal risks

In establishing an adequate sum insured, three areas need to be considered:

- a lump sum amount to meet costs at the time of premature death of the income earner
- a provision to meet the needs of dependants for the period of their dependency after premature death of the income earner
- a provision to meet the needs of dependants and the income earner in the event of disablement of the income earner.

Lump sum costs

At the time of death a number of expenses may arise and provision needs to be made to meet these costs. The more common items are burial and associated expenses, **estate** administration costs, legal expenses, taxes (e.g. death is a trigger to incur capital gains tax), final medical and associated care expenses, debt clearing and adjustment expenses.

estate
the deceased assets which have not been directly passed to beneficiaries

- Burial and associated expenses. These expenses will vary but an amount in the vicinity of $10 000 is reasonable. A check with a funeral director at the time of establishing a sum insured will help ensure adequacy. Keep in mind that provision is being made for an event in the future, so allow for inflation. It is common for many people to prepay for a funeral via means of a funeral bond. This type of bond is a form of investment fund that allows for the prepayment to increase in value to ensure that a rise in future costs is covered.
- Estate administration costs. The amount to be allowed here will vary according to the size and complexity of the estate. Allow not only for the estate administration costs but also for legal expenses, including any associated taxes or other costs. For example, the situation where one **beneficiary** is left property and another is left cash may result in an unfair distribution, since a future liability for CGT could arise in the case of the property. This can be overcome by providing for the CGT amount in the term life policy sum insured.
- Final medical and associated care expenses. The medical and care expenses associated with death can be considerable. Health insurance will reduce the costs but keep in mind that hospital and medical expenses covered under a health insurance policy will not always cover all costs. For example, specialised nursing supervision outside of hospital may be necessary, and the cost of obtaining the service may be greater than the cover provides for.
- Debt clearing. The repayment of debts and associated interest places an additional strain on the dependant's income. Having all outstanding debts paid at the time of

beneficiary
a person nominated to receive a payout from an insurance policy, a superannuation fund or the assets of an estate

death reduces the level of income needed to maintain the family's standard of living. These debts might include outstanding balance on mortgages, amounts owed on loans, and outstanding balances on credit cards and charge accounts. Remember that the amount being calculated is to provide for the future. Where there are future plans that involve debt, this should be allowed for also.

- Adjustment expenses. Following a death, the family members have to adjust to their new circumstances. This may involve a reduction in their standard of living. The adjustment to this new standard can be helped by a lump sum that supplements their income during, say, a 6-month transition period.

Provision for dependants

To this point, the discussion has related to providing for lump sum amounts that usually need to be met at the time of death. Provision must also be made for the needs of dependants. Two approaches are commonly used to calculate this amount — the multiple approach and the needs approach.

The multiple approach

This approach is quite a simple one and at times is used to calculate the entire amount of cover. As the lump sum needs can vary considerably from one person to another, that component is better calculated separately. The multiple approach simply seeks to replace the insured's income by providing an amount that, when invested, will produce for the dependants the amount of income the insured was earning. For example, in the event of the premature death of a person whose income is $50 000 p.a., and assuming a future investment rate of 6%, the necessary sum insured can be arrived at by dividing the salary by the interest rate, or 0.06 in this case. This produces a sum insured of $835 000. This amount, when invested at 6%, will provide an income of approximately $50 000 in perpetuity. A more sophisticated version of this approach involves a table which gives a range of multiples to be used. The table takes into account the age of the dependants and income.

The simplicity of the approach is its downfall. It assumes everyone's situation is the same and does not take into account the circumstances of the individual. It ignores the individual's resources and commitments, and relies on investment rates in the future being similar to those applying at the time the sum insured is calculated. Interest rates can vary considerably over time. Dependencies can last for 20 years or more. If the rate used to calculate the future investment return is high there is every possibility that in a future period these same rates will not be available, so the return will be less than initially planned, leaving the dependants in a difficult position. This approach also ignores the effects of inflation. Over time, the purchasing power of the income generated will diminish.

The preferred approach is to do a detailed analysis of the dependants' needs and establish more precisely the amount of cover needed. When using the multiple approach, there could well be a tendency to look on the amount estimated as being unduly high, but, by doing a detailed analysis, a family can see how that amount is compiled and the necessity for each item.

In order to be in a position to recommend a particular program to clients, financial advisers need to have a good understanding of their clients' financial and family circumstances. In chapter 1 you read that advisers need to comply with s. 961B of the *Financial Services Reform Act 2001* (FSRA), which requires that advisers need to 'act in the best interests of the client' so it is just as important to assess a client's needs for risk protection as it is to ascertain a client's tolerance of risk of investment.

The needs approach

The needs approach requires a more detailed analysis, including the compilation of a budget of the costs that would be incurred in the future. The position will, of course, continually change, so it is necessary to recalculate the figures periodically as a check to see that the amount remains adequate.

Keep in mind that what is being calculated is the provision to be made for the dependants. Those provided for under this heading are usually dependent children. Their financial needs will increase as they grow older.

In a two-income family, the income of the surviving partner is deducted from the income needed in each period. Also brought into account is any income received from pensions or benefits to which the surviving partner may be eligible, e.g. parenting payment, widow's pension. These benefits or allowances are subject to assets and income tests and, in most cases, those who have insurance cover to provide for such situations are not eligible. The benefit paid under the policy would exceed the limits set down in the assets test.

In a single-income family, the premature death of the non-earning partner needs to be considered. Provision must be made to cover the cost of employing someone to undertake the non-earning partner's contribution, for example, cooking, cleaning and child care.

This section has considered the provision of an income for the dependants. The amount provided will not be needed immediately so most of it can be invested, generating further income. This will be necessary as the buying power of the lump sum amount will be eroded over time with inflation. Through generating investment income, the effects of inflation will be offset. Under the multiple approach, the interest income is used to generate the dependants' income. As a result, that approach produces, over time, a diminishing income (in terms of buying power) as the effects of inflation set in.

ILLUSTRATIVE EXAMPLE 9.1

Deb McIntosh is aged 40 and earns $100 000 per annum. Ian McIntosh, her husband, is aged 38. Ian has part-time work and looks after the house and raises their two children (Hamish, aged 8, and Andy, aged 10). The McIntoshs own their house which has a value of $500 000 and a mortgage of $120 000. They have two cars, one of which is subject to a finance agreement and currently has $12 000 to be repaid. Other outstanding debts including credit cards amount to $13 000. Deb has $88 000 in a superannuation account and Ian has no money in superannuation. The McIntoshs have estimated that their monthly expenses are $3000 plus $750 per child. This figure has been adjusted to take into account rising costs as the children get older. This amount will be needed until the children are 25.

The expenses that are expected to arise at the time of Deb's death are:

- funeral and associated expenses $15 000
- legal and associated costs $3000
- emergency funds $12 000.

When the house mortgage was arranged, a term life cover of $180 000 was taken out for Deb.

»

»

Determining the sum insured for term life insurance for Deb using the multiple approach (assuming a 10% investment rate):

Item	Calculation	Amount
Replacement of income flow	$\frac{\$100\,000}{0.1}$	$1 000 000
Less term life insurance in force		($ 180 000)
Less superannuation		($ 88 000)
Sum insured		**$ 732 000**

Determining the sum insured for term life insurance for Deb using the needs approach:

Item	Calculation	Amount
Cost of dependency: Hamish	17 years × 12 months × $ 750	$ 153 000
Cost of dependency: Andy	15 years × 12 months × $ 750	$ 135 000
Cost of dependency: Ian[a]	27 years × 12 months × $3000	$ 972 000
Funeral and associated expenses		$ 15 000
Legal and associated costs		$ 3 000
Emergency funds		$ 12 000
Repay debts: mortgage		$ 120 000
Repay debts: car finance		$ 12 000
Repay debts: credit cards		$ 13 000
Total amount required		**$1 427 500**
Less term life insurance in force		($ 180 000)
Less superannuation		($ 88 000)
Sum insured		**$1 167 000**

a. This figure is based on Ian's dependency until age 65. Ian might remain dependent for less time and return to work once the children are older. Conversely if Ian does not return to work and the monthly costs do not include some provision for contributions to superannuation the period of dependency could be longer.

From the analysis above it is clear that the needs and multiple approaches can produce very different results. Both methods are highly contingent on the assumptions that underpin them, particularly the rate of investment return and the period of dependency.

Disablement

The discussion to this point has been in relation to the effects on dependants of the death of an income producer. However, if the income earner becomes disabled and unable to work, a similar problem arises but this time with the added need to provide for the income earner.

Disablement can vary from a minor injury or illness that incapacitates for a short period of time to one that is permanent. The costs that need to be met will vary, but can include the following.

- Medical expenses. If health insurance is in place, much of the cost may be met but policies do not cover all areas. There may, for example, be a need for specialised nursing that goes beyond the amounts provided by health insurance.
- Other costs associated with the disability. These may include the need for house alterations, the provision of prostheses, and the purchase of wheelchairs and other aids.
- Provision of an income to support the dependants. This will differ from the calculation for death, as provision will need to be made for the income earner.

The elimination of debts must be included in the calculation of a sum insured, as these will place a drain on the income. An amount to provide immediate funds to help during the adjustment period should also be included.

Two covers can meet these costs. A total and permanent disablement (TPD) extension on a term life insurance policy will meet the lump sum amounts, and an income protection policy can provide a regular monthly income.

Control measures for personal risks

Control measures look at what can be done to eliminate the occurrence of risks or to reduce the impact should the risk occur. In relation to personal risks, these measures are mainly lifestyle matters, such as keeping fit, eating sensibly and avoiding risk factors such as smoking and drinking too much.

Financing of personal risks

If, despite the control measures, a loss occurs, then provision needs to be made for the financing of those losses. These losses can be financed by retention or transfer.

Retention

With retention, losses are met from an individual's own resources. This approach is used for smaller losses that the person is able to afford. The most common method is to use an excess on an insurance policy. An excess is the amount of insurance risk which is retained by the individual rather than transferred through insurance.

Transfer

Transfer of risks involves passing financial responsibility for the loss to another party. The main form of transfer is by insurance. In return for a premium, the insurer agrees to meet the cost of certain specified risks. In relation to personal risks, the policies used are term life policies, disability policies and health policies. Term life insurance policies provide a lump sum amount in the event of death, TPD and specified traumas. Income-replacement policies provide a monthly income in the event of disability, even if it is temporary.

PERSONAL FINANCE BULLETIN

Life insurance gap reducing — industry must evolve to meet changing customer needs

Rice Warner's *Underinsurance in Australia Report 2012* reveals the underinsurance gap is narrowing.

The rapid growth of the life insurance market over the past few years means that, on average, life cover is now sufficient to meet the basic needs of Australians. However, the median level of life cover is still only 66% of basic needs and 41% of the amount required to ensure that family members and dependants can maintain their standard of living after the death of a parent or partner.

A significant gap also exists for disability insurance.

However, much of the progress made by the insurance industry, directly and through financial advisers and superannuation funds, has been through the provision of default insurance provided by superannuation. Whilst this has proved to be extremely successful in providing cheap cover, often with no medical checks or underwriting questions, this blanket approach can only ever be part of the solution.

Longer term, insurers and superannuation funds, either directly or through advisers, will need to switch to making tailored insurance offers to customers, based on a deep understanding of their insurance needs — true customer engagement.

As at June 2012, life underinsurance based on current median levels of cover is $2166 billion to maintain the living standards of family members after the death of a parent or partner, compared to $3073 billion at 30 June 2010 — a reduction of 30%.

Meanwhile, for total and permanent disability (TPD), the level of underinsurance is $7912 billion and income protection underinsurance is $589 billion.

Richard Weatherhead, Principal at Rice Warner, attributes this shift to continued strong growth in the life insurance market and, for disability insurance, the growing population of single people who often need greater financial support if they are unable to work.

'Apart from individual detriment, underinsurance also comes at a substantial cost to the government. Currently the total cost to the government of life underinsurance across Australia is calculated to be $76 million per year as publicly funded social security benefits fill the gap. Meanwhile, the situation regarding disability underinsurance is even more serious, costing the government nearly $1.5 billion per year!'

The report also provides a comprehensive breakdown of the Australian working age population by household type and income and determines insurance needs for each segment. This enables analysis of broad needs for customer segments.

Source: RiceWarner Actuaries, media release, 17 December 2012.

Term life policies

A term life policy was the original form of life policy. It paid the nominated death benefit when the person whose life was insured died during the period of insurance. In early times, the period of insurance would have been about a year.

A term life policy as it is offered today usually includes a terminal illness benefit as part of the basic cover. The terminal illness benefit provides that, in the event of the insured person being diagnosed with an illness or disease or sustaining an injury which is likely to lead to death within 12 months, the specified lump-sum benefit is payable. This lump sum is the same as the death benefit in the policy with one proviso — the company usually specifies a maximum amount it will pay in relation to all policies with that company. The amount varies, with most companies specifying $1 million. Any amount paid reduces the death benefit that will eventually become payable. The reasoning behind this premature payment of the death benefit is to make available funds that can help the family during such a trying time with medical and other costs.

Policy features

The basic term life policy has, over time, developed a number of features designed to make it more attractive to clients. Those described in the following sections are found in most policies.

Indexed sum insured

It is usual for policies to have the sum insured indexed so the insured has the option of an increase in the sum insured each year. The advantage of these increases is that they are automatic and do not need a medical examination. Companies generally provide that, in the event of the indexed increase being declined three times in succession by the insured, the automatic index benefit ceases. It can, on request, be reinstated at a future date but is subject to a medical check.

Special sum insured increase

Another benefit often found in policies is a provision that allows for an increase in the sum insured at other times, again without the need for a medical check. The ability to do this arises at the occurrence of certain specified events, such as marriage of the insured, the birth of a child or taking out a mortgage. The policy provision usually specifies minimum and maximum amounts for the increase and the frequency with which these increases can be made. The main value of this benefit lies in the fact that a medical check is not required. If, after effecting the policy, the insured acquires a condition that would be a bar from effecting further cover, this policy provision allows the insured to obtain sum insured increases.

Guaranteed renewal

This provision means the policy will remain in force continuously, subject to any specified age limit, with the insured having the right only to terminate the policy. This means that the cover cannot be altered or changed if the insured develops any adverse condition; this includes any premium increase related to the condition. Premium rates applied to all those insured are not guaranteed to remain unaltered from year to year as standard premiums can change according to the cost of risks as assessed by underwriters. However, once an adverse condition is experienced, such as the onset of diabetes, the insurance company cannot impose an additional loading to the normal premium.

Multiple lives

Most insurers will allow more than one life to be covered under the one policy. The benefit here is that only one policy fee applies. Where a husband and wife and other family members are all covered under the one policy, a saving in multiple policy fees can be made.

Policy duration

Generally the policy can be taken out for any period of time ranging from 1 day to a term that continues until the insured turns 65 years. Premiums are either stepped premiums or level premiums.

- Stepped premiums: these are calculated annually and rise each year in accordance with the increased death risk that results as the insured gets older. Table 9.1 shows typical term life insurance policy premiums at different ages for a professional person with a sum insured of $250 000. Premiums are given for both males and females and for smokers and non-smokers.

TABLE 9.1 Stepped premiums — professional person, $250 000 sum insured

Age	Male non-smoker	Male smoker	Female non-smoker	Female smoker
35	$ 240	$ 440	$200	$ 330
40	$ 290	$ 550	$230	$ 420
45	$ 400	$ 840	$300	$ 570
55	$1120	$2500	$820	$1420

- Level premiums: stepped premiums are good if the cover is needed for only a small number of years. The problem with a stepped premium is that if the insurance is needed for a long period of time, the premiums will rise each year in accordance with the increased risk of death (as seen in table 9.1). By the time the insured reaches 60 years of age, the premium will become quite large and may start to become unaffordable. The level premium offers a solution to this problem. The cost of the premium is averaged over the lifetime of the policy. In the early years, the amounts paid will be greater than the stepped premium for the same year, but in the later years the amount payable will be less. The amount paid in excess of the 'death risk' amount in the early years is invested and the interest along with the surplus is used to supplement the amount paid in the later years, so the full risk premium is still received by the insurer. Table 9.2 compares typical level and stepped premiums for a $500 000 term life policy.

TABLE 9.2 Comparison of stepped and level premiums — $500 000 term life policy

Age	Stepped premium	Level premium
30	$ 370	$600
40	$ 460	$600
50	$1200	$600
55	$2200	$600

The point that needs to be borne in mind is how long the insured expects to keep the cover in force. If a policy is effected to age 65 using level premiums and after 6 years the cover is cancelled, then the insured would have paid an excessive price for the policy.

Look at the amounts shown in table 9.3, where the two situations are compared. This would mean an overpayment of $1230 for the period in question. Although taking out a cover to age 65 spreads the premium burden and guarantees insurability, it may come at a price.

TABLE 9.3 Typical premium differences between stepped and level premiums over 6 years

Age	Stepped premium	Level premium
30	$ 370	$ 600
31	$ 380	$ 600
32	$ 390	$ 600
33	$ 400	$ 600
34	$ 410	$ 600
35	$ 420	$ 600
Total	$2370	$3600

Convertibility

There is generally a provision that allows you to convert the policy to any other type of policy with the insurer so long as the sum insured is the same. No medical examination is needed. This can be done at any time to age 65, and could be of value in a situation where a person's health deteriorates and a medical examination would mean that cover may not be attainable, or could be effected only at an increased premium. This provision allows people to change the cover to one that better suits their needs at the time. For example, the initial cover may be a term life policy with a stepped premium. People contracting an ailment that precludes them from obtaining further cover may wish to convert to a policy with a level premium so that, at a future time, the premiums do not become prohibitive.

Optional benefits

Companies provide a range of optional benefits as follows.

- Total and permanent disablement. This benefit is described in more detail in the next section on disability policies. Under this benefit, a lump sum is paid if the person insured becomes totally and permanently disabled.
- Trauma cover. This cover is also discussed in more detail in the section 'Disability policies'. Briefly, it provides for the payment of a nominated lump sum in the event of the person insured being diagnosed with any of a number of life-threatening or major illnesses or diseases that would change the person's life.
- **Future insurability**. The optional benefit future insurability gives the insured the opportunity to purchase more cover at future nominated dates without providing further evidence of health status. This is of particular value where an insured has developed a health condition which would preclude further cover being provided. There could be as many as five opportunities until the insured person's forty-fifth birthday. The dates on which the option can be exercised are nominated in the policy, but, in the event of certain nominated events such as a house purchase or birth of a child, the date may be brought forward. The benefit usually has a ceiling concerning the additional amount of cover.

future insurability
a clause in an insurance contract which provides the insured with the opportunity to purchase more cover at future nominated dates without providing further evidence of health status

Policy exclusions

In a term life policy, the exclusions are few. For example, most term life insurance policies will exclude suicide for the first 13 months of insurance coverage. Suicide is one exclusion that is common to all policies. Other exclusions vary between insurers.

- Terminal illness. Cover is not provided where the terminal illness is a result of an intentional self-inflicted injury or disease.
- Other exclusions. These are not found in all policies and, in fact, some insurers will have only the suicide exclusion. Other exclusions are:
  - war — the policy excludes death resulting not only from war and warlike activities but also from civil commotions and other similar events
  - pre-existing conditions — where a pre-existing condition that was not disclosed to the insurer before entering into the cover is the cause of death, the policy benefit will not be paid.

In both these situations, cover may not be granted on policies that do not have such exclusions. An insured going into a war zone could be regarded as non-disclosure of a material fact, due to the increased risk. Similarly, the non-disclosure of a pre-existing condition may fall into the same category.

Policy ownership

A term life policy can be:

- in the name of the life insured
- in the name of the life insured but with a beneficiary nominated for the proceeds to be paid to
- in the name of a person or company on the life of the person insured.

In the case of the policy being in the name of the life insured, the benefits are paid to the life insured's estate in the event of death. Thus, any distribution of funds needs to wait until probate is granted, which can be some time later. If a creditor has required the insured to effect a policy to cover a debt, the creditor may not ultimately receive payment as the estate debts may exceed the estate funds (including the term life policy proceeds).

Where a beneficiary is nominated, or the owner is a person other than the insured, then the proceeds are paid directly to that person. The advantage of this approach is that the benefit is paid straight away. In the case of creditors or a situation where the insured wants a certain party to receive the funds, the policy should be effected in the name of that party.

Disability policies

Life insurers and, in respect of some policies, general insurers offer a range of disability policies. The cover afforded by these policies revolves around the concept of incapacity as a result of injury or illness. Some provide cover by way of a lump sum, and others provide cover by way of monthly payments. Four covers are examined in this section:

- total and permanent disablement insurance
- trauma insurance
- income protection insurance
- business overheads insurance.

Total and permanent disablement (TPD) insurance

This cover is usually taken as an extension of a trauma or term life insurance policy. The benefit provides that, in the event of the person insured becoming totally and permanently disabled, the policy will pay the nominated amount. On payment of a TPD benefit, the remaining amount of cover is reduced by the amount of the benefit. The definition of total and permanent disablement is the critical aspect of the cover and the policy definition needs to be considered carefully. Not all policies are the same and some are quite restrictive. The more restrictive definitions usually carry a lower premium but this may be little consolation if, in the event of a claim, it is too restrictive to meet the loss.

An example of a commonly used definition of total and permanent disablement is where an applicant satisfies either:

- the total and permanent loss of any of:
  - the use of both hands
  - the use of both feet
  - the use of one hand and one foot
  - the sight of both eyes
  - the use of one hand and the sight of one eye
  - the use of one foot and the sight of one eye

  or
- injury or disease which, in the opinion of the insurer, has wholly prevented the insured person from performing the principal duties of their usual occupation for a continuous period of at least 6 months and which, despite the insured person receiving treatment or rehabilitation, will continue to prevent them from ever again performing those duties or the principal duties of any other full-time occupation that they were engaged in during the 5 years prior to the cessation of work. For the purpose of this definition, it does not matter if the occupation is paid or unpaid.

The definition is in two parts. If either part is satisfied, the benefit is payable.

The circumstances in which the benefit is paid occur infrequently. In the first part of the definition, two limbs or faculties are involved. Bear in mind that the phrase used is 'loss of use of'. If, for example, a foot is badly damaged so that it is not usable on its own, the courts have decided that this does not constitute loss of use if the foot is usable with a prosthesis. However, the wording of the latter part of the definition is quite important. It relates to the insured's usual occupation or one they have undertaken over the past 5 years.

The broadest definition is one referred to as the 'own occupation' definition. This is usually available only in professional white-collar occupations. It stipulates that the insured is unable to work in their occupation for at least 6 consecutive months and is so incapacitated that in the opinion of the insurer's professional adviser the insured is unlikely to be able to resume his or her own profession or occupation ever again. Under this definition for example, a surgeon who lost a hand would meet the definition requirements and therefore would be entitled to a payout under the policy and would still be able to lecture in surgery at a university.

The following is an example of a restrictive definition:

> Total disablement arising from illness, accident or injury, which we believe causes the insured person to be unable to engage in any occupation, employment or business for remuneration or profit.

This definition is extremely restrictive. The use of the words 'any occupation' leaves very few situations where the conditions of the definition could be met. Referring back to the earlier example the surgeon would not be able to make a claim.

Trauma insurance

The purpose of trauma cover is to provide a lump sum in the event of the diagnosis of any of the listed traumas. The cover can be purchased as an extension of a term life policy or as a stand-alone policy. The trauma cover is generally offered in two forms — basic trauma cover includes a few traumas only; broader trauma cover provides a more extensive list.

Basic trauma cover generally includes the following traumas:

- cancer — malignant tumours
- heart attack
- coronary artery surgery
- stroke
- terminal illness.

Some insurers will also cover paraplegia, quadriplegia and occupationally acquired HIV under their basic trauma cover. The list for broader trauma cover also varies between insurers. Of all claims reported, more than 90% are for traumas that are covered under the basic cover.

Problems arise because insurers differ in their definitions of trauma. The problems are further compounded by the complex medical terminology which is necessarily used to define the trauma but which will not mean a great deal to the average person.

Some benefits require qualifying periods; that is, the policy will not apply if the condition becomes apparent within 90 days of the commencement of the policy. In the list set out, cancer (malignant tumours), coronary artery surgery, heart attack and stroke may fall into this category. The insurer imposes the waiting period to eliminate any traumas that are present but have not yet become apparent at the time the cover is effected.

consumer price index (CPI)
an index used to measure inflation i.e. the general increase in prices

The benefits under the cover are usually indexed to the **consumer price index (CPI)** subject to a ceiling, which is usually set at around 5%. Cover is available from age 15 to 55, on renewal to 65. Premium payment can be stepped or level.

Trauma policies generally exclude suicide within 13 months of the policy commencement, intentional self-injury or intentional infection, and trauma from war or civil commotion.

Most companies seem to provide a maximum amount of cover of $1 million.

Combined term life, trauma and TPD policies

Life insurance, trauma insurance and TPD insurance can each be taken out as stand-alone (un-bundled) policies.

TPD insurance is frequently included as an additional benefit within a life insurance policy. This additional benefit is sometimes referred to as rider benefit. Combining two or more insurances into the one policy is generally referred to as bundling.

Trauma insurance can also be included as a rider benefit within a life insurance policy.

In a bundled insurance policy the sum insured under the rider benefit cannot exceed the death benefit specified in the life policy. Any payment under the rider will reduce the amount payable under the policy overall. For example a life insurance policy with a sum insured of $1m includes a trauma rider — if the insured subsequently makes a trauma claim of $200 000 the life insurance sum insured will now be limited to $800 000. Most insurers will provide the insured with the opportunity to buy back some additional coverage after a claim.

ILLUSTRATIVE EXAMPLE 9.2

Kong is single and has no dependants. He has no need for life insurance and therefore a bundled policy which includes life, TPD and trauma is probably not the best choice for him. He should consider TPD and trauma as stand-alone policies and/or he should consider an insurance policy which bundles TPD and trauma cover together.

Income protection insurance

Income protection policies provide cover in the event of the insured being unable to work as a result of accident or sickness.

Benefit

The policy provides a monthly income benefit if the person insured becomes totally disabled by injury or sickness. This benefit is agreed on at the time the policy is effected and is set at a maximum of 75% of pre-tax monthly income derived from personal exertion. Investment income is not taken into account as this will continue regardless of incapacity. As with other personal risk products, there are variations. Some insurers may offer a fortnightly benefit. The benefit payable under the policy is reduced by any sick-leave payment, workers compensation or motor accident compensation, or payments from other insurance for sickness or accident.

If the insured person's income has been erratic over the past 12 months the insurer may decide to issue an 'indemnity type' cover rather than the fixed benefit. Under this approach, the insurer will calculate the monthly benefit on the basis of 75% of the average monthly earnings over the past 12 months.

Benefit period

This is the length of time the insurer will pay the benefit for. The more common periods are 2 or 5 years or to age 65 years. This latter benefit is the one that should be most seriously considered. The main purpose of an insurance cover is to provide for a catastrophe. An event that disables for a long period of time completely changes a person's lifestyle and, in most cases, severely so. Where incapacity lasts for 5 years, in most cases it will be permanent.

In the case of a benefit to age 65, this is usually available only to low-hazard occupations such as white-collar professionals.

Waiting period

All policies have a waiting period where no cover is provided. The length of the waiting period is decided by the insured and can range from 14 days to 2 years. In deciding on a waiting period, people need to take into account the reason they are effecting the cover. Most accidents and illnesses are of short duration and, generally, people are able to manage for that time. Employees have sick leave, and self-employed people will, generally, be able to manage for a short time — they may have set aside an emergency fund for this purpose. The major problem arises when the illness is prolonged, because loss of income cannot be sustained for the long term. Each case needs to be judged on its merits, and people need to work out how long they could manage without an income before deciding on the length of the waiting period. The longer the waiting period the lower the premium.

Guaranteed renewal

The insurer guarantees renewal of the policy each year until some stated age. The premium rate is changed only if the premiums for the whole underwriting class are increased.

Total disablement

The benefit under the policy is paid in the event of the insured person becoming totally disabled during the policy period. An example of a commonly used definition in policies is that you are totally disabled if, due to injury or sickness, you:

- cannot do at least one of the income-producing duties of your occupation
- are not working and are under medical care.

For those in manual occupations, the definition used is that you are totally disabled if, due to injury or sickness:

- during the first 2 years, you cannot do at least one of the income-producing duties of your occupation
- after the first 2 years, because of the same injury or sickness, you are unable to perform any occupation for which you are reasonably suited by education, training or experience
- you are not working and are under medical care.

An even more restrictive wording, rarely seen today, states:

> You are totally disabled if, due to injury or sickness, you are unable to perform any occupation.

Care needs to be exercised in the choice of policy taken. The definition wording that indicates you will be considered disabled only if you are 'unable to perform any occupation' allows the insurance company greater scope in avoiding payment. Such policies will be offered at quite a cheap premium, but this is of little value if it does not provide the cover needed when a serious incapacity occurs.

Partial disablement

With rehabilitation, an insured person may be able to return to partial duties some time before a full recovery is made. Most policies recognise this position and provide a partial benefit in this event. Where the period of total disablement has existed for at least 14 days, after which the insured person is able to return to work in a reduced capacity, a proportionate benefit will be paid from the end of the waiting period. The benefit is calculated by a formula similar to the following:

$$\text{Benefit payable} = \frac{\text{Pre-disablement income} - \text{Post-disablement income}}{\text{Pre-disablement income}} \times \text{Monthly income benefit}$$

Consider the following example. Samantha is a television journalist. She fell and broke her arm badly. For 8 weeks she was unable to work, but after that she was able to undertake some light duties. Her pre-accident income was \$12 000 per month. Following the accident, her income dropped to \$4000. The monthly benefit under the policy is \$9000. Applying the formula results in a benefit payable of \$6000:

$$\begin{aligned}\text{Benefit} &= \frac{\$12\,000 - \$4000}{\$12\,000} \times \$9000 \\ &= \$6000\end{aligned}$$

Additional benefits

Insurers may add several extras to their coverage, including rehabilitation expenses, CPI indexation of benefits, and payments to cover superannuation contributions.

Business overheads (expenses) insurance

This cover is a variation of the income protection policy. Cover under both policies revolves around the fact that the insured person must be incapacitated by accident or illness. Where the income protection policy provides cover for loss of income, the business overheads policy provides cover for 'eligible' business overheads that accrue while the insured person is incapacitated, less any income received during that period. The amount payable, however, cannot exceed the monthly benefit figure nominated by the insured when the policy was taken out.

The policy defines eligible business overheads as recurring costs incurred in the normal day-to-day running of the business, such as, electricity, rent and lease costs. 'Eligible' expenses do not include costs such as capital expenditures and depreciation on land and buildings.

There are several important points to remember about the cover. Unlike the income protection policy, the amount paid is not the benefit stated in the policy. The benefit stated represents the maximum amount payable. The amount paid is the total of the eligible expenses that accrue in that month. Cover can be obtained for 100% of the 'eligible' expenses. Unlike the income protection policy, the benefits under this policy are paid only while the insured person is unable to work — no partial benefit is available.

Business overheads insurance seeks to protect the revenue of the business. Since the policy is for a revenue purpose, the premium will be tax deductible for the business; however, this also means that any payout from the policy will be taxable.

Health insurance policies

Health insurance in Australia is provided in two areas. The public system, Medicare, is available to all Australian residents. In addition to Medicare, there is private health insurance. This is available only to those who purchase insurance from a licensed health insurer.

Medicare

Medicare provides free treatment as a public patient in a public hospital and subsidised treatment by health professionals such as doctors, specialists and optometrists for certain services.

Medicare provides a range of medical and hospital benefits.

- Medical benefits. This includes fees for doctors, specialists, obstetricians, optometrists and other specified specialists, and the cost of X-rays and pathology tests.
- Hospital benefits. Cover is provided for Medicare patients (public patients) in a public hospital. This means that the patient is attended by doctors and specialists nominated by the hospital. Most of the cost is met by Medicare. This includes any physiotherapy, occupational therapy and pharmaceuticals provided by the hospital while the person is an in-patient at the hospital.

The benefit paid by Medicare is 85% of the schedule fee. The remaining 15% is met by the patient. Note that many doctors charge an amount greater than the schedule fee. In those cases, patients must bear the cost of the excess themselves.

Medicare is paid for by way of a levy on income and it is collected with a person's income tax. For a more detailed coverage of Medicare, visit its website at medicare.gov.au.

Private health insurance

Private health insurance provides greater flexibility in where and by whom a person is treated. It also provides cover for services not covered by Medicare.

With private health insurance, patients are able to choose the hospital to be treated in and the specialist who will provide the treatment. In addition, they have access to private wards and, if available, individual rooms.

Health insurers must be licensed and provide cover within the framework of the health insurance legislation. Health insurers must accept cover from all applicants, and the premium rates they apply, which must be approved by government, cannot be loaded for poor health. Waiting periods are imposed by funds for pre-existing or other conditions on first taking out health insurance, but this is for a maximum of 12 months.

Private health insurance covers a wide range of areas including hospital costs in a public or private hospital as a private patient. 'Extras' can be added which provide cover for dental treatment, chiropractic, ambulance, home nursing, podiatry and a range of therapies including physiotherapy, occupational therapy and speech therapy. In addition, private health insurance can cover the cost of prostheses, glasses and contact lenses.

In addition to providing the 'extras' cover, funds offer a range of different hospital covers that suit the needs of people and may allow them to obtain a lower premium. The hospital benefit provided can vary from one that meets the full cost to one where the patient pays a portion of the cost. In addition, covers are available that may exclude some conditions such as obstetrics, heart surgery or hip replacement.

Policies are also available that have an excess, i.e. the patient pays the initial amount of any claim. This is applied only in relation to hospital covers, where an excess of up to $500 for singles ($1000 for couples) a year can be taken.

Private health insurance is not cheap. Spiralling medical costs brought the cover to a near crisis point in the late 1990s. As costs rose, more people dropped out. Those who stayed in included the people who were in poor health. This meant that the claims costs were shared by fewer people and premiums rose further. At the same time, the people who withdrew were now using Medicare and the increased numbers were causing a strain on the public hospital system. Once the participation rate for private health insurance dropped to 30%, the government stepped in with measures aimed at stalling this drop.

Three measures were introduced: the health insurance rebate, the Medicare levy surcharge and the premium loading.

The federal government health rebate provides individuals and their families with a rebate of their health insurance premiums. The size of the rebate depends on age and income as shown in table 9.4.

TABLE 9.4 Federal government health rebate effective for the 2013–14 financial year

	Below threshold	Tier 1	Tier 2	Tier 3
Singles	$88 000 or less	$88 001–102 000	$102 001–136 000	$136 001 or more
Families	$176 000 or less	$176 001–204 000	$204 001–272 000	$272 001 or more
		Rebate		
Aged under 65	30%	20%	10%	0%
Aged 65–69	35%	25%	15%	0%
Aged 70 or over	40%	30%	20%	0%

The Medicare levy surcharge is in addition to the 1.5% Medicare levy. The surcharge is 1.0% and is applied to people without private health insurance who earn a 'high' income, as described in table 9.5. Income includes both taxable income and reportable fringe benefits and the threshold is indexed annually.

TABLE 9.5 Medicare levy surcharge 2013–14

	Below threshold	Tier 1	Tier 2	Tier 3
Singles	$88 000 or less	$88 001–102 000	$102 001 –136 000	$136 001 or more
Families	$176 000 or less	$176 001–204 000	$204 001–272 000	$272 001 or more
		Medicare levy surcharge		
Rate	0.0%	1.0%	1.25%	1.5%

A premium loading of 2% applies for each year a person delays joining a health insurance fund after they turn 30 years of age.

With the wide range of covers now available and the high premiums involved, choosing a cover can be a daunting task. This has led to the advent of health insurance advisers who research the market and provide guidance on the cover that best suits a person's needs and at the most competitive price. These advisers are often able to secure significant savings. One firm has a questionnaire on its website to assist in choosing the cover that best suits — see www.iselect.com.au.

PROFESSIONAL ADVICE

Choosing health insurance

As a financial adviser, you want to see your clients achieve their financial goals. As such, it can be tempting to encourage clients to insure for every possible contingency. Such a level of insurance will be expensive and limit the funds available to the client for investment and potentially day-to-day expenditure.

While you may have a personal view about whether health insurance is suitable for your own circumstances, it is important not to impose this view on your clients. In what circumstances is health insurance of value to a client?

Successive federal governments have introduced measures aimed at reducing pressure on the public hospital system primarily by encouraging individuals to

»

»

take out private health insurance and to use the private health system (although some commentators have questioned whether some of the changes will indeed achieve this objective).

Decisions with respect to health insurance go beyond purely financial considerations. Some clients will place a very high value on the choice that private health insurance generally provides. Some clients will be perfectly fit and make very little use of medical facilities over their lifetime, making health insurance less necessary. The problem, as with all insurance, is how can you tell, with foresight rather than hindsight, whether a client will need health insurance? This is easier to do for clients who have a history of medical problems or anticipate making more use of medical facilities in the future, in which case health insurance will have a higher value.

QUESTION

Your client, Kathy, is a healthy 29-year-old single female earning $100 000 a year. She has no private health insurance. What are the financial and non-financial arguments for Kathy taking out private health insurance? What would you recommend for this client?

Arranging personal risk management insurance through a superannuation fund

Some personal risk insurance policies, such as term life insurance, can be arranged via the individual's superannuation fund and paid out of pre-tax dollars rather than after-tax dollars.

ILLUSTRATIVE EXAMPLE 9.3

Labuki is 40 years old and wishes to take out a $1 million term life insurance policy. The annual premium on this policy is $2100. Labuki's marginal tax rate (MTR) is 40%. If Labuki was to pay for the policy from after-tax dollars she would need $3500 in pre-tax income ($2100/(1 – MTR)). Term life insurance premiums paid by individuals out of after-tax dollars are not tax deductible. If Labuki was to salary sacrifice $2100 to her superannuation fund and ask the superannuation fund to pay the premium she would need only $2100 in pre-tax income. Labuki is $1400 better off in pre-tax dollars or she might prefer to view the gain in after-tax dollars where she would be $840 better off ($1400 × (1 – MTR)). Labuki might use these savings to buy more term life insurance or she might just enjoy more cash in her pocket.

Term life insurance through superannuation

When a person first joins a superannuation fund, the balance will be quite small, but over time this will grow. Having the term insurance arranged through a superannuation fund ensures that in the event of death or serious disability there will always be an adequate amount in the fund to provide for dependants and beneficiaries. A minimum level of term life insurance is an automatic requirement of some funds.

ILLUSTRATIVE EXAMPLE 9.4

Bob is 35 years old and has $100 000 in superannuation. Bob also has a $900 000 term life insurance policy which he has arranged through his superannuation fund. If Bob were to pass away, $1 million would be available in his superannuation fund to provide for dependants and beneficiaries. When Bob is 45 years old he might have $400 000 in superannuation in which case he might reduce his term life insurance coverage to $600 000 — if he were to pass away, $1 million would still be available in the fund. The idea is that insurance coverage is higher when superannuation balances are lower (and insurance premiums are lower) and insurance coverage is lower when superannuation balances are higher (and insurance premiums are higher). Refer to figure 9.1.

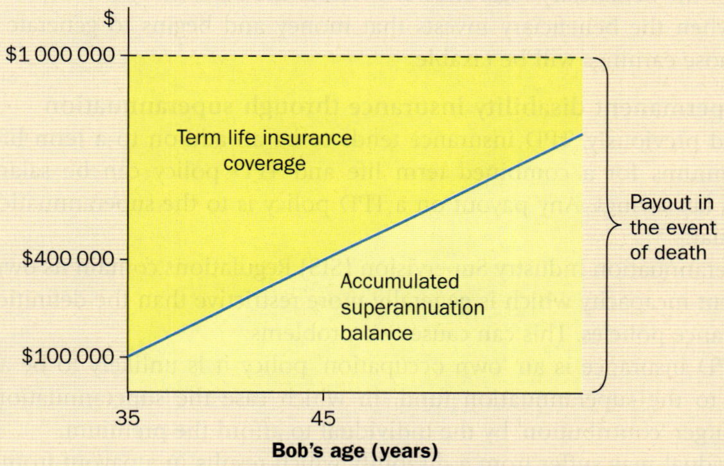

FIGURE 9.1 Term life insurance through superannuation

Pre-tax **salary sacrifice** contributions made to superannuation are normally taxed at 15%; however, when the 'contribution' is for the purpose of paying a term life insurance premium the contribution itself is not added to the taxable income of the superannuation fund. It thereby avoids tax which means the full 'contribution' can go to paying the term life insurance premium.

salary sacrifice where an employee asks their employer to take some of their income and redirect this to paying for a benefit on behalf of the employee; the most commonly salary sacrificed benefit is superannuation

When the term life insurance premium is paid by the fund, any payout on that policy as a result of the death of the individual is to the superannuation fund and not to the estate of the deceased. The death of the member is, however, a **condition of release** which allows the trustees of the superannuation fund to pay out the member's account balance which also includes the proceeds of the insurance payout. The trustees will either be bound to pay out the balance to a nominated individual because the deceased had made a binding death benefit nomination, or the trustees will use their discretion to pay out the account to an individual or to the deceased's estate.

condition of release criteria that, if satisfied, enable an individual to withdraw their money from superannuation

If the trustee pays out the account to a dependant of the member, the money will be received by the dependant tax free. If the trustee pays out the account to a non-dependant, tax will be payable. The amount of tax payable depends on the composition of the account. The account may comprise a tax-free component, a taxed component and an untaxed component. The taxation treatment of these components is discussed in chapter 11, which deals with retirement planning.

Given the taxation implications, if an individual seeks to save money by arranging their term life insurance through their superannuation fund, if possible, it would be better to leave this money to a dependant and redirect other estate assets to non-dependants. If an individual does arrange their term life insurance through their superannuation fund and this money is then left to a non-dependant, they should understand that some or all of their tax savings will be lost when the funds are paid out. Just how much is lost will be a function of the beneficiaries marginal tax rate and the composition of the superannuation account.

If an individual arranges their term life insurance outside a superannuation environment using after-tax dollars to pay the premium, any payout on the policy is not taxed in the hands of the beneficiary regardless of whether the beneficiary is a dependant or not. However, when the beneficiary invests that money and begins to generate investment earnings, those earnings will be taxable.

Total and permanent disability insurance through superannuation

As discussed previously, TPD insurance tends to be an add-on to a term life insurance policy. Premiums for a combined term life and TPD policy can be salary sacrificed resulting in tax savings. Any payout on a TPD policy is to the superannuation fund not the individual.

The Superannuation Industry Supervision (SIS) Regulations contain its own definition of permanent incapacity which is generally more restrictive than the definition found in many insurance policies. This can cause two problems:

1. If the TPD insurance is an 'own occupation' policy it is unlikely to be a deductible expense to the superannuation fund, in which case the superannuation fund will need a larger 'contribution' by the individual to afford the premium.
2. An individual may suffer from a disability which results in a payout from the insurer to the superannuation fund but the nature of the disability does not satisfy a condition of release from the superannuation fund. This could be a significant problem if the person is considerably younger than their **preservation age**. Preservation age is discussed in chapter 10, which deals with superannuation.

preservation age
the minimum age at which funds can be withdrawn from superannuation

If term life and TPD policy premiums are paid from after-tax dollars, they are not tax deductible for the individual, nor is any payout taxable. If term life and TPD premiums are paid via a superannuation fund, any TPD benefits paid to recipients over the age of 60 will be received tax free. If TPD benefits are paid to a recipient under 60 years of age some tax will be payable. The amount of tax payable depends on the composition of the superannuation account and whether the payout is a lump sum or an income stream.

Income protection through superannuation

An individual may decide to pay their income protection insurance premiums via pre-tax salary sacrifice contributions to their superannuation fund. Provided the income protection policy covers a period of temporary disability which lasts more than 2 years, the 'contributions' will be a deductible expense to the fund. As a consequence, the full contribution (premium) would pass through the superannuation fund to the insurer.

The individual would have to satisfy an SIS 'temporary incapacity condition of release' for benefits under the policy to pass through to the individual. Most insurers have aligned their policies to ensure the terms under which the income protection policy pays out are consistent with these SIS regulations.

Income protection premiums are tax deductible when paid by an individual out of after-tax dollars, so the tax savings previously discussed in relation to term life and TPD insurance are not applicable here.

Any payout on an income protection policy is assessable income for the individual regardless of whether the premium was paid by the superannuation fund or the individual. An individual may still decide to organise their income protection policy through their superannuation fund because the fund has some buying power with insurers, which means that the fund can achieve lower premiums than the individual could.

Term life, TPD and income protection policies are all designed to protect against a loss of future income. As such, for some people it makes sense to consolidate these policies and hold them all within a superannuation environment.

Group underwriting

Insurance policies can be either individually underwritten or underwritten as a group. A group policy occurs when individuals who have a specific relationship with each other are collectively underwritten. For example, an employer may take out a group policy for employees, or a superannuation fund trustee might take out a group policy which covers members of the fund. Where a group policy is taken out by an employer, the employer is generally the owner of the policy. Similarly, where a group policy is taken out by a superannuation fund trustee, the trustee is generally the owner of the policy. Group policies are available for term life, TPD and income protection. Many large superannuation funds provide a base level of group term life and TPD cover.

In **underwriting** a group policy, the insurer calculates the group's characteristics and sets premiums accordingly. Group insurance does not take into account the risk associated with particular individuals and, as such, it is a useful means by which individuals with particular health risks can achieve cover at a reasonable price. However, this means that group insurance involves some cross-subsidy from healthy to less healthy individuals. The insurer attempts to manage this risk by insisting on the following.

underwriting
the process by which the insurer assesses the risk associated with an individual or a group of individuals and provides insurance coverage at a price commensurate with the risk

- *A minimum rate of acceptance.* If only 10% of new members accept the group insurance, it is likely these would be 'unhealthy' people (attempting to take advantage of the reasonable price despite their individual health risks). This is often referred to as **adverse selection against the fund**. To avoid this adverse selection the underwriter might insist, for example, that at least 75% of new members accept the insurance.
- *Acceptance within a set time.* New members have a limited period of time to accept the insurance. If no time limit was specified, individuals may wait until they are 'unhealthy' before joining the fund.
- *The amount of insurance is fixed.* If the amount of insurance was not fixed, 'unhealthy' members could significantly increase their level of insurance and thereby make an adverse selection against the fund. Some superannuation funds allow individuals to buy additional units of insurance, but the number of additional units is usually limited. If an individual wishes to increase their insurance beyond this level, it would need to be done on an individually underwritten basis.

adverse selection against the fund
where individuals are able to make choices which alter the risk profile of a fund and which can potentially limit the fund's ability to meet its commitments and/or unfairly shift obligations between members

If a policy for an employer-sponsored group pays a benefit, the benefit is paid to the employer who in turn will pass this benefit on to the employee. The employee will receive the benefit in the form of an employment termination payment. If a policy for a superannuation fund trustee-sponsored group pays a benefit, the benefit is paid to the superannuation fund. The release of the benefit to members and the taxation treatment of the benefit are as previously discussed under the section on arranging insurance through a superannuation fund.

If an individual leaves a superannuation fund, they may not be able to transfer their insurance. This means they would need to take out new cover which might be assessed at their current age and health condition. This is an important consideration for anyone considering exercising their right of choice to move to a new superannuation fund. The promise of lower management fees in a new fund could be more than offset by a higher cost of insurance.

LO 4 House and contents risk management

This section discusses the identification and evaluation of house and contents risks, the control measures for house and contents risks and the financing of house and contents risks.

Identification of house and contents risks

A range of perils can cause damage to these assets, such as fire, storm, water damage, burglary, impact by vehicles and earthquake. Items of a more fragile nature are subject to breakage.

Evaluation of house and contents risks

In most cases, the value of an item can be easily ascertained. With a house, the value relates only to the building, and does not include the land, since the land will not normally suffer damage. The question to be asked is what amount will be needed to meet any loss. In the event of a total loss, the building will need to be replaced, so a sum sufficient to rebuild the property will be needed. This may well be greater than the market value of the building. As a building gets older its value will diminish, but maintenance and extensions can change this. What increases and keeps property prices increasing is principally the value of the land. With house contents, the same will apply. A 5-year-old washing machine will have a lower value than a new one. In the event of a loss there needs to be sufficient funds to purchase a new one.

Control measures for house and contents risks

Measures can be taken to minimise the damage that can occur, such as the use of smoke detectors which gain attention and facilitate summons of help to put out a fire. Burglar alarms, deadlocks and other fixed protection on the house reduce the risk of burglary. An important point to bear in mind is that, by making a house more difficult for a burglar to gain entry, the more likely it is that the burglar will move on to another property that is easier to gain access to.

Financing measures for house and contents risks

Control measures will not stop all losses occurring so there is the need to provide financing should a loss occur. This is generally achieved by insurance. Some amount of retention can be undertaken by using an excess. Care needs to be taken in arriving at a sum insured so that, in the event of a major loss, the sum insured is sufficient to replace the property that has been damaged or destroyed.

Two types of policies are available in the marketplace. The more common one is a replacement value policy (often referred to as a 'new for old' policy). In the event of a loss, this cover provides new items to replace those lost or destroyed, even though the items lost may be several years old. The same also applies to the house — the policy will provide a new house in the event of a loss. The other type of policy is an indemnity value policy. This cover, which was the original type of cover, pays only the value of the property at the time of the loss — depreciation is taken into account.

In arriving at a sum insured under the replacement value cover, the property covered by the policy needs to be included at its replacement value price. In the case of contents insurance, this will include all the contents of the client's house. It is necessary to do a detailed calculation to arrive at an adequate sum insured. The result invariably surprises. Keep in mind that, when calculating replacement value, you are using current prices even though the original purchase price may have been somewhat lower and the item is now several years old. Contents that were purchased some years ago for \$50 000 may well have a replacement value today of \$100 000. There is no shortcut to the calculation — it is necessary to go through the house room by room and calculate the total value. Some insurers have guides that list items commonly found in different rooms to help you calculate the total amount.

A builder will be able to give an indication of the replacement cost of a building. Working on a standard figure per square may not be accurate as it does not take into account the quality of the fittings and the finish to the house.

When considering policies, you must be aware that some policies incorporate a **co-insurance clause** (or average clause). The purpose of this clause is to penalise policyholders if they fail to insure for the full value of the property. The use by insurers of this clause is diminishing — many are electing not to include it in their policies. Where it is used, the effect of this clause is to reduce the amount of the loss in proportion to the amount of **underinsurance**. The calculation recognises the difficulty in arriving at an accurate sum insured, so the calculation is made on only 80% of the full value.

co-insurance clause a clause in an insurance contract which reduces the claimable loss in proportion to the amount of underinsurance

underinsurance where the payout from an insurance policy as a result of an event is not able to restore the individual to the financial position they were in prior to the event

The application of the clause is shown in the case where a house, the full value of which is \$300 000, is insured for only \$160 000, but the partial damage amounts to \$150 000. The calculation is as follows:

$$\frac{\$160\,000}{80\% \times \$300\,000} \times \$150\,000 = \$100\,000$$

The insurance company would cover only \$100 000 of the \$150 000 loss, leaving the owners of the house with an amount of \$50 000 to cover from their own resources.

Keep in mind that many insurers do not use this clause so check the policy before taking it out.

The importance of insurance and using an adequate sum insured must be stressed. Following major bushfires and widespread storm damage, the fact invariably emerges that many people have no insurance or are underinsured by as much as 50%. Particularly with bushfires, the outcome may be a total loss, so the owners are looking at a considerable shortfall in the policy payout. In the 2009 Victorian Black Saturday bushfires, tragically 173 people lost their lives and 2029 homes were destroyed. It has been estimated that 25% of the homes were uninsured. Of those homes that were insured, 80% were underinsured.

Domestic policies are usually offered in a package which includes house, contents and liability insurance.

House and contents insurance

There are broadly three types of policies used in the area of house and contents insurance. A brief description of each follows.

- A policy that covers 'All risks of loss or damage'. Its cover is very broad and the premium is more expensive.
- A policy that **lists the perils** to be covered. The following are included in most covers:
  - fire
  - explosion
  - lightning or thunderbolt
  - earthquake
  - theft
  - vandalism
  - water or other liquid
  - falling trees, branches or aerials
  - damage by animals
  - riot
  - storm, rain or flash flood
  - glass breakage.
- A policy that provides a cover for 'All risks of loss or damage' in relation to valuables only. This cover is taken in conjunction with the listed perils policy where a broader cover is required for property at and away from the premises.

listed perils
an insurance contract which lists the events (perils) covered. Therefore, events not listed are not covered.

The main policy exclusions include:

- damage when property has been left unoccupied for more than 60 days
- where the loss or damage is deliberately caused with intent to defraud
- damage caused by structural defects and faulty workmanship in the construction of the building or lack of maintenance to the building
- damage to property caused by tree lopping or the actions of trees, plants or their roots
- accidental damage to TV screens, ceramic stove tops, glass in picture frames, radios and clocks.

House cover

The cover on the house is usually for replacement value, and is often referred to as a 'new for old' cover. There are some variations of this in the marketplace. The original type of cover was an indemnity value policy which provided cover for 'market value'. In other words, depreciation was taken into account. The market value would, in most cases, be lower than the cost to rebuild the house. Since the point of replacement value cover is to provide the insured person with sufficient funds to rebuild the house, the market value or indemnity value policy would not achieve this.

Contents cover

Cover is normally provided on a replacement value basis (new for old). In addition to cover against the listed perils, the policy may also provide for temporary accommodation, where the insured premises are uninhabitable due to an insured peril. As well, cover is often provided for credit card fraud, food spoilage and burning out of electric motors.

Liability insurance

Public liability covers liability arising out of the ownership or occupation of the property and is usually for a fairly large amount, e.g. $10 million. Bear in mind that awards for bodily injury can run into several million dollars. One not unusual case concerned a tenant left paraplegic after he fell from an upper floor balcony of a block of flats where the external lighting was not working. The damages were assessed at $4 million and legal costs were around $600 000. Suddenly $10 million doesn't seem such a large amount after all.

LO 5

Motor vehicle risk management

This section discusses the identification and evaluation of motor vehicle risks, and the control measures and financing for motor vehicle risks.

Identification and evaluation of motor vehicle risks

There are two types of motor vehicle risks — damage to the vehicle itself and loss or damage to third parties or their property. The former is limited to the amount of the repairs and will probably not exceed the value of the vehicle. The latter can run into millions of dollars — serious bodily injury to a third party could result in very large losses if legal liability is established.

Control measures and financing for motor vehicle risks

Control measures involve fitting the vehicle with a car alarm and undertaking advanced driving courses to improve driving skills. Financing measures are mainly through the use of insurance policies. Retention would be considered in relation to small losses only; this can be achieved by taking an excess on the motor policy.

Types of motor vehicle insurance policies

There are four main types of motor vehicle insurance policies. Compulsory third party (CTP) insurance, as its name implies is compulsory by law. Comprehensive motor insurance (CMI), Fire, theft and third-party property damage insurance (FTTPPD) and Third-party property cover (TPPO) insurance are not compulsory. It is necessary to apply to an insurer for cover, with the insurer deciding acceptance in each case and advising the terms and conditions. Each of these policies is briefly described in the following sections.

Compulsory third party (CTP) insurance

This policy is compulsory by law and is effected, usually, at the same time as the vehicle's registration. The policy provides for the legal liability of the driver arising out of the use of the vehicle. The nature of the legal liability varies from state to state. In some states, the scheme is a 'no fault' one. This means that it is not necessary to prove fault on the part of the driver. It is necessary to show only that the injury arose out of the use of the vehicle. In other states, the scheme is fault-based or partially fault-based.

Regardless of the type of scheme, the compensation paid is by way of a weekly benefit. The injured party's medical and hospital expenses are met as well. Where compensation is sought for permanent impairment, the schemes will provide compensation only for 'serious permanent injury', which is defined by each state Act, and the amount payable is limited.

agreed value cover generally applies to motor vehicle insurance where the insured believes their vehicle is worth more than market value and therefore they reach an agreement with the insurer to insure the vehicle at a higher value with a commensurately higher premium

Comprehensive motor insurance (CMI)

This is the broadest of the policies and has two main sections.

1. Damage to the vehicle itself. This section provides cover for damage to the vehicle, whether for repairs or if the vehicle is a total loss. Under a motor policy, a total loss applies when the cost of repairs exceeds the value of the vehicle. As the vehicle gets older and its value reduces, a situation could arise where the vehicle is quite repairable but the cost of the repairs exceeds the value of the vehicle. The insurer's liability, however, is limited to the vehicle's value. Thus, the sum insured on a motor policy is usually expressed as 'market value'. The insurer uses the value of the vehicle in the market at the time of the loss. It is possible, however, to have an **agreed value cover**. This is used in a situation where the insured feels that the condition of the vehicle is such that its value is greater than that of similar vehicles in the market. In such a case, the insured and insurer agree on the value of the vehicle.
   Common exclusions in this section of the policy are:
   - contents of the vehicle other than standard tools and accessories
   - claims for loss of use or any consequential losses
   - wear and tear and mechanical or electrical breakdown.
2. Third-party liability. This section provides cover for the insured or the driver (driving with the insured's consent) for their legal liability in relation to property damage as a result of an accident arising out of the use of the vehicle. This section pays, in addition, legal costs incurred in defending the action. The amount of cover provided is large — $50 million is not unusual.
   The following provisions are the main ones that apply to both sections of the policy.
   - The driver must be licensed.
   - The blood-alcohol level of the driver must not exceed the limit permitted by law.
   - The driver must have the insured's consent to drive the vehicle. (If not, it would be theft, which is still covered, but the insurer could bring an action against the driver for the cost of the claim.)
   - The vehicle must not carry more passengers than is permitted by law (the number is specified in the vehicle registration).
   - The policy is subject to an excess. This is the initial amount of any loss that must be borne by the insured. There is a basic excess to which an age and/or new driver excess amount may be added.

Fire, theft and third-party property damage insurance (FTTPPD)

This cover contains the two sections of the comprehensive policy but the own damage section cover is limited to fire and theft of the owner's vehicle. This policy is used for an older vehicle where the value is lower. The premium is cheaper than the comprehensive cover.

Third-party property cover only (TPPO)

This policy provides cover for third-party property damage only. It also is used for older vehicles.

Uninsured motorists extension cover can also be included in either the FTTPPD or TPPO covers. It provides cover when the insured's vehicle is damaged as the result of an accident where the driver of the other vehicle is uninsured. If the insured is not at fault, and so long as the name and address of the other driver are supplied to the insurer, the damage to the insured's vehicle is covered up to a specified amount. This is usually around $3000.

LO 6 Other insurances

A range of other non-business general insurances are available including sickness and accident insurance, consumer credit insurance and travel insurance. Each of these insurances is discussed briefly below.

Sickness and accident insurance

This cover is a restricted form of an income protection policy provided by life insurers. The policy provides cover for both capital and weekly benefits. Capital benefits provide cover for death or total disablement as a result of an accident. The weekly benefits are provided in the event of temporary disablement as a result of accident or illness. In the case of illness, the incapacity must be of more than 7 days duration.

The main difference between this policy and an income protection policy is that the sickness and accident policy defines an accident as being of 'violent, accidental, external and visible means'. The income protection policy does not define 'accident' and is therefore much wider in the events it provides cover for. The sickness and accident policy usually has a maximum benefit period of 2 years for sickness. Another important difference relates to the cancellation provision. A sickness and accident policy contains a cancellation clause and must be renewed each year. The insurer can refuse renewal. Income protection policies cannot be cancelled by the insurer.

The main exclusions are injuries from war, nuclear weapons or radiation, deliberate self-injury, and conditions sustained while under the influence of alcohol or drugs, professional sporting activities, and flying other than as a passenger in a licensed plane.

Consumer credit insurance

This is a sickness and accident cover designed for a specific purpose. It provides protection for those who have entered into any type of consumer finance contract where they are required to make regular payments. The policy includes an unemployment benefit also.

The policy provides for the payment of the periodic instalment if the insured person is incapacitated by way of accident, sickness or unemployment. In the event of death, the policy will pay out the contract.

The main exclusions are:

- a deliberately self-inflicted injury
- drug or alcohol addiction
- the insured becoming voluntarily unemployed or if unemployment results from a contract expiring.

Travel insurance

Travel insurance policies are a collection of different covers in the one policy, including the following.

- *Luggage and personal effects*. This provides cover for loss or damage to the traveller's luggage and personal effects. The policy usually excludes damage to the baggage (not contents), including chipping, denting, and mechanical or electrical breakdown. The policy also generally excludes the loss of currency, travellers cheques and similar forms of payment. Lost or stolen items must be reported to the police within 24 hours and before a claim can be made.
- *Medical expenses*. This cover includes medical expenses incurred on a trip, including hospital, medical, surgical and associated treatment provided by a qualified

practitioner, as well as travel and accommodation expenses incurred as a result of illness or injury. Cover is also provided for the non-refundable section of the accommodation and travel costs in the event of the cancellation of the trip owing to the death or disablement of the insured or an accompanying traveller, the death in Australia of a specified person or the collapse of the tour operator.

- *Personal liability*. Included is a personal liability policy that provides cover for any negligent act involving bodily injury or property damage. The policy excludes damage to property in the insured's custody or control, the use of a motor vehicle, contractual liability and liability arising out of AIDS.

LO 7 Liability risk management

There are three broad areas from which a legal liability can arise.

- *Common law*. The most common area in which liability can be incurred here is due to negligence, e.g. where a financial adviser was negligent in giving advice.
- *Statute law*. This refers to liability arising under an Act of Parliament. For example, liability in relation to an injury resulting from a faulty product may exist under the *Competition and Consumer Act 2010*.
- *Contract*. People can make themselves liable beyond the areas covered by common law or statute law by agreeing under a contract to be liable for any loss or damage.

This section discusses the identification and evaluation of liability risks, and the control measures and financing for liability risks.

Identification and evaluation of liability risks

Liability at the personal level is increasing. People sustaining injury or suffering damage to property are more prepared to pursue a legal action. This is in part encouraged by the legal fraternity and firms that provide representation on a 'no win no fee' basis. A significant rise in the number of negligence actions has resulted in the liability crisis of recent years and large premium increases for liability insurance. The importance of having adequate liability insurance is now evident.

Control measures and financing for liability risks

With liability risks, an effective control measure is simply taking steps to minimise the chance of loss in relation to potential loss situations that have been identified. For example, in a financial planner's office, the use of a checklist helps ensure that nothing has been overlooked in gathering information in order to provide advice to a client. An area overlooked can result in incorrect advice and possible legal action. Because of the amounts that can be involved, insurance is the best means of handling liability risks. Liability losses do not occur often, but when they do the amounts involved are rarely small. To this end, retention is not usually appropriate.

Regulations of the *Corporations Act 2001* were amended in 2007 with respect to professional indemnity (PI) insurance. Holders of an Australian Financial Services Licence (AFSL) must have adequate professional indemnity insurance. ASIC Regulatory Guide RG 126 *Compensation and insurance arrangements for AFS licensees* provides guidance on the minimum requirements for PI insurance cover as follows:

> Where a financial services licensee has revenue from retail clients of less than $2 million they should have PI cover of at least $2 million which includes the ability to meet an

individual claim of up to $2 million. Where a financial services licensee has revenue from retail clients of more than $2 million they should have PI cover at least equal to their expected revenue from financial services which includes the ability to meet an individual claim of up to $2 million.

PI insurance is a form of business insurance to assist a business in meeting any claims which are made against it. The primary purpose of PI insurance is not to act as a form of consumer compensation scheme. In some cases a consumer may make a valid claim against a business; however, the claim is not covered by the terms of the PI insurance in which case the business will need to fund the compensation from their own resources. In some cases the amount paid out by the PI insurer may be less than the amount the business has to pay in settlement with the consumer, in which case the business will need to fund the difference. This problem is further compounded when the business has insufficient capital to fund the payment and in extreme cases where the business itself has collapsed. The collapse of high profile financial advisory firms such as Storm Financial, Opes Prime and Westpoint highlighted the need for advisers to have adequate PI insurance and also raised the issue over whether there should be a national compensation arrangement for consumers of financial services.

In 2010 the Federal Government commissioned a review of compensation arrangements for consumers of financial services and in 2011 as part of the FOFA reform process published that review. The review recognised the difficulty of trying to transform what is essentially a PI insurance service to business into an insurance compensation scheme for consumers. The review suggests a number of means by which consumers can be better protected within the current PI framework including strengthening the capital adequacy of financial advisers so that they have the financial capacity to meet claims as they fall due.

Whether the review of compensation arrangements for consumers of financial services will ultimately lead to legislative change remains to be seen. There is, however, considerable uncertainty associated with the broad scope of the FOFA reforms and uncertainty for insurers is generally reflected in higher premiums.

It is important to remember that PI insurance does not, in any circumstances, cover the adverse consequences for an investor of a significant downturn in investment markets.

LO 8 Implementation and review

With risks identified, control and financing measures are developed and implemented to enable the systematic management of the identified risks.

The next step, a very important one, is the ongoing review of the program. The changes people experience bring with them a need to change the financial plan. A financial planner needs to systematically revise a client's financial plan to take into account the effects of any changes in circumstances. A periodic review should be undertaken, and it is important to review the pure risk aspects of the plan at the same time. A common premium instalment date on the insurance covers is an ideal time to undertake the review.

Summary

It is worth reflecting on the case study of Simon and Vikki that we introduced at the start of this chapter. Risk management is a systematic approach to the identification and management of risks faced. Simon and Vikki need to identify and quantify the risks they face including personal and property risks. Having identified the risks they need to plan how to control and manage those risks. Simon spoke of controlling some of the property risks by having good security systems in place; nonetheless, some risk remains. Where risk remains it needs to be financed or transferred. Where a risk is relatively small it might be financed from the savings of Simon and Vikki; however, many risks will be too expensive to finance through personal savings and will need to be transferred via insurance. The death of Simon or Vikki would seriously compromise the capacity of the remaining partner to meet their mortgage commitments. However, insurance comes at a cost and a decision must be made over whether the cost is affordable and if it represents a fair trade for the risk being exchanged.

Simon and Vikki face a wide range of insurable risks. In this chapter we have reviewed the need for personal risk, property, motor vehicle and liability insurance policies as well as the main characteristics of these policies. To the extent that Simon and Vikki manage their risk exposure through insurance they will need to deal with insurers by acting with the utmost good faith. To do otherwise might result in the insurer not paying the claim and therefore leaving Simon and Vikki still exposed to risk.

Simon and Vikki should also consider arranging some or all of their personal insurance requirements through their respective superannuation funds in order to pay their premiums in the most tax-effective manner.

Having developed a risk management plan, the plan must be implemented and regularly reviewed. At the time that Simon and Vikki pay their annual insurance premiums they should review the adequacy of their insurance coverage in light of any changes in their circumstances.

We have discussed in this chapter some of the ways that risk can be controlled and financed without the use of insurance. Nonetheless insurance remains the principal means of providing for the potential of serious losses.

Professional application questions

9.1 What is the difference between pure and speculative risk? What are the main categories of pure risk?

9.2 The Bellamys, Ben and Laura, ages 38 and 35 respectively, have three children aged 8, 10 and 13. Ben is a manager at the local Safeway supermarket and Laura runs a secretarial service from home. Laura's business has been growing quite steadily and currently produces an annual income of $30 000. The Bellamys own their house, which is valued at $300 000. Their mortgage is $200 000. They have two cars, a current model Commodore and a 7-year-old Toyota. Identify and discuss the various risks to which the Bellamys are exposed.

9.3 What are the five main steps in any systematic risk management process?

9.4 What is risk pooling? How can insurers reduce the size of the pool in order to reduce the average level of risk within the pool? Is there any limit to how small the pool can be?

9.5 What is the difference between indemnity and non-indemnity insurance products?

9.6 Sally has a small amount of life insurance provided through her superannuation fund. She is thinking of applying for additional coverage but is worried about filling in an application form and/or having to attend a medical examination.

Six months ago Sally was diagnosed with hypertension and in response to this she gave up smoking. She is quite confident that her health has improved as a result although she has not been back to a doctor to confirm this. Given her improved health Sally's partner has suggested that she not mention the hypertension in any application, but Sally is unsure of the consequences of failing to declare her medical history correctly. Advise Sally.

9.7 How can insurers use severity limitations to reduce their risk exposure?

9.8 Your client, Nya, is 23 years old, single and a non-smoker. She has just received a quote from an insurance company for $1 million in term life insurance. The annual premium would be $1212. In your opinion, is it worth it?

9.9 Which policy is likely to attract the higher premium: a TPD 'own' occupation insurance or a TPD 'any' occupation insurance?

9.10 Fiona and Greg are both aged 35 years, both earn the same level of income ($80 000) and both work in the same occupation. Fiona is upset to learn that her quote for income protection insurance is more expensive than Greg's. The quotes the couple received were as follows. For a benefit of $60 000 p.a. (for each of Fiona and Greg), Fiona's quote was $634.80 for a 30-day delay before the insurance would be paid and $429.60 for a 60-day delay. Greg's was $368.40 for a 30-day delay and $203.40 for a 60-day delay. Provide reasons why Fiona's quote for income protection insurance is more expensive than Greg's.

9.11 Isamu has an annual income of $90 000. He has savings in a bank account of $300 and has accumulated 12 days of unused sick leave. What amount would you recommend Isamu takes as a monthly benefit under an income protection policy and what deferment period might he select before insurance cover would be provided? Give reasons for your answer.

9.12 Mio Striker has a 2007 Ford Falcon valued at $5000. She asks your advice as to which motor vehicle insurance cover she should have. Discuss the cover provided by the different types of motor policies and suggest one for Mio, giving your reasons.

Professional application exercises

Basic	*
Moderate	**
Challenging	***

9.13 Income protection insurance — partial disablement *

Under an income protection policy, Ellen Tucker, who has been disabled, is receiving $4000 a month. Ellen has made a good recovery and is now able to resume some duties. Her salary while working reduced hours is $4000 per month, whereas her pre-accident salary was $6000 per month. What partial disability benefit would be paid under the policy?

9.14 Co-insurance *

The market value of the Smiths' home and contents is $400 000. However, Mr Smith insured the home and contents for only $300 000. If fire caused $200 000 damage, what amount is the insurance company liable to pay if the policy included a co-insurance clause and the company required a market value of 80%?

9.15 Income protection insurance — agreed value versus indemnity policy *

Danni is earning $8000 per month and takes out a fixed benefit (agreed value) income protection policy for 60% of her monthly income. Six months after commencing the policy her income falls to $6000 per month. After several months of earning $6000 per month she falls ill and is unable to work.

(a) What will be the monthly benefit under the policy?

(b) If Danni had an indemnity policy rather than a fixed benefit policy what would be the monthly benefit under the policy?

9.16 Term life insurance premiums * *

KGB Insurance offer term life insurance under the following terms:

- guaranteed renewal
- cover to age 75
- sum insured remains constant.

The indicative monthly premiums for $1 million coverage are:

Age	21 to 34	35 to 39	40 to 44	45 to 49	50 to 54
Non-smoker	$101	$112	$148	$223	$387
Smoker	$161	$225	$285	$485	$808

(a) Why do the premiums increase as the age of the insured increases?

(b) In percentage terms, approximately how much more expensive is term life insurance for a smoker than a non-smoker?

(c) If the renewal of the policy was at the discretion of the insurer, would you expect the premiums to be higher or lower? Why?

(d) If the sum insured was indexed to CPI, would you expect the premiums to be higher or lower? Why?

(e) If the term of the insurance was to age 65 rather than age 75, would you expect the premiums to be higher or lower? Why?

(f) Ashleigh and her husband are both 45, non-smokers and considering term life insurance. Ashleigh believes she is being discriminated against by being asked to pay the same premium as her husband. Why does she hold this view? Do you agree?

9.17 Paying term life insurance through superannuation * *

(a) If a term life insurance premium is $1000 and the client decides to pay their premium out of after-tax dollars, how much pre-tax income will an individual need if their marginal tax rate is:

(i) 0%?

(ii) 19.0%?

(iii) 32.5%?

(iv) 37.0%?

(v) 45.0%?

(b) If a term life insurance premium is $1000, how much pre-tax income will an individual need if they decide to salary sacrifice their premium into superannuation?

(c) Besides the cost differential between (a) and (b), what are the advantages/disadvantages of paying term life insurance premiums through a superannuation fund versus paying for them out of after-tax dollars?

9.18 Stepped versus level premium * *

GAI Insurance are offering the following insurance premiums to a 30 year old male non-smoker with a sum insured of $1 000 000.

Age	Stepped	Level
30	$740	$1200
31	$750	$1200
32	$761	$1200
33	$773	$1200
34	$787	$1200
35	$803	$1200
36	$821	$1200
37	$842	$1200
38	$866	$1200
39	$894	$1200
40	$926	$1200
50	$2150	$1200
55	$4400	$1200

(a) Why do stepped insurance premiums differ from level insurance premiums?
(b) If your client is 31 and is unsure whether they have a long term need for life insurance should they take out a stepped or level premium policy?
(c) If your client was 50 should they take out a stepped or level premium policy?

9.19 Health insurance ✱✱✱

Longwei is 33 years old and single. He is looking to take out some health insurance coverage. Longwei earns $112 000 per year and he has not had health insurance coverage in the past. He has entered his personal details and preferences into the iselect.com.au website and has been given a quote of $178 per month before any loadings or rebates are applied.

(a) Given that Longwei is over 30 years of age how will premium loading be applied?
(b) How much health rebate will Longwei be entitled to?
(c) What will be the net annual cost of the insurance after allowing for (a) and (b) above?
(d) If Longwei decides not to take out health insurance how much Medicare levy surcharge will he have to pay?

9.20 The multiple approach to determining the sum insured ✱✱✱

Huan is married and has two teenage children. He has a detailed retirement plan in place. He is 40 years old and he hopes to retire in 20 years from now when he is 60, by which time his superannuation should be sufficient to afford a comfortable life in retirement for himself and his partner. He is, however, concerned that he has insufficient life insurance and he would like to ensure that he has sufficient to cover any loss of earnings caused by his death during that 20 year period. He currently earns $100 000 per annum.

(a) Using a simple multiple approach how much life insurance coverage will Huan need to cover his loss of earnings for the 20 year period?
(b) If Huan were to pass away in the first year and the amount calculated in (a) above was invested at 3% for 20 years what would be the present value of this insurance payout?

(c) If Huan were to pass away in the first year and the amount calculated in (a) above was invested at 3% for 20 years and the inflation rate was 3%, what would be the present value of this insurance payout?

(d) If the rate at which funds are invested is greater (less) than the inflation rate what implications does this have for the sum insured?

(e) Assuming that Huan does not pass away in the first year of insurance what implications does this have for the sum insured (see figure 9.1)?

CASE STUDY

Establishing personal insurance needs

Eddie and Kaye Turner, aged 39 and 37 respectively, have four children aged 4, 6, 8 and 10. They own their home, which has a current market value of $500 000, and have a mortgage of $150 000. Eddie is a self-employed butcher who employs three staff. Eddie and Kaye are in partnership and share profits equally. Eddie's annual income is $80 000. Kaye works part-time helping in the butcher's shop and also part-time as a school's teacher aide; she also receives $15 000 as a salary from the school.

Both Eddie and Kaye contribute to superannuation funds. Eddie has an accumulation fund which currently has a balance of $250 000. Kaye joined her fund more recently and has a balance of $100 500. Eddie has effected a term life cover on his life for $200 000 with Kaye named as the beneficiary. Kaye does not have any term life insurance cover.

Eddie and Kaye have assets which are mainly in the butcher's shop, totalling $150 000. The Turners have a car each. Eddie's is a 2014 model which is leased and has $30 000 outstanding on it at present. Kaye has a 2009 van so that she can transport the children to school and various sporting clubs. Her van is valued at $10 000 and is fully paid for. Personal loans, credit cards and other outstanding debts amount to $20 000.

The family's monthly expenses amount to $8000. The Turners feel that all their children should receive a university education and expect them to be dependent until they turn 21 years of age. They expect to contribute a total of $200 000 to the cost of the children's university education. As each child ceases to be dependent, the monthly expenses will reduce by $1000 a month. Eddie's life expectancy is 82 and Kaye's is 86.

QUESTIONS

1 Calculate the amount of cover required to provide for the family's future needs in the event of:

(a) Eddie's death

(b) Kaye's death.

2 You have advised the Turners of the amount of insurance cover they need. They find it hard to believe that such a large amount is needed. They say that, by insuring for a lower amount and investing the funds, the required amount could be achieved. Explain to them the problem with this approach.

3 Discuss the need for the following covers for both Eddie and Kaye.
   (a) Total and permanent disability
   (b) Trauma
   (c) Income protection

4 When talking about income protection insurance, Eddie and Kaye ask if there is some way they could cover their business overheads against a time when the butcher's shop would have to close for a month or so as a result of some unknown health risk. Explain business overheads insurance and advise the amount of cover that should be taken.

5 When completing the personal health questionnaire Kaye indicates that she has had no history of breast cancer. However, 3 months after completion of the contract, Kaye has tests which confirm some minor breast cancer tumours. Discuss whether Kaye's term life insurance is still valid.

6 Outline insurances other than the personal risk covers discussed so far in this case study that Eddie and Kaye should have as part of their overall risk protection plan.

References and further reading

InsuranceNEWS.com.au 2012, 'Flood definition becomes law', 18 June.

Miller, N. 2010, 'You bet your life: health insurer's cheap DNA test could prove costly', *Sydney Morning Herald*, 15 February, smh.com.au.

RiceWarner Actuaries 2012, 'Life insurance gap reducing — industry must evolve to meet changing customer needs', media release, 17 December, www.ricewarner.com.

Scriven, D. 2012, 'Life risk insurance', Australian master financial planning guide, CCH 2012/13, ch. 7.

Useful websites

Australian and New Zealand Institute of Insurance and Finance, theinstitute.com.au
Australian Prudential Regulation Authority, apra.gov.au
Australian Securities and Investments Commission, asic.gov.au
Comminsure (the insurance division of the Commonwealth Bank), comminsure.com.au
Financial Ombudsman Service, fos.org.au
Financial Planning Association of Australia, fpa.asn.au
Insurance Council of Australia, insurancecouncil.com.au
National Insurance Brokers Association, niba.com.au

10 Superannuation

LEARNING OBJECTIVES

After studying this chapter, you should be able to:

1. explain what superannuation is and why Australians need it
2. describe the 'three pillars' policy of superannuation
3. outline the main legislative provisions that regulate superannuation
4. differentiate between accumulation accounts and defined benefit schemes and discuss the major providers of superannuation funds
5. outline the historical development of the Australian superannuation system
6. differentiate between concessional and non-concessional contributions to superannuation
7. discuss the main investment constraints that apply to superannuation
8. demonstrate how superannuation funds are taxed
9. outline the various fees and charges which apply to superannuation
10. model how much a person might accumulate in superannuation.

CASE STUDY

Lucy is 28 years old and has been working as a university lecturer for the past 15 months. When she started work her superannuation contributions were automatically directed to a defined benefits superannuation plan. Her superannuation fund recently wrote to her explaining that she will soon need to decide whether to stay in the defined benefits plan or to swap to an accumulation plan and, once made, the decision will be irrevocable.

Lucy has asked her friends for advice about what she should do.

- Clare has suggested that she should stay in the defined benefits plan because there is zero risk; however, Lucy is not so sure about this.
- David suggested that she should swap into the accumulation plan because given her long-term investment horizon she should be able to achieve much better investment returns than those which are implicit in the defined benefits plan.
- Clara suggested that regardless of whether she stays in the defined benefits plan or moves to the accumulation plan, Lucy should salary sacrifice as much as possible so that she will be able to afford the life in retirement that she deserves and expects.
- Roger disagrees strongly with Clara and argues that a dollar in Lucy's pocket is much more valuable than a dollar locked away in superannuation. Lucy eventually will need to buy a house and this is much more likely to increase her wealth in the longer term than salary sacrificing into superannuation at the age of 28.

Asking her friends for advice hasn't really helped much. Some of the issues that Lucy needs to consider include the following.

- What is Lucy's attitude to investment risk? Do defined benefit plans cater for a different risk appetite than accumulation plans?
- How have the superannuation rules changed in the past? How are they likely to change in the future? How will these likely changes impact on Lucy?
- How long will her money be locked away inside superannuation and is there any way she can release it if her circumstances change?
- What does salary sacrifice actually mean and why do people recommend it as a way of contributing to superannuation? How much can Lucy salary sacrifice over and above what her employer currently contributes to superannuation?
- How does superannuation fit into Lucy's overall financial plans? How will she prioritise current expenditure over deferred expenditure i.e. expenditure in retirement?
- How much will she need to accumulate in superannuation to fund her retirement and how does this compare with what she is likely to accumulate given her current circumstances?

The issues facing Lucy in deciding how to approach superannuation are examined throughout this chapter.

Introduction

With more than 32 million member accounts and $1.6 trillion dollars invested, superannuation is of vital importance to Australians. We need to investigate what superannuation is and why it has become such a topic of interest in recent times.

In this chapter we will focus primarily on the individual superannuation fund member; however, it is impossible to do this without some overall understanding of the superannuation industry itself. Therefore, we need to scan the legislative environment within which superannuation operates.

Keeping up to date in a highly dynamic superannuation environment is difficult; however, anticipating changes is made easier by understanding the factors that have led us to the superannuation environment as it is today. To do this, we need to review the historic themes that have threaded their way through the evolution of the superannuation environment.

Funds enter the superannuation environment by being contributed. Once funds are contributed to superannuation they need to be invested to generate earnings for the member. Both contributions to superannuation and earnings inside a superannuation environment are subject to tax. We will review the means by which funds are contributed, invested and taxed inside a superannuation environment.

This chapter concentrates on the accumulation aspect (mode) of superannuation. The next chapter concentrates on the pension aspect (mode) of superannuation where money is withdrawn from a superannuation environment.

Figure 10.1 summarises the sequential development of material across chapters 10 and 11.

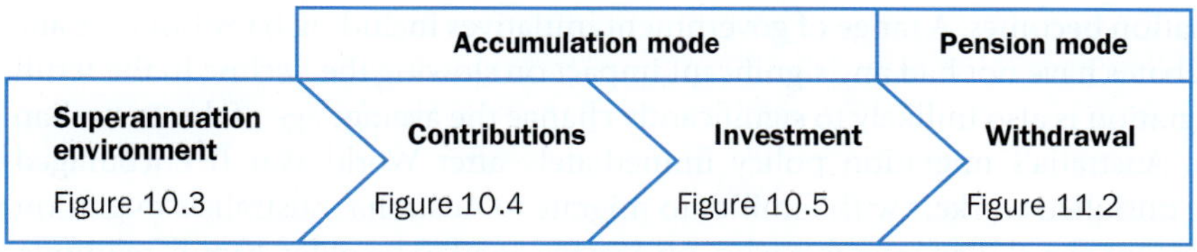

FIGURE 10.1 The sequence of material discussed in chapters 10 and 11

Figure 10.1 will be 'expanded' at the end of each section of our discussion; for example at the end of the discussion of the superannuation environment, figure 10.3 will briefly summarise that section. By moving between each of the expanded sections of figure 10.1 you will able to see the 'bigger picture' of superannuation and how the various components are linked.

LO 1 What is superannuation?

Superannuation is simply a means of saving and investing to accumulate wealth and then using that wealth to fund retirement, usually in the form of an income stream. Throughout this chapter and the next we will focus primarily on Australia's formal superannuation system, which is the product of government legislation and is subject to government supervision through a variety of agencies. Superannuation does not, however, have to be so formal — many individuals will make saving and investment decisions outside the superannuation environment as a way of building wealth for retirement. For example, an individual might invest in shares, managed funds or rental properties with the view to progressively selling these down to fund retirement in the future.

superannuation a means of saving and investing to accumulate wealth and then using that wealth to fund retirement

While the term superannuation is widely used in Australia, it is not so widely used overseas. Other countries describe such funds as pension plans, pensions, provident funds and deferred payment plans. Sometimes the name becomes very specific and has a clear meaning in one particular country. For example, US citizens talk about their 401k plans. Whatever it is called, the intent remains the same — a tax concessional environment designed to encourage people to save for their retirement.

Why the need for superannuation?

Australians are living longer and the baby boomers who were born in the years after World War II are now reaching retirement age. That is, Australia's population is getting older.

The tax revenue collected from people in the workforce helps the federal government to meet its social security commitments, particularly its commitment to pay the age pension.

In 1970, there were 7.5 people in the workforce for each person aged over 65. The federal government's third intergenerational report, *2010 Intergenerational Report*, predicts that in 2050 there will be only 2.7 people in the workforce for each person aged over 65 (Australian Government 2010). As a result, the government will not have the tax revenue base to afford its social security commitments unless changes are made. The key change required is to reduce the reliance on the age pension by encouraging individuals to invest more in their superannuation.

Other policy options are available; however, it is unlikely that they will have a significant impact. For instance, one option is to increase the number of people in the workforce to, in turn, increase the tax revenue base. However, fertility rates continue to fall, women are having fewer babies and women are having babies at a later age. The 'average' woman will have 1.9 babies — this, by itself, will not sustain the existing population. The 'average' woman will have her first child at 29 years of age and, as this age increases, the older our population becomes. A range of government initiatives including baby bonuses and childcare rebates have not had any significant impact on slowing the decline in the fertility rate.

Migration is also unlikely to significantly change the average age of the Australian population. Australia's migration policy immediately after World War II encouraged many young unskilled workers with families to migrate to Australia. Australia's migration policy now encourages skilled migrants who, on average, tend to be older. Family reunions as part of the migration policy, where older relatives from overseas join younger family members in Australia, will also increase the average age of migrants. Moreover, many of the countries that Australia has traditionally taken migrants from are experiencing the same ageing population problem as Australia and are therefore resistant to losing their skilled worker base.

To suggest that the public policy shift away from relying on the age pension and towards self-managed and self-funded retirement was entirely the result of concerns over the ability of national governments to meet their social security funding requirements is to oversimplify a long and ongoing public policy debate. The debate might be traced back to the 1980s in the United Kingdom when Margaret Thatcher was that country's Prime Minister. Many government businesses were privatised and the 'user pays' concept was very much in vogue — that is, the notion that the state will always provide was gradually being supplanted by the notion that individuals need to look after themselves. Providing for retirement was perhaps the greatest exemplar of this philosophy.

LO 2 The three pillars policy of superannuation

Superannuation policy has been a hot political issue for the past 25 years. Incumbent federal governments will bring out their new raft of superannuation promises prior to an upcoming election. Opposition parties, who by their nature must oppose the government, will bring out their own counter superannuation promises. Despite financial commentators and individual superannuation fund members crying out for stability in superannuation for many years, the hallmark of superannuation in Australia for the last 25 years has been constant change.

However, there is one key aspect of Australia's superannuation system which has bipartisan support — the three pillars (or tiers) policy of superannuation:

- Tier 1 — a tax-payer funded social security pension (a safety net) which is means tested
- Tier 2 — compulsory employer contributions to superannuation for employees
- Tier 3 — tax incentives for voluntary contributions to superannuation.

It is easy to criticise Australia's superannuation system — the age pension is too low, the rate of employer contribution is not high enough, the withdrawal of lump sums should not be allowed. However, the basic structure of Australia's three pillar system is highly regarded worldwide.

LO 3 The legislative context for superannuation

The federal government, through a clever use of its section 51 constitutional powers to control taxation, pensions and corporations, has effectively gained legislative control of superannuation in Australia. The cornerstone of this legislative framework is the *Superannuation Industry (Supervision) Act 1993* (SIS Act).

For a superannuation fund to be able to claim the tax concessions associated with being a superannuation fund it must be a complying superannuation fund. To be a **complying superannuation fund**, the fund must:

- be resident in Australia
- have made an irrevocable election to be regulated by the SIS Act
- meet the conditions for compliance as outlined in the SIS Act.

A superannuation fund is a form of trust and as such it is administered by **trustees**. Individuals can act as trustees. It is also possible to have a corporate trustee. The **fiduciary responsibilities** of trustees have been developed by the courts through common law principles over many years. Fiduciary means to act in good faith and to put the interests of others (members) ahead of your own. The fiduciary responsibilities of superannuation fund trustees have largely been **codified** by the SIS Act, although some common law principles still remain. Trustees have a wide range of responsibilities and the role of trustee should not be undertaken lightly. The SIS Act contains a range of penalties for trustees who breach specific provisions of the Act.

As a form of trust, a superannuation fund is governed by its trust deed. The trust deed of a superannuation fund will generally incorporate the terms of the SIS Act and the Superannuation Industry (Supervision) Regulations (SISR). Many trust deeds also include a provision which automatically incorporates any changes to the SIS Act and SISR in order to avoid the expense and inconvenience of the trust deed having to be changed every time the legislation or the regulations change. A trust deed can be 'narrower' than the SIS Act and the fund still be a complying superannuation fund; however, a trust deed cannot be 'broader' than the SIS Act and the fund still be a complying superannuation fund. That is, the trust deed cannot allow the fund to take an action which is prohibited by the SIS Act and still be a complying superannuation fund. A complying superannuation fund enjoys a range of tax advantages which will be outlined later in this chapter. A non-complying fund will have all its income taxed at the highest marginal tax rate.

complying superannuation fund
a superannuation fund which is resident in Australia, has made an irrevocable decision to be regulated by the SIS Act and meets the conditions for compliance as outlined in the SIS Act

trustee
a person who administers a trust fund; a superannuation fund is a form of trust fund

fiduciary responsibilities
to act in good faith and to put the interest of others (members) ahead of your own

codified
legal principles that have been developed by the courts (common law) and included in legislation

The SIS Act is based on a number of underlying principles which include the following.

- The trustees remain responsible for all decisions of the fund. The trustees might decide to delegate some decision making and/or outsource some functions but the trustees are ultimately responsible for all decisions made.
- Wherever possible, members of superannuation funds should participate in decision-making processes via elected membership on trustee boards. The SIS Act is also very prescriptive about the communication required by the fund with members as a means of encouraging their active participation in the fund.
- All investment decisions must be directed towards funding retirement. Superannuation should not be simply a tax haven.
- Superannuation is a regulated and controlled investment environment; however, compliance with the Act does not guarantee the performance or financial viability of the fund.

Four bodies are primarily charged with the regulation and control of the superannuation industry.

1. The Australian Prudential Regulation Authority (APRA) is the prudential regulator for deposit-taking institutions, insurance and superannuation. APRA is the prudential regulator for all superannuation funds other than self-managed superannuation funds. The term **prudential** generally means the monitoring of risk-taking behaviour. In this context, a very important part of APRA's role is to monitor the risk-taking behaviour of individual superannuation funds.

   prudential to monitor risk-taking behaviour

   All trustees of APRA-supervised superannuation funds must hold a Registrable Superannuation Entities (RSE) licence. The formulation of and adherence to a risk-management strategy is an important part of the licensing system.
2. The Australian Securities and Investments Commission (ASIC) regulates market conduct and disclosure. It is part of ASIC's role to ensure consumers are protected and that markets, including the 'market' for superannuation funds, are conducted in a fair, orderly and transparent manner.

   Superannuation funds are often called upon to give information to members. Where information stops and advice starts is often a difficult line to draw. A superannuation fund must decide whether to refer members to third parties for advice or to provide the advice themselves. If a superannuation fund provides financial advice it needs to be licensed to do so. Most large superannuation funds hold their own Australian Financial Services Licence (AFSL), which is issued by ASIC.
3. The Australian Taxation Office (ATO) performs a variety of roles including:
   - acting as the regulator of self-managed superannuation funds
   - collecting tax from superannuation funds and conducting audits to ensure that assessable income is properly disclosed
   - administering the tax concessions available to individuals
   - auditing employers to ensure that they meet their requirements under the *Superannuation Guarantee (Administration) Act 1992* (SGAA) (discussed later in this chapter)
   - collaborating with the state collectors of unclaimed superannuation funds.
4. The Superannuation Complaints Tribunal (SCT) deals with complaints by members against the decisions of trustees. Section 101 of the SIS Act requires that a complying superannuation fund has an established complaints resolution process. An individual member is obliged to use this process first. If unsuccessful, they have access to the SCT.

In determining a case, the SCT effectively substitutes itself for the trustee and in exercising the discretion of the trustee they may:

- agree with the original decision of the trustee
- refer the matter back to the trustee for further consideration based on advice from the tribunal
- modify the decision of the trustee, or
- cancel the decision of the trustee and substitute their own decision.

While we have primarily concentrated on the impact of the SIS Act and the SISR on superannuation, many other legislative provisions impact on superannuation. Superannuation trustees need to be particularly mindful of discrimination, privacy and family law legislation. However, changes to the superannuation environment can be driven by many factors. For instance, the *Same-Sex Relationships (Equal treatment in Commonwealth laws-Superannuation) Act 2008* had a significant impact on superannuation funds. Trustees need to be vigilant to ensure that they are up to date with the legislative environment within which superannuation sits.

LO 4 Types of superannuation funds and who provides them

Superannuation is a large 'industry' that can be viewed from a number of different perspectives. We will examine two views here. One view is to look at the types of accounts that are held by individuals. A second view is to examine the major providers of superannuation funds, that is, corporate, industry, public sector, retail and small superannuation funds.

Accumulation accounts and defined benefit schemes

The most common type of superannuation account held by an individual is an **accumulation account**. Contributions by an individual's employer and their personal contributions increase the balance of their accumulation account as do positive investment returns of the superannuation fund. Negative investment returns of the fund reduce the balance of the individual's accumulation account. The investment risk associated with the superannuation account is borne by the individual. The superannuation entitlement on retirement is simply the balance of the account. The term 'accumulation' is widely used in Australia; in the United States this style of account is often called a defined contribution account which emphasises that the amount contributed to the account is known but there is uncertainty as to the ultimate balance in the account. In Australia, approximately 80% of all superannuation assets for funds with more than four members are held in accumulation style accounts.

accumulation account a type of superannuation fund where the investment risk is borne by the member and in which contributions and positive earnings increase the accumulated amount and negative earnings reduce the accumulated amount

Less common, but still a significant part of the superannuation industry, are **defined benefit schemes**. Under these schemes, contributions are made by an employer into a pooled fund which is designed to cover the entitlements accruing to members. Sometimes such schemes are non-contributory for the employee, i.e. the employee makes no contribution to the fund. Sometimes such schemes require the employee as part of their industrial award or agreement to contribute a percentage of their pre-tax income to the scheme.

defined benefit scheme a type of superannuation account where the balance is determined by a formula which often includes salary and years worked; generally the investment risk is borne by the employer sponsor of the fund

The superannuation entitlement for an individual member of a defined benefit scheme is defined by a formula rather than by the balance of their account (as under an accumulation account). The nature of the formula will vary depending on the particular scheme. For example, a defined benefit entitlement might equal final average salary times a 'factor' times the number of years worked. Final average salary is usually calculated as the average salary over the last 3 years of working and the factor is often related to the amount of contributions made by the employee.

For example, Mahesh is in a defined benefit fund and has a final average salary of $100 000. He has worked for 20 years and contributed 5% of his pre-tax salary to superannuation which entitles him to a 'factor' of 17%. Mahesh will be entitled to a superannuation payout of $340 000 ($100 000 × 17% × 20).

actuarial calculations evaluate mathematically the likelihood of certain financial events and their associated costs; for example, what percentage of the total superannuation fund membership is likely to retire in the next 12 months and how much should be set aside to meet this likelihood

Detailed **actuarial calculations** are required to determine these formulae, including the factors embedded within them. If the actuaries get it right, the pool of funds which is a product of the contributions made and the investment earnings generated will match the entitlements accruing to members. If the actuaries get it wrong, and overfund the pool it is less of a problem than if the pool is underfunded. If the pool is underfunded, most defined benefit schemes require the employer to make good the shortfall, in which case the investment risk associated with superannuation has been completely transferred from employee to employer (in contrast to accumulation accounts).

Some defined benefit schemes have in their trust deed that the defined benefits can be reduced if the pool is underfunded, in which case the investment risk remains with the individual. Most defined benefit members were unaware that these provisions existed; however, the global financial crisis and the significant falls in the portfolios held by some defined benefit schemes have caused some funds to conduct actuarial reviews to ensure that their defined benefit schemes are adequately funded.

PERSONAL FINANCE BULLETIN

Defined benefit super also defines the problem

There are few guarantees in today's corporate Australia — a job for life being one of them — but the defined benefit (DB) superannuation schemes of another era live on. For a lucky few these plans, popular in the 1980s and early 1990s, effectively guaranteed an employee's final retirement payout decades in advance.

However, employers (and their actuaries) underestimated just how big such DB liabilities would grow because of increasing employee salaries, life spans and volatile investment performance.

'Certainly they [the funds] have been hit by poor returns in recent years due to the global financial crisis (GFC) — that's required additional contributions from employers', says Mercer's retirement, risk and finance senior partner David Knox, who also notes that less than 10 per cent of working Australians are still DB fund members.

The Rio Tinto pension plan, for example, held a net deficit of US$4.66 billion by the end of 2011 — a deterioration of more than US$1.4 billion in just 12 months as the GFC impacted its asset base. Such legacy DB funds continue to weigh on companies even though most were closed to new members by 2002 when the superannuation guarantee (SG) hit 9 per cent, forcing investors to ride the market's ups and downs in defined contribution (or accumulation) funds.

The situation is more pressing in the public sector where unfunded liabilities total in the hundreds of billions. Local governments — such as the City of Greater Bendigo in Victoria, Australia — need to find an extra A$453 million by 1 July next year to fully fund their DB liabilities.

Should investors in such schemes be worried? Generally not, according to Towers Watson senior consultant David McNeice.

'It's only a concern if an employer is in financial stress [but] there is an order that liabilities have to be settled if you move into liquidation and employee entitlements rank highly in that order.'

Governments, meanwhile, have a longer-term view on such debts and can continue meeting liabilities (although at the expense of other obligations).

While DB liabilities in Australia are challenging, there are even larger issues offshore. In June, troubled US car maker General Motors began restructuring its massive DB plan, including offering thousands of retirees a cash lump sum if they stopped taking monthly benefits, in an effort to strip US$26 billion from its liabilities.

Nonetheless, the Australian Prudential Regulation Authority (APRA) recently noted that several Australian DB funds were still in unsatisfactory financial positions and, while the majority of employers were injecting cash into them, employers are still keen to shift or convert DB fund members to accumulation plans.

'It's clearly the employers limiting their risk — it's an area fraught with legal problems and it's not one you would advise anyone to jump into', says Russell Mason, a partner at Deloitte.

DB members of UniSuper face a potential cut in their entitlements next year unless employers agree to increase their contributions. The unusual situation appears to have been promoted by a change in the fund's trust deed, which downplayed employers' traditional responsibility to meet DB liabilities. At 30 June this year UniSuper's vested benefits index had fallen to 85.3 per cent, well below the required 100 per cent funding level.

Switching employees from a DB plan to an accumulation plan is no small matter. Investors bear the risk in accumulation funds: their final retirement lump sum depends on how much they have saved and the investment return it generates.

But despite the fundamental differences between the two types of funds, DB funds have surprisingly been invested in similar assets. It is only in more recent times that DB funds have undergone a major shift away from riskier assets (such as equities and property, which can comprise 60 to 70 per cent of the portfolio), to less-volatile assets (such as cash and bonds) in the wake of the GFC and as the number of active members declines.

Source: Brendan Swift, *In The Black*, December 2012, pp. 68–9.

Major providers of superannuation funds

The Australian Prudential Regulation Authority (APRA), which oversees all superannuation funds in Australia other than self-managed superannuation funds, gathers and publishes data on the superannuation industry. APRA disaggregates the industry into five types of providers. Figure 10.2 highlights the assets held by each provider type.

In the past 10 years, industry, retail and small superannuation funds have significantly increased the value of the total assets under management. Over the same period, the value of funds under management in corporate superannuation funds has remained relatively constant, as some companies have closed down their superannuation schemes and transferred employees to retail funds. This trend in corporate funds has also been fuelled by some companies not wishing to retain the investment risk associated with defined benefit schemes.

fully funded scheme a superannuation fund where contributions and earnings have been set aside to meet the commitments to members as they fall due

Figure 10.2 includes only funded superannuation schemes. Funded means that contributions have been made progressively into the superannuation fund over the working lives of the individual members. All corporate, industry, retail and small superannuation funds are funded schemes.

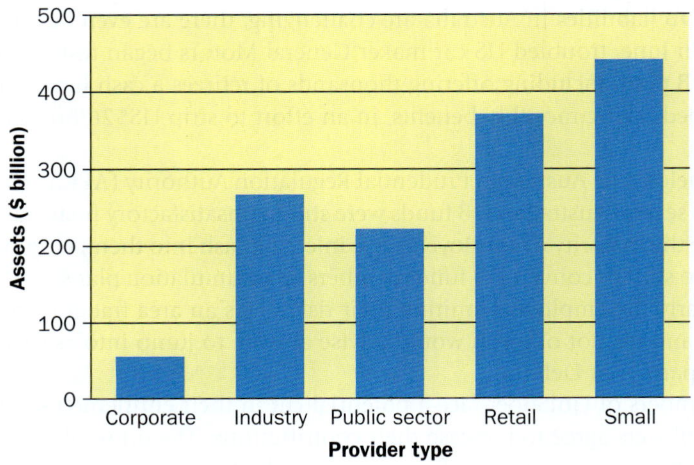

FIGURE 10.2 Superannuation assets ($ billion) held by provider type, June 2012
Source: APRA 2012, table 9.

However, not all public-sector schemes are **fully funded schemes**. It was estimated that at 30 June 2013 the federal government had an **unfunded** liability to pay public servants superannuation equivalent to $143 billion (Australian Government 2013). In July 2005, the Public Sector Superannuation Accumulation Plan was introduced and provides fully funded accumulation benefits for new civilian employees. However, the unfunded obligation to military personnel and public servants who joined their superannuation fund before July 2005 means that the total unfunded liability is expected to grow further. Successive federal governments have tried to reduce this unfunded liability — the Future Fund was established as a savings plan designed to accumulate wealth over time to offset this unfunded superannuation liability. Part of the privatisation proceeds from the sale of Telstra was paid into the Future Fund. At 30 June 2013, the Future Fund held $87 billion in assets (Australian Government 2013).

unfunded scheme a public-sector superannuation fund where contributions and earnings have not been set aside to meet the commitments to members as they fall due; the balance in a member's account is effectively only a promise to pay

LO 5 History of superannuation in Australia: how did we get to where we are today?

The history of superannuation can be told in a number of ways. The most traditional way of recalling a history is to recount events in chronological order; however, sometimes themes are more instructive than dates. Many themes run through the historical development of superannuation. These themes have led us to where we are today and are useful in providing an insight into where we might go in the future. When following a theme, sometimes the progression is logical and its direction is clear. At other times, public policy seems to have gone backward and forward on a particular issue making it difficult to predict a trend.

Some of the themes to consider in the development of the superannuation system in Australia include:

- the change from white collar to blue collar to no collar
- the need to stay at work longer
- taking lump sums from superannuation
- the tax-concessional environment — do we control the inputs or the outputs?
- is everybody treated equally?

From white collar to blue collar to no collar

The beginnings of formal employer-sponsored superannuation schemes can be traced back to the latter half of the nineteenth century in Australia. The schemes tended to be called provident funds rather than superannuation funds and were mainly confined to 'white collar' employees in the banks and public service. To be eligible for a payout from the provident fund, employees had to stay with the same employer until retirement — a concept which today seems quite alien. For the banks, the provident fund was also a means of ensuring good behaviour and character from their employees because conviction for an offence such as theft and/or dismissal would generally result in the employee forfeiting their payout from the fund. Superannuation is often referred to as a 'golden handshake' and sometimes less seriously as a 'golden handcuff' — which could be the case for employees whose entitlements are tied to staying with a job they may not particularly like doing.

By the mid 1980s, approximately 40% of the Australian workforce was covered by superannuation. Coverage was still largely confined to 'white collar' employees. Often women were excluded from superannuation schemes after they were married — again a concept which seems out of place today.

The federal government has commissioned four inquiries into superannuation — 1928, 1938, 1976 and the Cooper Inquiry of 2010. The 1928, 1938 and 1976 inquiries all supported the concept of a national contributory superannuation scheme; however, all three failed to generate the political impetus for such a scheme.

In 1985, the Australian Council of Trade Unions (ACTU), with the support of the Hawke/Keating government, petitioned the then Arbitration Commission for a 3% wage increase payable in the form of a superannuation contribution. The commission accepted the argument but left unions and individual companies with the responsibility of negotiating the superannuation contribution as a result of improved productivity on a case-by-case basis. The decision extended the reach of superannuation; however, the coverage of the workforce was still 'patchy' and inconsistent. In 1992, the Hawke/Keating government introduced the **superannuation guarantee** system, which obliged all employers to contribute 3% of each employee's income to superannuation. This rate of contribution was progressively increased to 9% by 2002. Superannuation coverage now extends to well over 90% of the workforce and includes both white and blue collar employees.

superannuation guarantee
an arrangement whereby employees are guaranteed that their employers will contribute to their superannuation funds a minimum of percentage of their ordinary times earnings

In 1997, the federal government introduced the eligible spouse rebate for superannuation. We will discuss the operation of the rebate later in the chapter; however, in financial terms, it provides a small tax rebate when a person makes a contribution for a low-income or no-income spouse. No income means not working, and the rebate is often seen as a signal that superannuation coverage needs to extend beyond the workforce and apply to all Australians. In 2004, the Howard/Costello government took this a step further by removing the work test for people under the age of 65, resulting in white collar, blue collar and no collar (not working) people being eligible to contribute to superannuation.

This broadening of the base of people eligible to contribute to superannuation appears to be a consistent trend — in an environment of an ageing population and concern over meeting the funding requirements of the age pension, it seems unlikely that public policy will narrow the base of people entitled to contribute to superannuation in the future.

The need to stay at work longer

The longer people work the more they accumulate to fund their retirement and the shorter the period of retirement that needs to be funded.

As discussed in more detail in chapter 13, in 1909 the age pension was introduced for men in Australia. To be eligible for the age pension you needed to be 65 years of age. Given that the life expectancy of males at birth in 1908 was approximately 55 years of age, only a very small percentage of the male population lived long enough to claim the pension. For the next 100 years, the entitlement age remained at 65; however, male life expectancy at birth increased to 79 which has resulted in a significant proportion of the male population reaching the entitlement age (Australian Government Actuary 2013). This increasing social security burden has been an important factor driving successive federal governments to create a superannuation environment which encourages us to work longer.

Policy initiatives include:

- a progressive increase in the age-pension entitlement age for women from 60 to 65
- an increase in the age-pension entitlement age from 65 to 67 for both men and women over the period 2017 to 2023
- the introduction of a **transition to retirement (TTR) income stream**
- the introduction of the **work bonus scheme**
- a progressive increase in the minimum age at which funds can be released from superannuation from 55 to 60
- superannuation changes by the Howard/Costello government in 2007 to encourage people to keep working until at least 60 years of age in order to release money from superannuation tax free
- public policy discussions about aligning the minimum age at which funds can be released from superannuation and the age-pension entitlement age.

transition to retirement (TTR) income stream a scheme which allows workers to continue to work part-time (or full-time) and supplement their income by drawing down some of their superannuation

work bonus scheme a scheme that encourages people over age pension age to continue working by allowing them to earn a higher amount of income before their age pension payments are reduced

Policy initiatives in recent years have consistently encouraged us to work longer. It is hard to see this trend changing. Based on the current rules, how old will you be before you can access your superannuation and be entitled to the age pension? Will the rules change before you get there?

Taking lump sums from superannuation

Many countries in the world do not allow individuals to take their money out of superannuation as a lump sum. Some might argue that the ability to withdraw superannuation as a lump sum is an 'Australian right' which cannot be interfered with. Others would argue that allowing individuals to withdraw their money in a lump sum, and possibly spend it quickly and ultimately rely on the age pension, is poor public policy. Nonetheless, it would certainly be a brave federal government that decided to remove the right to take money out of superannuation as a lump sum. This has not, however, stopped federal governments from taxing such lump sum withdrawals.

Prior to 1983, it was possible to take money out of superannuation as a lump sum and only 5% of the amount taken was taxable at the individual's marginal tax rate. Even if an individual's marginal rate was as high as 50% the effective tax rate on lump sum withdrawals was 2.5% (50% × 5%) which is hardly a disincentive to withdraw superannuation as a lump sum.

The Hawke/Keating government decided to tax superannuation accrued after 30 June 1983 and subsequently withdrawn as a lump sum at 15% after a particular tax-free threshold had been reached. Some would argue that 15% was not a sufficient tax penalty to discourage people from taking their money out of superannuation but it was more of a penalty than the pre-1983 regime. The Howard/Costello government in 2007 introduced the Simpler Super reforms, which allowed individuals over the age of 60 to withdraw their superannuation as a lump sum completely tax free.

Over the longer term, will we see a trend of taxing lump sums to discourage people from withdrawing them or a trend of allowing people to withdraw lump sums tax free? How will future federal governments deal with this issue? With likely significant budgetary pressures in the future, will governments be able to afford the tax revenue forgone by not taxing lump sums?

The tax-concessional environment — do we control the inputs or the outputs?

Superannuation is a tax-concessional environment designed to encourage people to save in order to fund, or at least partially fund, their retirement. A tax-concessional environment implies that the federal government is forgoing tax revenue it would have otherwise collected. Estimates of how much tax revenue is forgone vary wildly; however, there is no doubt that it amounts to billions of dollars a year and, as such, it has a significant budgetary impact.

The key policy issue is how 'concessional' does a tax-concessional environment need to be in order to entice individuals to save for their retirement? If the environment is too concessional, the federal government will lose significant tax revenue, which may compromise its ability to provide a full range of services. If the environment is not concessional enough, federal government tax revenues will be higher but people will be saving less for retirement, and the end result will be greater budgetary outlays in the future to meet the burden of increased social security payments.

How can people be encouraged to save enough to fund their retirement but not so much as to exploit the tax-concessional nature of superannuation? Essentially, either the amount of money flowing into superannuation must be controlled or the amount of money flowing out of superannuation must be controlled.

Prior to 2007, the limit for concessional contributions was a function of the individual's age. Concessional contributions occur where a tax deduction can be claimed for a contribution. We will discuss these in more detail later in the chapter. In 2006–07, for example, the employer of a person over the age of 50 could claim up to a $100 000 superannuation contribution as a tax deduction. This enabled people to build up significant superannuation balances. The government's response was to impose reasonable benefit limits (RBLs) which more heavily taxed money leaving a superannuation environment that was in excess of the RBLs. Effectively, the government was seeking to control the money coming out of a superannuation environment, which, in turn, would cause individuals to carefully monitor how much they put into the tax-concessional superannuation environment in the first place.

As part of the Howard/Costello reforms to superannuation, RBLs were abolished; however, a limit was placed on concessional contributions greater than $50 000 per year. Arguably, this is a shift from controlling money flowing out of superannuation to controlling money flowing into superannuation. The Rudd/Swann government subsequently reduced this $50 000 limit to $25 000.

Have we got the balance right? Is the superannuation environment concessional enough to attract contributions but not so attractive that it seriously reduces government tax revenue? Should we control the money going into superannuation, or out of superannuation or both?

Is everybody treated equally?

Prior to 1988, contributions to and earnings inside superannuation funds were not taxed. In 1988, a 15% tax was introduced on all contributions and earnings.

salary sacrifice
where an employee asks their employer to take some of their income and redirect this to paying for a benefit on behalf of the employee; the most commonly salary sacrificed benefit is superannuation

An individual who earns $200 000 might decide to **salary sacrifice** $10 000 into superannuation. If this $10 000 was taken as income, the individual would be taxed at their marginal tax rate of 45% and they would lose $4500 of this amount in tax. If, instead, the $10 000 was sacrificed into superannuation, the individual's employer would be able to claim this as a tax deduction and the full $10 000 would be remitted to the superannuation fund. The fund would then be obliged to deduct 15% in contributions tax; that is, the individual would lose $1500 in tax. By salary sacrificing the amount, the individual has saved $3000 in tax. We will discuss the process of salary sacrifice later in the chapter.

An individual who earns $37 000 might also decide to salary sacrifice $10 000 into superannuation. If this $10 000 was taken as income, the individual would be taxed at their marginal tax rate of 19% and they would lose $1900 of this amount in tax. If, instead, the $10 000 was sacrificed into superannuation, the individual's employer would be able to claim this as a tax deduction and the full $10 000 would be remitted to the superannuation fund. The fund would then be obliged to deduct 15% in contributions tax; that is, the individual would lose $1500 in tax. So, the individual has saved $400 in tax through salary sacrificing. Is it fair that a high-income earner saves $3000 in tax whereas the low-income earner saves only $400?

In 1996, the federal government introduced the superannuation surcharge. The surcharge added an extra 15% to the existing 15% contributions tax for high-income earners resulting in an effective tax rate of 30% on contributions. The surcharge was very unpopular — perhaps it was the political influence of those subject to the surcharge, or perhaps the superannuation environment was not sufficiently tax concessional anymore but either way the surcharge was removed in 2005. In 2013, however, the federal government effectively reinstated the surcharge by passing legislation which results in individuals who earn more than $300 000 paying contributions tax at the rate of 30%.

Another way of injecting more equity into the superannuation tax environment is to provide low-income earners with a contributions tax rebate. In 2012 the federal government introduced a rebate for low-income earners which effectively negated the contribution tax for people earning less than $37 000.

Figure 10.3 provides a brief summary of the superannuation environment we have discussed in this chapter.

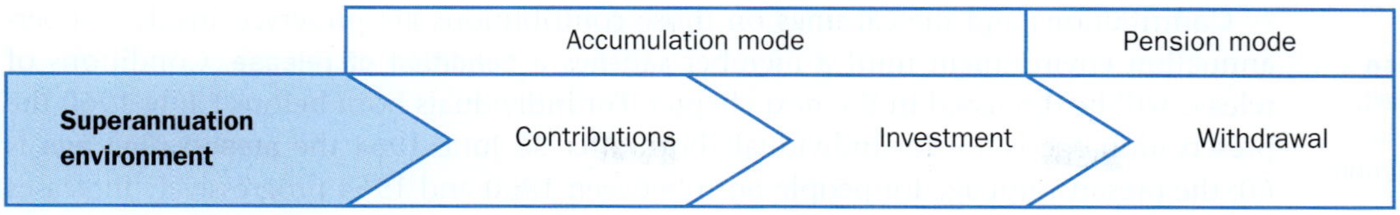

Australia's three pillars (or tiers) policy

Tier 1
A tax payer funded social security pension (a safety net) which is means tested.

Tier 2
Compulsory employer contributions to superannuation for employees.

Tier 3
Tax incentives for voluntary contributions to superannuation.

The legislative context of superannuation
The legislative environment is dominated by Federal legislation. While many Acts impinge on superannuation the cornerstone of this legislative framework is the *Superannuation Industry (Supervision) Act 1993*.

The legislative framework controls how funds are *contributed*, how they are *invested* and how they are *withdrawn* from superannuation.

The Regulators
- Australian Prudential Regulation Authority
- Australian Securities and Investments Commission
- Australian Taxation Office
- Superannuation Complaints Tribunal

Types of funds
Funds can be viewed from a number of different perspectives.

Superannuation funds are either accumulation funds (also known as defined contribution funds) or defined benefit funds. Most working Australians will have an accumulation fund(s).

Funds can also be viewed from the perspective of the provider of the funds. The main providers are:
- corporate funds
- industry funds
- pubic sector funds
- retail funds
- small funds.

Historical development of superannuation
The history of superannuation in Australia is full of recurrent themes. Understanding these themes helps in predicting where superannuation might go in the future.

FIGURE 10.3
Overview of the superannuation environment

LO 6 Superannuation contributions

A superannuation fund can accept contributions from people under the age of 65 without restriction. Between the ages of 65 and 75, the member needs to be gainfully employed at least on a part-time basis. Over the age of 75, the only contributions allowed are superannuation guarantee contributions and employer contributions which are mandated under an award.

condition of release criteria that, if satisfied, enable an individual to withdraw their money from superannuation

preservation age the minimum age at which funds can be withdrawn from superannuation

Contributions and the earnings on those contributions are preserved inside a superannuation environment until a member satisfies a **condition of release**. Conditions of release will be discussed in the next chapter. For individuals born before 1 July 1960 the preservation age is 55; for individuals born after 30 June 1964 the **preservation age** is 60; the preservation age for people born between 1960 and 1964 progressively increases from 55 to 60. The Henry Tax Review of 2010 recommended that the preservation age and the age at which people are entitled to the age pension be aligned. This would mean that the preservation age would become 65 and eventually 67. This was one of the first Henry recommendations to be rejected by the then Rudd/Swann government.

For most people, preservation means that superannuation is a very long-term investment and the lack of liquidity is an important consideration when people are considering voluntary contributions to superannuation. There are some extreme circumstances where money can be released prior to reaching preservation age and satisfying a condition of release. These include:

- permanent incapacity
- permanent departure from Australia
- severe financial hardship
- compassionate grounds.

Concessional and non-concessional contributions

concessional contribution a contribution to superannuation for which a tax deduction has been claimed

A **concessional contribution** to superannuation is a contribution for which a tax deduction has been claimed.

For example, if Jenny earns $100 000 per year and her employer contributes an additional $10 000 to her superannuation under its superannuation guarantee obligations, the employer is able to claim $110 000 as a tax deduction. If Jenny asks her employer to salary sacrifice $12 000 of her salary to superannuation, the employer will pay Jenny $88 000 and send $22 000 to her superannuation fund. Either way, the employer claims $110 000 as a tax deduction.

When a superannuation fund receives a concessional contribution, it deducts 15% in tax.

self-employed an individual who earns less than 10% of their income from employment-related activities

If a person is **self-employed**, the process works in exactly the same way. Any concessional contribution by a self-employed person up to the concessional contribution limit is tax deductible for the self-employed person. A self-employed person is an individual who earns less than 10% of their income from employment-related activities. The distinction between being engaged as an employee in employment-related activities and working as a self-employed contractor is discussed later in the chapter under the heading of the superannuation guarantee scheme.

Since 2009 concessional contributions have been limited to $25 000 per financial year. This figure is indexed to average weekly ordinary times earnings (AWOTE) but increments are accumulated until they reach $5000, which means that the limit will jump in $5000 steps at irregular intervals. Due to budgetary constraints, however, the cap was kept at $25 000 for the 2013–14 financial year with indexation due to resume in the 2014–15 financial year. The federal government did, however, increase the cap for people over the age of 50 to $35 000 effective from 1 July 2014. Excess concessional contributions which are not withdrawn are taxed at the individual's marginal tax rate plus Medicare levy.

Concessional contributions into accumulation accounts are reasonably easy for an individual to calculate to ensure that they stay below the concessional contribution limit. Concessional contributions into defined benefit schemes are more difficult to measure. To get around this problem, each superannuation fund offering a defined benefit plan will publish a notional taxed contribution (NTC) for each defined benefit member according to a prescribed formula. For example, a member who earns $100 000 might have an NTC of 17%, which means the concessional contribution is assumed to be $17 000. If the concessional contribution limit is $25 000 per financial year, the individual could salary sacrifice up to $8000 and stay below the limit. If they salary sacrifice too much and exceed the limit they will be subject to the excess concessional contributions tax discussed earlier.

A **non-concessional contribution** to superannuation is a contribution for which a tax deduction has *not* been claimed. That is, individuals have taken their after-tax dollars (capital) and placed these inside a superannuation environment. When a superannuation fund receives a non-concessional contribution, no tax is deducted.

non-concessional contribution
a contribution to superannuation for which a tax deduction has not been claimed (formerly known as undeducted contributions)

Non-concessional contributions are limited to six times the concessional contribution limit. Therefore they are limited to $150 000 per year, although this is calculated on a rolling 3-year basis, which means an individual can contribute $450 000 today but it would be 3 years before they could make additional non-concessional contributions. Excess non-concessional contributions are taxed at the highest marginal tax rate plus Medicare levy.

Concessional contributions

The superannuation guarantee scheme

The superannuation guarantee (SG) scheme is an arrangement whereby an employee is guaranteed that their employer will contribute to the employee's superannuation fund a minimum contribution. In 2012–13 this minimum was equal to 9% of the employee's ordinary earnings quarterly. In 2012 the federal parliament passed legislation which will progressively increase the rate from 9% to 12% in annual increments of 0.25%. Superannuation guarantee contributions are concessional contributions. The contributions are to be made at least quarterly, but may be made monthly. The ATO administers the scheme and, if employers do not contribute the required minimum amounts, they are liable to pay an SG charge which comprises the shortfall plus an interest and administration charge.

The legislation that established and governs the scheme are the *Superannuation Guarantee (Administration) Act 1992* (SGAA) and the *Superannuation Guarantee Charge Act 1992* (SGCA).

The SG scheme is a self-assessment scheme. Employers must ensure they have contributed at the required minimum levels or report the shortfall to the ATO and pay the SG charge.

Obviously, the definition of an employee is very important when the labour cost of a given employer can increase by between 9% and 12% immediately if a person is classified as an employee. Under the SGAA, 'employee' is defined within its ordinary common-law meaning as a person who works for salary or wages, but is expanded to include, among others, directors of companies and board members of associations (who are not normally employees), members of parliament and entertainers under contract to entrepreneurs and film producers. The difficulty lies, as it always has with taxation law, with employee-like persons such as independent contractors. True contractors normally work for many customers (who are not 'employers') and are running their own businesses.

Because of the importance of this definition in taxation law, it has been subjected to a great deal of judicial thought. Case law has concluded that there are many indicators to be considered in each case, but no one indicator is the deciding determinant. The following factors have been used and would tend to suggest a person is a contractor rather than an employee.

- The client has limited control over the worker's actions — the worker decides what to do and how to do it.
- The worker has their own business organisation.
- The worker has a large number of clients.
- The worker bears the risk of unsatisfactory work or results and of cost increases.
- The worker has the freedom to employ others.
- The worker provides their own tools.

The ATO has provided guidance on this issue with the Commissioner's view given in *Superannuation Guarantee Ruling SGR 2005/1*. A difficulty arises with people who work under genuine contracts but must perform the work themselves, provide principally their own labour, work with the employer/client's tools, machinery or assets, and are paid by time rather than outcome. The Commissioner regards these people as employees rather than contractors for the purposes of the SG scheme.

ILLUSTRATIVE EXAMPLE 10.1

Tim Jones is a local electrician. He does repairs and new work for householders. Is Tim an employee or a contractor for the purposes of the SG scheme? Clients tell him what needs to be done in general terms but do not normally stipulate where the wires should be run or how the job is to be carried out; he has a business structure; he works for many clients; when he gives fixed quotes, he bears the risk of cost increases and of rectifying his work; he may employ others; he provides his own tools. Therefore, Tim is an independent contractor and as such the people who engage him will not make a separate payment to cover the SG charge. It will be up to Tim whether or not he decides to contribute some of his personal income to superannuation.

ILLUSTRATIVE EXAMPLE 10.2

Brian Need is a computer programmer who specialises in complex shipping-industry design programs. He works for a small number of clients each year, sequentially rather than at the same time. He must use his own skills, works on large mainframe computers and is paid for hours worked fortnightly. The ATO considers him an employee for SG purposes and therefore people who employ Brian will also need to contribute the SG to his nominated superannuation fund.

ordinary times earnings (OTE) prescribed in legislation as including some items, e.g. earnings for ordinary hours worked, and excluding other items, e.g. overtime pay

The ATO website (ato.gov.au) contains a useful 'Employee/contractor decision tool'.

Employers are required to calculate their SG contributions on their employees' **ordinary times earnings (OTE)**. *OTE* are defined in the SGAA and include *inter alia*:

- total earnings for ordinary hours of work
- over-award payments
- shift loadings
- commissions.

OTE do not include *inter alia*:

- general bonuses
- overtime pay
- car allowances paid as cents/km
- fringe benefits
- maternity and paternity leave payments
- annual leave loadings
- payments in lieu of notice and redundancy pay.

A maximum income level per employee to which the SG contribution rate applies is prescribed. In 2013–14 this figure was $48 040 per quarter. This figure is subject to indexation. If for example an employee earns $50 000 in a particular quarter and the SG rate is 10% the amount payable by the employer would be limited to $4804 ($48 040 times 10%).

An employer may use a different measure than OTE to determine their superannuation contributions provided the resultant contribution is equal to or greater than the contributions applicable if the SG rate had been applied to the OTE. The ATO website contains a useful SG contributions calculator.

Some employees are outside the scope of the SG scheme. The mechanism to exclude these employees comprises exclusion of their salaries or wages. Hence, if an employee's earnings are excluded, there is no need for an employer to pay a percentage of those earnings to superannuation. Excluded employees include *inter alia:*

- employees receiving less than $450 per month (based on actual cash receipts in a month).
- part-time (less than 30 hours per week) employees under 18 years of age.
- people who do work of a domestic nature for not more than 30 hours per week. This work includes housework or cleaning, child care in the home, doing minor repairs and gardening.

The ATO website contains a useful superannuation eligibility decision tool.

The SGAA specifies that employers will be liable to pay SG charges if the level of superannuation support paid on behalf of an employee does not at least equal the required level of employer contributions. The SG charge for any employer who incurs a liability is the sum of the following.

- *The SG shortfall in contributions for the employee*. The SG percentage is applied against total wages or salary, not OTE. This can potentially increase the shortfall amount, as more components are included in wages and salaries than in OTE. This charge is not tax deductible, whereas the original contributions would have been deductible. This charge is collected by the ATO and passed on to the employee's superannuation fund.
- *The nominal interest component*. The interest charge is calculated at the rate of 10% p.a. The nominal interest component is a charge to compensate employees suffering shortfalls for the earnings their superannuation funds could have made if contributions had been received on time. This charge is collected by the ATO and passed on to the employee's superannuation fund.
- *An administration fee of $20 per affected employee*. The administration fee is retained by the ATO.

Once an SG charge debt is raised by the ATO, it is a debt due to the Commonwealth of Australia and the ATO may sue for recovery of the funds. Where employers become insolvent, unpaid superannuation contributions have the same priority as unpaid wages. Generally, employee entitlements rank behind secured creditors.

As interest and administration charges further increase employers' costs, presumably few employers knowingly underpay their employees' SG contributions. However, shortfalls do occur following errors in calculations, where employees have highly variable OTE and with firms having cash flow problems. The ATO does randomly audit employers' compliance with their SG obligations and generally there is a high level of compliance. Where it does find non-compliance, the ATO publishes a list of 'at-risk industries' on its website as a means of encouraging compliance. A perennial favourite is the café and restaurant business.

Salary sacrifice

An employee may decide to sacrifice some of their pre-tax salary as a contribution to superannuation. Because the contribution is a tax deduction for the employer, the contribution is a concessional contribution and the individual must ensure that they stay within their concessional contribution limit in order to avoid excess taxes. A decision to salary sacrifice must be made prospectively, i.e. before the income is earned. All concessional contributions are taxed at 15% when they enter the superannuation fund. The tax saving from salary sacrificing is a function of the employee's marginal tax rate (MTR) — the higher the MTR the higher the tax saving. This is illustrated in table 10.1.

TABLE 10.1 Income tax saving from salary sacrifice of $10 000 at various MTRs

Marginal tax rate	Cash in pocket	Money invested in superannuation — tax rate 15%	Saving
19.0%	$8100	$8500	$ 400
32.5%	$6750	$8500	$1750
37.0%	$6300	$8500	$2200
45.0%	$5500	$8500	$3000

A decision to salary sacrifice is a trade-off between current consumption and future consumption. A younger person might be less willing to trade current consumption for future consumption — they need disposable income to buy their first car and their first home. Indeed, buying their first home might be the first step to building wealth which will ultimately set them up for partially funding their retirement. An older person, however, who has accumulated assets and is possibly earning a higher income might find it easier to salary sacrifice. The older person may also see that they can access their superannuation within a reasonably short time frame as opposed to a younger person who might have to wait 30 years or more before they can access their superannuation.

Prior to the Howard/Costello government reforms in superannuation in 2007, the concessional contribution limit was a function of age. In 2006–07, the limit was $14 603 for people under 35 years, $40 560 for people between 35 and 49 years, and $100 587 for people over 50 years. This staged increase in the contribution limit was partially a reflection of the fact that younger people generally place more emphasis on current consumption, whereas older people are generally more able to trade-off current consumption for future consumption. As we have discussed, these graduated increases in the concessional contribution limit were replaced by the Howard/Costello Simpler Super reforms, which introduced a flat $50 000 concessional contribution limit for all Australians. The federal Labor government's changes to superannuation reduced this flat $50 000 to a flat $25 000 with periodic increases of $5000 to allow for inflation.

The ability under the old regime for individuals over the age of 50 to concessionally contribute $100 000 a year meant that superannuation could be 'topped up' very quickly later in a person's working life. The new flat contribution limits mean that this is no longer the case. If individuals are to accumulate enough superannuation to afford a comfortable retirement they need to start salary sacrificing more and earlier in their working lives; that is, younger people need to be convinced that forgoing current consumption for the sake of future consumption is worthwhile. Many younger people ignore the issue because it is too distant, too abstract and too complicated. Other younger people conclude that a dollar in their pocket is worth more than a dollar in superannuation.

PROFESSIONAL ADVICE

Salary sacrifice

Jess is 28 and works 4 days a week in a costume shop. Her employer contributes the standard superannuation guarantee amount into her nominated superannuation fund. Jess does not salary sacrifice into superannuation but her employer is happy to organise this if she wants. Jess has also been very successful in attracting a lot of contract costume work. Last year, Jess earned $20 000 more than the threshold at which the 37% marginal tax rate commences. She was annoyed that she lost $7400 in tax on this income. This year, she is determined not to let this happen and has decided to salary sacrifice into superannuation. The problem is that her income level fluctuates so much she is not sure how to organise this.

QUESTIONS

1. What advice can you give Jess with respect to the concessional contribution limit?
2. Is Jess likely to qualify as a self-employed person with respect to superannuation contributions?
3. If Jess is able to estimate the minimum amount she is likely to earn this financial year, how can you build a salary sacrifice strategy around this?
4. Can Jess wait until April/May when she has a clearer idea of how much she will earn in the financial year before implementing her salary sacrifice strategy?

Non-concessional contributions

As we discussed earlier, a non-concessional contribution to superannuation is a contribution for which a tax deduction has *not* been claimed. That is, individuals have taken their after-tax dollars (capital) and placed these inside a superannuation environment. When a superannuation fund receives a non-concessional contribution, no tax is deducted.

Non-concessional contributions are limited to $150 000 per year calculated on a rolling 3-year basis which means an employee could contribute $450 000 today but it would be three 3 years before they could make additional non-concessional contributions. Excess non-concessional contributions are taxed at the highest marginal tax rate plus Medicare levy.

Non-concessional contributions are a useful way for an individual to build their superannuation balance. Often non-concessional contributions are motivated by particular legislative provisions which in turn are generally tax driven. For example, non-concessional contributions might be made to derive the government co-contribution or the eligible spouse rebate or to take advantage of the proceeds from the sale of a small business. Non-concessional contributions are also a valuable tool for people with self-managed superannuation funds (SMSFs) who wish to make in-specie contributions, that is, contributions other than cash. SMSFs are discussed in more detail in chapter 12.

Government co-contributions

The government introduced the co-contribution scheme in 2003 to encourage low-income earners to build their superannuation balances by making a non-concessional contribution which would be matched by the government. Unfortunately constant government changes to the co-contribution scheme have resulted in a low level of public awareness and understanding of the co-contribution.

The amount of the government matching payment has varied over the years — in some years it has been $1 government co-contribution for each $1 of *eligible* non-concessional contribution; in other years it has been $1.50 for $1; and in one particularly generous year it was $3 for $1. Since 2012–13 *eligible* non-concessional contributions have been matched $0.50 for each $1 of contribution up to a maximum government co-contribution of $500.

This maximum government co-contribution is reduced by 3.333 cents for each $1 that the individual's income exceeds a particular level. In 2013–14, this level was $33 516. For example if an individual earned $43 516, their maximum non-concessional contribution *eligible* for matching would be reduced by $333 ($10 000 times 3.333 cents) to $167 ($500 – $333).

Therefore, if a person earning less than $33 516 makes an *eligible* non-concessional contribution of:

- $1000 it will be matched with a government co-contribution of $500
- $1200 it will be matched with a government co-contribution of $500 ($500 is the maximum government co-contribution)
- $800 it will be matched with a government co-contribution of $400 ($0.50 for each dollar contributed).

Therefore, if a person who earns $43 516 makes an *eligible* non-concessional contribution of:

- $1000 it will be matched with a government co-contribution of $167 (the maximum government co-contribution for someone with this income level)
- $334 it will be matched with a government co-contribution of $167 ($0.50 for each dollar contributed up to the maximum government co-contribution for someone with this income level)
- $300 it will be matched with a government co-contribution of $150 ($0.50 for each dollar contributed).

If a person's income exceeds $48 516 they will not be eligible for the government co-contribution.

Spouse rebate

The government provides a tax rebate of 18% for an individual who makes a non-concessional contribution for a low-income earning spouse. A $3000 non-concessional contribution limit is reduced by $1 for every $1 that the spouse earns in excess of

$10 800. For example, if Rachael contributes $3000 to her spouse Jason's superannuation and Jason earns less than $10 800 Rachael will be entitled to a $540 ($3000 × 0.18) tax rebate.

Proceeds from the sale of a small business

The federal government introduced a series of special capital gains tax (CGT) provisions for small business owners in recognition that many small business owners build up and reinvest in their businesses rather than in superannuation throughout their working lives. The provisions enable small business owners to remove or reduce their CGT liability which would otherwise arise from the sale of their small business while at the same time making contributions to superannuation in excess of the non-concessional contribution limit which would normally apply without tax penalty.

In-specie contributions

In specie means a contribution in kind rather than in cash. A self-managed superannuation fund (SMSF) is able to accept **in-specie contributions** provided its trust deed allows it and the investment rules that apply to the fund are complied with. For example, a member of an SMSF might contribute $100 000 in NAB shares to their fund. In-specie contributions are discussed in more detail in chapter 12.

in-specie contributions
contributions made in kind rather than in cash e.g. a self-employed person may contribute listed shares to their SMSF

Contribution splitting

An individual may split concessional superannuation contributions with their spouse. A concessional contribution will be received by the individual's superannuation fund and the 15% contributions tax deducted. The balance may then be split with their spouse.

Choice of fund

The Howard/Costello government announced in 1997 that employees would have a choice in the fund to which their employer contributions were made. This initiative had one of the longest gestation periods in recent history for a proposed government policy. It endured 8 long years of argument and counter-argument until it was finally put in place from 1 July 2005. This policy is important for a number of reasons. Firstly, being able to choose the fund in which an individual's employer contributions are invested is an incentive for each member to take an interest in superannuation, rather than ignoring it because contributions are invested in a fund of the employer's choice. Individuals now have control; they can compare funds, assess performance or earnings history, assess fee structures and compare risk. Secondly, choice of fund fosters competition between funds and thus encourages fund managers to examine their processes to gain efficiencies and cut fees, and to invest as well as possible to maximise returns and so retain existing and attract new members.

Some superannuation funds are for members of a defined group only; for example, TelstraSuper is open only to existing employees and their family members and former Telstra employees. A person who is not a member of the defined group cannot choose the fund. However, most industry funds and all retail funds are public-offer funds.

Employers must give employees a standard choice form within 28 days of commencing employment. The standard choice form nominates the **default fund** to which the employer will make contributions. Employers must also give employees a standard choice form within 28 days of a request for the form by the employee. An employee's right to change funds is limited to once every 12 months. However, employers may accept more frequent changes at their discretion.

default fund
an employer nominated superannuation fund where the member does not exercise their choice of fund

default investment option
a trustee nominated investment choice where the member does not exercise their investment choice

MySuper

Ironically, while most Australians have a choice of superannuation fund and a choice of investment options within that fund most people do not exercise that choice. Most Australians allow their employer and the 'system' to make perhaps the two most critical superannuation decisions on their behalf. Firstly the employer will have a default fund into which superannuation contributions will be made. Most people will simply accept this as their 'preferred' fund notwithstanding the fact that they have a choice of funds. Secondly the fund will have a **default investment option**, typically a balanced investment option. Again, most people will simply accept this as their 'preferred' investment option notwithstanding the fact that they have a choice of investment options.

Motivated in part by this superannuation 'apathy' the federal government introduced the MySuper reforms. The federal government's stronger super website claims that MySuper will result in '... a simple, low cost default superannuation product called MySuper which will improve the simplicity, transparency and comparability of default superannuation products' (www.strongersuper.treasury.gov.au).

Superannuation funds began offering MySuper accounts from 1 July 2013. Since 1 January 2014 employees who have not exercised their choice of fund will have had their contributions placed into a MySuper account as the default option.

Prior to the introduction of the MySuper reforms individual accounts with small balances, that is, balances of less than $1000 were protected from being eroded by administration fees. This protection was criticised by the Cooper Inquiry of 2010 on a number of grounds including the fact that it provided little incentive for individuals to consolidate their disparate superannuation balances. Most such small accounts will now end up in the default MySuper investment choice and therefore will be subject to a low cost standard fee environment. However, it is important to note that they are no longer protected from erosion by fees.

A range of criteria are used to determine if a superannuation account is inactive and lost and these are outlined on the ATO website (www.ato.gov.au). Not surprisingly small account balances are more frequently 'lost' than large account balances. Small account balances are periodically swept up and transferred to the ATO. Currently balances of less than $2000 which are 'lost' are transferred to the ATO. From 1 January 2016 this will increase to $2500 and from 1 January 2017 it will further increase to $3000.

Bankruptcy provisions

The High Court has affirmed that it is possible for all funds held in superannuation to be protected from creditors in the case of bankruptcy. However, the legislative response to the High Court's decision has been to allow creditors access to the superannuation funds of a bankrupt provided it can be 'proven' that the transfer of assets to a superannuation fund was done for the purpose of denying creditors their entitlements. The legislation also provides some guidance on how proof might be established, for example:

- if it can be reasonably assumed that the individual was insolvent at the time assets were transferred to the superannuation fund
- if a transfer to a superannuation fund was 'out of character', for example, it would generally be seen as out of character for a person who has, in the past, made no contributions to superannuation to make a $400 000 contribution the day before they declare bankruptcy.

Figure 10.4 summarises the types of contributions that can be made to superannuation.

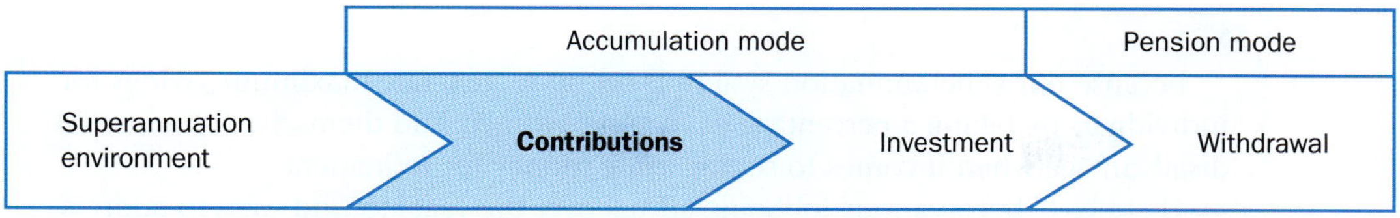

Concessional contributions

A contribution to superannuation for which a tax deduction has been claimed — for example employer superannuation guarantee contributions (*Tier 2*) or a salary sacrifice contribution (*Tier 3*).

Will be taxed at 15% inside the superannuation fund. If the amount contributed had been taken as salary instead it would be taxed at the individual's marginal tax rate.

Amount is generally limited to $25 000. Amount is indexed by average weekly ordinary times earnings — amount will jump in increments of $5000.
Concessional contributions include:
- superannuation guarantee
- salary sacrifice.

Non concessional contributions

A contribution to superannuation for which a tax deduction has *not* been claimed, that is, a contribution of after-tax money.

Will be *not* be taxed inside the superannuation fund.

Amount is limited to $150 000. Amount is six times the concessional limit.

Non concessional contributions include:
- government co-contributions
- spouse rebate
- proceeds from the sale of a small business
- in-specie contributions.

FIGURE 10.4
Overview of superannuation contributions

PERSONAL FINANCE BULLETIN

Bridging the super gap

Women finish their careers with less superannuation than men and they live longer, but it will take smart saving strategies — not government incentives — to address this inequity.

Based on the numbers, superannuation could be one of the starkest examples of a gender gap that there is. Women retire with almost half the super of men, a ratio that hasn't changed in more than a decade. Data shows that the mean super balance for women at retirement is $112 000 compared to $190 000 for men.

The reason for the difference is twofold — women are spending on average five or six years out of paid work to have children in what could be their prime earning years; meanwhile they are paid 18 per cent less on average than their male counterparts, according to figures compiled by the Australian Institute of Superannuation Trustees (AIST).

»

»

Because our superannuation system is set up to generate maximum savings for individuals by taking a percentage of income, women find themselves at a natural disadvantage when it comes to setting aside money for retirement.

There have been various lobbying efforts over the years to find ways to address the gap. The co-contribution scheme introduced in 2003 to help boost super balances of low-income earners has been gradually watered down over the years; meanwhile, the government's low-income super contribution scheme, that makes automatic payments up to $500 a year for low earners, is shaping up to be a decisive political issue leading up to the election.

The existing low-income super contribution scheme, which AIST president Cate Wood says effectively helps boosts the super account balances of around two million women who earn less than $37 000 a year, is not currently supported by the Coalition.

A chorus of voices, from the AIST, Women in Super (WIS) and the Financial Services Council (FSC), are calling for full super entitlements to be paid to all women when they take either their government-sponsored parental leave or employer-sponsored parental leave.

In AIST's recent budget submission, the association, which represents predominantly industry fund members, also asks the government to remove the $450 monthly income threshold for compulsory super payments, which it says can make it difficult for women in part time and casual work to build their retirement savings.

AIST also advocates for a 'return to work' payment or super credit for women who have been out of the workforce raising children. Yet despite the obvious disparity in super balances between males and females, there has been little progress towards any of these reforms. On the contrary, lobbyists admit that budget cuts targeting existing super tax concessions are far more likely.

Having more women appointed to super fund boards would help close the gender gap, says Wood, who is also chairperson of WIS, the national advocacy group.

'We believe that if more women are appointed to the boards of super funds, policy proposals aimed at addressing the gender gap will have more chance of being prioritised', she says.

The government this year provided a grant of $150 000 for AIST and WIS to run a 'board readiness' program aimed at increasing female representation on super fund boards.

Save early and save often

However, many see the gender savings gap as less about shortfalls in the superannuation system and more as a reflection of broader inequities in society, particularly relating to pay.

'You can't expect to retire with as much as someone who works full time and is paid more', says Susan Jackson, principal of Women's Financial Network, a Melbourne-based financial planning practice focused on the female market. 'You can't have it all — it's a compromise [having a career and a family] and super is part of that compromise.'

The best thing women can do to bridge the retirement savings gap is know it exists and plan to address their own gap from an early age, she says.

A woman's best strategy to bridge the gap is to make smart decisions that help stretch their savings dollar further, says Ipswich-based authorised representative with AMP Financial Planning Group, Diane Charman.

She says women in their mid to late 20s are now in the prime of their earnings lives and should be salary sacrificing to build their balances sooner. 'This is something I would normally say to someone in their 40s, but it applies in particular to women approaching the age when they are looking to start a family', Charman says, which in Australia is now about 31 years of age.

Under the current rules, individuals can add up to $25 000 a year into their superannuation and have it taxed at a concessional rate of 15 per cent.

The fact that women on average live longer than men makes it all the more important for women to think about their super earlier, Charman says.

The Australian Bureau of Statistics states a 65-year-old woman will on average live to 87 whereas a 65-year-old man can expect to live to 84. Actuarial estimates suggest people will be living an extra three years by the time the next generation enters retirement, which means women will need to ensure their retirement savings last them until at least the age of 90.

Annuities may be an answer

Because of this additional longevity risk, women might do well to look at purchasing products that guarantee an income over a pre-nominated period of time, or even the rest of a lifetime.

The most common of these insurance-style products are annuities, which begin paying an income immediately upon purchase, or deferred annuities, which have a cheaper upfront price tag but do not start paying an income until a future date (the birthday after the purchaser has surpassed the average life expectancy for their gender is a common choice).

Annuities have struggled to find acceptance in Australia; Challenger is the only vendor that's built anything like a scalable business out of the product.

One drawback is that annuities don't attract as many tax concessions as super — for instance the investment income earned by a deferred annuity before it converts to pension-paying mode is taxed at the purchaser's marginal income tax rate.

In something of a vicious circle, their lack of popularity also makes them expensive, because the risk to the issuer cannot be spread among enough customers.

But those that have embraced annuities have overwhelmingly been women — as of July 2012, 62 per cent of annuity beneficiaries in Australia were female according to the chief executive of Challenger's life insurance business, Richard Howes.

Aside from the additional 'longevity risk' to which women are exposed because they live longer than men, Howes says the more financially conservative nature of women attract them to the capital and income security the annuity affords.

Source: Matthew Smith, *BRW*, 7–13 March 2013, pp. 40–2.

Annuities are discussed in more detail in chapter 11 which deals with retirement income streams. Shortly after this article was written the federal government announced changes to the way investment income earned by deferred annuities is taxed to make it more attractive to investors/retirees.

LO 7 Investment and superannuation

Contributions to a superannuation fund need to be invested by the trustees of the fund. For members with accumulation style superannuation accounts, positive investment earnings will increase their account balances. For members of defined benefit schemes where the investment risk has been passed to the employer, the impact of short-term investment returns is of less consequence. Nonetheless, it is vital for the long-term viability of the fund that the trustees of defined benefit schemes also properly manage the investment of contributions.

Investment objectives and strategies

Trustees of superannuation funds must formulate an investment objective and supporting investment strategies pursuant to the SIS Act s. 52(2)(f). If a fund offers more than one investment choice, each must have its own objective and supporting strategies.

A published investment objective(s) helps members and potential members decide on which superannuation fund and which investment choice suits their needs. The objective also becomes a benchmark by which the actions of the trustees can be judged. For example, a fund might offer a balanced investment choice which aims to return 2% above the rate of inflation on a rolling 5-year basis.

Once an investment objective is established, the fund must formulate and implement strategies to support that objective. Specifically these strategies must address the following:

- risk and return — how will investments be chosen which are likely to produce the return specified in the objective while at the same time managing risk?
- diversification — how will investments be spread across different asset classes to reduce volatility?
- short-term liquidity — how will the fund manage its day-to-day cash flow?
- long-term liquidity — how will the fund invest its assets such that the assets release cash over the longer term to meet the needs of members who leave the fund and/or retire?

Investment choices

Most large superannuation funds offer a range of investment choices to accumulation account members. Most funds use fairly standard and conventional terms to describe their investment choices — typically the most conservative investment choice will be labelled 'Cash' and the most aggressive might be labelled 'High growth' and sitting somewhere in between will be a 'Balanced' investment choice. Sometimes more exotic labels are used by funds, so it is important for a member to look beyond the label and review the asset allocation strategy adopted by the particular investment choice.

Members have different investment needs and different attitudes to risk. High-growth investment choices tend to be more volatile and better suited to members with longer investment time horizons and a willingness to accept a degree of risk. Members closer to retirement or already retired may prefer a more conservative investment choice.

Typically, funds allow members to switch their investment strategy monthly. Some members do switch their investment choice frequently, which seems illogical given the long-term nature of superannuation as an investment. Conversely, some members never switch, which might mean they have accepted the long-term nature of superannuation and are happy with their investment choice, or it might mean that they have not given the matter any thought at all.

Investment restrictions

As there are significant tax benefits associated with superannuation, individuals/trustees might be tempted to use the superannuation environment for purposes other than providing for retirement. This may be particularly so in the case of SMSFs. The government has placed numerous investment restrictions on superannuation in an attempt to ensure that the superannuation environment is used for its intended purpose. These restrictions, described next, include the sole purpose test, the in-house assets rule, borrowings, loans and financial assistance to members and the need for transactions to be conducted on an arm's length basis. Individuals considering setting up their own SMSF need to balance these investment restrictions against the tax advantages on offer. It may be a rational choice for an individual to forgo some of the tax advantages of superannuation in order to have greater investment freedom. The investment restrictions faced by SMSFs are discussed in more detail in chapter 12.

Sole purpose test

Section 62 of the SIS Act requires that the trustee of a regulated fund must ensure that the fund is maintained *solely* for one or more of specific retirement-related issues such as:

- the provision of benefits upon retirement
- the provision of benefits upon reaching age 65
- the provision of benefits to dependants in the event of death.

Where an investment provides an incidental advantage to a member this will not automatically cause the fund to fail the sole purpose test. For example, a fund might own a ski chalet which is vacant for one weekend a year and it might let members stay there for that weekend at a reduced rate. This incidental advantage is unlikely to cause the fund to fail the sole purpose test. However, if the chalet is never rented out and provides no commercial return but members can use it free of charge any time they like, the regulator may well ask whether this advantage is more than incidental; that is, is the fund seeking to provide retirement benefits to members or is it seeking to provide them with cheap holidays partially funded by a concessionally taxed superannuation environment?

The regulator is concerned with the purpose of the investment not the type; that is, it is possible for a superannuation fund to invest in quite 'exotic' investments and still meet the sole purpose test, provided it can establish that the purpose of the investment was to provide for retirement benefits.

In-house assets rule

Trustees are not permitted to acquire assets from a 'related party' of the fund except where the acquisition of the asset will not result in the 'in-house' assets of the fund exceeding 5% of all assets. A superannuation fund is meant to provide for retirement benefits; it is not meant as a vehicle to invest in the business and other assets of members and associates. If a superannuation fund was to have substantial investments in a business related to the members, diversification is reduced, and if the business performs poorly a member might find both their job and their superannuation at risk.

There are two important exemptions to the in-house assets rule for SMSFs. The first is the business real property exemption, which we will discuss in more detail in chapter 12. The second exemption applies to listed securities purchased at their market value.

Borrowings

Superannuation is a controlled and regulated environment, making it a relatively 'safe' investment environment; however, it is important to remember that investment returns for accumulation account members are not guaranteed. Superannuation funds are not allowed to borrow money in order to gear up returns and this makes the superannuation environment 'safer'. Superannuation funds can, however, borrow small amounts of money for transactional purposes for periods up to 90 days.

Loans and financial assistance to members

Trustees are not allowed to lend money or provide financial assistance to members or relatives of members.

Transactions on an arm's length basis

All investments are to be made on an arm's length basis, that is, on strictly commercial terms. The purchase and sale price of an asset should always reflect the true market value. Income from assets should always reflect the true market rate of return.

In the case of *APRA v Derstepanian* [2005] FCA 1121 the defendant was a trustee of the Tunstall Bond Superannuation Fund. The defendant was also the sole director of Tunstall Bond Pty Ltd. The defendant transferred jewellery-making equipment as an in-specie contribution to the superannuation fund to satisfy their superannuation guarantee obligations on behalf of their employees.

In the accounts of the superannuation fund this equipment was valued at $285 000; however, the equipment was largely obsolete and had a real value of approximately $10 000. Had the transaction been conducted on an arm's length basis on commercial terms it would have been readily apparent that the jewellery-making equipment was not worth $285 000.

The Federal Court ruled that the defendant had breached arm's length rules and ordered that the defendant pay the $225 000 owing to employees, a further $70 000 to the ATO and a $100 000 fine.

Figure 10.5 opposite provides a brief summary of the superannuation investment environment.

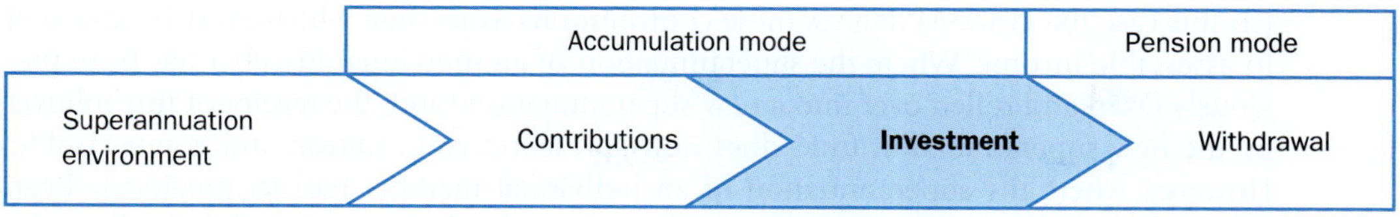

Investment objectives and strategies
Contributed funds and accumulated balances are invested. All superannuation funds must have a published investment objective and strategies to support that objective. The fundamental purpose of all investment is to build wealth.

Investment choice
Most Australians can choose which superannuation fund they contribute to.

Most superannuation funds offer a range of investment choices from very conservative to very aggressive. The individual member can select the investment choice which suits their risk profile.

Tax-concessional environment
Earnings are taxed at 15%. If these earnings had been made outside a superannuation environment they would be taxed at the individual's marginal tax rate.

Investment restrictions
The Federal Government provides tax concessions for superannuation and wants to ensure that this money is used to fund retirement. Therefore it imposes investment restrictions on superannuation money.

Investment restrictions include:
- the need for investments to be for the sole purpose of providing retirement benefits
- limits on assets acquired from members via the in-house asset rule
- limits on borrowings
- prohibition on loans and financial assistance to members
- the need to conduct transactions on an arm's length basis.

FIGURE 10.5
Overview of superannuation investment environment

LO 8 Taxation of superannuation funds

The taxation arrangements of superannuation funds are important because the tax paid effectively reduces the balances of members' accounts.

In Australia, the principal legislation governing the taxation of superannuation fund income and capital gains are the *Income Tax Assessment Act 1936* (generally known as the ITAA36) and the *Income Tax Assessment Act 1997* (generally known as the ITAA97). In 2007, the ITAA97 was amended by the *Tax Laws Amendment (Simplified Superannuation) Act 2007*.

The basic framework for taxing the income of superannuation funds is very similar to that used for individuals. That is, the superannuation fund must determine its assessable income and then subtract allowable deductions to result in the taxable income of the fund.

Assessable income

Income includes both ordinary income and statutory income but excludes exempt income. Income from investments, such as dividend income, will generally meet the description of ordinary income and will need to be included by superannuation funds in their assessable income.

The ITAA97 provides a full list of statutory income for superannuation funds. Concessional contributions are, in essence, a receipt of capital; however, the relevant legislation (in this case the ITAA36) defines these contributions as income which must be included in assessable income. Where the superannuation of an individual member has been previously taxed and rolled over into a new superannuation fund, the receipt of this rollover by the new superannuation fund does not represent a contribution and is not taxable. However, where the superannuation of an individual member has *not* previously been taxed and is rolled over into a new superannuation fund, the receipt of this rollover by the new superannuation does represent taxable income.

Capital gains from investments are also, in essence, capital; however, as with individuals, the superannuation fund must declare part of this gain as income. For assets bought after 21 September 1999, two-thirds of any gain is assessable income for a superannuation fund and one-third is exempt and does not have to be included in assessable income. Other exempt income for superannuation funds includes:

- contributions to superannuation where no tax deduction has been claimed, i.e. non-concessional contributions
- income attributable to investments which are dedicated to the purpose of paying current pensions.

Allowable deductions

Deductions are expenses necessarily incurred by a superannuation fund to earn assessable income. The legislative provisions about general deductions and specific deductions are set out in sections 8.1 and 8.5 of the ITAA97 and a table covering each particular deduction is in section 12.5 of the Act.

Some deductions are administrative in nature, for example, the costs of running an office and employing staff to answer member inquiries. Some deductions are more a function of how the fund operates, for example, contributions received by superannuation funds for the purpose of paying insurance premiums are generally deductible. Chapter 9, which deals with risk management and insurance, discusses the circumstances under which insurance premiums are deductible for a superannuation fund.

Taxable income

Taxable income is simply assessable income less allowable deductions. The taxable income of complying superannuation funds is taxed at 15%. A superannuation fund with a taxable income of $100 000 will have to pay $15 000 in tax; however, tax credits may mean that the actual tax paid will be less than $15 000. The two most important tax credits are as follows.

- *Dividend imputation credits*. Fully franked dividends, which provide 30% tax credits, are a valuable tool for trustees in managing their fund's tax liability. Imputation credits have the power not only to negate the tax payable on dividend income but to also reduce the tax otherwise payable on other sources of income.
- *Foreign tax credits*. Where an Australian superannuation fund holds investments overseas in a country with which Australia has a tax treaty, any tax paid in that country is offset against income from that country. Therefore, tax would be payable on this income only if the tax rate was less than 15%.

There are, however, occasions where additional tax will be payable by the superannuation fund, including the following.

- Where the individual member has not supplied a tax file number (TFN), the fund is obliged to tax any contributions received at the highest personal marginal tax rate. The TFN is a discrete identifier issued to taxed entities by the ATO to help reduce identity fraud. It is important to remember that an individual may have many superannuation funds and could claim concessional contributions for each of these funds. The matching of TFNs by the ATO is designed to prevent this abuse.

- Where an individual has made concessional contributions in excess of their concessional contribution limit and the excess has not been withdrawn.
- Where an individual has made a non-concessional contribution in excess of their non-concessional limit.
- Where a fund is 'non-complying', all taxable income will be taxed at the highest personal marginal tax rate.

ILLUSTRATIVE EXAMPLE 10.3

During the financial year, the Three Crows Superannuation Fund receives the following amounts. Three Crows is a complying superannuation fund.

Superannuation guarantee contributions	$200 000
Salary sacrifice contributions (includes $10 000 which are contributions received to pay for life insurance)	$100 000
Cash received from fully franked dividends	$ 84 000
Unfranked dividends	$ 20 000
Non-concessional member contributions	$ 80 000
Proceeds from sale of property (cost $140 000 in 2003)	$200 000
Income from investments used to fund pensions	$ 50 000

What is the assessable income of the fund and how much tax will be payable by the fund?

Assessable income		
Superannuation guarantee contributions (defined under the ITAA as assessable income)	$200 000	
Salary sacrifice contributions (defined under the ITAA as assessable income)	100 000	
Fully franked dividends (the cash received needs to be grossed up) $\frac{\$84\,000}{(1 - \text{company tax rate})}$	120 000	
Unfranked dividends	20 000	
Non-concessional member contributions (no tax concession has been claimed and therefore not taxed inside the fund)	0	
Capital gain from sale of property ($200 000 – $140 000) × 2/3 assessable (defined under the ITAA as assessable income)	$ 40 000	
Income from investments used to fund pensions (exempt income and not included)	$ 0	
Total assessable income		**($480 000)**

»

»

Allowable deductions	
Contributions received to pay for life insurance (defined under the ITAA as an allowable deduction)	(10 000)
Taxable income	**470 000**
Tax payable (taxed at 15%)	70 500
Less franking credits (grossed up amount less cash received = $120 000 – $84 000)	(36 000)
Net tax payable	**$ 34 500**

Relationship breakdown and the splitting of superannuation

Superannuation is often the most valuable non-housing asset owned by a couple. In many cases one member of the couple may have substantially more in superannuation than their partner. We have seen earlier in this chapter that men have on average substantially more in superannuation than women. In any division of assets resulting from relationship breakdown superannuation is a significant asset which needs to be considered.

The *Family Law Act 1975* and the *Superannuation Industry (Supervision) Act 1993* provide for the division of superannuation as a result of a relationship breakdown. The Act applies to spouses who are legally married and to spouses who are in de facto relationships whether they are opposite sex or same sex relationships.

Where spouses agree, they are able to enter into a superannuation agreement which if ratified by the Family Court outlines how their superannuation is to be divided. Where spouses are unable to agree the Family Court will need to make a determination as to how the superannuation should be divided. The Family Court may order an interest split or a payment split. An interest split is where the account is split immediately and one account becomes two — each party then independently manages their own separate superannuation account. A payment split is where the split occurs at the time of payment which is generally at retirement. In both interest splits and payment splits the components that make up the original superannuation balance are split proportionally. For example:

ILLUSTRATIVE EXAMPLE 10.4

Thelma has $500 000 in a superannuation account which comprises a $100 000 tax-free component (20%) and a $400 000 taxable component (80%). The Family Court determines that Thelma's superannuation should be split 60% to Thelma and 40% to Louise. After the split Thelma will have $300 000 in superannuation comprising a $60 000 tax-free component (20%) and $240 000 taxable component (80%). Louise will have $200 000 in superannuation comprising a $40 000 tax-free component (20%) and $160 000 taxable component (80%).

(The difference between tax-free and taxable components is discussed in chapter 11 which deals with retirement planning.)

Rather than an interest or payment split spouses may initiate, or the Family Court may impose, a flagging order. The flagging order is a form of injunction on the superannuation account and limits what actions can be taken until the flag is lifted.

Superannuation is often the most valuable non-housing asset owned by a couple and this can often cause problems for the Family Court in arriving at an equitable distribution of assets which meets the needs of both parties.

ILLUSTRATIVE EXAMPLE 10.5

Bonny and Clyde own a house that is worth $600 000 and Clyde has $400 000 in superannuation. Other than an everyday bank account with a very low balance they have no other assets. Bonny cares for their two children. The Family Court determines that the assets should be split 60% to Bonny and 40% to Clyde. Bonny gets to keep the house to assist with the raising of the children and Clyde gets to keep his superannuation. The problem for Bonny is that although she has the house she has very little cash flow and the problem for Clyde is that he cannot access his superannuation until he reaches his preservation age and nor can he use his superannuation as security for a loan — he too will have cash flow problems.

LO 9

Fees and charges

The financial planning industry has been subject to considerable criticism over the complexity and lack of transparency with respect to how fees are charged and this has led in part to the Future of Financial Advice (FOFA) reforms discussed in chapter 1. It is hoped that these reforms will over time simplify and make more transparent the way fees are charged on all financial investments including superannuation.

We discussed earlier under the heading of MySuper how apathy often results in individuals letting others make key superannuation decisions on their behalf. Where an individual makes their own superannuation decisions (or their employer or the MySuper system makes them on their behalf) no adviser service fees are applicable. However, on some occasions individuals will seek professional financial advice with respect to their superannuation and other investments. One of the key elements of the FOFA reforms is to eradicate conflicted remuneration. In the past product issuers would charge a 'product' fee and some or all of this fee would be rebated to the adviser. This arguably could influence the adviser to recommend a product that may not be in the best interests of the individual, hence the conflict. This product fee was in effect a contribution fee which meant that for every $100 contributed something less than $100 ended up in the superannuation fund. The FOFA reforms will lead to more fees being charged upfront as adviser service fees and less fees at the back end in the form of product fees which will hopefully reduce conflict and improve transparency. The initial adviser service fee may be charged as a flat dollar fee or as a percentage of the amount invested. Similarly, any ongoing fees may be charged as a flat dollar fee or as a percentage of the amount invested.

Superannuation fees and charges

Once funds are inside the superannuation environment, whether as a result of following professional advice or as a result of the action or inaction of the individual, they are subject to a range of fees and charges.

The fees and charges which apply to a superannuation account can have a significant bearing on the final amount accumulated in superannuation. Industry funds have run a very successful media campaign in recent years claiming that the fees they apply are on average substantially lower than the fees of other providers, particularly retail funds.

Fees and charges must be disclosed in the product disclosure statement associated with the fund. These documents can be long and complex, often making it difficult for the individual to understand what fees actually apply.

Fees for superannuation can be broadly disaggregated into direct and indirect fees. Direct fees are fees that are charged directly to the investor account when a given transaction occurs whereas indirect fees are usually expressed as a percentage of the funds under management and are subtracted from investment returns to produce an investment return net of indirect costs.

Direct fees

Direct fees include establishment fees, contribution fees, switching fees and withdrawal fees. This list is not exhaustive and different funds will use different terminology to describe the particular fees that apply to their funds.

Establishment fees are fees payable when money is initially contributed to superannuation. Contribution fees are payable when money is periodically contributed to superannuation. Many superannuation funds do not charge an establishment or contribution fee, but when they do the fees are typically charged as a percentage of the amount contributed. Establishment and contribution fees can have a significant impact on the dollar amount accumulated, depending on the percentage applied. If for example a superannuation fund charges a 2% establishment fee on the initial superannuation contribution and a 2% contribution fee on all additional contributions, the amount accumulated will be 2% less than for a comparable fund which does not charge these fees, all other things being equal. This 2% differential applied to a large superannuation balance as a person approaches retirement has a significant dollar effect.

A switching fee is usually charged when an individual wishes to change their selected investment option. For example, if an individual wishes to switch from a balanced option to a growth option this will incur a fee. Most funds will limit the frequency with which investors can change their investment option (typically this would be monthly). Most funds will also have an established cycle as to when switches take place and it is important for the individual to realise that having made the request to switch there may be some time lag before this switch takes place.

A withdrawal fee is generally payable when an individual seeks to withdraw a full or partial lump sum when they are in pension mode. This withdrawal fee will also often apply to rollovers to other funds and contribution splitting.

Indirect fees

Indirect fees include the annual management fee and all other fees which cannot be directly attributed to an individual member's account, including legal, accounting, auditing and other operational and compliance costs.

The annual management fee is often separately identified by the fund. The dollar amount incurred is aggregated, then expressed as a percentage of the funds under management. This measure is generally known as the **management expense ratio (MER)**. All other indirect fees — legal, accounting and so on — are similarly aggregated and expressed as a percentage of funds under management. If for example the MER was 1% and the other indirect fees were equal to 1% of the funds under management, the **indirect cost ratio (ICR)**, which is an aggregation of the MER and the other indirect fees, would be 2%. It is important to remember that the MER is a subset of the ICR and that the ICR is the most valuable fee-based measure by which funds can be compared.

management expense ratio (MER) a ratio of fees charged to the value of the assets under management

indirect cost ratio (ICR) an aggregation of all management costs (MER) and other indirect costs which cannot be attributed to individual member accounts expressed as a percentage of funds under management

For accumulation style superannuation funds the ICR is subtracted from the investment returns that would otherwise be credited to members' accounts. If the investment returns were a positive 7% before the application of the ICR and the ICR was 2%, this would mean that accounts would be credited with a net 5% return. Similarly, if investment returns were a negative 4% before the application of the ICR and the ICR was 2%, this would mean that accounts would be credited with a net 6% negative return.

For defined benefit style superannuation funds the indirect costs are effectively built into the formula which determines the defined benefit entitlement.

Once a superannuation balance gets reasonably large the indirect fees are a much more significant consideration than the direct fees.

ILLUSTRATIVE EXAMPLE 10.6

Jiang has done his research on where he wants his superannuation money to go and has narrowed the choice to two funds, A and B. He believes that both funds are very similar and that the only significant difference between them is that fund A has an ICR of 1% while fund B has an ICR of 2%.

If Jiang was to contribute $10 000 per year for the next 30 years and the investment return for each fund was 8% per annum before the application of the ICR, what would be the future value of Jiang's superannuation in each fund?

In Excel Future Value (FV) = (rate, number of periods, amount)

Fund A FV = $944 607 (7%, 30, 10 000)

Fund B FV = $790 581 (6%, 30, 10 000)

The promoters of Fund B may well argue that not all funds are equal. They may argue that they employ expert fund managers who are likely to outperform other funds and more than compensate for their higher ICR. They could also argue that they offer a greater range of services. The ICR is a very useful starting point in comparing funds; however, it is not the only factor to be considered.

LO 10 How much will I accumulate in superannuation?

There are a number of superannuation calculators available on the internet which will calculate how much you will accumulate in superannuation for a given set of assumptions. Sometimes these assumptions are quite explicit as the calculator prompts you to input your assumption; for example, the rate per annum you expect your income to grow over the next 10 years. Sometimes, however, the assumptions are implicit in the model and the model itself becomes a 'black box' where you feed data in one end and results come out the other end without you really understanding the calculations.

It is instructive to build your own model using a spreadsheet such as Excel. Building the model will force you to address all the assumptions and processes which underpin the model. The model itself does not have to be complicated; however, the assumptions can be more difficult. Some people consider the assumptions so difficult that they do no planning at all. However, a plan — even if some of the assumptions are mis-specified or need constant review — is better than no plan at all.

ILLUSTRATIVE EXAMPLE 10.7

Gina currently earns $60 000 per year and her employer contributes 10% of this amount to superannuation. She currently has $100 000 in superannuation. Gina would like to know how much she will accumulate in superannuation over the next 10 years. She makes the following assumptions.

- Her salary will grow by 5% per annum.
- Her investment choice inside superannuation will earn 7% return p.a. after fees but before tax.
- The inflation rate will be 3% per annum.

To make the modelling simpler, we will model in calendar years and assume that contributions are made in December each year so that they do not attract investment earnings in the current year.

The model might look like that shown in figure 10.6.

FIGURE 10.6 Gina's superannuation projection

Assumptions and data	
Salary	$ 60 000
Rate of growth of salary	5.00%
Opening balance of superannuation	$100 000
Earnings after fees but before tax	7.00%
Earnings tax	15.00%
Earnings after fees and after tax	5.95%
Employer superannuation contribution before tax	10.00%
Contribution tax	15.00%
Employer superannuation contribution after tax	8.50%
Inflation	3.00%

Workings

Salary	Year	Opening balance ($)	Earnings after fees and after tax $	Employer superannuation contribution after tax $	Closing balance ($)
(S)		(OB)	(Earn)	(Cont)	(CB)
			= OB × 5.95%	= S × 8.50%	= OB + Earn + Cont
63 000	1	100 000	5 950	5355	111 305
66 150	2	111 305	6 623	5623	123 550
69 458	3	123 550	7 351	5904	136 806
72 930	4	136 806	8 140	6199	151 145
76 577	5	151 145	8 993	6509	166 647
80 406	6	166 647	9 915	6834	183 397
84 426	7	183 397	10 912	7176	201 485
88 647	8	201 485	11 988	7535	221 008
93 080	9	221 008	13 150	7912	242 070
97 734	10	242 070	14 403	8307	264 781

If the assumptions hold true, Gina will have accumulated $264 781 in superannuation in 10 years. The problem for Gina is that she is not sure what $264 781 will buy in 10 years. She can see that her salary will increase significantly over this time but knows that part of this is due to inflation. The $264 781 superannuation balance is a nominal figure; that is, it includes an inflationary component. We can remove this inflationary component and convert it to a real figure.

Today, $100 in your pocket can buy a basket of goods worth $100. If you went to the supermarket the $100 might fill the shopping trolley. If that $100 stays in your pocket for 10 years it loses 3% of its value through inflation each year and can buy a basket of goods worth only $74 in today's prices — the shopping trolley would be only three-quarters full.

$$\frac{100}{(1 + 3\%)^{10}} = \$74.41$$

$$\frac{264\,781}{(1 + 3\%)^{10}} = \$197\,022$$

As the formula shows, Gina's superannuation in 10 years will buy the equivalent of what $197 022 will buy today. Is this enough? Does she need to start salary sacrificing? Should she be more aggressive in her investment selection? In the next chapter we discuss the difficult question of how much we need to accumulate in order to fund our retirement.

Summary

Superannuation is simply a means of saving and investing to accumulate wealth and then using that wealth to fund retirement, usually in the form of an income stream. Superannuation has progressed from humble beginnings in 1992 and the introduction of the superannuation guarantee to a trillion dollar business 20 years later. During that time there has been a perceptible shift in expectations from reliance on the state to provide for retirement to reliance on the individual to fund their own retirement. Individuals need to understand the different types of superannuation accounts available and the characteristics of the different providers of these accounts so that they can make informed choices about their superannuation.

The political and legislative context of superannuation is highly dynamic. Understanding how we have got to where we are today provides some insight into where we might go in the future. Individuals and their advisers need to be aware of history as well as have a keen eye for current and future developments.

There is one key aspect of Australia's superannuation system which has bipartisan support — the three pillars (or tiers) policy of superannuation: Tier 1 — a tax-payer funded social security pension (a safety net) which is means tested; Tier 2 — compulsory employer contributions to superannuation for employees; Tier 3 — tax incentives for voluntary contributions to superannuation. The federal government has effectively gained legislative control of superannuation in Australia. The cornerstone of this legislative framework is the *Superannuation Industry (Supervision) Act 1993* (SIS Act). For a superannuation fund to be able to claim the tax concessions associated with being a superannuation fund it must be a complying superannuation fund. Four bodies are primarily charged with the regulation and control of the superannuation industry: the Australian Prudential Regulation Authority (APRA), the Australian Securities and Investments Commission (ASIC), the Australian Taxation Office (ATO) and the Superannuation Complaints Tribunal (SCT).

The most common type of superannuation account held by an individual is an accumulation account. Less common, but still a significant part of the superannuation industry, are defined benefit schemes. Money needs to be contributed to superannuation. Concessional and non-concessional contributions are treated differently when they enter the superannuation environment and (as we will see in the next chapter) they are also treated differently when they leave the superannuation environment. Money needs to be invested by the trustees of superannuation funds. The rules for investment inside superannuation are quite different from those outside superannuation. Contributions and earnings are taxed and trustees always need to be mindful of the tax consequences of their actions.

Superannuation is often the most valuable asset owned by spouses besides the family home. Sadly therefore it is also an asset often in dispute when a relationship breaks down. In an ideal world both parties would have a similar amount 'tied up' in superannuation. However, as we have seen for tax and work-related reasons there is often a significant difference between the superannuation balances of each spouse. The Family Court is often called upon to determine how superannuation should be split between spouses.

Over the longer term fees and charges can have a significant impact on the amount ultimately accumulated in superannuation. Individual fund members should know the indirect fees they are being charged and make a conscious decision that the 'services' they receive from their fund justify the fees being charged. The advent of MySuper would suggest that there is a low level of public interest in superannuation and as a result most fund members would have very little understanding of the fees and charges they are currently paying on their superannuation.

A number of superannuation calculators are available on the internet which will calculate how much you will accumulate in superannuation for a given set of assumptions. It is instructive to build your own model using a spreadsheet such as Excel. A superannuation plan — even if some of the assumptions are mis-specified or need constant review — is much better than no plan at all.

Professional application questions

10.1 Given that we have the age pension in Australia, why do we need superannuation?

10.2 Feng, aged 38, has $250 000 to invest in order to help fund his retirement but is unsure how to do this. Assume each of the following investments are returning 5% per annum — superannuation, share portfolio and rental property. How would you advise Feng?

10.3 What is the three pillars policy? What tax incentives drive the third pillar?

10.4 Superannuation in Australia is primarily regulated by the *Superannuation Industry (Supervision) Act 1993*. What are the key underlying principles upon which this Act is based?

10.5 Distinguish between the roles of APRA, ASIC and the ATO with respect to the regulation and control of the superannuation industry.

10.6 Why has there been a shift away from defined benefit schemes and towards accumulation schemes in Australia?

10.7 Why are actuarial calculations and estimations critical to the viability of defined benefit schemes?

10.8 Distinguish between funded and unfunded superannuation schemes. How will the commitments to unfunded schemes be met?

10.9 What public policy initiatives have been introduced to encourage Australians to stay at work longer?

10.10 What is the difference between a concessional and a non-concessional contribution? What are the different tax consequences when these contributions enter the superannuation fund?

10.11 Why is it important to distinguish between an employee and a contractor? How do we distinguish between them?

10.12 Each investment choice within a superannuation fund must have investment objectives that must be supported by investment strategies. What are the key investment strategies which must be addressed?

10.13 How have the FOFA reforms shifted advice fees from the product to the adviser?

10.14 Distinguish between direct and indirect superannuation fees. In the longer term which fees are likely to have the most impact on the amount accumulated? Why might an individual 'choose' a fund that has higher indirect fees?

Professional application exercises

Basic	*
Moderate	* *
Challenging	* * *

10.15 Tax saving from concessional contributions *

Chitra is self-employed and earns $200 000 p.a. If she make a concessional contribution to superannuation of $8000, how much tax will she save?

10.16 Eligible spouse rebate *

Trish has an assessable income and reportable fringe benefits of $12 800. Her spouse, Philipe makes a non-concessional contribution of $3000 on her behalf. What tax rebate is Philipe entitled to?

10.17 Impact of fees on amount accumulated *

Jiang has received his Choice of Superannuation Funds form from his employer. He is undecided whether to contribute to the FlexE Superfund or the PeqSA Superfund. He believes that both funds are very similar and that the only significant difference between them is the FlexE Superfund has an ICR of 0.9% whilst the PeqSA Superfund has an ICR of 2.2%.

If Jiang was to contribute $5000 per year for the next 20 years and the investment return for each fund was 7% per annum before the application of the ICR, what would be the future value of Jiang's superannuation in each fund?

10.18 Excess concessional contributions — accumulation * *

Mark is 29 and earns $100 000 p.a. As part of the applicable industrial award, his employer contributes an amount equal to 12% of his salary to his nominated superannuation fund. If Mark salary sacrifices $20 000 into superannuation, how much contributions tax will he pay? How much would you suggest Mark salary sacrifices into superannuation?

10.19 Excess concessional contributions — defined benefit * *

Janice is 31 and earns $100 000 p.a. She is a member of her employer's defined benefit scheme. She has just received a notice from her superannuation fund which indicates that her notional taxed contribution is 17%. If Janice salary sacrifices $18 000 into superannuation, how much contributions tax will she pay? How much would you suggest Janice salary sacrifice into superannuation?

10.20 Determining SG obligation * *

Peter believes that his employer has not contributed enough in SG payments. The table shows what Peter has earned over the last financial year. If we assume a SG rate of 10%, how much should the employer contribute?

Earnings for ordinary hours of work	$40 000
Overtime pay	$ 6 250
Over award payments	$ 3 320
Loadings for night shift	$ 4 800
Annual leave loading	$ 500
Christmas bonus	$ 1 000
Total	**$55 870**

10.21 Government co-contribution — under the income threshold * *

How much government co-contribution will each of the following people be entitled to?

(a) Barnaby earns $30 000 p.a. and makes a non-concessional contribution of $1000.

(b) Pixie earns $30 000 p.a. and makes a non-concessional contribution of $700.

(c) Rufus earns $30 000 p.a. and makes a non-concessional contribution of $2000.

10.22 Government co-contribution — over the income threshold * *

How much government co-contribution will each of the following people be entitled to?

(a) Ed earns $40 182 p.a. and makes a non-concessional contribution of $1000.

(b) Darren earns $40 182 p.a. and makes a non-concessional contribution of $250.

10.23 Government co-contribution — an efficient co-contribution amount * *

Audrey earns $40 000 p.a. She wants to make the smallest non-concessional contribution possible and still get the maximum government co-contribution payment available. How much will she need to contribute?

10.24 Investment restrictions * *

The trustees of Uripper Superannuation fund have made the following investment decisions. As auditor of the Uripper Fund, advise the trustees as to whether you believe the decisions comply with the investment restrictions outlined in the *Superannuation Industry (Supervision) Act 1993* and its associated regulations.

(a) The trustees of the fund have bought a beach house for the exclusive use of members.
(b) The trustees have acquired shares in Uripper Pty Ltd which amount to 40% of the total assets of the Uripper fund. Uripper Pty Ltd is owned by two of the members of the Uripper Superannuation Fund.
(c) In order to fund a payout to a recently retired member the fund has borrowed $100 000 for a period of two years.
(d) The fund has loaned Kita, who is a member of the fund, $200 000 to help fund a new business venture. The loan has been offered on commercial terms.
(e) Masami, who is a member of the fund, has sold a parcel of vacant land to the fund at a price which is considerably below its market value.

10.25 Determining the taxable income of a superannuation fund * * *

During the financial year, the Stone Masons superannuation fund receives the following amounts. The Stone Masons fund is a complying superannuation fund.

SG contributions	$400 000
Salary sacrifice contributions (includes $20 000 which are contributions received to pay for life insurance)	$185 000
Cash received from fully franked dividends	$ 21 000
Unfranked dividends	$ 10 000
Non-concessional member contributions	$127 000
Income from investments overseas (includes $10 000 in tax withheld — the country has a reciprocal tax agreement with Australia)	$100 000
Proceeds from sale of property (cost $120 000 in 2009)	$210 000
Income from investments used to fund pensions	$ 40 000

What is the assessable income of the fund and how much tax will be payable by the fund?

10.26 Determining the balance of a defined benefit account * * *

Tran is a member of a defined benefit superannuation scheme. His superannuation entitlement is determined by the following formula:
Final average salary times years of service times a factor.
Final average salary is determined by taking the average salary over the last three years of work. His annual salary over the last three years has been $80 000.
Years of service is equal to the number of equivalent full time years he has worked for the firm. Tran has worked with the firm for over 25 years; however, some of that has been part-time work and there was also a period of six months where he took leave without pay. Tran has the equivalent of 18 years of equivalent full time service.
The factor which is relevant to Tran is determined by a number of variables. The key variable is the rate of salary sacrifice that Tran has made to the fund over the years. The choices for Tran were 0%, 5% and 7%. Tran has salary sacrificed 5% during his working career. As a result his factor is 15%.

(a) What is Tran's current superannuation balance?
(b) Tran has noticed that if his rate of salary sacrifice was 7% rather than the current 5% his factor would rise to 18% and this would give him a superannuation 'windfall'. Advise Tran on the benefits of increasing his rate of salary sacrifice.
(c) Tran has recently been offered a promotion which would increase his salary by 40%. The new position is highly stressful, however, and Tran is not sure how long he would be able to cope with the stress. Advise Tran on the arguments for and against taking the promotion.

CASE STUDY

Salary sacrifice to achieve an accumulation target

Belinda is an engineer who likes precision in everything she does. Belinda is 50 years old and wants to retire in 10 years. She has been doing some reading about retirement incomes. If Belinda was 60 years old today and was to retire today she has calculated that she would require $587 574 to afford the type of income stream she desires in retirement. However, Belinda is 50 years old, not 60 — she has 10 years to accumulate this amount. Belinda also knows that inflation over the next 10 years will mean that she will need to accumulate more than $587 574.

Belinda has worked out that $789 650 received 10 years from today has the same value as $587 574 today assuming an inflation rate of 3% per annum.

As her financial adviser, you explain that the broad scope of the assumptions which underpin such modelling mean that such precision is very difficult to achieve. Nonetheless, any plan is better than no plan even if it is necessary to come back to the plan from time to time and adjust the assumptions.

Belinda wants you to build a model which accumulates a nominal $789 650 in superannuation over the next 10 years. She has supplied you with the following information and assumptions.

- Her opening superannuation balance is $367 823.
- Her income is $70 000 per annum and will grow in nominal terms by 4% per year.
- Her investment choice inside her fund is expected to earn 6% nominal returns p.a. after fees but before taxes.
- Her employer contributes an amount equal to 12% of her income to superannuation.

To make the modelling simpler, we will model in calendar years and assume that contributions are made in December each year so that they do not attract investment earnings in the current year.

The missing variable is the percentage of salary sacrificed into superannuation. Belinda is happy to sacrifice as much as possible to achieve her goal provided she stays within her concessional contribution limit. Belinda uses spreadsheets a lot in her work and has found the GOALSEEK function very useful in trying to solve problems like this. Construct a model similar to figure 10.6 and answer the following questions.

QUESTIONS

1. What percentage of her salary must Belinda sacrifice into superannuation in order to accumulate $789 650 in nominal terms in 10 years?
2. Explain to Belinda how salary sacrificing represents a trade-off between current consumption and future consumption and the factors she should take into account in determining the appropriate level of salary sacrifice.
3. What other factors besides salary sacrificing might Belinda alter in order to achieve her accumulation goal?
4. If Belinda was 15 years from retirement rather than 10 years, would her goal of accumulating a real amount of $587 574 in superannuation alter if her desired retirement income stream remained the same? Would her goal of accumulating a nominal amount of $789 650 in superannuation alter?

References and further reading

APRA 2012, *Annual superannuation bulletin*, June, apra.gov.au.

Association of Superannuation Funds of Australia (ASFA) 2013, www.superannuation.asn.au.

ATO 2010, *Superannuation guarantee — how to meet your super obligations*, July, ato.gov.au.

Australian Government 2010, *2010 Intergenerational Report*, treasury.gov.au.

Australian Government Budget Paper Number 1 2013, www.budget.gov.au/2013–14.

Australian Government 2013, *Stronger super*, www.strongersuper.treasury.gov.au.

Australian Government Actuary (AGA) 2013, *Life expectancy tables*, www.aga.gov.au.

Australian Securities and Investment Commission (ASIC) 2013, www.moneysmart.gov.au.

CCH 2012, *Australian master financial planning guide 2012–13*, 15th edition.

CCH 2012, *Australian master superannuation guide 2012–13*, 16th edition.

Inspector General of Taxation 2010, *Review of the ATO's administration of the SGC*, March 2010.

Smith, M 2013, 'Bridging the gap: how women can catch up on super', *Business Review Weekly*, 7–13 March, pp. 40–2.

Swift, B 2012, 'Defined benefit super also defines the problem', December, *In The Black*, pp. 68–9.

11 Retirement planning

LEARNING OBJECTIVES

After studying this chapter, you should be able to:

1. explain why it is important to plan for retirement
2. outline the three phases of retirement
3. calculate how much is needed to fund a particular income stream
4. differentiate between ordinary money and superannuation money
5. outline the tax consequences of withdrawing a lump sum from superannuation to fund retirement
6. differentiate between the different types of retirement income streams
7. calculate the deductible amount of an income stream
8. contrast and compare account-based and non-account based income streams
9. explain the tax advantages associated with transition to retirement income streams
10. discuss what constitutes an adequate retirement income.

CASE STUDY

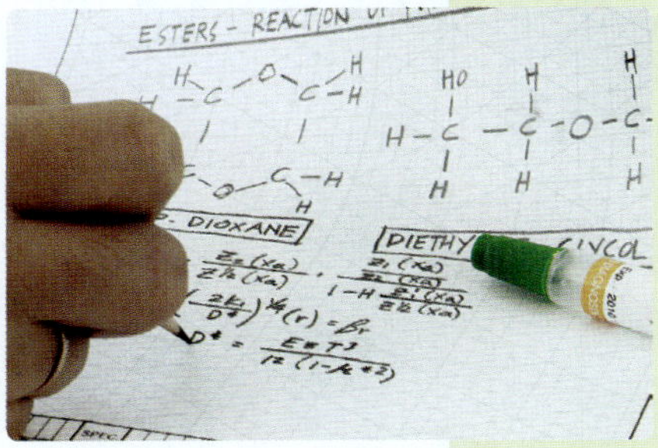

Lisa is a 63-year-old chemical engineer. She works full-time and earns around $100 000 p.a. Lisa rarely takes holidays — she has 6 months accumulated leave that she has not used. Her work often involves travel and long hours at the office in order to meet the demands of clients.

Lisa would like to retire or, at the very least, cut back on her work commitments and start to ease into retirement; however, she is worried that she may not have saved enough to retire.

Lisa has a holiday home which she estimates to be worth $300 000 and a negatively geared share portfolio which is currently valued at $80 000, although its value has been highly volatile in recent times. Lisa also has $220 000 in superannuation.

Some of the issues that Lisa needs to consider include the following.

- If she was to retire immediately how would she replace the sense of belonging and achievement that often comes through working?
- Should she retain her highly volatile share portfolio as she approaches retirement?
- How will her income needs change throughout the various phases of retirement?
- How will she 'enjoy' her retirement savings while ensuring that she does not outlive her retirement savings?
- If she continues to work, should she commence a transition to retirement income?

These issues will be explored in this chapter.

Introduction

If a person makes poor investment choices when they are working, one option is to work harder or longer in an attempt to recoup those losses. When a person is retired, however, this strategy is not an option. Accumulating enough money to fund a comfortable retirement is a key concern for those approaching the end of their working life. While this chapter focuses primarily on the financial aspects of retirement, we will also briefly consider some of the non-financial aspects of retirement.

Planning generally leads to better outcomes than not planning. Too many Australians leave retirement planning too late. Retirement planning cannot commence on the day a person retires; it cannot commence a year before they retire. Retirement planning is a long-term process. In this chapter, we will review each of the component parts of a long-term retirement plan.

Part of retirement planning is determining how much a person needs to accumulate in order to fund their desired lifestyle in retirement. This is often an iterative process where what is desirable is traded off against what is achievable.

Having accumulated sufficient funds for retirement, decisions need to be made about how these funds are used. Should the individual take a lump sum or an income stream? If the individual takes an income stream then what type of income stream should they take?

This chapter concludes by reviewing the question of what constitutes an adequate retirement income. Can an adequate level of income be generally prescribed or is the level different for each individual? If the level is different, what factors make it different?

LO 1 What is retirement planning?

Planning involves making choices. Retirement planning requires an individual to make many choices — some of them very difficult choices.

In accumulating wealth to fund retirement, an individual must consider the following.

- How much current consumption am I prepared to forgo in order to fund future consumption?
- How aggressive should my investment strategy be?
- Should I accumulate wealth inside or outside a superannuation environment?
- How long should I seek to accumulate wealth as opposed to using that wealth to enjoy my retirement?
- How much do I need to accumulate in order to fund my desired lifestyle in retirement?

Having 'retired' there are still many choices to be made, including:

- What does retirement actually mean? Does it mean stopping work or working less? How will I know when I am retired?
- How will I manage the change in lifestyle associated with being retired? Will I be happy in retirement? What if I change my mind?
- How do I access my retirement savings?

Individuals' needs in retirement

An individual's basic needs do not change in retirement; however, the post-retirement lifestyle within which those needs are fulfilled does change, and it does so dramatically. Individuals need to plan for this change such that their needs are fulfilled.

Maslow (1987) identified a hierarchy of individual needs. One of the key aspects of Maslow's hierarchy is that higher level needs cannot be satisfied unless lower level needs in the hierarchy have been satisfied first.

At the base level, we all have physiological needs that must be satisfied, for example, for water, food, shelter and basic health. In Australia, we are fortunate that most people have these basic physiological needs satisfied. Health issues are of particular concern to retirees. People who plan to become fit and healthy when they retire are likely to be disappointed — for this to occur, changes to lifestyle patterns need to occur well before retirement if they are to be enduring and effective. Increased life expectancies mean that most people will enjoy longer and more active retirements. However, as people age, it is reasonable to expect that health concerns and health costs will increase.

Moving up the Maslow hierarchy are safety needs, for example, feeling safe at home and outside of the home. As people get older, security concerns become more prominent — many people decide to defend themselves via deadlocks, alarm systems and gated communities; however, we also want to live in a society where such defensive measures are not required.

All people have the need for belonging and love, for example, to sustain personal and family relationships, and to be members of their communities. Many people form significant relationships at work and lose some contact with these friends when they retire. Developing new friendships can be difficult. Some retirees intend to join groups when they have more time in retirement; if at all possible, it would be better to join these groups while working and increase participation once retired. (It is no good waiting until you are retired to take up golf only to find that you don't like the game.) Many retired Australians participate in voluntary work both as an aide to the community and as a means of maintaining belonging to the community. The death or loss of a partner is generally recognised as one of the most significant psychological events in a person's life. Sometimes the end of a long-term relationship coincides with retirement because unpreparedness for retirement compounds the effect of other difficulties in a relationship. Such events cannot really be planned for but their effects on the need for love and belonging can be mitigated somewhat by a good support network of family and friends.

Everyone has the need for self-esteem and to be respected by others. One of the first questions often asked by a new acquaintance is 'what do you do?' In many ways, work defines who we are. This can lead to difficulties in retirement — work provides people with the opportunity to complete a task well and to earn the respect of others for doing so, an opportunity that can be difficult to replicate in retirement.

All people have what Maslow calls self-actualisation needs, for example, to be creative, to acquire knowledge and enjoy the aesthetic. Retirement often provides people with the time they need to pursue these needs. It is important, however, that retirement also provides people with the money they need to do so — to stand in front of the pyramids is a joyous experience, but it costs money.

LO 2 The three phases of retirement

The concept of retirement is relatively new. Up until the end of the nineteenth century, people expected to work until they died. If a person was unable to continue working for any reason, there was an often an extended family to provide some level of support.

The average Australian retiring today might reasonably expect a retirement period of 20 to 30 years. Over that period, the individual might go through a number of phases. The phases can be categorised in a number of ways, including as active, passive and support phases. There are no clear boundaries between these phases, for example, the transition from active to passive may take a number of years, and the age at which these transitions take place will depend on the individual.

The active phase of retirement

The traditional notion of the workforce made up of mainly men working for a single employer for many years, retiring, having a going away party, receiving a gold watch and never again working in paid employment was always a fairly cumbersome generalisation. Nonetheless, in the past it did reflect some aspects of the working life of many Australians. However, today, female participation in the workforce is much higher, and people change jobs more frequently, move between full-time and part-time work for the same or different employers more often, and provide consulting services or start small business from home more commonly. As a result of these and other changes, today many people find it hard to identify if and when they have retired. Maybe a new term needs to be invented that means 'working less'.

The active phase might also include more time for pursuits that were previously constrained by full-time work such as hobbies, sport, travel and voluntary work. Surveys of retirees highlight the importance of these pursuits in helping the individual ease from full-time work to part-time work to no work.

The income generated from part-time work can provide a useful supplement to other retirement income. Conversely, active retirement can involve expensive outlays such as for overseas travel which will place greater demands on retirement savings.

The passive phase of retirement

Generally, in the passive phase, the individual will no longer be working in paid employment, although many older Australians still participate in voluntary work. Hobby and sporting interests are likely to be somewhat less energetic than during the active phase and more expensive pursuits such as travel are likely to be reduced.

In the passive phase, the individual is capable of caring for themselves in their own home although they may need some support such as Meals on Wheels or home nursing care.

The support phase of retirement

In the support phase, the individual is no longer able to care for themselves in their own home, even with the support services. The individual may need to move into an aged-care facility or nursing home. Provision needs to be made in any retirement plan to cover the costs associated with moving into such alternate accommodation.

LO 3 Funding retirement

The active, passive and support phases of retirement all need to be funded. Surveys of retirees show that their number one concern is whether they will have adequate wealth to fund their desired retirement lifestyle.

Perhaps the best way to answer the question of how much wealth is adequate to fund retirement is to start with a simple example and then make it slightly more complex (and realistic). For example, Kate is 60 years old and is retiring today. She wants an income stream of \$50 000 per year for the next 10 years. Kate needs to save \$500 000 to afford this income stream. She can place the \$500 000 under her bed and each year she can reach down under her bed and take out \$50 000 to fund her retirement lifestyle.

This approach, however, has a number of problems. First, \$50 000 in year 1 will have a much higher purchasing power than \$50 000 in year 10 because of the effects of inflation. We might adjust for this by increasing the desired income stream by the rate of inflation each year. If we assume inflation of 3% p.a., Kate would need an income of \$51 500 in year 1, \$53 045 in year 2 and so on. To afford this income stream, Kate would need to put \$640 390 in total under her bed.

Most retirees do not, however, put their money under their bed. They consume some of their capital in the current year as 'income' and invest the remaining capital. The investment returns on unused capital mean that Kate can start with a smaller accumulated amount and still achieve the income stream she desires. If we assume that Kate invests her unused capital at 7% p.a. and she draws down her income at the end of the year she would need \$407 907 to afford her desired income stream. This is illustrated in table 11.1 (overleaf).

Kate, however, is only 60 years old. She has estimated that she will require her retirement income stream for 10 years; however, there is every likelihood that she will outlive this income stream. The risk that the individual will outlive their retirement income/savings is generally referred to as **longevity risk**. Table 11.2 illustrates the **life expectancy** of men and women aged 55 to 70.

longevity risk
the risk that the individual will outlive their retirement income/savings

life expectancy
how long a person is expected to live based on their gender and current age as determined by the Australian Government Actuary's life expectancy tables

TABLE 11.1 Kate's retirement funding

Year	Opening balance ($)	Earnings (invested at 7%) ($)	Income drawn down (adjusted for 3% inflation p.a.) ($)	Closing balance ($)
1	407 907	28 553	51 500	384 961
2	384 961	26 947	53 045	358 863
3	358 863	25 120	54 636	329 347
4	329 347	23 054	56 275	296 126
5	296 126	20 729	57 964	258 891
6	258 891	18 122	59 703	217 311
7	217 311	15 212	61 494	171 029
8	171 029	11 972	63 339	119 662
9	119 662	8 376	65 239	62 800
10	62 800	4 396	67 196	0

TABLE 11.2 Male and female life expectancies

Age(years)	Life expectancy (years)	
	Male	Female
55	26.95	30.53
56	26.08	29.61
57	25.20	28.70
58	24.34	27.79
59	23.48	26.89
60	22.63	26.00
61	21.79	25.11
62	20.96	24.23
63	20.14	23.35
64	19.34	22.48
65	18.54	21.62
66	17.76	20.76
67	16.99	19.92
68	16.24	19.08
69	15.49	18.24
70	14.76	17.42

Source: Extracts from Australian Government Actuary 2013, *Life expectancy tables 2005–07.*

Kate has a life expectancy of another 26 years. If we were to extend table 11.1, Kate would need \$809 380 to afford her desired income stream for 26 years rather than 10 years. However, Kate might still outlive her income stream; life expectancies are just that, they are not certainties. In contrast, Kate might die before her life expectancy and might have wished that she had enjoyed more of her savings during her life.

An alternative to creating a spreadsheet like the one shown in table 11.1 to determine how much a client needs to accumulate to fund their retirement is to use the present value (PV) function, either in a financial calculator or a spreadsheet. The PV function requires three inputs. Once the inputs are determined, the amount a client needs to accumulate in retirement savings in order to afford their desired income stream in retirement can be estimated.

1. *The real rate of return.* This is a function of the nominal rate of return and the rate of inflation. Generally, the more aggressive the investment strategy the higher the nominal rate of return. However, it is important to remember that the client is now in **pension mode** rather than **accumulation mode** and not able to recover from investment losses by working harder/longer. Therefore, their investment strategy is likely to be less aggressive. In Kate's example, 7% is the nominal rate of investment return including an inflationary component. If the inflation rate is 3% then the real rate is approximately 4%. More precisely, to allow for a small compounding effect the real rate is 3.88%:

$$\frac{(1 + \text{nominal})}{(1 + \text{inflation})} - 1$$

2. *The number of periods.* How much longevity risk does Kate wish to bear? In this case, we have assumed 26.
3. *The payment required.* It is important for the client to determine whether this payment is relative to how much they earned prior to retirement or more of an absolute figure. The Association of Superannuation Funds of Australia (ASFA) has a Retirement Calculator which determines the cost of living in retirement (www.superannuation.asn.au). In March 2013, a single person was estimated to need \$41 169 income p.a. for a comfortable lifestyle in retirement. In Kate's case, we have assumed \$50 000 p.a.

   As a result:

$$PV = (\text{rate, number of periods, desired income})$$

$$PV = (3.88\%, 26, \$50\,000) = \$809\,380$$

If Kate was to use the ASFA assumptions, she would need to accumulate:

$$PV = (3.88\%, 26, \$41\,146) = \$666\,310$$

If Kate was some years away from retiring, she would need to build an accumulation strategy that would achieve the equivalent of \$666 310 in real terms by the time she retired. This process is discussed in the section 'How much will I accumulate in superannuation?' in chapter 10. Often the process is an iterative one. The client may have unrealistic retirement income expectations, the adviser will calculate the amount that needs to be accumulated to fund this income, and it will become clear that the client will not be able to accumulate this amount during their working life. The client will often need to both boost the amount they accumulate and modify their retirement income expectations.

pension mode where an individual is no longer contributing to superannuation and has begun drawing down their superannuation in order to fund their retirement

accumulation mode where an individual is still contributing to superannuation

In undertaking this planning process, it might be useful to provide the client with a scenario analysis. The financial planner must decide which variables to vary.

Changing one variable at a time provides the client with a one-dimensional view of the data which can be displayed as a list.

Changing two variables at a time provides the client with a two-dimensional view of the data which can be displayed in a table format. Figure 11.1 below varies the nominal rate of return and the number of periods the income stream will last for Kate. The client can then see the impact of the individual variable as well as its interaction with the other variable.

Changing three variables at one time provides the client with a three-dimensional view of the data. Results of this analysis cannot be displayed in a single table; a series of tables would be needed. Moreover, understanding the interactions between the three changing variables becomes more complex.

Any number of variables can be varied at one time but it becomes increasingly difficult to display and interpret the results for both the client and the financial planner.

Kate's retirement								
Income of: $41 146								
Assume inflation rate of: 3.00%								
Nominal	3.00%	4.00%	5.00%	6.00%	7.00%	8.00%	9.00%	10.00%
Real	0.00%	0.97%	1.94%	2.91%	3.88%	4.85%	5.83%	6.80%
Periods								
15	$617 190	$571 779	$531 007	$494 317	$461 227	$431 317	$404 223	$379 628
20	$822 920	$744 684	$676 594	$617 123	$565 001	$519 161	$478 710	$442 895
25	$1028 650	$909 435	$808 833	$723 507	$650 775	$588 469	$534 833	$488 435
30	$1234 380	$1066 416	$928 949	$815 666	$721 672	$643 152	$577 118	$521 216
35	$1440 110	$1215 994	$1038 052	$895 500	$780 271	$686 296	$608 978	$544 813

FIGURE 11.1
Scenario analysis for Kate's retirement

The table in figure 11.1 highlights that higher nominal returns mean less has to be accumulated to afford the desired income stream. Higher nominal returns means higher risk and the client should identify what level of risk they are comfortable with. The table also highlights that the longer the desired income stream is expected to last the more that has to be accumulated.

Kate might believe that 6% nominal return is as risky as she should go. Kate might also be worried about longevity risk and choose an income stream for 30 years. This means she would need to accumulate $815 666 in retirement savings in real terms by the time she retires. However, if Kate has only $550 000 accumulated in retirement savings, only the shaded cells in figure 11.1 represent achievable outcomes — Kate will need to modify some combination of the total amount she accumulates, the nominal return she seeks, the desired term of her income stream, and the desired amount of her retirement income stream.

LO 4 Ordinary money versus superannuation money

In chapter 10, we recognised that individuals can accumulate wealth to fund their retirement both inside and outside of a superannuation environment. If money is accumulated outside of a superannuation environment it is known as **ordinary money**. If money is accumulated inside a superannuation environment, it is known as **superannuation money**. It is likely that most individuals will have some combination of ordinary money and superannuation money available to fund their retirement.

ordinary money money held outside a superannuation environment

superannuation money money held inside a superannuation environment

Ordinary money is after-tax money. It could be held in many forms, including cash, shares and property. One of the advantages of using ordinary money to fund retirement is that it does not have to be 'released' from a superannuation environment before it can be used for retirement purposes. If, for example, an individual wishes to withdraw some of their cash to fund an extended overseas holiday, the decision is entirely up to the individual. That is, no other conditions need to be satisfied and no tax has to be paid to release the funds.

Superannuation money is money held inside the tax-concessional superannuation environment. This money must be maintained (**preserved**) in a superannuation environment until a minimum age is reached.

preserved money must be maintained in a superannuation environment until a minimum age is reached

- For individuals born before 1 July 1960 the preservation age is 55.
- For individuals born after 30 June 1964 the preservation age is 60.
- For individuals born between 1960 and 1964 the preservation age progressively increases from 55 to 60.

For money to be withdrawn from a superannuation environment a **condition of release** must be satisfied. A condition of release can be satisfied by one of the following situations.

condition of release criteria that, if satisfied, enable an individual to withdraw their money from superannuation

- The individual has reached age 65.
- The individual is aged between 55 and 60 and has reached preservation age. Also the normal employment arrangement must have ceased and the superannuation trustee must be convinced that the individual does not intend to work more than 10 hours per week in the future.
- The individual is aged between 60 and 65 and has reached preservation age. Also the normal employment arrangement must have ceased. The individual must declare their intention to the superannuation trustee not to work more than 10 hours per week in the future; however, there is no onus on the trustee to verify the truth of this assertion.
- The individual is permanently incapacitated or suffering from a terminal medical condition.
- The individual dies.

If, for example, an individual wishes to use some of their superannuation money to fund an extended overseas holiday they must ensure that they have satisfied a condition of release from superannuation. In some circumstances, taxes will be payable on the release of the funds. The amount of tax payable will be a function of three factors:

1. the 'type' of superannuation money held in the individual's account
2. the age of the individual
3. whether the money is withdrawn as a lump sum or as an income stream.

taxed superannuation money
money held inside a superannuation environment which has been subject to the 15% contributions and earnings tax

untaxed superannuation money
money held inside a superannuation environment which has not been subject to the 15% contributions and earnings tax

non-concessional contribution
a contribution to superannuation for which a tax deduction has not been claimed (formerly known as undeducted contributions)

Superannuation money can be held in one of three forms:

- **Taxed superannuation money** is where money has been contributed and the standard 15% contribution tax has been deducted. For most Australians, this represents the major portion of their superannuation money.
- **Untaxed superannuation money** is where the standard 15% contribution tax has not been deducted. In some unfunded public-sector schemes the employer contribution is often made as a lump sum contribution the day before the individual retires. In these circumstances, the superannuation fund generally has the discretion to immediately deduct the 15% contributions tax and treat the money as taxed superannuation money or to not deduct the 15% contributions tax and treat the money as untaxed superannuation money. As public-sector schemes move towards being fully funded, the prevalence of untaxed superannuation money is likely to decrease.
- **Non-concessional contribution** is after-tax money that individuals have contributed to superannuation.

Various federal governments have introduced policies aimed at keeping people in the workforce longer. A number of these were discussed in chapter 10. The Howard/Costello changes to superannuation included superannuation tax concessions for people who waited until they were 60 years of age before accessing their superannuation.

LO 5

Withdrawing a lump sum in order to fund retirement

As we discussed earlier in this chapter, withdrawing a lump sum from ordinary money in order to fund retirement is a simple and straightforward process — this is after-tax money (capital) over which an individual has complete and unfettered control.

tax-free component
that part of superannuation which is exempt from tax

Withdrawing superannuation money as a lump sum is less straightforward. The process is made more difficult because sometimes different words are used to describe the same process. It is important to separate taxable superannuation money from non-taxable superannuation money. The non-taxable component is also known as the exempt or **tax-free component**. We will use the term *tax-free component*. Non-concessional superannuation money is after-tax money that has been contributed to superannuation and forms part of the tax-free component. Individuals who have a work history that extends prior to 1983 might also have some superannuation attributable to this period — this will also form part of the tax-free component. All superannuation money which is not tax free is taxable. Table 11.3 and the following illustrative examples illustrate the tax implications of withdrawing a lump sum from superannuation.

TABLE 11.3 Taxed superannuation money — withdrawing a lump sum

Type of superannuation money	Age	Tax consequences
Tax free	Not applicable	Tax free
Taxable (taxed)	Over 60	Tax free
	Under 60	Up to the low-rate threshold[a] tax free Above the low-rate threshold[a] taxed at 15%

[a]The low rate threshold for 2013–14 was $180 000.
Source: Australian Taxation Office.

ILLUSTRATIVE EXAMPLE 11.1

Sally is 59 years old and has $500 000 in superannuation. Her superannuation comprises a tax-free component of $100 000 and a taxed superannuation component of $400 000. Sally has satisfied a condition of release from superannuation and would like to withdraw a $240 000 lump sum. Money must be withdrawn from a superannuation environment in proportion to the components that exist within the individual's superannuation fund. Sally's superannuation fund consists of a tax-free component of 20% ($100 000/$500 000) and a taxable component of 80% ($400 000/$500 000). Any lump sum that Sally withdraws must therefore be 20% tax free and 80% taxable. If Sally withdraws $240 000 as a lump sum, $48 000 (20%) will be tax free and $192 000 (80%) will be taxable. Sally will need to pay $1800 in tax to release a $240 000 lump sum from superannuation as shown below.

Component	Amount released	Tax payable	Note
Tax-free component	$ 48 000	0	Tax free
Taxable component	180 000	0	Low-rate threshold — tax free
	12 000	$1 800	Taxed at 15% ($12 000 × 15%)
Total	$240 000	$1 800	

If Sally was to wait until she was 60 years of age, the taxable component would also be tax free and no tax would be payable. This reflects the Howard/Costello 2007 changes to superannuation where individuals over the age of 60 years with taxed superannuation money are able to withdraw their superannuation money entirely tax free.

If an individual has untaxed superannuation money, the tax treatment associated with withdrawing a lump sum (shown in table 11.4) is not quite so generous. This reflects the fact that the government has not received taxes on contributions and taxes on superannuation fund investment earnings from the individual's superannuation fund during the accumulation phase.

TABLE 11.4 Untaxed superannuation money — withdrawing a lump sum

Type of superannuation money	Age	Tax consequences
Tax free	Not applicable	Tax free
Taxable (taxed)	Over 60	Up to the untaxed plan cap* taxed at 15% Above the untaxed plan cap taxed at 45%
	Under 60	Up to the low-rate threshold taxed at 15% Above the low-rate threshold but below the untaxed plan cap taxed at 30% Above the untaxed plan cap taxed at 45%

*The untaxed plan cap for 2013–14 was $1.315 million.

Source: Australian Taxation Office.

ILLUSTRATIVE EXAMPLE 11.2

Ben is 59 years old and has $500 000 in superannuation. His superannuation comprises a tax-free component of $100 000 and an untaxed superannuation component of $400 000. Ben has satisfied a condition of release from superannuation and would like to withdraw a $240 000 lump sum. Ben will need to pay $30 600 in tax to release a $240 000 lump sum from superannuation as shown in table 11.5.

TABLE 11.5 Ben's tax payable on lump sum withdrawn from superannuation at 59 years

Component	Amount released	Tax payable	Note
Tax-free component	$ 48 000	0	Tax-free
Taxable component	180 000	$27 000	Low-rate threshold — taxed at 15% (180 000 × 15%)
	12 000	3 600	Above the low-rate threshold but below the untaxed plan cap — taxed at 30% ($12 000 × 30%)
Total	$240 000	$30 600	

If Ben was to wait until he was 60 years, the tax consequences would be as shown in table 11.6.

TABLE 11.6 Ben's tax payable on lump sum withdrawn from superannuation at 60 years

Component	Amount released	Tax payable	Note
Tax-free component	$ 48 000	0	Tax-free
Taxable component	192 000	$28 800	Up to the untaxed plan cap — taxed at 15% (192 000 × 15%)
Total	$240 000	$28 800	

Superannuation death benefits payable as a lump sum

The tax consequences of leaving a superannuation lump sum to a beneficiary depend on whether the beneficiary is a dependant or non-dependant. A dependant in this case is a person who is:

- a spouse of the deceased
- a child of the deceased under the age of 18
- a person who was financially dependent on the deceased
- a person who had an interdependency relationship with the deceased.

If the beneficiary is a dependant, any lump sum will be tax free. If the beneficiary is a non-dependant, any lump sum will be divided into a tax-free and a taxable component. If the taxable component contains taxed superannuation money, this will be taxed at 15%. If the taxable component contains untaxed superannuation money, this will be taxed at 30%.

The trustees of a superannuation fund have discretion as to who a superannuation death benefit is payable to unless the superannuation fund member makes a binding death nomination. In estate planning terms, it might be wise to make a binding death nomination in favour of a dependant to reduce the amount of tax that would otherwise be payable. If other non-dependants need to be provided for, non-superannuation assets might be distributed to non-dependants via the individual's will.

Rolling over a superannuation lump sum

An individual may decide to move their superannuation money from one superannuation fund to another — this is known as rolling over superannuation and does not constitute a lump sum withdrawal. Normally such transfers are immediate; however, if an amount is withdrawn and not rolled over within 30 days it might be deemed a withdrawal and lump sum withdrawal taxes might apply.

Splitting the lump sum as a result of divorce or separation

The *Family Law Act 1975* allows the Family Court to split superannuation between separating couples. Where the superannuation money is held in an accumulation style account the splitting process is relatively straightforward — the components of the old superannuation account are split proportionally into two new accounts.

ILLUSTRATIVE EXAMPLE 11.3

Ray and Janice recently divorced. As part of the Family Court's determination, Ray's superannuation of $400 000 is to be split 70% to Ray and 30% to Janice. Ray's superannuation includes a $100 000 tax-free component.

After the split, Ray will have $280 000 in superannuation which includes a tax-free component of $70 000. Janice will have $120 000 in superannuation which includes a tax-free component of $30 000. Both Ray and Janice are now free to manage their superannuation as they wish.

Where the superannuation money is held in a defined benefit account, the process of splitting is more complex. Defined benefit accounts have a notional balance which is a function of the formula that defines the benefit — the assets which underwrite the benefit are pooled by the superannuation fund. In these cases, the court might order a payment split; that is, the funds will remain in the defined benefit account until the current owner of the account retires, at which time part of the payment received will pass to the other party.

Recontribution of a lump-sum withdrawal

We have already seen that there are certain tax advantages associated with having a tax-free component in superannuation. We will see shortly that in some circumstances a larger tax-free component can also have tax advantages for income streams.

recontribution
the process by which some funds are withdrawn from superannuation and then contributed back into superannuation in order to boost the tax-free component

One strategy developed by financial planners to increase the amount of the tax-free component of superannuation is called recontribution. **Recontribution** involves taking out a lump sum from superannuation and paying a small amount of tax or no tax and then recontributing it as a non-concessional contribution.

ILLUSTRATIVE EXAMPLE 11.4

Barney is 58 years old and has $800 000 in superannuation which includes a tax-free component of $400 000 and a taxed superannuation component of $400 000. Therefore, 50% of Barney's superannuation is tax free and 50% is taxable.

Barney has satisfied a condition of release from superannuation and decides to withdraw $360 000 as a lump sum and then immediately recontribute this $360 000 as a non-concessional contribution.

The money must be withdrawn in proportion to the components of his superannuation:

- $180 000 (50% × $360 000) is tax free
- $180 000 (50% × $360 000) is taxable — the first $180 000 (the low-rate threshold in 2013–14) of the taxable component is tax free.

Therefore, Barney can release a lump sum of $360 000 from his superannuation and pay no tax.

If Barney then recontributes this $360 000 as a non-concessional contribution, his $800 000 in superannuation will now comprise:

- $580 000 (72.5%) tax-free component ($400 000 – $180 000 + $360 000)
- $220 000 (27.5%) taxable component ($400 000 – $180 000).

Barney has increased the tax-free component of his superannuation at no cost via his recontribution strategy. If Barney had withdrawn more than $360 000 and/or if less of his superannuation was initially tax free, some tax would be payable to release the lump sum from superannuation. The skill for the financial planner is to determine how much tax would be payable by withdrawing a lump sum and then trading this off against the benefits of increasing the tax-free component of superannuation.

Employment termination payments (MTP)

Employees sometimes receive a payment associated with the termination of their employment. While this might occur at any stage during a person's working life it is more likely to occur as a person approaches retirement. Any such payment is effectively a lump sum.

Employment termination payments in the past were frequently referred to as ETPs. While the title of such payments has not changed the abbreviation has — employment termination payments now tend to be abbreviated to MTP. Part of this change of abbreviation is to recognise that MTPs post-2007 are treated quite differently from ETPs prior to 2007. In the old ETP system it was possible for some ETPs to find their way directly into the superannuation account of the recipient; in the new MTP system all payments occur completely outside the superannuation environment. If the individual does receive an MTP they might have to pay some tax and then they would be left with after-tax money. The individual might then decide to spend it, save it or contribute it to superannuation as a non-concessional contribution.

MTPs are prescribed in the *Income Tax Assessment Act 1997* (ITAA 97) and include:

- payment in lieu of notice
- payment for unused sick leave
- golden handshakes
- severance or termination payments
- redundancy payments in excess of the tax-free amount.

Individuals who receive a redundancy payout are entitled to a tax-free amount of $9246 (2013–14) plus $4624 (2013–14) for each year of service.

ILLUSTRATIVE EXAMPLE 11.5

Marge is aged 63 and has worked for her employer for 10 years. She has just received a redundancy payout of $100 000. Therefore Marge will be entitled to a tax-free amount of $55 486 ($9246 + [10 × $4624]).

This will leave Marge with an MTP of $44 514 ($100 000 – $55 486).

The ITAA97 also prescribes those payments that are not considered MTPs and which include:

- payment for unused annual leave
- payment for unused long service leave
- compensation for personal injury.

Payments which are not considered MTPs have their own individual tax treatment.

MTPs are divided into tax-free and taxable components. If the employee has some work history before June 1983 and part of the MTP can be attributed to that period, that amount will be considered tax free. For most people receiving an MTP the entire amount will be taxable. The taxable amount up to the low-rate threshold is treated in a tax concessional manner. In 2013–14 the low-rate threshold was $180 000.

MTPs are also divided into life benefit termination payments (LBTP) where the employee is alive to receive the payment, and death benefit termination payments (DBTP) where sadly the employee is not alive to receive the payment.

Life benefit termination payments (LBTP)

The tax-free component of a LBTP is exempt from tax. The taxable component is taxed as follows:

- If the recipient is above their preservation age the amount up to the low-rate threshold is taxed at 15%.
- If the recipient is below their preservation age the amount up to the low-rate threshold is taxed at 30%.
- Amounts in excess of the low-rate threshold are taxed at the individual's marginal tax rate.

ILLUSTRATIVE EXAMPLE 11.6

Continuing from illustrative example 11.5, given that Marge has worked for her employer for 10 years all her work must have been after June 1983. As a result, all her MTP represents a taxable component. At age 63 Marge is past her preservation age and will need to pay $7073 ($47 154 × 15%) in tax on her MTP. Marge is then free to spend this money, save it or contribute it to superannuation as a non-concessional contribution.

Death benefit termination payments (DBTP)

The tax payable on a DBTP depends on who is the recipient of the DBTP. Dependants are treated more generously than non-dependants. For dependants:

- the tax-free component of a DBTP is exempt from tax
- the taxable component up to the low-rate threshold is also exempt from tax. Amounts in excess of the low-rate threshold are taxed at the highest marginal tax rate.

For non-dependants:

- the tax-free component of a DBTP is exempt from tax
- the taxable component up to the low-rate threshold is taxed at 30%. Amounts in excess of the low-rate threshold are taxed at the highest marginal tax rate.

LO 6 Sources of income streams in retirement

Many Australians see the ability to withdraw all their money from superannuation as a lump sum, once a condition of release has been satisfied, as a 'right'. In contrast, most countries with retirement savings schemes do not allow individuals to withdraw all their money as a lump sum, although some do allow limited lump sum withdrawals.

Most Australians, however, do not withdraw all their superannuation as a lump sum. During their working lives, an individual earns a regular income, pays bills that come in each month, and basically budgets their expenditure in this way. People see retirement in much the same way and therefore often seek to create an income stream in retirement.

Commencing an income stream means moving from accumulating wealth for retirement to using wealth in retirement. In superannuation terms, it is often referred to as moving from accumulation mode to pension mode.

Source of income

Income can come from a variety of sources in retirement, including:

- part-time work
- the age pension
- from owning a business
- the use of capital.

Capital can be used in a number of ways. The individual might decide to draw down the capital only, live off the investment earnings only, or use some combination of capital draw down and investment earnings to fund their retirement.

Draw down of capital

In this extreme case, the client does not invest their capital, they effectively place the capital 'under their bed' and withdraw an amount for retirement income purposes until the capital is exhausted.

For example, Tracey places $100 000 under her bed. Each year she takes $10 000. Tracey does not face any investment risk — investment returns might go up or down but this has no impact on the amount of Tracey's capital. Tracey does, however, face longevity risk — if she takes $10 000 each year, in 10 years her capital will be exhausted and she will be faced with the task of funding the remainder of her retirement. Tracey will also a suffer a fall in the real value of her retirement income — inflation will ensure that $10 000 taken in 10 years will not have the same buying power as $10 000 taken in the first year.

Investment earnings only

In this case, the client invests their capital and uses the investment earnings only to fund their retirement income stream. Clients with a large amount of accumulated wealth may be able to afford this type of retirement income stream.

If Tracey was able to invest her $100 000 at 10% p.a., this would produce an income stream of $10 000 per year. In this case, Tracey has removed longevity risk — as long as investment returns remain at 10% and she draws down $10 000 each year, the situation could continue indefinitely. The downside for Tracey is that she is now subject to variations in investment returns. The other downside is that the real value of her $10 000 in earnings will reduce over time due to the effects of inflation.

Combination of capital draw down and investment earnings

Most Australians will fund their retirement by drawing down some capital and using some investment earnings.

If for example, Tracey invested her $100 000 at a real rate of return of approximately 7.8%, this would generate a real income of $10 000 per year for 20 years.

Tracey remains exposed to the risks associated with fluctuating investment returns. Higher returns will mean that her income stream will last longer than 20 years; lower returns mean it will last less than 20 years — longevity risk, compared with the capital draw down only discussed previously, has been reduced but not completely removed.

The higher the investment returns and/or the lower the income stream drawn down, the longer the income stream will last. Conversely, the lower the investment returns and/or the higher the income stream drawn down the less time the income stream will last.

Where individuals decide to take an income stream from superannuation rather than a lump sum the superannuation system effectively forces the individual to take an income stream as a combination of capital draw down and investment earnings.

Life expectancy

The Australian Government Actuary periodically publishes life expectancy tables.

Table 11.2 earlier in the chapter shows the life expectancies for males and females aged 55 to 70 years from the most recently published tables. Table 11.7 shows a selection of male life expectancies over the past century.

TABLE 11.7 Selected male life expectancies

Age (years)	1901–10	1946–48	1965–67	1985–87	2005–07
0	47.20	66.07	67.63	72.74	79.02
10	48.86	59.04	59.50	63.74	69.55
20	40.58	49.64	49.98	54.13	59.75
40	26.50	31.23	31.44	35.40	40.71
60	13.77	15.36	15.27	18.13	22.63
65	11.06	12.25	12.16	14.60	18.54

Source: Australian Government Actuary 2013.

We can see from the table that life expectancy at all age levels has increased significantly over the last 100 years. A male born in 1910 had a life expectancy of

47 years, whereas a male born in 2007 has a life expectancy of 79 years. More recent statistics gathered by the Australian Bureau of Statistics and actuaries working for major Australian superannuation funds suggest that current life expectancies exceed those shown in table 11.7. Increased longevity means a longer retirement period needs to be funded.

We can also see a survivor bias in the table. This is evident in each of the time periods but most pronounced in the 1901–10 figures. For example, a baby born in 1910 was expected to live, on average, to 47 years. However, a baby that survived to the age of 10 had a life expectancy of another 49 years which means that they would live, on average, to 59 years. In other words, less developed health systems and higher rates of infant mortality meant that if you were able to survive this period your life expectancy would increase.

In modelling retirement income streams it is important to allow for this survivor bias. In the 2005–07 life expectancy tables, a 60-year-old male is expected to live for another 22.63 years on average; that is, they are expected to live until 82.63 years of age. It is important to remember that if your 60-year-old client comes back to see you 5 years later when they are 65, this does not mean that their life expectancy is 17.63 years (22.63 – 5) and they are still expected to live to 82.63 years. Rather, they have survived another 5 years and the life expectancy of a 65-year-old male is 18.54 years which means they are expected to live, on average, to the age of 83.54 years.

It is also important to remember that life expectancies are averages. If we have 100 males at age 65 their average life expectancy is 18.54 years. We would expect approximately 50 of these males to still be alive at 83, we would expect 20 to be alive at age 90 and 10 to be alive at age 93. Should individuals be encouraged to spend their money while they can just in case they die before their life expectancy or should they be encouraged to be more frugal just in case they are one of the 10% who live to 93?

LO 7 Assessable income

We discussed earlier that income can come from a variety of sources in retirement. Income from part-time work, income from the age pension and income from owning a business all fit the Income Tax Assessment Act (ITAA) definition of income and are therefore taxable.

Income generated from the use of capital is more complex. To initially generate capital, income must be earned and taxes must be paid on that income. The after-tax money effectively becomes capital. It follows that if an individual subsequently consumes part of this capital in funding their retirement, it would be unfair to tax this capital a second time as income. Therefore, all 'income' which is effectively a consumption of capital is not taxable.

ILLUSTRATIVE EXAMPLE 11.7

Stan is 59 years old and has $500 000 in ordinary money (capital). He takes his $500 000 to an income-stream provider and the provider agrees to pay Stan $43 592 p.a. for the next 20 years. The provider will invest Stan's $500 000 and the income stream provided to Stan will be a combination of investment earnings and a return of Stan's capital.

The Australian Taxation Office (ATO) will take the view that Stan's capital is returned in equal instalments over the term of the income stream. Stan will be able to claim a **deductible amount** of $25 000 ($500 000/20). His **assessable income** for tax purposes is therefore $18 592 ($43 592 – $25 000).

If Stan had chosen instead to buy a **life expectancy income stream**, the income-stream provider would be obliged to pay the income stream for the fixed term of 23.48 years (see table 11.2). In this case, his deductible amount would be $21 295 ($500 000/23.48).

If Stan had chosen to buy a **lifetime income stream**, the income-stream provider would be obliged to pay the income stream for as long as Stan lives. The best estimate of how long this will be is 23.48 years. In this case, his deductible amount would still be $21 295 ($500 000/23.48).

deductible amount
that amount of an income stream which represents a return of capital

assessable income
income that is assessable or recognised and measured under taxation law

life expectancy income stream
a fixed-term income stream where the term is determined by the Australian Government Actuary's life expectancy tables

lifetime income stream
an income stream that will last as long as a person lives

ILLUSTRATIVE EXAMPLE 11.8

Wilma is 59 years old and has $500 000 in superannuation money. This includes a tax-free component of $200 000. A tax-free component is effectively capital parked inside a superannuation environment. We noted earlier that non-concessional contributions which form part of the tax-free component are after-tax money that has been contributed to superannuation. We also noted that when withdrawn as a lump sum, a tax-free component is exempt from tax.

Wilma takes her $500 000 to an income-stream provider and the provider agrees to pay her $43 592 p.a. for the next 20 years.

The ATO will take the view that Wilma's capital (in this case her tax-free component) represents 40% of her total superannuation ($200 000/$500 000) and therefore 40% of any income stream she receives is a return of capital and is received tax free. Wilma will be able to claim a deductible amount of $17 437 ($43 592 × 40%). Her assessable income for tax purposes is $26 155 ($43 592 – $17 437).

If Wilma was to buy a life expectancy or lifetime income stream, 40% of any income received would be free from tax regardless of how much income she receives. If Wilma was to commence an account-based pension, discussed shortly, which allows the individual to vary the amount of income they take each year, the deductible amount will still be 40% of the total amount of income.

To summarise what can be a complex area: when 'income' includes a component which is actually a return of capital, that part which represents the return of capital is not taxed. For ordinary money, the amount divided by the term of the income stream equals the non-taxable part (deductible amount). This deductible amount is fixed in dollar terms. For superannuation money, the tax-free component divided by the total superannuation amount equals the tax-free percentage. This percentage when applied to the amount of income received equals the non-taxable part (deductible amount). This deductible amount is fixed in percentage terms. Total income less the deductible amount equals the assessable income.

LO 8 Account-based versus non-account based income streams

There are two types of income stream available in Australia today: account-based income streams and non-account based income streams. Both types of income stream are based on the individual using a combination of their investment income and the draw down of capital to fund their retirement.

account-based income stream where an individual owns and maintains an individual account from which an income stream is drawn

non-account based income streams where an individual gives their retirement savings to an income-stream provider who pools those assets and promises an income stream in return

An **account-based income stream** places the individual in charge of their retirement account in much the same way that most individuals are in charge of their superannuation accumulation account during their working lives. Account-based income streams are the most popular type of income stream for Australians who convert their accumulated superannuation into an income stream.

Non-account based income streams involve contracting with either a superannuation fund or a life office to provide an income stream. These income streams are often referred to as pensions or annuities, with the terms used interchangeably. Usually an income stream from a superannuation fund is called a pension and an income stream from a life office is called an annuity.

The characteristics of account-based and non-account based income streams are shown in table 11.8.

TABLE 11.8 Comparing account-based and non-account based income streams

Characteristic	Account-based income streams	Non-account based income streams
Superannuation or ordinary money	Can be purchased only with superannuation money	Can be purchased with superannuation money or ordinary money
Investment assets	Held in the name of the individual	Pooled by the income-stream provider
Investment selection	Made by the individual	Made by the income-stream provider
Investment risk	Borne by the individual	Borne by the income-stream provider
Income level	Prescribed minimum annual payment which is a function of age. No maximum. (see schedule below)	Amount is contracted with provider Can be a fixed amount each year or can be subject to indexation Can be contracted that income reverts to a dependant on death, usually at a lower rate (e.g. 60% of the original pension payment is paid to the surviving spouse)

Age	Up to 2007–08	2008–09 to 2010–11	2011–12 to 2012–13	2013–14
Under 65	4%	2.0%	3.00%	4%
65–74	5%	2.5%	3.75%	5%
75–79	6%	3.0%	4.50%	6%
80–84	7%	3.5%	5.25%	7%
85–89	9%	4.5%	6.75%	9%
90–94	11%	5.5%	8.25%	11%
95 and over	14%	7.0%	10.50%	14%

Characteristic	Account-based income streams	Non-account based income streams
Longevity risk	Borne by the individual	If a fixed-term income stream then borne by the individual If a lifetime income stream then borne by the income-stream provider
	(See discussion of minimum income levels for account based income streams later in the chapter.)	
Taxation on fund earnings	Investment earnings are exempt from tax	When purchased with superannuation money investment earnings are exempt from tax.
Taxation on income if individual is over 60 years of age	Tax free if funded by taxed superannuation money	Tax free if funded by taxed superannuation money. If purchased with ordinary money income is fully assessable less any deductible amount.
	(See discussion of taxation of retirement income streams later in the chapter.)	
Commutation[a]	Can be commuted at any time	Generally not possible to commute
Move back to accumulation mode	Additional contributions cannot be made in pension mode; however, a separate accumulation account could be started. Individual could commute current pension account and rollover into new accumulation account.	Income-stream provider will not accept additional contributions; however, a separate accumulation account could be started. Individual generally cannot commute; therefore, they are locked in to their income stream.
Consequence of death	The balance in the account forms part of the estate.	If a fixed term income stream, the present value of remaining payments is paid to the estate. If a lifetime income stream with a guarantee period, the present value of the remaining payments within the guarantee period will be paid to the estate. If a lifetime income stream with no guarantee period or the guarantee period has expired, the remaining capital is forfeited.
	(See discussion of tax of retirement income streams on death later in the chapter.)	

[a]Commutation is the conversion of an income stream back into a lump sum.

Minimum income levels for account-based income streams

From table 11.8 we can see that the minimum percentage that must be drawn down by the individual as an account-based income stream increases with the individual's age. This is designed to encourage individuals to progressively use their superannuation, both investment earnings and capital, to fund their retirement. The federal government provides generous tax concessions when individuals are in pension mode (e.g. earnings inside the superannuation fund are tax exempt). The government does not want individuals to simply park excess capital in this tax-concessional environment. Rather, it wants this money used for retirement funding, and the minimum draw down requirements are designed for this purpose. In response to the global financial crisis (GFC), the federal government halved the minimum percentages shown in table 11.8 for the 2008–09 to 2010–11 financial years. Most retirees with account-based retirement income streams had seen a dramatic fall in their account balances as a result of the GFC. To have insisted in this environment that retirees further draw down their accounts would have resulted in many retirees crystallising further losses. With the recovery in world economic markets post-GFC the federal government has indicated its intention to increase the minimum percentages back to their pre-GFC levels.

Taxation of retirement income streams

If the individual uses taxed superannuation money to fund their retirement income stream and they are over 60 years of age, the tax consequences are very simple: no tax is payable. This provides a powerful incentive to stay working and accumulating wealth until at least the age of 60. The tax consequences for individuals who do not meet these criteria are more complex. Some scenarios are outlined in table 11.9.

TABLE 11.9 Retirement income tax consequences

Scenario	Rebate	Client	Tax consequence	
Taxed superannuation money and individual is under 60 years of age	15%	Client has $1 000 000 which includes $400 000 (40%) tax-free component; takes an income stream of $80 000.	Total income	$80 000
			Less deductible (40%)	32 000
			Assessable income	48 000
			Tax payable 2013–14	7 147
			Rebate (15%)	7 200
			Net tax payable	0
Untaxed superannuation money and individual is over 60 years of age	10%	Client has $1 000 000 which includes $400 000 (40%) tax-free component; takes an income stream of $80 000.	Total income	$80 000
			Less deductible (40%)	32 000
			Assessable income	48 000
			Tax payable 2013–14	7 147
			Rebate (10%)	4 800
			Net tax payable	2 347
Untaxed superannuation money and individual is under 60 years of age	0%	Client has $1 000 000 which includes $400 000 (40%) tax-free component; takes an income stream of $80 000.	Total income	$80 000
			Less deductible (40%)	32 000
			Assessable income	48 000
			Tax payable 2013–14	7 147
			Rebate (0%)	0
			Net tax payable	7 147
Ordinary money regardless of age	0%	Client has $1 000 000 and buys a fixed-term income stream of $80 000 p.a. for 20 years; the deductible amount equals $50 000 ($1 000 000/20).	Total income	$80 000
			Less deductible ($)	50 000
			Assessable income	30 000
			Tax payable 2013–14	2 242
			Rebate (0%)	0
			Net tax payable	2 242

All of the scenarios outlined in table 11.9 are underpinned by the following basic concepts:

- total income less deductible amount equals assessable income
- all assessable income is taxed at marginal rates
- for some income streams, the amount of tax otherwise payable will be reduced by a rebate which is applied to assessable income.

Taxation of retirement income streams on death

A retirement income stream can **revert** only to a dependant. The tax-free component is exempt from tax. The amount of tax payable on the taxable component is a function of whether the:

- money used was taxed or untaxed
- deceased was under or over 60 years of age
- dependent beneficiary was under or over 60 years of age.

This is shown in tables 11.10 and 11.11.

reversion
where the recipient of an income stream dies, the income stream then passes to a dependant

TABLE 11.10 Taxation of taxed death benefits

Age of deceased	Age of dependant < 60 years	Age of dependant > 60 years
< 60 years	Taxable at marginal rates with 15% rebate	Tax free
> 60 years	Tax free	Tax free

TABLE 11.11 Taxation of untaxed death benefits

Age of deceased	Age of dependant < 60 years	Age of dependant > 60 years
< 60 years	Taxable at marginal rates	Taxable at marginal rates with 10% rebate
> 60 years	Taxable at marginal rates with 10% rebate	Taxable at marginal rates with 10% rebate

Any unused retirement income stream which is payable to a non-dependant is taxed as a lump sum as per our earlier discussion of the taxation of 'superannuation death benefits payable as a lump sum'.

Choosing between an account-based and non-account based income stream

As can be seen from table 11.12 (overleaf) many factors need to be traded off against each other in deciding between an account-based or non-account based income stream.

It is important to remember that an individual, who has sufficient funds, might commence both an account-based and a non-account based income stream in order to best manage their individual circumstances.

TABLE 11.12 What type of income stream is preferred?

Characteristic	Prefer an account-based income stream	Prefer a non-account based income stream
Managing investment risk	More confident	Less confident
Fluctuations in investment returns	More prepared to accept	Less prepared to accept (See discussion of implicit non-account based income stream returns later in the chapter.)
Longevity risk	Less concerned	More concerned
Might still draw a lump sum	Possible	Not possible
Potential to re-enter the workforce and move back to accumulation mode	Easy	Difficult
Potential to leave unused retirement savings to beneficiaries upon their death	Easy	Depends on income stream chosen (not possible for a lifetime income stream beyond guarantee period)

The use of annuities to provide retirement income

As we noted above individuals may decide to use their superannuation money to buy an annuity from a life office. These income streams effectively include an insurance component in their offer.

While the number of life offices offering annuities has declined in recent years the range of 'features' associated with the annuities on offer have increased considerably, making direct comparisons between annuity products more difficult.

Annuities can be as short as one year or for as long as a person might live if they purchase a lifetime annuity. Other features that some annuity products include are as follows.

- Income which is:
  - fixed each period or indexed to some measure which is typically movements in the CPI
  - paid for the agreed term (fixed term annuity) or paid for as long as a person lives (lifetime annuity)
  - paid to the owner of the annuity only (single life) or with reversion to a spouse on the death of the owner of the annuity (joint lives)
- Capital which is:
  - completely or partially returned at the expiration of the fixed term of the annuity (residual capital value)

- entirely consumed during the fixed term of the annuity (residual capital value is zero)
- returned to the estate if the owner of the annuity dies within a guarantee period or forfeited if there is no guarantee period or the guarantee period has expired (lifetime annuity).

By agreeing to pay a fixed or indexed income stream regardless of how financial markets are performing, life offices are effectively insuring the individual against the volatility of investment markets. Similarly by offering lifetime annuities life offices are insuring the individual against the prospect of living beyond their life expectancy. This insurance component within annuities means that an individual should expect the rate of return on these income products to be less than the rate of return on similar income products which do not offer this insurance component.

Because of this insurance component life offices generally do not disclose the rate of return implicit in the income streams they provide. Instead, they might disclose their offer in the following terms; for example, for every $100 000 invested, a 60-year-old male can buy a life expectancy income stream of $6151 per annum.

Using a financial calculator or the RATE function in Excel it is possible to work out the rate of return implicit in a fixed-term non-account based income stream.

If a 60-year-old male commences a life expectancy income stream, it will have a fixed term of 22.63 years. If they invest $400 000 in the non-account based income stream and receive an annual payment of $24 604 ($6151 × 4), the implicit rate of return is 3%.

$$\begin{aligned} Rate &= (Number\ of\ periods,\ Payment,\ Present\ value) \\ 3\% &= (22.63, -\$24604, \$400000) \end{aligned}$$

If the 60-year-old male commences a lifetime income stream rather than a life expectancy income stream, we cannot be sure how long the income stream will last and therefore cannot be certain of the rate of return implicit in the income stream. If the individual lives to 120 years of age, the implicit rate would be much higher; if they die before their life expectancy, the implicit rate would be lower. Historically annuities provided by life offices have had relatively low implicit rates of return. The provider needs to manage the investment risk including the insurance-type risk associated with lifetime income streams. The provider pools the available funds and tends to select relatively conservative portfolios which tend to be dominated by fixed interest-type investments.

Since the global financial crisis there has been a significant increase in individuals buying short-term annuities with their superannuation to fund their short-term retirement income needs. Life offices have been successful in marketing the relative safety of annuities in uncertain economic times and how individuals can insure against a rapid reduction in income and capital levels precipitated by another GFC by buying an annuity. Individuals have been prepared to accept the very low implicit rates of return associated with these short-term annuities in return for the income and capital certainty they provide.

It is important to remember that buying a short-term annuity keeps funds within the tax concessional superannuation environment. If an individual were to withdraw their money from superannuation and buy for example a fixed term deposit with a bank, the interest on that capital would be taxable. Buying a short-term annuity also gives the individual some time to determine how to best fund their long-term retirement income needs.

While the GFC and the economic uncertainty which has followed has seen a significant increase in individuals buying short-term annuities with their superannuation, it has not seen a significant increase in individuals buying long-term annuities, including lifetime annuities. Arguably the implicit rates of return in long-term annuities are just too low, even allowing for the insurance aspect, to entice individuals into buying. In 2012 sales of lifetime products reached $75m.

APRA statistics reveal that in 2012 Australians withdrew approximately $35 billion dollars from superannuation in the form of pensions and spent approximately $2 billion dollars on annuities, which means that the annuity market, particularly the lifetime annuity market, remains a small fraction of the overall retirement income market.

At its peak 15 life companies in Australia were selling annuities. Annuities are now issued by only two providers, Challenger and Comminsure. Both providers are regulated by APRA.

PERSONAL FINANCE BULLETIN

Deferred annuities

At the start of 2013 the US Government introduced the 'Qualified Longevity Annuity Contract' or QLAC.

Basically the contract allows a person to use some of their retirement savings to buy an annuity now which will not commence paying an income stream until a pre-determined time in the future. For example a 65-year-old man might buy a QLAC now with the income stream to commence at age 85 — effectively he is buying an insurance policy which will pay him an income stream if he lives beyond his life expectancy. The purchase price of the annuity can be quite low as the insurer will be able to invest the money for 20 years and will have to pay the income stream only if the buyer lives beyond their life expectancy. This gives the buyer of the annuity the comfort of knowing that longevity risk has been provided for and they can then plan how to use the balance of their retirement funds to finance their retirement over the period of their life expectancy.

There has been strong support in the Australian superannuation industry for the introduction of a similar 'deferred annuity' product; however, current rules and regulations have limited their market appeal. Recent announcements from the federal government, including the proposed extension of the tax-free status of earnings from assets which support superannuation pensions, is likely to see their market appeal increase.

PROFESSIONAL ADVICE

Income streams

Your client is Blanche, aged 72. Blanche has been through a difficult period. Both her parents recently died and her husband Bob also passed away leaving her to care for her three stepchildren: Barry, aged 14, Paula, aged 11, and Carly, aged 9. Bob had managed all the financial affairs of the couple and Blanche does not feel comfortable making investment decisions. Blanche now finds herself with $500 000 in superannuation and would like the security of an income stream.

QUESTIONS

1. What advice can you provide Blanche with respect to longevity risk? Given her circumstances, how is she likely to be affected by longevity risk?
2. Blanche is concerned that she does not have the skills to manage the investment decisions associated with the $500 000 in superannuation. Does this effectively rule out an account-based pension as an option?
3. Based on Blanche's circumstances, would you advise that she commence an account-based income stream or a non-account based income stream?

LO 9 Transition to retirement income streams

Prior to changes in superannuation in 2007, an individual had to completely retire in order to gain access to their superannuation. This made it difficult for individuals who wanted to reduce their working hours but not completely retire and still enjoy a reasonable income level during their part-time working years. The federal government responded to this dilemma by introducing the **transition to retirement (TTR) income stream**. The introduction of the TTR had additional benefits, including the following.

- It encouraged skilled workers to stay in the workforce longer.
- It enabled individuals to accumulate more for their retirement.
- It reduced the number of retired persons relative to the number of working persons and thereby reduced some pressure on the funding of the social security system.

transition to retirement (TTR) income stream a scheme which allows workers to continue to work part-time (or full-time) and supplement their income by drawing down some of their superannuation

A TTR is very similar to an account-based pension. The main differences are as follows.

- The individual must draw down the same minimum income level as a normal account-based pension holder; however, the maximum income draw down for a TTR is limited to 10% of the account balance.
- The individual is still able to contribute to superannuation.
- The balance of the account which funds the TTR cannot be commuted until a condition of release has been satisfied.

TTRs for individuals 55 to 59 years old

We noted in chapter 10 that for superannuation purposes a person born before 1 July 1960 has a preservation age of 55. If a person born before 1960 commences a TTR at the age of 55, any earnings inside superannuation are tax free and any income stream drawn from superannuation will benefit from the tax-free component and a 15% rebate.

ILLUSTRATIVE EXAMPLE 11.9

Stephen was born in 1959 and at age 55 commences a TTR. He has $400 000 in his superannuation account which comprises a $300 000 taxed component and a tax-free component of $100 000. Twenty-five per cent of Stephen's superannuation is tax free ($100 000/$400 000). Therefore, 25% of any income stream he takes will be tax free.

TTRs for individuals 60 years and over

When a person commences a TTR after the age of 60 or continues with a TTR and turns 60 the tax advantages become more generous. All earnings inside the superannuation fund are tax free and all TTR income is also received tax free.

ILLUSTRATIVE EXAMPLE 11.10

Continuing from illustrative example 11.9, Stephen has now turned 60 years of age. Assume that his account has grown to $500 000 and has just generated 10% gross returns. The mix between the taxed superannuation component and the tax-free component is immaterial for TTR purposes as all TTR income will be received tax free.

The fund has generated $50 000 in returns. In accumulation mode this would have been taxed at 15% resulting in $7500 tax being paid. In TTR pension mode this tax is not payable. If Stephen takes a TTR of 4% this would result in $20 000 in income — all of which would be tax free.

Financial planners often recommend combining salary sacrifice with a TTR in order to maximise the tax benefits. If Stephen earned $20 000 more than the threshold at which the 30% marginal tax rate commences and he decides to salary sacrifice $20 000 at the same time as drawing down a TTR of $20 000, what are the tax savings available?

The savings are shown in table 11.13.

TABLE 11.13 Tax savings of a TTR and salary sacrificing

Item	Rate	Tax saving (cost)
Salary sacrifice (PAYG)	30% × $20 000	$6 000
Contributions tax	15% × $20 000	($3 000)
Earnings tax	15% × $50 000	$7 500
Total		$10 500

Several conclusions can be drawn from Illustrative example 11.10.

- The higher the individual's marginal tax rate the higher the PAYG savings.
- The amount that can be salary sacrificed is constrained by the concessional contribution limits. If these limits are exceeded then any TTR tax savings will be very quickly eroded.
- In the example, we have made the amount sacrificed equal to the TTR. There is no reason why these two numbers need to be the same. If the client has sufficient cash resources they might decide to sacrifice more than their TTR and build up their superannuation balance. Ironically, many people in full-time employment have found TTRs a useful tax-saving device. Conversely, if the client does not have sufficient cash resources, perhaps because they have dropped back to part-time employment, they might decide to draw a TTR which is greater than the amount sacrificed or they may choose not to sacrifice at all.
- Income-stream providers will charge an annual fee for providing a TTR and this fee must be balanced against the tax savings associated with TTRs.
- Moving to a TTR does not have to involve any change in the investment strategy by the individual. The gain to be received from a TTR is not as a result of increased investment risk. Rather, the gain is derived from a reconfiguration of the individual's income into a more tax-effective outcome and as such deserves serious consideration, particularly for individuals over the age of 60.

PERSONAL FINANCE BULLETIN

Award winning retirement income products

Awards for innovative financial products can be a bit like gold medals on wine bottles — you wonder how such an ordinary tasting wine can have so many gold medals until you check the independence, or lack thereof, of the party making the award. That is not to say that there are no reputable organisations making awards for financial product innovation and delivery — there are. However, it is very much a case of 'buyer beware'.

The *Superannuation Industry (Supervision) Act 1993* and the *Tax Laws Amendment (Simplified Superannuation) Act 2007* establish the broad framework for compliant retirement income products; however, the breadth of the specifications gives scope for product providers to innovate. Such innovation is generally seen as a good thing as it enables product providers to better fit products to clients. It also enables product providers to adapt to changing social, demographic and economic conditions.

In 2012 Challenger introduced their Challenger Care Annuity. The product is aimed at people who may be moving into residential care and wish to protect the value of their capital while at the same time maximising their social security entitlements. Some of the product features include that:

- it provides a regular source of income
- capital can be withdrawn at any stage during the first 10 years
- capital is payable to the estate if the person dies within the first 10 years

»

»

- it can assist in reducing income tested aged care fees
- it receives concessional treatment under the age pension income and assets test
- it can be converted into an annuity for life after the tenth year; however, capital can no longer be withdrawn.

The Challenger Care Annuity was one of the winners of the CANSTAR Innovation Excellence Awards for Financial Services in 2012. Advisers can expect more innovation. While innovation is to be applauded in that it helps us fit the right retirement product to the client, it does bring with it a considerable burden in terms of keeping up to date with the inherent complexities of these new products. It is vital that the adviser and their client look beyond the glossy brochures and be thoroughly familiar with the terms and conditions associated with these products as outlined in the relevant product disclosure statement.

The age pension

Most retiring Australians will need to supplement their self-funded retirement income with a full or part pension provided by Centrelink.

In 2013–14 the federal government spent approximately $39 billion dollars supporting the 75% of Australians 65 or over who rely on a full or part pension to fund their retirement income needs. Over the last 10 years the percentage of the population receiving the full age pension has decreased, particularly in the 65 to 70 age bracket, as retirees are now using some of their accumulated superannuation to fund their retirement needs. This, however, has provided very little relief to the overall budget spend on pensions as the Australian population continues to age.

In the 2013 Federal Budget Treasury estimated that superannuation tax concessions cost the federal government close to $35 billion in tax revenue forgone, therefore the federal government would expect to see some reduction in reliance on the age pension, all other things being equal. Combining the age pension and tax concessions means that the total budget 'spend' on retirement incomes in 2013–14 was $74 billion. Not surprisingly the amount spent on retirement incomes is a hot political topic, with many commentators concerned about Australia's capacity to meet its future commitments.

Australians can access their superannuation at age 55 if born before 1 July 1960 and at age 60 if born after 1 July 1964 if they have satisfied a condition of release. However, they are not currently eligible to access the age pension until the age of 65 (for females, the access age is dependent on birth date). The eligibility age for both males and females will progressively increase to age 67 by 2024. There has been some discussion in the financial media about bringing the age eligibilities into line; that is, allowing individuals to access their superannuation and the age pension at the same age. Most of the discussion has emphasised lifting the preservation age for superannuation so that it is in line with the age pension entitlement age. This would be a difficult political move for any party to make and the likelihood is that the disparity will remain for some time. As such, individuals will continue to access and use some (or all) of their superannuation before being entitled to the age pension.

APRA statistics reveal that in 2012 retired Australians withdrew approximately $70 billion from superannuation, $35 billion of which was in the form of lump sums. The withdrawal and use of lump sums prior to reaching the age pension entitlement age increases an individual's pension entitlement. This process has been called 'double-dipping' and clearly places additional strain on the federal government in funding its retirement income responsibilities.

The Household Income and Labour Dynamics in Australia (HILDA) survey is a comprehensive survey of Australian households. In the 2010 HILDA data for households aged 50 to 64 years the level of property-related debt increased by 123% when compared to 2002 levels after adjusting for inflation. One view is that this spike in debt has been fuelled by people approaching retirement who are borrowing to fund a current lifestyle they would not otherwise be able to afford who are 'comforted' by the fact that they can withdraw some of their superannuation as a lump sum to extinguish this debt in retirement.

By 2016–17 it is estimated that the federal government will spend $48 billion on the aged pension and $51 billion on superannuation tax concessions for a total projected spend of $99 billion (Australian Government Budget Paper Number 1, 2013).

Centrelink applies both an assets and an income test to an individual to determine age-pension entitlements. The following discussion concentrates on superannuation held in accumulation style accounts, which are the most commonly held form of superannuation. The Centrelink treatment of defined benefit style accounts is slightly different and outside the scope of this chapter.

Assets test

When the individual is above the age-pension entitlement age, superannuation is an assessable asset. When superannuation (or ordinary money) is used to fund the purchase of an income stream, Centrelink recognises that over time the underlying capital is consumed and therefore it periodically depletes the value of the asset for assets test purposes.

ILLUSTRATIVE EXAMPLE 11.11

Helen spends $600 000 to buy a 20-year income stream. Centrelink will assume that $30 000 p.a. is periodically depleted ($600 000/20). When the income stream is first purchased, Centrelink will assume the asset has a value of $600 000. After the first year, Centrelink will assume it has a value of $570 000; after the second year, $540 000 and so on.

Income test

Income received from an income stream, whether that income stream was funded by superannuation or ordinary money, is assessable income for Centrelink purposes. Centrelink, like the ATO, recognises that some income received is actually a return of capital. If the income stream is funded by ordinary money, the Centrelink and ATO approaches coincide.

- The purchase price divided by the term equals the deductible amount.
- Total income less the deductible amount equals the assessable income.

If the income stream is funded by superannuation, the Centrelink and ATO approaches differ. For Centrelink the situation is as follows.

- The purchase price divided by the term equals the deductible amount.
- Total income less the deductible amount equals the assessable income.

For the ATO the situation is as follows.

- The tax-free component divided by total superannuation equals the tax-free percentage.
- The income stream multiplied by the tax-free percentage equals the deductible amount.
- Total income less the deductible amount equals the assessable income.

ILLUSTRATIVE EXAMPLE 11.12

Claude had $500 000 in superannuation which comprised an untaxed component of $300 000 and a tax-free component of $200 000. He used this money to buy a 20-year income stream of $40 000 p.a.

Centrelink would assess Claude's assessable income for income-test purposes as follows:

$$\text{Deductible amount} = \frac{\$500000}{20} = \$25000$$

$$\text{Assessable amount} = \$40000 - \$25000 = \$15000$$

The ATO would assess Claude's assessable income for tax purposes as follows:

$$\text{Tax-free percentage} = \frac{\$200000}{\$500000} = 40\%$$

$$\text{Deductible amount} = \$40000 \times 40\% = \$16000$$

$$\text{Assessable income} = \$40000 - \$16000 = \$24000$$

Where an income stream is for fewer than 5 years, Centrelink does not attempt to measure the actual income. Instead, it considers the underlying assets to be financial assets and therefore applies the rules of deeming to these assets. Deeming is considered in more detail in chapter 13.

Figure 11.2 provides an overview of how funds are withdrawn from a superannuation environment.

Reverse mortgages

For older people with a large amount of equity in their family home but with little disposable income, reverse mortgages provide a valuable means by which equity can be turned into *income*. We have used the word income in italics because it is not income as such; it is actually a progressive consumption of capital. Indeed some providers prefer to use the term home equity conversion loans.

reverse mortgage an arrangement to mortgage a home in order to receive payments from the fund provider in return for a percentage ownership in the home or an accumulated debt to be paid when the home is sold

Under a **reverse mortgage**, the home owner borrows a sum of money secured against the family home. Rather than paying regular amounts of interest (and principal), the interest accrues and the total interest accrued and the principal are paid as a lump sum from the sale proceeds of the family home once it is eventually sold.

The terms and conditions which apply to reverse mortgages can be very complex and difficult to understand. There can also be an incentive for commission-based sellers of these products to encourage clients to borrow more than is prudent for their circumstances.

	Accumulation mode		Pension mode
Superannuation environment	Contributions	Investment	**Withdrawal**

Ordinary money

While we have concentrated on superannuation it is important to remember that many people build wealth outside a superannuation environment and then use this ordinary money to fund their retirement. This money does not have to be withdrawn as such.

Superannuation money

Superannuation money is money that is held inside a superannuation environment and needs to be withdrawn (released) to fund retirement. Superannuation money can be held in one of three forms: taxed, untaxed and non concessional.

Taxed and untaxed superannuation money

For most Australians their concessional contributions and earnings are taxed at 15% — this results in taxed superannuation money.

For some Australians their concessional contributions and earnings are *not* taxed — this results in untaxed superannuation money.

Taxed and untaxed money form what is known as the **taxable component.**

Non concessional superannuation money

Where an individual has made an after-tax contribution to superannuation.

Non concessional superannuation money is combined with superannuation which is attributable to superannuation that was accrued prior to June 1983 to form what is known as **the tax-free component.**

Tax payable on withdrawal of money from superannuation

The amount of tax payable is a function of four factors:

1. whether the taxable component contains taxed or untaxed money
2. the size of the tax-free component relative to the taxable component
3. the age of the individual — persons over the age of 60 are treated more generously than persons under the age of 60
4. whether the individual wishes to take a lump sum, an income stream or some combination of both.

Lump sum or income stream from superannuation

A range of factors need to be taken into account in deciding whether to take a lump sum, an income stream or some combination of both. These factors are outlined in the chapter.

If an income stream is selected then should the individual take an account-based income stream, a non account-based income stream or some combination of both?

Interaction with Centrelink

All Australians who meet the qualifying requirements are entitled to the aged pension *(Tier 1).* One of the qualifying requirements is that the retiree meets the asset and income tests. Withdrawing money from a superannuation environment and/or using ordinary money to fund retirement will have an impact on Centrelink entitlements.

FIGURE 11.2
Overview of the withdrawal of funds from a superannuation environment

ILLUSTRATIVE EXAMPLE 11.13

Gran is a 70-year-old widow. She lives in the family home which is worth $500 000. She relies on the single age pension for income. She would like to release some of the equity in her home to provide some additional 'income'. She decides to borrow $200 000 against the equity in her house using a reverse mortgage. The current rate of interest on the reverse mortgage is 8%. Assume that her home increases in value by 4% per annum. Figure 11.3 outlines Gran's equity in her home.

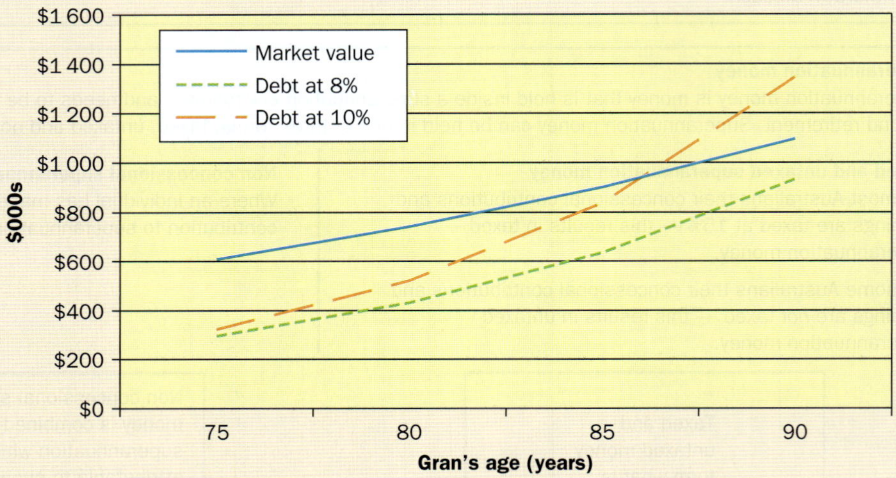

FIGURE 11.3
Gran's reverse mortgage

The blue line represents the market value of Gran's home over time. The green line represents the accumulated debt. Because the interest cost of 8% is greater than the rate of appreciation of the value of the home of 4% the two lines begin to converge over time. That is, the amount of equity Gran has in her house diminishes. At the age of 75 and 80 Gran still has a considerable amount of equity in her home; however, by the time she turns 90 her equity is seriously diminished. If she needs to sell the family home in order to fund moving into other accommodation she may not have enough left to do so after repaying the loan.

The orange line represents an interest rate on the loan of 10%. If Gran's loan is a variable-rate loan and if interest rates suddenly jump to 10% soon after she enters the loan agreement then the solid and dashed lines will converge more quickly and equity will be lost more rapidly.

no negative equity guarantee (NNEG)
a guarantee that the accrued interest and principal obligations under a reverse mortgage will not exceed the value of the real estate pledged as security

On 18 September 2012 the federal government legislated to ensure that all reverse mortgages issued from that date had a **no negative equity guarantee (NNEG)**. Individuals who have taken out a reverse mortgage prior to that date need to check their loan contract to see if it includes a NNEG clause.

Individuals also need to be aware that the cash/income provided by a reverse mortgage may affect their age pension entitlement. The family home is exempt from the age pension asset test; however, the cash released via the reverse mortgage is not exempt. The cash released will also be subject to deeming and will therefore have age pension income test consequences. See chapter 13 which discusses deeming and the age pension assets and income tests.

The ASIC website MoneySmart also has a warning with respect to property options. Property options are similar to reverse mortgages in that they release cash from real estate in order to provide additional income; however, they also have important differences. A property option establishes a base value for real estate and then shares any increase in value between the property owner and the property option promoter. For example, the property owner might receive an amount equal to 2% of the value of the property in cash each year. If the property increases in value by more than 2% each year then the property option promoter will capture this gain when the property is eventually sold. The MoneySmart website warns that property options are unlikely to be covered by credit or financial services laws.

PROFESSIONAL ADVICE

Reverse mortgages

People often have strong views on reverse mortgages without much understanding of what they entail. One view is expressed below:

> People spend much of their working lives trying to pay off their mortgage so that they can fulfil the Australian dream and own their home. The day that they make that last mortgage payment and legal title passes from the bank to the homeowner is often a very special day in people's lives. Reverse mortgages are an insidious thing — they undo all that hard work, they turn that psychology upside down — you end your days living in a house owned by the bank. I saw an article in the paper the other day that said 'Reverse mortgages aren't for everybody', well I would go further — I would say that 'Reverse mortgages aren't for anybody'.

There is no doubt that in Australia many people have a strong desire to own their own home. Most people feel that they own their home when they move in, notwithstanding the fact that they are still paying off their mortgage. The final mortgage payment is an important symbolic event; however, most people will feel at that point that they have already owned their own home for a long period of time. To suggest that taking out a reverse mortgage would make people feel that their home is now not theirs might be overstating the argument somewhat. Nonetheless, re-establishing a mortgage after years of trying to extinguish a mortgage does represent a significant psychological hurdle for many people.

»

»

Interest on reverse mortgages is not paid on an annual basis. Instead, it compounds. The younger the person taking out a reverse mortgage, the longer the compounding period. For instance, a female at age 65 has a further life expectancy of 22 years. This is a long time for interest to compound and the amount of debt ultimately accumulated could be substantial, leaving little or no equity in the family home. The older the client, the less the effect of compounding interest and the lower the amount of debt ultimately accumulated.

The age pension provides a very basic level of income support. If a person lives in a $1 million home but has no other means of income besides the age pension they would generally be referred to as asset rich and income poor. In this case, a reverse mortgage may release some valuable *income* for the individual, and because they are asset rich they may still retain substantial equity in their home even after allowing for the amount of accumulated debt. However, if a person lives in a more modestly valued home, the amount of equity left in their home might be substantially reduced by the amount of accumulated debt under a reverse mortgage.

With increasing life expectancies and fewer people living in an extended family environment, many Australians will now move into alternative accommodation in old age. The sale of the family home is often used to help fund this alternative accommodation and it is important that the sale proceeds, net of any reverse mortgage payout obligation, are sufficient to fund this accommodation. Many people also see the family home as an asset that should be passed on to dependants unencumbered by reverse-mortgage obligations.

If you have a 95-year-old client who is living in a $5 million house who is not too worried about any inheritance they might leave and whose only source of income is the age pension, the argument in favour of the client taking out a reverse mortgage is fairly strong. This is as long as they can overcome the psychology of owing the bank money again.

In summary, to say that 'reverse mortgages aren't for anybody' is perhaps an overstatement. However, reverse mortgages are not for everybody. Financial planners need to balance a number of variables in determining whether or not a reverse mortgage is suitable for a client.

QUESTIONS

What would be your advice to each of the following clients, who all own their own home and rely on the age pension as their only source of income?

1. Roger is 65 and his home is valued at $350 000.
2. Tony is 90 and his home is valued at $350 000.
3. Bianca is 65 and her home is valued at $2 million.
4. Blair is 90 and her home is valued at $2 million.

Pensions loan scheme

The Department of Human Services offers a pensions loan scheme which has some similarity to a reverse mortgage. If an individual satisfies the requirements to be eligible for the age pension but they are not entitled to the age pension due to the assets test or they are entitled only to a part pension, they may be able to take out a pension loan.

This loan tops up any part age pension payment so that the individual receives an amount equivalent to the full age pension. It is not possible to borrow more and increase the level of income beyond the full age pension. This loan needs to be secured against real estate and does not have to be repaid unless the property is sold or the individual passes away. The amount borrowed and the associated interest continues to accumulate in much the same way as the balance of a reverse mortgage accumulates.

LO 10 What is an adequate retirement income?

Most people who rely on the age pension as their only source of income in retirement will tell you that the age pension is not adequate.

We referred earlier to the ASFA modelling which suggested a comfortable retirement for a single person in March 2013 requires \$41 146 per annum. Is this adequate?

Is an adequate income stream a fixed amount or is it a relative number? If it is a relative number, what is it relative to?

Some commentators suggest that retirement income should relate to a person's pre-retirement income. That is, someone who earns \$200 000 p.a. prior to retirement will have higher expectations in retirement relative to someone who earns \$50 000 per year. Various percentages have been suggested over time. For instance, former prime minister Paul Keating suggested '65 at 65'; that is, individuals should aim for a retirement income of 65% of pre-retirement income at age 65. A retirement income of less than 100% of pre-retirement income reflects the fact that generally less tax is paid in retirement and often other financial commitments are lower.

Should retirement income be relative to your friendship group? You want to eat out, travel and socialise with your friends in retirement. Should retirement income be a function of your commitments? If the mortgage still has to be paid and if dependent children are still at home, there are considerable commitments that still need to be met.

The federal government recognises that the superannuation guarantee system will not, in its current form, produce an adequate income in retirement and as a result has legislated to increase the superannuation guarantee contribution (SGC) rate from 9% to 12%. The SGC rate is 9.25% in 2013–14 and will progressively increase by 0.25% per year.

In their report 'How much super do Australians really have?' Challenger provides a series of estimates of superannuation balances. One of the difficulties of estimating the superannuation balances of individuals is that some individuals have many superannuation accounts. Challenger estimates that in June 2010 the average superannuation balance for males aged 60 to 64 was \$198 000 and for a female of the same age range it was \$113 000.

If we assume that the average retirement age is 62 and the average real rate of return in retirement is 3% then:

PMT = (rate, number of periods, amount)
Male: PMT = (3%, 20.96, \$198 000) = \$12 862
Female: PMT = (3%, 24.23, \$113 000) = \$6 628

These income levels are unlikely to produce an adequate retirement lifestyle.

It is important to remember that we are using superannuation only as the basis for modelling retirement incomes. Some households will have additional wealth not held in superannuation which can assist in funding retirement incomes. The HILDA survey 2010 estimated wealth for households aged 50 to 64 years was approximately $130 000 excluding superannuation and housing; however, it also estimated that the level of household debt was approximately $148 000 in which case the 'average' Australian is unlikely to have significant non-superannuation wealth to assist them in funding their retirement.

It is also important to remember that we are dealing with averages. At the lower limit, the amount of wealth created to fund retirement is zero; however, there is no upper limit. The average wealth balances will be impacted by these very high balances. The end result is that significantly more than 50% of the male retirement population will have accumulated less than $198 000. Challenger estimates that the median aggregate superannuation balance for males aged 60 to 65 is $127 000; that is, half the male population in the 60 to 65 age bracket have superannuation balances of less than $127 000. For females the median balance for the 60 to 65 age bracket is $90 000. As we mentioned earlier in the chapter there is still a very heavy reliance on the aged pension in Australia and this reliance looks set to continue for many years yet notwithstanding the introduction of the SGC, the increase in the SGC from 9% to 12% and the tax incentives encouraging us to save for our retirement.

ILLUSTRATIVE EXAMPLE 11.14

Jodie is 60 years old and has just retired. Her gross income in the last year prior to retirement was $140 000. She would like to receive 65% of this figure as a retirement income, that is $91 000 for her life expectancy. She would also like the real value of this $91 000 income stream maintained over time. She estimates that she will be able to invest her unused superannuation at a real rate of 2%, that is, a rate over and above the rate of inflation. How much superannuation does she need to fund her retirement income desires?

$$PV = (2\%, 26, \$91\,000) = \$1\,831\,000$$

While the concept of adequacy can be discussed at great length, the reality is that most retirees in the near and medium term are unlikely to produce the level of retirement income they desire.

ILLUSTRATIVE EXAMPLE 11.15

At the beginning of this chapter, we introduced the case of Lisa. Lisa was working full-time and long hours. For Lisa to retire immediately would represent a dramatic change in lifestyle. Work for many people provides a sense of belonging that might be hard to replicate in retirement — it is not clear how much retirement planning Lisa has done. Many people these days seek to ease themselves into retirement rather than retire immediately, but this is not always possible — Lisa has been dealing with demanding clients who may not appreciate that she no longer works full-time.

Lisa is 63 years old and earns around $100 000 per annum. If Lisa wanted to generate a real income of 65% of her pre-retirement income (and we assume real investment returns of 2%) she would need to have accumulated around $1.2 million in wealth [PV = (2%, 23.35, $65 000)]. At the moment her accumulated wealth is $600 000 ($300 000 + $80 000 + 220 000). This would produce an income stream of $32 410 per year [PMT = (2%, 23.35, $600 000)] which is approximately 32% of her pre-retirement income. Lisa will also be entitled to a small part age pension. It is unlikely that Lisa will see this as an adequate retirement income.

Lisa might need to work beyond the age of 63 — this has a twofold benefit. Firstly, the existing accumulated wealth is not eroded and hopefully is increased through additional contributions and positive investment returns. Secondly, the period of retirement to be funded is shorter. An extra 5 years of work can have a significant impact on the level of retirement income that is achievable — nonetheless Lisa might also have to modify her retirement income expectations.

If Lisa continues to work beyond the age of 63 she should seriously consider starting a transition to retirement income stream and combine this with a concessional contribution strategy in order to maximise the tax benefits available.

Financial considerations need to be blended with non-financial considerations. The thought of working five more years in the same job might be completely unacceptable to Lisa — health, lifestyle and social issues all need to be factored into the planning.

Summary

Planning does not guarantee a good outcome; however, most people concede that planning generally produces better outcomes than not planning. Retirement is a significant life event and it needs to be planned. Retirement planning has many dimensions.

We all have needs in our life — Maslow describes them as a hierarchy of needs. These needs must be satisfied in our working lives and in our retired lives. Retirement provides a different context within which these needs must be satisfied — retirement planning must address issues such as how we will maintain our sense of belonging and self-esteem in retirement.

There are active, passive and support phases of retirement. Most retirement income modelling assumes a uniform income flow over the retirement period; however, maybe more income should be directed to the active phase and less to the passive phase, while at the same time ensuring there is a sufficient safety net for the support phase.

Retirement income can be funded by ordinary money or superannuation money or some combination of both. Inside a superannuation environment money can exist in one of three forms: taxed, untaxed and non-concessional. Understanding the characteristics of each helps the client and the financial planner determine the tax consequences of withdrawing money from a superannuation environment.

Money can be withdrawn from a superannuation environment as a lump sum or an income stream or both. A person over the age of 60 with taxed superannuation money (the most common form of superannuation money) can withdraw a lump sum or an income stream from superannuation tax free. Where a person is under the age of 60 and/or has some untaxed superannuation money some tax may be payable on withdrawal.

Most Australians withdraw their superannuation in the form of an income stream. The individual must then decide whether to commence an account-based income stream, a non-account based income stream or some combination of the two. Account-based income streams are distinctly different from non-account based income streams and it is important to match the needs of the individual to the characteristics of the income stream.

Retirement income can also be funded by a variety of other means including releasing cash from property through the use of reverse mortgages and downsizing the family home.

Federal government budget papers highlight that most Australians will not be able to achieve an 'adequate' self-funded retirement income for many years yet in which case self-funding will still need to be supplemented by the age pension. However, the modest income support provided by the age pension is unlikely to satisfy the average Australian's needs for an adequate retirement income, so working Australians need to reassess their wealth accumulation and retirement income strategies in an iterative process until an achievable outcome is obtained.

This chapter has largely concentrated on the financial dimensions of retirement; however, it is wrong to assume that a person with a large amount of accumulated wealth leading into retirement will automatically have a 'happy' retirement — just as it is wrong to assume that a person with little accumulated wealth leading into retirement will have an 'unhappy' retirement. Retirement planning has many dimensions and these dimensions stretch far beyond financial considerations alone. Nonetheless, surveys of retirees and those approaching retirement consistently highlight their number one concern as having insufficient financial resources for retirement.

Retirement planning should be one aspect of a comprehensive financial plan which is commenced long before retirement.

Professional application questions

11.1 What is the difference between superannuation money and ordinary money?

11.2 When can money be 'released' from superannuation?

11.3 Differentiate between taxed, untaxed and non-concessional superannuation money.

11.4 For the purposes of superannuation who is considered a dependant?

11.5 What is a binding death nomination?

11.6 Outline the types of risks each of the different types of income streams listed below are exposed to.

(a) Draw down of capital only

(b) Investment earnings only

(c) Combination of capital draw down and investment earnings

11.7 The life expectancy tables demonstrate a survivor bias. What is survivor bias? How does this impact on modelling for a client?

11.8 For a person under the age of 60 who is drawing a retirement income, the ATO subtracts a deductible amount from the individual's total income in order to determine their assessable income. Why does the ATO do this?

11.9 Outline the main differences between account-based and non-account based income streams.

11.10 What is the difference between a lifetime income stream and a life expectancy income stream?

11.11 The federal government insists that individuals in pension mode must draw down a minimum pension income. Why?

11.12 Why do annuities have relatively low implicit rates of return?

11.13 What is a deferred annuity? How can deferred annuities be used to manage longevity risk?

11.14 Outline the tax advantages associated with transition to retirement income streams.

11.15 If a retirement income stream is funded by superannuation money, Centrelink and the ATO use slightly different methodologies to determine the deductible amount. Distinguish between the two approaches.

11.16 The withdrawal and use of lump sums from superannuation prior to reaching age pension entitlement age is often referred to as double dipping. What does this mean and should people be allowed to double dip?

Professional application exercises

Basic	*
Moderate	* *
Challenging	* * *

11.17 Present value function *

Using the present value function in Excel or a financial calculator, how much would an individual need to accumulate in superannuation in order to fund a real retirement income of $60 000 p.a. for 20 years if the real rate of return was 4%?

11.18 Impact of divorce: lump sum split *

Brendan and Annie recently divorced. As part of the Family Court determination it has been decided that Brendan's superannuation of $400 000 should be split 60% to Brendan and 40% to Annie. Brendan's superannuation includes a $300 000 taxed component and a $100 000 tax-free component. What will be the component parts of Brendan's and Annie's superannuation after the split?

11.19 Using the rate function *

Using the rate function in Excel or a financial calculator, what is the implicit rate of return if a 60-year-old female commences a life expectancy retirement income stream of $50 000 p.a. based on a purchase price of $700 000?

11.20 Using the PMT function *

Using the PMT function in Excel or a financial calculator, how much retirement income can be generated for a 60-year-old male wishing to have a lifetime income stream assuming $400 000 to invest and a real rate of return of 4%?

11.21 Reverse mortgage * *

Your client Chris is a 75 year old male. He currently lives independently in his own home and hopes to do so for another 10 years. He currently relies on the single aged pension as his only source of income. He estimates that his home is currently worth $600 000. He would like to commence a reverse mortgage to release some cash; however, he wants to ensure that in 10 years at least half the equity in his house remains so that he can leave this as an inheritance for his grandchildren and/or afford to move to alternative accommodation. If we assume that house prices will increase by 5% and the interest rate on the reverse mortgage is 10% how much would be a prudent amount for Chris to borrow?

11.22 Lump sum taxes: taxed superannuation money * *

Kim is 57 years old and has $500 000 in superannuation. Her superannuation comprises a tax-free component of $150 000 and taxed superannuation money of $350 000. Kim has satisfied a condition of release from superannuation and would like to withdraw a $300 000 lump sum. How much lump sum tax would be payable?

11.23 Lump sum taxes: untaxed superannuation money * *

Adam is 58 years old and has $700 000 in superannuation. His superannuation comprises a tax-free component of $100 000 and untaxed superannuation money of $600 000. Adam has satisfied a condition of release from superannuation and would like to withdraw a $250 000 lump sum. How much lump sum tax would be payable?

11.24 Income stream: ordinary money deductible amount * *

Murray is 57 years old and has $450 000 in ordinary money. He takes his $450 000 to an income-stream provider and the provider agrees to pay Murray $52 350 p.a. for the next 15 years. The provider will invest Murray's $450 000 and the income stream provided to Murray will be a combination of investment earnings and a return of Murray's capital.

What will be Murray's assessable income for tax purposes?

11.25 Income stream: superannuation money deductible amount * *

Petra is 59 years old and has $700 000 in superannuation money. This includes a tax-free component of $200 000 and a taxed superannuation component of $500 000. Petra takes her $700 000 to an income-stream provider and the provider agrees to pay her $54 322 p.a. for the next 25 years.

(a) What will be Petra's assessable income for tax purposes?

(b) Will Petra be entitled to a tax rebate?

11.26 Transition to retirement * *

Paul is aged 57. He has $600 000 in his superannuation account which comprises a $400 000 taxed superannuation component and a tax-free component of $200 000. What tax advantages will Paul receive if he commences a transition to retirement income stream?

11.27 Recontribution strategy * * *

Chuck is 56 years old and has $800 000 in superannuation which includes a tax-free component of $200 000 and a taxed superannuation component of $600 000. Chuck has satisfied a condition of release from superannuation and decides to withdraw $260 000 as a lump sum and then immediately recontribute this $260 000 as a non-concessional contribution.

(a) Will Chuck be subject to any lump sum withdrawal tax?

(b) What will be Chuck's tax-free component after the recontribution takes place?

(c) Why might Chuck be seeking to increase his tax-free component?

(d) Can you suggest a more tax-efficient amount for Chuck to withdraw and recontribute?

CASE STUDY

Retirement income streams

Peter is 59 years old and has just been made redundant from his job. Peter is married to Maggie. They have two grown-up daughters who live away from home and are financially independent. Both daughters are engaged to be married with weddings likely in the next 18 months.

For the past 12 years, Peter has worked as an insurance assessor. In his last year of work, he earned $100 000. Peter's mate Dave has offered him work as a landscape gardener which would generate about $50 000 p.a. for a 5-day working week. Dave thinks it would be a great change for Peter and also give him the chance to build up his retirement savings, particularly if he starts a transition to retirement income stream to supplement his lower income. Peter is not so sure — the landscape work is full-time and he was hoping to cut back on work or maybe stop altogether.

Peter currently has $500 000 in superannuation which includes a tax-free component of $120 000 and a taxed component of $380 000.

Peter has been looking at the various annuities on offer in the market. He is particularly attracted to the offer made by XYZ Life, which for a $100 000 purchase price offers:

- a lifetime income
- a guarantee period of 10 years
- single life, that is, no reversion
- payment of $6500 p.a.
- nil increase, that is, the payment is not indexed.

Peter has also been considering the life expectancy annuity offered by XYZ Life, which for a $100 000 purchase price offers:

- payment of $7500 p.a.
- nil increase, that is, the payment is not indexed.

Dave thinks Peter is mad to be considering a non-account-based income stream. Dave thinks if Peter will not follow his advice and join the landscaping business and commence a TTR, he should commence an account-based income stream and generate some decent returns which he will not get if he goes with the non-account-based income stream approach.

QUESTIONS

Part A: TTR

If Peter decides to join Dave in the landscaping business and we assume:

- Peter uses his $500 000 in superannuation to commence a TTR.
- Peter's superannuation generates earnings of 5% in the first year of the TTR.

»

»

- Peter draws down a TTR of $10 000.
- Peter's marginal tax rate is 30%.

1 What will be the annual tax savings of the TTR for Peter at age 59?

2 How will the tax savings for Peter change when he turns 60?

Part B: Lifetime income stream — non-account based

If Peter decides to commence a lifetime income stream and we assume:

- Peter uses his entire $500 000 superannuation balance.
- All payments are received at the end of the year.

3 How much income will Peter generate?

4 What will be Peter's assessable income at age 59?

5 What will be Peter's assessable income at age 60?

6 What rate of return is implicit in his income stream?

Part C: Life expectancy income stream — non-account based

If Peter decides to commence a life expectancy income stream and we assume:

- Peter uses his entire $500 000 superannuation balance.
- All payments are received at the end of the year.

7 How much income will Peter generate?

8 What rate of return is implicit in his income stream?

9 Why is the rate of return implicit in the life expectancy income stream higher than the rate implicit in the lifetime income stream?

Part D: Account-based income stream

If Peter decides to commence an account-based income stream and we assume:

- Peter uses his entire $500 000 superannuation balance.
- Peter's superannuation generates earnings of 5% in the first year.
- At the end of the first year of having the account, Peter withdraws an income stream equal to 7% of the account balance.

10 How much tax will be payable on the 5% earnings inside the fund?

11 What will be Peter's assessable income at age 59?

12 What will be Peter's assessable income at age 60?

Part E: Summary

13 In your opinion, are options B, C and D above likely to provide Peter with an adequate retirement income?

14 How might the TTR option be supplemented by a salary-sacrifice strategy to improve the outcome?

15 Besides tax savings, how does the TTR help Peter increase his retirement income?

16 What other factors need to be taken into account in determining the appropriate income stream for Peter?

References and further reading

Agnew, J 2013, *Australia's retirement system: strengths, weaknesses and reforms*, Center for Retirement Research Boston College, April 2013, number 13-5.

Association of Superannuation Funds of Australia (ASFA) 2013, www.superannuation.asn.au.

Australian Financial Review (AFR) 2012, 'Why retirees overlook lifetime annuities', 30 May 2012.

Australian Government Actuary (AGA) 2013, *Life expectancy tables*, www.aga.gov.au.

Australian Government Budget Paper Number 1 2013, www.budget.gov.au/2013–14.

Australian Prudential Regulation Authority (APRA) 2013, www.apra.gov.au.

Australian Securities and Investments Commission (ASIC) 2013, www.moneysmart.gov.au.

Bewley, R 2012, *A pension or an annuity*, CPA Intheblack, 13 September 2012.

Canstar 2013, Innovation Excellence Awards — Financial Services, www.canstar.com.au.

CCH 2012a, *Australian master financial planning guide 2012–13*, 15th edition.

CCH 2012b, *Australian master superannuation guide 2012–13*, 16th edition.

Challenger 2013, www.challenger.com.au.

Challenger Retirement Income Research 2012, 'How much super do Australians really have?', April 2012.

CPA Australia 2012, *Household savings and retirement*, October 2012.

Household, Income and Labour Dynamics in Australia (HILDA) 2013, www.melbourneinstitute.com/hilda.

Maslow, AH 1987, *Motivation and personality*, 3rd edition, Harper & Row, New York.

Money Management 2012, 'Can retirement income products make the savings last?', www.moneymanagement.com.au.

National Information Centre on Retirement Investments Inc (NICRI) 2013, www.nicri.org.au.

Rice Warner 2012, *Reforming the Age Pension*, August 2012.

12 Self-managed superannuation funds

LEARNING OBJECTIVES

After studying this chapter, you should be able to:

1. describe the history and growth of SMSFs
2. outline the major steps involved in setting up a SMSF
3. describe the contribution opportunities provided by SMSFs
4. outline the investment opportunities and constraints faced by SMSFs
5. explain the process by which SMSFs can pay tax-free benefits to members
6. explain the strategies that can be employed by a SMSF to improve estate planning outcomes
7. describe the role of the SMSF auditor and other SMSF professionals in delivering services to SMSFs
8. model a cost–benefit analysis to determine whether establishing a SMSF structure is warranted
9. explain compliance and penalties.

CASE STUDY

Simone is 52 years old and is separated. She has twin daughters who are 18 years old and who still live at home.

Over the years Simone has built up a very successful business selling clothes and fashion accessories from a shop in her local shopping strip. Simone owns the freehold on the shop. She purchased the shop in 2001 for $200 000 and it is currently valued at $800 000.

Currently Simone has $100 000 in an industry superannuation fund. Over the years there have been many opportunities for Simone to contribute more to superannuation; however, when she has had spare cash she has tended to put this back into her growing business.

Simone has recently attended a 'high pressure' seminar about self-managed superannuation funds. Simone is keen on the idea of setting up a SMSF although she is concerned about tying up all her money in superannuation just when her daughters are about to go to university.

Simone has discussed the idea of setting up a SMSF with her friends, most of whom think it is a good idea. However, her friends have slightly different ideas on how she should go about it.

- Robbo thinks it's a great idea and that she should contribute her real business property to the SMSF.
- Margie went further than Robbo and suggested that Simone should run her clothing shop business from inside her SMSF to take advantage of 'all those tax concessions'.
- Ernest thought it was a good chance to do some estate planning and manage the eventual transfer of the clothing shop to her two daughters, both of whom have expressed an interest in continuing the family business.
- Julie was the only one to express a note of caution. She was concerned that 'mixing super and family' might cause problems down the track.

Some of the issues that Simone needs to consider include:

- Should Simone roll over her $100 000 industry fund account into her SMSF?
- What is real business property and how can it be contributed to superannuation? What impact will this have on the need to hold a diversified portfolio of assets within the fund?
- What are the contribution limits and will a contribution of her real business property fit within these limits?
- How can Simone ensure that if she establishes a SMSF all her money is not tied up in superannuation and that she will have sufficient cash available to assist her daughters as they commence their university education?
- Will Simone be allowed to run her business inside the SMSF as Margie suggests?
- How can a SMSF be structured to facilitate the eventual transfer of the clothing shop real business property to her two daughters?
- Should she include her two daughters as members and trustees of the SMSF? What are the dangers of 'mixing super and family'?

The issues facing Simone in whether or not to establish a SMSF are examined throughout this chapter.

Introduction

In chapter 10 we discussed the shift in public policy away from reliance on the aged pension and towards self-managed and self-funded retirement. The growth of small superannuation funds, particularly self-managed superannuation funds (SMSFs), are perhaps the best exemplar of this policy shift. This chapter will concentrate on SMSFs.

A **small superannuation fund** is a fund with four or less members. Throughout this chapter, all other funds, that is, funds with five or more members, will be referred to as large funds.

small superannuation fund
fund with four or less members

There are two main types of small funds: small APRA funds and self-managed superannuation funds (SMSFs).

Small APRA funds, as the name implies, are supervised by APRA. APRA provides a list of approved **trustees**. An individual or a group of up to four people can arrange for an approved trustee to run a small fund on their behalf. At 30 June 2012, there were 3201 small APRA funds representing approximately 6000 individual accounts with $1.8 billion invested (APRA 2012, tables 1, 3 and 9).

small APRA fund
fund with four or fewer members that is supervised by APRA

trustee
a person who administers a trust fund; a superannuation fund is a form of trust fund

Self-managed superannuation funds (SMSFs) are supervised by the ATO. In SMSFs the members are the trustees or directors of the trustee company. At 31 March 2013, there were 503 320 SMSFs representing 958 095 individual accounts with $496 billion invested (ATO 2013b).

self-managed superannuation fund
a fund with four or fewer members that is supervised by the ATO

SMSFs have always dominated the small funds market. In the last decade, small APRA funds have continued to decline in number while SMSFs have seen significant growth.

In this chapter we will outline how individuals establish a SMSF. Important decisions, including what type of trustee structure the SMSF may use, need to be made very early.

We will also examine how funds are contributed to and invested by the SMSF. In many ways SMSFs and large funds are *similar* with respect to how funds are contributed and invested. We will not spend much time in this chapter discussing these similarities and instead presume that the reader is familiar with the material in chapter 10 (Superannuation). We will concentrate on how SMSFs are *different* to large funds with respect to contributions and investment.

Ultimately benefits will need to be paid to members. Again this chapter will concentrate on the *differences* between SMSFs and large funds and presume that the reader is familiar with the material in chapter 11 (Retirement planning).

LO 1 The history and growth of small superannuation funds

Small superannuation funds are often thought of as being a relatively recent phenomenon; however, their history can be traced back over 100 years. In 1915 the *Income Tax Assessment Act* provided a tax exemption for superannuation funds established for the benefit of employees of any business, which effectively included small business owners who were employees of their own business. Where these funds had fewer than five members they were known as 'excluded funds'.

In 1997 the federal government commissioned the Wallis Inquiry into financial services. The Wallis Inquiry made a number of recommendations including:

> *The Inquiry considers that self-managed funds provide a worthwhile and competitive option for superannuation investors. However, as self-managed funds they should not be subject to* ***prudential*** *regulation. To apply prudential regulation in such circumstances is impracticable.*

prudential
to monitor risk-taking behaviour

> *Moreover, it should be made clear that such schemes are conducted entirely at the risk of the beneficiaries — in relation to financial safety, there should be no regulatory assurance attaching to such schemes.* (Wallis p. 333)

Given that Wallis did not believe prudential regulation was required, the Wallis Inquiry went on to recommend that the regulation of excluded funds should pass from the Australian Prudential Regulation Authority (APRA) to the Australian Taxation Office (ATO).

In 1999 legislation was passed which re-categorised excluded funds into self-managed superannuation funds (SMSFs) and small APRA funds (SAFs), with the regulation of SMSFs passing from APRA to the ATO.

compliance acting in accordance with established guidelines, specifications, or legislation

The ATO is quite clear that it does not provide for the prudential regulation of SMSFs, but instead applies **compliance**-based regulation. The distinction, however, is sometimes difficult to draw as the ATO also declares that its role includes the regulation of SMSFs 'to safeguard the retirement savings for Australians who choose to manage their own super' (ATO 2013a, p. 6). The growth of SMSF tax rulings and guidance releases from the ATO would suggest that they are an active regulator of SMSFs and the distinction in terminology between prudential and compliance seems of little practical consequence. Nevertheless there are still some significant differences in the regulation of SMSFs and other (APRA regulated) funds, including the following.

- SMSFs are not protected by government or industry compensation if they suffer losses through the fraudulent behaviour of trustees.
- SMSFs have no access to the Superannuation Complaints Tribunal.
- SMSFs are subject to less rigorous reporting requirements under the *Superannuation Industry (Supervision) Act* (SISA) 1993.

Managing a SMSF can be a complex and time consuming business; however, the rate of growth of SMSFs, particularly in the last decade, has been significant. Surveys of individuals asking why they decided to establish a SMSF identify three prominent reasons:

- control — particularly investment control
- flexibility — including the flexibility to accept in-specie contributions; that is, contributions other than cash
- cost — notwithstanding the fact that small funds can cost several thousand dollars to establish and cost several thousand dollars a year to run, there is a tipping point where control, flexibility and the amount of funds to be invested make the small fund an attractive option.

Figure 12.1 shows the number of SMSFs has basically doubled in the last ten years and the amount of assets under management has increased by a factor of five. SMSFs now have $496 billion in assets under management and this is projected to increase to more than $2 trillion by 2030. Ten years ago assets held by SMSFs represented approximately 10% of all superannuation assets in Australia. In 2013 assets held by SMSFs represent approximately one-third of all superannuation assets in Australia.

Males and females are relatively evenly represented in SMSFs. Most SMSFs have one or two members; only 8% of funds have three or four members.

Compared to large superannuation funds, SMSF members tend to:

- be older — approximately 60% of SMSF members are over 55
- have larger superannuation balances — the average balance per member is more than six times the average account balance of large funds
- invest more of their assets directly — we will review the statistics associated with investment later in the chapter (see 'Investment trends' later in this chapter).

The average balance per member for a SMSF was approximately $517 000 in March 2013. Approximately half of all SMSF individual account balances, however, are less than $300 000. Figure 12.1 shows that 11% of SMSFs have less than $100 000 in assets under management, while at the other end of the spectrum, 9.4% of funds hold between $2m and $5m in assets and 2% of funds hold more than $5m in assets.

	Dec 03	Mar 13
Total number of SMSFs	252 854	503 320
Total number of SMSF members	480 191	958 095
Assets held	105 718 000 000	496 204 000 000
Average balance per member	220 158	517 907
Percentage of SMSF members under 35		4.4%
Percentage of SMSF members over 55		61.5%
Percentage of funds with 1 member		22.5%
Percentage of funds with 2 members		69.1%
Percentage of funds with 3 members		4.1%
Percentage of funds with 4 members		4.3%
Average number of members per fund		1.9
Percentage of funds with less than $100 000 in assets		11.0%
Percentage of funds with more than $2m and less than $5m in assets		9.4%
Percentage of funds with more than $5m in assets		2.0%

FIGURE 12.1 SMSF selected facts and figures

Source: Extracted from ATO 2013b.

SMSFs are not without their critics. Some commentators have criticised SMSFs as tax havens for the rich and an unsustainable burden on taxpayers. Politicians seeking to balance budgets in difficult economic times often cast an eye towards SMSFs to see if any tax dollars can be clawed back. Whether you are a fan or a critic of SMSFs, their importance in the Australian economic and political landscape cannot be denied.

LO 2 Setting up a self-managed superannuation fund

Setting up a SMSF starts with getting the 'right' advice. The key legal document to establish the SMSF is the trust deed. To prepare this document, decisions need to be made about what trustee structure will be used and who will be admitted as members. Once this is done an investment and insurance plan needs to be developed. Regulators will also insist that the assets of the fund are distinguishable from the assets of the members.

Getting advice

People are often attracted to SMSFs by the notion that they can do it all themselves and in the process save a significant amount in fees that would otherwise be payable to advisers. However, very few people have the breadth of tax, accounting and legal knowledge necessary to establish a SMSF.

In many cases the idea of establishing a SMSF arises in discussion with an accountant at tax time. Before 1 July 2013 accountants were able to provide advice about the set up and closure of SMSFs without the need to hold an Australian Financial Services Licence (AFSL). However, this exemption is currently being phased out and will finish on 30 June 2016. In its place, accountants (and other advisers) have been able to apply for a limited AFSL since 1 July 2013. This limited licence enables the holder to give their clients advice on their current superannuation arrangements and on SMSFs.

The rapid growth in the funds under management by SMSFs has resulted in a corresponding growth in the number of professionals who offer advice and assistance in the establishment of SMSFs, including financial advisers and legal practitioners. In engaging financial advisers it is vital that they hold an AFSL and that the individual does their due diligence in choosing the 'right' adviser.

With $500 billion invested the SMSF market is vulnerable to exploitation by unscrupulous 'advisers'. This exploitation can range from bad (and conflicted) advice through to clearly fraudulent activity.

The advent of limited recourse borrowing (which is discussed later in the chapter) has encouraged a number of property 'spruikers' to run workshops where individuals are encouraged to consider setting up their own SMSF and to borrow to fund the purchase of property within that SMSF. In many cases these individuals may not have sufficient funds to justify the creation of a SMSF and if they then do create a SMSF they may find that the resulting fund is highly illiquid and impracticable when it comes time to creating an income stream.

Other fraudulent activity has included what are called 'boiler room' operations, where SMSF members are cold called by call centres and encouraged to invest in overvalued or sometimes non-existent assets. Some of the schemes can be very elaborate, where individuals are encouraged to make a small investment which then appears to make very high returns. Encouraged by this level of return individuals are encouraged to invest more of their funds and not surprisingly the high returns quickly disappear.

SMSF scams tend to hit the headlines and therefore the extent of truly fraudulent activity may appear greater than it actually is. It is likely that bad advice and fraudulent activity is no more prevalent in SMSFs than it is within the broader advice industry. That does not make it acceptable, however, and as the SMSF industry grows it is likely to become more of a target of so-called 'advisers' pursuing their own interest at the expense of the client's interest.

PERSONAL FINANCE BULLETIN

Superannuation scam

Kim was desperate to pay off her car loan and her huge credit card debt. She knew there was $30 000 sitting in her super fund. She really wanted to get that money now, not in years to come. Kim saw an ad in her local paper saying she could get hold of her superannuation money now and phoned the number.

Greg answered her call and said all she needed to do was to sign some papers to transfer the money into his SMSF. Then Greg could give Kim 90% of the $30 000 and he would take only 10% commission. Kim thought this was a great idea so she signed the papers.

A few weeks later Kim had still not received the $27 000 that Greg said he would give her. She thought this was strange but decided the money would come soon. Then Kim got a call from the Australian Taxation Office letting her know she was up for a big tax bill as she had accessed her super.

She also got a call from an ASIC investigator who had received complaints from other people in Greg's SMSF who had not received any of their money. The investigator told Kim it was illegal to get hold of super funds before you had retired and she was questioned about her dealings with Greg.

The investigator then sent her the real bank statements from Greg's fund. Greg had withdrawn all her money and there was nothing left.

The truth was that Greg had a gambling problem and ran the scam to fund it. Greg was already bankrupt so there wasn't much hope that Kim would get her money back.

Source: https://www.moneysmart.gov.au/scams/superannuation-scams/case-study-superannuation-scam, accessed 24 July 2013.

Establishing the trust deed

The key legal document in any SMSF is the trust deed.

The trust deed effectively sets out the rules by which the fund will be conducted. It is a complex legal document that requires careful drafting and therefore usually requires specialised legal assistance.

The trust deed will:

- state the objective of the fund
- outline how trustees can be appointed and removed
- describe who is eligible to be a member of the fund
- explain how contributions can be made to the fund
- outline how and when benefits can be paid from the fund.

The trust deed works in conjunction with the relevant superannuation legislation, particularly the Superannuation Industry (Supervision) (SIS) Act to direct the actions of the trust. As we noted in chapter 10 the trust deed of a superannuation fund will generally incorporate the terms of the SIS Act and the Superannuation Industry (Supervision) Regulations (SISR). Many trust deeds also include a provision that automatically incorporates any changes to the SIS Act and SISR in order to avoid the expense and inconvenience of the trust deed having to be changed every time the legislation or the regulations change.

Regardless of how the trust deed is structured, the SIS Act contains a number of covenants that **codify** the common law responsibilities of trustees and which are automatically included in all superannuation funds' trust deeds. These responsibilities include:

- to act honestly in all matters
- to exercise the same care, skill and diligence as an ordinary prudent person
- to act in the best interests of the fund members.

codify
legal principles that have been developed by the courts (common law) and included in legislation

For a SMSF to be able to claim the tax concessions associated with being a superannuation fund it must be a complying superannuation fund. To be a complying superannuation fund, the fund must:

- be resident in Australia
- have made an irrevocable election to be regulated by the SIS Act
- meet the conditions for compliance as outlined in the SIS Act.

A trust deed can be 'narrower' than the SIS Act and the fund can still be a *complying* superannuation fund; that is, a trust deed might prevent a trustee from acting in a manner that normally would be permitted under the SIS Act and SISR. However, a trust deed cannot be 'broader' than the SIS Act; that is, the trust deed cannot authorise the trustee to act in a manner that goes beyond the scope of what is permitted under the SIS Act and SISR.

The trust deed must be signed and dated by all trustees and properly executed under the relevant legal jurisdiction.

Trustee structure

If a SMSF has between two and four members, all members must be trustees and all trustees must be members. Rather than having individuals as trustees, the SMSF may decide to have a corporation act as the trustee. In this case, all members of the fund must be directors of the trustee company and all directors must be members.

If a SMSF has a single member, the individual cannot be the only trustee as the legal and equitable notion of 'trust' has not been established. A single-member SMSF must have two individual trustees, one of whom is the member. An individual can, however, establish a separate company with the individual as the sole director of the company. This company can then act as the corporate trustee of the single-member fund. In this case, the notion of 'trust' has been established because the corporate trustee has a separate legal identity from the member.

Trustees are not allowed to be paid for the services they provide to the fund as a trustee.

Any person over the age of 18 can be a trustee provided they are not a disqualified person. A person is disqualified if they:

- have been convicted of an offence involving dishonesty, or
- have been subject to civil penalty under the superannuation laws, or
- are an undischarged bankrupt, or
- have been disqualified by APRA or the ATO to act as a trustee.

Any person under the age of 18 cannot be a trustee of a fund, in which case a parent or guardian will usually act as a trustee on their behalf.

SMSF members are usually connected in some way; for example, family members or business partners might join to form a SMSF, although there is no requirement in the legislation for any such connection.

No member (and therefore trustee) of a SMSF is allowed to be an employee of another member of the fund unless they are a relative. The reason for this is that participation on the trustee board of the fund implies that all parties participate equally in the decision-making processes of the fund. If a trustee is an employee of another trustee, it may make it difficult for the employee to participate equally in decisions made by the trustee board. The exemption for relatives recognises that many small businesses employ family members; for example, the owners of a local milk bar might employ their children casually to work in the business. To deny these families the right to enjoy the benefits of a SMSF would be unfair, notwithstanding the fact that the 'power' relationship is somewhat unequal. Traditionally, self-employed professionals and small business owners have been the main users of SMSFs.

ILLUSTRATIVE EXAMPLE 12.1

Ling and Jiangou own the local newsagency. They have two long-standing employees, their son Peng and Migzhu. Migzhu has worked for Ling and Jiangou for so long she feels like one of the family. Ling and Jiangou want to establish a SMSF which includes themselves and Peng and Migzhu. Is this permissible under SISA?

No person who is an employee of a member is allowed to be a member of a SMSF unless they are a relative. Peng will be allowed to join the SMSF but Migzhu will not.

The choice between individual and corporate trustee is a critical decision in setting up a SMSF. Seventy-five per cent of SMSFs opt for the individual trustee structure and for most people this works out well. However, in the case of *Shail Superannuation Fund and the Commissioner of Tax [2011] AATA 940* a husband and wife set up a SMSF as individual trustees. The husband withdrew over $3m from the fund contrary to the rules of the fund and subsequently disappeared. The ATO declared the fund non-complying and as a result the fund incurred tax payable in excess of $1.5m. The wife, who all agreed was the innocent party in this event, was left with a $1.5m tax bill for which she was personally liable as an individual trustee. The wife would not have been personally liable if the fund had used a corporate trustee structure instead.

Who should be members?

As we mentioned earlier there is no need for members of SMSFs to have any familial relationship, although overwhelmingly they do. Two person SMSFs are dominated by couples, and three and four person SMSFs are typically funds that include parents and one or two children. Children tend to be older children, with fewer than 1% of SMSF members under the age of 25.

There are significant advantages in having the 'family' within the SMSF, including:

- a larger pool of funds increases the investment opportunities for the fund
- cost savings in running one fund rather than multiple funds
- assets, particularly small business assets, can be effectively transferred between generations without incurring capital gains and other transactional costs.

There are, however, also significant risks. Superannuation is a long-term investment and commitment. Families can go through difficult times and sometimes these difficult times are made more complex because of membership of a SMSF. Some examples are as follows.

- Nearly 70% of all SMSFs are two person SMSFs and this group is dominated by couples. Couples do separate and divorce, sometimes acrimoniously. If both parties are individual trustees of the fund they will remain trustees, notwithstanding the fact that they have separated.
- Where a fund has parents and adult children as members it is possible that the married partner of one of the children has a claim against the assets of the fund in any separation proceedings, notwithstanding the fact that the party is not a member of the fund.
- There may be disagreement over investment decisions including decisions that impact on small business assets which are held as part of the fund.

In the case of *Katz v Grossman [2005] NSWSC 934* the fund had two trustees, a father and a daughter. The father also had a son who was not a trustee of the fund. The father died and in his will directed that his $1m in superannuation be left equally to his son and daughter. When he died the daughter decided that she should receive the entire $1m. The NSW Supreme Court held that she was entitled to take this action under the fund's trust deed and therefore the will had no effect.

Setting the investment objectives/strategies

As part of setting up a SMSF trustees must develop and officially record a clear investment objective and strategies to support that objective.

Where a fund has one member, a single investment objective and supporting strategies need to be developed. The objective will be strongly influenced by the individual's circumstances. For example, if the individual is close to retirement the investment objective might be more conservative.

Where a fund has multiple members and all assets are managed within a single pool the fund will need to develop a single investment objective and supporting strategies. This could be relatively straightforward if all members had similar characteristics; however, it becomes more complex when members have divergent characteristics; for example, if one member is retired, one is approaching retirement, one is 40 years old and one is 12 years old. As a result a SMSF may choose to forgo some of the efficiencies associated with the pooling of assets for all members and have separate investment 'pools' for each member, in which case each pool will need its own investment objective and supporting strategies.

Supporting strategies need to address how the fund will manage risk and return, diversification, short-term liquidity requirements and longer term liquidity requirements as members seek to withdraw their money from the fund.

In outlining how the fund will address risk and return the fund may specify what types of assets it will and won't invest in. In addressing diversification it may then attribute weighting to various asset classes. In addressing liquidity it may develop specific rules; for example, the fund will keep at least $10 000 cash in an at call account at all times.

A clearly articulated and regularly reviewed investment plan which includes objective(s), strategies and rules is likely to avoid or minimise disputes between members as to how assets are invested and will also make it easier to justify investment decisions to auditors and regulators.

Building an investment strategy

When devising an overall investment strategy it is very tempting to start at the top by establishing an investment objective and then cascade downwards into strategies, asset allocation and ultimately specific investment rules. However, often the best strategies are built from the ground up, with the investment objective emerging as the end result of a systematic process.

The bottom-up process might begin by capturing some demographic and other data, for example:

- age
- work status
- what superannuation will be rolled over into the SMSF
- what level of contributions are likely to be made to the SMSF and whether this will include in-specie contributions
- anticipated years to retirement.

Investors in a SMSF could then complete a risk profiling questionnaire. This profile can then be linked to a suggested degree of exposure to growth assets.

If the fund is to have separate investment pools for each member this exposure to growth assets can then be used to drive the asset allocation decision for each pool.

If the fund is to have a single investment pool this exposure to growth assets could then be weighted by each member's contribution to the investment pool to assist in determining an overall asset allocation for the fund.

The historical returns table below is compiled from a number of sources and highlights the historical performance of various asset classes over time. The asset classes have been classified into growth assets, that is, assets that provide the opportunity for capital appreciation over time, and income assets, that is, assets that provide a regular income flow but generally do not provide the opportunity for capital appreciation.

In figure 12.2 fixed interest investments have been classified as income assets. If a SMSF adopts a buy and hold strategy for fixed interest investments where they simply receive the interest income and redeem the principal at the end of the term, there is no price volatility and therefore no chance of making a capital loss/gain, in which case they are 'income' assets. If, however, a fund seeks to trade in fixed interest investments it is possible to make a capital loss/gain through unfavourable/favourable price movements, in which case, they might be regarded as 'growth' assets.

Columns 2 and 4 in figure 12.2 show the historical average 41 and 10 year nominal returns respectively. Nominal means the rate of return includes an inflationary component and is the usual way rates of return are quoted and discussed. Most investors, however, are seeking returns over and above the rate of inflation and as such are generally more interested in real returns; that is, returns over and above the rate of inflation. Columns 3 and 5 show the average 41 and 10 year real returns respectively.

1	2	3	4	5	6	7	8
Time frame	1971 to 2012 (41 years)		2003 to 2012 (10 years)		1971 to 2012 (41 years)		
Asset class	Average nominal return	Average real return	Average nominal return	Average real return	Best annual return	Worst annual return	Likelihood of negative return every . . .
Inflation		*5.8%(1)*		*2.8%(1)*			
Growth assets							
Australian equities	14.2%	8.0%	11.8%	8.8%	86.1%	–44.4%	4.2 years
International equities	10.9%	4.8%	1.6%	–1.2%	92.9%	–33.5%	3.3 years
Listed property	12.6%	6.4%	6.4%	3.5%	53.3%	–58.2%	9.5 years
Business real property — performance will depend on the individual asset(s)							
Other investments (e.g. collectables) — performance will depend on the individual asset(s)							
Income assets							
Cash	8.3%	2.4%	5.4%	2.5%	19.1%	3.4%	0
Australian fixed interest	10.1%	4.0%	6.4%	3.5%	25.7%	–6.2%	37.2 years
International fixed interest	11.0%	4.9%	7.7%	4.8%	35.7%	–2.6	69.1 years

(1) Australian Bureau of Statistics 6401.0 — consumer price index, Australia
Data in columns 2, 6, 7 and 8 CCH MFPG p. 634
Data in column 4 CCH MFPG p. 639

FIGURE 12.2
Historical returns: how various asset classes have performed over time

From figure 12.2 we can see that growth assets in comparison to income assets:

- produce higher real returns (although the evidence over the last 10 years is more mixed)
- are more volatile:
  - the gap between the best and worst annual return can be very large
  - there is a higher probability of a negative return in any one year.

ILLUSTRATIVE EXAMPLE 12.2

Imagine that a couple, Chantelle and James, wish to set up a SMSF. Chantelle has $1.4m in assets that she wants to rollover and/or contribute to the fund. This includes business real property of $320 000. James currently has $200 000 in superannuation which he wants to roll over to the new SMSF. Chantelle and James have decided that they want all their assets held within a single investment pool.

James and Chantelle have both completed a risk profile survey. James recorded a low rating whereas Chantelle was rated as high. They might decide to allocate their funds between growth and income assets as follows.

Risk profile	Percentage of growth/ income assets	Growth	Income
Conservative	0%/100%		
Low (James $200 000)	20%/80%	40 000	$160 000
Medium	40%/60%		
High (Chantelle $1 400 000)	60%/40%	840 000	$560 000
Aggressive	80%/20%		
Total ($1 600 000 = 100%)		$880 000 = 55%	$720 000 = 45%

This information then needs to be transformed into an overall asset allocation strategy.

James and Chantelle want to hold *growth* assets of approximately 55% of their portfolio. The business real property currently represents 20% of the overall asset pool ($320 000/$1 600 000). Traditionally SMSFs have been reluctant to invest in international equities and therefore they may choose to spread their growth investments between Australian equities and other growth assets.

James and Chantelle want to hold *income* assets of approximately 45% of their portfolio. Post the global financial crisis, SMSFs have held large cash balances and this trend continues. Again, the SMSF may wish to diversify by holding some Australian fixed interest investments. As with international equities, SMSFs have also been reluctant to invest in international fixed interest. Income assets tend to be more liquid than growth assets and as such will assist the fund in meeting their liquidity requirements.

Most SMSF investment strategies will specify a range for each asset class to give trustees the flexibility to adjust their portfolio as circumstances change. For example, in figure 12.3 Chantelle and James will seek to hold 25% of their funds in Australian equities. There may be times, however, when they hold as little as 20% or as much as 50%. The ATO as regulator is looking for an investment policy with a clear sense of direction and purpose, in which case declaring that the funds holding of Australian equities might be between 0 and 100 per cent is unlikely to satisfy the regulator.

1	2	3	4	5
Asset class	Range	Target	41 year average real return	Weighted average real return (3 * 4)
Growth				
Australian equities	20–50%	25%	8.0%	1.99%
International equities	0–10%	0%	4.8%	0.00%
Listed property	0–25%	10%	6.4%	0.64%
Business real property	0–50%	20%	5.0%(1)	1.00%
Other investments including collectables	0–10%	0%	5.0%(1)	0.00%
Total growth		55%		
Income				
Cash	0–50%	25%	2.4%	0.60%
Australian fixed interest	0–30%	20%	4.0%	0.81%
International fixed interest	0–10%	0%	4.9%	0.00%
Total income		45%		
Total growth and income		100%		5.03%

(1) The values in column 4 have been assumed for the sake of the illustration.

FIGURE 12.3
Chantelle and James: recommended asset allocation

In figure 12.3 column 4 reports the 41 year average real returns for each asset class. Column 5 then weights these returns by the targeted amount to be allocated to this asset class. Summing up column 5 results in a real rate of return for the overall investment portfolio of 5.03%. This figure can then be used by James and Chantelle in shaping their investment objective.

James and Chantelle might like to express the overall investment objective for the fund as:

'To achieve a 4% real rate of return per annum on funds invested on a rolling five year basis'.

The '4%' appears achievable given their asset allocation and the historical performance of these asset classes. The 'rolling five year basis' recognises that returns are volatile, particularly with respect to growth assets and that there may be years when returns are less than 4%, including years when the overall return could be negative. Over any five-year window selected, however, real returns would be expected to average 4%.

Having commenced the process from the bottom up rather than the top down and culminating in a draft investment objective, the financial adviser then needs to ensure that the overall investment strategy is consistent with the investor's goals and aspirations.

Ultimately the 'official' investment strategy is likely to revert to a top down publication:

- investment objective
  - investment strategies
    - growth versus income
      - asset allocation
        - fund-specific investment rules.

Finally, a word of caution: average past returns are 'past', that is, they in no way guarantee future returns. If past returns are used as a guide then a decision needs to be made as to which 'window' of time should be used. Income assets over the last 41 years have produced fairly consistent real returns regardless of which time window is used. However, growth assets, particularly international equities and listed property, have been relatively disappointing in the last 10 years.

Establishing the insurance plan

It is estimated that less than 15% of SMSF members have life insurance.

Legislative changes in response to this low level of life insurance means that trustees are now obliged to consider the type and level of insurance for each fund member. This consideration needs to be formally recorded either in the fund's investment strategy or in the minutes of the trustee meetings.

In chapter 9 we discussed the group underwriting of life insurance. A group policy occurs when individuals who have a specific relationship with each other are collectively underwritten. For example, a trustee of a large superannuation fund might take out a group policy that covers members of the fund. In underwriting a group policy, the insurer calculates the group's characteristics and sets premiums accordingly. Group insurance does not take into account the risk associated with particular individuals and, as such, it is a useful means by which individuals with particular health risks can achieve cover at a reasonable price. If an individual decides to roll over their superannuation from a large fund to a SMSF they cannot take their life insurance coverage with them, in which case they will need to seek out new insurance cover. For an insurer to provide insurance coverage for four members or less means that each of those members needs to be individually risk assessed by the insurer and the premiums determined accordingly. In some cases insurance may not be available and in other cases it may be available but at a much higher premium. This is an important factor to take into account before the rollover decision is made.

Issues concerning totally and permanently disabled (TPD) and trauma insurance are essentially the same for SMSFs and large funds, and these are discussed in chapter 9.

Assets owned by the fund also need to be insured, particularly collectables and artwork. Similarly property owned by the fund needs to be insured, including property which is subject to a limited recourse borrowing arrangement.

Holding assets

It is important that the resources of the fund are kept separate and distinct from the personal assets of the individual members.

All investments should be held in the name of the fund, for example:

- if the fund has individual trustees — Fred and Wilma Rubble as trustees for the Bedrock Superannuation Fund

- if the fund has a corporate trustee — Bedrock Pty Ltd as trustee for the Bedrock Superannuation Fund.

Where ownership is shared between a SMSF and other parties the assets should be held as tenants in common rather than as joint tenants.

With **joint tenants** each tenant effectively owns the whole property and the death of one tenant means that the property is now owned by the surviving tenant. Most couples own their home as joint tenants, that is, the death of one tenant (spouse) means that the surviving tenant (spouse) now owns the whole property. Because the ownership interest is not severable the ownership of assets through joint tenancy is not appropriate for a SMSF.

joint tenant
where ownership is shared between tenants and the death of one tenant means that ownership passes to the surviving tenant

With **tenants in common** each tenant owns a share of the property and in this case a superannuation fund could be one of the tenants in common. The trustee(s) will need to decide whether the ownership interest is one which could be reasonably severed without damaging the interests of the fund.

tenants in common
each tenant owns a defined share of an asset which does not automatically pass to another tenant upon death

ILLUSTRATIVE EXAMPLE 12.3

Arun and Lucy have their own SMSF.

Arun and Lucy, as private individuals separate to the superannuation environment, each own 33.3% of a warehouse. The remaining 33.3% of the warehouse is owned by their SMSF. With respect to the warehouse, Arun, Lucy and their SMSF are tenants in common.

The trustees of the SMSF, in this case, Arun and Lucy, are free to sell the SMSF's share of the warehouse at any time. However, if in practice the ownership interest could be severed only by a 'fire sale' of the relevant asset then this is unlikely to be in the interests of the fund.

In the above example the SMSF was a common tenant with two individuals who also happened to be trustees of the SMSF. The SMSF could just as easily have been a common tenant with other parties who were unrelated to the fund.

The fund should also have its own bank account. If an individual member pays for an expense of the fund then this could be deemed a contribution unless an immediate reimbursement is claimed. Conversely, if an individual member receives cash that belongs to the fund then this could be deemed a withdrawal. If the member is not entitled to make withdrawals from the fund this could lead to serious consequences for the fund.

Auditors are required to report to the ATO whenever there is insufficient separation between the assets of the fund and the assets of the individual. Moreover the creditor protection afforded by holding assets inside the fund might be put at risk where there is some uncertainty as to whether assets are assets of the fund or assets of the individual member.

LO 3

Contributions

For a SMSF to receive contributions it is essential that each member has supplied their tax file number (TFN), otherwise additional contributions tax will be payable. Where members are claiming contributions as tax deductions (**concessional contributions**) they need to notify the fund in writing of their intention do so.

concessional contribution
a contribution to superannuation for which a tax deduction has been claimed

Contributions to SMSFs are essentially bound by the same rules, regulations and tax incentives as apply to large superannuation funds. There are, however, some important differences we should review, including the:

- ability to make in-specie contributions
- distinction between selling and contributing to a SMSF
- tax concessions available to small business owners.

In specie

in-specie contributions contributions made in kind rather than in cash; for example, a self-employed person may contribute listed shares to their SMSF

A SMSF is able to accept in-specie contributions provided its trust deed allows it and the investment rules that apply to the fund are complied with. **In specie** means a contribution in kind rather than in cash.

In-specie contributions are limited to:

- ASX listed securities
- widely held managed funds
- real business property
- cash-based investments such as bonds and debentures.

A member of a SMSF might for example contribute their personal holding of $20 000 in National Australia Bank Ltd (NAB) shares to their fund.

An in-specie contribution might be claimed by the individual as a tax deduction, that is, as a concessional contribution, or it might be made on an after-tax basis, that is, as a **non-concessional contribution**. In-specie contributions are subject to the same limits as cash contributions.

non-concessional contribution a contribution to superannuation for which a tax deduction has not been claimed

As explained earlier, assets might be owned as tenants in common with one of the tenants being the SMSF. This strategy is often employed when the SMSF has insufficient resources to buy the asset and/or contributing the asset would breach the contribution limits. Alternatively the individual member might consider setting up a company or unit trust structure to own the asset, thereby simplifying the progressive contribution or sale of shares or units to the SMSF in the future.

An in-specie contribution is a disposal of an asset and the member, therefore, needs to be mindful of the CGT consequences.

ILLUSTRATIVE EXAMPLE 12.4

self-employed an individual who earns less than 10% of their income from employment-related activities

Kevin is a 38-year-old **self-employed** carpenter. Kevin is always very careful to ensure that he earns less than 10% of his income from employment-related activities so that he can maintain his self-employed status.

Kevin's marginal tax rate is 40%. He has a share portfolio which he purchased in 2004 for $60 000 which is currently worth $85 000. He wishes to make an in-specie contribution of this portfolio to his SMSF in the most tax-effective way possible.

- Kevin has held the portfolio for more than 12 months so the assessable capital gain is $12 500 (($85 000 – $60 000)/2).
- Kevin will pay $5000 in CGT ($12 500 × 40%).
- Given his age, Kevin can make a concessional in-specie contribution of up to $25 000 and this will save him $6250 in tax:
  - He can claim the $25 000 as a deduction against his personal income which will lower his tax bill by $10 000 ($25 000 × 40%)

- His SMSF will have to pay a contributions tax of $3750 ($25 000 × 15%)
- Kevin needs to understand that while he has saved tax his money is now preserved within a superannuation environment.

- Kevin can contribute the balance of the shares value $60 000 ($85 000 less $25 000) as a non-concessional contribution.

It is important to remember that if Kevin had earned more than 10% of his income from employment-related activities he would not be considered self-employed and his SMSF would not have been able to accept his concessional contribution regardless of whether it was a contribution in cash or in kind (in specie).

Contribution versus sell

It is important to distinguish an in-specie contribution from a purchase by the SMSF. For example, if the member makes a non-concessional contribution of $20 000 in NAB shares, then these shares are subject to the non-concessional contribution limit and the member receives nothing in return for their contribution other than having their account credited with the $20 000 contribution. Alternatively, the member might decide to sell the shares to their SMSF. In this case, the non-concessional contribution limit does not apply because it is not a contribution and the member will receive $20 000 in cash from the SMSF as the proceeds from the sale.

All SMSF investments are required to be made on an *arm's length basis*, that is, on strictly commercial terms. The purchase and sale price of an asset should always reflect the true market value. Tax Ruling 2010/1 states that when a 'fund acquires an asset for less than market value the difference between market value and actual purchase price is deemed to be a superannuation contribution'.

Small business and CGT

Small business owners are able to make 'special' contributions to superannuation that are linked to capital gains tax concessions.

A small business is defined as a business which has an annual turnover of less than $2m or the CGT assets of the business are less than $6m.

Small business owners are able to access:

- a 15 year active asset exemption
- a small business retirement exemption.

These exemptions recognise that many small business owners build up and reinvest in their businesses rather than in superannuation throughout their working lives.

15 year active asset exemption

An active asset is an asset that satisfies the active asset test as prescribed under the relevant legislation. The 15 year active asset exemption allows the capital gain arising from the sale of active business assets to be exempt from CGT provided the individual is over 55 and retires. The small business owner can then, if they choose, move some or all of this gain into superannuation through the use of the CGT cap. To be eligible for the 15 year active asset exemption the assets must have been held for at least 15 years and been active for at least half of the last 15 years, that is, for a minimum of seven and a half years.

In 2013–14 the CGT cap was $1 315 000. This cap is subject to indexation. The cap is a lifetime limit which means that it can be used only once and any unused portion can be carried forward to offset future gains. The cap can be used in conjunction with the non-concessional contributions cap of $150 000 per year or $450 000 over a rolling three-year period to increase the amount that can be contributed to superannuation.

ILLUSTRATIVE EXAMPLE 12.5

Tania is 62 years old and is planning to retire. Fifteen years ago she purchased a shop in the main street and commenced running a coffee shop. She did this for five years before leasing out the shop for seven years. Three years ago she resumed running the coffee shop. The coffee shop will be considered an active asset for eight of the last fifteen years in which case it will satisfy the 15 year active asset exemption.

ILLUSTRATIVE EXAMPLE 12.6

Alan is 61 years old and is planning to retire. He has just sold his small business for $1.6m which includes a capital gain of $1.2m. The sale satisfies the conditions associated with the 15 year active asset exemption. Alan will receive this gain tax free and he can then decide if he wants to contribute this money to superannuation. If Alan does decide to contribute the $1.2m gain to superannuation as an after-tax contribution he is still below the $1 315 000 CGT cap. Indeed Alan may decide to contribute the entire $1.6m sale proceeds in which case he will need to utilise $1.2m of the $1 315 000 CGT cap plus the $400 000 of the non-concessional cap.

The CGT cap applies to contributions to all superannuation funds. The extensive use of SMSFs by small business owners means that the cap is primarily used in a SMSF context.

Small business retirement exemption

A small business owner may dispose of a business asset but not satisfy the requirements of the 15 year active asset exemption.

The small business retirement exemption allows the first $500 000 of a capital gain arising from the disposal of business assets to be exempt from tax. This $500 000 is a lifetime limit and is not subject to indexation.

If the small business owner is over 55 years of age the individual can decide whether they want to keep this gain or contribute it to superannuation. If the small business owner is under 55 years of age the gain will remain CGT exempt only if it is contributed to superannuation.

ILLUSTRATIVE EXAMPLE 12.7

Steve is 60 years old. He has just sold his small business and made a $1.2m capital gain. Steve has owned the business for six years and therefore does not satisfy the requirements of the 15 year active asset exemption. Given that Steve has owned the small business for more than 12 months he will be entitled to the 50% CGT discount which means his net gain is $600 000. Steve will be able to claim the small business retirement exemption which will reduce his assessable gain to $100 000. Steve can then choose whether or not to contribute the $500 000 he has claimed as the small business retirement exemption to his superannuation fund. He is not obliged to contribute and he could contribute less than the full amount.

If Steve had been 52 years old rather than 60 he would have been obliged to contribute the full $500 000 to superannuation.

LO 4

Investment

'Investment choice and control' is typically cited by SMSF members as the number one reason for why they have established a SMSF. SMSFs do not, however, have a completely free investment choice — there are many investment restrictions. Nonetheless, in the trade-off between investment restrictions and the tax advantages of having a complying SMSF, the tax advantages tend to win as evidenced by the rapid growth in the number and size of SMSFs.

SMSFs also have some investment choices which are not available to large APRA supervised funds. These choices when combined with the ability to make in-specie contributions can make establishing a SMSF a very attractive option. In fully exercising these investment choices the trustees of SMSFs invest their funds differently to the trustees of large superannuation funds.

Trustees also need to ensure that their investments are protected. A SMSF can face a massive tax bill if they lose their residency status. Similarly an 'unplanned' bankruptcy for one of the trustees can have a significant impact on a SMSF.

Investment restrictions

The investment restrictions that apply to SMSFs, with a few notable exceptions discussed later in the chapter, are very similar to the restrictions that apply to large funds.

A SMSF must be maintained *solely for the purpose* of providing retirement benefits to members or to their dependants if the member dies. Breaching the sole purpose test can lead to the trustee facing both criminal and civil penalties. Penalties can include up to five years imprisonment and a fine up to 2000 penalty points, with each point currently worth $110. A breach of the sole purpose test is also likely to result in the fund being deemed non-complying, in which case both current and past tax concessions can be reversed, leading to a significant tax bill. It can be very tempting for the trustees of a SMSF to invest in assets that provide current benefits to members, but in so doing they are putting their compliance with the sole purpose test in jeopardy. It is important to note, however, that the regulator, in this case the ATO, is concerned with the purpose of the investment, not the type of investment. A SMSF might invest in some quite exotic investments and still comply with the sole purpose test.

Trustees are permitted only to acquire assets from a 'related party' of the fund where the acquisition of the asset will not result in the 'in-house' assets of the fund exceeding 5% of all assets. Related parties include members, trustees and employers who contribute to a fund. Related parties also include relatives of members. SISA s 10(1) and Pt 8 outline who are related parties. SMSFs are, however, allowed to acquire **business real property** from related parties which exceeds 5% of all assets.

business real property property that is used wholly and exclusively for business purposes

Superannuation funds are *not allowed to borrow* longer term funds in order to gear up returns. SMSFs can, however, use a separate trust to undertake leveraged investments.

Trustees are *not allowed to lend money* or provide financial assistance to members or related parties.

All transactions are to be made on an *arm's length basis*, that is, on strictly commercial terms. The purchase and sale price of an asset should always reflect the true market value. Income from assets should always reflect the true market rate of return.

The relationship between trustees and members in SMSFs means that members are in a position where they may try to push the investment restriction boundaries — sometimes beyond what the auditors and regulators deem is acceptable. While members of large superannuation funds might be also tempted to breach the investment rules, in reality the separation between trustee and member in large funds is such that members are not really in a position to breach the rules.

Investment choices

SMSFs basically have the same range of investment choices as large funds; however, there are three very important investment opportunities available to SMSFs that are not available to large funds.

SMSFs can:

- invest in collectables and personal use items
- leverage their investment portfolio through the use of **instalment warrants**
- invest in business real property without the constraint of the 5% in-house asset rule.

instalment warrant where an investor pays a deposit on an asset and then pays off the balance by one or more instalments

Collectables and personal use items

As noted earlier one of the key attractions of establishing a SMSF is the investment freedom they provide, particularly when compared to large superannuation funds. This freedom extends to investing in collectable and personal use items.

Section 62A of the SIS Act outlines the rules associated with investing in collectables. Regulation 13.18AA (1) lists the collectable assets, which include:

- artwork
- jewellery
- antiques
- coins, medallions or bank notes
- postage stamps or first day covers
- rare folios, manuscripts or books
- memorabilia
- wine or spirits
- motor vehicles.

The use by SMSF members of collectable and personal use assets owned by the fund does raise questions of compliance with the sole purpose test. In response to the uncertainty associated with permissible use and clear cases of inappropriate use, the SIS Act was amended effective from 1 July 2011 with respect to the use of collectables and personal use assets by members of SMSFs.

If a SMSF held investments in collectables and personal use assets prior to 1 July 2011 it has until 1 July 2016 to comply with the new rules. All acquisitions of collectables and personal use assets after 1 July 2011 must comply with the new rules. The new rules require that:

- assets must not be leased to any related party of the fund
- assets must not be stored or displayed in the private residence of any related party of the fund
- trustees make a written record of the reasons for the decisions on where to store the assets and keep the record for 10 years
- collectables and personal use assets cannot be used by any related party of the fund.

For those unsure about what investments constitute collectables and personal use assets and how those assets are impacted by the change of rules, the ATO has an excellent question and answer section on their website, www.ato.gov.au.

ILLUSTRATIVE EXAMPLE 12.8

Amy's aunt has had her jewellery independently valued at $50 000. Amy's aunt is prepared to sell it to Amy's SMSF at its market value with the only proviso being that she gets to wear the jewellery on very special occasions.

Amy's aunt is a related party of the SMSF and as such she cannot use any of the assets of the fund. Even if Amy's aunt promises not to make use of the jewellery Amy needs to be careful that all the other investment restrictions are complied with, including the limitation that in-house assets, that is assets acquired from related parties, do not exceed 5% of the total assets.

Instalment warrants and leveraged investment

An instalment warrant is where an asset is purchased via a series of payments which effectively extinguish a loan which is used to finance the purchase. There has been significant growth in the purchase of residential and commercial property using instalment warrants by SMSFs in recent years.

If a SMSF buys an investment asset financed through borrowing, the legal title to the asset must be held in a trust separate to the SMSF. This separate trust is usually called a **bare trust**. However, all the cash flows associated with the investment asset such as interest payments, rent, maintenance and so on pass through the accounts of the SMSF in the same way as the cash flows associated with investment assets that are fully owned by the SMSF pass through the accounts of the SMSF.

In addition to creating a bare trust, trustees must ensure:

- the SMSF has the right to acquire legal ownership by making a series of payments (instalments)
- the lender's **recourse** against the SMSF is limited to the underlying asset, that is the lender has no recourse to the other assets of the fund
- the investment is in line with the fund's investment objective and strategies.

bare trust
a separate trust to the SMSF that can hold the legal title of an asset until the debt incurred in buying the asset has been extinguished

recourse
where the lender can seize a particular asset pledged as security for a loan if the borrower defaults on their payments; an unsecured loan is a nonrecourse loan

The ATO's *Self-managed superannuation funds ruling (SMSFR) 2009/2* outlines what constitutes 'borrowing' for a SMSF. A SMSF can purchase an instalment warrant issued over any asset that a SMSF can normally purchase; however, the asset must be 'a single acquirable asset'. A portfolio of shares is not a single acquirable asset; however, the shares of an individual company would be. It is important to remember that the other investment restrictions discussed earlier still apply, including the prohibition against acquiring assets from related parties which exceed 5% of the total assets.

The superannuation community is divided over whether borrowing should be allowed by SMSFs. Some argue that the 'safe' superannuation environment is being jeopardised by gearing. Others argue that when a superannuation fund purchases investments, which are themselves highly geared, they are in fact 'gearing up' and that instalment warrants are no different. For example, it could be argued that a superannuation fund is 'gearing up' when it buys shares in a listed company which has high levels of debt.

A SMSF can invest in all types of property, including residential, commercial, industrial, and listed and unlisted property.

There are a number of restrictions and disadvantages of holding a leveraged residential or commercial property inside a SMSF. These include the following.

- The increased complexity of the lending arrangements combined with the limited recourse nature of the loan means that lenders will limit the amount that they will lend. Typically residential property would be limited to 75% to 80% of the property value. For commercial property it might be limited to 60% to 65% of the property value. Lenders are also likely to charge higher fees initially and insist on higher interest rates than would apply outside a SMSF environment.
- A SMSF can purchase an investment asset and maintain that asset. The SMSF can also use their own funds (as opposed to borrowed funds) to improve the asset. However, the SMSF cannot improve an asset to the point where a replacement asset is created. If a replacement asset was created the trustees would effectively be running a business inside their SMSF. SMSFs are created for the purpose of holding investment assets, not as a tax shelter for running a business. For example, a SMSF might buy a residential property and improve that property by adding another bedroom without creating a 'replacement asset'. However, if a SMSF bought an old house, knocked it down and built two townhouses on the site this is likely to be seen as creating a replacement asset and therefore is not permissible.
- A SMSF must be careful to not infringe the investment restrictions that apply to superannuation funds. A purchase of a property from a related party is likely to breach the in-house asset rule unless it is covered by the business real property exemption. Similarly renting the property to a related party is likely to be in breach of the investment restrictions.
- If a rental property is negatively geared i.e. the annual expenses are greater than the annual revenue then the tax shield associated with these annual losses is only equal to the tax rate applicable to superannuation funds, namely 15%. Therefore an annual pre-tax loss of $1000 on the property effectively becomes an $850 post-tax loss.
- Tax advantages rarely turn a bad investment into a good investment. A poorly selected property is likely to produce disappointing results both inside and outside a SMSF environment. Selecting the 'right' property is really a first order decision and determining the 'right' tax vehicle is a second order decision.

These restrictions need to be balanced against the potential advantages of holding a leveraged residential or commercial property inside a SMSF, which include:

- An individual may not hold sufficient cash resources outside the superannuation environment to enter into a leveraged property investment.
- The legal title to the property sits in a bare trust funded in part by a limited recourse loan. If the SMSF was to default on the loan the other assets within the SMSF are protected from the lender as are the other non-superannuation assets of the individual members of the SMSF.
- If the rental property is positively geared i.e. the annual revenue is greater than the annual expenses then the taxable income is taxed at only 15%. Therefore an annual pre-tax gain of $1000 on the property effectively becomes an $850 post-tax gain.
- Other income derived by the fund can be used to reduce the principal on the loan. For example, concessional contributions that are taxed at 15% inside the superannuation fund can be used to reduce the principal on the loan. If the property was held outside a SMSF environment the investor would need to pay their marginal tax rate of up to 46.5% to release these funds to help extinguish the principal.
- If the investment asset is sold during the accumulation phase the asset will be subject to capital gains tax. As discussed in chapter 10 the effective rate on capital gains for a superannuation fund is 10% (2/3 of 15%) compared to capital gains made outside a superannuation fund where the rate could be as high as 23.25% (1/2 of 46.5%).
- If the investment asset is sold during the pension phase the asset will not be subject to capital gains tax. However, if the gains were made outside a superannuation fund the rate could still be as high as 23.25%.

It is therefore not surprising that SMSFs have been eagerly acquiring residential and commercial property. The ability to extinguish the principal with dollars that have been taxed at 15% and the opportunity to sell the investment during retirement and incur no capital gains have been the primary drivers of this 'boom'.

Business real property

As we noted earlier trustees are permitted to acquire assets from a related party of the fund only where the acquisition of the asset will not result in the in-house assets of the fund exceeding 5% of all assets. SMSFs are, however, allowed to acquire business real property from related parties which exceeds 5% of all assets. This exemption to the in-house asset rule is primarily aimed at small business owners who have effectively built up wealth in their business in order to fund their retirement and now wish to move some of that wealth into a superannuation environment.

Business real property is defined in the ATO SMSF Ruling 2009/1. Business real property is property that is used wholly and exclusively for business purposes. The property must be unencumbered by loans unless the property is acquired via the use of instalment warrants discussed earlier. The SMSF is allowed to own the property and then lease the property on commercial terms. Often the property is leased back to the member so that they can continue to run the small business. It is important to note that the real business property exemption allows the fund to own the property inside the fund but it does not allow the business to be run from inside the fund. To run the business from inside the fund would be seen by the auditor and regulator as a breach of the sole purpose test.

ILLUSTRATIVE EXAMPLE 12.9

Cassie is a sole trader who owns and runs a hairdressing salon. Cassie purchased the business premises 12 years ago for $250 000. The premises are currently worth $900 000 and Cassie wishes to contribute the premises to her SMSF.

Cassie's SMSF currently has $500 000 in assets, including $200 000 in cash. Cassie has realised that to contribute the entire $900 000 of real business property will exceed her contribution limits and therefore decides to partly contribute and partly sell the business real property to the SMSF.

The contribution of the premises is effectively a disposal of the asset so the disposal will be subject to capital gains tax. The capital gain is $650 000; however, the premises have been owned for more than 12 months so only $325 000 of the capital gain is assessable. Cassie is able to use the small business retirement exemption of $500 000 that we discussed earlier to completely extinguish her CGT liability.

Cassie is then able to make an in-specie contribution of her real business property of $900 000 by:

- using the $325 000 small business retirement exemption
- making a non-concessional contribution of $450 000
- receiving the balance in cash from the fund of $125 000 as proceeds from the part sale ($900 000 – $325 000 – $450 000 = $125 000).

In order to continue running the hairdressing business Cassie will need to pay a commercial rent to the SMSF for the use of the real business property.

If we assume the rent is $1000 per week then this is income to the fund that is then taxed at 15% inside the fund. If Cassie had not contributed the business real property to the fund she would have saved this $1000 and reported a higher personal income which would have been taxed at marginal rates. It might be tempting for Cassie to pay a higher than commercial rent to in effect shield some income inside the tax concessional superannuation environment. However, excessive rent is likely to be viewed as a contribution and will therefore be subject to contribution limits. Conversely, if Cassie's hairdressing business is going through difficult economic conditions Cassie might be tempted to pay less than a commercial rate of rent. As discussed earlier all investments must be undertaken on an arm's length basis and income from assets should always reflect the true market rate of return.

Business real property also includes property that is used for primary production purposes. Where the property includes a residence which occupies no more than two hectares the property can still be considered business real property.

While for small business owners the real business property exemption provides considerable tax advantages, it does sometimes cause concern with respect to the investment objectives of diversification and liquidity. Real business property could constitute 100% of the SMSFs assets, in which case the fund is not diversified and is highly vulnerable to changes in the value of a single asset. If the fund has more than one member and some members are approaching retirement then a single, large, non-divisible asset presents challenges in terms of releasing cash to pay retirement incomes.

Investment trends

Table 12.1 compares the investment choices made by large superannuation funds supervised by APRA with SMSFs supervised by the ATO. Unfortunately APRA and the ATO use a slightly different methodology in collecting and reporting their data. Nonetheless table 12.1 does highlight differences in the choice of investments between large and small funds.

Large APRA funds generally employ specialist fund managers and have significant investments in overseas shares while SMSFs have minimal investments in overseas shares. Large APRA funds have approximately 15% of their funds invested in fixed interest securities whereas SMSFs have less than 1%. SMSFs have approximately 15% of their funds directly invested in real property whereas large funds tend to hold their property in the form of listed and unlisted property trusts.

Large APRA funds hold significantly less cash (8.9%) compared to SMSFs (27.8%). The global financial crisis (GFC) of 2007–08 caused a significant movement into cash for all superannuation funds, but as the impact of the GFC has receded large APRA funds have rebalanced their portfolios and reduced their cash holdings. SMSFs, however, have continued to hold large cash balances.

It is also worth noting that SMSF investment in artwork and collectables is 0.2 of 1%. For all the publicity and discussion it generates, investment in artwork and collectables nonetheless represents a very small percentage of the overall investment portfolio of a SMSF.

TABLE 12.1 Superannuation investments

APRA statistics	ATO	Large APRA	SMSF ATO
Table 18 Asset allocation of default investment strategy, *Annual superannuation bulletin*, June 2012	Statistical report, Self-managed superannuation fund, 31 March 2013	30 June 2012	31 March 2013
Australian shares	Listed shares	27.5%	32.6%
International shares	Overseas shares	23.2%	0.4%
	Other managed investments		4.8%
Listed property	Listed trusts	2.3%	4.2%
Unlisted property	Unlisted trusts	7.8%	9.2%
Australian fixed interest	Debt securities	8.6%	0.7%
International fixed interest		5.4%	
Cash	Cash and term deposits	8.9%	27.8%
	Non-residential real property		11.3%
	Residential real property		3.5%
	Artwork, collectables, metal or jewels		0.2%
Other assets	Other assets	16.3%	5.3%
		100.0%	100.0%
Total assets in default strategy		$393 218 000 000	
Total assets		$917 431 000 000	$496 203 000 000

Source: ATO, Self-managed super fund statistical report, March 2013.

PERSONAL FINANCE BULLETIN

Keeping score for your SMSF

Football teams have an advantage over trustees of self-managed super funds. When the siren sounds at the end of a game they know if they have won or lost; whether they have been competitive or thrashed.

That is particularly valuable information for football clubs and supporters alike.

Progress can be charted even with losing performances — hope springs eternal when seemingly the gap between the top teams and those aspiring to join them is narrowed with a spirited performance. Melbourne Football Club supporters aspire to such losses at some stage in their pre-retirement years.

It is important — as coaches are prone to expound — for a club to 'know where you are at'.

The same is true for your self-managed super fund and courtesy of some rule changes going forward we are going to get a better sense of how self-managed funds really are performing.

It is one of the great ongoing debates of the super industry — do SMSFs perform as well or better than the professional fund managers?

Trustees of SMSFs certainly think so and there is a reasonable amount of data from the likes of APRA and the tax office plus independent analysis that suggests that SMSFs as a sector hold their own with the professionals.

But in many ways the question is redundant because by their very nature every SMSF will perform differently and the only person that really cares is you — the fund's trustee and ultimate beneficiary.

So as trustee of your SMSF do you know how your fund's investment portfolio has performed for the past financial year?

If that seems a slightly absurd notion, particularly as we head into annual tax return time and the start of a new financial year, it is perhaps worth pausing and considering that calculating net performance results accurately on your fund's investment portfolio in a comparable way to large retail and industry super funds is not as straightforward as it may first appear.

Most trustees will be making regular contributions into the fund so comparing account balances from one financial year end to another will be simply misleading — albeit probably in a positive way.

Then there is the issue of valuing illiquid assets which is where a new requirement from the ATO will come into play for next financial year.

For many trustees this will hopefully not be that big a change because pricing fund assets at market value has long been regarded as best practice. From the start of the 2013 financial year though it becomes a legal requirement.

For investments like shares, ETFs and most managed funds this is an easy thing to do because you can simply look at the closing price on the sharemarket on any given day or in the case of unlisted funds there will be monthly or quarterly valuation statements from the fund manager.

Where it becomes more difficult is in the area of illiquid investments and for SMSFs the challenge will be on residential property.

A straightforward way to do it is to get an annual valuation by a third party but that is a cost and property values may often be flat for several years. The requirement is not that onerous because trustees may conclude, based on market assessment of comparative properties for example, that the value has not changed significantly.

In the past it was not uncommon at investor seminars to hear SMSF trustees openly discuss that they had bought a property years ago and never revalued it — the argument being that the only value that really mattered was when they sold it when they retired.

But valuing assets at market prices is important to be able to calculate individual member's benefits. Where it becomes more critical though is in the pension phase where minimum withdrawal rules apply.

In a worst case scenario if a property was significantly undervalued and the ATO challenged it through the audit process it has the power to apply a different valuation methodology and revalue the investment.

If the revaluation is significant, that could see the SMSF being in breach of the minimum pension payments and the fund could lose its tax-free status — something of a nuclear strike penalty.

So if you are running your own SMSF it definitely pays to know where you are at — even if your football team has no clue.

Source: Robin Bowerman, www.vanguardinvestments.com.au, 14 June 2013, accessed 19 June 2013.

Resident status

Earlier we mentioned that a SMSF must make an irrevocable election to be a complying fund under the SIS Act. In order to be complying, a fund must be 'resident' in Australia. Residency requires that the:

- fund was established in Australia
- fund satisfies the active asset test
- central management and control of the fund remains in Australia.

Trustees (and members) of SMSFs are able to travel overseas for periods of up to two years without jeopardising the residency status of their SMSF. If the trustee returns to Australia for a period of at least 28 days they are then able to travel overseas for a further two-year period without jeopardising the residency status of their SMSF. This process could be repeated a number of times.

If a trustee travels overseas and their return date is uncertain or they remain away for more than two years, then determining the residency status of their SMSF becomes more complex.

The ATO will employ an 'activity' test. If a person who is a resident (including a resident who is travelling overseas) contributes to their SMSF in the current financial year they are an 'active' member and their accounts will represent 'active' assets. The SMSF can satisfy the activity test by having:

- no active members and therefore no active accounts, or
- more than 50% of the fund's assets held in 'active' accounts.

With careful management the trustees might comply with the active asset test, but they also need to be mindful that extended stays overseas may cause the ATO to question whether the central management and control of the fund remains in Australia. A stay overseas in excess of two years does not automatically mean that the ATO will deem the central management and control is no longer in Australia. The ATO will look at the individual circumstances of the fund and how it is being administered. The ATO will be more concerned about where the higher level strategic decisions are being made rather than where more routine operational tasks are performed. Therefore having locally based accountants and administrators performing operational tasks is unlikely to satisfy the ATO management and control requirements. The trustees might consider establishing an enduring power of attorney which passes management and control to an Australian-based representative. The ATO will, however, want to be reassured that the 'attorney' has real management and control and is not simply acting under instruction from the trustees.

private binding ruling
an individual is able to ask the tax office for a ruling on how they would judge a particular course of action by the individual before that action is undertaken. The tax office will then supply the individual with written advice and is then bound by that advice (ruling).

In some cases trustees might foreshadow their actions and ask the ATO for a **private binding ruling** in order to avoid problems later on.

If, however, some of the SMSF members lose their resident status and more than 50% of the fund's assets become inactive and/or the ATO deem that the central management and control of the fund no longer remains in Australia, the fund will be declared a non-resident fund and therefore non-complying. The SMSF will then have its *assets* (less any non-concessional contributions) taxed at 46.5% and any income it receives while it remains non-resident and non-complying will also be taxed at 46.5%.

ILLUSTRATIVE EXAMPLE 12.10

Sue and Greg established their SMSF in 2002. Their SMSF currently has $500 000 in assets, including non-concessional contributions of $300 000.

Greg and Sue have lived and worked in the United Arab Emirates for the past four years. Their fund has just been declared a non-resident and therefore non-complying fund. How much tax will be payable to the ATO?

- $500 000 (total SMSF assets) less $300 000 (non-concessional) equals $200 000 taxable value of assets
- $200 000 (taxable value of assets) × 46.5% = $93 000 tax payable.

If the trustees of a SMSF anticipate problems with the residency status of their fund they should consider pre-emptively changing the trustee structure of their SMSF, or rolling over their superannuation into a small APRA fund or a large public offer fund.

Bankruptcy

undischarged bankrupt
a person who has been declared bankrupt under the provisions of the Bankruptcy Act and has not been discharged from the bankruptcy

personal insolvency agreement
where a person enters into an agreement with their creditors without being made bankrupt

If an individual becomes an **undischarged bankrupt** or enters into a **personal insolvency agreement** with creditors then superannuation legislation deems they are a disqualified person and prohibited from being an individual trustee of a SMSF or a director of a SMSF corporate trustee. For a disqualified person to continue to act as a trustee would risk the compliance status of the fund and expose the individual to civil and criminal prosecution.

If an individual foresees that they are likely to become bankrupt they need to plan how to relinquish their trustee status. If plans are not in place the regulator generally gives the individual six months to rectify the situation.

The individual might roll over their superannuation into an industry or retail superannuation fund, or they may convert their SMSF into a small APRA fund.

As we noted in chapter 10, the High Court has affirmed that all funds held in superannuation while the individual is in *accumulation* mode are protected from creditors in the case of bankruptcy. However, the legislative response to the High Court's decision has been to allow creditors access to the superannuation funds of an undischarged bankrupt provided it can be proven that the transfer of assets to a superannuation fund was done for the purpose of denying creditors their entitlements. The legislation also provides some guidance on how proof might be established, for example:

- if it can be reasonably assumed that the individual was insolvent at the time assets were transferred to the superannuation fund
- if a transfer to a superannuation fund was 'out of character'. For example, it would generally be seen as out of character for a person who has, in the past, made no contributions to superannuation to make a $400 000 contribution the day before they declare bankruptcy.

If the individual is in *pension* mode there is less protection from creditors. If the individual's total annual income including pension income is above a prescribed amount, half of the excess can be claimed by creditors until such time as the individual is discharged from their bankruptcy. In March 2013 this amount was $50 332 for a person with no dependants (ITSA). This amount increases with the number of dependants and increases in March and September each year through indexation. Lump sum withdrawals while in pension mode remain protected from creditors.

ILLUSTRATIVE EXAMPLE 12.11

Kim is 62 years old, has no dependants and is an undischarged bankrupt. In anticipation of bankruptcy Kim rolled over her superannuation from her SMSF to an industry fund. Kim is in pension mode, she has an account-based pension and she has $1.8m in her account. The minimum draw down rules means that she must withdraw at least 4% of the account balance as income, which is $72 000. This is $21 668 greater than the prescribed amount of $50 332, which means that half of this figure, $10 834, could be claimed by creditors.

It is important to note that bankruptcy is not, of itself, a **condition of release** from superannuation. Bankruptcy may, however, lead to satisfying the financial hardship provisions which are a condition of release. If early access is given to superannuation then any lump sums withdrawn as a result, provided they occur after the date of bankruptcy, will be protected from creditors.

condition of release criteria that, if satisfied, enable an individual to withdraw their money from superannuation

accumulation mode where an individual is still contributing to superannuation

pension mode where an individual is no longer contributing to superannuation and has begun drawing down their superannuation in order to fund their retirement

LO 5 Paying benefits to members

We have seen how funds are contributed to and invested by SMSFs. Eventually fund members will wish to move from **accumulation mode** to **pension mode**.

In accumulation mode funds are locked away in a preserved environment and concessional contributions and investment earnings are generally taxed at 15%.

preservation age
the minimum age at which funds can be withdrawn from superannuation

In pension mode the member is no longer allowed to contribute; however, funds are now no longer preserved and any earnings on funds left within the SMSF are exempt from tax.

To move from accumulation mode to pension mode the member must satisfy a condition of release, for example the member has reached their **preservation age** and has now stopped working and does not intend to return to work in the future. At age 65, regardless of work status, a member may elect to move from accumulation mode to pension mode. However, people's circumstances do change and it is not unusual for a member to have more than one account in a SMSF, one of which is in pension mode and another which is in accumulation mode.

In establishing a SMSF trustees need to decide whether to have separate investment pools for each member or whether all investments should be placed in a single pool. This has implications for the payment of pensions.

Trustees also need to decide what pension options are open to members and the members themselves will need to decide what type of pension and/or lump sum payments meet their retirement needs.

Pooling and segregation

One of the advantages of having separate investment pools is that the assets attributable to that member are clearly segregated — as the fund moves from accumulation mode to pension mode it is relatively easy to identify which assets and the resulting earnings from those assets are exempt from tax.

ILLUSTRATIVE EXAMPLE 12.12

Jiro and Midori have a SMSF with separate investment pools. Jiro's pool includes shares and other assets that have a value of $600 000. Midori's pool includes the business real property associated with their dry cleaning business and other assets with a value of $1.2m. Jiro has satisfied a condition of release and has decided to move into pension mode and therefore any earnings resulting from the investment of his $600 000 will be received by the fund tax free.

If Jiro and Midori had decided instead when they established their SMSF to place their assets into a single pool this does not prohibit them from segregating the assets once Jiro or Midori satisfies a condition of release. Jiro and Midori will need to engage an actuary to determine what percentage of the fund's assets are dedicated to paying pensions. This percentage is then applied to the fund's income. This percentage will need to be re-determined each year.

Assuming Jiro and Midori established their SMSF using a single investment pool the actuary may determine that 33.3% of the fund's assets are dedicated to paying pensions. If the fund income is $100 000 then $33 333 would be exempt from tax and $66 666 would be taxable at 15%.

Careful consideration needs to be given as to how and when capital gains are realised. In the case of Jiro and Midori the $100 000 fund income might include some capital gains. If Jiro and Midori had established their fund with separate accounts and if the capital gain had been made on assets held by Jiro, the gain would have been 100% tax free because Jiro is in pension mode. However, with a single pool 66.6% of the gain would be taxable.

Types of pensions

Income streams can either be **account-based** or **non-account based**.

With an account-based income stream the individual has an 'account', the balance of which represents their superannuation entitlement. The balance of the account will increase as a result of positive investment returns and will decrease with negative investment returns and as the individual draws down a retirement income. The individual can vary the amount of income drawn down to suit their particular circumstances.

A non-account based income stream involves contracting with either a large superannuation fund or a life office to provide an income stream. Income streams can be for a defined period, for example for 20 years, or they can be for an individual's **lifetime**. The income level for each year is determined at the commencement of the contract and cannot be varied. The investment risk associated with funding this income level is borne by the income-stream provider. Where an income stream is for a lifetime there is a risk that the individual will outlive their life expectancy. This risk is known as longevity risk. Longevity risk is also borne by the income-stream provider. Income-stream providers factor these risks into the level of income they are prepared to offer for a given purchase price.

Provided it is permitted under the fund's trust deed, SMSFs can provide account-based pensions and **transition to retirement** account-based pensions. These types of accounts are popular with SMSF members because they maintain the flexibility in pension mode that the members enjoyed in accumulation mode. The member does not have to change the investment portfolio as they move from accumulation to pension mode. For example, they may choose to continue to own the business real property and other assets they acquired during the accumulation phase, or conversely they may choose to change their investment allocation to a more conservative allocation in keeping with their pension mode status.

As part of enjoying the tax-free status on earnings inside the fund, the federal government does insist on a minimum draw down each year in order to ensure that the funds really are used for retirement purposes.

Income drawn from the fund where the individual is under 60 years of age is subject to taxation; however, the level of taxation is reduced by the **deductible amount** and tax rebates. Income drawn from the fund where the individual is over 60 years of age is tax free.

account-based income stream
where an individual owns and maintains an individual account from which an income stream is drawn

non-account based income streams
where an individual gives their retirement savings to an income-stream provider who pools those assets and promises an income stream in return

lifetime income stream
an income stream that will last as long as a person lives

transition to retirement (TTR) income stream
a scheme that allows workers to continue to work part-time (or full-time) and supplement their income by drawing down some of their superannuation

deductible amount
that amount of an income stream which represents a return of capital

ILLUSTRATIVE EXAMPLE 12.13

Clara is 57 years old and has decided to retire and commence an account-based pension from her SMSF. Her account has a balance of $510 000, which comprises a tax-free component of $160 000 and a **taxable component** (taxed superannuation money) of $350 000. In the current financial year she wishes to draw down the minimum income stream.

- 31.4% of Clara's income stream will be deductible ($160 000/$510 000 = 31.4%)
- The minimum income draw down for someone aged under 65 is 4%
- 4% of $510 000 is $20 400
- 31.4% of $20 400 is $6400 (deductible amount)
- $20 400 less $6400 is $14 000 (assessable income)
- Because the income stream is funded by taxed superannuation money and Clara is under 60 years of age, the assessable income will be subject to a 15% tax rebate.

taxable component
money held inside a superannuation environment which has been subject to the 15% contributions and earnings tax

reversion when the recipient of an income stream dies, the income stream passes to a dependant

commute convert an income stream back into a lump sum

Account-based pensions other than transition to retirement account-based pensions also allow the individual to withdraw tax-free lump sums when the individual is over 60 years of age. Lump sums can also be withdrawn in specie rather than in cash if required.

Account-based pensions can also be paid to a **reversionary** beneficiary on the death of a member, provided the reversionary beneficiary is also a dependant.

SMSFs were allowed to pay defined benefit (non-account based) pensions prior to 2004. At that time they were particularly popular because of very generous Centrelink concessions. However, SMSFs cannot now pay defined benefit pensions although pensions which were in place prior to 2004 can continue to be paid. If a SMSF member now wishes to have a non-account based pension, the SMSF must purchase this pension on their behalf from a life insurance company. This is not a very popular option for SMSF members because of the inability to **commute** the income stream and the associated loss of investment control which was often the key reason they established the SMSF in the first place.

ILLUSTRATIVE EXAMPLE 12.14

The Clarke family SMSF has three members, one in accumulation mode and two in pension mode. The Clarke family SMSF pools all investment funds into a single pool.

During the current financial year the fund has received the following cash flows:

SG contributions	$25 000
Salary sacrifice contributions	$40 000
Non-concessional contributions	$300 000
Cash received from fully franked dividends	$55 000
Proceeds from the sale of property (cost $200 000 in 2004)	$290 000

The actuary has determined that 70% of the fund's assets are dedicated to paying pensions. How much tax will be payable by the fund?

Contribution income	
SG contributions	$25 000
Salary sacrifice contributions	$40 000
Non-concessional (not assessable income)	$ –
Subtotal	*$65 000*

Earnings income	
Cash from fully franked dividends	$55 000
Franking credits = ($55 000/(1 – 0.3)) – $55 000	$23 571
Capital gain (2/3 of $90 000)	$60 000
Subtotal before exempt earnings	*$138 571*
Less exempt earnings (70%)	–$97 000
Subtotal after exempt earnings	*$41 571*
Total income ($65 000 + $41 571)	$106 571
Tax payable @ 15%	$15 986

LO 6 Estate planning

Superannuation death benefits can be paid to a beneficiary or to multiple beneficiaries, or to an estate. Where there is no **binding death benefit nomination** in place the trustees of the SMSF have discretion as to who will be the recipient of the superannuation death benefit.

binding death benefit nomination a declaration by a superannuation fund member that on their death the balance of their superannuation must be paid to a nominated person; the trustees are bound to follow this direction

Superannuation death benefits can be paid as a lump sum or as an income stream to a dependant. A number of strategies can be employed within a SMSF to improve estate planning outcomes.

Death benefit lump sum

Superannuation *lump sum* death benefits are received tax free by dependants. A financially independent adult child is not a dependant for the purposes of receiving a superannuation death benefit, in which case the benefit received will have to be split into a tax-free and a taxable component.

As outlined in chapter 11, the taxable component can include:

- taxed superannuation money, that is, funds for which the 15% contributions tax and the 15% earnings tax has been taken away, or
- untaxed superannuation money, that is, funds for which the 15% contributions tax and the 15% earnings tax has *not* been taken away, or
- some combination of taxed and untaxed superannuation money.

For most Australians the taxable component is completely comprised of taxed superannuation money.

The taxable component (taxed superannuation money) received by a non-dependant will be taxed at 15% plus the Medicare levy.

ILLUSTRATIVE EXAMPLE 12.15

Andrew had $500 000 in his SMSF which comprised a tax-free component of $200 000 (40%) and a taxable component (taxed superannuation money) of $300 000 (60%). He made a binding death nomination in favour of his estate. Andrew recently passed away and his will leaves equal shares of his superannuation to his two daughters, Christine aged 24 and Angie aged 16.

Christine is financially independent. Her $250 000 will need to be divided into a tax-free component and a taxable component:

- $100 000 tax free (40% of total)
- $150 000 taxable (60% of total) at 15% will result in $22 500 tax payable.

As a financial dependant Angie will receive $250 000 tax free.

Death benefit income stream

The taxation of superannuation income-stream death benefits is covered in chapter 11. Income streams cannot revert to non-dependants and must be converted into a lump sum.

If an income stream is funded by a tax-free component and a taxable component (taxed superannuation money), and the deceased *and* the dependant to which an income stream reverts are both under 60 years of age, the income stream (net of any deductible amount) will be taxable at the marginal rate of the dependant; however, the tax payable will be reduced by a 15% rebate.

If an income stream is funded by a tax-free component and a taxable component (taxed superannuation money) and the deceased is older than 60 years of age *or* the dependant is older than 60 years of age the income stream will be received by the dependant tax free.

It is estimated that approximately 90% of superannuation death benefits are left to financially independent children, in which case some tax will be payable.

SMSF estate planning strategies

A number of strategies can be employed within the SMSF to improve the estate planning outcome on the death of one of the SMSF members, including the following.

1. *Ensuring where possible that superannuation is left to dependants* and that non-superannuation assets are left to non-dependants. This might be achieved by some combination of a binding death nomination and directions left within a will.
2. *By increasing the tax-free component* through a **recontribution** strategy.

recontribution
the process by which some funds are withdrawn from superannuation and then contributed back into superannuation in order to boost the tax-free component

ILLUSTRATIVE EXAMPLE 12.16

Alberto is 58 years old and has $700 000 in superannuation, which includes a tax-free component of $180 000 and a taxable component (taxed superannuation money) of $520 000. Alberto has satisfied a condition of release from superannuation and decides to withdraw $250 000 as a lump sum and then immediately recontribute this $250 000 as a non-concessional contribution. What will be Alberto's tax-free and taxable component after the recontribution?

- 25.7% of Alberto's superannuation is currently tax free ($180 000/$700 000) and 74.3% is taxable ($520 000/$700 000)
- $64 286 of the lump sum withdrawal will be tax free ($250 000 × 25.7%) and $185 714 will be taxable ($250 000 × 74.3%)
- $5714 of the lump sum will be taxable ($185 714 less the low-rate threshold 2013–14 of $180 000)
- $857 tax will be payable ($5714 × 15%)
- 52.2% of Alberto's superannuation will be tax free after the recontribution:
  - before recontribution tax free was $180 000
  - less $64 286 withdrawn
  - add $250 000 recontributed
  - equals $365 714 ($180 000 – $64 286 + $250 000)
  - $365 714/$700 000 = 52.2%
- 47.8% of Alberto's superannuation will be taxable after the recontribution:
  - before recontribution taxable was $520 000
  - less $185 714 withdrawn
  - equals $334 286 ($520 000 – $185 714)
  - $334 286/$700 000 = 47.8%
- The higher the tax-free component the lower the tax bill for any non-dependant who inherits Alberto's superannuation.

ILLUSTRATIVE EXAMPLE 12.17

Megan is 63 years old and has just commenced an account-based pension with her SMSF. When she commenced her pension her account had a value of \$800 000, which included a tax-free component of \$200 000 and a taxable component (taxed superannuation money) of \$600 000. Megan decides to withdraw \$250 000 and then recontribute this amount to superannuation. What will be Megan's total tax-free and taxable component inside the superannuation environment after the recontribution?

Megan is in pension mode so she cannot contribute money to her pension account; however, she can commence a separate accumulation account.

- 25% of Megan's superannuation is currently tax free (\$200 000/\$800 000) and 75% is taxable (\$600 000/\$800 000).
- \$62 500 of the lump sum will be withdrawn from the tax-free component (\$250 000 × 25%) and \$187 500 will be withdrawn from the taxable component (\$250 000 × 75%).
- Because Megan is over 60 years of age the taxable component of the lump sum can be withdrawn tax free.
- 48.4% of Megan's superannuation will be tax free after the recontribution:
  - before recontribution tax free was \$200 000
  - \$62 500 withdrawn
  - total tax free inside pension account equals \$137 500 (\$200 000 – \$62 500)
  - add \$250 000 recontributed to a separate accumulation account
  - total tax free inside superannuation equals \$387 500 (\$250 000 + \$137 500)
  - \$387 500/\$800 000 = 48.4%
- 51.6% of Megan's superannuation will be taxable after the recontribution:
  - before recontribution taxable was \$600 000
  - less \$187 500 withdrawn
  - equals \$412 500 (\$600 000 – \$187 500)
  - \$412 500/\$800 000 = 51.6%
- The higher the tax-free component the lower the tax bill for any non-dependant who inherits Megan's superannuation.
- Megan might be tempted to withdraw all her superannuation as a lump sum in order to maximise her tax-free component as part of a recontribution strategy; however, she needs to be mindful of the contribution limits that apply, both in terms of dollars and age.

3. *Regularly selling assets when in pension mode* when there is no CGT payable and if necessary buying those assets back again. The repurchased assets will then have a higher cost base which means that if they need to be sold to release cash for the payment of a death benefit the fund will have minimised the amount of CGT it will have to pay.
4. *Using a corporate trustee* to ensure the current trustee arrangement can stay in place on the death of one member. Given that many funds have two members, typically a husband and wife, consideration should also be given to admitting an adult child to the fund as the husband and wife age to assist any surviving spouse on the death of their partner and/or granting an enduring power of attorney.

5. *Determining how assets might be transferred between generations.*

ILLUSTRATIVE EXAMPLE 12.18

Lochan owns a florist shop. She decides to transfer the ownership of the business real property associated with the florist shop to the family SMSF. This property is worth $500 000 and this value is recorded in the SMSF account of Lochan. Lochan would like to retire in five years and her children are keen to take over the family business. Lochan and her children need to ensure that there are sufficient other resources in the SMSF besides the business real property when Lochan retires so she can take her superannuation benefit without the need to sell the business real property.

6. *Maximising taxation entitlements.* The federal government introduced the 15% tax on contributions in 1988. At the time the tax was criticised for disadvantaging dependants who might subsequently receive a death benefit lump sum. The government responded by introducing an 'anti-detriment' deduction which effectively refunded contributions to the fund.

ILLUSTRATIVE EXAMPLE 12.19

Kasen has passed away. Kasen had paid $15 000 in contributions tax via his SMSF. The SMSF will now be entitled to a tax deduction which will effectively negate the impact of the contribution tax. The anti-detriment formula and process can be complicated, but if we assume for simplicity that the fund is allowed to claim an additional $100 000 as a tax deduction as a result of Kasen's death, this would reduce the amount of tax otherwise payable by the fund by $15 000. It may be that Kasen's fund does not have sufficient income for the full deduction to be claimed, in which case the unclaimed amount will become a future tax benefit.

LO 7

Auditors, actuaries and other SMSF professionals

SMSFs are often referred to as DIY superannuation. There are, however, some functions by law that the trustee cannot do themselves.

All SMSFs must appoint an auditor. The auditor needs to examine the SMSF's financial statements and assess the SMSF's compliance with the relevant legislation.

Auditors need to be a registered company auditor or a member of a designated organisation such as CPA Australia or the Institute of Chartered Accountants of Australia. Since 1 July 2013 auditors also need to complete a competency exam which is administered by ASIC.

The auditor needs to:

1. provide the SMSF with an annual audit report
2. notify the trustees of the SMSF of any concerns raised through the auditing process
3. notify the ATO of any serious contraventions of the relevant law.

In the year ended 30 June 2012 the ATO reported that 90% of SMSF audits cost less than $1000.

If a SMSF has more than one member and if some member(s) are in accumulation mode and some member(s) are in pension mode and all the investment assets are held in a single pool, the SMSF must appoint an actuary to produce an annual actuarial certificate. The certificate will determine the amount of fund income which is exempt from tax.

Virtually all other supporting roles can be performed on a DIY basis; however, this obviously depends on the expertise of the trustees and the time they have available to devote to fund-related tasks. These supporting roles include accounting, legal, administration and investment advice and services. Many SMSF trustees rely heavily on the services provided by their 'local' accountant, particularly during the start-up phase. However, as the SMSF legislative landscape becomes more complex some small accounting practices are finding it uneconomic to keep up to date and are moving out of this work altogether, or acting instead as a conduit between their client and specialist providers.

As the amount of funds under management by SMSFs has grown so too has the specialist advice and support services available. A range of providers offering outsourced fund administration services now operate in the Australian market, including some overseas-based providers.

LO 8 The cost of establishing and running a SMSF

Establishing a SMSF typically costs $1000 to $4000. For $1000 the SMSF is likely to have individuals acting as trustees, with almost all the preparatory work being done by the individuals themselves. Having a corporate trustee adds approximately $1000 in establishment costs.

Once a fund is established annual running costs will be a combination of fixed costs, semi-variable costs and variable costs. To the extent that costs are fixed or semi-variable a SMSF becomes cheaper in percentage terms the larger the sum invested.

SMSFs have to pay an annual supervisory levy to the ATO which in 2015 is approximately $260. This is a fixed annual cost.

SMSFs need to engage auditors each year and this cost is largely fixed. However, as the fund gets larger and its operation more complex, the audit fee will reflect this, in which case this cost will become more of a semi-variable cost. Most other professional advisory services will also charge in this way.

Some costs such as the transaction costs associated with buying and selling investments are essentially a function of the volume of transactions. All things being equal, you would expect a fund with more funds under management to have more such transactions, in which case this would be a variable cost.

Figure 12.4 (overleaf) shows the average annual cost of running a SMSF with a balance of $50 000 in 2011 was $4145, which in percentage terms is 8.3%. A balance of $50 000 is not enough to justify the establishment and maintenance of a SMSF when other providers in the market, for example industry funds, can provide significantly cheaper services, albeit without the flexibility provided by SMSFs. A small balance for a short period of time could perhaps be justified if it is part of some longer term strategy to build up the funds under management in the SMSF.

The ATO also report that SMSFs with balances in excess of $2m incurred annual running costs of approximately $8200 or 0.2%. Clearly SMSFs with large balances can achieve lower running costs than other providers in the market and therefore, when combined with the flexibility provided by SMSFs, they become a very attractive option for investors.

$1–$50k	8.3%
>$50k–$100k	4.0%
>$100k–$200k	2.8%
>$200k–$500k	1.4%
>$500k–$1m	0.7%
>$1m–$2m	0.4%
>$2m	0.2%

FIGURE 12.4 Average operating expense ratios to assets by SMSF fund size

Source: Extracted from ATO, Self-managed super fund statistical report, March 2013.

The figure quoted as to when a SMSF becomes a viable option is often $250 000. The ATO reports that a fund with $250 000 invested will incur annual costs of $3500 or 1.4%. It is important to remember that we are discussing averages — a trustee who undertakes more of the tasks themselves will incur fewer costs than a trustee who relies heavily on the professional advice and services of others. It is also possible that SMSF trustees are prepared to pay a premium for the flexibility provided by having their own SMSF.

PROFESSIONAL ADVICE

Helen is a 31-year-old nurse who lives in a rented apartment in inner Brisbane. At the age of 18 her father encouraged her to invest a small amount of money in shares and over the years she has actively and successfully traded her share portfolio to the point where it is currently valued at $450 000. The cost base of her portfolio for CGT purposes is $380 000.

Helen currently has $72 000 in her industry-based superannuation fund. On her last statement from her superannuation fund Helen noticed that the indirect cost ratio was 0.88% and this amounted to a $634 deduction from her account. Helen is also charged a flat fee of $120 per annum regardless of the balance in her account. All other fees are based on the activity associated with her account — the fund charges $80 for switching investment choices but does not impose any charges on rollovers and contributions.

Helen is considering establishing a SMSF but is unsure whether the costs of establishing and running a SMSF would be less than the costs charged by her industry fund.

If Helen does establish a SMSF she would like to contribute her share portfolio as an in-specie contribution which she would continue to actively manage inside her SMSF. She also has an uncle who knows a bit about accounting but nothing about SMSFs who has offered to help Helen set up and run her SMSF.

QUESTIONS

1 If Helen was to sell the share portfolio and contribute the full sale proceeds to her industry fund as a non-concessional contribution what would be the approximate annual cost applied by the industry fund to Helen's account?

2 What are the CGT consequences of contributing the share portfolio to the SMSF?

3 Will Helen be able to contribute her share portfolio to the SMSF and be able to avoid excess contribution tax penalties?

4 What factors are likely to impact on the cost of establishing and running a SMSF for Helen?

5 What factors besides costs does Helen need to take into account in determining whether or not she should establish a SMSF?

6 What would be your advice to Helen?

LO 9 Compliance and penalties

As seen in this chapter and the two previous chapters superannuation can be a complex business. SMSF trustees remain liable for the actions of their fund regardless of whether certain tasks are delegated or outsourced.

The ATO as regulator of SMSFs encourages:

- self-management
- self-regulation, and
- self-assessment.

The ATO sees itself as working with SMSF trustees in a cooperative environment to assist them in achieving their retirement goals within the prescribed legislative framework. Where a trustee identifies a problem which may lead to their fund being non-complying they are encouraged to contact the ATO to see if collaboratively the problem can be solved.

As part of their compliance SMSFs are expected to keep detailed records including:

- records of financial transactions
- an annual operating statement and statement of financial position
- copies of all of the audited annual returns lodged with the ATO
- minutes of trustee meetings
- copies of reports to members.

These records need to be readily available to the ATO during any compliance review or audit.

Figure 12.5 (overleaf) lists the type and prevalence of contraventions reported to the ATO between 2005 and 2012.

Loan to member/financial assistance	20.90%
In-house assets	18.30%
Administrative-type contraventions	12.00%
Separation of assets	12.90%
Operating standard-type contraventions	8.30%
Borrowings	8.00%
Sole purpose	7.80%
Investments at arm's length	7.50%
Other	2.80%
Acquisition of assets from related parties	1.50%
Total	**100.00%**

FIGURE 12.5
Types of contraventions reported to the ATO (2005 to 2012)
Source: Extracted from ATO, Self-managed super fund statistical report, March 2013.

Where a potential non-compliance is identified the ATO may:

- accept a written undertaking from the trustee that outlines how they intend to rectify the non-compliance
- remove or disqualify the trustee(s)
- freeze the assets of the SMSF pending further investigation and action
- prosecute the trustee and seek the application of civil and/or criminal penalties
- declare the fund non-complying and therefore subject all fund income to the highest marginal tax rate which can apply retrospectively, depending on the nature of the non-compliance and when the non-compliance first occurred.

If the ATO decides to take civil action the maximum penalty is \$220 000. If the ATO decides to take criminal action the maximum penalty is 5 years in prison. Some actions by trustees could lead to both civil and criminal prosecution for the same 'offence'.

For less serious offences that don't jeopardise the SMSF's compliance, for example, failing to lodge returns on time, the ATO can apply a range of administrative financial penalties.

ILLUSTRATIVE EXAMPLE 12.20

At the start of the chapter we introduced Simone, who was thinking of establishing a SMSF but had a number of concerns.

Simone owned the freehold of a clothing shop from which she ran the family clothing and fashion accessories business. A contribution of the real business property to a SMSF would constitute a sale for CGT purposes. The property cost \$200 000 and if valued at \$800 000, would result in a gain of \$600 000. Because Simone has owned the property for more than 12 months only half of the gain — that is, \$300 000 — would be assessable for CGT purposes. Simone will be eligible for the small business retirement CGT exemption of up to \$500 000 provided she contributes an amount at least equal to the assessable gain to superannuation.

Simone wishes to keep the clothing shop in the family so that eventually her two daughters can run the business. Therefore she needs to contribute the entire $800 000 property to the fund. Simone is able to claim the small business retirement exemption of $300 000 and she is also able to make a non-concessional contribution of up to $450 000 every three years, giving her a capacity to make a contribution of up to $750 000 without incurring an excess contribution tax penalty.

Simone is also concerned about tying up all her money in superannuation. Simone might decide to roll over her $100 000 industry superannuation fund balance into her SMSF. She can then partially contribute and partially sell her real business property to her SMSF. For example, she might contribute $700 000 in real business property and sell $100 000 real business property to her SMSF. The fund will receive real business property to the value of $800 000 and Simone will receive $100 000 in cash and recognition in her superannuation account of a $700 000 non-concessional contribution.

Simone will not be allowed to run her business inside her SMSF as Margie suggests. SMSFs are designed for the sole purpose of providing retirement benefits to members and any attempt to run the business inside the fund is likely to risk the complying status of the fund and leave Simone vulnerable to civil and criminal prosecution by the regulator.

A SMSF does, however, provide Simone with valuable estate planning opportunities. Initially the fund's assets will be dominated by the real business property associated with the shop and this will cause diversification and flexibility problems in the short term. However, over time other assets will be accumulated by Simone and her daughters, so Simone may be able to retire and draw a retirement income from the fund without the need to sell the shop.

Simone's friend Julie did raise the issue of 'mixing super and family'. Simone will need to carefully consider what type of trustee structure she uses in setting up her SMSF and if/when she would invite her two daughters to be members of the fund.

Summary

This chapter considered how SMSFs are established and how funds are contributed to, and invested by, SMSFs. The ways in which SMSFs pay benefits to members was also reviewed.

When an individual has a significant sum of money to invest, cost savings is often put forward as the main reason for establishing a SMSF. However, cost savings is only one factor. There are a number of other advantages in establishing a SMSF.

- SMSFs allow the trustee to control their investments. The trustee can directly invest, invest in some quite exotic assets if they wish to, gear up through the use of instalment warrants and invest in real business property.
- SMSFs give trustees considerable flexibility. Members can make in-specie contributions, small business owners can take advantage of CGT concessions and careful estate planning can ensure that estate assets are well managed for current and future generations.

The advantages of SMSFs do, however, need to be balanced against some disadvantages:

- There is considerable responsibility in being a trustee of a SMSF. Trustees remain personally liable for their actions. If a fund is declared non-complying it will face significant tax penalties and the trustees could be liable to civil and criminal prosecution.
- SMSFs can have up to four members and generally members of SMSFs have family linkages. Sometimes family members do not agree and family disputes may spill over and impact on the operation of the SMSF. Conversely disputes over how the SMSF is managed might cause difficulties within the family.
- SMSFs do have some investment opportunities that are not available to large funds, nonetheless small and large funds still operate within a number of investment constraints that would not apply if the funds were invested outside a superannuation environment. The individual needs to balance these constraints against the tax concessions available within a superannuation environment.
- SMSF trustees need to engage a range of specialist advisers and service providers, so are vulnerable to the quality of advice and service given. The growth in the amount of funds under management by SMSFs has encouraged some less than reputable 'advisers' into the market.

The growth in SMSFs both in terms of the number of funds and the amount of funds under management shows no sign of abating and most commentators predict this trend will continue for some time yet.

Professional application questions

12.1 What is the difference between a small APRA fund and a SMSF?

12.2 Distinguish between owning an asset as joint tenants and owning an asset as tenants in common. How should superannuation funds own assets?

12.3 In establishing a SMSF the trustees must decide whether to include all investment assets into a single pool or create separate pools for each member. What are the advantages and disadvantages of each approach?

12.4 Are accountants allowed to provide SMSF advice?

12.5 What factors need to be taken into account in deciding whether to use an individual trustee structure or a corporate trustee structure?

12.6 The trustees of a SMSF bought a bungalow in a golf-course precinct ostensibly as a rental house as part of the investment strategy for the fund. Purchase of the property brought with it membership and playing rights in the associated golf club, which the trustees found attractive and intended to use. How do you think the ATO as regulator would view this investment?

12.7 What are some of the advantages of holding a leveraged residential or commercial property inside a SMSF?

12.8 What are some of the restrictions and disadvantages of holding a leveraged residential or commercial property inside a SMSF?

12.9 What type of income streams can SMSFs pay?

12.10 What strategies can be employed within the SMSF to improve the estate planning outcome on the death of one of the SMSF members?

Professional application exercises

Basic	*
Moderate	* *
Challenging	* * *

12.11 Self-employed status *

Hung is a 43-year-old electrician. He does household repairs and occasionally does the wiring for new homes. Clients tell him the work that needs to be done but he then decides the best way to achieve the outcome required. He uses his own tools and equipment and provides his clients with fixed quotes for his work. Hung bears the risk of cost increases and rectifying his work. This financial year Hung has earned $120 000 from his electrical work. This financial year Hung has also run some classes at the local TAFE where he has earned $20 000. The TAFE also paid $2000 in SG payments into Hung's SMSF — this is the only concessional contribution that has been paid into his account this year.

The end of the financial year is rapidly approaching and Hung is keen to make the maximum concessional contribution he can to his SMSF. Advise Hung.

12.12 Investment restrictions *

Bob's uncle has offered to sell to Bob's SMSF his classic Mustang 66 convertible on the proviso that once in a while he can come around and take it for a 'spin'. The Mustang has recently been valued at $60 000. Bob is certain that the Mustang is a good investment — three years ago similar cars could be purchased for $40 000. Bob doesn't think he will have too much trouble convincing the auditor that it meets the sole purpose test as long as he can keep his uncle away from the car. Currently Bob's SMSF has $400 000 in investments which includes $100 000 in cash. Advise Bob.

12.13 Estate planning *

Qiang has $750 000 in her SMSF, which includes a tax-free component of $120 000 with the balance being taxed superannuation money. She has made a binding death nomination in favour of her financially independent daughter Rou. If Qiang was to pass away and leave the $750 000 as a lump sum to Rou, how much tax will Rou need to pay?

12.14 Bankruptcy *

Mal-Chin is 68 years old, has no dependants and is an undischarged bankrupt. Mal-Chin is in pension mode, he has an account-based pension and he has $1.6m in his account. Mal-Chin draws down the minimum income. How much of his income could be claimed by creditors?

12.15 Contributions * *

Troy is a 40-year-old self-employed plumber. His marginal tax rate is 40%. Earlier this financial year he bought $40 000 in ANZ shares which are now valued at $42 000 and he is considering contributing these shares to his SMSF. Should Troy contribute these shares as a concessional or non-concessional contribution and what are the CGT consequences of making such a contribution?

12.16 Small business active asset exemption * *

Vina is 45 years old and has owned and operated her dry cleaning business for the last 20 years. She has decided to sell the business in order to fund her retirement. She has just accepted an offer of $2m for her business and this includes a $1.5m capital gain. Vina qualifies for the 15 year active asset exemption and she would like to contribute as much of the sales proceeds as possible to her superannuation fund.

Vina has made non-concessional contributions to her SMSF in the past and currently has the capacity to contribute another $220 000 without exceeding the non-concessional contributions limit. Vina has not made any concessional contributions to her SMSF in this financial year.

How much of the sales proceeds is Vina able to contribute without exceeding any caps or limits?

12.17 Income stream ✱✱

Adam is 58 years old and has decided to retire and commence an account-based pension from his SMSF.

His account includes a tax-free component of $220 000 and a taxable component (taxed superannuation money) of $400 000.

In the current financial year he wishes to draw down the minimum income stream.

How much of his income stream will be assessable for tax purposes and is Adam entitled to any tax rebate?

12.18 SMSF income tax payable ✱✱✱

The Smalltime SMSF has four members, three in accumulation mode and one in pension mode. The Smalltime SMSF pools all investment funds into a single pool.

During the current financial year the fund has received the following cash flows:

SG contributions	$30 000
Salary sacrifice contributions	$20 000
Cash received from fully franked dividends	$50 000
Unfranked dividends	$10 000
Cash received from fixed income investments	$6 000
Proceeds from the sale of property (cost $100 000 in 1999)	$220 000

The actuary has determined that 30% of the fund's assets are dedicated to paying pensions.

(a) What is the income of the fund?

(b) How much tax will be payable by the fund?

(c) If the fund had separate investment pools for each member and the member who was in pension mode had held the property which was sold for a capital gain (above) and this was their only asset, what impact would this have on the amount of tax payable by the fund?

12.19 Recontribution: client under 60 years of age ✱✱✱

Matthew is 57 years old and has $600 000 in superannuation, which includes a tax-free component of $100 000 and a taxable component (taxed superannuation money) of $500 000. Matthew has satisfied a condition of release from superannuation and decides to withdraw $300 000 as a lump sum and then immediately recontribute this $300 000 as a non-concessional contribution.

(a) Will Matthew be subject to any lump sum withdrawal tax?

(b) What will be Matthew's tax-free component after the recontribution takes place?

(c) Why might Matthew be seeking to increase his tax-free component?

12.20 Recontribution: client over 60 years of age ✱✱✱

Moubani is 63 years old. She retired 2 years ago and commenced an account-based pension with her SMSF. When she commenced her pension her account had a value of $700 000 which included a tax-free component of $150 000 and a taxable component (taxed superannuation money) of $550 000. Good investment returns have outweighed the income drawn down so that the current account balance is $720 000.

Moubani recently started working again part-time. She would like to withdraw $200 000 as a lump sum and then recontribute this amount to her SMSF.

You need to advise Moubani on how she could achieve this and what the tax implications will be.

CASE STUDY

Estate planning and the intergenerational transfer of assets

Tony and Maria are both in their early sixties. They continue to run a successful greengrocer business from a shop in the main street of Triple Bay. They have three financially independent children — Isabella, Sofia and Teresa who is the youngest of the three.

Ten years ago Tony and Maria established a SMSF as individual trustees and all the assets of the fund were contributed to a single investment pool. The SMSF has the following assets and liabilities.

Assets

- Business real property (the shop in Triple Bay) $1 400 000. The property was valued at $500 000 when it was initially contributed to the fund.
- Shares $100 000
- Cash $20 000
- Total assets in pool = $1 520 000

Liabilities

- Tony's accumulation account $800 000 (10% taxable and 90% tax free)
- Maria's accumulation account $720 000 (15% taxable and 85% tax free)
- Total liabilities of the fund = $1 520 000

Tony and Maria are keen to admit their children to the SMSF but understand that a SMSF can have no more than four members. Tony and Maria's plan is that they will admit the two eldest daughters and provide for the third daughter through their respective wills.

Tony and Maria would like to retire and Isabella would like to take over the responsibility of running the family business. Tony is concerned that the fund

»

»

will not have sufficient cash flow to pay a retirement income to Maria and himself without selling the shop. If the shop is to be sold it is possible that Isabella could lease the premises from the new owners, but there is no guarantee that this will be possible and Tony is worried that there will be a huge CGT bill as a result of any sale.

Tony, Maria and their daughters need your advice.

1. If the business real property has to be sold would it be better to do this before or after they retired and before or after the two eldest daughters are admitted to the SMSF?
2. How might Isabella and Sofia bring liquid assets into the fund to assist in providing Tony and Maria with a retirement income?
3. What other sources of income is the SMSF likely to have to assist in providing Tony and Maria with a retirement income?
4. How will the SMSF find the cash to pay a death benefit if either Tony or Maria pass away?
5. If Tony or Maria pass away and the death benefit is payable to their daughters, what rate of tax will they pay on the death benefit?
6. The youngest daughter, Teresa, is concerned that she is being left out of the decision-making process and that a will may not sufficiently protect her interests. What advice can you give Teresa?

References and further reading

Australian Bureau of Statistics 2013, 6401.0 — Consumer Price Index, Australia, www.abs.gov.au.

APRA 2012, *Annual superannuation bulletin*, www.apra.gov.au.

ATO 2010, *Running a self-managed super fund*, June, www.ato.gov.au.

ATO 2011a, *Thinking about self-managed super*, November, www.ato.gov.au.

ATO 2011b, *Setting up a self-managed super fund*, August, www.ato.gov.au.

ATO 2013a, *How your self-managed super fund is regulated*, March, www.ato.gov.au.

ATO 2013b, *Self-managed super fund statistical report*, March, www.ato.gov.au.

Bowerman, R 2013, 'Keeping score for your SMSF', July, www.vanguradinvestments.com.au.

Castillo, J 2010, *The rise and rise of self-managed superannuation in Australia*, www.asb.unsw.edu.au.

CCH 2013, *Australian master financial planning guide*, 2013–14, 16th edn.

CCH 2012, *Australian master superannuation guide*, 2012–13, 16th edn.

ITSA 2013, *Insolvency and Trustee Service Australia*, www.itsa.gov.au.

Moneysmart 2013, *Superannuation scams*, www.moneysmart.gov.au.

SPAA 2012, *SMSF Generations Report*, March www.spa.asn.au.

Wallis, S 1997, *Financial System Inquiry Final Report.*

13 Social security

LEARNING OBJECTIVES

After studying this chapter, you should be able to:

1. explain briefly the history of and rationale for social security in Australia
2. outline the role of the Department of Human Services in the delivery of social security services
3. provide an overview of the range of benefits available under social security
4. outline pension and allowance benefit entitlements and eligibility rules
5. outline the assistance provided to retirees
6. explain the means testing regime for eligibility for the age pension
7. outline the assistance provided to families raising children
8. outline the assistance provided to people with disabilities
9. explain the support provided for those undertaking study or an Australian apprenticeship
10. outline the taxation of pensions and allowances
11. describe the accommodation alternatives in retirement.

CASE STUDY

Jack and Judy are aged 65 and 59 respectively. Jack has just retired from the workforce and the couple is wondering what their social security entitlements may be, if any. The couple own their home, but are looking to move into a granny flat on their daughter's property next year. They plan to sell their home, pay their daughter $300 000 for the cost of building the granny flat and gift the balance equally between their three children.

The couple's assets consist of the following.

Home	$520 000
Contents	$50 000
Cars	$35 000
Caravan	$12 000
Bank account	$80 000
Managed funds	$60 000
Australian shares	$240 000
Superannuation — Judy	$100 000
Superannuation — Jack	$350 000

Other relevant issues include that the couple has no liabilities and that Judy is still working part-time, earning $15 000 p.a. Their investments generate the following returns:

- bank account 2.5%
- managed fund 8%
- shares 3.5% fully franked
- superannuation 6.5% for both Jack and Judy.

Some of the issues for the couple to consider include.

- Is the couple entitled to the age pension or any other social security entitlements?
- Are any strategies available to Jack to help increase his age pension entitlement?
- What are the tax and social ramifications of the couple selling their home and gifting funds to their three children?
- What are the social security ramifications of the couple moving into a granny flat with their daughter?

Illustrative examples used throughout this chapter relate to the information contained within this case study.

Introduction

The social security system in Australia is the means by which the government provides a level of care and assistance to people in society who need help. Over time, the range of benefits provided by Australian society has been extended dramatically, although in recent years rationalisation has taken place to reduce the number of specific benefits available and to better target those in need.

In 2013–14, the Australian Government is expected to spend $138.1 billion or 36% of total budgeted revenue on social security and welfare. Assistance is provided to the aged, veterans and their dependants, people with disabilities, families with children, the unemployed and the sick, youth and Indigenous people. In this chapter we will examine in some depth the three areas of social security which between them account for more than 80% of the annual funding: assistance to the aged (37%), families with children (27%) and people with disabilities (16%) (Treasury 2013).

LO 1 History of social security in Australia

Since the early 1900s, Australian governments have passed legislation to support a basic standard of living for virtually all citizens through a range of social security policies. Before 1900, voluntary charitable organisations accepted responsibility for care of the destitute. However, the effects of the 1890s depression, the emergence of the political power of the trade union movement through the Labor Party, the recognition that welfare policies could play a part in consolidating the gains of the industrialisation era, and the desire to avoid workhouses for the poor (which constituted the welfare policy of Britain) all combined to produce policies which accepted state responsibility for alleviation of financial distress which was beyond the control of the individual. In the early 1900s, Australia was a world leader in social reform.

The first legislation centred on the provision of assistance to alleviate financial hardship of the unemployed elderly. It is of interest to note, however, that the first steps were somewhat tentative, as the qualifying age of 65 years for the **age pension** for men (established from 1 July 1909) was in fact older than the average life expectancy of men at the time. Additionally, the legislators of the time could not escape the social morality of the period — help was made available only to those who were considered deserving. For instance, people could be disqualified from receiving the age pension if they were not of good character or if they had deserted their spouses without just cause.

age pension
a pension paid to eligible members of the community based on their age and subject to an income and assets test

The social security safety net was expanded in the 1940s. In 1942, the widow's pension was introduced and, from 1 July 1945, the government introduced a suite of unemployment, sickness and special benefits. These benefits were aimed at supporting an active working population. The 1980s saw another period of expansion of benefits with carers' and sole parents' pensions either introduced or reformed and several other allowances introduced. The home and community care program was also introduced during this period.

However, despite the extension of the types of benefits, there has been rationalisation during the past 10 years to reduce the number of specific benefits in favour of more generally applicable benefits. Additionally, conditions of eligibility have been tightened to try to ensure only the needy have access to community support.

Rationale underlying the provision of social security

The reasons that a community allocates taxation revenue to the payment of social security benefits vary from the lofty and philosophical to the mundane and practical. The philosophical reasons include:

- altruism — support for others who are worse off than oneself is considered to be one facet of a civilised society
- humanitarianism — enjoyment of basic necessities of living is a fundamental human right and all societies should strive to provide these for all members
- utilitarianism — individuals' marginal utility (happiness) derived from the expenditure of money decreases as expenditure increases, so redistribution from the better-off to the worse-off will increase the total stock of happiness in a society.

Practical arguments include:

- economic — help given to the needy at relevant times (e.g. the unemployed or temporarily disabled) may facilitate their recovery to become productive members of society and thus the continuation of their contribution to society
- reduction in crime — needy people given community support do not need to resort to crime to survive, thus protecting the assets of the better-off.

There are, of course, people who are against the provision of social security and they refute most of the arguments described above. Their views usually centre around the notion that financial help reduces work incentives for both the helped and the helpers and that it is economically inefficient to continually levy the high-fliers with increased taxation to help the poor.

LO 2 Centrelink and the Department of Human Services (DHS)

Centrelink
the federal government agency which administers the payments of government pensions and allowances

In 1997, the federal government restructured the way social security services were delivered to Australians and established the Commonwealth Services Delivery Agency, more commonly known as **Centrelink**. Centrelink is the access point for social service beneficiaries. Social security and compensation payments are also provided to defence-service veterans and their dependants by the Department of Veterans' Affairs (DVA) either directly by DVA or through Centrelink.

Centrelink is managed through a federal government department (a department which has been the subject of continual change), the Department of Human Services (DHS). The DHS is responsible for the development of service delivery policy and provides access to social, health and other payments and services. The *Human Services Legislation Amendment Act 2011* integrated the services of Medicare Australia, Centrelink and CRS Australia on 1 July 2011 into the DHS. The creation of Centrelink as an agency can be seen as part of a broader shift to the use of market-like mechanisms in the running of public programs. The work is increasingly carried out under an agreement or contract even though those agents are themselves public service organisations.

The other main government department involved in the development and provision of social policy outcomes is the Department of Families, Housing, Community Services and Indigenous Affairs (FaHCSIA). It is responsible for integrated service delivery to the Australian public of a wide range of Commonwealth programs and manages about one-fifth of the federal budget.

Table 13.1 gives details of the estimated costs of social security and welfare payments.

TABLE 13.1 Social security estimates and projections, 2012–13 to 2016–17

	Estimates			Projections	
	2012–13 $m	2013–14 $m	2014–15 $m	2015–16 $m	2016–17 $m
Assistance to the aged	50 984	54 754	57 620	61 648	66 251
Assistance to veterans and dependants	7 046	7 006	6 880	6 795	6 635
Assistance to people with disabilities	23 873	25 479	27 208	29 156	32 396
Assistance to families with children	35 256	34 945	35 534	36 353	37 158
Assistance to the unemployed and the sick	8 559	9 550	10 559	9 830	9 859
Other welfare programs	1 663	1 637	1 649	1 687	1 763
Assistance for Indigenous Australians nec	1 145	1 043	939	928	1 053
General administration	3 861	3 731	3 631	3 513	3 365
Total social security and welfare	**132 388**	**138 145**	**144 021**	**149 911**	**158 479**

Source: Data derived from Treasury 2013.

The main growth area in estimated and projected payments is the income support for seniors (age pension), which is estimated to grow by 5.7% in real terms from 2012–13 to 2013–14 and 12.5% in real terms from 2013–14 to 2016–17. The expected increase in expenses is associated with home care, home support, and the residential and flexible aged care programs, reflecting demographic factors.

LO 3 The range of social security benefits

The DHS has reported that it pays more than 140 different types of benefits. Table 13.2 lists a number of the main social security benefits available and explains the purpose of each benefit. To obtain a current list of benefits and their eligibility conditions, refer to the website of the DHS (humanservices.gov.au).

TABLE 13.2 The main benefits available from DHS

Type of benefit	Purpose of benefit
For aged people	
Age pension	Ensures that elderly people receive a minimum level of income to meet their retirement income needs.
For people raising children	
Family tax benefit (A)	Assists families with the cost of raising children and is paid per child. Eligibility requirements relate to the age of the children and satisfying an income test.
Family tax benefit (B)	Provides extra assistance to single-parent families and families with one main income. Eligibility requirements relate to the age of the children and satisfying an income test.
Baby bonus	Assists with the costs of a newborn or adopted child where the eligibility requirements for Family Tax Benefit for the child are met.
Child care benefit	Assists with the cost of approved and registered child care. Eligibility criteria based on the child attending approved or registered child care, and the parent or carer being liable to pay child care fees and satisfying an income test.

(continued)

TABLE 13.2 *(continued)*

Type of benefit	Purpose of benefit
For people who are ill, injured or disabled	
Disability support pension	Provides minimum level of payments to people who are unable to work because of a physical, intellectual or psychiatric impairment.
Sickness allowance	Paid to a person who is 21 or older but under age pension age and who is temporarily incapacitated for work; must have a job or full-time study to return to when recovered.
For people who are unemployed looking for work	
Newstart allowance	Payments to a person who is registered as unemployed and is over 21. Person must be capable of undertaking work, be available for work or be actively seeking work, or be temporarily incapacitated for work.
Youth allowance	Provides income support for full-time students and apprentices aged 16–24. Job seekers aged under 21 must be looking for work, or combining this with part-time study, or undertaking any other approved activity. Paid also to 15-year olds who have left school and are living independently.
For people caring for others	
Carer payment	Income support to a person who provides constant care for an adult and that adult's dependent child; a person who has a physical, intellectual or psychiatric disability; a profoundly disabled child; or two or more disabled children who need care for an extended period.
Carer allowance	Payments to a person who provides daily care and attention to a person with a disability who is a family member aged 16 or over or a dependent child under 16.
For students	
Youth allowance	Provides income support for full-time students and apprentices aged 16–24. Job seekers aged under 21 must be looking for work, or combining this with part-time study, or undertaking any other approved activity. Paid also to 15-year olds who have left school and are living independently.
Austudy payment	Payment to a person who satisfies the activity test by undertaking qualifying study or a full-time apprenticeship and who is 25 years or over.
ABSTUDY	Payments to students who are Aboriginal Australians or Torres Strait Islanders and are studying an approved course of study at an approved education institution or undertaking a full-time apprenticeship.
Concession cards	
Pensioner concession card	Concession card that provides fringe benefits to persons in receipt of certain pension and allowance support. The card provides concessions on pharmaceutical prescriptions, a telephone allowance and access to a number of state, territory and local government concessions.
Health care card[a]	Concession card that is issued to persons who do not qualify for a pensioner concession card but who are receiving a number of other government income support payments or for those people on low incomes. The card provides concessions on pharmaceutical prescriptions and access to a number of state, territory and local government concessions.
Commonwealth seniors health card[a]	Concession card that is targeted at self-funded retirees of age pension age who do not qualify for an age pension due to assets or income levels. To qualify, the person must have an adjusted level of income of less than $50 000 for singles and $80 000 for couples. The card provides concessions on pharmaceutical prescriptions and access to the seniors supplement.

a. Entitlements to the health care card for low-income earners and to the Commonwealth seniors health card are based on an adjusted taxable income which comprises taxable income plus: the value of any adjusted fringe benefits, target foreign income, total net investment losses and reportable superannuation contributions.

LO 4 Pension and allowance benefit entitlements and eligibility rules

It is important to note that benefit entitlements and eligibility rules change on a regular basis and the rates provided in the text below may not be the most current available. While the latest rates and eligibility rules are obviously important, these can be readily looked up through the DHS website (humanservices.gov.au).

What is more important is an understanding of the entitlements available for individuals in need of income support and the principles governing their application.

Pension and allowance benefit entitlements

The rate of payment for the majority of **government pensions** is shown in table 13.3.

TABLE 13.3 Maximum pension entitlements (effective to 19 September 2013)

Status	Maximum payment per fortnight
Single	$808.40 including the maximum Pension and Clean Energy supplements
Couple (each)	$609.40 including the maximum Pension and Clean Energy supplements

Source: Department of Human Services 2013a.

The **pension supplement** is an extra payment received by those in receipt of a pension or other form of eligible income support. The **clean energy supplement** is a tax-exempt payment that provides assistance to meet the ongoing impacts of carbon pricing on living expenses.

Table 13.4 illustrates the maximum allowance entitlement for a number of **government allowances** including the Newstart allowance, sickness allowance and widow allowance.

TABLE 13.4 Maximum allowance entitlements (effective to 19 September 2013)

Status	Maximum benefit per fortnight
Single, no children	$497.00
Single, with children	$537.80
Single, aged 60 and over, after 9 months on allowance	$537.80
Couple (each)	$448.70

Source: Department of Human Services 2013a.

government pension
income support payments for persons in need of medium to long-term assistance

pension supplement
additional support paid to those in receipt of a pension and replacing a number of individual allowances and supplements

clean energy supplement
additional support to those in receipt of a pension to cover the impact of carbon pricing

government allowance
income support payments for persons in need of short-term assistance

Pension and allowance benefit eligibility rules

Means testing

Social security pensions are subject to a **means test** to ensure they are paid only to people most in need. The means test is based on a person's assets and their income. A person's pension entitlements are based on the test that produces the lowest payment. Means testing will be considered in further detail later in the chapter.

means test
a test that reduces a person's entitlement to a pension or allowance based on exceeding certain asset and income thresholds

Residence requirements

To qualify for a social security pension, a person must be a permanent resident by being:

- an Australian resident for at least 10 years with more than 5 years of continuous residence, with the exception of refugees
- in Australia at the time of applying.

An Australian resident residing outside of Australia, but residing in a country with which Australia has entered into an international social security agreement, may still be eligible for payment.

LO 5

Assistance provided to retirees

To ensure that retirees have an adequate level of income in retirement, the government provides retirees in need with access to income support and a range of concessions. The main form of income support for retirees in need is known as the age pension. The age pension is administered through Centrelink and is paid on the basis of a retiree satisfying certain eligibility criteria.

The age pension is paid fortnightly and is reviewed twice yearly, in March and September, to keep in line with the greater of the consumer price index (CPI) and changes in the male total average weekly earnings (MTAWE). Commencing from March 2010, the age pension is indexed against the MTAWE at a rate of 27.7% for singles and 41.76% for couples combined.

Age test eligibility for the age pension

age test
a test that requires persons to reach a certain age before being eligible for the age pension

As well as satisfying residency requirements and a means test qualification, retirees accessing the age pension are also required to satisfy an **age test**. Men must have reached 65 years before they are eligible to apply for the age pension. Historically, the age pension eligibility age for women was 60, but this has been progressively increased over the years so that from 1 July 2013, women must also have reached 65 years of age.

One of the recommendations of the 2009 Henry Review looking into Australia's future tax system was that the age pension age should be lifted further. The following is an extract from that report.

> The age at which pensions become available should be responsive to the increase in life expectancy and longevity. For a century, the Age Pension age has been 65 years for men. To support system sustainability, and fairness, and to ensure that social policies adapt to changes in the life circumstances of people, the Age Pension age should rise modestly and gradually to age 67 years. This would provide a strong social signal about work and retirement expectations and their link to increasing life expectancies. The increase in the Age Pension age should be part of a suite of polices to increase the social and workforce participation of older Australians (Commonwealth of Australia 2009, pp. 16–17).

This recommendation was adopted by the government and as a result, the age pension age for men and women will be increased progressively to age 67 commencing in 2017, as detailed in table 13.5.

TABLE 13.5 Increase in pension age eligibility for the age pension

Effective from	Age pension age
1 July 2017	65.5 years
1 July 2019	66 years
1 July 2021	66.5 years
1 July 2023	67 years

Source: Australian Government, *Guide to social security law*, 2013.

The age service pension is the equivalent of the age pension but is paid to eligible ex-defence-service claimants. The age requirements are the same as for the age pension.

LO 6 Means testing

In order to determine how much benefit is paid to an applicant, a means testing system is generally used. The means testing regime considers both an asset test and an income test subject to some important exceptions. Each test comprises a threshold level and an upper limit with a shade-out zone between these levels. For applicants with incomes or assets levels which are less than the thresholds, the benefit payments are made at the maximum or full rates. Where incomes or assets are greater than the thresholds, the benefits are reduced, and where the upper limits are exceeded no benefits are payable.

The principal rules for the application of the assets and incomes tests are as follows.

- Both tests are applied to *pension* applications. Asset and/or income levels that exceed a lower threshold reduce the level of pension payment. The test on assets or income that produces the lower benefit is ultimately applied.
- Both tests are applied to *allowance* applications. However, under the assets test, the lower threshold is a cut-out point which causes the payment to be decreased to zero. No allowance is payable where the person's holding of assets exceeds this lower threshold.
- Some other types of payments are not means tested or are not subject to the assets test (e.g. baby bonus)

As part of its 2009–10 budget, the federal government announced a number of significant changes to the pension system under its Secure and Sustainable Pension Reform. These changes included an increase in the rate of payment for age pensioners and the introduction of the **work bonus scheme** and a pension supplement. As a result of these changes, some pensioners experienced an actual reduction in their pension payment. To prevent any reduction in benefits, the government introduced a transitional pension rate based on the old income and assets tests for those pensioners who were disadvantaged. Where pensioners are paid a transitional rate of pension, DHS will switch the pension over to the new rules rate once this becomes the same as or higher than the transitional rate. Over time, all transitional-rate pensioners will be converted to the new pension system.

work bonus scheme
a scheme that encourages people over age pension age to continue working by allowing them to earn a higher amount of income before their age pension payments are reduced

Assets test

The values applied under the assets tests differ according to the applicant's home ownership status and whether they have a partner. Table 13.6 provides the threshold and upper limits effective to 19 September 2013.

TABLE 13.6 Assets test thresholds and upper limits effective to 19 September 2013

Value		Homeowner	Non-homeowner
Threshold for full benefit	▪ single	$192 500	$332 000
	▪ couple	$273 000	$412 500
Upper limit for part benefit	▪ single	$731 500	$871 000
	▪ couple	$1 086 000	$1 225 500

Source: Department of Human Services 2013a.

From the data in the table, it can be seen that a single pensioner who owns their own home may have up to $192 500 in assessable assets and receive the full age pension. Where a person's assessable assets exceed the lower threshold, the maximum pension entitlement is reduced by a reduction factor. The reduction factor is calculated as a reduction in the maximum pension entitlement of $1.50 for singles (75 cents for each member of a couple) for every $1000 of assets up to the upper limit. Once assessable assets exceed the upper limit or threshold, no pension is payable.

You may notice that the difference between the allowable values for homeowners and non-homeowners for each component in the test is $139 500. This is the notional value of a house. You might think this is a pretty low value for a house in, say, Sydney and, in fact, it might well be impossible to buy a house in any major centre for this price. Setting a fair value for a house Australia-wide is a very difficult task. The notional value of a house has increased only slightly over the years.

Assessable assets

The most important questions in relation to an assets test is 'what assets are counted?' followed by 'how are they valued?' The answer to the first question is 'almost all assets are counted', but there are some limited exemptions from assessment. The main exemption from the asset test is a person's 'principal home'. Other exempt assets include:

- prepaid funeral expenses and funeral bonds (up to $11 750 per person)
- superannuation assets if under age pension age (exemption ceases after reaching age pension age)
- life interests in assets created by others excluding the applicant's partner
- gifts of up to $10 000 per person or couple in a 12-month period provided no more than $30 000 has been gifted in the last 5 years (see gifting rules)
- accommodation bonds paid to an aged care hostel (low-care facility)
- the proceeds of the sale of a principal home for up to 12 months, as long as the proceeds are used to buy another home.

The assets taken into account and assessed include both financial and physical assets. Financial assets are investments such as term deposits, shares, units in managed funds or insurance policies with surrender values. Physical assets include cars, home contents and businesses. Other than the above exemptions, most other assets and investments are assessed.

Superannuation accounts are exempt under both the assets and income tests for social security purposes until a person reaches age pension age. Withdrawals of superannuation by persons under age pension age are also not assessable under either test. The exemption of superannuation from both the assets and income tests may provide opportunities for couples to structure their affairs in order to minimise their asset assessment. Thus, where one member of a couple is under age pension age, for example where the husband is aged 65 and the wife is aged 59, funds may be transferred from the husband into the wife's superannuation account and be exempt under both the assets and income tests. However, the amount of the transfer/contribution is subject to normal super contribution limits.

Principal home

The most significant assets test exemption is the principal home. The principal home may be a house, unit, flat, houseboat, caravan or shack — there is no limit placed on the value. It could be a **life interest** gained under a will in a home owned by someone else. It might also be a $6 million mansion, but it is unlikely such an owner would be applying for the

life interest
an interest in property for the remaining life of the owner or occupant

age pension. Included within the principal home category are permanent fixtures such as garages, swimming pools and garden features, carpets and fixed internal fittings such as dishwashers and stoves. Also included with the house is up to 2 hectares of land on a single title. Some people with a larger area of residential land on more than one title currently have an exemption on this greater area. This is known as the 'private land use test'.

From 1 January 2007, rural applicants have benefited from a concession in that land areas greater than 2 hectares may be exempted, provided:

- the land is on one title
- the applicant has had a long-term (20-year) continuous attachment to the land and house
- the applicant must be making effective use of the land within their physical capacity to do so.

General asset valuation methodology

The general rule for asset valuations including real estate and businesses is net market value. Net market value is fair market value less any debts owing on the asset. Thus, an investment house is valued at market value at the time of the estimate less any debt owing. The DHS generally asks clients to make these valuations, but can call in registered valuers if required to make required estimates.

Special rules apply to home equity conversion loans. Home equity conversion loans, commonly known as **reverse mortgages**, are a loan product whereby a homeowner can convert some home equity to immediate cash by taking out a loan on which both interest and principal repayments are deferred until death or the owner voluntarily leaves the house. If a single lump sum is withdrawn under the loan contract, the first $40 000 is exempt from the assets test for 90 days. Any amount after $40,000 not spent becomes an assessable asset. Any excess loan over $40 000 is assessable as an asset from the time of receipt. If the loan is taken out in the form of regular payments, the payments are not assessable under the assets or income test as long as they are spent immediately on the costs of living.

reverse mortgage
an arrangement to mortgage a home in order to receive payments from the fund provider in return for a percentage ownership in the home or an accumulated debt to be paid when the home is sold

ILLUSTRATIVE EXAMPLE 13.1

Referring to the case study presented at the start of this chapter with Jack and Judy, the couple's assessable assets would consist of the following.

Asset	Value	Status
Family home	$520 000	Exempt
Contents	$ 50 000	Assessable
Cars	$ 35 000	Assessable
Caravan	$ 12 000	Assessable
Bank account	$ 80 000	Assessable
Managed funds	$ 60 000	Assessable
Shares	$240 000	Assessable
Superannuation — Judy	$100 000	Exempt (under 65 years of age)
Superannuation — Jack	$350 000	Assessable
Total assessable assets	**$827 000**	

Income test

Like the assets test, the income test also imposes limits on the amount of income that can be earned for eligibility to either full or part benefits. The income test differs between pensions and allowances. Table 13.7 shows the income limits for the full and part pension for singles and couples.

TABLE 13.7 Income limits for the full and part pensions effective to 19 September 2013

Status	Full pension per fortnight	Part pension per fortnight
Single, no dependent children	152.00	1768.80
Couple, no dependent children	268.00	2705.60

Source: Department of Human Services 2013a.

The pensions payable under the income test are reduced by 50 cents per fortnight for every dollar of income in excess of the full-pension limit for single pensioners (25 cents each for every dollar of income in excess of the full-pension limit for each member of a couple). Thus, for a married couple with a combined assessable income of $1 800 per fortnight, the reduction in their maximum age pension benefit would be ($1800 − $268) × 0.25 = $383 per fortnight each.

Assessable income

For social security purposes, assessable income includes income derived from most sources. It includes income derived from both inside and outside Australia and, if you have a partner, their income and assets are taken into account when working out payment rates. The following is a list of the types of income generally assessable for social security purposes:

- gross income from wages and salaries, including fringe benefits and amounts that are salary sacrificed into superannuation
- income from carrying on a business
- net rental income
- family income trust distributions
- total losses from rental property
- long-term income derived from income-stream products, such as pensions and annuities (short-term income-stream products are subject to deeming rules (discussed in the next section))
- **deemed income** earned from financial assets (discussed in the next section).

deemed income
a notional rate of earnings used by DHS to calculate the investment returns from assets of eligible age pensioners

Deeming of income from financial assets

To discourage the practice of pensioners holding large sums in low-earning accounts, such as cheque accounts, in order to minimise assessable income and thus maximise pension payments, the government introduced deeming provisions in 1996. Deeming provisions apply predetermined rates of return on all financial investments held by a pensioner to determine assessable income regardless of the actual return generated. In other words, the values of all financial assets are added together and it is assumed that they earn certain set rates of return. People are free to invest their money wherever they like, but they have an incentive to invest in assets which earn at least the deeming rates. Any return earned above the deeming rates is non-assessable.

Table 13.8 shows the deeming rates and thresholds effective to 19 September 2013. The thresholds are changed periodically, as are the deeming rates (in line with market interest rates).

TABLE 13.8 Deeming rates for benefit recipients effective to 19 September 2013

Status	Initial rate (%)	Threshold ($)	Upper rate threshold (%)
Single	2.5	45 400	4.0
Couple	2.5	75 600	4.0

Source: Department of Human Services 2013b.

Financial investments generally include most forms of investments held by a pensioner such as bank accounts, shares, managed funds and short-term income streams. However the following are excluded:

- life insurance policies
- rental properties, holiday homes and other real estate
- long-term income-stream products, such as pensions and annuities, with a term of 5 years or more (pensions and annuities having a term of 5 years or less are subject to deeming rules).

As discussed previously, superannuation fund balances for those aged under age pension age are exempt under both the assets and income tests. Once a pensioner reaches age pension age, superannuation is treated as a financial investment and is subject to deeming rules.

ILLUSTRATIVE EXAMPLE 13.2

Referring to the case study presented at the start of this chapter with Jack and Judy, the couple's financial assets and income would consist of the following.

Financial investments	
Bank account	$ 80 000
Managed funds	$ 60 000
Shares	$240 000
Superannuation — Jack	$350 000
Total	$730 000

As Judy is below age pension age, her superannuation account balance is exempt under both the assets and income tests.

Deemed income	
First $75 600 assessed at 2.5%	$ 1 890
Balance of financial investments ($654 400) assessed at 4.0%	$26 176
Total deemed income	$28 066

»

»

Income assessed for taxation purposes	
Bank account — $80 000 @ 2.5%	$ 2 000
Managed funds — $60 000 @ 8%	$ 4 800
Shares — $240 000 @ 3.5%	$ 8 400
Plus imputation credit — 30/70	$ 3 600
Total	**$18 800**

Judy's salary of $15 000 would need to be added to the above figures for both social security and taxation purposes.

As can be seen, while the couple's income for tax purposes, excluding Judy's salary, would be assessed at $18 800, the DHS would assess the couple's income at nearly $10 000 more than this amount. The main reason is that Jack's superannuation account is treated as a financial investment and subject to deeming rates.

Is this difference likely to encourage Jack and Judy to sell their investments in favour of higher yielding investments? Probably not — it depends on the capital gain they would make, the associated capital gains tax and the outlook for the shares held. Is the couple able to do anything with Jack's superannuation account to reduce the income that is assessed by the DHS? As will be seen in a later section in this chapter, rolling over the superannuation into some sort of retirement income stream, such as an account-based pension, is likely to reduce the income that is assessed by the DHS.

Exempt income

home equity conversion (HEC) loan (reverse mortgage) a loan or an amount by which a home owner may draw funds based on the equity or ownership value of the home

The income test exempts some cash flows which are not really income but are payments of capital (such as **home equity conversion (HEC) loans** or **reverse mortgages**), as well as income flows paid by government and the non-cash estimated value of any free board and lodging. Cash inflows exempt under the income test include:

- lump sums received as home equity conversion loans
- general insurance receipts from claims for damage to property
- capital gains realised on the sale of assets
- rent subsidies and most other government transfer payments, such as child support payments and carer allowances
- emergency relief payments
- medical benefits.

In relation to home equity conversion loans, the lump sum received as a loan is exempt as income. However, if the amount is deposited into a bank account and interest is earned, the income will be assessed under deeming rules.

When only one member of the couple is entitled to the age pension

Situations may arise when only one partner is entitled to an age pension. This may occur when only one of the partners satisfies age requirements. In such cases, all of the couple's combined assets and income are used to determine eligibility under the assets and income test regardless of which partner owns the assets or receives the income. Pension payments and reduction factors are based on individual partner rates.

ILLUSTRATIVE EXAMPLE 13.3

Based on the case study involving Jack and Judy provided at the commencement of this chapter, Jack's age pension entitlement would be calculated as provided below. As only Jack satisfied the age eligibility requirement, his pension entitlement will be based on the individual partner rate as will all reduction factors.

Assets test

The couple's assessable assets total \$827 000 (see illustrative example 13.1):

Pension payable under assets test

Jack's pension entitlement is calculated as the maximum pension entitlement less a reduction factor.

$$\begin{aligned}\text{Pension entitlement} &= \$609.40 - [(\$827\,000 - \$273\,000)/\$1000 \times 0.75] \\ &= \$609.40 - \$415.50 \\ &= \$193.90 \text{ per fortnight}\end{aligned}$$

Income test

Based on the calculations determined earlier (see illustrative example 13.2), the couple's financial investments total \$730 000 and generate deemed income of \$28 066. Total assessable income is determined as follows:

Wages	\$15 000
Deemed income	\$28 066
Total income	\$43 066

Their fortnightly income is \$43 066 ÷ 26 weeks = \$1656.38 per fortnight.

Pension payable under income test

Jack's pension entitlement is calculated as the maximum pension entitlement less a reduction factor.

$$\begin{aligned}\text{Pension entitlement} &= \$609.40 - [(\$1656.38 - \$268) \times 0.25] \\ &= \$609.40 - \$347.10 \\ &= \$262.30 \text{ per fortnight}\end{aligned}$$

Pension payable

The test that provides the lowest pension applies. In this case, the age pension payment under the assets test (\$193.90 p.f.) will apply.

Gifted assets

Gifted assets are assets that have been disposed of for less than market value or given away. Pension applicants may be tempted to give away some of their cash or other assets to family members and then claim higher pension entitlements due to a lower holding of assessable assets and/or income earned. The **gifting rules** allow an applicant to give away, without affecting the pension entitlement:

- a maximum of \$10 000 annually, and
- a maximum of \$30 000 over a 5-financial-year rolling period.

gifting rules the rules that restrict the amount of assets able to be given away by pensioners before their age pension entitlements are affected

Any amounts given away above these limits are assessed as assets and income in the hands of the applicant and continue to be so assessed for 5 years. Any gifts made in the 5-year period prior to the initial application for a pension will also be assessed.

PERSONAL FINANCE BULLETIN

Tips for revving up your age pension

At less than $390 a week, Australia's age pension won't provide a flashy retirement amid today's soaring living costs, so claiming every possible cent is vital.

This week the federal government will increase its fortnightly payments to 3.5 million pensioners by up to $17.10, taking the pension for a single person to $772.60. The maximum pension for a couple will rise to $1164.80 a fortnight.

Many pensioners missed out on the benefits of employer superannuation payments, which became compulsory only in the 1990s and have been at the current 9% rate for only a decade.

Some retirees may not have qualified for a pension previously but falling asset values may now make a part-pension possible. People near retirement can ensure they collect the maximum pension through some careful planning.

'The more pension you get, the less you have to draw down on your own retirement savings', says Commonwealth Bank advice senior technical manager Kim Guest. Here are five ways to boost age pension payments or qualify for one.

1. Move money to a spouse's super.
   Assets held in super are exempt from income and assets tests if a person is under pension age.
   AMP financial planner Darren James says a retiree over 60 can cash out their own super tax-free and then inject it into their younger spouse's fund. 'The downside is that this will lock up most of your super until the younger partner reaches the age at which they can access this', he says.
2. Gifting can be good.
   James says pensioners are able to gift up to $10 000 a year, but no more than $30 000 over five years, to stay under the assets test limit.
   'This may assist with a slight increase in age pension entitlements, or potentially enable someone who is not currently eligible', he says.
   Guest says people who plan ahead can gift money years before applying for the pension. 'If it's five years before you apply, that doesn't count (for the tests)', she says.
3. Value assets correctly.
   AustralianSuper head of member advice Frank Ceravolo says when quoting to Centrelink the value of non-investment assets such as home contents and motor vehicles, you need only the estimated current value.
   'While the replacement or insured value of your home contents might be $50 000, if you sold them all this weekend what would they sell for? It might be only $2000–$5000 — this is the value Centrelink is concerned with', he says.

4. Prepay funeral costs.
   Ceravolo says prepaying for your funeral or buying a funeral bond can reduce your level of assets for the Centrelink test. 'Burial plots are not included in assessable assets, and prepaid funeral expenses will not be assessed provided there is a contract in place that sets out the services to be undertaken and no more expenses need to be paid', he says.
   James says funeral bonds are exempt from the asset and income tests up to $11 250.
5. Account-based pension
   Account-based pensions are not just tax free for retirees. They also have a more favourable income test than other financial assets.
   'You can draw up to the non-assessable portion each year without it being assessed as income', James says. 'The non-assessable portion is the commencement account balance divided by your life expectancy at commencement.'

Source: Anthony Keane, News.com.au, 17 September 2012.

The assessment of income streams

Upon retirement, a retiree will normally look to use their superannuation to acquire a financial product that pays them a regular income stream to cover their living costs. In return for providing a lump sum, income-stream products covering pensions and annuities provide a regular income flow to the recipient. While many income-stream products are typically acquired with a person's superannuation account balance, some income-stream products can also be acquired with non-superannuation monies, such as with personal savings or through the sale of an investment property.

The issue that needs to be determined is how retirement income-stream products are assessed for social security purposes.

The assessment of retirement income-stream products for the purposes of the assets and income tests falls under one of the following three categories:

1. **asset-test-exempt income streams** — non-commutable income streams that have a nil residual value
2. asset-tested income streams (long-term) — long-term (more than 5-year) income streams which are assessed on the account balance (such as account-based pensions)
3. asset-tested income streams (short-term) — short-term (less than 5-year) income streams which are assessed on the account balance (such as short-term annuities).

asset-test-exempt income stream
an income-stream product where part or all of the account balance is exempt under the assets test

Rules of assessment under the assets test

For asset-test purposes, most income-stream products under category 2 and 3 above are generally assessed on the actual account balance at any point in time. However, asset-test-exempt income streams (category 1), such as lifetime or life expectancy pensions and annuities and term-allocated pensions, are exempt under the assets test as follows:

- 100% exempt if purchased before 20 September 2004
- 50% exempt if purchased on or after 20 September 2004 and up to 19 September 2007.

All income-stream products acquired after 20 September 2007 are fully assessable.

For pensions and annuities for which there is no account balance, such as with a lifetime pension or annuity, the value of the asset is calculated under a method called

residual capital value (RCV)
the capital amount payable on termination of a pension or annuity

the *original purchase price depletion method*. This method calculates the value of the asset based on the original purchase price reduced periodically for income payments made by the product provider. The following formula is used where income payments are made to the recipient more than once a year and there is no capital sum returned at the end of the term, that is, there is no **residual capital value (RCV)**.

$$PP - \left(\frac{PP}{RN \times 2} \times \text{Completed half years}\right)$$

where: PP = purchase price of the income stream

RN = the relevant number of the income stream. Where the income stream does not have a specified term, for example a lifetime pension, the relevant number used is the member's life expectancy at the time of taking out the income stream. Where the income stream does have a specified term, say a 10-year fixed annuity, the relevant number is the term of the contract.

Completed half years = the number of half years that have passed since the commencement of the contract.

Rules of assessment under the income test

Income-stream products provide regular income payments to the member. In return for providing a capital sum at the commencement of the income stream, the product provider pays the member an ongoing income stream. For each payment made to the member over the term of the income stream, part of the payment will consist of income earned within the fund while part will represent a return of the original purchase price (capital) to the member. For all longer-term income-stream products greater than 5 years (categories 1 and 2), while income earned within the fund is assessable for social security purposes, that part of a payment that relates to the return of capital is exempt.

The deduction for the capital component, known as the deductible amount, is calculated by apportioning the whole of the initial capital invested or the purchase price over the term of the contract or the life expectancy of the beneficiary. The annual income is thus determined as the gross income received less the deductible amount. It should be noted that the deductible amount is determined at the date of original acquisition of the pension and remains fixed thereafter. Thus, assessable income is determined as follows:

$$\text{Gross anual income } \textit{less } \frac{\text{Purchase price}}{\text{Life expectancy or term of pension or annuity}}$$

Current life expectancy tables can be found on the Australian government website 'Social security and family assistance legislation and policy guides' (http://guidesacts.fahcsia.gov.au/guides_acts/ssg/ssguide-4/ssguide-4.9/ssguide-4.9.5.html).

This method for determining the assessable income generally applies to all retirement income-stream products. However, short-term income products (category 3) taken out for less than 5 years, are generally assessed under deeming rules.

On 5 April 2013, as part of the superannuation reform announcements, the government proposed extended the deeming provisions to all superannuation-based income streams. Grandfathering provisions, which ensure that only income streams commencing on or after 1 July 2015 would be caught under this proposal, were also outlined. If this legislation is passed, all account-based pensions will be assessed under the deeming rules for income test purposes.

ILLUSTRATIVE EXAMPLE 13.4

Continuing on from the case study based on Jack and Judy, assume that Jack decides to roll over his superannuation account balance of $350 000 into an account-based pension. Jack's life expectancy at the time of acquiring the income stream at age 65 is 18.54 years.

In two years, with Jack aged 67, how will the income stream be assessed for DHS purposes given that the balance of the account-based pension has risen to $360 000 and Jack takes an income withdrawal of $30 000 for that year? The value of the asset for age pension purposes is calculated as the current balance of the account-based pension, that is, $360 000.

Jack's assessable income under the income test for age pension purposes is calculated as:

$$\$30\,000 - \frac{\$350\,000}{18.54} = \$11\,122$$

Note that the deductible (tax-free) amount is based on the original amount of the account-based pension and the life expectancy at the time that the account-based pension was first acquired. In other words, the deductible amount remains the same each year.

Work bonus

From 20 September 2009, those eligible to receive an age pension may be entitled to disregard some of their employment income under the income test. The work bonus allows those eligible to receive an age pension to disregard the first $250 per fortnight of assessable employment income. For those not working, the entire fortnightly work bonus amount of $250 is saved and added to the individual's work bonus balance. The work bonus balance can reach a maximum of $6500.

The work bonus replaced the pension bonus scheme, which was closed to new entrants from 20 September 2009. Those registered with the pension bonus scheme prior to 20 September 2009 continue to receive this bonus payment.

Means testing of allowances

Allowance recipients use the same assets test thresholds as shown in table 13.6. However, unlike pension payments, no allowance is paid where the level of assets exceeds the lower threshold. The income test for the payment of allowances is slightly more complicated. Table 13.9 (overleaf) shows the threshold and upper-limit rates for a number of allowances including the Newstart, widow, partner and sickness allowances. Fortnightly income in excess of $62 and up to $250 reduces the payable benefit by 50 cents per dollar, and income above $250 reduces the benefit by 60 cents in the dollar.

TABLE 13.9 Income test limits for allowances to 19 September 2013

	Limits ($ per fortnight)	
Status	Full allowance	Part allowance
Single, no dependent children	62	935.67
Single, dependent children	62	1004.84
Partnered (each)	62	853.84
Single, principal carer with dependent children	62	1429.25

Source: Department of Human Services 2013a.

LO 7

Assistance provided to families raising children

family tax benefit income support paid to eligible families to assist them with the cost of raising children

adjusted taxable income (ATI) adjustments made to taxable income to determine eligibility for a number of family assistance and DHS payments, and tax offsets and rebates

The DHS provides assistance to families through a range of benefits. The chief benefits are **family tax benefit** part A, family tax benefit part B, baby bonus, maternity immunisation allowance, child care rebate and parenting payment.

For the purposes of satisfying an income test for eligibility to a number of family benefits, including family tax benefits, child care benefit and baby bonus, an income test based on **adjusted taxable income (ATI)** is used.

An individual's ATI is made up of:

- taxable income
- the value of any adjusted fringe benefits (total reportable fringe benefit amounts multiplied by 0.535)
- reportable employer superannuation contributions
- target foreign income
- total net investment losses
- tax-free pension or benefit.

Family tax benefit part A

The family tax benefit part A provides assistance to low- and medium-income families for the cost of raising children. Residency and income testing eligibility rules apply, but some allowance is made when a family may be required to live temporarily overseas. Claimants must be living in Australia on a permanent basis and be Australian citizens, holders of permanent visas, New Zealand citizens or holders of one of some specific temporary visa. The benefit is payable to families with dependent children under 16 years of age, dependent children aged 16 or 17 years and completed a Year 12 or equivalent qualification, or for children aged 16–19 years (up to the end of the calendar year they turn 19) and undertaking full-time education or training in an approved course leading to a Year 12 or equivalent qualification.

The child or student will not be classified as a dependant if they are receiving some sort of government pension or benefit, are not studying full-time and their annual income is $14 078 or more effective 1 July 2013. Payment is made for each dependent child. The payment is not assets tested. The maximum rates of benefits are shown in table 13.10.

TABLE 13.10 Maximum rate of family tax benefit part A payable, effective 1 July 2013

For each dependent child	Payment per fortnight	Payment p.a. (includes supplement of $726.35)
Under 13 years	$172.20	$5215.85
13–15 years	$224.00	$6566.35
16–19 years, secondary student	$224.00	$6566.35
16–17 years, completed year 12	$55.16	$2164.45

Source: Department of Human Services 2013a.

The supplement is paid after the end of the financial year once a tax return has been lodged. Maximum family benefits are payable where family adjusted taxable income is less than $48 837 p.a. (effective 1 July 2013). Part payments are available as family income rises. Where income levels are above $48 837 p.a., entitlement to the maximum benefit reduces by 20 cents for each dollar above $48 837 until the payment reaches the 'base rate' of family tax benefit part A. The base rate is $55.16 per fortnight for each child, or $2164.45 p.a. for each child including the supplement. The base amount of family tax benefit part A will reduce by 30 cents for every dollar of adjusted taxable income over $94 316 p.a. (plus $3796 p.a. for each child after the first) until payment reaches nil.

Family tax benefit part B

The government has extended assistance to single-income families with children and to families with one main income earner where one parent chooses to stay at home to look after the children through the family tax benefit part B. To be eligible for a part B benefit, a family must have a dependent child under the age of 16 or have a qualifying dependent full-time student up to the age of 18 (who does not receive a youth allowance or a similar benefit).

The maximum amount of family tax benefit part B payable depends upon the age of the youngest child as shown in table 13.11.

TABLE 13.11 Maximum rate of family tax benefit part B payable, effective 1 July 2013

Age of youngest child	Payment per fortnight	Payment p.a. (includes supplement of $354.05 per family)
Under 5 years	$146.44	$4171.95
5–15 years (or 16–18 years if a full-time student)	$102.20	$3018.55

Source: Department of Human Services 2013a.

The supplement is paid after the end of the financial year once a tax return has been lodged.

Income test for sole-parent families

Sole parents will receive the maximum part B benefit if they have an income of $150 000 or less.

Income test for two-parent families

The maximum part B benefit will be payable where the higher income earner in a couple has an income of $150 000 or less. The income of the lower income earner determines how much part B benefit the family will receive. The lower income earner can earn up to $5183 p.a. before the maximum part B benefit is reduced. The maximum benefit is reduced by 20 cents for each dollar of income earned over $5183 p.a.

A couple will still receive some part B payment if the income of the lower income earner is less than:

- $26 390 p.a. where the age of the youngest child is under 5 years
- $20 532 p.a. where the age of the youngest child is aged between 5 and 18 years.

The payment is not assets tested.

Schoolkids bonus

The purpose of the schoolkids bonus is to provide assistance for families and students in relation to the payment of education costs. Eligibility for the bonus is based on the family or student receiving the Family Tax Benefit Part A for a dependent child who is in primary or secondary education, or a primary or secondary student turning 19 years or younger in the calendar year, who receives certain government payments. There is no asset test and the income test is based on eligibility to the Family Tax Benefit Part A.

Families will not have to apply for the bonus. Eligible families will receive the schoolkids bonus in two instalments as follows:

- for each child in primary school — $205 each instalment (total of $410 each year)
- for each child in secondary school — $410 each instalment (total of $820 each year).

Baby bonus

The baby bonus assists parents with the costs associated with the birth (including stillbirth) or adoption of a child. The payment is income tested but not subject to an assets test. The bonus is paid where eligibility requirements for the Family Tax Benefit for the child are met within 26 weeks of the child's birth. The full amount is paid for each child in multiple births. For the period from 30 June 2013, the benefit is $5000 for the first child and all multiple births and $3000 for all subsequent children. The income test is based on a combined adjusted family income of $75 000 or less in the 6 months following the birth or adoption.

Claims must be made within 52 weeks of a child's birth or coming into claimants' care. The payment is paid in 13 fortnightly instalments.

Child care benefit

approved child care
child care that has been approved by the Australian government for child care benefit purposes because it meets certain standards and requirements

registered child care
child care provided by relatives, friends or other persons who are registered as child carers with the Family Assistance Office

A child care benefit is paid to parents who use approved or registered child care. **Approved child care** is normally offered by long day care, family day care, before- and after-school care and vacation care centres. **Registered child care** is usually offered by nannies, relatives or friends and can include care provided by private preschools, kindergartens and some outside-school-hours care services. Registered carers must be registered with the Family Assistance Office.

Eligibility for the Child Care Benefit is based on the following:

- using approved or registered child care
- being responsible for paying the child care fees for the child
- the child being immunised (or on an immunisation catch-up schedule) or is exempt from the immunisation requirements
- meets the residency requirements.

Parents who use approved child care can receive up to 24 hours of child care benefit per child per week. Parents using approved child care and who are working, looking for work, studying or training for at least 15 hours a week can claim up to 50 hours of child care benefit per child per week.

For parents using registered care, up to 50 hours per child per week of child care benefit is available if parents are working, training or studying at some time during the week.

The maximum rate for approved care for a non-school child is $199.50 for a 50 hour week. The maximum rate for registered care for a child is $0.666 per hour up to $33.30 per week (from 1 July 2013).

Income test for approved care

If the family income is less than $41 902 (from 1 July 2013), the parent will receive the maximum rate of child care benefit. Once family income rises above the income limits shown in table 13.12, payment will be reduced to zero. However, if the benefit is reduced to zero due to the application of the income test, parents may still be eligible for the child care rebate. Registered care is not subject to an income test.

TABLE 13.12 Maximum income limits beyond which approved child care benefit is not payable, from 1 July 2013

Number of children in approved care	Income limits
1	$145 642
2	$150 914
3	$170 404 + $32 219 for each child in care after the third

Source: Department of Human Services 2013a.

Registered care has no asset or income test.

Child care rebate

A child care rebate is available for parents who:

- use approved child care
- are eligible for child care benefit (at a rate of zero or more)
- are working, looking for work, training or studying (no minimum number of hours is required).

The rebate covers 50 per cent of out-of-pocket child care costs up to an annual cap of $7500 per child per year (2013–14). Out-of-pocket costs include amounts paid after the child care benefit has been taken out.

There is no income test for the child care rebate.

LO 8 Assistance provided to those with a disability or impairment

A number of support services are available to people with disabilities and to carers of people with severe disability. These services include the disability support pension, sickness allowance and carer payment.

disability support pension
a pension paid to people who have a physical, intellectual or psychiatric impairment

Disability support pension

The **disability support pension** provides a level of income for people who have a physical, intellectual or psychiatric impairment assessed under impairment tables at 20 points or more. To qualify for a disability support pension, a person must:

- be over 16 but less than age pension age
- be unable to work for 15 hours or more per week for the next 2 years as a result of the impairment
- meet the requirements for Australian residency and the income and assets tests for pensions
- be unable to undertake a training activity due to the impairment which would equip the person for work within the next 2 years, or
- be permanently blind.

In situations where a person has been working and has suffered an injury as a result of the working environment, a range of other factors are taken into account before any disability support pension may be payable.

The rate for the disability support pension is the same as the age pension (detailed earlier in this chapter), except where the claimant is aged less than 21 years and has no children. The benefit is means tested under the assets and income tests as a pension payment.

Sickness allowance

The sickness allowance is paid to eligible claimants aged 22 years and over but under age pension age who are temporarily incapacitated for work or full-time study. They must have a job or student place to which they can return when well. Illness must be verified by a medical certificate. Applicants must be Australian residents and have been in Australia for at least 2 years. The allowance is paid at Newstart allowance rates and is means tested as an allowance.

Carer payment

The carer payment is payable to eligible carers who provide daily care for either an adult or child who is being nursed at home. The carer payment is paid at the same rate as the age pension.

The person being cared for must:

- require care in their home or in hospital
- meet an income and assets test unless they receive an eligible pension or benefit paid from DHS or the Department of Veterans Affairs
- meet the residence requirements, and either
  - be an adult 16 years or over with a medically assessed physical, intellectual or psychiatric disability, or frail aged, or
  - be an adult 16 years or over with a medically assessed physical, intellectual or psychiatric disability, or frail aged, with a dependent child in their care.

The carer must:

- personally provide constant care, in the home, to someone with a disability or medical condition, or who is frail aged
- meet the income and assets tests
- be living in Australia and meet residence requirements.

LO 9 Support for those undertaking study or an Australian apprenticeship

The government pays a number of allowances to support those undertaking study or an apprenticeship.

Austudy

Austudy provides income support to students aged 25 years or over undertaking qualifying study or a full-time Australian apprenticeship. Courses approved for Austudy payment include secondary education, undergraduate courses, graduate courses (excluding most Masters Degrees and all doctorates), TAFE courses and associate diplomas. Full-time students under the age of 25 may be eligible for the youth allowance.

Austudy
an Australian education assistance scheme that provides financial support to those aged 25 years and over and studying or undertaking an Australian apprenticeship full-time

The basic rate of payment from 1 July 2013 is:

- $407.50 per fortnight for a single or partnered person with no children
- $533.80 per fortnight for a single person with children
- $447.40 per fortnight for a partnered person with children.

Assets and income means tests

The assets means test is the same as for pensions and a number of other allowances.

Under the income test, the full benefit under Austudy will be paid where the student's or apprentice's income is less than $405 per fortnight (from 1 July 2013). Income above the income-free area reduces payment by 50 cents in the dollar.

Austudy students are also allowed to accumulate up to $10 000 of any unused portion of their $405 fortnightly income-free area which can be used to offset against income earned in excess of $405. Australian apprentices can accumulate up to $1000 of any unused portion of their income-free area. This is known as the income bank.

Youth allowance

The **youth allowance** is payable to full-time students and Australian apprentices aged between 16 and 24 or students who are temporarily incapacitated for full-time study aged 22–24. Job seekers under 22 years, either looking for work or combining part-time study with job search, or undertaking other approved activity or temporarily incapacitated for work or study, may also be eligible. Those aged 25 and over may also qualify if they were receiving the youth allowance immediately before turning 25.

youth allowance
financial support for young people who are studying, undertaking training or an Australian apprenticeship, looking for work or sick

If the recipient is not independent, a parental income test and a family assets test will apply. Otherwise the recipient will be subject to personal income and assets tests. If not independent, the rate reduces if the parents' income exceeds the income threshold of $47 815. If the recipient is independent, the personal income test applies. The income-free area is $143 per fortnight for job seekers and $405 per fortnight for students and Australian apprentices.

Rates of payment (from 1 July 2013) include:

Single no children	
– aged under 18 and at home	$223.00 pf
– aged under 18 and away from home	$407.50 pf
Single with children	$533.80 pf
Partnered with children	$447.40 pf

LO 10 Taxation of pensions and allowances

The taxation of social security benefits introduces more complexity to the social security field. Some pensions and allowances are taxable and some are not. In addition, some social security benefits attract a tax offset to reduce a person's overall tax liability. A tax offset directly reduces the tax payable by taxpayers on their taxable income, whereas a tax deduction reduces taxable income and therefore the tax payable.

Some of the more common taxable pensions and allowances are:

- age pension
- age service pension
- Austudy
- bereavement allowance
- carer payment with some exceptions
- disability support pension — for person of age pension age
- Newstart allowance
- parenting payment
- sickness allowance
- widow allowance
- youth allowance.

Some of the more common non-taxable pensions and allowances are:

- carer allowance
- carer payment — if both carer and the cared-for are under age pension age
- child care benefit
- disability support pension — if under age pension age
- disaster relief
- double orphan pension
- Family tax benefit (A) and (B).

Newstart allowance an allowance paid to unemployed persons while they are looking for work

The benefits that are taxable are, in the main, those which are paid in substitute of employment income. For example, **Newstart allowances**, age pensions and disability support pensions are paid to people as a result of their inability to find work or because they are regarded as too old to work. In contrast, benefits that are not taxable are those designed to top up other income and give individuals and families specific financial assistance for special purposes such as maternity, pharmaceuticals, rent and living in a remote area.

Seniors and pensioners tax offset (SAPTO)

The senior and pensioners tax offset (SAPTO) is payable to persons of age pension age who are self-funded retirees. The tax offset provides a tax concession for those retirees on a low income who satisfy eligibility for an Australian government pension but who do not qualify because of the application of the means test. Each member of a couple is tested separately for SAPTO eligibility.

The rebate amount and thresholds for 2013–14 are detailed in table 13.13:

TABLE 13.13 The SAPTO tax offset and thresholds for 2013–14

Family status	Maximum tax offset	Shade-out threshold	Cut-out threshold
Single	$2230	$32 279	$50 119
Couple (each)	$1602	$28 974	$41 790
Couple (separated due to illness)	$2040	$31 279	$47 599

The shade-out threshold is the level of income at which individuals will be entitled to the maximum tax offset. The tax offset reduces by 12.5 cents for each dollar of rebate income in excess of the shade-out threshold.

The income test for SAPTO is based on income known as 'rebate income' which includes:

- taxable income
- adjusted fringe benefits (that is, the total reportable fringe benefits amount multiplied by 0.535)
- reportable employer superannuation contributions and deductible personal superannuation contributions
- total net investment loss.

LO 11 Accommodation in retirement

One of the considerations that persons need to make as they grow older is the need for some form of alternative accommodation. This is an important issue when planning a retirement strategy not only because of the emotional stress of moving, but also because of the costs and charges levied with the alternative accommodation and the effect that moving will have on social security entitlements.

The various accommodation options available to a person in retirement include:

- remaining in their principal residence
- special residence options
  - retirement villages
  - granny flats
- aged care accommodation options
  - low-level care
  - high-level care.

The Australian government spends more than $11 billion annually on residential aged care facilities. Two levels of residential aged care are provided in Australia. These are low-level (hostel) services and high-level (nursing home) services. These aged care services are quite separate from the facilities provided in retirement villages and granny flats, which constitute a different segment entirely of the housing market.

Special residence

Retirement villages

Retirement villages generally accommodate people, both singles and couples, aged over 55. Some complexes include both retirement villages and aged care homes, which may include low-level care and sometimes high-level care. Retirement villages are funded by residents' payments, loans or donations (also known as entry contributions) and by ongoing fees and charges. The amount of entry contribution required will vary according to the retirement village and the kind of accommodation chosen. Some villages base their entry contribution on the actual purchase price or market value of a unit in the facility. Residents of a retirement home also need to pay ongoing fees and charges for services and facilities. Fees for those residents living in a self-care or serviced unit are set by the retirement village. There is no government legislation that sets these fees. A departure or exit fee is normally also payable on leaving the retirement village and is usually determined by a formula that takes into account entry costs, sale proceeds and years of occupancy. This fee will vary between retirement villages.

Granny flats

Under the *Guide to social security law* (para. 4.6.4.50) a granny flat is defined as:

A life interest or right to accommodation for life where:

- the person 'pays' for a life interest or right to accommodation for life, AND
- the life interest or right to accommodation for life is in a private residence that is to be the person's principal home.

A granny flat interest does not include where a person is the owner or part-owner of the property. In this case, the person has the right to live in the property because of their ownership. The assessed value of a granny flat interest is normally the same as the amount paid for the interest and could include the value of the transfer of the title of their home, the costs paid for the construction and fit out of premises, or where a property has been purchased in another person's name in return for a life interest or the right to accommodation for life.

Social security implications of entering special residences

One of the issues in moving into special residences, such as a retirement village or granny flat, is how any age pension entitlement will be affected. For DHS purposes, the amount of the entry contribution to a retirement village or granny flat determines whether the age pension recipient is assessed as a homeowner or non-homeowner. Where the entry contribution paid to enter a special residence is greater than the difference between the pension single/couple asset test threshold for a homeowner and that of a non-homeowner ($142 500 as at 1 July 2013), the person will be assessed as a homeowner under the assets test. The amount of the entry contribution in this case will not be assessed as an asset. If the entry contribution is less than $142 500, the person will be considered a non-homeowner under the assets test. In this case, the entry contribution will be considered an assessable asset but not subject to deeming rates.

If a person is living in a special residence and retains their former principal home, the home will be assessable under the assets test and any rental income will be assessable under the income test. Where a person's former principal home is sold, the proceeds from sale will be treated as an assessable financial investment and subject to deeming rates. If some or all of the proceeds are to be used to pay for the entry contribution to the special residence, the amount will be treated as an exempt asset for up to 12 months until payment is made. However, the whole proceeds will still be subject to deeming rates.

The other issue of particular concern for granny flats is whether the amount paid for the accommodation is reasonable and whether the gifting rules have been breached. In these cases, a reasonableness test is applied.

Aged care accommodation

Following the reforms introduced by the *Aged Care Act 1997*, hostels and nursing homes were brought under one regulation regime. The residential aged care system now has two levels of care — low and high. Hostels generally provide low-level residential care and nursing homes provide high-level care for people who have been assessed by an aged care assessment team (ACAT) as needing those levels of assistance. Many establishments specialise in one level of care but others provide both high- and low-level care so that residents may enter under hostel arrangements and later move on to higher level nursing-home care in a different section of the same establishment.

ACATs assess people in terms of their ability to cope with their clinical needs, personal hygiene, daily living, communication, and social and emotional support structures. Clients are currently assessed on a scale containing eight grades.

A summary of the costs involved in aged care accommodation is shown in figure 13.1. These costs are discussed in further detail later in this chapter.

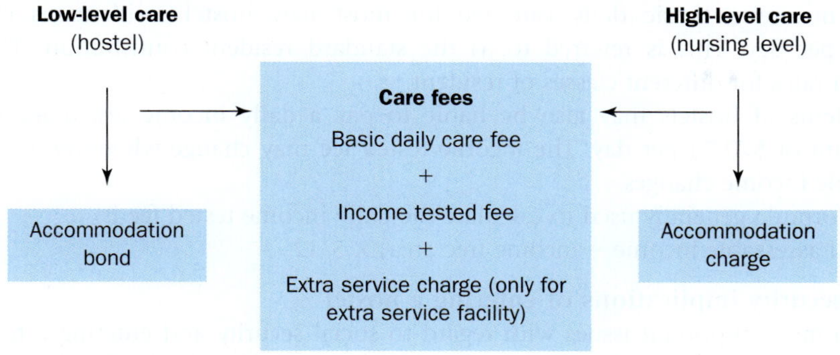

FIGURE 13.1 Summary of the costs involved in aged care accommodation

Hostel accommodation

Residents in **hostel accommodation** generally require a lower level of care than residents of a nursing home. Hostel residents can pay up to three types of fees:

- accommodation bond
- basic daily care fee
- income tested fee.

hostel accommodation aged care accommodation that provides low-level care places for people who need some help

Hostel construction is paid for by means of accommodation bonds. New residents make a refundable payment in the form of an interest-free loan, to the managers of the hostel as well as paying daily care fees.

An accommodation bond is a fixed amount paid on entry to a hostel. It can be paid as a lump sum, in periodic payments or a combination of the two. The hostel retains a monthly amount from the bond for up to 5 years which must not exceed $331 per month for bonds in excess of $39 720 and $171 per month for bonds of no more than $20 520 (to 30 June 2014). The amount of the accommodation bond less a monthly retention amount is repaid to the resident upon them either moving to high-level care, where they pay an accommodation charge, or paid to the resident's estate upon their death. Accommodation bond repayment is guaranteed by the government.

The size of the accommodation bond is determined by the hostel management and is based on the value of assets owned by the new resident. DHS and the DVA assess the ability of new residents to pay a bond. This measure was introduced to provide consistency of assessment between providers. Currently, the government intervenes in this process only by stipulating that hostels cannot charge accommodation bonds of an amount that would leave residents with less than $43 000 in assets (from 1 July 2013). This figure is based on 2.25 times the maximum annual single basic age pension rounded to the nearest $500. Where a resident has assets less than $43 000, the hostel provider receives a full rate of government assistance.

Operators cannot force new entrants to pay accommodation bonds during the first 6 months of residence, although residents may choose to do so. However, where a bond is not paid immediately after it is determined, interest may be charged on the outstanding amount of the bond until it is paid. Residents may choose not to pay the bond but to pay the interest that such a lump sum would have earned if invested. Alternatively, some residents choose to pay part lump-sum bond and part interest on the outstanding amount. The maximum permissible interest rate is 6.82% (to 19 September 2013).

Care fees

In addition to the entry contribution, residents pay daily care fees and may be required to also pay a daily income tested fee. These fees contribute to the ongoing costs of nursing, personal care, meals, laundry, light, heating/cooling etc. Daily care fees are charged at stepped rates, depending on residents' means.

The maximum basic daily care fee for most new hostel residents is currently $43.22 per day. This is referred to as the standard resident contribution. There are different rates for different classes of resident.

Residents of hostels may also be liable to pay a daily income tested fee up to a maximum of $70.74 per day. The income tested fee may change whenever a resident's assessable income changes.

The formula generally used to calculate the daily income tested fee is:

(Total assessable income − income free area) × 5/12

Social security implications of entering a hostel

The two most important issues with regard to social security and entering a hostel are how accommodation bonds and the value of former principal homes are treated in the calculation of pension entitlements.

Thresholds for the income free area change periodically. Lump sum accommodation bonds paid by residents in aged care homes are exempt from the pension assets test. Where a resident retains their principal home, they will be assessed as a homeowner. The former principal home is exempted from the pension assets test for 2 years for all people entering residential care. While the home is occupied by a partner, spouse or dependent child, it is classed as an exempt asset. Additionally, this exemption will remain in force for 2 years after the second member of a couple leaves the home. If the home is retained and rented out to assist in paying for the accommodation bond, which is being paid by way of periodic payments, the home and the rental income will be exempt from the pension assets and income tests for as long as the periodic payment continues.

PROFESSIONAL ADVICE

Negotiating aged care accommodation bonds

Donna is single, has become too frail to continue living in her home and is looking to move into a residential facility near her family. Donna's family have looked at a number of facilities around the area and have chosen one that has been newly renovated and has a good reputation.

After discussions with the manager of the facility, the family are advised that the accommodation bond required to be paid is set at a minimum of $500 000 and may be higher based on the size of the room required and the resident's level of assessable assets.

Donna's family has undertaken a number of strategies over the past few years, with the result that Donna has been left with her home and contents worth $420 000 and $60 000 contained in some bank accounts and term deposits. The ACAT team have provided Donna with an asset assessment form which Donna completes and sends into to the DHS. The DHS will verify the information in the form to calculate her level of assessable assets and the maximum bond she is eligible to pay. The maximum bond is calculated as the assessable assets less $43 000 (up to 19 September 2013). Donna's assessable assets amount to $480 000 and she receives a letter from the DHS stating the maximum bond she can pay is $437 000.

A week later, Donna's family receives a phone call to say that a place has become available and an appointment is made to discuss the opportunity for her to move in.

However, the facility is firm that the minimum bond is $500 000. To admit Donna, they would need to accept a lower bond.

QUESTIONS

1 Does the facility have to offer Donna a place based on an accommodation bond of only $437 000?

2 If the facility demands an accommodation bond of $500 000, is it too late for Donna's family to gift funds to Donna to bring her assessable assets up to $500 000?

3 How will the accommodation bond be assessed under the asset and income test for age pension purposes?

Nursing home accommodation

Nursing home accommodation residents generally require a higher level of care than residents of a hostel. The government's policy on charging residents of nursing homes is extremely liberal. There is no ongoing lump-sum accommodation bond as there is for entry to a hostel. There is, however, an accommodation charge for some entrants. The accommodation charge is a periodic charge which is payable on entry to a nursing home that meets the government's minimum building and care standards.

nursing home accommodation aged care accommodation that provides high-level care for people who need 24-hour nursing assistance

In addition to a range of fees, as discussed below, residents who enter care with assets in excess of $43 000 (to 19 September 2013) may be asked to pay an accommodation charge. This means that the accommodation charge for people with assets of $43 000 or less is zero. The amount of the accommodation charge is based on the value of the assets held by the resident. Where the resident's assets at entry are at least $112 243.20, the daily accommodation charge will be assessed at the maximum applicable rate, which is $33.29 per day. On asset levels of less than $112 243.20, DHS will advise the fee. The aged care provider can be asked to defer payment or have the payment taken from the entrant's estate upon their death. If this is agreed to by the aged care provider, the provider will be entitled to charge interest on the unpaid amount at no more than double the lowest pension deeming rate applicable at the time of the entrant entering the home, which is currently 5% (to 19 September 2013).

In addition to the accommodation charge, nursing home residents can pay up to three types of fees:

1. basic daily care fee
2. income-tested fee
3. extra services fee (only charged by extra services nursing homes).

The first two fees were covered above.

Social security implications of entering a nursing home

The social security implications of entering a nursing home involve the assessment of the former principal home and the entitlement to rent assistance. The assessment of the former home involves the same conditions and issues as assessment of the former home for hostel entrants. Aged care residents who pay an accommodation charge are able to rent out their former home without the value of the home or the rental income affecting their aged care fees and, if applicable, their pension.

The former home is exempted from the pension assets test for 2 years for all people entering residential care. While the home is occupied by a partner, spouse or dependent child, it is classed as an exempt asset.

Summary

The provision of social security measures has expanded dramatically during the last century in Australia although the eligibility requirements are gradually being tightened. Protagonists argue that helping our fellow community members financially is one mark of a civilised society and there are also humanitarian, utilitarian and economic arguments for such expenditures. The range of possible social security benefits is wide and has grown to include benefits designed to assist a diverse community in almost any form of need. About one-third of Australia's population receives some form of income assistance, to a greater or lesser extent.

The government's purse, however, is not bottomless, even in these times of relative prosperity. Thus, there is a comprehensive system of means testing for most benefits. Means testing involves both assets and income testing to ensure that benefits are only paid to those in need. Even so, the upper limits of assets and income for some benefits are particularly liberal.

Age pension benefits have been part of Australian culture for over 100 years and currently form the basis of retirement income for 70–80% of the retired population. The work bonus scheme and the Commonwealth Seniors Health Care card supplement the age pension as mechanisms to assist the aged.

Families raising children enjoy a comprehensive set of financial benefits to help compensate them financially for the extra costs they bear in raising children who, to some extent, provide population benefits to the whole of our society. These family based benefits include general benefits such as the family tax benefits and baby bonus, and specific benefits such as the child care benefit and the maternity immunisation allowance.

People with disabilities who are unable to work to support themselves are able to apply for the disability support pension if they are likely to be disabled for at least the next 2 years, while those with temporary sickness or disability may apply for the sickness allowance. There are also other allowances to assist disabled people.

The taxation of government pensions and allowances is a complex area. Some pensions and allowances are taxed at normal rates and others are not. Generally, the benefits that are taxed are those which are substitutes for employment income, while those untaxed include supplements to employment income.

With regard to the issue of housing for the aged who can no longer live in their own home, a number of different alternatives exist including special residence and residential aged care, depending upon the ability of the person to care for themself. The government provides funding for residential aged care at two levels — low and high care. In addition, government funding is available for home and community care to keep people at home as long as possible. There are social security implications for both low- and high-care residents.

Professional application questions

13.1 Should every person reaching the age of 65 be entitled to receive a certain amount of age pension based on the fact that they have paid taxes all their working life?

13.2 Should employment income be assessed in a concessionary fashion for age pension entitlement purposes to encourage ongoing worker participation?

13.3 Why are there still so many Australians receiving the age pension when most employees have been receiving a superannuation guarantee contribution since 1992?

13.4 Should the government place a cap on the amount of the family home that is exempted from the social security assets test?

13.5 What are the implications for an aged pensioner gifting $20 000 in a financial year to their family?

13.6 How is an account-based pension assessed for social security purposes?

13.7 For the purposes of maximising an age pension entitlement, is it better for a pensioner to retain their retirement funds in superannuation or roll over their funds into a retirement income stream? Discuss.

13.8 Margaret sells her family home and pays her son an amount of $320 000 to acquire an interest in a granny flat behind her son's house. The granny flat has a market value of $250 000. What issues might DHS have with the amount paid by Margaret for the granny flat?

13.9 What is included within the definition of 'adjusted taxable income' and why do you believe the government introduced this concept as a means of determining eligibility to family assistance?

13.10 Is it fair that an older person might be forced to sell their family home in order to fund an accommodation bond? Explain.

Professional application exercises

Basic	*
Moderate	* *
Challenging	* * *

13.11 Asset test assessment *

Peter is single and aged 69 years. He lives in his own home and has $350 750 in various assessable assets. How much would the assets test reduce his age pension per fortnight?

13.12 Income test assessment *

Betty is a single age pensioner. She has just sold her house and entered an aged care hostel. After paying her mortgage loan and the accommodation bond, she is left with total assets of $180 000 in cash. Regardless of where she holds these funds, what is her annual deemed income?

13.13 Age pension entitlement *

Bert is a single age pensioner. His assessable assets total $520 000, which includes $240 000 of financial investments. Bert still works part-time and earns a salary of $15 000 p.a. Calculate Bert's age pension benefit entitlement on the basis that he is a homeowner.

13.14 Gifting rules ✱

Dom and Bernie are age pensioners and have assets of $300 000. They wish to gift their son, Roberto, an amount of $40 000 to help him acquire a new home. How should they do this without affecting their age pension entitlement?

13.15 Aged care accommodation ✱

Cassie is an age pensioner who owns a unit worth about $340 000. She is assessed by an aged care assessment team (ACAT) and enters an aged care hostel. She also has $30 000 in cash. What is the most likely assessed accommodation bond? Why?

13.16 Assessment of retirement income streams ✱✱

Yin Ling is aged 67 and has an expectation of a long life. However, she does not want to commit her superannuation to a lifetime annuity at her stage of life and would prefer to invest her $220 000 in an account-based pension fund. On the basis that she withdraws an income of $25 000 p.a. from the account-based pension, how will this income stream be treated under the assets and income tests?

13.17 Age pension entitlement ✱✱

Geoff and Hilary are age pensioners and have the following assets:

Home	$600 000
Contents	$50 000
Car	$15 000
Investment property — net rental income of $10 000	$420 000
Shares — dividend yield of 4%	$100 000
Bank account —interest rate of 2%	$10 000
Superannuation — return of 6%	$200 000
Term deposit — interest rate of 4%	$50 000

Calculate their entitlement for the age pension.

13.18 Age pension entitlement ✱✱

Mr and Mrs Wu are a pensioner couple. They own their own home and have no dependants. Their home is valued at $380 000 and needs repair, and they have the following assets:

Superannuation — Mr Wu	$200 000
Bank account, interest rate 2.5% p.a.	$140 000
Balanced managed fund, income return 5.5% p.a.	$150 000
Shares, actual dividends $5000	$80 000
Funeral bonds	$8 000
Total	$578 000

Mr Wu has just retired. Mrs Wu still works on a casual basis with her son and earns a salary of $15 000 p.a. During the year, the couple gave their daughter $20 000 to help with buying a new car.

Calculate the couple's entitlement to the age pension. Suggest ways the couple might be able to improve their pension entitlement.

13.19 Aged care accommodation ✱✱

Gina is an age pensioner who enters an aged care hostel and pays a $222 000 accommodation bond.

(a) What is the value of this bond for assets test purposes after the expiry of 12 months?

(b) How is this asset treated under the income test?

(c) What are the implications for social security purposes if Gina retains her former family home?

13.20 Family Tax Benefit ✱✱✱

Samantha and Tim are a young married couple. Samantha, aged 41, earns a salary of $35 000 plus the 9.25% employer superannuation contribution. Tim is aged 44 and earns a salary of $52 000 after salary sacrificing $6000 into his superannuation account. He also has $8000 of reportable fringe benefits. The couple has three children aged 5, 8 and 15. Calculate the couple's family income for the purposes of determining eligibility for the family tax benefit part A and determine whether the couple would be eligible for any benefit under the Family Tax Benefit part A.

13.21 Assessment of retirement income streams ✱✱✱

Jasmin is aged 60 and still working while James aged 66 is a self-funded retiree. They own their home and the couple's combined income consists of Jasmin's employment income of $40 000, income from an account-based pension held by James as well as dividends and bank interest. James acquired the account-based pension at age 64 for $480 000 and it is currently worth $400 000. James withdraws an income from his pension account of $35 000 p.a. The couple's share portfolio is valued at $560 000 and generates a dividend yield of 4% p.a. The couple also has a term deposit of $200 000 which earns an interest rate of 5% p.a. and a savings account holding $50 000 earning 2% p.a.

(a) Calculate how the account-based pension would be assessed under the asset and income tests.

(b) How would DHS's treatment of the income from the retirement income stream differ from its treatment for income tax purposes?

(c) Will the couple be entitled to any age pension? Calculate.

(d) Explain any strategies the couple might consider using to reduce their assessable assets and income for social security purposes.

(e) If the couple were not able to receive any age pension entitlement, are there any other social security benefits or tax concessions they may be entitled to?

CASE STUDY 1

Age pension entitlements

Mark and Brigitte have been married for 31 years. Mark is aged 66 and Brigitte is aged 59. Mark retired last year from his part-time job where he had been working with his son for the past 6 years helping with the bookkeeping. Brigitte is still employed as a hairdresser running her own business and earns a net taxable income of around $32 000 p.a. The couple does not have any dependent children living at home.

»

»

The couple's assets and liabilities consist of the following.

Assets	**$**
Home	700 000
Contents	60 000
Cars	32 000
Bank account — joint account	50 000 — interest of 3% p.a.
Shares — Mark	160 000 — fully franked dividend of 2.8% p.a.
Rental property — Brigitte	340 000 — net income after expenses of 3% p.a.
Superannuation — Brigitte	190 000 — average return of 5.5% p.a.
Account-based pension — Mark	380 000 — income stream of $20 000 p.a.
Liabilities	
Mortgage on rental property	140 000
Credit cards	8 000

Other information is as follows.

- Mark's account-based pension was acquired 2 years ago from a superannuation account balance of $500 000. At that time, 22% of the superannuation account represented a tax-free proportion.
- The couple's annual living needs total around $60 000. This includes a joint donation to charities of $500, a fee of $1000 for preparation of the couple's tax returns (split 50/50) and $2000 for payment of private health insurance.
- Brigitte is in good health but Mark is a smoker and has not been well of late.
- Brigitte's mother has recently died and the couple expects to receive an inheritance of around $100 000.

QUESTIONS

1. Calculate the couple's assessable assets and income for the purpose of assessing their eligibility for the age pension.
2. Calculate whether Mark and/or Brigitte will be entitled to an age pension.
3. Determine the couple's after-tax income for the current year from all sources and determine whether this meets the couple's income needs.
4. What will be the ramifications on the couple's age pension entitlement upon receipt of the inheritance of $100 000?
5. Are there any strategies that you can suggest to assist the couple in maximising their age pension entitlements?

CASE STUDY 2

Aged pension and assessment of granny flats

Joan is single and aged 72 and has been receiving the aged pension for the past few years. Joan has a nice comfortable house but the garden is quite large and Joan is no longer able to properly manage it. Joan is in good health and quite active and would like to continue with some gardening. She has looked at a few houses in the area but the houses are either too large, have no garden or the property is not near public transport which she is reliant upon.

Joan's daughter Abby has suggested that her mother move in with her family into a granny flat which they would build for her.

Joan has the following assets and income:

Asset	Current market value	Income return
Home	$430 000	Nil
Contents	$60 000	Nil
Bank account	$25 000	2% p.a.
Term deposit	$80 000	4% p.a.
Account-based pension	$300 000	6% p.a. (withdraws an income of $30 000 p.a.)
Share portfolio	$100 000	3% p.a. (fully franked)
Prepaid funeral expense	$9 000	nil

It has been agreed that in return for the transfer of her home to Abby, Joan will receive ownership of the granny flat and a cash amount of $100 000. The value of the granny flat when completed is expected to be $280 000.

QUESTIONS

1. Calculate the cash income *and* taxable income of Joan prior to the granny flat arrangement.
2. Calculate Joan's aged pension entitlement prior to the granny flat arrangement proceeding.
3. Describe the impact that the granny flat arrangement between Joan and Abby is likely to have for social security purposes.
4. Based on the granny flat arrangement proceeding as detailed above, calculate the impact on Joan's aged pension entitlement.
5. Joan is wondering whether she is able to add the $100 000 received from her daughter into her existing account-based pension or into a new superannuation account. Discuss. What other investment options does Joan have if she wants to minimise the impact of the funds on her income assessed for aged pension purposes?

CASE STUDY 3

Financial implications of entering a hostel

Mr Pope, aged 72, is a widower and due to his poor health has decided to move into residential aged care. Mr Pope has been offered a place at the Green Valley Hostel, which is located 10 minutes away from where his daughter lives. Mr Pope owns his home worth $420 000 and has other assets of around $180 000.

After considerable negotiations, the hostel provider agrees to charge Mr Pope an accommodation bond of $380 000. Mr Pope is worried that if he pays a lump sum for the full accommodation bond, he will be left with very few funds to cover the hostel daily care fees, emergency payments and other cost of living expenses. He would also need to sell his home which he does not want to do. Mr Pope has been told by the hostel owner that he can pay the bond by way of a lump sum, in periodic payments or a combination of both. The owner explains that Mr Pope is able make the periodic payments either monthly or fortnightly.

Mr Pope agrees to pay a lump sum of $190 000 towards the cost of the accommodation bond and pay the remaining $190 000 balance by way of regular payments. To pay for the periodic payments, Mr Pope has decided to rent out his home which he believes should be able to earn a net amount of around $250 per week.

Unfortunately, after 4 years, Mr Pope dies. Mr Pope's entire estate is to be left to his daughter.

QUESTIONS

1 What is the maximum accommodation bond that Mr Pope could have been asked to pay by the hostel provider?

2 In terms of maximising his age pension benefit, would Mr Pope have been better paying the total amount of the accommodation bond as a lump sum or by way of a mixture of a lump sum and periodic payments?

3 Mr Pope wants to minimise his monthly outgoings. Calculate the minimum monthly periodic payment that Mr Pope is likely to have to pay on the $190 000 owing on the accommodation bond.

4 How will the following items be assessed for social security purposes: the accommodation bond; Mr Pope's former home that is being rented out; and the rental income generated?

5 Upon Mr Pope's death, how much of the accommodation bond is likely to be refunded to Mr Pope's daughter?

References and further reading

Australian Government 2010, *2010 Intergenerational Report*, treasury.gov.au/igr/igr2010/.

Australian Government 2013, *Guide to social security law*, http://guidesacts.fahcsia.gov.au/guides_acts/ssg/ssg-rn.html.

Commonwealth of Australia 2009, *Australia's future tax system, the retirement income system: report on strategic issues*, May, taxreview.treasury.gov.au.

Department of Human Services 2013a, A *Guide to Australian Government payments*, http://www.humanservices.gov.au/corporate/publications-and-resources/a-guide-to-australian-government-payments.

Department of Human Services 2013b, 'Deeming', http://www.humanservices.gov.au/customer/enablers/deeming.

Secure and Sustainable Pension Reform, 2010 Budget Overview, Treasury, Commonwealth Government, Canberra, http://www.fahcsia.gov.au/seniors/news/2011/secure-and-sustainable-pension-reform-package.

Treasury 2013, *Budget paper no. 1: Budget strategy and outlook*, Commonwealth Government, Canberra.

Useful websites

Department of Human Services, humanservices.gov.au.

Department of Families, Housing, Community Services and Indigenous Affairs (FaHCSIA), fahcsia.gov.au.

Department of Health and Ageing, health.gov.au.

Family Assistance Office, familyassist.gov.au.

14 Estate planning

LEARNING OBJECTIVES

After studying this chapter, you should be able to:

1. understand the importance of estate planning and the role of the financial planner in helping clients achieve their estate planning objectives
2. understand the role of a valid will within estate planning
3. explain the consequences of dying without a valid will
4. analyse the impact of taxation on distributions from deceased estates
5. understand the role and benefits of testamentary trusts in the minimisation of taxation and protection of assets
6. understand the rules applicable to superannuation death benefits
7. discuss the purpose of a power of attorney.

CASE STUDY

Maria, aged 62, died last month leaving an estate valued at $1.5 million. Maria separated from her husband 3 years ago and they divorced. Maria has a will in place that was drawn up 10 years ago leaving 50% to her husband and 50% to her son Michael. Maria's daughter Felicity, aged 26, was left out of Maria's will as the two were not on speaking terms. Felicity left her parents' house at age 17 with a child and has not spoken to her parents since that time. Felicity is currently a single mum and is struggling financially.

At the date of Maria's death, her estate consisted of the following:

House and contents (cost price $200 000 in 1982)	$550 000
Car	$20 000
Fixed interest	$100 000
Investment property (cost price of $250 000 in 1990)	$380 000
Share portfolio (cost price of $145 000 in 2001)	$160 000
Managed funds (cost price of $50 000 in 2005)	$70 000
Life insurance policy (owned in Maria's name)	$100 000
Superannuation fund	$300 000
Total	**$1 680 000**

The investment property is jointly owned with Maria's sister.

Maria does not have a death benefit nomination in place within her superannuation fund.

Michael is married and has 2 children under the age of 12.

Some of the issues that need to be considered include the following.

- What effect does separation and divorce have on a will? Will Maria's ex-husband be entitled to a share of Maria's estate?
- Under what circumstances might Felicity be able to successfully challenge her mother's will and receive a share of her estate?
- Which of Maria's assets are covered by her will?
- What is the ramification of Maria not having a death benefit nomination in place within her superannuation fund?
- If upon inheriting the home and contents and the share portfolio, Michael subsequently sold them 9 months later, would there be any capital gains tax implications? If so, how much tax would be payable?

Illustrative examples used throughout this chapter will relate back to the information contained within this case study.

Introduction

Traditionally, the **will** has been the major focus of **estate planning**. Although it is important to ensure clients have valid and up-to-date wills, client needs in estate planning must be viewed more broadly as a means of protecting and maximising net assets available for distribution to chosen beneficiaries and ensuring those beneficiaries receive the assets in a tax-effective manner. Increasingly, a significant portion of a person's wealth is held in superannuation, insurance and business structures that are not directly owned by the person. These assets may not form part of a will but are still an important consideration in estate planning. The area of estate planning is dynamic and affected by legislative changes in the areas of wills, taxation and superannuation, and by societal changes in attitudes to inheritance and increasing amounts of wealth to pass on.

will
a legal document which directs how a willmaker's assets are to be distributed or disposed of upon their death

estate planning
the planning and management of a person's estate following their death

LO 1 Obligations of the financial planner

Estate planning is part of the overall financial planning process and a financial planner has an important role to play in ensuring that the estate planning objectives and needs of a client are met. As with any other financial product or service, financial planners have an obligation to ensure that their advice is appropriate to the client's circumstances and complies with the statutory best interest provisions brought in under the FOFA reforms. While much of the work in estate planning may need to be undertaken in conjunction with other professionals, such as lawyers and accountants, financial planners are in a unique position of having a detailed understanding and comprehension of the client's overall goals and needs. Some of the needs and concerns of the client might consist of the following.

- I'm getting too old to properly manage my finances.
- Do I need a will and what are the ramifications of not having one?
- How do I leave money to a particular beneficiary?
- How can I ensure that children from a previous marriage are protected upon my death?
- What happens to my superannuation account balance upon my death?
- How can I best protect the interests of a disabled child upon my death?
- How can I minimise the tax payable by beneficiaries in receipt of an inheritance?

It is useful to think of estate planning in terms of the before- and after-death stages, and financial planners can provide important guidance to their clients in both areas. The following are major considerations for financial planners in estate planning.

1. *Identify objectives and wishes.* Identifying a client's objectives and wishes is the first step in the estate planning process. Who does the client want to benefit from their estate and how much is to be left to each **beneficiary**? Are there any specific objectives, such as maintaining lifestyle of dependants in the event of early death, supporting a spouse in retirement, or passing on control of any family businesses? Are there any special circumstances which need consideration, such as disabled beneficiaries or beneficiaries who are financially at risk? Is a beneficiary likely to be exposed to bankruptcy and potentially lose an inheritance to the trustee in bankruptcy? Another example of a beneficiary at risk is a drug-dependent beneficiary who may easily be taken advantage of and use the inheritance to pay for drugs.
2. *Identify assets available to the estate for distribution and non-estate assets.* What is the value of the deceased's estate and how are the assets to be distributed among

beneficiary
a person nominated to receive a payout from an insurance policy, a superannuation fund or the assets of an estate

beneficiaries? For those assets not forming part of the will, how will ownership be passed to the intended beneficiary? Who will benefit from any insurance policies and/or superannuation assets?
3. *Identify any tax implications on the estate plan.* Tax planning is an important element of estate planning, both to maximise the amount of assets available for distribution and to minimise the amount of tax to be paid by the estate and individual beneficiaries.
4. *Ensure a valid and up-to-date will is executed.* A current legal will helps to ensure that the client's assets go where intended. Consideration needs to be given to any potential claims on the estate by disgruntled potential beneficiaries. Selection of an appropriate executor is also important as this is the person who will carry out the instructions contained in the will.
5. *Establish an enduring power of attorney.* An **enduring power of attorney** is especially important if a client becomes ill and is unable to act on his or her own behalf. Different forms of enduring powers of attorney may need to be considered for different situations that might arise, such as managing the financial affairs of a person, or making medical and accommodation decisions on behalf of the person. To illustrate, when a person is assessed as needing high-level care the enduring power of attorney has the power to arrange such accommodation needs by locating and arranging the placement of the person into the facility providing the high-level care. Powers of attorney are discussed in more detail later in this chapter.

enduring power of attorney
a power of attorney (POA) is a legal document given by a person (donor) that authorises another person (attorney) to act on their behalf; an enduring POA continues to be valid even after the donor becomes mentally incompetent

While legislation in most states prohibits persons other than legal practitioners from providing legal advice, financial advisers are ideally placed to assume a facilitator role and coordinate the various professionals involved in the estate planning process to ensure proper execution of the plan.

LO 2 The role of a will within estate planning

A will specifies how property is to be dealt with after the willmaker's death. It provides directions about who the willmaker wants to distribute their assets to, how much each beneficiary is to receive and nominates the person responsible for finalising the affairs of the deceased in accordance with the directions of the will. Although there are many reasons why having a valid will is important, it is not required by law.

Drawing up a valid will

A will is a legal document that must be made in accordance with the relevant legislation applicable in the place where it is made. In Australia, making a will falls under state jurisdiction and each state has its own legislation dealing with wills. Although there are many similarities between the states, there are some differences. This chapter deals with making a will in general terms and does not examine the differences in state legislation.

The person making the will is known as the willmaker or testator. Wills must be in writing and signed by the willmaker in the presence of witnesses. Generally, there needs to be at least two witnesses who are independent of the willmaker and must not be beneficiaries. The number of witnesses required and who is allowed to witness wills differs between states. Although it is not a requirement, it is preferable that the willmaker and witnesses use the same pen when signing. Otherwise, the validity of the will may be open to challenge on the basis that the witnesses and willmaker were not present at the same time. It is important that the willmaker sets out all his or her wishes in the body of the will.

Any details written in another place and not referred to in the main body of the will, or any instructions appearing after the signatures, may not form part of the will. Some people make a separate list of belongings and nominate the person they want to leave them to. Although this list may be useful, unless it is referred to in the will it may not be legally enforceable if a dispute over any of the nominated items arose among the beneficiaries.

A willmaker does not have to engage a solicitor to prepare the will. There are many do-it-yourself will kits available that can be used to construct a valid will. However, a will is a very important document and must be validly constructed and executed. In all but the simplest cases, it is well worth getting advice from a solicitor to ensure that no mistakes are made. Remember, if there is no valid will, the willmaker's assets may not go to the people intended to have them.

When a person wants to make a minor adjustment to a will they can prepare a **codicil** (a 'little will'). The codicil will contain the minor amendments but needs to be witnessed in the same manner as a normal will. If major changes are to be made then it is advisable to prepare a new will.

codicil
a legal document that amends an existing will without revoking the will in its entirety

While most people consider drawing up a will to be an important matter to ensure that their family is adequately looked after upon their death, there are many examples of unusual wills in existence. Take the case of Harry Houdini. The renowned master escapee and daredevil died in 1926 on Halloween. Towards the end of his life, Houdini had become interested in the afterlife and spiritual mediums. Houdini left his wife, Bess, a 10-digit secret message that only she would know, to silence naysayers when she eventually reported his presence (she never did). His last will and testament also stated that a séance should be held each anniversary of his death. Bess held the séance for 10 years, without any appearance from Houdini. In another interesting case, California rancher Thomas Shewbridge's last will and testament turned over shareholder rights of his estate to his two dogs. They became the owners of 29 000 stock shares in the local electric company. The dogs regularly attended stockholders' and board of directors' meetings (*Source:* 'Weird and wacky wills', *Wealth Professional*, 21 June 2013, http://www.wealthprofessional.com.au/news/weird-and-wacky-wills-176499.aspx).

Who can make a will?

Anyone over the age of 18 years can make a will, providing they have **testamentary capacity**. Testamentary capacity can be difficult to define, but a useful guide is that the willmaker should:

testamentary capacity
the mental capacity required of a willmaker to be able to make a valid will

- understand the nature of making a will
- understand the extent and character of the property left in the will
- understand the claims of potential beneficiaries such as family
- have no mental disorders which may influence the decision.

A will made by someone who does not have testamentary capacity is invalid and can be challenged. Any potential beneficiaries who think they should have been left more in a will may challenge the will on the grounds that the willmaker did not have testamentary capacity at the time of making the will.

The existence or otherwise of testamentary capacity is a growing area for concern today because people are living much longer and there is increasing incidence of dementia. Solicitors and financial planners taking instructions from elderly clients or clients who have suffered from mental illness are well advised to establish testamentary capacity. In such cases, it is a good idea to have the will signed in front of a solicitor, who can then give evidence if the will is challenged. Additionally, a statement from the client's doctor attesting to the client's testamentary capacity at the time of making the will should be attached to it.

In some states, the court can allow a minor to make a will and can authorise a will to be made for a person who does not have testamentary capacity.

The need to update a will

To ensure that a will continues to accurately represent the wishes of a willmaker, it is essential that the will be reviewed and updated on a regular basis. There may be a range of situations which necessitate the need to update a will, including the birth of children, the death of dependants, disputes with beneficiaries, windfalls, starting a business, and divorce and marriage.

Generally a will is cancelled upon the marriage or remarriage of a person. The only exception to this is if the will is made in contemplation of the marriage. While a divorce in most states of Australia does not automatically cancel a will, it will cancel any distribution to the ex-spouse as well as cancelling their appointment as an executor, trustee or guardian of children.

Appointing an executor

executor
the personal representative or manager of a deceased person's estate

The person appointed in the will to look after and distribute the assets in accordance with the willmaker's wishes after death is called the **executor**. Some of the tasks usually undertaken by the executor are:

- organising the funeral
- managing the legal and financial affairs of the estate
- obtaining grant of probate
- locating, protecting (such as changing the locks) and insuring estate assets
- paying outstanding debts from the estate
- distributing the remaining assets in accordance with the will
- defending the will if there is a challenge.

Grant of probate

probate
the process of proving and registering in the Supreme Court the last will of a deceased person

Obtaining the grant of **probate** confirms the last will and testament and provides the executor with authority to proceed to collect the assets and distribute them to the beneficiaries. Probate simply means 'proof of the will'. On death, the assets of a person are frozen and cannot be dealt with by anyone other than the personal representative upon production of a document stating grant of probate. The grant of probate is awarded by the Supreme Court, which undertakes an assessment of the validity of the will, confirms the appointment of the executor(s), and confirms the major assets and liabilities owned by the estate. When estates are of relatively low value (such as $25 000), grant of probate may not be required.

Letters of administration apply when, for example, an executor has died and no replacement has been named in the will. Letters of administration are also granted by a court when a person dies without a will. Letters of administration give court authority to a person to carry out the functions of administering the estate.

The role of the executor is a very important one and the person chosen should be carefully considered. Some of the questions that should be considered in the selection of the person include the following.

- Is the person likely to outlive you?
- Is the person competent to undertake the tasks required?

- Does the person have the time to carry out the tasks required of an executor?
- Will the person be impartial if a dispute arises between the beneficiaries?
- Is the person trustworthy?

It is usually best to check that the person chosen both understands the duties and is happy to accept the role. The executor should also be told where the will and other important documents are kept. It is a good idea to appoint an alternative executor in case the first one is unable to do the job when the time comes.

What can you leave in your will?

It may seem unnecessary to say that any assets that a willmaker owns or is entitled to at the time of their death can be left in the will. However, many willmaker's may be surprised to learn that some of their major assets cannot be left in their will. For estate planning purposes, it is useful to classify a person's assets into two categories.

1. **Estate assets**. These are assets owned solely and independently by the willmaker. These assets form part of the willmaker's estate and their distribution to beneficiaries is determined in accordance with the will.
2. **Non-estate assets**. These are assets that are either owned jointly or are owned and controlled through an independent tax structure, such as a family company or trust, or a superannuation fund. The distribution of non-estate assets is not determined by the will of the deceased and will require other forms of estate planning over and above the preparation of the will document.

estate assets
assets owned in the personal name of the willmaker which are capable of being disposed of by a will

non-estate assets
assets that are not owned in the personal name of the willmaker and their distribution is not governed by a will

As noted, only estate assets are governed by the terms of a will. Examples of non-estate assets that fall into the second class are:

- bank accounts in joint names
- jointly owned property
- superannuation accounts
- some life insurance policies where there is a nominated beneficiary
- assets held in a family company or trust.

Jointly owned property can be divided into two categories: **joint tenancy** and **tenancy-in-common**.

joint tenancy
a form of ownership of an asset where two or more persons each hold the rights over the entire asset and in which the surviving tenant receives total ownership of the asset

In the case of *joint tenancy*, both parties own the entire asset. Upon the death of one of the owners, ownership automatically passes to the surviving owner and does not form part of the deceased's estate. For example, in the case of a husband and wife who have money in a joint bank account, if the husband were to die, the whole account balance would be transferred to the surviving wife. The same is true for a jointly owned family home.

tenancy-in-common
a form of ownership of an asset where two or more people each have a distinct share in the ownership of an asset and in which the share of the deceased's interest forms part of their estate

For assets owned as *tenants-in-common*, each party owns a separate, defined portion of the asset, typically with respect to property. In this case, the willmaker is able to leave his or her share of the property to a chosen beneficiary in their will and hence, these are estate assets. For example, two brothers may each hold a 50% interest of an investment property valued at \$500 000 under a tenants-in-common arrangement. If one of the brothers was to die, their 50% interest in the property (\$250 000) would form part of their estate and the terms of the will would determine the distribution to their beneficiaries.

The assets owned within a family company structure are not estate assets nor are assets held in a family trust structure. The assets held within these structures are owned by the respective entities, not the individual. However, the actual shares held by the shareholder of a company structure are an estate asset and can be transferred to a beneficiary under a will. Similarly, units held in a unit trust are estate assets and, accordingly, the ownership of the units can be transferred to a beneficiary through the will of the deceased. While shareholdings and ownership of units in a trust can be transferred to a beneficiary in a will, the entity and its assets remain in existence. The distribution of superannuation will be discussed in a later section.

PERSONAL FINANCE BULLETIN

Who inherited Princess Diana's estate?

Diana, Princess of Wales, died in a car crash in Paris on 31 August 1997 aged 36 years. Her estate when she died was valued at around US$35.6 million, consisting of cash (US$28.8 million) from her divorce settlement with Prince Charles, and jewellery, dresses and other personal belongings valued at approximately US$6.8 million. After taxes, the estate available for distribution to beneficiaries was nearly US$22 million.

The Princess of Wales left a last will and testament which she had originally completed on 1 June 1993, which was modified by a codicil nearly three years later on 1 February 1996. Princess Diana's mother, Frances Ruth Shand Kydd, and her sister, Lady Elizabeth Sarah Lavinia McCorquodale, were appointed as executors and trustees of the Princess' estate. Upon the death of Princess Diana, her mother and sister as executors of her will were able to obtain a variation order from the High Court of Justice in December 1997 in order to vary the terms of the will.

The final provisions of her will provided for the following.

1. She wished to be buried.
2. If any of her children were under-age upon her death and that of her husband, the Princess' mother and brother Earl Spencer were to be appointed as guardians of that child. The will expressed the desire that should the Princess predecease her husband, that he would consult with her mother with regard to the upbringing in education and welfare of their children.
3. Princess Diana's former butler, Paul Burrell, was to receive US$82 000.
4. Certain personal effects were to be left to Princess Diana's 17 godchildren. However, the Princess made this specification in a 'letter of wishes', not in her will. This distribution caused considerable controversy.
5. A Discretionary Fund was established for the benefit of Prince William, Prince Harry, their respective future descendants and spouses, and charities as selected by the trustees. The Discretionary Fund received a number of assets of the estate including intellectual property rights, all wearing apparel, US$170 000, and accumulated income earned by the fund's assets.
6. The bulk of Princess Diana's estate, around US$21.3 million after taxes, was to be held in trust in equal amounts for her two sons, Prince William and Prince Harry. The shares were to be held in trust until each prince reached the age of 30. However, when each prince turned 25, he was to be given access to all of the income from his trust.

Rights of beneficiaries

In general, beneficiaries have the right to have the estate administered properly and the right to their allocation in accordance with the instructions in the will. While the estate is in the hands of the executor, the beneficiaries have no claim to the assets or income of the estate, even if they are left a specific bequest or legacy. Beneficiaries are not entitled to borrow against assets of the estate until it is settled and proper title has passed to them.

However, if the executor makes a distribution to a beneficiary but then realises that an estate debt has not been paid, the executor cannot demand the beneficiary return the distribution. The executor would have to pay the debt personally.

Beneficiaries can bring the executor to court to apply for a grant of probate if the executor fails to lodge the application with the Probate Office within the statutory time frame.

Beneficiaries have the ability to challenge a will if they feel they have been inadequately provided for or they believe the will is invalid.

Contesting a will

As a general principle, people can leave their estate to whomever they wish. There is no obligation at law, for example, for willmakers to treat their children equally or fairly. However, a disgruntled beneficiary, or potential beneficiary, has some scope to challenge a will. There are two main situations where an estate could be contested:

1. if the validity of a will is challenged
2. if inadequate provision has been made in the will for a beneficiary.

It should be noted that when a will is challenged, the executor(s) is entitled to pay for the estate's legal costs from the estate's funds. If costs become extensive and the challenge to the will is drawn out, there will be less available to distribute to beneficiaries.

Challenging the validity of a will

The validity of a will can be challenged on any of the following grounds:

- lack of testamentary capacity
- **undue influence**
- incorrect execution.

If beneficiaries/potential beneficiaries believe that the willmaker did not have testamentary capacity at the time the will was executed, they can challenge it. If potential beneficiaries believe the willmaker was unduly influenced by another person when giving instructions for a will, they can mount a challenge to the will.

If there is an omission or error in drafting and/or executing a will, it may be voided. For example, if the willmaker signed the will and then later took it to work to have a colleague witness their signature, the will would be void as it was not witnessed appropriately at the time of signature. However, in some states, the court has discretion to rectify a will that does not fully comply with legal requirements if the court is satisfied that the document was intended by the willmaker to be his or her last will.

If the court finds that the will is invalid on any of these grounds and it does not use its discretion to validate it, the estate will be distributed in accordance with any earlier valid will. If there is no earlier valid will, it will be distributed in accordance with the applicable laws of **intestacy**. (The laws of intestacy are examined later in the chapter.) This may mean, of course, that disgruntled beneficiaries may not necessarily be any better off, even if their challenge is successful.

undue influence
a situation that arises where one person is able to take advantage of a position of power over another person

intestacy
the situation that arises when a person dies without having a valid will and, as a result, their assets are distributed in accordance with a government formula

The time limits for contesting a will vary from state to state. For example, in Victoria and Western Australia claims against an estate must generally be commenced within six months of the date of the grant of probate, while in New South Wales and the ACT claims against an estate must generally be commenced within 12 months of the date of death.

Inadequate provisions for certain beneficiaries

The second ground for contesting a will stems from the notion that the family members of a deceased person should be properly maintained and supported out of the proceeds of the estate, wherever possible. The laws in each state differ in terms of the classes of people who have the right to make claims for a share, or an increased share, of the estate. Such proceedings are called testator's family maintenance (TFM) proceedings.

In general, the classes of potential claimants are restricted to various family members, including former spouses. However, which family members are eligible to make claims differs between states. For example, same-sex spouses are eligible claimants in some states but not all. New South Wales and Victoria extend eligible claimants beyond family members. In New South Wales, a person who has been a member of the deceased's household and partly or wholly dependent on the deceased can make a claim. In Victoria, the class of eligible claimants is broad and includes 'anyone for whom the deceased had responsibility to make provision'; thus the pool of people eligible to challenge the will can be quite large.

To help prevent TFM proceedings, it is important that financial planners alert willmaker's to the possibility of a challenge to their will. One suggestion for anyone thinking of omitting a family member is to make a small provision in the will for that person. This may reduce the chance of a successful challenge to the will. In addition, the reasons for the omission should be documented and kept with the will to be used if a challenge is mounted. A letter prepared by the willmaker and left with the will which explains why a family member has been left a smaller entitlement under the will may be an effective means to reduce a likely challenge to a will. Although adoption of these strategies will not guarantee the failure of any challenge, a judge will at least understand the willmaker's reasoning for excluding the particular person from the will or for leaving that person only a small amount, and can make a decision in the light of that knowledge.

ILLUSTRATIVE EXAMPLE 14.1

As noted in the case study at the start of this chapter, Maria's daughter Felicity was left out of Maria's will as the two were not on speaking terms. Felicity is currently a single mum and is struggling financially. Felicity may decide to challenge her mother's will on the basis that she has not been appropriately maintained and supported from her mother's estate. The success of any challenge may depend upon the extent to which a judge is able to understand Maria's reasoning for excluding Felicity from the will.

Given the increasingly complex family structures that exist in today's society, a common concern often raised is, how can a person safeguard the interests of their children in the event of their spouse re-marrying after they die?

In determining whether or not provision should be made for a dependant or applicant, the Court will consider a range of factors including the relationship between the deceased person and the dependant; the nature and length of the relationship between the parties; the extent to which the deceased had obligations or responsibilities towards the dependant or any other persons; the size and nature of the estate; and the needs of the beneficiary or other parties.

The foundation case governing this issue was established in 2004 in the case of *McKenzie v Topp* ('McKenzie'). In this case, the Victorian Supreme Court was required to consider the rights and entitlements of an adult son who was making a claim against the estate of his deceased stepmother. The applicant's father had previously passed away, leaving everything to the applicant's stepmother. The applicant contested his stepmother's will on the basis of not being adequately provided for. The court took into consideration not only the time and effort that the applicant put into caring for his elderly stepmother, but also the fact that the stepmother had a moral obligation to provide for the adult son in these circumstances. The judge noted that while it was appropriate for the father to provide for his wife above other dependants, it was appropriate that children from a previous marriage should rank for their fair share.

LO 3 Dying intestate

If a person dies without a valid will they are said to have died intestate. In such cases, the estate will be distributed in accordance with the individual state's intestacy laws. The fundamental principle is that the estate will pass to the deceased's next of kin. The state laws prescribe the precise order of persons who will share in the estate. For example, under Victorian intestacy rules:

- the entire estate goes to the surviving spouse if there are no children
- if there are both a surviving spouse and children:
  - if the total estate is less than $100 000, the entire estate goes to the spouse
  - if the total estate is more than $100 000, the spouse receives the first $100 000 and the remaining estate is split one-third to the spouse and two-thirds equally between the children
- if there are children but no spouse, the children share the estate equally
- if there are no children and no spouse, then any surviving parents receive the estate
- if there are no children, no spouse and no surviving parents then any surviving siblings receive the estate
- if there is no family or next of kin, the property of that person is passed to the Crown.

Naturally, intestacy laws are unlikely to match precisely the wishes of the deceased, and dying intestate may mean that the deceased's assets are distributed to people who he or she would not have wanted to have them.

Dying intestate can have even worse ramifications in the case where both parties to a marriage die at the same time. It is a generally accepted rule of law that if it is not possible to determine the actual time of death, the older person is presumed to have died first. In this event, the estate of the older spouse will pass firstly to the younger one. The estate of the younger spouse will then include both of the couple's assets. It is possible that these will then be distributed to the younger partner's next of kin and nothing will pass to the family of the older spouse. (This scenario depends on the relevant state laws. In Victoria, for example, a beneficiary must survive for 30 days before he or she can inherit.)

The NSW Trustee and Guardian provide a number of real-life examples on its website of how things can go wrong when a valid will is not in place.

- A reclusive woman decided to write her own will. The only relative with whom she had contact was a niece. However, after writing her own will, she asked the niece's husband to sign the will as her witness. On her death she left an estate worth $400 000, but unfortunately the niece was not able to inherit the estate due to the fact her husband had signed the will as a witness. The will fell into intestacy as a spouse of a beneficiary should not be a witness. The estate was distributed to the next of kin and the niece received nothing.
- An 18-year-old man had been living with his girlfriend for only 6 months when he died without a will. The court decided that his girlfriend was his legal de facto spouse, and she received his entire, substantial estate. The man's parents received nothing.
- Jim had looked after his uncle Wayne for many years and had been assured that he was included in the will. When Wayne died, Jim searched the house for a will but to no avail. He checked all the local solicitors, banks and anyone else who might have dealings with his uncle. There was no evidence of a will anywhere or anything to suggest Wayne ever made a will. Under the laws of intestacy, Jim shared his uncle's estate with several other nieces and nephews who barely knew their uncle and never attended to any of his needs.
- A 21-year-old girl with no will was killed in a motor vehicle accident during the course of her employment. There was $200 000 accident cover. The estate passed to her mother and father equally on intestacy but the father had deserted the family weeks before she was born. He had had no contact since but was entitled to $100 000.
- A 'family' consisting of three stepchildren fought for three years over the division of old 'antique' furniture which was valued at $6000. Legal costs incurred by the children amounted to $55 000.

PERSONAL FINANCE BULLETIN

Amy Winehouse didn't have a will after all but did have millions

Shortly after Amy Winehouse passed away from accidental alcohol poisoning at the age of 27 . . . reports surfaced that she not only had a will, but she had the foresight to update her will after her divorce from ex-husband, Blake Fielder-Civil. These early reports have recently been proven wrong.

Probate records were recently filed showing that Winehouse died intestate, meaning without a valid will. The estate value is listed as £4 257 580 (worth about $6.7 million US) in total assets, but taxes and other debts reduce the value to £2 944 554, or $4.66 million, US. Many believed her estate would be worth much more, perhaps as high as $15 to $20 million.

But, let's not jump to conclusions so quickly. The assets passing through probate court are those left in her individual name when she died. So anything held jointly with someone else, or that had a beneficiary designation (like a life insurance policy), would pass outside of probate, directly to the other person. Also, if Winehouse had a trust — which is unlikely, considering she didn't have a will — anything held in the trust would also avoid probate. None of these types of assets would be included in her estate value as listed in the probate documents.

What of her ex-husband, Fielder-Civil, who has been serving a lengthy jail sentence for burglary related to his drug addiction? As an ex-spouse, he gets nothing. Some have speculated that Winehouse still loved him and would have left him something if she had a will. Whether that's true or not, it doesn't matter at this point, because there is no will. That's the biggest problem with procrastinating with estate planning; you have no say over 'who' receives 'what' when you die. For example, did Winehouse want her older brother, Alex, to inherit anything? He doesn't, because she had no will.

Instead of money passing to her brother or to her ex-husband, it will all go to Winehouse's parents, Mitch and Janis. Mitch is the estate administrator, according to the probate documents.

It's too bad that the earlier reports of Winehouse having done proper estate planning have proven to be inaccurate. We previously applauded the foresight that a 27-year-old would have had in updating her will after her divorce. By having no will at all, despite earning millions of dollars in her short career, Winehouse joined the dozens of other famous celebrities who procrastinated with their estate planning.

This has many pitfalls, for celebrities and non-celebrities alike. Without a will, you have no say about who inherits your legacy, and you also lose control over how and when they receive it. In addition, wealthier individuals lose the ability to do estate-tax avoidance planning. For many families, probate court can often be a breeding ground for family fights, and this is especially true when there is no will.

Wills do not cost much to have prepared the right way, by an experienced estate planning attorney. No adult with any level of assets should be without one, especially someone with millions — no matter what their age. In fact, for most people a will is only the beginning of a comprehensive estate plan, but it's a good start.

Source: Danielle and Andy Mayoras, Forbes online, accessed 28 March 2012, http://www.forbes.com/sites/trialandheirs/2012/03/28/amy-winehouse-didnt-have-a-will-after-all-but-did-have-millions/.

LO 4 Estate planning and taxes

The basics of taxation have already been covered in chapter 3. This section examines some of those concepts and discusses their relevance to and implications for estate planning. The area of taxation in estate planning is highly technical and complex. This section covers the main areas that financial planners should be aware of, but it is not meant to be a definitive statement on taxation law. In cases where complex taxation issues arise, financial planners are advised to refer their clients to a tax specialist.

Most willmakers will be concerned to minimise the impact that income tax and Capital gains tax is likely to have on estate assets that are left to beneficiaries. The main areas of tax consideration in relation to estate planning are:

- capital gains tax
- the '3-year rule'
- **testamentary trusts**.

testamentary trust a trust established under the terms of a will that comes into effect upon the death of the willmaker

It is important to note that there is no inheritance tax in Australia and no tax is payable by beneficiaries upon receipt of estate assets. However, tax consequences may arise when the beneficiary disposes of an inherited asset.

Capital gains tax

Capital gains tax (CGT) (refer to chapter 3) is an important consideration in estate planning. For CGT purposes, the death of the owner of an asset does not constitute a CGT event; that is, it is not considered to be a disposal of the asset for CGT purposes. However, it does constitute an acquisition by the beneficiary inheriting the asset. Hence, there is no CGT paid at the time of death, but CGT may be levied at some later date when the asset is sold by the beneficiary. Table 14.1 provides a summary of the CGT position on the inheritance of certain assets.

TABLE 14.1 CGT position on the inheritance of certain assets

Asset type inherited	CGT consequences
Family home	CGT-free if sold within 2 years of date of death or the home continues to be used as the principal residence of the beneficiary.
Investment assets (e.g. shares and property)	**Purchased by deceased before 20 September 1985** The cost base to the beneficiary is the market value at date of death of the deceased and CGT will be payable at the time of sale by the beneficiary on any gain since date of death. The 50% CGT discount will apply only where the disposal takes place more than 12 months after the deceased acquired the asset. **Purchased by deceased after 19 September 1985** The beneficiary takes on the original cost base of the deceased at the date of death. CGT is payable at the time of disposal by the beneficiary on any gain made from date of acquisition by the deceased to the date of sale, either by the estate or the beneficiary. The asset must be held for a total of 12 months (by the deceased and/or the beneficiary) to attract the 50% discount.
Personal assets (e.g. cars, jewellery, furniture)	CGT-free (unless they are collectibles, e.g. antiques, art work, expensive jewellery).

In estate planning, as in other applications of CGT, the date an asset is acquired determines how the asset will be treated for CGT purposes. Assets can be categorised into two time periods:

1. assets acquired before 20 September 1985
2. assets acquired after 19 September 1985.

Assets acquired before 20 September 1985

Assets acquired by the deceased before 20 September 1985 will incur CGT only when sold by the beneficiary or executor. The CGT payable will be on gains made from the date of death of the deceased to the date of disposal by the beneficiary. The cost base will be the market value of the asset at the date of death of the deceased. For the CGT discount to apply, the disposal must take place at least 12 months after the death of the deceased.

Assets acquired after 19 September 1985

Similarly, assets acquired by the deceased after 19 September 1985 will incur CGT only when sold by the beneficiary or executor.

The method used for calculating CGT on assets acquired from a deceased estate is determined upon the date of death of the deceased. Where the deceased died between 19 September 1985 and 20 September 1999, the CGT rules allow owners to choose to calculate their capital gain by either the indexation method or the discount method, whichever gives the better result. Where the deceased died after 20 September 1999, the CGT discount method must be used to determine the capital gain. However, for the CGT discount to apply, the disposal of the asset must occur at least 12 months after the deceased acquired the asset.

CGT exemptions

The principal residence of the deceased is normally exempt from CGT upon disposal by the beneficiary providing one or more of the following conditions are met.

- The property is used by the beneficiary as their principal residence for the entire period of ownership.
- The residence is disposed of by the beneficiary within 2 years of the date of death of the deceased.
- While the residence is under the control of the executor, it is the principal residence of the deceased's spouse.

A partial CGT exemption will apply if the property was used as the principal residence of the deceased for only part of their period of ownership, but not at the date of death, or the property was used for part of the period of ownership by the beneficiary as their principal residence. The partial exemption is based on the total period of time for which the property was used as a principal residence relative to the total period of ownership.

The 3-year rule

The *Income Tax Assessment Act 1936* allows executors up to 3 years to finalise an estate. During this period, the estate itself is taxed as if it were an individual. The estate is entitled to a tax-free threshold and will be taxed at normal adult marginal tax rates for amounts in excess of the threshold. Depending on the tax position of the beneficiaries, this may provide some scope to minimise the tax paid on distributions from the estate. For example, if there are two beneficiaries entitled to all of the estate assets, both of whom are on the highest marginal rate, the executor can choose to retain the assets within the estate and delay distribution until towards the end of the 3-year period. The effect of this is that the estate will have paid tax only on income above the tax-free threshold for those 3 years and, depending on the size of the estate, at lower marginal tax rates. If the estate had been distributed promptly, the beneficiaries would have paid tax on the full amount of income at the highest marginal tax rate.

ILLUSTRATIVE EXAMPLE 14.2

Refer to the case study presented at the start of this chapter.

Part of Maria's estate consists of the managed funds that were acquired in 2005. The managed funds were acquired for $50 000 and, at the date of Maria's death, their value had increased to $70 000. Assume that her son Michael inherits the managed funds and subsequently sells them for $80 000 nine months after Maria's death.

»

» What will be the CGT ramifications of the sale of the managed funds by Michael?

The managed funds are not subject to an exemption and so the disposal by Michael will be subject to CGT. For the purposes of determining the CGT payable, Michael will need to determine the cost base of the managed funds. As the managed funds were acquired by Maria after 19 September 1985, Michael's relevant cost base will be the same as that of Maria's, that is, $50 000.

Thus, the capital gain upon disposal would be $30 000 ($80 000 – $50 000).

As the managed funds had been held for a period greater than 12 months since the date of acquisition by Maria, Michael will be entitled to the 50% CGT discount upon disposal. Accordingly, the assessable capital gain forming part of Michael's taxable income for the year will be $15 000 ($30 000 less 50%).

Stamp duty

Under state legislation, stamp duty is typically payable on the transfer of assets between entities or individuals based on the value of the asset. Assets subject to stamp duty include real estate and shares. However, stamp duty is usually not levied on assets where they are distributed to beneficiaries under the terms of a will. Full stamp duty is payable where dutiable property is transferred while the deceased is still alive or where an asset is distributed to a beneficiary not in accordance with a will.

LO 5 Estate planning and trusts

Two of the more important objectives in effective estate planning lie in:

1. establishing a tax-effective structure by which estate assets and income are able to be distributed to intended beneficiaries
2. providing the willmaker with control over how their estate assets will be distributed and managed after their death.

One of the commonly used tools to achieve these objectives is the establishment of testamentary trusts established through a will.

A trust is a unique legal entity, recognised by law, which involves separation of the legal and beneficial ownership of an asset. There are two main types of trusts in the context of estate planning: a living trust, also known as an **inter vivos trust** (established during a person's lifetime) and a testamentary trust (established by will after the death of the person), sometimes referred to as a will trust. A testamentary trust is established by a will and comes into effect only upon the death of the willmaker. Assets of the estate are passed into the testamentary trust rather than being paid directly to the beneficiary. It is the use of trusts — both testamentary and living (inter vivos) — that provides for more effective estate planning. For example, through a trust, a willmaker is able to leave the assets of an estate to at-risk nominated beneficiaries (or classes of beneficiaries) without giving them actual access to the capital.

inter vivos trust
a trust established during the lifetime of a person

Essential elements of a trust

A trust has the following essential elements.

- *A settlor* — the person who settles a sum of money or property to establish the trust. Usually a trust created during a person's lifetime is established by a settlor, who starts by placing a small amount of money in trust. The settlor is usually a lawyer, accountant or friend who settles the trust with a small sum (usually $10). A settlor should never be a beneficiary of the trust. Note that for a testamentary trust, the willmaker (as future settlor) is able to instruct their legal representative in the appointment of the trustee for the trust. The willmaker can also nominate the trustee under his/her will.

- *An appointer* — a person nominated by the settlor to appoint a trustee for the trust. The appointer has ultimate control of the trust (i.e. they can appoint and discharge the trustee).
- *A trustee* — the person or party who holds trust property on behalf of beneficiaries and who has the personal obligation attached to that property. The trustee is appointed and manages the trust in accordance with the conditions set out in the trust deed. The trustee can be one or more persons or a corporation.
- *A beneficiary* — the person or persons nominated to receive the beneficial interest in the trust property; they are entitled to receive distributions of income and/or assets from the trust.
- *Trust property* — the property held in the trust; trust property is legally vested in the trustee.
- *A personal obligation* — the trustee has a personal obligation and a fiduciary duty to deal with trust property for the benefit of the beneficiaries. A fiduciary duty means that the standard of care that a trustee should exhibit in carrying out their responsibility for the beneficiaries is at a higher standard than simply showing a normal duty of care. It is highlighted by concepts of good faith and loyalty. It implies that there is no conflict of interest in carrying out the duties of trustee. The trustee's powers, rights, duties and obligations are determined by a combination of factors, including:
  - the contents of the trust deed, if any; the trust deed records the terms and conditions of the trust
  - specific legislation regulating trusts, such as the *Trustee Act 1958* (Vic)
  - common law rights, obligations and duties imposed on trustees.

How a trust is controlled

For a living trust, once the settlor has created the trust, the person who wants the trust established nominates an appointer who can appoint and can dismiss the trustee of the trust at any time. If the trust is created by the will then the trustee may be named either in the will or by the executor of the will.

A trustee has control over the trust assets and authority to distribute the income and capital of the trust in accordance with the trust deed. The person with ultimate control over the trust and its assets is the person who controls the trustee; that is, the appointer of the living trust. For a testamentary trust, the executor or legal representative takes the role of appointer and can remove the trustee if necessary.

Types of trusts

Trusts can also be described in a number of different ways, for example, in accordance with the entitlements of the beneficiaries, such as a fixed or discretionary trust. A fixed trust (or unit trust) gives beneficiaries a fixed entitlement in respect of the income and capital of the trust in proportion to the number of units they hold. Whenever a distribution is made from the trust, the beneficiary must receive this proportion of the available income.

A discretionary trust gives beneficiaries an entitlement to distributions from the trust but does not give them a right to distributions. The trustee has complete discretion on how any income is to be distributed among the beneficiaries. A testamentary trust is normally established as a discretionary trust in order to provide the trustee with this discretion.

Trusts can also be named in accordance with their purpose, for example, family trusts, charitable trusts and child support trusts.

Use of trusts in estate planning

There are four significant reasons why a business, assets or investments may be preferred to be held in a trust rather than in individual names:

1. tax minimisation
2. asset protection
3. succession
4. provision for minor and/or disabled dependants.

These reasons apply to both inter vivos (living) trusts and testamentary (or will) trusts. The discussion here focuses on the use of trusts in estate planning, which includes both preserving assets available to the estate before death and protecting assets after death.

Tax minimisation

Trusts can provide significant tax-minimisation benefits. Trusts do not generally pay income tax because the trustee distributes all the trust's net income to beneficiaries. Income distributed from a trust retains its original character on distribution to the beneficiaries. The establishment of a discretionary trust provides a significant degree of flexibility in the way that income is distributed and split between the potential beneficiaries of the trust. In a discretionary trust, the trustee has complete discretion over how trust income is distributed each year. The receipt of trust income by beneficiaries is taxed at their marginal tax rate. One of the major benefits of a trust is the ability to divert income to beneficiaries, such as family members, on a lower marginal tax rate. This can be achieved through the use of either an inter vivos trust whilst still alive or a testamentary trust that is established upon death. Upon the death of the person, the establishment of a testamentary trust allows income to be distributed across a range of beneficiaries, such as a spouse and children, rather than being left directly to the spouse and them earning all their income in their individual name.

Taxation of minors

Rather than distributing income to adult beneficiaries, significant tax benefits may arise where income is able to be distributed to children. As discussed in chapter 3, penalty tax rates apply to the 'unearned income' of minors. 'Unearned income' up to $416 p.a. is tax free. Any amount above this is taxed at penalty rates of tax.

One of the main considerations in distributing income to a minor is that 'unearned income' is taxed at these penalty rates of tax. However, an exemption from this penalty tax rate is given to any income derived from an estate which is held and distributed through a testamentary trust established under a will. Income distributed from a testamentary trust to minor beneficiaries is taxed at normal adult tax rates, thereby providing an opportunity to gain significant tax advantages in cases where estate assets can be left to minors. Accordingly, each minor is able to receive $18 200 of trust income tax free. One of the important issues to note when distributing income to minors is that the minor has a legal entitlement to any amount distributed to them.

ILLUSTRATIVE EXAMPLE 14.3

Refer to the case study presented at the start of this chapter.

Upon the death of Maria, a testamentary trust was established for the benefit of Michael. During the current year, the trust derives the following classes of income:

- fully franked dividend income: $8000 p.a.
- rental income: $15 000 p.a.
- interest income of $7000 p.a.

The trustee is able to distribute the income to beneficiaries in the most tax-effective way possible. Rather than assets being distributed directly to Michael and him paying tax on the total income at his marginal tax rate, assets can be distributed into a testamentary trust with the result that any investment income earned within the testamentary trust can be distributed equally between Michael's two minor children who would be taxed on the income at normal adult resident marginal tax rates. As each child's share would be less than $18 200 (assuming no other income), they would not be subject to any tax on the income received.

If all the income had been received by Michael in his personal name, the investment income of $30 000 would be added to Michael's other income for the year and subject to tax at his marginal tax rate, which could be at 37% plus the Medicare levy.

The tax effectiveness of distributing income to Michael's 2 children through a testamentary trust can be illustrated through the following figure:

	Situation 1	Situation 2	
Assets distributed to:	Michael ↓	Testamentary trust ↓	
Assets held in name of:	Michael ↓	Trust fund ↙ ↘	
Investment income of $30 000 received by:	Michael	Child one	Child two
Taxable income of beneficiary:	$30 000	$15 000	$15 000
Tax payable on $30 000	At Michael's MTR of 37% = $11 100	No tax payable as each child's income is below tax-free threshold	
Overall tax saving		$11 100 p.a.	

Asset protection

The separation of legal and beneficial ownership protects trust assets from claims made on the beneficiaries by third parties. For example, many professionals prefer not to own assets in their own name because of the possibility of a negligence claim arising from their work. Any such claim could result in assets held in their own name being liquidated to pay any damages awarded. A negligence claim can greatly reduce the assets available to an estate.

A discretionary trust can be used to protect assets from creditors. When a person places assets into a trust, legal ownership of the assets vests in the trustee. If the person is subsequently declared bankrupt, the trust assets may not be available to the trustee in bankruptcy (provided the beneficiary has only a contingent interest or mere expectancy). Recent changes to bankruptcy law increase the reach of creditors in bankruptcy to trust assets in certain circumstances. These changes relate to the right to 'claw back' contributions to trusts within a certain time frame prior to a person being declared bankrupt.

From an estate planning perspective, a testamentary trust can also be used to protect assets from beneficiaries who have problems such as drug or gambling addictions or who are spendthrifts. Often these people are in need of parental support, and parents may wish to continue to provide such financial support after they die. Leaving an inheritance to people with these problems may result in the money disappearing quickly to support their lifestyle or habit. Leaving the assets in trust under the control of a trustee provides a way of leaving the benefits of the inheritance to the child and providing ongoing financial support without giving the beneficiary access to a large amount of money.

Succession

The separation of legal and beneficial ownership of trust assets can also assist in preserving an estate for intended beneficiaries and future generations. Potential claims against beneficiaries could arise as a result of bankruptcy, litigation or family breakdown. The ownership of assets within a trust structure helps to protect assets from claimants, ensuring the assets are available to future generations.

One application of this is protecting assets from 'inadequate provision' claims. With the broadening of the class of potential Testator Family Maintenance (TFM) claimants in some states, a growth in such claims can be expected. One way to prevent TFM claims and ensure assets go to the intended beneficiaries is to place the assets into a trust during the willmaker's lifetime (an inter vivos trust). Assets held within a trust cannot be contested. Under the trust deed, the trustee would be obliged to hold assets for the intended beneficiaries after the death of the settlor. However, as opposed to an inter vivos trust, a testamentary trust is established under a will, and therefore assets forming part of the deceased's estate are able to be contested under a TFM claim prior to them being transferred into the testamentary trust.

Discretionary trusts, both inter vivos and testamentary, can also offer protection from any potential divorce settlement. Division of assets as a result of divorce can substantially reduce the assets available to an estate. The use of a testamentary trust can protect assets inherited by one spouse from claims by the other in a divorce settlement. The benefit of trusts to thwart divorce settlements, however, is somewhat minimised as the Family Court has broad powers in determining divorce settlements. Although Family Court judges are not always able to access trust assets for distribution, they do take into account any access to trust assets and distributions available to the parties when making their judgements. This can result in the spouse who is entitled to trust assets and distributions being awarded a smaller proportion of other family assets.

Provision for minor and/or disabled dependants

Discretionary trusts are also useful vehicles to provide for minor and/or disabled dependants who are unable to manage their affairs. Under a testamentary trust, the assets are preserved and distributions from the trust can be applied for the benefit of the dependant(s). The taxation benefits associated with testamentary trusts for minors were discussed earlier in this chapter.

In formulating an estate plan, the client in conjunction with the financial planner and other professionals, need to establish whether it is preferable to keep assets out of an estate and paid directly to a beneficiary or rather left within an estate so as to allow for assets to be transferred into a testamentary trust. Issues to consider include:

- the likelihood of the estate being challenged
- the costs v benefits of establishing a testamentary trust
- how quickly probate may take
- the need to control estate assets for 'at-risk' beneficiaries
- potential tax savings.

LO 6

Superannuation death benefits

For many people, superannuation will be one of the largest assets they have to pass on to their beneficiaries. In addition to the increasing popularity of superannuation as a retirement savings vehicle, many people are being advised to hold their life insurance within their superannuation funds. Accordingly, the way in which superannuation balances are distributed upon the death of a member will be of increasing importance. However, for many people, their superannuation may never pass through their estate and, therefore, may not be distributed through their will.

Binding death benefit nominations

Amendments to the *Superannuation Industry (Supervision) Act 1993* (SIS Act) gave trustees the option of introducing **binding death benefit nominations**. These nominations enable superannuation fund members to give a binding nomination regarding the distribution of their superannuation account upon death. Strict provisions apply to the effective execution of these nominations — they must be signed and witnessed by two witnesses, are valid for normally 3 years only and must be confirmed or renewed at that time. A number of funds have started to offer non-lapsing binding nominations which do not need to be reviewed every 3 years.

binding death benefit nomination
a declaration by a superannuation fund member that on their death the balance of their superannuation must be paid to a nominated person; the trustees are bound to follow this direction

As previously stated, superannuation is not normally treated as an estate asset and its distribution upon the death of the member is not generally governed by the terms of the deceased's will. On the death of a member, the superannuation fund trustee will determine and have some discretion as to which of the deceased's dependants will receive a share of the super death benefit, unless a binding death benefit nomination is in place. Members can also make a non-binding nomination where the superannuation fund trustee will take the member's nomination into account when distributing the super funds, but is not compelled to. When a member joins a super fund, they will be given the opportunity of completing a binding or non-binding death benefit nomination form and can amend the nomination form at any time.

Who can you leave your superannuation to?

Upon the death of a member, superannuation funds must be paid to dependants, as defined by the SIS Act, or to the estate of the deceased. Both the SIS Act and the Income Tax Assessment Act (Tax Act) have similar definitions of 'dependants', but there are some differences. Both definitions include: spouse (including de facto spouses); children, both adopted and ex-nuptial; any person who is financially dependent on the deceased at the time of death; and a person in an interdependent relationship with the deceased just before death.

Under the Tax Act, the following differences exist:

- a spouse includes not only a current spouse or de facto spouse but also a former spouse or former de facto spouse
- a child of the deceased is included but only if they are under 18 years of age.

Under the Tax Act, a child over the age of 18 would be classified as a non-dependant, unless they could show financial dependence on the deceased.

An interdependent relationship between two people is one in which:

- they have a close personal relationship
- they live together
- one or each of them provides the other with financial support
- one or each of them provides the other with domestic support and personal care.

People in such a relationship can receive the death benefit of a deceased fund member.

Rather than having superannuation death benefits paid directly to a beneficiary, there may be circumstances where it may be preferable to have the death benefit paid directly into the estate of the deceased. This might arise where a will provides for the establishment of a testamentary trust and tax benefits would be derived from having superannuation death benefits transferred to a testamentary trust rather than being paid directly to a beneficiary. To allow for superannuation death benefits to be paid into the deceased's estate, superannuation funds may allow a member to nominate that their superannuation death benefit be paid to their **legal personal representative**.

legal personal representative the person responsible for managing the estate of a deceased who is appointed through either being named as the executor in a will or, if there is no will, by being appointed administrator of the estate by the Supreme Court

Taxation of superannuation death benefits

Taxation of superannuation death benefits depends on whether the money is distributed to a dependant as defined under the Tax Act. Different tax rates apply to the various superannuation components and to different categories of beneficiaries.

The definition of a dependant by the Australian Taxation Office is somewhat more restrictive than that adopted under the SIS Act. As previously noted, a tax dependant is defined to include:

- the person's spouse, including a de facto or former spouse or de facto
- a child of the person under the age of 18
- any person who was financially dependent on the deceased at the time of death
- any person with whom the person has an interdependency relationship.

A death benefit can generally be paid to a tax dependant in the form of a lump sum and/or a super pension (such as an account-based pension). The main restriction relates to the payment of an income stream to a child. Where a child is over 18 and under 25 years of age, a pension can only be paid where the child was financially dependent on the deceased at the date of death. All income streams paid to a child cease when the child turns 25 and then must be paid out as a lump sum to the child.

On the death of a member, a superannuation benefit is completely tax free if paid to a tax dependant. On the other hand, the taxable component of a superannuation death benefit paid to a person who is a non-tax dependant of the deceased, such as an adult child, is assessed as a death benefit lump sum and taxed at 15% plus the Medicare levy. Note that the tax-free component will always be tax free. Table 14.2 indicates the tax levied on death benefits paid either as a lump sum or as a pension.

Note that, under the changes to the rules from 1 July 2007, an existing superannuation pension is not able to be paid to a non-dependant on death; rather, death benefit payments to non-dependants must be paid as a lump sum.

TABLE 14.2 **Summary of tax treatment for superannuation death benefits (taxable component — taxed element)**

Lump sums	Dependant	Tax treatment
Death benefit	Tax dependant	Nil
	Non-tax dependant	15%[a]
Income stream (tax dependants only)		
Death pension	Either the deceased or the dependant is age 60 or above	Nil
	Both the deceased and dependant are under age 60	Marginal tax rates[a] with a 15% tax offset.

a. plus Medicare levy

Source: Information derived from Treasury 2013.

For a superannuation fund member aged 60 and above, the tax position of their superannuation account is not particularly relevant as all lump sum withdrawals and income payments are tax free. However, the tax components become relevant upon the death of the member where death benefits are to be paid to non-tax dependants. As previously detailed, the taxable component of a lump sum death benefit paid to a non-tax dependant will be subject to a 15% tax rate plus Medicare levy. Accordingly, estate planning and superannuation strategies remain a critical issue throughout the life of a person to ensure that wealth is passed on to beneficiaries in the most tax-effective manner possible. Thus, a member aged 60 and over may still be interested to ensure that the tax-free proportion of their superannuation account balance is maximised so as to minimise tax payable on super death benefits distributed to non-dependants upon their death. An interesting issue that provides some scope for strategic planning is that while a 15% tax rate plus Medicare levy is payable on super death benefits paid to non-tax dependants, no tax is payable by the member aged over the age of 60 who withdraws any funds from their super account or account-based pension prior to their death. A member might consider gifting some of their super monies to their beneficiaries prior to death, especially where there are non-tax dependants, in order to avoid the dependants paying the 15% tax plus Medicare levy.

ILLUSTRATIVE EXAMPLE 14.4

Refer to the case study presented at the start of this chapter.

When Maria died, her superannuation benefit amounted to $300 000 with a tax-free proportion of 20%. As Maria did not have a binding death benefit nomination in place, the trustee of Maria's superannuation fund will determine how her funds are to be distributed. Assume that the trustees decide to split the superannuation balance 50% to Maria's husband and 25% to each of her two children Michael and Felicity.

The lump sum superannuation death benefit would be taxed in the hands of the beneficiaries as follows.

- Death benefit received by Maria's husband of $150 000 — as he would be a tax dependant (former spouse), all of the lump sum death benefit would be tax free in his hands.
- Death benefit received by Michael and Felicity of $75 000 each — as the two adult children would be non-tax dependants due to their age, the taxable component of the death benefit received would be subject to a tax rate of 15% plus Medicare levy.

That is:

Tax-free component = $75 000 × 20% (tax-free proportion) = $15 000
Taxable component = $75 000 − $15 000 = $60 000
Michael and Felicity would be subject to a tax rate of 17% (including Medicare levy) on the taxable component — $10 200 each.

PROFESSIONAL ADVICE

Binding death benefit nominations for self-managed superannuation funds (SMSF)

To ensure that the benefits are distributed in accordance with the member's wishes, a valid binding death benefit nomination should be put in place.

The Australian Taxation Office's determination SMSFD 2008/3 states that a member of an SMSF can make a valid binding death benefit nomination if it is permitted by the fund's trust deed. The ruling also states that the binding nomination does not have to satisfy certain requirements of the SIS Act, including the need for it to be:

- witnessed by two individuals
- updated every three years.

This means that SMSFs can offer binding nominations that do not have to be updated on a regular basis to remain valid, that is, non-lapsing binding nominations. A non-lapsing binding nomination remains valid until the member changes it or revokes it.

If the member dies and there is no valid binding nomination directing how the benefit is to be distributed, the trustees must refer to the trust deed. Generally, the trust deed includes one of the following options.

- The trustees identify all potential dependants and decide to whom the benefit should be paid. The trustees can also decide to pay the benefit to the deceased member's estate.
- Automatic payment is made to the deceased member's estate.

An SMSF's trustees are likely to be closely related and emotional issues may impact how decisions are made if death benefits are paid without a valid binding nomination.

Example

Jason has two children, Grace and Jack. Grace works with Jason in the family business, is a member of Jason's SMSF and is also his LPR (legal personal representative). Jack is neither a member of the fund nor an LPR.

Jason passes away and, before his death, did not think it worth completing a binding death benefit nomination. Jason wanted his share of the SMSF to be distributed equally between his two children upon his death.

Source: Adapted from Miles 2009.

QUESTIONS

1. Why is there a need to consider binding death benefit nominations for members within an SMSF when all members are also required to be trustees of the fund?
2. What persons are able to be nominated as beneficiaries within a binding death benefit nomination?
3. Discuss the ramifications of Jason's death in terms of control over the funds of the SMSF and the potential distribution of Jason's superannuation death benefits.
4. If a dispute was to arise in the distribution of Jason's death benefits, what means of redress would SMSF beneficiaries have?

LO 7

Power of attorney

A power of attorney is a legal document that authorises another person to act on your behalf. The person delegating the power is known as the donor, and the person receiving the power is known as the attorney. The attorney has the same power as the donor and can sign legal documents on behalf of the donor, which are binding on the donor. A power of attorney therefore gives the attorney extensive powers to act on behalf of the donor, such as to buy and sell property, invest and enter into contracts on behalf of the donor. The only legal act an attorney is unable to do on behalf of the donor is make the donor's will.

The granting of powers of attorney comes under state legislation, and the legislation differs between states. Power of attorney granted in one state does not give the attorney power to act in any other state.

Types of powers of attorney

In general, there are three types of powers of attorney: (1) limited power of attorney, (2) general power of attorney, and (3) enduring power of attorney. Although each authorises the attorney to act on behalf of the donor, there are differences in the extent and duration of the powers.

Limited power of attorney

A limited power of attorney is usually granted to cover certain specified transactions or events or a specified period of time. For example, if you were negotiating to purchase a property and were required to travel overseas before finalising the deal, a limited power of attorney could be granted to authorise someone to act on your behalf in finalising the property purchase. If you were travelling overseas on an extended holiday, you might grant a limited power of attorney for the duration of your holiday, so that someone could attend to your affairs, such as paying bills, registering your car and investing money on your behalf during your absence. A limited power of attorney will lapse after completion of the transaction it covers or at the expiration of the specified time period. It will also lapse if the donor dies or becomes mentally incompetent. Donors can cancel the power of attorney at any time.

General power of attorney

A general power of attorney authorises the attorney to stand in your place and make any financial and legal decisions for you. It will remain in force until it is specifically cancelled by the donor. The power of attorney will also lapse if the donor dies or becomes mentally incompetent.

Enduring power of attorney

An enduring power of attorney grants the same extensive powers to an attorney as a general power of attorney. One significant difference between an enduring power of attorney and other powers of attorney is that an enduring power of attorney remains in force even if the donor is unable to make decisions due to mental incompetence.

In addition to these 'financial' powers of attorney, there are medical powers of attorney which empower the attorney to make decisions about what medical treatment the donor should receive. Powers of guardianship empower the guardian to make lifestyle and accommodation decisions on behalf of the donor. (See the appendix at the end of this chapter for information on the legislation and where to access sample forms.) It is important to realise that enduring powers of attorney do not apply only to elderly people. One never knows when misfortune may strike with a consequence of not being able to make decisions for oneself.

Executing a power of attorney

The laws relating to powers of attorney are complex, differ between states and do not transcend state boundaries. For example, a power of attorney issued in one state may not give the attorney power to act on behalf of the donor in transactions conducted in other states. As we have seen, the granting of a power of attorney gives the attorney broad powers to act on behalf of and legally bind the donor. For these reasons, it is recommended that professional legal advice be sought before granting a power of attorney.

Cancelling a power of attorney

A power of attorney becomes valid as soon as the legal document is signed and witnessed and continues to be valid until it is revoked. In most cases, a power of attorney can be cancelled verbally simply by telling the attorney that his or her authority to act has been cancelled. The problem with simply telling the attorney is that there is no evidence of the cancellation and those who have been dealing with the attorney may not be aware that authority has been withdrawn. It is wise to cancel the power of attorney in writing and to inform those people who have been dealing with the attorney of the cancellation. All copies of the power of attorney, including the copy held by the attorney, should be destroyed.

If the donor wishes to alter the power of attorney, this can be done either by simply amending the original one or by cancelling it and making a new one. The second option is preferable, as amending the original power of attorney could result in it becoming messy and confusing.

A power of attorney is valid only while the donor is alive and automatically ceases when the donor dies. Therefore, granting a power of attorney is not a substitute for making a will.

Choosing a power of attorney

Granting a power of attorney gives extensive power to the attorney to make decisions that are legally binding on the donor. Although powers of attorney can be very useful, they should be used carefully and the attorney must be chosen carefully. The chosen attorney should be someone the donor can trust completely, who is likely to outlive the donor and who is competent and has the time to undertake the tasks required. The person chosen must understand the nature and effect of the power of attorney, and understand the need to be trustworthy. The attorney cannot delegate the powers to anyone else.

Who should have a power of attorney?

It is normally beneficial for husbands and wives to hold an enduring power of attorney for each other. This would enable each spouse to take control of and make financial and legal decisions about the assets held by his or her partner in the event of loss of mental competence of either of them. Additional problems can arise where the family has made use of business structures for asset protection and tax minimisation purposes. These structures can cause difficulty and hardship when the person owning or controlling the structure becomes mentally incompetent and cannot deal with legal and financial affairs. The person's family may find that they do not have access to the income and assets intended for their benefit. An enduring power of attorney prevents the added hardship of being denied access to vital financial resources in such tragic times.

Appointment of each spouse as the sole attorney for the other may not always provide the outcome sought. Consider the ramifications of both the husband and wife becoming mentally incompetent at the same time, for example, if both partners were involved in a serious accident leaving them both in a coma for a period of time, or they both became old and incompetent. In the case of either of these events, family members would be in a much better position to provide for the couple if another attorney had been appointed. The role of an attorney is similar to that of an executor of a will. The same questions should be considered in making such an appointment. These include the following.

- Does the person understand the role required?
- Does he or she have the time to carry out the tasks required?

- Does the person live close by; are they located conveniently for day-to-day requirements?
- Will the person act in the best interests of the donor?

In many cases, the attorney may be a son or daughter (or two together) so that the duties can be shared.

Summary

Estate planning is an important part of the wider financial planning discipline. A thorough estate plan looks beyond the need for a valid will to potential threats to the assets of the estate both before and after the death of the willmaker. There can be potential challenges to the will from disgruntled beneficiaries (and potential beneficiaries). Taxation has an impact on estate distributions and estate assets may be passed to outside claimants in the event of bankruptcy or divorce. An effective estate plan deals with both estate and non-estate assets, including superannuation fund distribution. Assets can be protected from vulnerable beneficiaries while still allowing them access to the benefits of those assets.

The establishment of a testamentary trust within a will can provide a number of potential benefits in minimising the imposition of tax on beneficiaries and in the protection of the assets of an estate. One of the important decisions to be made within estate planning is the extent to which assets should form part of a deceased's estate. Some of the issues to be considered include the size of the estate, the ability to transfer estate assets into a testamentary trust and the potential for estate assets to be contested.

As superannuation is increasingly likely to form a significant part of the assets of deceased estates, proper planning can ensure that death benefits are distributed to the beneficiaries of choice in the most tax-effective manner.

An important consideration in the estate planning of a person is the appointment of a power of attorney. This is an important document for all persons, but especially as a person starts to age and finds it increasingly difficult to properly manage their affairs.

Through careful estate planning, a financial planner can help clients identify their estate-planning goals and objectives, and put in place a plan to build and preserve assets for their estates, and ensure those assets will be distributed to the intended beneficiaries.

Professional application questions

14.1 What are the key estate planning matters that financial planners should identify when advising clients?

14.2 What are some of the circumstances that might require a person to update their will?

14.3 Describe the difference in treatment of assets upon the death of a person between those that are jointly owned compared with those held in a tenancy-in-common arrangement.

14.4 After hearing the contents of his mother's will, Maurice felt upset that his sister, Jocelyn, was to receive the family home valued at $350 000, whereas he was to receive only a cash sum of $50 000. Is Maurice able to contest the will, and, if so, on what basis? Give reasons why Jocelyn might argue that the distribution was fair.

14.5 Jasmine receives a distribution from her father's estate which includes a property. Jasmine sells the property four years later and wants to know if there are any CGT implications. Discuss.

14.6 What is the purpose of a binding death benefit nomination? What are the consequences and risks of having a non-binding death benefit nomination?

14.7 Discuss the circumstances by which it would be preferable for a person's superannuation death benefits to be paid to their estate, rather than directly to a dependent, and explain how this could be achieved.

14.8 Janelle, a widow, is updating her will and has heard from one of her friends that she should establish a family trust for her three adult children. Explain to Janelle the type of trust that would be provided for in a will and discuss the possible benefits of Janelle's estate being transferred to the trust upon her death.

14.9 Bill was an invalid for the last 5 years of his life and was cared for by his brother, Frank. Bill was a widower and is survived by his 2 children who live overseas and have not had any contact with Bill for the past 7 years. Upon his death, Bill wanted his estate to be distributed to Frank and a small donation made to the Cancer Council Australia. However, a valid will could not be found for Bill and accordingly he was deemed to have died intestate. Explain how Bill's estate is likely to be distributed and whether Bill's estate planning objectives are likely to be satisfied.

14.10 Lisa is looking to amend her will and has an estate worth approximately $2m. She wants to leave $1m to her eldest daughter Gail and $500 000 each to her other two children, Sheena and Adrian. Under what circumstances would Sheena and Adrian be able to challenge the will and how could Lisa ensure that her wishes are adhered to as far as possible?

14.11 Travis is aged 47, single and is updating his will. He wants to know how the difference in the definition of 'dependant' between the Tax Act and the SIS Act would affect funds paid from his superannuation fund to the following beneficiaries upon his death: his mother; his sister aged 44 and living with her husband; and his child, Beatrice, aged 14 and living with his former wife but supported by Travis through child maintenance payments.

14.12 Explain the purpose of a Power of Attorney including the difference between a general and enduring power of attorney.

14.13 What factors should be taken into account when considering the appointment of an executor of a will?

Professional application exercises

Basic	*
Moderate	**
Challenging	***

14.14 Wills *

Why is it important to differentiate estate assets from non-estate assets when drafting a will? Other than a will, is there any additional estate planning that may be required by a person in dealing with the distribution of their assets to intended beneficiaries?

14.15 Power of attorney *

Graeme and Anne are aged in their eighties and concerned about who will look after their daughter, aged 36, upon their death. Their daughter has a major disability and there are no other family members able or prepared to look after her when they die. What are the couple's options?

(Visit the site of the Office of Public Advocate publicadvocate.vic.gov.au and review the information relating to guardianship.)

14.16 Estate planning ✱✱

Barbara and Ewan Poulter come to you for financial planning advice. They are in their late fifties and are about to sell their business and retire. They have two children — David, aged 34, and Sarah, aged 31. Sarah is mentally disabled and is living in supported care. She receives a disability pension, and Barbara and Ewan provide further financial support. Sarah's needs are quite simple and inexpensive, but Barbara is anxious to ensure that Sarah is adequately provided for after Ewan and she die. Although David has a family of his own and runs a plumbing business, he is a wonderful support to his parents and sister.

Advise Barbara and Ewan of the issues they need to consider in their estate planning and give guidance on how they can best provide for Sarah upon their death.

14.17 Death benefits ✱✱

Joe is aged 58 and has a terminal illness. Joe has a superannuation account worth $500 000 of which 18% represents a tax-free proportion. His binding death benefit nomination states that his superannuation death benefit is to be distributed equally between his two adult children.

Joe seeks advice from a financial planner who advises him that a significant amount of tax will be payable by his beneficiaries from the superannuation death benefit they receive.

(a) Calculate the tax payable by Joe's beneficiaries upon receipt of the superannuation death benefit.

(b) What strategies could be implemented by Joe prior to his death to reduce the amount of tax payable by his children upon receipt of the superannuation death benefit?

14.18 Death benefits ✱✱

Tony has just died leaving an estate worth $2m. Part of his estate includes a superannuation account totalling $1.6m which contains a $600 000 superannuation balance and a $1 million life insurance policy. Components of the total super account balance are as follows:

Tax-free component	$300 000
Taxable component	$1 300 000
Total	**$1 600 000**

Assume the following:

Tony leaves behind a spouse and three children. The eldest child, Louise, aged 26, is married and lives with her family; Trent is aged 20, lives at home and goes to university; and Carol is aged 17, lives at home and goes to school.

Advise what the tax implications would be on each member of the family if they were to receive a share of Tony's $1.6m superannuation balance.

14.19 Intestacy ✱✱

Janine and Rick are living in a de facto relationship. Janine is 37, a widow and has two children — Meg, aged 8, and Jack, aged 6. Rick, aged 35, has three children who live with his former wife. They were divorced 4 years ago.

Janine and Rick have been living together for 3 years. Neither Janine nor Rick has a will. Janine owns the house (valued at $450 000) that they are living in, and has $20 000 in the bank and $80 000 in her superannuation fund. Rick has $5000 in a bank account and $70 000 in his superannuation fund. Janine and Rick have a car accident and Janine is killed instantly. Rick is seriously injured and lies in a coma for 5 weeks before he dies. Describe what will happen to the estate under intestacy laws in your state.

14.20 Estate distribution and CGT ✱✱

Barbara has the following assets at date of death.

Asset	Cost and date of purchase	Market value at date of death
Home	Acquired in May 1986 for $220 000	$650 000
Holiday house (50% share held under a tenancy-in-common arrangement with sister)	Acquired in July 1980 for $180 000	$300 000
Bank account		$40 000
Shares	Acquired in 1993 for $80 000	$90 000
Investment property	Acquired in 1990 for $300 000	$450 000
Superannuation account death benefit nomination to her daughter Shana (comprises 20% tax free component)		$200 000
Life insurance, owned in the name of Shana		$300 000

In her will, Barbara leaves everything to her daughter Shana.

For the next 12 months, Shana retains all of the inherited assets and uses her mother's home as her primary residence.

After 12 months, Shana decides to sell the following assets that she inherited:

Asset	Market value at date of disposal
Home	$700 000
Shares	$85 000
Investment property	$480 000

You are required to provide details on the following issues:

(a) At the date of Barbara's death, explain whether Shana would have been liable to any tax upon the distribution of the inherited assets.

(b) If a testamentary trust had been established within Barbara's will, which of her assets would have been able to be transferred into the trust structure?

(c) Calculate the amount of CGT likely to be payable by Shana upon the disposal of the inherited assets.

14.21 Estate planning ✱ ✱ ✱

Nick and Foula were recently married, each for the second time after knowing each other for about 4 years. Nick lost his wife 5 years ago and Foula divorced 7 years ago. Both Nick and Foula have children from their first marriages, and each has a will in place that was drawn up during their first marriage. As part of the process of starting a new life, they sold their respective homes and bought a new one as tenants-in-common.

As part of their estate planning needs, the couple has the following questions for you:

(a) Given their recent marriage, how would their respective estates be distributed under current circumstances?
(b) How could Nick and Foula ensure that, upon the death of either of them, the other could continue to live in the house for the remainder of their life?
(c) How are the interests of Nick and Foula's children able to be best safeguarded upon the death of either parent?
(d) Upon his death, how would Nick's account-based pension be treated for tax purposes if there was a desire for it to be paid to his adult daughter?

14.22 Testamentary trusts ✱ ✱ ✱

Denis is an electrician and has a $500 000 life insurance policy in place owned by his wife Sally. Denis also has $700 000 held in his superannuation account with a non-binding death benefit nomination in place leaving 50% of the funds to his two adult children and 50% to his cousin who is mentally disabled and cannot adequately look after himself. The cousin is currently receiving an income support pension from the government. The couple's home is jointly owned by Denis and Sally, as is the couple's share portfolio. Denis has a will in place that provides for the establishment of a testamentary trust upon his death and Denis is seeking to maximise the amount of his estate that is able to be held in the testamentary trust. Discuss the following issues:

(a) How is each of Denis's assets likely to be distributed upon his death?
(b) What modifications would be required to help Denis achieve his objective of maximising the amount of his estate held in the testamentary trust?
(c) What potential problems could be faced by the cousin upon the distribution from Denis's superannuation fund and can you suggest any solution?

CASE STUDY 1

Michael and Amy have made an appointment with you to discuss their financial planning needs. They provide the following information:

Michael is aged 58 and Amy is aged 56. Michael works as an accountant and earns $120 000 p.a. including the SG contribution. Amy works 2 days a week and earns $30 000. The couple have one child from their marriage, Catherine aged 14. The couple have been married previously and both have children from their first marriage. Michael has two children from his first marriage, Peter and Jack. Both are aged in their early thirties. Jack is severely disabled and needs full-time care. Michael pays support towards Jack's ongoing medical and care costs. Peter is married with 2 children but is experiencing some marriage problems. Amy has one child from her previous marriage, Sharon aged 26. Sharon was very upset when her mother re-married and Amy and Sharon have little contact.

The couple have the following assets and liabilities (current market value):

	$
Home and contents	720 000
Cars	35 000
Bank account	20 000
Holiday home	380 000
Shares	120 000
Superannuation accounts	
— Michael	410 000
— Amy	180 000
Life and TPD policy	
— Michael	500 000
— Amy	250 000
Liabilities	
Home mortgage	200 000

Michael and Amy advise that their objectives are as follows:

- Michael hopes to be able to retire in 4 years.
- They would like the home mortgage paid off as soon as possible.
- The couple would like to continue to send Catherine to a private school for the next 4 years.
- In the event of their death, the couple would like to ensure the following distribution of their estate:
  - Michael — Amy and Catherine to receive 25% each of his estate, his son Jack to receive 35% and his other son Peter to receive the remaining 15%. Michael is particularly concerned to ensure that Jack is looked after in the event of his death.
  - Amy — her daughter Sharon to receive a fixed amount of $100 000. The balance of her estate to be split equally between Michael and Catherine.

Other issues raised:

- In the event of Michael's death, Amy would sell the holiday home and the shares. In the event of Amy's death, Michael would sell the holiday home. The holiday home is jointly owned by the couple and its cost was $120 000 in 1990. The shares were acquired by Michael in 2006 for $150 000.
- Both Michael and Amy would like each other to make all of their financial and medical decisions in the event that either of them was unable to do so.
- Michael advises that he has just been notified from his superannuation fund that his death benefit nomination is about to lapse.

»

»

QUESTIONS

1. To be able to properly analyse the couple's estate planning needs, what additional information would be needed and why?
2. Explain to Michael what a death benefit nomination is and its purpose. What advice would you give to Michael about the type of death benefit nomination that he should establish and who he can and should nominate as his dependants?
3. In the event of Michael's death, what recommendations can you provide as to how any financial distribution to his son Jack should be structured to ensure that Jack's best interests are looked after?
4. In the event of Michael's death, how would the CGT legislation affect the amount of funds inherited by Amy? If Amy was to sell the holiday home and shares at their current market value, how much CGT would she be liable to pay?

CASE STUDY 2

Estate planning

Frank and Sandra are in their mid-fifties and have three children from their marriage: Andrew, aged 23; Felicity, aged 17; and Scott, aged 15. Frank has been married before and has one child from that marriage — Amy, aged 26. Amy has no contact with her father and blames him for the financial hardships that her mother has experienced since their divorce.

Frank is self-employed in his engineering business while Sandra is an employee within a medical practice. The couple's assets, at current market value, consist of the following:

	$
Home and contents (home acquired for $450 000 in 1992)	600 000
Bank account	30 000
Shares (acquired for $20 000 in 1986)	130 000
Holiday home (acquired for $280 000 in 1998)	380 000
Managed funds (acquired for $80 000 in 2006)	60 000
Life insurance policy	800 000
Engineering business	200 000

Land and building used to conduct the business (acquired for $450 000 in 2001)	600 000
Self-managed superannuation fund — total (Frank and Sandra)	250 000
Superannuation account — Sandra	60 000

Frank has suffered bad health for some time. The couple raise the following issues:

- All of the couple's assets are jointly owned between Frank and Sandra, except for the engineering business and the land and building used within the business (see below).
- The couple gave Amy $180 000 to establish a business 3 years ago on the basis that she has no further claim on Frank's estate. However, the couple is convinced that Amy will nevertheless contest Frank's will upon his death.
- Frank's life insurance policy is owned by Sandra.
- Sandra's individual superannuation fund contains a $150 000 life and TPD policy and Sandra has decided to retain this account in order to preserve the insurance policy. Sandra completed a binding death benefit nomination 4 years ago nominating 100% to be paid to Frank in the event of her death. Both Frank and Sandra have completed binding death benefit nominations within their SMSF.
- The couple each has a will in place leaving everything to each other. They have each nominated their son Andrew as executor of their respective estates. Frank and Sandra have appointed each other as their respective general power of attorney.
- Frank's engineering business and land and buildings are owned within a family trust. Frank and Sandra are trustees of the trustee company. The trust deed states that in the event of the death of the appointer of the trust, currently Frank, the new appointer is the deceased's legal personal representative; that is, the executor named in the will.
- Sandra's mother, aged in her mid-eighties, owns and manages a small apartment block in Queensland. However, the mother is in bad health and no longer wants to manage the properties. The mother is looking to gift the property to Sandra. The property cost $130 000 in 1989 and has a current market value of $410 000.
- The couple's son, Andrew, has been married for the past 3 years but Andrew and his spouse have experienced marriage problems for some time. Frank and Sandra would like to gift Andrew $50 000 to use as a deposit on a house, but given the marriage problems, do not want the money to be lost in a divorce.
- The couple would like the family assets distributed in a tax-effective manner upon their death.

QUESTION

Frank and Sandra are looking to review their wills and seek some advice from you on how best to structure their estate-planning needs. You are required to analyse the couple's situation and detail relevant issues and recommend advice that the couple should consider.

CASE STUDY 3

Estate planning

William and Ruth are aged 66 and 64 years respectively and have both just retired from running a furnishings shop together for many years. They intend to become 'grey nomads' for the next 12 months and tow a caravan around Australia. However, before they set off on their journey they decide that they had better get their personal estate plans put into action. They make an appointment to see Maurice, the financial planner whom they have consulted with over the past few years, to review their finances and to make plans in the event that they die while on their trip.

Maurice prepares notes based on the information provided by William and Ruth. They tell him the following.

- Their home is valued at $520 000 and has no debt. It was purchased in 1980 for $160 000.
- They own an investment property currently valued at $480 000 but they still owe $100 000 on the property. The property cost them $180 000 in 1996.
- They have a share portfolio currently valued at $240 000. The portfolio was purchased in two lots: $40 000 was acquired in 1982 with the proceeds of a distribution from Ruth's aunt; and $100 000 was invested in 1998 when they sold a separate part of their business to another family.
- The couple plan to fund the bulk of their retirement income with account-based pensions paid to each of them from the ABC Master Superannuation Fund. William's balance is $500 000 (30% tax free and 70% taxable) and Ruth's balance is $250 000 (100% taxable).
- All assets except for the balances held in the superannuation fund are held in joint names.

Maurice does some calculations based on the couple's account-based pensions, their share dividends and the rent that they receive from their investment property and after allowing for various expenses calculates an approximate income that they can expect to receive while they are away. William and Ruth are happy about that as it meets the travelling expenses that they have estimated as well as using the savings of an extra $10 000 that they have accumulated in a savings account for the specific purpose of the 'round Australia trip'.

Maurice is reminded that William and Ruth have three adult children, all of whom are married and are living independently. With thoughts about estate planning, Maurice specifically asks about whether the marriages of the children are happy or not. William and Ruth both express some concern about two of the marriages and admit that they would not be surprised if divorce were the outcome. Maurice uses the opportunity to ask about whether they would like to put in place some plans for their estates.

William and Ruth tell Maurice that they want to ensure that their children are treated equally on their death and that their funds are passed on for the benefit of their children and grandchildren. Maurice explains the implications of property settlement when a couple decides to separate and that the assets are likely to be split equally between the two parties. William and Ruth foresee that if they do not plan for their estate then some portion of their accumulated assets may be taken away from the family by one or more marriage dissolutions.

Through their discussions with Maurice, William and Ruth are prompted to look at what would happen if they were both to die in a car accident on their trip around Australia next year. The couple proposes that upon their death, all of their assets (including their home) are sold and converted to cash and the proceeds distributed to their beneficiaries accordingly. They also assume that the balances held in the superannuation fund would be paid by the trustees to their estate prior to distribution to beneficiaries. William and Ruth plan to make Shirley and Len, the two children who live in the same city as them, the executors of their will as their third child, Maureen, lives interstate.

Maurice suggests that he write some notes based on their conversation and then brief an estate-planning lawyer to whom he can refer them. William and Ruth agree that Maurice can assist them with this matter and even take up his offer to attend the meeting with the lawyer when they meet to discuss the estate plan.

QUESTIONS

1. Suppose the share portfolio containing the parcel of shares acquired in 1982 for \$40 000 is now valued at \$80 000 and regarded as a quality stock. If the three children agreed not to sell the shares but to split the shareholding of those shares equally between them:
   (a) Describe the CGT impact on such a proposal at the time of the inheritance.
   (b) Are the three children able to request that the shares not be sold as proposed by William and Ruth? Explain how this may be done.
2. Identify the taxation impact on the sale of each of the assets forming part of the couple's estate.
3. Determine the likely amount to be distributed to each of the children after taxes have been paid.
4. Consider how a testamentary trust might be used by William and Ruth to help protect the family assets if a divorce occurred with any of their children.
5. Describe how the establishment of three separate testamentary trusts, one for each child, may provide a better outcome than the creation of only one testamentary trust covering all of their children.

References and further reading

Catalano, T 2007, 'Anna Nicole Smith — some of the doubt is due to a lack of estate planning', cleardocs.com.

CCH 2013, *2013–14 Australian master financial planning guide,* 16th ed., CCH Australia Limited, Sydney.

CCH 2007, *Guide to estate planning,* 2nd ed., CCH Australia Limited, Sydney.

Glomb, K 2010, 'The new intestacy law in NSW — what your client needs to know', *The Australian Journal of Financial Planning,* vol. 5, no. 1, jofp.com.au/section/5.

Hacker, A, 2012, 'Estate planning pitfalls and how to avoid them', *Money Management,* 7 December, moneymanagememt.com.au.

Miles, A 2009, 'Tax strategies for SMSFs in estate planning', *Money Management,* 21 July, moneymanagement.com.au.

Perkins, M & Monahan, R 2005, *Estate planning,* LexisNexis Butterworths, Sydney.

Stewart, M & Flynn, M 2012, *Death and taxes: tax-effective estate planning,* 5th ed., Thomson Reuters, Sydney.

Stewart, T, 2013, 'Financial advisers and estate planning — a perfect fit', *Money Management,* 8 February, moneymanagement.com.au.

Wealth Professional, 2013, 'Weird and wacky wills', 21 June, wealthprofessional.com.au.

Useful websites

law4u.com.au provides plain English legal information on states and territories in Australia.

https://www.moneysmart.gov.au/life-events-and-you/over-55s/wills-and-power-of-attorney provides some basic information on estate planning.

http://www.australianestatelawtoday.com.au/estate-planning/ provides a range of interesting articles on estate planning.

http://www.mtaoptima.com.au/resources/15mistakes.pdf describes in plain English a number of estate planning mistakes that are commonly done in practice.

APPENDIX

Powers of attorney

In Australia, the law regarding powers of attorney is made by the individual states and territories. All of this legislation may be found on the internet at austlii.edu.au.

The relevant state Acts are:

State	Legislation
Australian Capital Territory	*Powers of Attorney Act 2006*
New South Wales	*Powers of Attorney Act 2003*
Northern Territory	*Powers of Attorney Act 1980*
Queensland	*Powers of Attorney Act 1998*
South Australia	*Powers of Attorney and Agency Act 1984*
Tasmania	*Powers of Attorney Act 2000*
Victoria	*Instruments Act 1958*
Western Australia	*Guardianship and Administration Act 1990* Guardianship and Administration Regulations 2005

Sample forms may be found on the internet, usually on state justice departments' websites. In Queensland, for example, a sample form may be found at the Department of Justice and Attorney-General website (justice.qld.gov.au). However, as this 'short form' comprises 20 pages of form and instructions, it is not reproduced here. Look on the internet for your state justice department's site to see if a sample form is available.

15 Development of a statement of advice

LEARNING OBJECTIVES

After studying this chapter, you should be able to:

1. understand the disclosure requirements for the provision of a financial product
2. outline the key principles behind the provision of financial advice
3. explain when a statement of advice is required and its purpose
4. explain the circumstances under which a statement of advice is not required
5. outline the main types of statement of advice documents used in the marketplace
6. appreciate the importance of effective communication in a statement of advice
7. understand the importance of the planner–client relationship
8. explain the six-step financial planning process used to prepare a statement of advice
9. understand the various ethical and legal compliance issues involved in developing a financial plan
10. appreciate the important components of a statement of advice.

CASE STUDY

Cory and Amy are seeking financial advice. You are employed as a para-planner with Good Advice Financial Planners and are just about to enter the first meeting with the clients and the practice's financial planner. Cory and Amy have supplied the practice with some preliminary financial information prior to the meeting. A summary of the information is provided below.

Cory is aged 33 and Amy is aged 29. Cory works as a self-employed builder while Amy is a physiotherapist. Cory earns an annual net income from his business of around $80 000 before tax and Amy earns a salary of $72 000 p.a. including the employer SG contribution. The couple is currently renting and after paying all their living costs, have a disposable income of $35 000 p.a. The couple's investments currently consist of:

- a savings account of $20 000 earning 2% p.a.
- a share portfolio of $25 000 paying a fully franked dividend of 2% p.a.
- superannuation accounts: Cory has a balance of $40 000 invested in the CBUS Industry Super Fund (conservative investment option) while Amy's superannuation is invested with the ABC retail super fund with an account balance of $35 000 (conservative balanced investment option).

The couple's superannuation accounts are invested as follows:

Cory: cash 10%; Australian fixed interest 35%; property 10%; Australian shares 30%; international shares 15%

Amy: cash 7%; Australian fixed interest 28%; property 10%; Australian shares 35%; international shares 20%

The couple is hoping to buy a home in the next 6 months and have seen a property worth around $650 000 which they like. The couple is seeking some advice on how best to save for a deposit, what deposit amount they need to accumulate for the purchase and how much they can afford to borrow from the bank. The couple is also looking to go on an overseas trip in 4 years and will need to save an amount of $20 000. They want to know how they should also save for this cost.

The couple has specifically requested that they do not want advice in respect of any other aspect of their financial circumstances. They have asked for information on how the financial planning practice charges for their advice.

Some of the issues to consider in this case include:

- the matters that should be discussed with the couple at the first meeting and the documentation required to be provided to the couple at the various stages of the financial planning process
- how a financial planner deals with the situation where a client wants to limit the scope of the advice sought
- the disclosure requirements in respect of the provision of financial advice
- the different charging options available to a financial planning practice and what disclosure requirements, if any, are required with the provision of financial advice.

The illustrative examples used throughout this chapter will relate back to the information contained within this case study.

Introduction

Personal financial planning provides a framework for people to effectively manage their finances to satisfy their goals and objectives. This is manifested in the design, implementation and review of a personal financial plan that incorporates an integrated set of actions and transactions that best achieves and maintains the financial goals and well-being of the individual.

The financial planning process should provide the basis for a systematic and organised approach to preparing a financial plan for a client. The planning process should detail the client's goals and objectives, put forward appropriate strategies and recommendations, describe the manner in which the recommendations will achieve the client's agreed goals and establish a framework from which the planner intends to put the plan into action. However, to be effective, it is vital that there is clear communication with the client throughout all stages of the process.

Personal financial planning encompasses many different disciplines, including investment, business structure, insurance, taxation, superannuation, retirement and estate planning. A comprehensive analysis of all these disciplines will need to be considered in a typical financial plan, in the context of the client's circumstances and requirements.

As a result of the implementation of Part 7.7 of the *Corporations Act 2001*, a financial plan is now formally referred to as **statement of advice (SOA)**. Section 946A provides that financial advisers must give a client a SOA when required and ss. 947B and 947C detail the main disclosure requirements of a SOA. The regulations prescribe a range of issues that need to be addressed within a SOA to ensure that a client can make an informed decision.

statement of advice (SOA) a written personal financial plan prepared for a client by a financial adviser

A SOA is the means by which a financial planner's advice and recommendations are communicated to a client in a clear, concise and effective manner. However, a SOA has a much greater role to play than simply setting out recommended advice, strategies and financial products to a client. An effective SOA should provide the planner with the opportunity to communicate with the client, to educate and inform them, and, importantly, to encourage client engagement with and ownership of their SOA.

LO 1 Disclosure requirements for the provision of a financial product

Part 7.7 of the Corporations Act and Regulatory Guide (RG) 175 and 168 set out the various disclosure documents that are required to be provided by a planner prior to the purchase of a financial product by a retail client. The three main documents are:

- financial services guide — who the financial planner is and what financial services are able to be provided
- statement of advice — a statement setting out the advice and recommendations provided by the planner
- product disclosure statement — details on the financial product that is being acquired by the client.

These obligations are designed to ensure that retail clients receive appropriate advice about financial products so they are able to make informed decisions.

Financial services guide (FSG)

Prior to the provision of financial advice, a client must be provided with a financial services guide (FSG). The FSG provisions (ss. 941–943 of the Corporations Act) are designed to ensure that retail clients are given sufficient information to enable them to decide whether to obtain financial services from the financial planner. The FSG is required to provide information to a client concerning:

- who is providing the service
- what financial services are being offered
- who the service provider is acting for
- details of how the planner is remunerated
- details of any potential conflicts of interests.

The financial planner must provide the client with a copy of their FSG at the earliest possible opportunity prior to any advice being given.

Statement of advice (SOA)

A retail client provided with personal advice from a financial planner must be issued with a SOA in such a way that they are able to make an informed decision about whether to act on the advice given and whether to acquire a financial product. The SOA must be provided to the client when, or as soon as practicable after, that advice is provided. A SOA must include various information, including:

- the name of the party providing the advice
- a statement setting out the advice
- the reasoning or basis that led to that advice
- the remuneration and other benefits received by the provider of the advice
- all conflicts of interest that may affect the advice.

Product disclosure statement (PDS)

A PDS is prepared by the financial product issuer and must contain sufficient information to enable a retail client to be able to make an informed decision about whether to purchase a financial product (Pt 7.9 of the Corporations Act). Briefly, a PDS includes information such as:

- fees payable in respect of a financial product
- risks of the financial product
- benefits of the financial product
- significant characteristics of the financial product.

A PDS is generally required to be provided to a retail client at or before the time a recommendation is made to buy a financial product. Since 2011–12, shorter PDSs have been permitted to be issued by product providers for most superannuation funds, simple managed funds and margin lending facilities. The length of the shorter PDS is generally restricted to around eight pages and its purpose is designed to make it easier for retail clients to find and understand key financial information.

ILLUSTRATIVE EXAMPLE 15.1

What can Cory and Amy expect from the first meeting with the financial planner and what documentation are they required to be provided with?

The first meeting provides an opportunity for both the financial planner and client to establish whether there is confidence and a rapport between themselves and whether the two parties are likely to be able to work effectively together to help the client achieve their goals and objectives. The meeting provides the planner with an opportunity to detail who they are, what services they can provide, how they're able to service the needs of the client and how they're remunerated. It also provides the client with an opportunity to see whether the planner is likely to be able to assist in satisfying their requirements and in adding value.

One of the disclosure obligations imposed on the planner is to provide the client with a financial services guide (FSG). A financial planner is required to provide a client with a FSG at the earliest possible opportunity, before any advice is provided or recommendations made.

LO 2

The legal obligations relating to the provision of financial advice

The financial planner's obligations relating to disclosure and conduct obligations are detailed within Pt 7.7 of the Corporations Act. Part 7.7A deals with the 'best interest' obligations now imposed on financial planners that arose out of the FOFA reforms introduced in 2012 (*The Corporations Amendment (Future of Financial Advice) Act 2012* and the *Corporations Amendment (Further Future of Financial Advice Measures) Act 2012* (FOFA Acts)).

On 13 December 2012 ASIC released guidance on the best interests duty in an update to Regulatory Guide (RG) 175 Licensing: Financial product advisers — conduct and disclosure. The key obligations are shown in figure 15.1.

Relevant section of the Corporations Act	Obligation imposed	How the obligation would be satisfied
s. 961B	Act in the best interests of the client	▪ Identify the objectives, financial situation and needs of the client. ▪ Identify the subject matter of the advice sought by the client. ▪ Make reasonable inquiries to obtain complete and accurate information. ▪ Assess whether the advice provider has the expertise required to provide the advice sought. ▪ Conduct a reasonable investigation into the financial products and assess the information gathered in the investigation. ▪ Base all judgements on the client's relevant circumstances. ▪ Take any other step that would be in the best interests of the client.
s. 961G	Providing appropriate advice	Advice must only be given if it is reasonable to conclude that it is appropriate for the client.
s. 961H	Warning the client if advice is based on incomplete or inaccurate information	The client must be warned if it is reasonably apparent that the advice is based on incomplete or inaccurate information about the client's objectives and needs.
s. 961J	Prioritising the interests of the client	Advice providers are required to prioritise the interests of the client over their own interests.

FIGURE 15.1
Key obligations contained in Regulatory Guide (RG) 175
Source: Regulatory Guide (RG) 175 Licensing: Financial product advisers — conduct and disclosure.

Best interest obligations

The best interest obligations mean that a planner has three separate duties:

1. a duty to act in the client's best interests
2. a duty to provide advice that is appropriate
3. a duty to prioritise the client's interests in the event of a conflict.

The term 'best interests' is not defined in the Corporations Act or RG 175, although ASIC interprets it to mean advice provided that would leave the client in a better position. The standards used to assess whether a client would be left in a better position are based on what a 'reasonable advice provider' would believe if the client followed the advice. The assessment of client's position would need to consider the following factors:

- the position the client would have been in if they had not followed the advice
- the subject matter of the advice sought by the client
- the client's objectives, financial situations and needs
- the features of a financial product that the client particularly values, provided that the client understands the cost of, and is prepared to pay for, those features
- if the client follows the advice, the benefits they receive are more than trivial.

It is important to note that RG175 does not expect a planner to give 'perfect advice' in establishing whether the client is likely to be in a better position.

The above factors require the planner to undertake an appropriate and reasonable level of investigation into both the client's situation (know your client) and the financial products (know your product) to ensure that the advice provided is fit and appropriate to meet the needs and requirements of the client.

The financial planner must be able to demonstrate compliance with these requirements and accordingly the planner's records must be able to support and provide evidence of the work undertaken in analysing both the client and the financial products recommended. Failure to provide appropriate personal advice is an offence under the Corporations Act.

PROFESSIONAL ADVICE

A client approaching retirement meets with an advice provider (financial planner) to seek advice on what to do with their superannuation when they retire. They have been told that SMSFs are an easy way to maximise the value of their superannuation. The client has a healthy superannuation balance because they have been contributing to their superannuation for the past 35 years. They have no experience with investing.

The client's existing employer-sponsored superannuation fund has no pension option. The client understands that they need to start making some decisions about their superannuation but, because they have no previous investment experience, they are nervous about this process. They want a simple, cost-effective solution that they can easily understand and does not require too much of their time. They are looking forward to retirement and do not want the burden of watching the market every day, as they have seen some of their colleagues do.

The advice provider recommends a SMSF and reassures the client that they do not need to be too involved because the advice provider will look after it for them.

Source: Example 21 RG 175: Licensing: Financial Product Advisers — Conduct and Disclosure.

QUESTIONS

1. What factors might account for why the financial planner might have recommended the establishment of a SMSF for the client?
2. There has been a significant growth rate in the establishment of SMSFs over the past decade. What are some of the reasons that might explain this growth?
3. Is the advice likely to be in the best interests of the client?

LO 3

When is a SOA required and what is its purpose?

Part 7.7 of the Corporations Act sets out the financial service disclosure requirements in respect of the provision of financial services or advice. Included within these provisions is a requirement that, when providing advice to a client, a financial planner must provide the client with a SOA at the same time as, or as soon as practicable after, the advice is provided (s. 946A) (see also RG 175.151).

The purpose of a SOA is to communicate advice and recommendations concerning the financial affairs of a client. To be effective, a SOA must disclose sufficient information to enable a person to make an informed decision about whether the advice is appropriate to their situation and whether they should act upon the advice. RG 175.157 sets out the information that is required to be disclosed within a SOA.

The title 'statement of advice' is required to be disclosed on the cover or at the front of the SOA. Other issues requiring disclosure include:

- the name and contact details of the holder of the Australian Financial Services Licence (AFSL)
- the name and contact details of the financial planner and the organisation that they work for
- a statement setting out the advice and the basis for the advice
- information about remuneration or other benefits that the adviser may receive arising from the advice
- information about any conflicts of interest that may prejudice the advice
- a warning that the advice provided by the financial planner may not be suitable or totally appropriate for the client's circumstances if information supplied by the client is incorrect or where the client is seeking limited advice only.

There has been ongoing concern within the financial planning profession about the appropriate length of a SOA and the amount of detail that needs to be provided within the document given the detailed regulatory disclosure requirements. There is no set rule that governs the appropriate length of a SOA. The level of detail provided is important in determining whether the financial plan is likely to be of value in helping the client to make informed decisions concerning their financial situation. In determining the suitability of a SOA, what is important is the extent to which the plan is tailored to the needs of the client while taking into account the client's level of financial literacy and the complexity of the advice provided.

LO 4 When is a SOA not required?

Although a SOA is generally required to be provided whenever personal advice is provided to a client, the Corporations Act provides for a limited number of situations where a SOA does not need to be provided (see RG 175.153 (ASIC 2012)). They are:

- when the client is not a retail client
- where the advice relates to a general insurance product, a cash management trust, basic deposit products, non-cash payment products related to a basic deposit product or traveller's cheques
- when providing further advice to a client
- when providing personal advice to clients having a small amount of funds to invest (less than $15 000)
- where the advice does not involve the purchase of a financial product and where the entity providing the advice does not receive any remuneration.

The obligations relating to the provision of further advice

In situations where a client is provided with further advice, RG175.198 and s. 946B of the Corporations Act sets out the circumstances where a SOA may not be required to be provided. The circumstances prescribed include:

- the client had previously been given a SOA by the adviser setting out the client's personal circumstances in relation to the advice
- the client's personal circumstances in relation to the further advice have not significantly changed
- the basis of the advice is not significantly different from the advice in the previous SOA.

record of advice (ROA) an alternative advice document to the SOA able to be used when providing further advice to existing clients

In these circumstances, the planner may provide the client with a **record of advice (ROA)** instead of a SOA. A ROA must be given to the client when the advice is provided or as soon as practicable after the advice is given. The ROA must include as a minimum:

- a brief description of the recommendations made and the basis on which the recommendations are made
- if the advice includes a recommendation that the client replace one financial product with another, information on the extent of any benefits lost, any charges made and any other significant consequence for the client
- information about the remuneration the adviser will receive and details concerning any conflicts of interest.

In situations where an adviser provides further advice to a client, there is no prescriptive format for the ROA. Although the ROA may simply be a record in the files of the planner in the form of a summary and bullet points, a written advice statement may be more practical and reliable in demonstrating that the financial planner has discharged their responsibilities.

Small investments

Under s. 946AA of the Corporations Act, a record of advice can also be used in place of a SOA where the total investments to which the advice relates is less than $15 000. For superannuation, managed investment schemes and non-derivative instalment warrants, the $15 000 threshold includes the cost of the initial investment plus any other amounts that the client is committed to invest in the future.

The advice does not involve the purchase of a financial product

In some situations, the financial planner may be asked to provide advice to a client that does not involve the acquisition or disposal of a financial product. Remember that a financial product is defined broadly under the Corporations Act and includes:

- making a financial investment
- managing a financial risk, or
- making non-cash payments.

For example, a client may seek advice relating to the feasibility of establishing a self-managed superannuation fund or salary packaging options. A SOA would not need to be prepared in these circumstances as long as the financial planner does not receive any remuneration or benefit in relation to the advice provided. The planner is, however, required to keep a record of the advice (s. 946B(9)).

ILLUSTRATIVE EXAMPLE 15.2

As Cory and Amy are looking to save costs in respect of the financial planning advice they are seeking, and wish to limit the advice to a 2-page letter, would the financial planner be able to provide the clients with a ROA instead of a SOA?

A ROA can be provided only in circumstances where the advice is provided to an existing client and where the client had previously been given a SOA setting out their personal circumstances. As Cory and Amy are new clients, a SOA would need to be prepared in accordance with all the regulatory requirements regardless of the wishes of the client. The client should be aware that the disclosure requirements are designed to protect their interests and the planner is not permitted to disregard their legal obligations.

LO 5 Types of SOAs

Three types of SOAs are generally used by financial planners:

1. no-advice statement
2. a limited SOA (known as scaled advice)
3. a comprehensive SOA.

In certain circumstances, the financial planner may be asked to execute a particular transaction, but not to provide any advice. An example is where the planner is asked to transfer a client's superannuation balance from one fund to another. It is prudent in such circumstances for the planner to ask the client to sign a **no-advice statement** — this is in the form of a disclaimer document where the client confirms that they have not sought financial advice. This is important in order to protect the planner against future claims that the client acted upon the advice of the planner (see appendix 15A).

no-advice statement a document signed by a client stating that no advice was given by a planner in respect of a transaction

Financial advisers can give scaled advice under the FOFA reforms. One of the goals behind the FOFA reforms was the removal of barriers to the affordability of financial advice. The Future of Financial Advice (FoFA) legislation addressed the need to expand the availability of low-cost simple, single issue, personal advice, to improve access to and affordability of financial advice to retail clients. Scaled advice is personal advice that is limited in scope, either by being in response to a limited range of issues or by addressing a specific area of the investor's needs. ASIC has clarified that all advice is scaled in some way.

scaled advice advice about a specific area of an investor's needs or about a limited range of issues

Scaled advice is often sought and requested by clients seeking financial advice on a particular issue or specific circumstances, for example, an investigation into negative gearing strategies, the investment of an inheritance or the effectiveness of a salary packaging arrangement (see appendix 15D).

Consultation paper 183: Giving information, general advice and scaled advice (para. 70) sets out what planners need to do in order to discharge their legal obligations when giving scaled advice under the best interest rule. The planner is required to:

- use their judgement and training to decide whether, by limiting the scope of the advice, they can provide personal advice that meets their legal obligations
- adjust the level of their inquiries to reflect the complexity of the advice being provided
- implement systems that will help them decide what advice the client requires
- communicate clearly to the client the type of advice service they are offering.

It is worth noting that, under s. 945B of the Corporations Act, clients must be provided with a warning where advice is based on incomplete or limited information. If a financial planner is aware, or ought to be aware, that personal advice is based on incomplete or inaccurate information, the financial planner must provide a warning to the client about the limitations of the advice and its appropriateness for the client.

A comprehensive SOA considers all aspects of the client's personal circumstances and situation. It is also known as holistic advice. The planner needs to complete a thorough fact finder, analyse all aspects of the client's circumstances and produce a comprehensive set of integrated solutions that helps to achieve all of the client's goals, needs and objectives.

PERSONAL FINANCE BULLETIN

Scaled advice to provide pay certainty

ISN-commissioned research predicts that advisers and clients will make a marked shift towards scaled advice to make the most of FoFA changes.

As clients become aware of the cost of advice, those who are not regularly serviced by advisers (around 40%), will switch to receiving scaled advice on a piece-by-piece basis, says the Rice Warner report.

Advisers will also be making the shift to cover remuneration gaps left by FoFA. The average cost of advice is expected to reduce from $2046 to $1163, and the overall reduction in adviser remuneration is expected to be $2.7 billion by 2027.

Rice Warner predicts that the number of advisers giving purely scaled advice will grow from 350, to almost 1500 by 2020 and 2729 by 2027. On the other hand, advisers giving full advice — including scaled advice — are expected to drop from 17 746 to 15 689 in 2020, and 14 926 in 2027.

Many full advisers rely on substantial trail commissions and platform rebates to sustain their business, says the research. Remuneration structures for scaled advice will be very different, with a fixed salary and possibly a bonus depending on quality of work rather than sales and retention.

Dealer Groups are likely to offer scaled advice models, and are also expected to take a higher share of the adviser fee, as it will be more difficult to hold an adviser to a particular platform — their fee will be paid irrespective of the fund chosen. 'This could lead to higher adviser fees but lower platform fees.'

The skills required for scaled advice will be different as it is more automated and provided over the phone rather than face-to-face. However, the selection and training is an on-going issue, according to Rice Warner. 'The market has a shortage of appropriately skilled individuals with the desired profiles to provide assistance.'

The report states that the different type of work is 'likely to lead to different people entering advice jobs and some existing financial advisers leaving theirs'.

What does scaled advice look like?

Scaled advice models have been structured around single issues, 'based on the assumption that clients at similar life stages will often have similar goals and objectives'.

Typical groups are:

- Young singles starting out in life — Require budgeting debt management and superannuation co-contributions
- Young married couples — Targets for voluntary super contributions and life insurance
- Asset builders — Possible targets for salary sacrifice and higher levels of insurance
- Mature people — May need to increase their superannuation
- Transitional era — Require transition to retirement strategy
- Retirees — Retirement income strategies

The price for scaled advice can vary anywhere between $200 and $1500, but the research predicts an average cost of $275.

Source: Kathleen Payne, *Wealth Professional*, 24 July 2013, www.wealthprofessional.com.au/news/scaled-advice-to-provide-pay-certainty-177473.aspx.

LO 6 The importance of effective communication in a SOA

A SOA should provide detailed strategies and projected outcomes for each of the recommendations raised and how these will meet the client's stated objectives. Once again, care should be taken to ensure that all strategies and discussions contained in the body of the SOA are specific to the client's circumstances.

To ensure that the client fully understands the strategies outlined to them by the planner, it is important that the SOA is written in plain English and prepared with the client's level of financial sophistication in mind. In this way, the planner helps to ensure that the client 'owns' the plan and commits to its realisation.

It is important to note that the SOA should be used both for communication and as an educative tool to set out and explain the planner's recommendations. The SOA should not be used as a compliance tool or a mechanism to protect the planner against liability.

In terms of the communication and disclosure of information to a client, a SOA is only as good as the client's understanding of the information provided within the SOA. Accordingly the financial planner needs to ensure that the information presented is tailored to the client's particular level of financial literacy. Where a client's level of financial literacy and understanding is low, information needs to be presented in such a way as could reasonably be understood from a layperson's point of view. For clients having a more sophisticated level of understanding, the level of detail and form of explanation may be expanded upon. The planner needs to carefully balance the need for illustrating the technical aspects of the strategy against the need for the client to understand what is being recommended. The central focus of the SOA should always be the client and not the financial planner's display of technical skills.

Good Disclosure Principles principles promoted by ASIC to help promote good disclosure outcomes for clients

RG 168 *Disclosure: Product Disclosure Statements (and other disclosure obligations)*, contains ASIC's **Good Disclosure Principles** to help product issuers and financial planners comply with the disclosure requirements and also promote good disclosure outcomes for consumers (ASIC 2010). The Good Disclosure Principles (RG 168.4) consist of the following:

(a) disclosure should be timely;
(b) disclosure should be relevant and complete;
(c) disclosure should promote product understanding;
(d) disclosure should promote product comparison;
(e) disclosure should highlight important information; and
(f) disclosure should have regard to consumers' needs.

LO 7 The importance of the planner–client relationship

Having excellent technical knowledge and a comprehensive knowledge of financial products will not be sufficient on its own to ensure an effective working relationship between the client and the financial planner. Many clients face difficulty opening up and confiding personal information to a planner, don't feel that their needs and best interests are being looked after, or fail to understand and engage with the strategies and recommendations developed by the financial planner. Communication is a critical aspect in both establishing and maintaining effective client relationships. A planner needs to exhibit excellent communication skills in order to develop a thorough understanding and appreciation of the client's personal, financial and emotive situation. In addition, an effective planner also needs to exhibit competence in communicating strategies and concepts in terms that are understood by the client and in a way that encourages the client to appreciate the importance of acting upon the advice.

Jaffe & Grubman (2011, p. 1) argue that the 'the most effective and successful advisers in the industry are ones who can truly listen, build trust, interview effectively, make the client feel understood, and manage the delicate issues money can evoke'.

A significant body of research has looked into some of the more important factors that determine an effective client–professional relationship. The financial planning discipline is no different to other professions, with the key attributes being the ability to communicate well and the ability to develop trust. A report by Wharton University entitled *Bridging the Trust Divide: The Financial Advisor–Client Relationship* found that three types of trust are important:

- trust in technical competence and knowhow — investors are primarily looking for someone whose level of competence and experience inspires trust
- trust in ethical conduct and character — does the client associate with the personal character and ethics of the planner and do these attributes instil trust that the planner will look after the client's best interests?
- trust in empathic skills and maturity — does the client have trust in the adviser to handle personal issues and sensitive information with empathy and tact?

Obligations at the initial client meeting

Prior to engaging the services of a financial planner, an introductory meeting between the financial planner and the client is normally arranged and serves a number of purposes:

- to establish the relationship between the planner and the client
- to provide the planner with an opportunity to learn about the client, the client's circumstances and needs, and to determine what the client is hoping to accomplish from the relationship
- to provide the client with an opportunity to learn about the planner and the services they offer and whether the planner is likely to be able to satisfy the client's requirements.

The initial meeting or interview provides the means by which a financial planner and client are able to ascertain the extent to which they have the confidence and trust to work constructively together. If either party does not feel comfortable with the relationship, the financial planning process should not continue.

The meeting allows the client to learn about the planner and their practice, the services the planner offers and how the client will be charged for the services provided. The client should be prepared to ask questions that will allow them to judge the ability of the planner to appropriately manage their client's finances and to act in their best interests. The initial meeting also provides an opportunity for the planner to learn about the client, their goals and concerns, their plans for the future and their personality. At the first meeting, the planner would normally provide the client with a copy of their FSG, run through the main provisions of the document and give the client an opportunity to ask questions and seek clarification on any issues.

Once the client and planner have agreed to commence the financial planning process and work towards the preparation of a SOA, a planner may decide to issue an engagement letter setting out the parameters of the engagement.

One of the important disclosure obligations imposed on the planner is to provide the client with a financial services guide (FSG). A financial planner is required to provide a client with a FSG at the earliest possible opportunity, before any advice is provided or recommendations made. The FSG is normally provided at the initial meeting between the planner and client. The provision of a FSG provides the client with the opportunity to learn about the planner, including their qualifications and experience, the type of services and advice offered, how the planner charges for their service and the mechanisms in place for complaint resolution. To provide evidence that the client has been provided with a FSG, many planners will ask the client to sign a written acknowledgement or statement that they have received a copy of the planner's FSG.

The information that would typically be found in a FSG includes:

- the identity of the holder of the Australian Financial Services Licence (AFSL), known as the dealer or licensee, as well as details of the financial planner operating under that licence, known as the authorised representative
- the range of investment advisory services offered
- the method and extent of fees charged
- the details of the licensee's dispute resolution procedures.

Another obligation imposed on the planner relates to the *Anti-money Laundering and Counter-Terrorism Financing Act 2006* (AML/CTF Act). The AML/CTF Act contains a number of compliance obligations imposed on the planner as part of the process of preventing and detecting money laundering and terrorism activities. These obligations relate to customer identification and identity verification, recordkeeping, and ongoing client due diligence and reporting. A planner should not provide a client with financial advice until they are able to personally identify and verify the identity of the client. This will require the planner to verify and keep on file documentation relating to the client's identification, such as a driver's licence or passport, and to report any suspicious activity or situation.

LO 8

The six steps of the financial planning process

In preparing a SOA for a client, a financial planner will normally follow a structured process to help understand the needs and requirements of the client and facilitate the design and implementation of appropriate strategies. While the process should be carried out in a logical sequence and will be similar for most clients, the depth and flexibility of the process will vary depending on the complexity and needs of the client.

The Financial Planning Association of Australia (FPA) generally recommends a six-step financial planning process; however, other formats and processes may equally be relevant and appropriate in compiling a client-specific SOA. The six-step process is discussed in detail next, but can be summarised as in figure 15.2.

Step 1: Gather client information

Client information is normally gathered in a data-collection questionnaire (also referred to as a fact finder) and forms the basis for the preparation of the SOA (see appendix 15B). Completing a data collection questionnaire is one of the key means by which a financial planner is able to demonstrate that they have made reasonable enquiries into the personal circumstances of the client (RG 175.281–287) and satisfied the 'best interests' obligations imposed under s. 961B of the Corporations Act.

It is important for the client to be made aware that the planner is unable to provide thorough and effective advice unless the client provides accurate and comprehensive information concerning their personal and financial circumstances. Some clients may not wish to disclose certain information about their circumstances, and in these cases the planner may need to limit their advice to certain issues or areas, such as superannuation, insurance or redundancy.

Throughout the data-gathering stage, the financial planner needs to look beyond the quantitative information provided by the client and ensure that qualitative issues are also considered. This is where the experience and expertise of the planner comes into play in terms of the types of questions they ask, their ability to build a relationship and ensuring that the client fully understands the questions in the data-collection questionnaire. Some of the qualitative issues that the planner may be interested in exploring may include the client's needs, objectives, concerns, health, degree of financial literacy and understanding, and any preconceptions the client may have, such as the relevance of income protection insurance.

Step 1	Gather client information	Gather all relevant information, both financial and non-financial, through data collection forms and questionnaires.
Step 2	Establish financial goals and objectives	Identify and establish the specific goals of the client. Assist the client in quantifying and prioritising competing goals.
Step 3	Analyse data and identify financial issues	Identify the strengths and weaknesses of the client's financial situation as it affects the ability of the client to achieve their goals and objectives.
Step 4	Prepare and develop the SOA	Develop a set of recommendations and strategies that are tailored to the client's specific requirements.
Step 5	Implement the agreed-upon recommendations	Put in place an agreed plan of action to determine how the recommendations are to be implemented and who is to perform the actions.
Step 6	Review and revise the SOA	Evaluate and review the plan at regular intervals to ensure that the recommendations remain appropriate for the client. Review changes in the client's circumstances.

FIGURE 15.2
The financial planning process

At this stage, the planner normally also assesses the client's risk profile. There are many ways this can be achieved, as discussed in the next section (see appendix 15C). Risk profiling is also an integral part of the 'know your client' process. Once the client's risk profile (i.e. attitude to risk) is identified, the weighting of the client's current and proposed asset allocation can be determined and matched against their profile. The asset allocation should incorporate all investments including superannuation but exclude all personal and lifestyle assets.

ILLUSTRATIVE EXAMPLE 15.3

You have assessed the risk tolerance of Cory and Amy and have determined them as moderately aggressive, with a recommended investment allocation weighted 75% to growth oriented investments (shares and property) and 25% to defensive investments (cash and fixed interest).

From the information provided, prepare both a current and recommended asset allocation.

Current asset allocation

Investment	Cash	Aust. fixed interest	Property	Australian shares	International shares	Total
Savings account	20 000					20 000
Share portfolio				25 000		25 000
Superannuation — Cory	4 000	14 000	4000	12 000	6 000	40 000
Superannuation — Amy	2 450	9 800	3500	12 250	7 000	35 000
Total $	26 450	23 800	7500	49 250	13 000	120 000
Total %	22.0%	19.8%	6.3%	41.1%	10.8%	100%

The current asset allocation is weighted 41.8% defensive and 58.2% growth oriented. The overall weighting is not consistent with their risk profile of the couple and accordingly needs to be amended. Options to amend the asset allocation of the couple to an appropriate 25/75 weighting may be to allocate excess cash to more aggressive investments or otherwise adjust the weighting of the couple's superannuation accounts. In this case, we may assume that the couple wish to retain their cash holding but are happy to amend their superannuation accounts. One way of achieving an appropriate asset allocation for the couple may be illustrated through the following table.

Recommended asset allocation

Investment	Cash	Aust. fixed interest	Property	Australian shares	International shares	Total
Savings account	20 000					20 000
Share portfolio				25 000		25 000
Superannuation — Cory	1 000	5000	7 000	14 000	13 000	40 000
Superannuation — Amy	1 000	4000	6 000	13 000	11 000	35 000
Total $	22 000	9000	13 000	52 000	24 000	120 000
Total %	18.3%	7.5%	10.8%	43.4%	20.0%	100%

By re-allocating the couple's superannuation accounts, the couple's investment allocation is now consistent with their risk profile. The couple should be made aware that some capital gains tax may be payable on the disposal of the fixed interest investments within their superannuation accounts.

Assessing the risk tolerance of a client

As part of the process of complying with the best interest obligations, the financial planner is required to first determine a client's relevant personal circumstances in respect of the advice to be given and then make reasonable inquiries about those relevant personal circumstances (s. 961B(2)). An important consideration when investigating the client's personal circumstances relates to the issue of risk and assessing the risk tolerance of the client. Valentine (2003) divides the assessment of risk into two aspects. Firstly, the planner needs to understand and provide the client with information on the various risks associated with investments. Secondly, the planner needs to establish the risk profile or risk tolerance of each client and ensure that all recommendations are consistent with the risk profile of the client. Risk tolerance can be differentiated from risk capacity, which refers to the amount of money that an individual could afford to lose without putting their financial goals at risk. Both risk tolerance and risk capacity are important issues for a planner formulating appropriate advice for a client.

Reconciling a client's risk profile is not always an easy and straightforward process, especially where the client consists of a couple with differing tolerances to risk. In the end, it is up to the client to decide what risk they are prepared to accept and feel comfortable with. The planner can play an important role in educating the client about what risk tolerance is and what its impact might be in terms of the potential returns from investments and the ability to achieve certain goals and objectives. A client may need to be made aware that a certain tolerance to risk may not enable a client to achieve their goals and objectives.

While an assessment of the client's risk profile is an integral part of the financial planning process, there is no generally accepted view within the industry on how it should be assessed or applied in formulating appropriate advice for a client. Many advisers use some form of risk profiling questionnaire and an example is provided in appendix 15C. Under this approach, a series of questions is drawn up for the client to answer, either developed by the financial planner or supplied through their financial planning software. The answers the client provides to these questions are analysed by the planner and used to indicate the level of risk that a client is generally prepared to accept with their investments and, leading on from this, what would be an appropriate asset allocation. An alternative approach used by some planners within the industry is a psychological risk assessment, which attempts to ascertain how psychologically receptive an individual is to decisions involving risk. Whatever methodology is used to assess the risk tolerance of a client, the planner will need to ensure that the tool used is valid, thorough and justifiable.

In compiling an appropriate asset allocation and recommending specific investments for a client, the planner will attempt to compile the lowest risk portfolio that will meet a client's objectives and then compare the level of risk inherent in that portfolio with the client's risk tolerance and financial risk capacity.

Despite each person possessing different goals and differing abilities to cope with risk, it is generally accepted that investors can usually be grouped into a number of risk classifications or core profiles.

Table 15.1 provides an illustration of how an asset allocation can be determined based on the various risk classifications.

TABLE 15.1 Examples of asset allocations for different risk and return profiles

	Conservative	Moderate	Balanced	Growth	High growth
Cash	25%	15%	10%	5%	5%
Fixed interest	55%	45%	30%	25%	15%
Property	5%	10%	10%	10%	10%
Australian shares	10%	20%	30%	35%	40%
International shares	5%	10%	20%	25%	30%
Overall asset allocation (growth/defensive)	20/80	40/60	60/40	70/30	80/20
Investment term	2 years	3 years	5 years	7 years	7+ years

Step 2: Establish financial goals and objectives

During this stage, the planner's role is to help the client define and prioritise their personal and financial objectives. Each client will have different goals, objectives and time frames and it is up to the financial planner to determine the extent to which the client's objectives are achievable, realistic or optimistic.

ILLUSTRATIVE EXAMPLE 15.4

Cory and Amy are looking to acquire a family home in 6 months for a cost of around $650 000. Is this objective and expectation realistic and how might a planner deal with this?

Part of the financial planner's role is to educate the client on expectations and order of priorities. The financial commitments required in owning a property would need to be discussed with the client as well as their ability to fund an appropriate deposit on the purchase and repay mortgage repayments. Issues that the planner should cover with the client might include:

- what additional acquisition costs are likely to exist with the purchase (such as stamp duty and legal costs)?
- what amount of deposit is the couple able to provide?
- how much can the couple afford to commit towards annual mortgage and interest repayments?
- what deposit is a financial institution likely to require before they will provide any funding? If borrowing for an amount of greater than 80% of the worth of the property, will the couple be liable for mortgage insurance?

Given their accumulated savings and investments, it is highly unlikely that the couple will be able to afford to purchase a property worth $650 000 within the next 6 months. Part of the planner's role would be to put in place a savings/investment plan to assist the client accumulate a reasonable deposit on the home that they could afford and help them determine what annual mortgage repayment they could afford to repay.

As clients have different objectives, each financial plan needs to be tailored to fit the individual circumstances of the client. The planner's role is to help clients develop and clarify their objectives in terms of whether they are short term (e.g. taking a holiday, paying off credit cards), medium term (e.g. saving a deposit for a car or a home) or long term (e.g. estate or retirement planning).

Client objectives need to be clear, specific and measurable. An effective objective statement should contain a well-defined target that is expressed in a time frame that is achievable and details how the objective is to be funded. For example, the client is seeking to accumulate $60 000 in savings towards putting a deposit on a house in 5 years.

The financial planner then needs to identify any problems or conflicts that might arise between the client's objectives and the possible strategies and recommendations. Some of the issues that may arise include:

- analysing opportunity costs
- agreement on trade-offs
- decisions about priorities
- confronting ethical issues.

Step 3: Analyse data and identify financial issues

Having obtained all the necessary information relevant to the preparation of a comprehensive personal SOA, the financial planner then undertakes a detailed analysis of the client's quantitative and qualitative data and clarifies all areas of doubt regarding the client's perceptions and intentions.

This analysis will help the financial planner to determine what strategies may be appropriate to overcome problems or weakness in the client's financial position. Every area of financial planning has to be considered in the context of the client's circumstances for appropriate strategies to be developed. For example, in the area of tax planning, strategies such as negative gearing, salary sacrifice, income splitting, business and investment ownership structures, franking credits and capital gains and losses all need to be examined when relevant to the client's situation. Unless all of the client's circumstances are fully analysed, appropriate recommendations and strategies cannot be determined and put in place. This is consistent with the best interest duties required of financial planners under s. 961B(2) of the Corporations Act.

The following would normally form part of a comprehensive analysis of a client's situation:

- ascertaining cash inflows and outflows to determine saving capacity
- assessing income tax obligations
- assessing the appropriateness of the asset allocation
- determining the extent to which the current wealth creation of a client is likely to generate sufficient funds for retirement
- assessing social security entitlements
- determining whether personal insurance cover is adequate and appropriate
- comparing proposed strategies and investment products with the client's risk tolerance and objectives.

To assist in the analysis and interpretation of the client's position, the planner may prepare a set of personal financial statements from the data gathered. This normally consists of a balance sheet, income statement and cash flow statement. Financial planners may use a range of analytical techniques to monitor and review the data — for example, the use of financial ratios as discussed in chapter 2. The analysis will indicate such things as:

- what investments the client owns
- whether the investments are held in the most beneficial name or structure for tax purposes
- the amount and nature of the liabilities
- whether there is a cash deficit (to be rectified) or a cash surplus (investment opportunities)
- the tax position.

The planner may also undertake financial modelling to determine whether the client's goals are likely to be achieved based on existing conditions. For example, is the client likely to achieve their desired income upon retirement? Once the client's personal data is analysed, it can be related to the client's goals and objectives to determine possible problem areas. For example, a client may desire to invest some funds to achieve a high rate of return with low risk and low tax. Such an objective may prove impossible and require a trade-off between competing wishes. The planner would need to discuss the issues involved with the client to reach a compromise and a more achievable objective. Other examples of problems may include inadequate holdings of liquidity to fund a holiday; spending in excess of income levels; inadequate funds to support retirement at age 55; and inadequate levels of insurance to pay out all debts and provide for dependants in the event of the premature death of the main income earner.

Step 4: Prepare and develop the SOA

Once the client's personal situation has been comprehensively analysed, the planner can develop appropriate financial planning recommendations and strategies. One of the key skills and obligations of a planner is to be able to communicate their recommendations effectively and in a manner that will enable a client to make an informed decision. This is facilitated through the preparation and presentation of a comprehensive and detailed SOA.

Within the SOA, careful planning is needed to ensure that the plan is well structured, clear and concise. The strategies need to be sufficiently articulated so that a client is able to determine what is being proposed, the rationale for the proposal, the amounts involved, any tax implications, and the risks and benefits. The client should not have to go searching through different sections of the financial plan to determine what the recommendations are or be left guessing exactly what is being proposed.

A financial planner's recommendations are often based on a number of assumptions. It is important that all of these assumptions are clearly stated and attached to the plan. Only those issues that relate to future events that cannot be verified (e.g. economic indicators and expected returns) should be assumed. However, the assumptions need to be both reasonable and justifiable at the time they are made.

The following represent some of the assumptions that would normally be included in a SOA:

- tax rates (i.e. use current year's tax rates)
- inflation (e.g. assume an annual CPI increase of 3.5%)
- interest rates
- income and capital investment returns
- life expectancy of the client.

Step 5: Implement the agreed-upon recommendations

The SOA has to be formally agreed upon, signed and consented to before it can be implemented. The SOA should describe in a clear manner the implementation process and the agreed-upon recommendations. This may take the form of a chronological list of actions to be undertaken. It is most important that the client fully understands the contents of the plan so that they become a 'shared owner' of the ideas and are satisfied that implementation of the recommendations are in their best interests.

Implementation procedures will normally include the following documents for the client to sign:

- an 'action to proceed' section within the SOA
- an 'authority to proceed' document
- application forms to complete for the financial products recommended.

The 'action to proceed' section should indicate clear responsibilities and a time line for implementation.

For example:

Action	**When**	**Who**
Client to salary sacrifice	Immediately	The client to organise through their employer $1500 per month into their superannuation fund

The purpose of an 'authority to proceed' is for the client to be able to confirm acceptance of the strategies detailed within the plan and to confirm all product recommendations that have been proposed, including the name of the product, in whose name the product is to be acquired and the amounts involved. The authority also provides the opportunity for the client to confirm that they have received a SOA and a financial services guide (FSG). The authority to proceed document should be signed by the client and held in the planner's file.

Once the client's consent is obtained, the financial planner should take full control of time lines, check and network with all parties involved, and monitor the implementation stage. The planner and client should agree on *who* is going to implement *what* and *when*. The financial planner should be vigilant in every aspect of the implementation and processing stages and closely monitor the various steps of the action plan in an agreed-upon process. As part of this process, the planner may need to refer the client to other professionals, such as solicitors for estate planning matters, stockbrokers for the purchase of equities, and accountants for setting up business structures and tax advice.

Step 6: Review and revise the SOA

Periodically, the client's financial position should be reviewed to ensure the recommendations and strategies developed under the SOA remain appropriate. This should normally occur on a 6-monthly basis, although it could also be undertaken quarterly, annually or as required depending on the type of client and the level of service that has been agreed upon. The financial planner should describe the process of review, the frequency proposed and the charges for providing this service.

A review is much more than just a current valuation of the portfolio. It also evaluates whether the existing plan continues to meet the client's needs or requires adjustment. A review should therefore include consideration of the appropriateness of the portfolio in the context of any changes to the client's personal or family situation, new liabilities or changes to their goals and objectives.

It is important to note the distinction between monitoring and reviewing. The term 'monitoring' implies a 24-hour vigil, with prompt corrective action implemented in accordance with the client's prior consent. Some financial planning practices may well have the infrastructure and facilities to accommodate such a demanding service. This type of monitoring service, for instance, may well suit a stockbroking house. The review process undertaken by most financial planners, however, is normally done on a periodic basis, as required, and is more realistically achievable within a typical practice.

As discussed previously, the requirements of Part 7.7 of the Corporations Act requires that a written advice document be provided to a client each time financial product advice is given. One of the issues arising from this obligation is whether a comprehensive SOA is required to be prepared each time a review of a client is undertaken and, as a result, whether the planner is required to duplicate information already contained in an earlier SOA. Where the recommendations and strategies continue to meet the needs of the client and no significant changes have occurred in the client's financial circumstances or in the recommended financial products, the review may take the form of a ROA as previously discussed. Otherwise a new SOA will need to be issued.

LO 9 Ethical and legal compliance issues

Financial planners must be familiar with all regulatory requirements as well as their professional obligations if they are members of a professional association. Members of the Financial Planning Association (FPA) are required to comply with the Code of Professional Practice ('the Code') which includes three enforceable components: Code of Ethics, Practice Standards and Rules of Professional Conduct. Members of the Association of Financial Advisers (AFA) are similarly required to adhere to a code of ethics as well as a code of conduct, entitled the Principles of Practice.

Both sets of codes are based on the planner having a fiduciary obligation to look after the best interests of the client without bias or conflict and in a manner that establishes a relationship of trust, confidence and discretion.

Client records

It is important that all information contained within a client's file is stored safely and kept confidentially. This includes records such as SOAs, ROAs, letters, authorities to proceed, client invoices and receipts. A 7-year period is specified by the FPA for retention of client records (refer to FPA Rule 120). A prudent planner will, however, keep those records for longer periods than specified. Regular backups of electronic and other physical data should be made and stored at remote premises.

Financial planners must also strictly adhere to the guidelines of the *Privacy Act 1988*. (The website of the Office of the Privacy Commissioner, privacy.gov.au, has further information on the Act.) The aim of the privacy provisions is to ensure that organisations that collect information about people retain the information responsibly. The provisions set out how organisations should collect, use, keep, secure and disclose personal information. Individuals are also given a right to know what information an organisation is holding about them and a right to correct that information if it is wrong.

Access to client records

The courts and the Australian Securities and Investments Commission (ASIC) have the right to access client records as part of any investigation. The dealer or licensee will also have access to the client files of their financial planners and will check client records on a periodic basis to ensure that the planner is adhering to all regulatory and compliance issues. The licensee is responsible for the actions of their authorised representatives and for any breaches that put the licensee at risk.

Ownership of client records

Clients have the right, at all times, to be able to identify the licensee who bears the ultimate liability for the advice provided. As such, the ownership of the client's records lies with the licensee and not the planner. In the event that a financial planner moves to another licensee, the client's records remain the property of the original licensee unless the client decides to move with their planner. However, for years the financial planning industry has worked on the unwritten rule that the planner 'owns' the client, and, in the event that a planner leaves a licence holder, the client moves with the planner. From time to time, this arrangement has been challenged and planners who leave their licensees are discovering that it is not so easy to gain access to clients, even those who were brought into the licensee's business by the planner from a previous business arrangement.

Regardless of one's stance on such a contentious issue, it is vital to remember that clients are the people who decide whether they stay with the licensee or follow the adviser. The client's decision will be determined by their assessment of who has offered them the best value and the best advice.

Disclosure of remuneration

The issue of the disclosure of fees and remuneration received by financial planners has become an important and contentious issue within the financial planning profession. Consumers are demanding an increasing level of integrity, honesty and transparency from their planners.

Financial planners have an ethical and legal obligation to disclose all fees, commissions and any material interests that may result from their recommendations. Regulatory Guide RG 182 requires that various costs, fees, charges, expenses, benefits and interests related to the planner's remuneration, costs related to the purchase of a financial product or other costs incurred by the client as a result of the planner's recommendations be stated in dollar amounts in a SOA and Product Disclosure Statement (ASIC 2008).

The financial planning industry has traditionally relied upon commissions to pay for services provided to clients. However, in recent years there has been a shift towards a fee-based model. The range of remuneration models varies considerably within the financial planning industry and includes the following.

- *Commissions* — this remuneration model is based upon the product provider, such as a fund manager, paying a fee directly to the planner (a **commission**) out of the product costs charged to the client. Different product providers pay different levels of commissions to planners. While the client does not pay a fee to the planner directly, they do pay for the service indirectly through product charges. The problem with this remuneration model in the past was that the client may not have known what commissions they were actually paying to the planner. As well as an initial commission paid upon an investment into a fund, the planner is likely to be also paid an annual 'trail' commission by the product provider. These commissions are normally ongoing and are paid for as long as the client retains their funds within the managed fund. For example, a product provider might pay a planner a fee of 2% for recommending the product to the client and an ongoing trail of 1% p.a.

commission
a fee paid to a planner by a product provider for recommending a particular product to a client

fee-for-service
a remuneration model where the client is billed directly by the financial planner for the service they provide based on an agreement with the client

- *Fee-for-service* — under a **fee-for-service** model, amounts are charged by the planner based on an agreement with the client. The client may pay the fee directly or, more commonly, the product provider might execute or pay the fee on behalf of the client out of client's funds. The fee is negotiated with the client and may be based on an agreed level of service, the complexity of the advice or the size of the investment (i.e. amount of funds under management). For example, a planner might negotiate an initial fee for the provision of the SOA plus an ongoing fee of 1% p.a. based on the amount of the client's funds that are managed by the planner.
- *Hourly rate* — under this model, the client is charged an hourly rate based on the amount of time spent by the planner. For example, a planner may charge a fee of $150 per hour for advice provided to a client in respect of the establishment and operation of a self-managed superannuation fund.

The commission basis of remuneration has been around for many years and proponents have long argued that, as the client does not pay a fee directly to the planner, the model is an affordable way for clients to pay for financial advice. However, the true cost and value of advice has been the subject of an increasing level of community debate over past years and the spotlight has increasingly been placed on the remuneration models adopted within the industry. Concerns have been raised about the lack of transparency that can exist with commission payments being lumped together with product costs, as well as the potential for a conflict of interest arising due to product providers paying different rates of commission. After considerable community scrutiny, debate and consultation, the FPA has decided to move away from commission-based remuneration. Effective from 2012, the ability of members of the FPA to charge a commission will be removed and members will be required to adopt a fee-based model (FPA 2009). However, for the time being, commission payments will continue to be approved for risk and insurance products. Subsequent to the stance taken by the FPA, the Commonwealth Government announced a number of reforms to the financial planning industry as part of the *Future of financial advice* package released in 2010. The package represents the government's response to the Ripoll *Inquiry into financial products and services in Australia* in 2009 (Commonwealth of Australia Parliamentary Joint Committee on Corporations and Financial Services 2009). The government's reforms ban conflicted remuneration structures, including commissions and volume-based payments from 1 July 2013. The ban currently excludes insurance products held outside of a member's superannuation accounts.

LO 10 Important components of a SOA

A client must be provided with a SOA when, or as soon as practicable after, advice is provided and before any action is taken associated with that advice. As previously stated, each SOA needs to be tailored to the specific needs of the client. Every client has different needs, objectives and therefore strategies, and accordingly each SOA must be specifically tailored to the individual client and take into account their level of financial literacy and general understanding.

It is important to note that while there is no set format or template for a SOA, s. 947B(2) of the Corporations Act does set out a range of issues that are common to every SOA. The test applied by ASIC is based on what a person would reasonably require for the purpose of deciding whether or not to act on the advice.

To illustrate how a SOA might be constructed, the following section provides reference to two different scaled (limited) SOAs. The first example has been provided by ASIC in RG 90, *Example Statement of Advice: Scaled advice for a new client*, which was re-issued in August 2013. The example SOA has been kept deliberately short and concise with the focus being on the key sections that help clients make informed decisions about the advice given. The ASIC example SOA provides a guide to industry best practice. However, this is only one example of an acceptable format; many other and different formats are acceptable and being used throughout the industry. What is important is that the disclosures are in accordance with prescribed regulations, the strategies are appropriate for the client's needs and objectives, and the information is communicated in a clear and concise manner.

The second example (scaled) SOA provides an alternative format for consideration. The client's background personal and financial information has been made available, as has the client's objectives, and the information forms the basis of the recommendations contained within the SOA. The example SOA is provided in appendix 15D.

The main components of a SOA

The main components of a SOA are outlined next.

Covering letter

A covering letter should always accompany any client correspondence. The covering letter that accompanies a SOA may contain some or all of the following:

- references to the meeting(s) with the client, the attached SOA, and the FSG provided at the first meeting with the client
- a request that the client review the SOA, make further inquiries if needed, check the accuracy of their personal details and bring any inaccuracies to the attention of the financial planner
- a summary of the main recommendations
- an offer to help with implementing the SOA
- recommendations as to a time frame for the SOA and its validity, that is, a sunset clause (which is a date limit for the recommendations to remain valid)
- a suggestion of a date and time for a follow-up appointment.

In all correspondence with a client, it is important that the following details are provided:

- licensee's identification, including name, licence held, address and contact information
- planner's identification, including name, authority held, address and contact information.

Contents page

Given the comprehensiveness of the SOA presented to a client, the pages should be numbered and an easy-to-follow contents or index page should be included to facilitate referencing. The client can then see at a glance the various components of the SOA.

Cover page

The cover page introduces the nature of the report, whether a SOA or ROA, and sets out basic information the client needs to know before they read the contents of the SOA, including the name of the providing entity and their contact details, what the SOA is about and why the client should read it.

Executive summary

An executive summary is normally included at the front of most SOAs and should include in a simple, clear and concise way the following aspects:

- the main strategies recommended
- the risks and benefits associated with each of the strategies
- how the strategies meet the needs of the client
- fees and charges
- how to proceed.

These elements should be viewed from a *macro* point of view, with details provided within the body of the SOA. The executive summary should normally be no more than one page and is designed to be a quick summary for the client.

Scope of the advice

scope of the advice the nature of the advice sought by the client, including any client or planner limitations

To ensure that both parties are clear as to the nature and coverage of the advice sought, the SOA should detail the extent to which the plan is limited or restricted in any fashion. This is known as the **scope of the advice**. Limitations may arise in terms of the information provided by the client, areas of the client's circumstances that are to be excluded from the review, or restrictions placed by the licence holder on the planner's ability to recommend certain financial products. Where the advice is based on incomplete or inaccurate information provided by the client, the planner is required to warn the client that they should consider the appropriateness of the advice having regard to their personal circumstances (s. 961H of the Corporations Act).

Important information about the client

The financial planner must ensure that the client's present position, financial circumstances, attitude and risk are clearly identified and form an integral part of the SOA. A current balance sheet and cash flow statement is normally provided here. The current asset allocation of the client should also be detailed and analysed in terms of the client's risk profile to establish a target or direction for the asset allocation going forward. This information should be organised and displayed in an easy-to-follow manner.

As the SOA's strategies and recommendations are based on the information gathered from the client, it is imperative that the information is accurate. Clients should be encouraged to review their particulars in the SOA carefully and refer any errors or omissions immediately to the planner.

What the client wants to achieve

Under this section, the client's goals and objectives are listed. The objectives should be prioritised, quantified where possible and categorised into time periods.

The advice to the client

The SOA needs to detail specific strategies to meet the clients' specific needs and objectives. The SOA needs to be sufficiently detailed and specific for the client to be able to clearly determine what is recommended, the basis for the recommendation, how much, with who and when. However, the planner needs to be mindful of not overloading the SOA with so much detail that the nature of the advice itself is lost.

The recommendations should enable the client to understand and determine exactly:

- what the advice is
- why the advice is appropriate

- the benefits of the advice
- the risks and disadvantages associated with the advice
- how the advice enables the client to achieve their goals and objectives.

To facilitate understanding and comprehension, advice may best be illustrated through the use of graphs, tables, diagrams and charts. The wording and detail of the information provided will be determined largely by the financial literacy of the client.

It is important that the advice provided to a client covers all aspects of the client's circumstances. Any issue that is omitted leaves the financial planner open to possible litigation. Any restriction or limitation to the advice provided or sought should be detailed in the scope of the advice section.

ILLUSTRATIVE EXAMPLE 15.5

As part of your comprehensive analysis of Cory and Amy's circumstances, you identify that the couple are significantly underinsured for life, trauma and income protection insurance. You discuss this issue with the couple at a meeting and the ramifications that a premature death or disability would have on their family's lifestyle. The couple agree they probably need more insurance, but state that they cannot afford the cost of the premiums at this stage and therefore do not require any recommendations on their insurance needs within their SOA.

Should the planner still refer to the client's insurance shortfall and provide recommendations within the SOA regardless of the client's request to ignore this issue, or can the planner safely ignore the insurance needs of the client within the plan?

Despite Cory and Amy stating that they cannot afford the cost of insurance premiums for any level of insurance coverage or for the level of coverage recommended by the planner, the planner should still provide what they believe is appropriate for the client and in their best interest. Imagine if the planner made no reference to the insurance needs of the client and 2 months later the client was killed in a car crash. The planner would have to try to explain to the family why they had not tried to educate the client on the importance and benefits of taking out appropriate insurance. Unless there was some documentary evidence to show that the advice was actually provided but that the client chose to ignore the advice, the planner would also be potentially exposing themself to possible litigation on the basis of not providing advice appropriate to the client's needs. A lawsuit for the lost income of the client to age 65 could run into many hundreds of thousands of dollars. In the end, it is up to the client to determine whether they take up the insurance or not. However, the planner does have a responsibility to raise the issue with the client and provide advice that is in the client's best interests.

Other disclosure requirements

The cost of the advice and how the planner is paid

Under this section, all costs, fees, commissions and potential conflicts of interest associated with the SOA need to be detailed to the client.

With respect to the purchase or replacement of a financial product, all product costs need to be disclosed. These may include brokerage costs and stamp duty in respect of the purchase of shares, management expense ratios (MERs), entry and exit costs and buy/sell spreads for managed funds, and stamp duty and legal expenses for the purchase of property. For specific details on the costs of the financial products recommended, the client should be provided with a copy of the product disclosure statement (PDS) of the financial product or, if appropriate, provide the client with a link to the product's website.

Any potential tax implications associated with the purchase or disposal of a financial product, such as CGT payable, should also be referred to in the SOA, However, as an adviser is not a tax expert, the client should always also be referred to their accountant or tax adviser.

The legal requirement to disclose the remuneration of the planner (such as costs, fees, expenses, benefits, interests and commissions) in the SOA, is contained in both the Corporations Act and RG 175. Remuneration may be charged by the planner for preparing a SOA, implementing the recommendations contained within a SOA and for the provision for ongoing advice and review. The regulations prescribe that, no matter what form the remuneration takes, the planner is required to disclose all fees, costs, benefits, charges and interests as a dollar amount within the SOA. The planner is also required to detail whether they have any financial interest or conflict of interest in any of the investments recommended within the SOA. Regulatory Guide (RG) 181 *Licensing: Managing conflicts of interest* provides three mechanisms that licensees would generally use to manage conflicts of interest. These relate to controlling, avoiding and disclosing any conflicts of interest (ASIC 2004).

An example of the disclosure of fees is provided in illustrative example 15.6.

ILLUSTRATIVE EXAMPLE 15.6

The following disclosure is illustrative of the type of disclosure that might be provided on the planner's remuneration within the SOA.

ABC Financial Planners will charge you a fee of 1% plus GST on the establishment of your investment plan. This fee will be deducted by the investment manager from your investment account and paid to ABC Financial Planners in the form of a fee as shown in the following table. ABC Financial Planners will rebate all upfront commissions back to you, the investor. ABC Financial Planners will also charge an ongoing fee of 0.5% p.a. plus GST based on the amount of funds under management.

	Amount invested	Establishment fee		Ongoing fee	
Investment	**($)**	**(%)**	**($)**	**(%)**	**($)**
MNO Master Trust	120 000	1.1	1 320	0.55	660
DEF Retail Fund	80 000	1.1	880	0.55	440
Total	200 000		2 200		1 100

These fees and commissions are inclusive of the goods and services tax (GST).
Note: As the holder of the AFSL, XYZ Financial Planners receives all fees, retains 10% and pays the balance to us as the financial planner. This equates to the licence holder receiving $220 p.a. of the initial fee and $110 p.a. of the ongoing fees.

Specific disclaimers

Disclaimers are often used within a SOA in an attempt to restrict the liability of the planner for situations outside of the planner's direct control. There are certain statutory obligations that cannot be disclaimed, such as the fiduciary obligation imposed on financial planners under common law to act in the best interests of their clients and to exercise a duty of care. However, in the preparation of a SOA, and in dealings with the client, specific disclaimers can be used to assist in clarifying the role and responsibility of the planner and client.

The following are examples of such disclaimers.

- No responsibility is given to any person other than the client(s) addressed in the SOA.
- No guarantees are provided on future performances.
- Taxation issues should be referred to the client's tax accountant.
- A sunset clause (i.e. a date limit for the recommendation to remain valid).
- The plan is prepared from information provided by the client, to suit their particular needs and objectives. If the information is not accurate, the onus is on the client to bring it to the planner's attention.

How to proceed

The client should fully understand the agreed-upon recommendations and the implementation process going forward, including responsibilities, time lines and amounts. Where referrals to other professionals are required in order to implement the plan, these should be detailed in the plan and it is the financial planner's responsibility to facilitate and coordinate the process. The client should be asked to check the accuracy of the information contained within the SOA and to notify the planner if the information is incorrect or has changed so that the strategies can be reviewed and amended if necessary.

The SOA has to be formally agreed upon, signed and consented to before it is implemented. The client should be asked to sign and return an 'authority to proceed' in order to signify acceptance of the recommendations contained within the SOA.

Summary

The practice of financial planning encompasses many disciplines — investments, retirement planning, superannuation, insurance, taxation planning, portfolio management, social security, debt management and financial analysis, to name a few. The objective of the financial planning process is to analyse these aspects in the context of the client's circumstances and provide recommendations and strategies in the form of a compliant and comprehensive SOA that meets the needs and requirements of the client. All personal advice must comply with the 'best interest' obligations detailed in the Corporations Act.

The Corporations Act sets a requirement that, when providing advice to a retail client, a financial planner must provide the client with a statement of advice (SOA). While this may be in the form of a comprehensive SOA, increasingly clients are seeking scaled advice in relation to a limited range of issues. The nature of the arrangement with the client and the type of advice sought will determine which of these SOAs will be appropriate.

The Corporations Act also provides for an alternative advice document in a limited number of situations, known as a record of advice (ROA).

While it is important that the planner be technically competent and be able to provide detailed strategies, the advice and recommendations will be of little use if the client does not fully understand the strategies and the rationale for them. Effective communication and trust is vital if the client is to accept and act upon the advice provided by the planner. Without an open, trusting and honest relationship between the planner and client, it is unlikely that the goals and objectives of the client will be satisfied. The first meeting between the planner and client is not only important for establishing this relationship, but the regulations also impose a number of requirements on the planner, including the need to provide the client with an FSG, and obligations relating to the prevention and detection of money laundering and terrorism activities.

The six-step financial planning process provides a framework for the development of a SOA and highlights the compliance issues imposed on the financial planning profession.

A considerable number of regulations have been imposed on the financial planning industry to ensure that clients are given appropriate and reasonable advice at a fair price. Financial planners have a professional and fiduciary obligation to look after the interests of a client without bias or conflict, be compliant with all regulations and act in a manner that is transparent and ethical.

Finally the various components of a SOA were outlined, including reference to two example scaled SOAs.

This chapter aims to apply the knowledge and skills acquired from earlier chapters to the preparation, presentation, implementation and review of a SOA. This case study approach is used to help foster and develop those skills considered essential for the professional financial planner — critical thinking, analysis and interpretation, and problem solving.

Professional application questions

15.1 When must a FSG be provided to a client? List five items in a FSG that convey information about the planner to a client.

15.2 'Knowing your client' is of paramount importance if a financial planner is to be able to satisfy the best interests obligations imposed under the Corporations Act. How might a planner develop a comprehensive insight and level of knowledge about the client in order to be able to provide appropriate advice?

15.3 What is 'scaled advice' and what are the advantages and risks for a client?

15.4 How does the planner demonstrate to a client that the advice provided is feasible and achievable and meets the client's objectives?

15.5 Does a disclaimer in a SOA assist the client in any way? If so, how? In what way might a disclaimer be used to assist the financial planner?

15.6 In practice, it is common for a financial planner to disclose their recommendations and provide a SOA by using a practice template. What advantages and disadvantages can you foresee with this practice?

15.7 There is often a disagreement between the licensee and the financial planner about who 'owns' the client. Why does this happen? Who do you think owns the client? Discuss your answer from the view of the licence holder, the financial planner and the client.

15.8 A SOA should be developed to accommodate a client's aims and goals. On the basis that these goals are likely to change over a client's lifetime, by what means can a financial planner ensure the goals continue to be achieved?

15.9 Explain the importance of the planner keeping appropriate file notes on all dealings with clients.

15.10 Explain some of the methods that a planner may adopt to present their recommendations in a way that engages the client.

15.11 Explain the purpose of an executive summary in a SOA.

15.12 When discussing a particular strategy or investment within a SOA, how does the planner determine how much general information and description should be included?

15.13 What are the conditions that allow a ROA to be prepared instead of a SOA?

Professional application exercises

Basic	*
Moderate	* *
Challenging	* * *

15.14 Compliance and regulatory obligations *

David seeks some financial advice for his cousin Isaac who is migrating to Australia in 3 months. David provides information about Isaac's personal circumstances and provides an assessment of what he thinks is likely to be Isaac's risk tolerance. David states that Isaac wishes to invest $10 000 into a particular managed share fund and asks whether you will accept cash. What are some of the issues or obligations that you should consider in providing financial advice to David's cousin?

15.15 Analysing issues and developing strategies *

Jamal seeks some assistance from you in respect of buying a property. At this stage he is unsure whether he will live in it straight away or use it as an investment property initially and then move into it in a few years. Jamal has $30 000 sitting in a cash management account and $20 000 held in a managed fund and will borrow the rest. Jamal advises that he is looking to buy a property worth around $450 000 and is keen to get into the market as soon as possible as he believes property will start to boom given historically low interest rates. Jamal is single and earns a salary of $70 000 p.a. plus SG contributions.

(a) What are some of the issues you would raise with Jamal about the purchase of a property and the related borrowing?

(b) If Jamal decided to wait a few years before purchasing a property, what investment options would you recommend to help him save for a deposit?

15.16 Type of disclosure advice statement * *

Jonathon is an existing, long standing client aged 49. In 2007 you established a self-managed super fund for Jonathon with recommendations documented in a SOA dated 23 February 2007. The fund now has $500 000 of assets. In 2007, Jonathon stated that he intended to retire in 10 years time and that he would not expect to access the funds before then. The plan provided an asset allocation strategy for the fund. Jonathon was made aware at the time that there may be a need to change some of the managed funds from time to time.

Since 2007 you have provided Jonathon with a review of the managed funds every 6 months. These reviews have included changes to the investment portfolio by way of portfolio re-weighting and changing fund managers from time to time. The risk profile and asset allocation strategy has not changed.

For each of the following situations, explain whether you could provide the client with a ROA or whether a SOA would be required.

(a) In July 2014, the fund has available cash of $40 000 to invest. You recommend that Jonathon allocates the cash among his existing investment products based on maintaining his agreed asset allocation.

(b) In August 2014, your research provider issues a sell on the State Australian Share fund. During your next review you recommend that Jonathon sells his holding in the share fund, worth $50 000, and invest the proceeds into the Capital Australian Share Fund which hasn't been used before.

(c) In September 2014, during discussions with Jonathon he expresses a desire to reduce the tax he pays and undertake some sort of gearing strategy (he hasn't previously geared before). You recommend a protected structured loan through the ANZ.

(d) In November 2014, upon turning 55 years of age, you recommend to Jonathon that he implements a transition to retirement strategy. This involves him rearranging his affairs to salary sacrifice to the super fund and to commence drawing a pension from the fund.

15.17 Satisfying the needs of a client ✱✱

Mary has sought advice from you on her financial position. Mary is aged 38 and married and the couple's combined earnings are around $160 000 p.a. The couple's home is worth $800 000 and they have a $500 000 outstanding mortgage owing. The couple also has $20 000 owing on one of their cars. The couple is both in good health but you note that there is a history of heart-related issues within Mary's family. You complete a SOA providing advice on the couple's superannuation funds, managed fund portfolio and their personal insurance cover. You recommend that the couple each take out a $1m life and TPD cover, an income protection insurance policy for up to 75% of their salary and a trauma policy for an amount of $200 000 each.

At a meeting that you have with the client prior to the presentation of the SOA, the couple appears happy to accept your recommendations on the superannuation and managed funds but raises concerns about the level of insurance cover that you have recommended and the cost of the premiums. They advise that they would want only half the amount of insurance that you have recommended.

(a) What sort of issues would the financial planner likely have taken into account in determining an amount of $1m for the couple's life and TPD coverage?

(b) How should the planner deal with the situation where the client wants only half the amount of personal cover that has been recommended? Should your advice provided in the SOA reflect the client's preferences?

(c) Discuss the importance of requiring a client to sign an 'authority to proceed' document prior to the implementation of the recommendations.

15.18 Regulatory obligations and developing strategies ✱✱

My name is Sarah, I am 51 years old and a widow. I am employed to run exercise programs for senior citizens. My gross salary is $55 000 p.a. plus a 9.25% SG contribution. Together with investment income of $1500, I am left with a disposable income of $6000 p.a. I have one child who lives independently. I am currently renting a flat near where I work and have decided to sell my family home which is some 2 hours drive from my work. I have rented out the family home for the past 7 years but now have decided to sell the property and buy another one closer to work as I expect to stay in the area in which I am now living. I receive $10 000 p.a. from renting the property after payment of all ongoing property expenses. My assets consist of the following: family home,

$600 000 (no mortgage); bank deposits, $10 000; managed share portfolio, $30 000; and superannuation, $120 000 invested in a balanced fund. I purchased the family property 21 years ago for $180 000 but have been advised that because I have been away from the family home for over 6 years I cannot claim a full exemption from capital gains tax. I am told that it is exempted from capital gains tax for the time that it was my principal place of residence, but I must pay capital gains tax on that proportion of the gain accrued during the remainder of the time when it was rented to another party. After selling the family home, buying another property and paying all costs and taxes, I expect to have surplus funds of approximately $100 000. I require some advice on how best to invest the funds.

(a) What issues should be covered with Sarah in the initial meeting?
(b) In order to reduce costs, is the planner able to provide Sarah with a ROA detailing strategies and recommendations?
(c) Determine Sarah's likely capital gains tax liability if she sells the property and uses the CGT discount method to determine the CGT liability.
(d) What are the advantages and disadvantages of contributing the proceeds from the sale of the property into her superannuation fund? Are there any restrictions on the amount of the proceeds that can be contributed into Sarah's superannuation account this year?
(e) If, as a result of the extra funds, Sarah decides to salary sacrifice an amount of $50 000 into her superannuation fund this year, what would be the tax consequences for both her employer and herself?

15.19 Analysing issues and developing strategies ✱✱

Ian approaches you for advice concerning his superannuation fund account. He is aged 38, earns a gross income of $80 000 p.a. and has $95 000 invested in superannuation. His super fund is invested in a conservative investment option and has achieved an average return of 5.5% p.a. over the past 3 years. Ian is attracted by a number of television advertisements that promote returns for an industry superannuation fund that, because of lower fees, has achieved an average return of 7.5% p.a. over the past 3 years.

(a) Ian wonders why his fund may have underachieved compared with the one advertised on the television. Explain.
(b) What factors would you need to discuss with Ian if he was considering transferring his superannuation account to the industry fund?
(c) What factors might you consider to determine Ian's risk tolerance?
(d) If Ian wanted more control over his superannuation fund with greater investment choice and the ability to acquire direct shares, what type of superannuation structure might be recommended for Ian?

15.20 Analysing issues and developing strategies ✱✱

My name is Amir and I am aged 25. My fiancée, Karima, is aged 24. I am still living at home and expect to remain there until our marriage in 9 months. My fiancée is currently living with her parents. Two years ago, I used $70 000 that I had saved and borrowed $250 000 from a bank and bought an investment property for $320 000. Apart from $10 000 in a savings account, I have no other investments. My fiancée has $20 000 invested in fixed-term deposits. We are unsure what our living arrangements will be once we marry. We could sell the investment property and use the proceeds to buy a home, or use our savings as a deposit and borrow further funds to acquire a home to live in, or we could live in the investment property for a couple of years before selling it and buying a bigger home. Alternatively, we could rent a property for the next 5 years and continue to invest our savings.

(a) What are some of the qualitative issues that you may discuss with Amir and Karima in helping them with their decision?
(b) What capital gains tax issues need to be considered if they were to sell the investment property?
(c) If the couple chose to use their savings to buy their own home and retain the investment property, what factors would you need to consider before recommending that the couple further increase their debt levels?
(d) Why might the couple decide to rent and, if they do decide to rent, do you consider renting to be a viable long-term solution to a client's housing needs?

15.21 Analysing issues and developing strategies * *

Kim works as a retail assistant in a large department store. She earns $42 000 p.a. after salary sacrificing $5000 into her superannuation fund. Kim is also entitled to a 9.25% SG contribution on her total remuneration package of $47 000. Kim also earns $3000 of interest income. Kim's husband recently retired, aged 59, and has a taxable income of $9500 for the year. Kim is looking to retire next year when she will be aged 56. Kim is interested in contributing further funds into her superannuation account in order to maximise taxation benefits and entitlements and has considered investing $2000 of savings into her superannuation fund so that she can claim the government co-contribution. However, one of her colleagues has told her that she would be better off salary sacrificing the amount into her superannuation account while another friend has told her about contributing the funds into her spouse's superannuation account in order to claim the superannuation contributions spouse tax offset. Kim comes to you for your advice.

(a) Is Kim entitled to make a superannuation contribution and claim a tax benefit or concession under the three alternatives? Explain.
(b) Which of the three alternatives would you recommend for Kim in terms of maximising her tax benefits and concessions? Provide calculations to justify your answer.
(c) Once Kim retires, she will need to receive an income stream from her superannuation fund account. What type of income-stream product is Kim able to choose from and what would you recommend?
(d) Assume that upon her retirement, Kim's superannuation balance amounts to $250 000 including a tax-free component of $60 000. If Kim rolls the super money into an account-based pension and withdraws an income of $35 000, how much tax would be payable on her taxable income? You can assume Kim continues to receive interest income of $3000.

15.22 Compliance and regulatory issues * * *

Fiona recently visited a financial planner to help sort out her financial affairs. After two short interviews, one being over the telephone, the planner sent her a 6-page financial plan. Fiona received no other documentation from the financial planner nor did she complete any forms. She says she is uncomfortable with some of the recommendations and does not understand a number of the strategies. When she asked about the fees, the planner replied that the plan was absolutely free and there was no charge to her. Fiona is aged 38, divorced and has two primary school-aged children. She earns $48 000 p.a. and has around $200 per month available to invest. She owns a house and is paying off a mortgage of $80 000. She has $20 000 invested in a savings account which her parents have given her for emergency expenses and to help with the education of her children. Fiona's financial planner has recommended that she takes out something called a margin lending facility totalling $80 000 to invest in an international equity fund. Fiona says she does not understand what a margin loan is and she is not sure whether investing in an international share fund is suitable for her. One of her friends told her that the fund has performed poorly over the past 5 years and has a very high fee structure.

(a) How appropriate do you think a margin lending strategy is to Fiona? Discuss.
(b) Describe the various methods of remuneration available to financial planners.
(c) Suppose the PDS of the international share fund indicates that the entry fee is nil, but there is an exit fee of 5% if the investor withdraws the investment in the first year of investment and that an exit fee will be charged on a sliding scale for up to 5 years. The PDS also indicates that the financial planner would receive commission of 4% on placement of the investment and an ongoing commission of 0.4% each year. In addition, the margin lender would pay the planner a commission of 1% upon commencement of the lending facility. Prepare a table to indicate what fees the financial planner should have included in the financial plan given to Fiona.
(d) It is obvious that the financial planner has breached several ethical, professional and legal obligations. Discuss the various areas of non-compliance by the financial planner.
(e) Discuss some of the ways in which financial planners can seek to limit their exposure to possible litigation and breaches of their ethical, professional and legal obligations.

15.23 Analysing issues and developing strategies ***

Paul and Anne are both 59 years of age. They are considering whether to commence a transition-to-retirement pension (TTR). They operate a family business and pay themselves a salary of $90 000 p.a. each. They are considering a proposal to salary sacrifice $25 000 each into their respective superannuation accounts, receive a cash salary of $65 000 and both commence withdrawing a TTR pension of $19 100. They each have $450 0000 in superannuation funds which they will roll over into a TTR pension. Assume that their superannuation and pension funds earn a 6% return.

(a) Calculate the amount of personal income tax that Paul and Anne are currently paying. Prepare a table to illustrate their income and taxation liability.
(b) Prepare another table to illustrate the taxation effect of the proposal for each of the couple to salary sacrifice $25 000 each into superannuation and commence a TTR pension with an income of $19 100 each. You can assume that the taxable proportion of their superannuation is 100%.
(c) How will the salary sacrifice/TTR strategy impact upon the couple's accumulated wealth when they retire at age 65? Determine the future value of the couple's combined superannuation accounts and TTR pension accounts to age 65.
(d) Given the salary sacrifice/TTR strategy, explain the taxation impact on their income when they both turn 60 years of age.
(e) Describe any other benefits that may be derived with the couple undertaking the TTR strategy.

CASE STUDY 1

The development of strategies

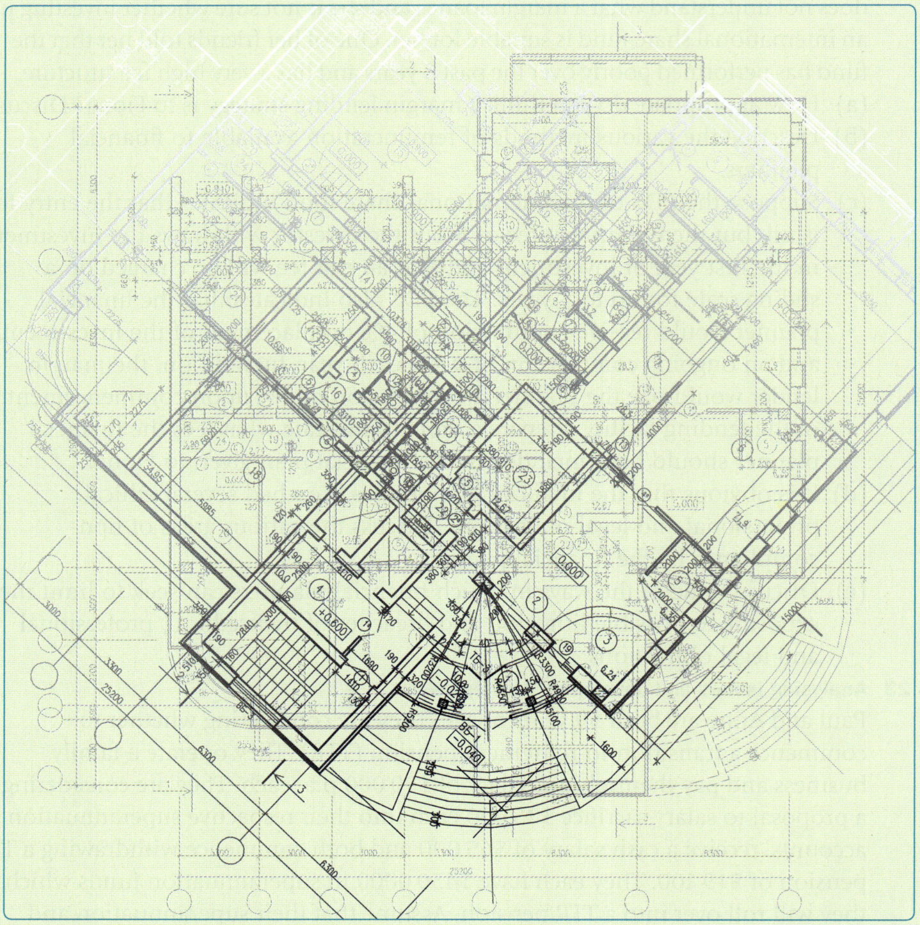

Phil, a new client, has approached your financial planning practice seeking some advice. The practice's financial planner had a telephone conversation with Phil last week. The planner asks you to undertake a few tasks as part of the process of providing advice and recommendations for Phil and his wife.

After speaking with Phil, the financial planner provides you with the following information concerning the couple's financial situation.

1. Personal situation

Phil is aged 37 and his wife Jill is aged 36. Phil is a self-employed architect while Jill works 2–3 days a week as a solicitor.

They have 2 children, Tessa aged 11 and Matthew aged 10. The couple would like the children to attend a private school from age 14 which is expected to cost around $15 000 p.a. in total.

2. Assets and liabilities consist of the following:

Assets:

Home (joint ownership) $900 000, contents (joint ownership) worth $80 000, 2 cars (one car in each name) worth approximately $60 000, savings account with Westpac Bank for $6000 (in name of Phil), shares (in name of Phil) with a current market value of $70 000 (cost price of $90 000 acquired in May 2006), superannuation balances — Phil $120 000, Jill $70 000.

Phil acquired the shares 3 years ago on the advice of a friend. However, the shares have never done well and Phil has no interest or time in following the share market.

The couple do not take an active interest in their investments.

Liabilities:

Eighteen year home mortgage of $590 000 with a variable interest rate of 6.5% p.a., monthly repayments of $4712.

Five year car loan of $15 000 with a variable interest rate of 7.6% p.a., monthly repayments of $310.

Credit card average monthly balance of $6000 (used to pay for living expenses).

The couple are finding that a lot of their monthly income is going towards paying off their large amount of debt. They are worried that they have taken on too much debt and would like to reduce outstanding debt as fast as possible.

3. Cash income and expenses consist of the following:

Income:	**$ p.a.**
– salary	40 000
– net profit from business	130 000
– bank interest	120
– fully franked dividends (cash receipt)	2 250
– unfranked dividends (cash receipt)	400
Payments:	
Living expenses (excluding loans and interest charges)	40 000
Mortgage and loan repayments	60 264
Private health insurance	3 200
Professional membership fees	
– Phil	700
– Jill	800
Travel expenses for work purposes:	
– Jill	400
Tax preparation (split 50/50)	2 000
Donations (split 50/50)	1 500
Holidays and entertainment	10 000

The couple feel they pay an excessive amount of tax and are looking at ways of minimising tax payable as far as possible.

»

»

4. The couple's superannuation accounts consist of the following:

Phil:	
(i) Australian Industry Super Fund	$20 000
– invested in the balanced option	
– includes death and TPD cover for $50 000	
(ii) Self-managed superannuation fund	$100 000
– invested 50% in shares and 50% in cash	
– includes death and TPD cover for $50 000	
Jill:	
(i) Invested with Australian Industry Super Fund	$60 000
– invested in the balanced option	
(ii) Self-managed superannuation fund	$10 000
– invested 50% in shares and 50% in cash	

Other than detailed above, the couple have no other personal insurance cover.

The couple's self-managed superannuation fund (SMSF) was established 4 years ago by their accountant. However, they have no real understanding of how the SMSF works or what the benefits are in contributing.

Jill's current employer contributes her 9.25% SGC into the Australian Industry Super Fund. Phil contributes to his SMSF on an irregular basis when he remembers to contribute or his accountant happens to mention it before the end of the year. However, Phil has not taken an active interest in his superannuation affairs and has not contributed for the past 2 years.

The asset break-up of the Australian Industry Super Fund balanced fund account is approximately as follows:

Cash	5%
Australian fixed interest	15%
International fixed interest	5%
Australian shares	35%
International shares	23%
Property	10%
Alternative investments	7%

The couple now feel that they need to take a more active interest in their wealth creation and retirement planning but are not sure how best to go about it. Their objective is to retire when Phil turns 58 so that they can travel around Australia. Accordingly, they have sought the advice of your financial planning practice.

The financial planner had a brief telephone conversation with Phil at the start of July 2014 and the client emailed the above details. The financial planner has asked you to prepare some appropriate strategies for Phil that will assist in meeting his goals and needs.

You are required to provide a discussion and explanation of the broad strategies that you would recommend for the couple taking into account their objectives and assumed risk profile, and explain how your recommended strategies meet the objectives of Phil. For each broad strategy, you should also detail the main benefits and risks to the client.

CASE STUDY 2

Establishing a framework for constructing a limited advice financial plan

The aim of this case study is to help the reader apply the financial planning principles and practices that have been covered in this book by analysing a typical client situation and providing appropriate recommendations and strategies.

Given that there is, in most cases, more than one appropriate solution to achieving a client's objectives in a dynamic and ever-changing financial environment, and that financial planners take different approaches when forming recommendations, the authors do not provide solutions to the questions arising from the case study. Rather, the reader is provided with a framework and a methodology within which a limited advice SOA can be constructed.

The case study on Fui Ling and Tin Nguyen is dealt with by applying the six steps of the financial planning process. Students are encouraged to refer to ASIC's *Example Statement of Advice (SOA) for a limited financial advice scenario for a new client* (RG 90) or to the Example Statement of Advice provided in Appendix 15D and use the examples as the basis to prepare a suitable SOA for Fui Ling and Tin.

Fui Ling Nguyen is a prospective client who phones your financial planning practice. She says she is approaching you as a financial planner to seek financial guidance and to ask you to prepare a financial plan for a particular matter. She would like to make an appointment to see you and has sent you the following letter detailing the couple's background.

Dear financial planner

I am 30 years old and my husband Tin is 32. We both have well-paying secure jobs. We have no children and are not planning to have any for at least 3–4 years. We both have very busy work and social lives that leave little time to organise our finances. There is a mortgage on our house, but we are gradually reducing the amount owing as we have been paying extra amounts to get it paid off sooner. We own two cars and have a loan on one of them. There is very little else I can tell you except that we have not been able to invest much at all despite our reasonably high income levels. However, we now want to start building up a managed fund portfolio of Australian shares by borrowing funds. We are not sure whether we should use some of the equity in our home now that we own more than half of the house; whether we should use margin lending; or whether we should start an instalment gearing plan. We tend to favour the idea of an instalment gearing plan to get us started. What do you think and can you advise us on the gearing options?

»

»

The financial planning process

First, you send Tin and Fui Ling your financial services guide (FSG), identifying the fact that you are acting as an authorised representative of an Australian Financial Services Licence holder, and providing information on the advisory services you offer, your experience, specialisations, remuneration details and complaints-handling mechanism. You also send a confidential client questionnaire and ask them to read the two documents, to complete as much as possible of the client questionnaire and bring it along with supporting documentation to the first appointment.

In developing an appropriate SOA for the couple, you should refer to the financial planning process discussed earlier in this chapter, specifically the six steps. Your plan must comply with all legal, professional and ethical standards that have been outlined in this chapter.

Step 1: Gather the clients' data

At the first appointment you should do the following.

- Introduce yourself and your organisation and ask if Fui Ling and Tin have any questions arising from the FSG.
- Briefly introduce the couple to the financial planning process and explain how you normally go about preparing your recommendations, the follow-up meetings, the implementation process, reviews, remuneration and so on.
- Discuss the terms of your engagement, scope of advice and legal ramifications of accepting the engagement and providing advice.
- Develop a rapport with the clients to gain an understanding of their circumstances and to assist them to relax and feel comfortable about openly discussing financial matters.
- Extract a more detailed account of the couple's circumstances to complete the client questionnaire — even though you have been requested to consider only one aspect of their financial circumstances.
- Maintain a professional image and presentation at all times.

From the results of the client questionnaire, you can summarise the clients' situation as follows:

Personal information

- Tin Nguyen — Date of birth: 10 May 1982
- Fui Ling Nguyen — Date of birth: 9 August 1984
- Contact information: Address, telephone and facsimile numbers were recorded.
- Children/dependants: None
- Employment details:
  - Tin Nguyen, Chemical engineer — Gross income: $95 000
  - Fui Ling Nguyen, Osteopath — Gross income: $65 000
- Other information
  - Both enjoy good health and are non-smokers.
  - Neither Tin nor Fui Ling has a will in place.
  - They are fully insured for their home contents, cars and medical costs. However, they have not thought about taking out any personal insurance coverage as they both have term life insurance and income continuance insurance within their superannuation funds.

Income and expenses

Cash flow reveals the following:

	Tin	Fui Ling	Combined
Income[a]	$70 000	$48 000	$118 000
Less expenses			$ 83 000
Net surplus			$ 35 000

[a]After tax and superannuation contributions

Note: A detailed and itemised expenditure list was not provided. The couple have been allocating extra amounts from their surplus to reduce their mortgage.

Assets at market value

Home and contents	$510 000	
Cars	$ 55 000	
Bank savings account	$ 6 500	earning 2% p.a.

Superannuation

Tin	$106 000	Balanced fund earning 5.5% p.a.
Fui Ling	$ 55 000	Balanced fund earning 5% p.a.

Liabilities

Home mortgage	$280 000
Credit cards	$ 15 000
Car loan	$ 20 000

Immediate financial goals

- Pay off credit card debt within 12 months.
- Commence an investment plan using borrowed funds.
- Go on an overseas holiday in 3 years — estimated cost $15 000.
- Perhaps start a family in 3–4 years.
- Pay off car loan within 3 years.

Personal investment preferences

- They do not require any further income from the proposed investment plan. They are mainly seeking capital growth over a long-term time frame. They intend to reinvest any dividend payments received.
- They prefer to have a reasonable amount of liquidity on hand to cover emergencies — say, a minimum of $5000.
- They are seeking a real rate of return of at least 6% from the investments.
- They are prepared to accept a reasonably high level of risk in order to obtain a reasonable rate of return.
- Tin and Fui Ling have no problems with any of the classes of investments suggested in the questionnaire. They feel comfortable about borrowing money to invest.
- They realise that the share market is subject to volatility and are prepared to invest for the long term.
- The client questionnaire was duly signed and dated by both Tin and Fui Ling and by the financial planner.

»

»

Step 2: Identify the clients' goals

The couple's short- and medium-term goals and objectives should be detailed as specifically as possible and, where appropriate, expressed in dollar terms. These goals should be confirmed in the executive summary to the client.

Short-term goals	Medium-term goals
▪ Pay off credit card debt within 12 months. ▪ Commence an investment plan in Australian shares.	▪ Go on an overseas holiday in 3 years — estimated cost $15 000. ▪ Maybe start a family in 3–4 years. ▪ Pay off car loan within 3 years.

The long-term plans of Fui Ling and Tin do not need to be considered at this stage as the couple has specifically asked about their short-term proposal of investing in shares using borrowed funds. Comments about the longer term may be confined to the projected amounts and issues concerned with the investment plan as proposed.

Step 3: Analyse the clients' financial position and identify financial problems

Having gone through the personal investment (risk profile) questionnaire (appendix 15C) with Tin and Fui Ling, you identify their risk profile to be that of a moderately aggressive type. This means that they accept volatility in both income and capital returns, they look for capital appreciation more than an income stream, and they have a long-term investment time frame.

At this point, all information about the client should be restated to ensure that strategies are based on accurate information. The analysis of the clients' financial position will cover some of the following areas.

- A balance sheet is compiled and the current net worth of the clients is established.
- A cash flow statement is drawn up based on the clients' details. An itemised expenses list has not been provided but it has been revealed that:
  - The car loan will be paid off in 3 years.
  - The credit cards will be paid off over the next 2 years.
  - The home mortgage requirement is $2500 per month but they have been paying up to $4000 per month in some months.
- Relevant personal financial ratios should be calculated.

The objective of the analysis should be to highlight potential problem areas in the clients' situation and to identify possible recommendations and strategies.

Step 4: Prepare written recommendations

It is important at this stage to detail the assumptions used in the SOA. All assumptions used must be reasonable and justifiable in the circumstances. Following are some of the assumptions that should be referred to in this case:

- the latest tax rates
- inflation is assumed to be 3.5% p.a.

- projected investment earnings for the various asset classes should be detailed, together with the type of returns the clients can expect to earn
- the couple will remain in secure employment for the foreseeable future.

The financial planner needs to ensure that facts concerning the clients are not assumed. The specific focus of the SOA needs to be examined in depth. The benefits of establishing an appropriate investment plan should be explained to the clients, including the principles of investing. You need to consider each of the proposed borrowing types and discuss the advantages and disadvantages of each. Items to consider include franking credits, capital gains, interest rate on borrowings and capacity to repay the interest.

Fui Ling and Tin favoured an instalment gearing plan and so (assuming you agree with them) you should explain how such a plan works and provide some projections of the plan. You should also indicate the flexibility of the plan and any other specific features to help them understand how the plan works. Critical issues to address are the benefits, risks and costs of the recommended plan (and financial product selected) and the suitability of the plan and products for your clients' circumstances. You will also need to detail the managed funds that will be acquired with the borrowings including such information as fees, past performance, fund profile, amounts to be invested, fund ratings and the rationale for the recommendation. The recommendations need to be considered in light of the client's risk profile and target asset allocation.

You may comment upon their current strategy of reducing non-tax-deductible personal debt as a worthwhile pursuit. You may also question their level of expenses and whether they can be reduced, with any surplus used to go towards the investment plan or to reduce the mortgage.

You may also comment about the areas of a financial plan that you have not addressed, and indicate that you could do so in a more comprehensive SOA. Such areas include: risk management and insurance coverage, retirement planning and estate planning.

You will need to ensure that all costs and fees associated with the recommendations are detailed in the plan including your remuneration. This will need to be expressed in dollar terms and include any fees and commissions for preparing the plan and implementing the plan, as well as any fees received from the instalment gearing provider.

Step 5: Implement the agreed-upon plan

The SOA should set out how the financial planner will put the recommendations into place and will include a breakdown of responsibilities. The plan will include an authority to proceed, together with an appropriate step-by-step action plan.

Step 6: Review, revise and maintain the SOA

The plan must indicate benchmarks for the clients' current financial position and expected position at the time of the review. The planned reviews and the frequency should be indicated in the original plan, together with the types of services offered and the associated costs.

References and further reading

ASIC 2004, *Licensing: Managing conflicts of interest*, Regulatory Guide 181, August, asic.gov.au.

ASIC 2008, *Dollar disclosure*, Regulatory Guide 182, June, asic.gov.au.

ASIC 2011, *Disclosure: Product Disclosure Statements (and other disclosure obligations)*, Regulatory Guide 168, October, asic.gov.au.

ASIC 2012, *Licensing: Financial product advisers — Conduct and disclosure*, Regulatory Guide 175, December, asic.gov.au.

ASIC 2012, *Giving information, general advice and scaled advice*, Consultation Paper 183, August, asic.gov.au.

ASIC 2013, *Example Statement of Advice: Scaled advice for a new client*, Regulatory Guide 90, August, asic.gov.au.

Australian Government, Corporations Act 2001.

Bowen, C (Australian Government, The Treasury) 2010, Media Release No. 36, *Overhaul of financial advice*, April, ministers.treasury.gov.au.

CCH 2013, *Australian master financial planning guide 2013–14*, 16th edn, CCH Australia Ltd, Sydney.

Collett, J 2010, 'Free advice a super idea', *The Age*, 15 September.

Commonwealth of Australia Parliamentary Joint Committee on Corporations and Financial Services 2009, *Inquiry into financial products and services in Australia*, November.

Financial Planning Association of Australia Ltd 2009, *Transitioning to fee-based remuneration for financial planning advice*, May, fpa.asn.au.

Jaffe, D. T. & Grubman, J. 2011, 'Core techniques for effective client interviewing and communication'. *Journal of Financial Planning*. October.

Payne, K 2013, 'Scaled advice to provide pay certainty', *Wealth Professional*, 24 July.

Valentine, T 2003, 'The treatment of risk in financial planning', *Journal of Law and Financial Management*, vol. 2, no. 1.

Wharton University of Pennsylvania, Bridging the Trust Divide: The Financial Advisor–Client Relationship.

APPENDIX 15A

No advice statement

The following adaptation is an example of a no advice statement, provided by Integrity Financial Planners Pty Ltd.

Integrity Financial Planners
AFSL #110099

The Directors
XYZ Financial Planners Pty Ltd
319 East Doncaster Road
Melbourne 3109

Dear Sirs
I/we confirm that I/we do not seek your advice in relation to the amount specified below, and that I/we do not require you to make any investigation or recommendation in relation to any other of my/our assets nor do I/we require a full analysis of my/our financial situation.

I/we request that you purchase/sell on my/our behalf the following:

Amount $ market price
Details 1000 units of Telstra Direct Shares at market price + brokerage

Name(s) Mr John Citizen and Mrs Ann Citizen
2 McKeons Drive
Mulgrave 3170

Signature(s) ....

....

Date ..../............/............ ..../............/............

Declaration by authorised representative

No advice is given, on the basis of your specific instruction that you do not wish me to make a full analysis of your financial situation but wish me to execute on your behalf the purchase/sell of 1000 **Telstra Direct Shares** as per your instructions.

Authorised representative: Josette Chikhani CFP

Signature: .... **Date** ..../............/............

Note: All parties must sign this disclaimer, with a copy being retained by each.

APPENDIX 15B

Confidential client questionnaire

The following adaptation is an example of a confidential client questionnaire, provided by Integrity Financial Planners Pty Ltd.

Name: Mr & Mrs Mark Stephan
Date ..../............/............
Adviser: David M. Smart
Referred by Mr Joe Stephan

CONFIDENTIAL CLIENT QUESTIONNAIRE

Important notice to client

In order for an adviser to make an investment or insurance recommendation, the adviser must have reasonable grounds for making that recommendation. This means that the adviser must conduct an appropriate investigation as to the investment objectives, financial situation and particular needs of the person concerned.
The information requested in this form is necessary to enable a recommendation to be made on a reasonable basis and will be used for that purpose only.

You should allow 1–2 hours to complete this questionnaire. We cannot stress how important that time will be in properly planning your future standard of living. If you have any queries or do not understand a question, then ask your adviser for an explanation.

Please note that you have a 14-day cooling-off period from the time your managed investment transaction confirmation is received by you, or 5 days after your units are issued, to notify the funds in writing that the investment does not suit your needs.

XYZ Financial Planners Pty Ltd
ABN 24 069 537 855
Holder of an Australian Financial Services Licence

What is your main reason for seeking advice?

....

....

....

....

....

Personal information

Name .... **Date of birth** ....

Partner's name .... **Date of birth** ....

Contact information

Telephone H ( ) .... **W ( )** ....

Mobile .... **Fax ( )** ....

Street address ....

....

.... **Postcode** ....

Postal address ....

....

.... **Postcode** ....

	Children/Dependants Name(s)	Date of birth	Dependant? Y/N
1	....	....	....
2	....	....	....
3	....	....	....
4	....	....	....

Employment details

Client's occupation ....

Business name .... Start date ..../........../..........

Business address ....

Tax file number (optional) ....

Retirement age .... Date ..../........../..........

Partner's occupation ....

Business name .... Start date ..../........../..........

Business address ....

Tax file number (optional) ....

Retirement age .... Date ..../........../..........

Health

Client — Are you in good health? Y/N
(If no, please give details on last page)

Are you a smoker? Y/N

Partner — Are you in good health? Y/N
(If no, please give details on last page)

Are you a smoker? Y/N

Legal details

Client's will Last updated ..../........../.......... Held by ....

Testamentary trust? Y/N Power of attorney? Y/N

Solicitor's name ....

Solicitor's address ....

....

.... Postcode..............................

Income and expenses/cash flow

Estimated income per annum, net after tax:

Client $ .... Partner $ ....

Your projected or regular expenses per annum

(please attach list) $ ....

Net surplus/(shortfall) per annum $ ....

Do you expect any significant change in income or expenses in the next year? Y/N

Description ....

....

....

....

ASSETS

Should insufficient space be provided, please supply details on a separate attachment.

General assets	Description	Original cost of investment	Owned by (client, partner or jointly)	Original date invested	Current income per annum	Current value
Home						$
Business				/ /	$	$
Motor vehicles				/ /	Insured value	$
				/ /		$
Home contents						$
Investments				/ /		$
Property				/ /	$	$
Shares				/ /	$	$
				/ /	$	$
				/ /	$	$
Unit trusts				/ /	$	$
				/ /	$	$
Insurance bonds				/ /		$
				/ /		$
Other bonds: Investment value of insurance policies				/ /		$
				/ /		$
				/ /		$
				/ /		$
				/ /		$
Bank accounts, term deposits, debentures etc.				/ /	$	$
				/ /	$	$
				/ /	$	$
Private pensions/ annuities				/ /	$	$
				/ /	$	$
				/ /	$	$
Superannuation account				/ /	$	$
				/ /	$	$
Other investments or assets (e.g. boat)				/ /	$	$
				/ /	$	$
				/ /	$	$
Other assets and investments as per attachment				/ /	$	$
Total general assets and investments					$	$

LIABILITIES

Short term: (personal loans, credit cards, leases etc.)

Description	Rate of interest % p.a.	Owned by (client, partner or jointly)	Repayments per month	Amount owing
			$	$
			$	$
			$	$

Long term: (mortgages, investment loans etc.)

Description	Rate of interest % p.a.	Owned by (client, partner or jointly)	Repayments per month	Amount owing
			$	$
			$	$
			$	$

Explanatory notes ....

....

....

....

Financial goals, objectives and extraordinary expenses

What financial goals and needs do you have?

For example, children's education, home renovations, overseas travel, new home, new car, luxury items, savings targets, retirement, gifts.

Short term (less than 3 years)	**Estimated costs**
$	$ ....
$	$ ....
$	$ ....
Medium term (3–5 years)	
$	$ ....
$	$ ....
$	$ ....
Long term (more than 5 years)	
$	$ ....
$	$ ....
$	$ ....

Your personal investment preferences

We need to understand how you feel about investments.

1. Do you need any income from your investments to help you meet your day-to-day living expenses?	Yes Details:	No
2. Do you have a loan payment or other financial commitment that requires a fixed amount from your investments in the future?	Yes Details:	No
3. What is the main objective for your investments?		
4. What is the time frame for your investment program?		
5. What level of funds do you prefer in investments that can be accessed at short notice (less than 7 days)?		

You should spend time with your adviser in completing this section.

6. What do you believe would be a realistic real return on these different asset classes? Your adviser will explain the risks associated with each type of investment.	Cash Fixed interest Property Shares			
7. How comfortable are you with the following investments? (1 = uncomfortable, 4 = very comfortable)	**1**	**2**	**3**	**4**
Shares: Australian				
regional/international				
Direct property				
Indirect property				
Cash				
Fixed interest: term deposits				
bonds				
debentures				
Speculative investments				

8. What do you feel about borrowing to fund your investment portfolio?	Uncomfortable ☐ Neutral ☐ Comfortable ☐ Very comfortable ☐	
9. What type of investor do you see yourself as?	Client	Partner
Conservative: capital secure, stable income stream		
Moderately conservative: capital security but with aspects of growth		
Balanced: moderate growth over a spread of investments		
Moderately aggressive: higher growth potential from a spread of growth assets		
Aggressive: high level of capital growth and volatility		

Existing insurance program details

We need to know about your existing personal insurance program.

1. Existing life/trauma insurance details

Policy details (co., commencement date & policy no.)	Owner's name	Type	Premium	Sum insured (death, TPD, trauma)	Reason for cover

2. Existing disability income insurance details

Policy details (co., commencement date & policy no.)	Owner	Premium (per month or per annum)	Benefit payable (per month)	Benefit period (accident/ illness)	Waiting period	Benefit ceasing age

I have requested to be insured for the amounts specified:	
Death cover	Sum insured $ ....
Total and permanent disability cover	Sum insured $ ....
Trauma cover	Sum insured $ ....
Income protection	Monthly benefit $ ....

Special planning considerations

What is your desired annual retirement income (in today's dollars)?

$ ....

Do you, your partner or children expect to receive an inheritance in the near future? Y/N

If yes, please provide details ....

....

....

....

Other information for consideration (e.g. expected changes to your income or debt level, proposed sale of assets, tax liability)

....

....

....

....

....

Superannuation and tax considerations

So that we may clarify your superannuation and tax, please complete the following.

Superannuation (please attach copies of statements)

Fund manager	Personal/employer/ SGC	Start date	Contributions per annum	Current value
			$	$
			$	$
			$	$
			$	$

If you are about to leave your job, please list the payments you expect to receive. Please attach copies of statements.

	Client	Partner
Superannuation account balance	$	$
start date	$	$
preserved amount	$	$
Redundancy payments ex gratia	$	$
other	$	$
Long-service leave (net after tax)	$	$
Annual leave (net after tax)	$	$
Other payments	$	$
Expected payment date		

Client statement/acknowledgement

	Yes (initial please)	No (initial please)
The information provided in this form is complete and accurate to the best of my knowledge	....	....
OR I have chosen to only disclose a limited amount of information shown in this form	....	....
OR I have chosen and requested that no formal analysis is to be conducted for my circumstances.	....	....

Detailed insurance analysis form

You may wish to complete the following insurance needs calculator for your own purposes.

Death, permanent disability and trauma insurance calculator			
Balance outstanding on:	**Client**	**Partner**	**Example**
Home mortgage	$	$	$50 000
Other investment loans	$	$	$20 000
Credit cards	$	$	$ 1 000
Business loans	$	$	Nil
Foreseen one-off capital requirements	$	$	$ 10 000
			$ 81 000
Future income needs	**Client**	**Partner**	**Example**
Annual income requirement	$	$	($25 000 × 15) = **$375 000**
How long can the family go without regular income? (e.g. 14, 30, 90 days)	$	$	nil
Subtotal (a) Total commitments	$	$	**$456 000**

Each partner does contribute to household income even if one partner is not earning an income. As a rule of thumb, it will be necessary to convert your surviving partner's income needs into a lump sum. In this example, we have multiplied the family income needs by 15, i.e. $25 000 × 15 = $375 000. (This number takes account of your age and would be higher if you were younger.)

Less	**Client**	**Partner**	**Example**
Net value of existing assets (excluding family home)	$	$	$ 50 000
Current level of cover	$	$	$250 000
Subtotal (b)			**$300 000**
Subtract (a) from (b) **Surplus/(Shortfall)**	$	$	**($156 000)**

General information

1. We need to know of any circumstances that may, or may have in the past, affected an application for insurance on your life. Things to consider may include your own health, your parents' health, any participation in hazardous sports, previous illnesses or accidents, or if you have ever been declined insurance cover. Please provide details.

2. As a life broker representative, by law we are required to operate in your best interests, which means that we shall choose insurance products designed to meet your needs. There are a range of features contained in risk products which, by way of our experience and training, would allow us to tailor an insurance program to *best fit* your needs as determined by the information you have provided to us within this form.

   If you are happy to accept our recommendations with this in mind, please tick the Yes box. If not, we shall be happy to provide a detailed table and an explanation of product features.

   Yes ☐ No ☐

3. Additional information or explanatory notes

....

....

....

....

I understand and acknowledge that by not completing a fact finder analysis/ questionnaire, advice may not be appropriate to my needs and objectives.

....	....
Client signature	**Partner signature**
Date ..../............/............	Date ..../............/............
....	............/............/............
Adviser signature	**Date**

ADDITIONAL INFORMATION

....

....

....

....

....

....

....

Future financial plan reviews: quarterly 6-monthly annually

APPENDIX 15C

Risk tolerance classifications

There are a number of risk tolerance classifications used by financial planners. Chapter 15 outlines the features of a risk profile questionnaire, and the example below provides a classification of risk based on a client's likely attitude towards risk.

However, it is important to note that the definition of the degree of risk tolerance is more important than the classifications used. Risk classifications can differ markedly depending on the design and terminology used within the questionnaire. It is recommended that advisers look beyond the terminology and understand the underlying meaning assigned to the classifications. This appreciation is very important because of its impact on the determination and design of an appropriate asset allocation model for the client.

Questions to ask yourself to determine your risk profile

1. Do you like to make all your investment decisions yourself?
2. Do you expect to leave your investments where they are for the next 5–10 years?
3. When considering long-term investing, do you aim to maximise returns accepting the possibility of short-term declines in the value of your investment?
4. Is your major investment objective to grow your investment portfolio quickly?
5. Do you want your investments to significantly outpace inflation?
6. Have you ever put money into shares or other volatile investments?
7. If the value of one of your investments fell by 15% 6 months after you bought it, would you consider buying more?
8. Do you decide on your investments quickly before the opportunity is gone?
9. Does the opportunity of increasing the value of your investments outweigh concern about market fluctuations?
10. Would you be willing to consider an investment which returned 50% in a good year and −25% in a bad year?

Count how many times you answered yes to these questions and choose the risk profile which fits your answers.

You have answered yes to 1 or 2 questions

Conservative investor

You are a conservative investor and you typically select investments with little or no risks associated with capital loss, such as fixed-term deposits. You are willing to accept other risks to avoid capital loss, such as a rate of return that does not keep pace with inflation.

You have answered yes to 3 or 4 questions

Moderately conservative investor

You are a moderately conservative investor and you are willing to accept a slightly higher risk of capital loss than a conservative investor but you still focus on avoiding potential capital losses and volatility. Typically, you are most comfortable with investments that normally have less severe and less frequent changes in their value.

You have answered yes to 5 or 6 questions

Moderate investor

You are a moderate investor and you are willing to tolerate more possibilities of suffering capital losses. Typically, you are 'middle of the road' with regard to both potential risks and rewards. You do not mind some fluctuations but will stay away from investments that have more dramatic or frequent changes. You are not as concerned as a more aggressive investor with investment timing and are less willing than a conservative investor to accept risks associated with inflation and reinvestment. Your portfolio will often have some investments that fluctuate in value, balanced with investments subject to less frequent fluctuation.

You have answered yes to 7, 8 or 9 questions

Moderately aggressive investor

You are a moderately aggressive investor and you are willing to tolerate a greater chance of capital loss and will be more comfortable with market fluctuations than a more conservative investor. You will usually have some investments that are subject to greater fluctuation than those of a more conservative investor. Your portfolio will be made up of a combination of direct investments in shares and property.

You have answered yes to all questions

Aggressive investor

You are an aggressive investor and you are willing and usually eager to accept a greater chance of capital loss in return for potentially higher returns. You sometimes focus on short-term market timing as opposed to long-term investing. You are comfortable accepting a high level of risk in the hope of greater opportunity for returns. Typically, you are less concerned with the rate of inflation and ability to reinvest earnings at the same rate. Your investment portfolio will typically include Australian shares, investment property, a direct investment in a private company and exposure to overseas markets.

APPENDIX 15D

Example Statement of Advice

The following case study provides an example of a SOA prepared to industry standards. Client information is provided on Jack and Jill Smith who are seeking assistance in relation to their income needs in retirement as well as their social security entitlements.

We gratefully acknowledge the assistance and support provided by Integrity Financial Planners — a dealership and financial planning practice based in Melbourne.

Client information

Jack and Jill Smith seek some assistance from the financial planning practice that you are employed with. The couple is an existing client of the practice and you have previously provided advice in respect of Jill's retirement and the commencement of an account-based pension, as well as the couple's eligibility for the age pension. Jack is now looking to retire as well and is seeking advice on what should be done with his existing superannuation account to provide an income upon his retirement, as well as to re-calculate the couple's Department of Human Service entitlements as a consequence of Jack's retirement.

The Smiths provide you with the following information in respect of their financial situation.

Ages:	Jack is aged 68 and Jill is aged 66.		
Children:	The couple has three children and they are all financially independent.		
Cash inflows:	Jack was previously a technician but is currently on long service leave leading to retirement and receives a weekly amount of $303. Jill currently receives income from an account-based pension of around $909 per month. The couple is also currently receiving an age pension payment of $528 per fortnight each.		
Cash payments:	The couple's living costs amount to approximately $42 000 p.a.		
Assets:	**Item**	**Owner**	**Market value**
	Home	Joint	$490 000
	Home contents	Joint	$5 000
	Motor vehicles: Ford Falcon Holden Astra	 Jack Jill	 $10 000 $6 000
	Netwealth superannuation Netwealth account-based pension	Jack Jill	$67 836 $218 234
Liabilities:	None		
Insurance:	The couple is fully covered for private health insurance.		
	The couple has no other personal insurance coverage.		

(continued)

Primary objectives:	■ Jack to retire at age 68
	■ To maximise social security entitlements
	■ To determine how to structure Jack's superannuation account to provide an income upon his retirement
	■ To target a combined retirement income of at least $42 000 p.a. in today's dollars.
	■ To have an investment portfolio that is easy to manage and provides flexibility.
Other information:	■ After completing a risk profile for the couple, you have assessed their risk tolerance as balanced with a target asset allocation of 60% allocated to growth investments and 40% allocated to defensive investments.
	■ The couple both have up-to-date wills as well as enduring power of attorney documents.
	■ The couple is seeking limited advice in relation to Jack's superannuation account and age pension entitlements only.
	■ The couple do not wish you to consider any other aspect of their financial situation other than issues that relate to the goal of making the most effective use of Jack's superannuation upon his retirement.

ACE Financial Services

25 September 2013

Mr J & Mrs J Smith
23 Bona Vista Road
BAYSWATER VIC 3153

Dear Jack & Jill,

Thank you for allowing us to present the enclosed recommendations.

Our recommendations are based on information you have previously provided. If this information does not in any way accurately reflect any part of your current situation please let us know so that we can check whether any part of the plan needs to be modified.

Attached is our most recent Financial Services Guide. If you have any questions about this guide please do not hesitate to contact us.

Our aim is to maintain an ongoing relationship with you as a client by providing an exceptional level of service now and in the future. Please take time to read through the enclosed plan in detail and contact us if you wish to discuss any matters further. We look forward to receiving your instructions to proceed.

Please note that you should not act on any advice in this plan after 45 days from the above date without first checking with us that the advice remains appropriate.

Yours sincerely,

Gayle Jones
Jones Private Clients Pty Ltd
Authorised Representatives of Ace Financial Services
Australian Financial Services Licence #225051
65 Main Street, Melbourne 3000

Statement of Advice

Prepared for:

Mr J & Mrs P Smith
23 Bona Vista Road
BAYSWATER VIC 3153

Prepared by:

Gayle Jones
Jones Private Clients Pty Ltd
Authorised Representatives of
Ace Financial Services
Australian Financial Services #225051

25 September 2013

Our contact details
You can contact us on: **(03) 9999 1111**
Our email address: **Gaylej@jonesfp.com.au**
Postal address: **65 Main Street, Melbourne 30000**

Contents

Executive summary

Recommendations

- Convert Jack's superannuation account held with Netwealth Investments to an account-based pension drawing the minimum level of income which will be $282 per month.
- Nominate Jill as reversionary beneficiary on the new pension. This would allow Jill to continue to receive an income from the account-based pension in the event of Jack's death.

Why my advice is appropriate

- You will have sufficient income to support you through your retirement.
- You will maximise your eligibility for a Department of Human Services pension.
- Your superannuation portfolio will be easy to manage, simple to administer and will enable you to retain investment flexibility. The portfolio asset allocation is in line with your risk profile, which will assist you to meet your financial goals.
- Nominating each other as reversionary beneficiary on your pension accounts will ensure that your partner has an ongoing income in the event of your death.

What are the risks associated with my advice?

- Your pension account may diminish, not increase. We have recommended you both withdraw the minimum from your pension accounts. However, this means your account would need to generate a return of at least 5.0% p.a. to prevent dipping into the capital.
- Projected superannuation returns will depend on movement of markets. Over the long run, in our projections we have assumed your investments will generate a return of at least 6%. While we do not believe this is unreasonable, this is by no means guaranteed.
- Legislation changes. The government may decide to change the superannuation rules again in the future — for instance, increase the tax rates on pension accounts.

Fees and commissions

Based on your current combined superannuation/account-based pension account balance of $286 070, our fee will be $3147 per year of which Ace Financial Services will receive $630 and Jones Private Clients will receive $2517.

The fund manager or responsible entity operating the recommended investments will charge other ongoing fees and/or deduct expenses for managing the investment. These fees and expenses are generally applied prior to the manager declaring a unit price or rate of return.

Confidential Personal Financial Plan for Jack Smith and Jill Smith 25 September 2013
Prepared by Gayle Jones

What to do next

As you are reading this plan please write down any questions that you may have about the information provided. We will attempt to satisfactorily answer your questions and you can indicate any changes that you wish to make to the recommendations outlined earlier. You should read any other information given to you and let us know if you have any queries.

Jack, you will need to sign the authority to proceed and return it to us.

Scope of advice

What is the scope of our advice?

Jack and Jill, you have sought our advice in relation to the following specific issues:

- review the investment of Jack's superannuation assets now that he is retired and there are no longer any further contributions going into your superannuation fund
- recalculate your Department of Human Service entitlements as a consequence of Jack's retirement.

We understand that you have provided us with complete information in relation to the above specific issues. Please note, as the advice in this report is limited to these specific issues, it does not address other areas of your financial circumstances such as:

- estate planning
- insurances
- non-superannuation assets.

As we have not reviewed your entire situation, you must decide whether it is appropriate to proceed with this advice in light of your total situation.

It is perfectly reasonable to seek advice regarding specific issues as you have done. You should be aware that by limiting advice in this way you risk neglecting issues of significance and that you could incur financial loss in relation to issues not covered by this advice. Where we become aware of such issues we will bring them to your attention; however, we are limited in our capacity to do so by the information you have provided. If you wish to undertake a broader analysis of your financial affairs you should let us know before proceeding with this advice.

If you believe we have misinterpreted or overlooked some relevant information, it is your responsibility to bring this to our attention before proceeding with this proposal. You should be aware that if you have not disclosed information that is relevant to this advice you risk making a financial decision that may not be appropriate to your needs and circumstances.

Confidential Personal Financial Plan for Jack Smith and Jill Smith 25 September 2013
Prepared by Gayle Jones

Jones Financial Planners is licensed to provide advice on a range of financial products as set down in the financial services guide we previously provided. We are not licensed to provide advice on derivatives (futures and options), nor on general insurance products such as car or household insurances.

We do not provide advice regarding every financial product that is available. We can only recommend products that are on our approved product list which generally only includes products that have been assessed by our chosen external professional researchers. Please refer to the Investment Research Appendix for further information relating to the products that we are licensed to advise on.

Section 1 Your current situation and objectives

Current situation

Before we provide you with recommendations, it is appropriate that we reflect on your current situation. Please check the following information carefully to ensure that no detail has been omitted or is inconsistent with your understanding. If the advice provided in this report has been based on incorrect information, it may be inappropriate for you.

Personal details

	Jack	Jill
Date of birth	14 Feb 1945	26 Sep 1947
Age last birthday	68	66
Marital status	Married	Married
Health	Good	Good
Smoker	Non-smoker	Non-smoker
Employment status	Long service leave	Retired
Occupation	Technician	Supervisor

Children and dependants

You have 3 children — Catherine, 40, Robert, 39 and Jamie 35 — who are not financially dependent on you.

Confidential Personal Financial Plan for Jack Smith and Jill Smith — 25 September 2013
Prepared by Gayle Jones

Assets as at 18 September 2013

Lifestyle assets

Description	Owner	Market value
Real estate — principal residence	Joint	$490 000
Contents/personal property (DHS market value)	Joint	$5 000
Motor vehicle — Ford Falcon 4dr auto	Jack	$10 000
Motor vehicle Holden Astra 4dr auto	Jill	$6 000
Total		**$511 000**

Financial assets

Description	Owner	Market value
Netwealth superannuation	Jack	$67 836
Netwealth account-based pension	Jill	$218 234
Total		**$286 070**

Cash flow

Based on the information that you provided during our meeting, we estimate your present fortnightly income situation is as follows:

	Jack	Jill	Total
Income			
Long service leave ($303 per week)	$606		$606
DHS age pension	$528	$528	$1056
DHS carer allowance	$114		$114
Netwealth pension ($909 per month)		$420	$420
Total fortnightly income	**$1248**	**$948**	**$2196**

Your objectives and goals

Jack and Jill, you have stated that your primary objective is to restructure your investments to provide an ongoing income now that you have both retired.

Confidential Personal Financial Plan for Jack Smith and Jill Smith — 25 September 2013
Prepared by Gayle Jones

Beyond this goal, your other short- and long-term objectives are:

- You would like to know more about your potential eligibility for any Department of Human Services benefits both now and in the future.
- You wish to receive ongoing advice and guidance in relation to the maintenance of your overall financial strategy to fulfil your financial goals.
- You wish to structure your investments in the most tax-effective means available and wish to spread your investments to maximise the benefits of diversification.
- You wish to maintain control of your financial affairs but require professional help planning and putting plans into action. You don't wish to take on the burden of managing your affairs on a daily basis.

Risk profile

For the purpose of developing a suitable investment strategy we discussed your understanding of, and tolerance to, risk and investment return volatility, as well as the types of investments you already hold and are familiar with.

There are two main areas in which your money can grow — shares and property. The other asset classes, cash and fixed interest provide you with income and minimal capital growth.

The important issues to consider when deciding on an appropriate level of risk for your circumstances are:

- You are at a stage in your life where you are relying on your superannuation investments to support your cost of living.

Given the above, we recommend you have a mixture of all asset sectors within your portfolio with a balance of income producing and growth investments. We recommend an asset allocation of 50% in defensive asset classes and 50% in the growth-oriented asset classes such as shares and property. This will enable your portfolio to focus on providing you with sufficient income to fund your retirement, while generating a moderate amount of capital growth without taking excessive risk to counter the effects of inflation.

Investment theory

Numerous research studies show that diversification across all asset classes will reduce risk and improve long-term returns. Risk is increased when a portfolio is too heavily exposed to any one sector.

Confidential Personal Financial Plan for Jack Smith and Jill Smith 25 September 2013
Prepared by Gayle Jones

Investment theory states that returns over the long term will be greatest for shares, property, fixed interest [bonds] and cash in that order. While past returns and risk are no indication of future performance these facts should be kept in mind. There are other ways of reducing risk within your investment portfolio and this is to include different investment styles within each asset sector [mainly the growth sectors].

Another risk reduction tool is to blend together investments that do not follow the same pattern i.e. some investments can be expected to underperform or in fact fall in value in the short term while still providing good long-term returns. It is important to diversify investments so that when one is suffering from short-term underperformance other investments, subject to different economic influences, are outperforming to compensate.

Asset allocation

Asset allocation and security selection are the two fundamental decisions in the implementation or realisation of investment objectives.

Asset allocation involves making the decision of how much to invest within each asset class or investment sector.

Investment selection involves making the decision of how to invest within each asset class.

Considering the above information regarding risk and returns, and that your investment needs are to provide income with some capital growth over the longer term, we recommend the following asset allocation for your portfolio:

	Target	Range
Cash	10%	0–20%
Australian fixed interest	30%	20–60%
Alternative income	10%	0–35%
Australian property	20%	15–40%
Australian shares	25%	5–35%
International shares	5%	0–15%

The above allocation provides you with a spread over all asset sectors with 50% of your funds invested in growth-oriented investments. You need to note that a

Confidential Personal Financial Plan for Jack Smith and Jill Smith 25 September 2013
Prepared by Gayle Jones

portfolio that has 50% of its funds invested in growth investments statistically is likely to have 1 year of negative returns in a 12-year period.

Your exposure to asset classes may differ from the long-term benchmark portfolio because of adjustments based on the latest research of medium-term risks and to account for individual considerations.

As investment markets move, profits should be taken periodically to rebalance the portfolio back to the desired asset allocation to ensure you are not over-exposed to any one asset sector and to increase exposure to sectors which may be under-valued. In this way, the risk of exposure to over-valued market sectors is reduced and long-term returns are improved.

We will review your risk profile and your asset allocation with all major changes in your circumstances and objectives that you inform us of, as well as discussing any concerns that you have during our regular review meetings.

If you do not feel that this description is an accurate reflection of your risk profile you should let us know. Please feel free to raise any queries you may have.

Section 2 Analysis of strategies and recommendations

Convert Jack's superannuation to an account-based pension

Earlier this year, we provided you with a statement of advice to convert Jill's superannuation to an account-based pension. Now that Jack has retired and will no longer be receiving an income from long service leave, we feel it is an appropriate time to also convert Jack's superannuation to a pension.

The information following has been previously provided to you; however, we have repeated it here so that you understand the process and can discuss any queries you have with us prior to proceeding.

What is an account-based pension?

An account-based pension is a retirement income stream that is drawn from an investment in a superannuation fund. An account-based pension has no guaranteed term or return. Exactly how long the pension payments will last is dependent on the performance of the underlying investments and the amount withdrawn from your pension account (either as pension payments or lump sums).

Confidential Personal Financial Plan for Jack Smith and Jill Smith 25 September 2013
Prepared by Gayle Jones

Advantages of account-based pensions

Account-based pensions are a secure, tax effective and flexible way of drawing down income in retirement. They provide flexibility, both in terms of investment choice and the amount of income drawn. Investment in an account-based pension provides you with many important advantages:

Flexibility

You are able to vary the income you receive, and you will have the option of monthly, quarterly, bi-annual or annual payments. Currently, account-based pension investors can also withdraw (commute) lump sums from their account at any time.

Tax concessions

- The commencement of an account-based pension counts as a rollover, so lump sum tax does not apply.
- The returns generated within your account-based pension account are entirely free of tax.
- As you are already over the age of 60, any pension payments or lump sum withdrawals from your account-based pension will be completely free of personal tax.
- If any assets are sold down within your pension account, they are exempt from capital gains tax.

No mortality risk

Importantly, there is no mortality risk with an account-based pension. If you die before the capital (plus any investment earnings) is exhausted, the balance can be paid to your nominated beneficiary.

Department of Human Services (DHS)

Your account-based pension may contain a portion of income which is exempt from DHS's income test. The exempt component each year is based on the balance of the account and your life expectancy at the commencement of the pension.

Jack, based on the current account balance of your superannuation — $67 836 — we have calculated that the amount of income that will be exempt under the DHS income test is $4181 pa. Therefore, for the next financial year, a total amount withdrawn from your pension account up to this amount will not be included under the DHS income test.

Pension payments

Pension payments must be made at least annually and are required to be above a set minimum amount which varies depending on your age at the 1st of July each year. These amounts are recalculated at the start of each financial year.

Confidential Personal Financial Plan for Jack Smith and Jill Smith — 25 September 2013
Prepared by Gayle Jones

The minimum amount that must be withdrawn each year is as follows:

Age	Minimum percentage of pension
Under 65	4.00%
65–74	5.00%
75–79	6.00%
80–84	7.00%
85–89	9.00%
90–94	11.00%
95 and over	14.00%

The minimum payment amount is imposed to ensure that there is no unreasonable build-up of assets in the tax-free environment.

Jack, as you are 68 years of age, the minimum pension that you are currently required to draw is 5.00% of your account balance. It is important to note that this is a minimum amount; no maximum limit is set. You do need to be aware, however, that your account balance is not guaranteed to last you for the rest of your life.

The minimum amount is adjusted on a pro rata basis for the year of purchase and must be recalculated at the start of each financial year to reflect the current balance of your account and your current age.

Therefore, based on your current account balance of $67 836, the minimum account balance you would be required to withdraw for this financial year is $3392 ($130 per fortnight), however, this will be pro-rated since you have not commenced your pension at the start of the financial year.

Superannuation vs pension — what's the difference?

The big difference is the tax rate. In the super accumulation phase, earnings are taxed up to 15%. In pension phase, the tax rate on earnings is zero.

The following example, using Jack's current super balance, helps to illustrate the potential savings:

In super accumulation phase	
Balance at beginning of year	$67 836
Add:	
Distributions/dividends @ 6%	$4 070
Capital gains made @ 3%	$2 035
Less:	
15% tax on distributions/dividends	$610
10% CGT on capital gains made	$204
Balance at end of year	**$73 127**
In pension phase	
Balance at beginning of year	$67 836
Add:	
Distributions/dividends @ 6%	$4 070
Capital gains made @ 3%	$2 035
Less:	
0% tax on distributions/dividends	$0
0% CGT on capital gains made	$0
Balance at end of year	**$73 941**
Difference = $814 over one year	

Recommendation

Jack, we therefore recommend that you convert your new Netwealth personal superannuation fund to a Netwealth account-based pension, drawing the minimum level of income which will be $282 per month.

Binding death benefit nomination or reversionary benefit nomination

As superannuation does not form part of your will, you need to nominate whom you wish to receive your superannuation monies in the event of your death.

When you commence an account-based pension you have the option of making either a binding death benefit nomination or reversionary benefit nomination.

Binding non-lapsing death benefit nomination

This type of nomination directs the superannuation company to pay out the balance of your account to the person you have nominated. It is binding and therefore cannot be challenged except under extreme circumstances. As it is non-lapsing it will not expire, and will not change unless you make a new nomination.

This type of nomination can be made only to a dependant; this is either your partner, children or someone who is financially dependent upon you at the time of your death.

Reversionary benefit nomination

The other type of nomination you can elect is a reversionary benefit. In this situation, the account would continue on as is, but be transferred into your nominated beneficiary's name. The pension would continue to be paid until either the funds run out or other instructions are provided by the beneficiary.

Recommendation

Jack, we would recommend that you make a reversionary benefit nomination in Jill's name. This is the option taken when Jill's superannuation was converted to an account-based pension earlier this year. This would allow Jill to continue to receive an income from the account-based pension in the event of your death.

Department of Human Services (DHS) age pension

You are both currently receiving the DHS age pension; however, when Jack's long service leave stops being paid, you will be reassessed. At this time your fortnightly payment should increase since you will be earning less under the income test.

How much age pension will you receive?

After Jack's income ceases, we believe DHS will calculate your entitlement as follows:

Assets test

Description	Owner	Market value	Included for assets test?
Real estate — principal residence	Joint	$500 000	No
Contents/personal property (Centrelink value)	Joint	$5 000	Yes
Motor vehicle — Ford Falcon	Jack	$10 000	Yes
Motor vehicle — Holden Astra 2000 4dr auto	Jill	$6 000	Yes
Netwealth account-based pension	Jack	$67 836	Yes
Netwealth account-based pension	Jill	$218 234	Yes
Total:		**$807 070**	

A couple can hold a total value of $273 000 in assets before the fortnightly pension amount is reduced by $1.50 per fortnight for every $1000 above the threshold.

Therefore, under the assets test, we believe you will be entitled to approximately ***$1168 per fortnight*** from DHS (this includes the pension supplement). Note that DHS will also include the value of your current bank accounts in their calculations so this might reduce our estimate slightly.

Income test

DHS includes all financial assets in their calculations when estimating your entitlement under the income test. This includes superannuation and any bank account balances which are deemed to earn a certain level of income, whether they actually earn this income or not. In the instance of superannuation, as mentioned earlier, if you convert your superannuation account to a pension, they will allow you a discounted amount.

We believe they will calculate your income as follows:

Description	Owner	Market value	Included for income test?
Real estate — principal residence	Joint	$500 000	No
Contents	Joint	$5 000	No
Motor vehicle — Falcon	Jack	$10 000	No
Motor vehicle — Astra	Jill	$6 000	No
Netwealth super	Jack	$67 836	Yes
Netwealth account-based pension	Jill	$218 234	Yes
Total:		**$807 070**	

As your combined income is less than the minimum income threshold, we believe you will be entitled to the maximum payment of approximately ***$1219 per fortnight*** combined from DHS (this includes the pension supplement). Note that DHS will also include the value of your current bank accounts in their calculations so this might reduce our income test estimate slightly but it is unlikely to change your overall pension entitlement since we believe you will be assessed under the assets test.

New DHS age pension amount

As DHS will pay the lower amount under both the income and assets tests, we believe you will receive a combined payment of ***$1168 per fortnight*** combined and be assessed under the assets test. As the value of your personal bank accounts has not been included in this calculation, this estimate might change slightly.

Confidential Personal Financial Plan for Jack Smith and Jill Smith 25 September 2013
Prepared by Gayle Jones

Summary of the recommended strategy

- Convert Jack's superannuation to an account-based pension.
- Nominate Jill as reversionary beneficiary on the new pension.

Other strategies considered

- We considered leaving Jack's superannuation in the accumulation phase. This alternative was not recommended as converting to pension phase is the most tax-effective outcome and would also allow you to maximise your DHS entitlement.
- We considered taking a larger amount of income from Jack's pension account. By taking the minimum you will be leaving a larger amount in the account, allowing this to grow. If you decide that you don't have enough income you can increase this level of income at any time or take a lump sum withdrawal from either of your pension accounts.
- We considered a binding nomination for Jack's pension account instead of reversionary. A reversionary nomination will ensure that Jill has an ongoing income in the event of Jack's death. Upon death, a binding nomination would move the pension back to superannuation phase and cease the monthly pension payment.

Outcomes of the recommended strategy

By implementing the recommendations made in this document:

1. You will have sufficient income to support you through your retirement.
2. You will maximise your eligible DHS pension.
3. Your superannuation portfolios will be easy to manage, simple to administer and will enable you to retain investment flexibility. The portfolio asset allocation is in line with your risk profile; this will assist you to meet your financial goals.
4. Nominating each other as reversionary beneficiary on your pension accounts will ensure that your partner has an ongoing income in the event of your death.

After the recommendations have been implemented, a revised estimate of your fortnightly income should appear as follows:

	Jack	Jill	Total
Income			
Centrelink age pension	$584	$584	$1 168
Centrelink carer allowance	$114		$114
Netwealth pension	$130	$420	$550
Total fortnightly income	**$828**	**$1 004**	**$1 832**
Total annual income	**$21 528**	**$26 104**	**$47 632**

Confidential Personal Financial Plan for Jack Smith and Jill Smith — 25 September 2013
Prepared by Gayle Jones

What are the risks associated with my advice?

Naturally there are risks associated with any financial planning strategy. Here are some of the more specific ones that relate to our advice for you:

- Your pension account may diminish, not increase. We have recommended you both withdraw the minimum from your pension accounts. Jill you are currently withdrawing $10 912 p.a. from your pension account which represents approximately 5.0% of your current balance. This means that your account would need to generate at least a return of this to prevent dipping into the capital. Jack, we have recommended you withdraw the minimum which is currently 5.0% of your balance. This means your account would need to generate at least a return of 5.0% p.a. to prevent dipping into the capital.
- Projected superannuation returns will depend on movement of markets. Over the long run, in our projections we have assumed your investments will generate a return of at least 6%. While we do not believe this is unreasonable, this is by no means guaranteed.
- Legislation changes. The government may decide to change the superannuation rules again in the future — for instance, increase the tax rates on pension accounts.

Section 3 Implementing the plan

What to do next

As you are reading this plan please write down any questions that you may have about the information provided.

We will attempt to satisfactorily answer your questions and you can indicate any changes that you wish to make to the recommendations outlined earlier.

You should read any other information given to you and let us know if you have any queries.

Jack, you will need to sign the authority to proceed and return it to us.

Implementation

Action required?	By who?	When?
Sign the enclosed authority to proceed (ATP)	Jack	Now
Convert Jack's Netwealth super wrap to an account-based pension	Jack and Jones Private Clients (JPC)	After ATP has been received
Notify changes to the Department of Human Services	JPC	After pension has commenced

Confidential Personal Financial Plan for Jack Smith and Jill Smith — 25 September 2013
Prepared by Gayle Jones

Disclosure of fees and commissions

Financial planning document

As you are an existing client you will not be charged for the preparation of this report.

Implementation

No fees are payable on the implementation of our recommendations.

Ongoing fees and commissions

Jones Private Clients will charge a fee for ongoing advice and review of your portfolio. This fee will be:

- 1.10% per year of your investment balance, up to a balance of $500 000;
- 0.825% on the amount from $500 000 to $750 000;
- 0.55% on the amount from $750 000 to $1 000 000; and
- 0.33% on the amount above $1 000 000.

Based on your current combined account balance of $286 070 this fee would be $3147 per year. Of this amount, the licence holder, Ace Financial Services, will be paid an amount of $630.

For your investments in Netwealth this fee will be deducted from your account each month and paid to Jones Private Clients (JPC).

Some investments held within Netwealth will pay JPC an ongoing commission. This commission is normally paid by the manager from their resources; **it is not deducted from your account**.

The following table shows an estimate of JPC's ongoing fees and commissions for the first year.

Investment	Account balance	Administration fees (paid from your account to manager)		Adviser fees (paid from your investment to Jones)	
	$	%	$	%	$
Netwealth pension — Jack	67 836	0.81	551	1.1	746
Netwealth pension — Jill	218 234	0.81	1773	1.1	2401
Total	**286 070**		**2324**		**3147**

Confidential Personal Financial Plan for Jack Smith and Jill Smith 25 September 2013
Prepared by Gayle Jones

The amounts shown in the table opposite will vary over time according to the mix of investments and changes to the account balances. The amount shown is only an estimate for the first year.

GST

The above fees and commissions are inclusive of the goods and services tax (GST).

Adviser's interest

You have been provided advice by Gayle Jones in her capacity as an Authorised Representative and Director of Jones Private Clients Pty Ltd.

Jones Private Clients pays Ace Financial Services a fee for the provision of services such as licensing, research, training etc.

Gayle Jones is owner of Jones Private Clients and will benefit from income and profits earned by Jones Private Clients.

Other costs

The table opposite shows charges deducted from your account and ongoing commissions paid to JPC.

The fund manager or responsible entity operating the recommended investments will charge other ongoing fees and/or deduct expenses for managing the investment. These fees and expenses are generally applied prior to the manager declaring a unit price or rate of return. They are not deducted from your account but will impact on the returns from your investment.

The indirect cost ratio (ICR) is an estimate of the total of these fees and expenses expressed as a percentage of the funds held. The ICR is used rather than showing a list of all fees and expenses to enable meaningful comparisons between products.

These fees are not paid to your adviser or Ace Financial Services.

In addition, investment products often have a spread between the buying and selling price of the investment. This represents a cost for trading investments which will occur only when units in the investment are bought or sold. This cost usually does not exceed 2% and is generally less than 0.5% of an investment's unit price.

We have not attempted to itemise these costs for each investment. You should refer to the product disclosure statements accompanying this statement of advice to determine the actual costs for particular products recommended. If you have any questions regarding this information please ask us.

Section 4 Disclaimer and authority to proceed

Disclaimers

The law requires that recommendations made to clients are consistent with their financial needs and objectives and have a reasonable basis. This statement of advice is based on information that you have provided. If you believe we have misinterpreted or overlooked some relevant information, it is your responsibility to bring this to our attention before proceeding with this proposal.

The scope of this advice is limited to areas defined in the statement of advice. No responsibility is accepted in relation to any other aspect of your financial circumstances. You are warned that there may be issues beyond the scope of this advice which may impact on outcomes. We have made reasonable efforts to identify such issues, where it is in our power to do so. If there is any information that has not been provided to us, or about which you have not sought our advice, you risk making a financial decision that may not be appropriate to your needs and circumstances and financial loss may occur.

In preparing this plan, we have relied on information supplied to us by you and by others, which, where reasonable, we have assumed to be correct. While reasonable efforts have been made to substantiate such information, no responsibility can be accepted if the information is incorrect or inaccurate.

This advice is prepared solely for the use of the client to whom it is addressed and we do not accept any liability whatsoever to third parties.

Advice in this report is based on current information and should only be considered current for one month from the date of this report. After that time you should not act on any of the recommendations without further reference to us.

In the event that any advice or other services rendered by the Company constitute a supply of services to a consumer under the Trade Practices Act 1974 (as amended), then the Company's liability for any breach of any conditions or warranties implied under the Act shall not be excluded but will be limited to the cost of having the advice or services supplied again.

While every effort has been made to include relevant tax and social security considerations, you are advised to discuss your annual tax liability and the tax and social security implications of this advice with your tax adviser as the estimates contained herein are intended as a guide only.

Estimates of income and capital growth are based on assessments of current and likely future economic conditions, as well as investment past and likely future performances. Such figures are purely estimates and may vary with changing circumstances. They are not guaranteed to occur.

Each paragraph of this disclaimer shall be deemed to be separate and severable from each other. If any paragraph is found to be illegal, prohibited or unenforceable, then this shall not invalidate any other paragraphs.

Authority to proceed

I hereby authorise Gayle Jones Authorised Representative of Jones Financial Planners Pty Ltd, to arrange for the implementation of the recommendations specified in the statement of advice dated 25 September 2013, and as per the attached summary.

I have read the statement of advice, agree that the client information on which it is based is complete and accurate and accept the advice provided.

I acknowledge that every care has been taken to ensure the accuracy of information included in this document and that neither Jones Financial Planners nor its representative will accept responsibility for any errors or omissions made by me regarding the information we have provided.

I understand that no guarantee is given that investments will meet the expectations stated in this report and that adverse market conditions may result in a reduction in the capital value of my investments.

At my instruction, advice has been limited to the funds, circumstances and issues specified in the statement of advice. I do not require advice regarding any other aspect of our financial affairs. I understand that, by limiting the advice in this manner, I risk making an investment or purchase that may not be appropriate to my overall needs and objectives.

I understand that I will be charged a fee for ongoing services which will not currently exceed 1.10% per year (inc. GST) of the value of my portfolio.

I have also been provided with a Financial Services Guide (FSG).

I authorise Jones Financial Planners Pty Ltd to retain my tax file numbers while acting on my behalf and to quote my tax file number to the Australian Taxation Office and to investment companies when making investments on my behalf.*

I wish to advise that my tax file number is ____ ____ ____ **(Jack)**

*(*Please note, you do not have to provide your tax file number nor authorise its use. Please delete these paragraphs if you do not wish us to retain your TFN)*

Signed: ______________________ Date:____/____/____

Jack Smith

Confidential Personal Financial Plan for Jack Smith and Jill Smith 25 September 2013
Prepared by Gayle Jones

Glossary

A-REIT a property fund listed on the Australian Securities Exchange *228*

account-based income stream where an individual owns and maintains an individual account from which an income stream is drawn *460, 517*

accumulation account a type of superannuation fund where the investment risk is borne by the member and in which contributions and positive earnings increase the accumulated amount and negative earnings reduce the accumulated amount *401*

accumulation mode where an individual is still contributing to superannuation *447, 515*

active investing an investment approach which is based on an investment manager selecting and trading in securities with the goal of outperforming an index *272*

actuarial calculations evaluate mathematically the likelihood of certain financial events and their associated costs; for example, what percentage of the total superannuation fund membership is likely to retire in the next 12 months and how much should be set aside to meet this likelihood *402*

adjusted taxable income (ATI) adjustments made to taxable income to determine eligibility for a number of family assistance and DHS payments, and tax offsets and rebates *552*

adverse selection against the fund where individuals are able to make choices which alter the risk profile of a fund and which can potentially limit the fund's ability to meet its commitments and/or unfairly shift obligations between members *379*

agent insurer's representative who directly organises insurance for clients *352*

age pension a pension paid to eligible members of the community based on their age and subject to an income and assets test *8, 535*

age test a test that requires persons to reach a certain age before being eligible for the age pension *540*

agreed value cover generally applies to motor vehicle insurance where the insured believes their vehicle is worth more than market value and therefore they reach an agreement with the insurer to insure the vehicle at a higher value with a commensurately higher premium *384*

allowable deductions expenses incurred by the taxpayer which are deducted from assessable income to derive taxable income *96*

approved child care child care that has been approved by the Australian government for child care benefit purposes because it meets certain standards and requirements *554*

assessable income income that is assessable or recognised and measured under taxation law *94, 317, 459*

asset-test-exempt income stream an income-stream product where part or all of the account balance is exempt under the assets test *549*

Austudy an Australian education assistance scheme that provides financial support to those aged 25 years and over and studying or undertaking an Australian apprenticeship full-time *557*

balance sheet a statement of assets and liabilities; the net result is the owner's value *49*

bare trust a separate trust to the SMSF that can hold the legal title of an asset until the debt incurred in buying the asset has been extinguished *507*

basis risk the risk that the risk-management product used does not exactly match the risk that is being hedged *332*

benchmark normally an index or other measure against which the performance of a managed fund or other investment portfolio is measured *278*

beneficial interest the entitlement to receive benefits generated by assets held in the name of another entity *264*

beneficiary a person nominated to receive a payout from an insurance policy, a superannuation fund or the assets of an estate *100, 359, 575*

best interest duty the obligation placed upon the financial planner to act in the best interests of the client *113*

binding death benefit nomination a declaration by a superannuation fund member that on their death the balance of their superannuation must be paid to a nominated person; the trustees are bound to follow this direction *519, 593*

broker insured's representative who determines the client's insurance needs *352*

business real property property that is used wholly and exclusively for business purposes *506*

call option a security that gives the buyer (holder) of the option the right but not the obligation to buy something in the future at a fixed price *335*

capital gain a gain that arises when the price of an asset increases *317*

capital gains tax (CGT) a tax applied when a profit is made on the disposal of a capital asset *109*

Centrelink the federal government agency which administers the payments of government pensions and allowances *536*

clean energy supplement additional support to those in receipt of a pension to cover the impact of carbon pricing *539*

co-insurance clause a clause in an insurance contract which reduces the claimable loss in proportion to the amount of underinsurance *381*

codicil a legal document that amends an existing will without revoking the will in its entirety *577*

codified legal principles that have been developed by the courts (common law) and included in legislation *399*

codify legal principles that have been developed by the courts (common law) and included in legislation *493*

commission a fee paid to a planner by a product provider for recommending a particular product to a client *635*

commute convert an income stream back into a lump sum *518*

compliance acting in accordance with established guidelines, specifications, or legislation *490*

complying superannuation fund a superannuation fund which is resident in Australia, has made an irrevocable decision to be regulated by the SIS Act and meets the conditions for compliance as outlined in the SIS Act *399*

concessional contribution a contribution to superannuation for which a tax deduction has been claimed *410, 501*

condition of release criteria that, if satisfied, enable an individual to withdraw their money from superannuation *377, 410, 449, 515*

constitution a set of rules and regulations that govern the conduct of an entity *268*

consumer price index (CPI) an index used to measure inflation i.e. the general increase in prices *370*

contract for difference (CFD) an agreement between a buyer and seller to exchange the difference in value of an underlying asset *329*

cost base the various costs of an asset that are included in the calculation of a taxable capital gain; these include the initial cost of the asset plus any other costs that are added to the initial cost *234*

coupon securities fixed-interest securities that pay interest at set periods of time during the life of the contract *188*

creditor a person to whom money is owed *359*

deductible amount that amount of an income stream which represents a return of capital *459, 517*

deemed income a notional rate of earnings used by DHS to calculate the investment returns from assets of eligible age pensioners *544*

default fund an employer nominated superannuation fund where the member does not exercise their choice of fund *417*

default investment option a trustee nominated investment choice where the member does not exercise their investment choice *418*

defined benefit scheme a type of superannuation account where the balance is determined by a formula which often includes salary and years worked; generally the investment risk is borne by the employer sponsor of the fund *401*

dependant a person who relies on another, financially, emotionally or in some other capacity *357*

derivative a financial product that has no inherent value; its value or price is derived from some other asset *329*

disability support pension a pension paid to people who have a physical, intellectual or psychiatric impairment *556*

discount method a method of determining a capital gain by including a percentage of the gain as assessable income *317*

discount rate the rate of return required by an investor from an investment *58*

discount securities fixed-interest securities are priced to include interest which is not paid in separate payments *187*

distributions the amounts distributed from an investment to unit holders; it can include both income and capital gain *228*

diversification the spread of different assets held in a portfolio *325*

dividend imputation a system in which shareholders are entitled to tax credits for the relevant amount of tax paid by a company on its profits *104*

efficient frontier the curved line that represents the optimal mix of return and risk for a portfolio of investments given a required level of risk *155*

endowment warrant where an investor pays a deposit on a share and borrows the rest to finance its purchase; the investor then uses the dividend income stream as the means by which to pay off the balance owing *338*

enduring power of attorney a power of attorney (POA) is a legal document given by a person (donor) that authorises another person (attorney) to act on their behalf; an enduring POA continues to be valid even after the donor becomes mentally incompetent *576*

equity the client's capital as opposed to borrowed funds *318*

estate the deceased assets which have not been directly passed to beneficiaries *359*

estate assets assets owned in the personal name of the willmaker which are capable of being disposed of by a will *579*

estate planning the planning and management of a person's estate following their death *575*

excess the amount of insurance risk which is retained by the individual rather than transferred through insurance *357*

exchange traded fund (ETF) a fund listed on a stock exchange that has the objective of managing investments on behalf of investors based on tracking a particular index *282*

executor the personal representative or manager of a deceased person's estate *578*

exempt income income that is not counted by the ATO and not taxed *317*

family tax benefit income support paid to eligible families to assist them with the cost of raising children *552*

fee-for-service a remuneration model where the client is billed directly by the financial planner for the service they provide based on an agreement with the client *636*

fiduciary responsibilities to act in good faith and to put the interest of others (members) ahead of your own *399*

financial counsellor a person who is not a financial planner, but who assists people who have difficulties with managing their money *12*

fixed-rate loan a loan whereby the interest rate is fixed by a length of time and/or by a fixed interest rate *248*

forward rate the interest rate that is required to be achieved in a later year when choosing between a short-term and longer-term fixed-interest investment *76*

fraudulent misrepresentation an inaccurate statement made knowingly believing it to be untrue, or an inaccurate statement made recklessly *354*

fringe benefits tax (FBT) a tax applied to the taxable amount of non-cash benefits provided to an employee *121*

frozen method a method of determining a capital gain using CPI index numbers from the date of purchase and the date of sale *317*

fully funded scheme a superannuation fund where contributions and earnings have been set aside to meet the commitments to members as they fall due *404*

future insurability a clause in an insurance contract which provides the insured with the opportunity to purchase more cover at future nominated dates without providing further evidence of health status *367*

future value an amount of money at some future time *58*

futures contract a futures contract is an agreement to trade something in the future, either to buy or sell a specific amount of a specific asset *332*

gearing the use of borrowed money to assist in the purchase of assets *311*

gearing ratio the ratio of debt to capital *316*

gifting rules the rules that restrict the amount of assets able to be given away by pensioners before their age pension entitlements are affected *547*

Good Disclosure Principles principles promoted by ASIC to help promote good disclosure outcomes for clients *624*

goods and services tax (GST) an indirect tax imposed on the purchase of goods and services at a flat rate of 10% *93*

government allowance income support payments for persons in need of short-term assistance *539*

government pension income support payments for persons in need of medium to long-term assistance *539*

growth at a reasonable price (GARP) an investment management style that incorporates both growth and value styles *289*

growth funds managers an investment management style where investments are selected and traded on the basis of superior future growth *288*

hedge to use a financial product to reduce or eliminate a risk to which an investor is currently exposed *311*

home equity conversion (HEC) loan (reverse mortgage) a loan or an amount by which a home owner may draw funds based on the equity or ownership value of the home *249, 546*

hostel accommodation aged care accommodation that provides low-level care places for people who need some help *561*

hybrid fund an investment fund that provides the benefit of both income and capital gains from a variety of sources *231*

in-specie contributions contributions made in kind rather than in cash e.g. a self-employed person may contribute listed shares to their SMSF 417, 502

income splitting shifting income from a person on a high marginal tax rate to a person or entity in a lower tax bracket *114*

income tax a tax levied on individuals and companies in proportion to the level of income earned *92*

indirect cost ratio (ICR) an aggregation of all management costs (MER) and other indirect costs which cannot be attributed to individual member accounts expressed as a percentage of funds under management *430*

information ratio a measure that considers the extent to which a fund has outperformed its benchmark after adjusting for risk *296*

initial public offer (IPO) the first offer of shares to the public; sometimes referred to as a 'float' of shares *191*

innocent misrepresentation an inaccurate statement made without fraudulent intent *353*

instalment warrant where an investor pays a deposit on a share and then pays off the balance by one or more instalments *338, 506*

Intermediaries those who arrange insurances for a client; that is, agents and brokers *352*

internal rate of return the rate of return at which the cash inflow and cash outflow of an investment is zero *73*

inter vivos trust a trust established during the lifetime of a person *588*

intestacy the situation that arises when a person dies without having a valid will and, as a result, their assets are distributed in accordance with a government formula *581*

investment-style warrant a warrant which is less actively traded and held for a relatively longer period of time as compared to a trading-style warrant *338*

investment scam an investment opportunity that is promoted to investors which has no substance other than to benefit the promoter of the investment *169*

joint tenancy a form of ownership of an asset where two or more persons each hold the rights over the entire asset and in which the surviving tenant receives total ownership of the asset *579*

joint tenant where ownership is shared between tenants and the death of one tenant means that ownership passes to the surviving tenant *501*

legal personal representative the person responsible for managing the estate of a deceased who is appointed through either being named as the executor in a will or, if there is no will, by being appointed administrator of the estate by the Supreme Court *594*

leverage use a small amount of capital to access a larger amount of an asset *310*

life expectancy how long a person is expected to live based on their gender and current age as determined by the Australian Government Actuary's life expectancy tables *446*

life expectancy income stream a fixed-term income stream where the term is determined by the Australian Government Actuary's life expectancy tables *459*

life interest an interest in property for the remaining life of the owner or occupant *542*

lifetime income stream an income stream that will last as long as a person lives *459, 517*

listed investment company (LIC) an investment company listed on a stock exchange that has the objective of managing investments on behalf of investors *281*

listed investment trust (LIT) an investment trust listed on a stock exchange that has the objective of managing investments on behalf of investors *281*

listed managed funds managed funds that are listed and traded on a stock exchange *281*

listed perils an insurance contract which lists the events (perils) covered. Therefore, events not listed are not covered *382*

loan-to-valuation ratio (LVR) the amount of debt expressed as a percentage of the total asset value *316*

longevity risk the risk that the individual will outlive their retirement income/savings *446*

managed investment schemes (managed funds) investment schemes where funds are deposited with a fund manager to manage on behalf of investors *108*

management expense ratio (MER) a ratio of fees charged to the value of the assets under management *273, 430*

marginal tax rates the percentage of tax paid on each additional dollar of income earned *98*

margin call where a lender asks for an additional contribution by a borrower because the current level of the security they are offering has fallen below an agreed threshold *324*

margin lending lending for investment where the loan is secured by the investment *321*

marking to market constantly reassessing the financial obligations of buyers and sellers as the market price of an asset changes *334*

master fund an investment fund which enables investors to invest in a number of funds via the one fund; sometimes referred to as a fund of funds or as an administration fund manager *179, 285*

material fact a fact that would influence a reasonable and prudent insurer in accepting a risk or in setting a premium given those particular facts *353*

means test a test that reduces a person's entitlement to a pension or allowance based on exceeding certain asset and income thresholds *539*

Medicare levy a levy on the taxable income of an individual taxpayer to help fund Australia's health system *101*

mezzanine fund a fund that offers a higher rate of return to investors based on a higher rate of return charged to borrowers — typically, borrowers invest in property development and are unable to borrow the full extent of the funds needed; hence they offer a higher return to investors to obtain more funds but the returns are subject to the developers' aims being achieved *230*

mortgage a contract between a lender and a borrower which pledges real estate as security for a loan *318*

mortgagee the person who receives the mortgage — the lender *318*

mortgage fund an investment fund in which the assets are based on first mortgages over property *230*

mortgagor the person who offers the mortgage — the borrower *318*

multiple asset-class investing a mixture of asset classes in an investment portfolio *163*

National Financial Literacy Strategy a body established by the federal government to act as a clearing house for resources to assist in the education of consumers about financial issues *12*

negative gearing a situation where the total deductions associated with an investment, including the interest charge, exceed assessable income generated from the investment; in this case, the loss can be claimed as a tax deduction *120, 314*

net present value the present value of a stream of income payments after deducting the cost of the stream of income payments *72*

Newstart allowance an allowance paid to unemployed persons while they are looking for work *558*

no-advice statement a document signed by a client stating that no advice was given by a planner in respect of a transaction *621*

non-account based income streams where an individual gives their retirement savings to an income-stream provider who pools those assets and promises an income stream in return *460, 517*

non-concessional contribution a contribution to superannuation for which a tax deduction has not been claimed (formerly known as undeducted contributions) *411, 450, 502*

non-estate assets assets that are not owned in the personal name of the willmaker and their distribution is not governed by a will *579*

no negative equity guarantee (NNEG) a guarantee that the accrued interest and principal obligations under a reverse mortgage will not exceed the value of the real estate pledged as security *474*

novation to replace an existing contractual obligation with a new contractual obligation *331*

nursing home accommodation aged care accommodation that provides high-level care for people who need 24-hour nursing assistance *563*

option an agreement that gives the buyer (holder) of the option the right but not the obligation to buy or sell something in the future at a fixed price *334*

ordinary money money held outside a superannuation environment *449*

ordinary times earnings (OTE) prescribed in legislation as including some items, e.g. earnings for ordinary hours worked, and excluding other items, e.g. overtime pay *412*

over the counter markets (OTC) informal arrangements where non-standardised financial products are traded, as opposed to the trading of standardised financial products on exchanges such as the ASX *329*

passive investing an investment approach which is based on selecting investments within a portfolio based on replicating an index *272*

pay as you go (PAYG) a system for paying instalments towards a taxpayer's expected tax liability *98*

pension mode where an individual is no longer contributing to superannuation and has begun drawing down their superannuation in order to fund their retirement *447, 515*

pension supplement additional support paid to those in receipt of a pension and replacing a number of individual allowances and supplements *539*

personal insolvency agreement where a person enters into an agreement with their creditors without being made bankrupt *514*

physical position when an investor is currently exposed to a financial risk *331*

positive gearing a situation where the assessable income generated from the investment exceeds total deductions incurred, including the interest charges; in this case, the tax is payable on the profit *120, 313*

premium the cost of taking out insurance *350*

present value an amount of money at today's value *59*

preservation age the minimum age at which funds can be withdrawn from superannuation *378, 410, 516*

preserved money must be maintained in a superannuation environment until a minimum age is reached *449*

principal the amount of a loan which is outstanding *318*

private binding ruling an individual is able to ask the tax office for a ruling on how they would judge a particular course of action by the individual before that action is undertaken. The tax office will then supply the individual with written advice and is then bound by that advice (ruling) *514*

probate the process of proving and registering in the Supreme Court the last will of a deceased person *578*

product disclosure statement (PDS) an offer document designed to provide information about a managed investment scheme to investors, including its risk, cost, return objectives and other information *267*

property an investment into the asset class that covers real estate in its many forms *145*

prudential to monitor risk-taking behaviour *400, 489*

public unit trust a trust that issues units to the general public for the purpose of investing monies raised *263*

pure risk where there is chance of loss or no loss, for example, your house might burn down this year or it might not *349*

put option an agreement that gives the buyer (holder) of the option the right but not the obligation to sell something in the future at a fixed price *337*

real estate investment trust (REIT) an investment trust listed on a stock exchange that has the objective of managing a portfolio of property on behalf of investors *281*

recontribution the process by which some funds are withdrawn from superannuation and then contributed back into superannuation in order to boost the tax-free component *454, 520*

record of advice (ROA) an alternative advice document to the SOA able to be used when providing further advice to existing clients *620*

recourse where the lender can seize a particular asset pledged as security for a loan if the borrower defaults on their payments; an unsecured loan is a non-recourse loan *325, 507*

registered child care child care provided by relatives, friends or other persons who are registered as child carers with the Family Assistance Office *554*

reportable employer superannuation contributions (RESCs) additional superannuation contributions salary sacrificed by an employee or made on behalf of an employee that are included in the definition of income for the purposes of determining entitlement to government benefits and obligations for government taxes and levies *127*

residential property property which is designed for and occupied by residents as a home *227*

residual capital value (RCV) the capital amount payable on termination of a pension or annuity *550*

responsible entity (RE) a public company that holds an Australian Financial Services Licence authorising it to operate and manage a registered managed investment scheme or managed fund *268*

retail managed funds funds that are targeted at individual retail investors with small amounts of money to invest *284*

reversed out taking out an equal and opposite contract which effectively cancels out the original obligation *334*

reverse mortgage an arrangement to mortgage a home in order to receive payments from the fund provider in return for a percentage ownership in the home or an accumulated debt to be paid when the home is sold *12, 63, 472, 543*

reversion when the recipient of an income stream dies, the income stream passes to a dependant *463, 518*

risk management a branch of management that provides a systematic approach to the management of pure risk *349*

safety margin a margin of security which must be maintained above the level required to meet the outstanding value of the loan *323*

salary sacrifice where an employee asks their employer to take some of their income and redirect this to paying for a benefit on behalf of the employee; the most commonly salary sacrificed benefit is superannuation *120, 377, 408*

scaled advice advice about a specific area of an investor's needs or about a limited range of issues *622*

scope of the advice the nature of the advice sought by the client, including any client or planner limitations *638*

security the promise of assets, including real estate, in the case of loan default *318*

self-assessment regime a system whereby the ATO initially accepts taxation information provided by a taxpayer for the purposes of assessing the taxpayer's tax liability *94*

self-employed an individual who earns less than 10% of their income from employment-related activities *410, 502*

self-managed superannuation fund a fund with four or fewer members that is supervised by the ATO *489*

shares an investment holding in a company *146*

Sharpe ratio a measure of the risk-adjusted performance of a managed fund that considers the size of the return relative to the risk undertaken *296*

small APRA fund fund with four or fewer members that is supervised by APRA *489*

small superannuation fund fund with four or less members *489*

speculating using a financial product purely to achieve financial gain, that is, not to reduce or eliminate a risk *311*

speculative risk where there is a chance of a loss or gain, for example, in gambling or investing *349*

spread or **bid-offer spread** the difference between the buying and selling price of units in a managed fund or other security *279*

standard deviation a measure of the riskiness of an investment *149, 295*

statement of advice (SOA) a written personal financial plan prepared for a client by a financial adviser *615*

strike price the price at which an option contract will be transacted if the option is exercised *335*

subprime mortgage fund a fund that holds mortgage assets that are of low quality; that is, the mortgages have been given to people who are in danger of not being able to make repayments on their mortgage *21*

superannuation a means of saving and investing to accumulate wealth and then using that wealth to fund retirement *397*

superannuation guarantee an arrangement whereby employees are guaranteed that their employers will contribute to their superannuation funds a minimum of percentage of their ordinary times earnings *405*

superannuation money money held inside a superannuation environment *449*

systematic risk the risk associated with the overall market and which cannot be eliminated by diversification *271*

taxable component money held inside a superannuation environment which has been subject to the 15% contributions and earnings tax *450, 517*

tax-free component that part of superannuation which is exempt from tax *450*

tax offsets or rebates reductions in tax payable provided by the government to support or assist individuals or activities *100*

tax shield where the net deductible expenses of an investment reduce the amount of tax payable *314*

tenancy-in-common a form of ownership of an asset where two or more people each have a distinct share in the ownership of an asset and in which the share of the deceased's interest forms part of their estate *579*

tenants in common each tenant owns a defined share of an asset which does not automatically pass to another tenant upon death *501*

testamentary capacity the mental capacity required of a willmaker to be able to make a valid will *577*

testamentary trust a trust established under the terms of a will that comes into effect upon the death of the willmaker *585*

tracking error a measure which looks at how closely the returns of a managed fund follow the returns of the index to which it is benchmarked *295*

trading-style warrant a warrant which is traded actively for a relatively short period of time as compared to an investment-style warrant *338*

transition to retirement (TTR) income stream a scheme which allows workers to continue to work part-time (or full-time) and supplement their income by drawing down some of their superannuation *406, 467, 517*

trust a legal structure where property is nominally owned and held by a trustee on behalf of beneficiaries *118*

trust deed a legal document used to establish and regulate the operation of a trust *265*

trustee a person who administers a trust fund; a superannuation fund is a form of trust fund *100, 399, 489*

underinsurance where the payout from an insurance policy as a result of an event is not able to restore the individual to the financial position they were in prior to the event *381*

underwriting the process by which the insurer assesses the risk associated with an individual or a group of individuals and provides insurance coverage at a price commensurate with the risk *379*

undischarged bankrupt a person who has been declared bankrupt under the provisions of the Bankruptcy Act and has not been discharged from the bankruptcy *514*

undue influence a situation that arises where one person is able to take advantage of a position of power over another person *581*

unfunded scheme a public-sector superannuation fund where contributions and earnings have not been set aside to meet the commitments to members as they fall due; the balance in a member's account is effectively only a promise to pay *404*

unlisted managed funds managed funds that are not listed on a stock exchange *278*

unlisted property trust (UPT) a property trust that is not listed on the Australian Securities Exchange *229*

unsystematic risk the risk associated with individual securities and which can be eliminated through diversification *272*

untaxed superannuation money money held inside a superannuation environment which has not been subject to the 15% contributions and earnings tax *450*

utmost good faith under the *Insurance Contract Act 1984* both parties to an insurance contract must display the highest degree of honesty *353*

value funds managers an investment management style where investments are selected and traded based on the extent to which they are believed to be under- or overpriced *288*

variable loan a loan that may vary in terms of interest rate charged to the borrower *248*

warrant a leveraged investment that gives the investor the right to buy or sell a particular asset *338*

wholesale managed funds funds that are targeted at institutional investors or individual investors that are deemed to be professional or financially sophisticated with large amounts of money to invest *284*

will a legal document which directs how a willmaker's assets are to be distributed or disposed of upon their death *575*

work bonus scheme a scheme that encourages people over age pension age to continue working by allowing them to earn a higher amount of income before their age pension payments are reduced *8, 406, 541*

wrap account an administration service that provides access to a range of different managed funds and other direct investment options and wraps the various investments into the one account for an investor *285*

yield curve a line representing the interest rates for different time frames of investment *183*

youth allowance financial support for young people who are studying, undertaking training or an Australian apprenticeship, looking for work or sick *557*

Index

H

I

Q

R

T

U

V